Strategic Management

Strategic Management

Shamsher Singh
Associate Professor
Banarsidas Chandiwala
Institute of Professional Studies
New Delhi

TECHSAR™
NEW DELHI

Published and Printed by

Techsar Pvt. Ltd.
4435-36/7, Ansari Road, Daryaganj,
New Delhi–110 016 (India)
E-mail: tech_info@techsarworld.com
Website: www.techsarworld.com

ISBN 978-93-82332-69-5

Reprint 2026

Preface

Strategic Management is the unique field of knowledge as it deals with the functions and role of the top management of an organisation. The strategies adopted by the organisation shapes the future course of and the survival of the organisation. The evaluation of strategic management as a subject stated as early as 1911, when "Business Policy' as a capstone course for the business administration programme was introduced in Harvard Business School. In fact, the course focused on integrating the functional areas of business administration like accounting, management, marketing, human resource, finance and production. Originally, this course aimed to provide practitioners and learners the ability to apply the knowledge learned in previous courses to solve problems in business organisations. As such the business policy course provided formal training and experience in handling issues affecting the business environment and systematic and analytical thinking in resolving problems affecting the performance of organisations.

The strategic management as a subject has gone through various ups and down and finally it has been accorded a place it deserves in the management education. All the management courses at either graduate or postgraduate levels in India and elsewhere has been included this paper as a core subject. The objective of the course is to develop an understanding of the Strategic Management process in a dynamic and competitive global environment so that students are able to perform in the changing environment of the business. The strategic management is the process of understanding the role and the functions of the top management, how it plans and implement different strategies. As such the strategic management is one of the important function of the management and understanding the subject is very important for the management students.

Strategic management is an ongoing process that evaluates and controls the business and the industries in which the company is involved; assesses its competitors and sets goals and strategies to meet all existing and potential competitors; and then reassesses each strategy annually or quarterly [i.e. regularly] to determine how it has been implemented and whether it has succeeded or needs replacement by a new strategy to meet changed circumstances, new technology, new competitors, a new economic environment., or a new social, financial, or political environment.

The textbook will help in understanding how the strategic management has evolved over a period of time, what strategies have been adopted by the different organisation around the world during the last and present century and what lesson students can learn from the approaches adopted by the different strategist and the organisations . The main objective of the textbook is to present the strategic management concepts, issues and processes in a simplified, logical and sequential manner.

Many books of Indian and foreign authors available in the market dealing with Strategic Management, still there is no comprehensive book which covers the syllabus of leading Indian universities and the professional institutions offering master degree in Management/Business Administration. Keeping in view this fact, there was a need to write textbook which can cover the syllabus of such courses. The textbook will cover the MBA syllabus of Guru Govind Singh Indraprastha University (GGSIPU) New Delhi, Gautam Budha Technical University and Mahamaya Technical University (formerly UP Technical University) and MD University Rohtak. The intended audience is the postgraduate students of MBA/PGDM in India. In majority of books, the entire syllabus is not covered and students have to refer different books and many a times the required text may not be available in any of the book. It will act as textbook which covers entire syllabus and hence they need not to look for other books while studying this subject. The present book is an attempt in this direction.

Shamsher Singh

Acknowledgements

Writing a textbook is a arduous task that requires enormous perseverance, endurance and sustained commitment over a long period of time. It also involves incredible sacrifices of other opportunities, social occasions, family leisure and social gathering not only for me but also for entire family especially my wife Ms Rajkumari and children Raveena and Ravish, making this book in its real sense our book rather than my book. I would like to extend my sincere gratitude to my all family members for their continuous support and inspiration.

The motivation to write the book is entirely goes to my students to whom I have taught this subject several times. I would like to extend my sincere thanks to all of them as well as to all those students who will be my future students.

The subject matter of this book has been adopted from various Indian and foreign books, professional journals, magazines, other publications and the Internet. However, while adopting the relevant subject matter, the emphasis has been given on its relevance in Indian context. I thank all those writers and researchers whose thoughts and theories have been helpful in bringing out this book. Their contribution has been duly acknowledged . My deep gratitude and sincere thanks to all of them, without their contribution this book would not have been possible. I am grateful to all of them.

I owe a debt of gratitude to my professionals colleague for their support. A special note of thanks is due to my publisher and their staff in extending their wholehearted support and encouragement.

I am thankful to numerous readers of the book and welcome their suggestions. Last but not the least I should thank God, for this grace and inspiration, word of thanks appear so inadequate. I eagerly look forward to receive your valuable comments feedback and suggestion for further improvement of the book at shamsher_1965@rediffmail.com, for which I would be highly grateful.

Shamsher Singh

Contents

Case Studies

1 Introduction

1.1 INTRODUCTION

Harvard Business School of USA in 1911 introduced Strategic Management as an integrative course in management aimed at providing general management capability and it was known as business policy. The course was primarily based on case studies, which had been in use at the Harvard Business School for instructional purpose since 1908. The objective of the course was to integrate the knowledge of the different functional areas of business management such as marketing , finance & accounting, human resource, production, etc., into one specifics area of knowledge so that students and practitioners are able to understand the interrelationship and linkages of each of the functional areas with the operations and management of the entire organisation. However, the different changes in the business environment had forced many organisations to make structural changes to cope with the rapid dynamics of the business environment. Managers and Chief Executive Officers (CEOs) of large corporations adopted some or part of knowledge in strategic management and found potential benefits to their organisations. Therefore, the purpose of this chapter to provide learners an understanding of the field of strategic management, the historical perspective, changing business dynamics and the potential advantages and benefits of strategic management to organisations.

1.2 EVOLUTION OF STRATEGIC MANAGEMENT

The evolution of strategic management as a subject started as early as 1911, when "Business Policy' as a capstone course for the business administration programme was introduced in Harvard Business School. In fact the course focused on integrating the functional areas of business administration like accounting, management, marketing, human resource, finance and production. Originally, this course aimed to provide practioners and learners the ability to apply the knowledge learned in previous courses to solve problems in business organisations. As such the business policy course provided formal training and experience in handling issues affecting the business environment and systematic and analytical thinking in resolving problems affecting the performance of organisations.

The real stride in the growth of strategic management in the United States came after the publication of two reports in 1959, the Gordon and Howell Report sponsored by the Ford Foundation. Based on their research and the advantages and benefits derived from the business policy course, the Gordon and Howell Report recommended that the business policy course be made a core course in the business administration curricula to all the universities in the American Association of Colleges of School of Business Administration (AACSB). Since then, the business policy course has been the major thrust of the business administration programmes at the undergraduate and postgraduate levels.

1.3 DEVELOPMENT FROM BUSINESS POLICY TO STRATEGIC MANAGEMENT

There are two perspectives in the development of the business policy course. First, from the perspective of the changing emphasis in the contents of the course, and the second one is from the management planning perspective.

1.3.1 Changing Emphasis in Business Policy Contents

The business policy course underwent different changes since its introduction as a core subject. The contents of the course had changed to cope with the changes in the dynamics of the business environment. The emphasis in the course is attributed to the varying needs of the business and non-business organisations in coping with the changing environmental concerns. There are four major factors contributing to the changing emphasis in the business policy course:

(i) Changing managerial roles in the organisation;
(ii) Rapid changes in business and non-business environment;
(iii) Emphasis on the case study method in learning; and
(iv) Other concerns affecting organisational performance.

When the business policy course was introduced at Harvard University, the perspective adopted was that of the top management view of the organisation. In other words, in trying to understand various issues in the organisation, participants in the course were asked to take the role of the Chief Executive Officer/General Manager of an organisation, and see how they would react to the varying issues affecting the organisation. While this perspective was required to have an overall view of things in an organisation, the perspective would also provide learners to relate various functional areas in an organisation and how it could affect the overall organisation. Further, this perspective would provide learners the interrelationship of external factors and their effects and impact on the management and performance of the organisation.

Getting the top management perspective of an organisation was found to be necessary but not sufficient towards better performance in an organisation. The participative management concepts and empowerment in management was found to be also important in ensuring organisational success and performance. Subsequently, the roles of middle management and first level management (that is, top down and bottoms-up) in handling various managerial issues was more important. Thus, vertical and lateral managerial perspective became important in trying to resolve managerial concerns in an organisation. Thus, the managerial roles and expectations were changing to cope with the impending needs of the environment.

The rapid changes in the business and non-business environments resulted in the change in emphases and contents of the business policy course. External factors, such as economic, social, political and technological, seemed to have evolved much in the last two decades. The industrial renaissance of the 1980s affected the management of business and non-business organisations in several ways. One major change was the information technology revolution which promoted the development of new ways of doing business. The increasing concerns for social responsibility, ethics, and the environment, for example, concerns over pollution, poorly managed health system and social discrimination, also contributed to the changing expectations of society towards organisational performance. Finally, the changing micro-management expectations of the stakeholders like corporate governance, transparency and social equity in organisational management also contributed to the change in business and non-business environments. In recent years, learning about organisations had changed much with the new developments in pedagogy and the interrelated tools. Case studies of organisations had been found to be effective in learning better about organisations and it was the major approach used in Harvard University, INSEAD and leading business schools throughout the world. The case study approach was found to be most effective in trying to reach the learners understanding of real business world problems and provide practical solutions. Consequently, this approach had been widely used in business policy courses worldwide.

The impending globalisation trends and liberalisation of trade barriers also had an effect on the curriculum of strategic management that is from an inward looking of one country to that of an international and global perspective. This had led to the concern for a more proactive or 'strategic' approach in handling complex business and non-business issues affecting organisations. Consequently, the name of the course had to be changed to 'strategic management' to reflect these changes in the environment.

1.3.2 Changing Management Planning Perspective

In the field of organisational management, one of the major functions of management process is planning. The management literature has often focused on the importance of planning in managing organisations more effectively and efficiently. Traditional management planning emphasises on the need to have a clear goal and objectives and preparing the necessary budgets for resource allocation. The rapid changes in the business environment has forced managers to make the necessary adjustments in management planning and thus raised the development of a 'strategic' approach in management planning. In other words, the changing managerial planning perspective has also contributed to the development in the field of business policy to 'strategic management'.

1.4 PHASES OF DEVELOPMENT IN STRATEGIC MANAGEMENT

As per the views of Gluck, the development of strategic management began when the managers started using planning techniques. Initially, managers started day-to-day planning, then moved to anticipate the future though preparations of budgets and using control techniques such as capital budgeting and management by objectives. However, these techniques could not adequately address the role for the future, long range planning came to the centre stage. The long range planning was replaced by strategic planning and in the present scenario we saw the emergence of strategic management — a term that is currently used to describe the process of strategic decision making. Strategic management is the theoretical framework of business policy courses today. According to Gluck et al. (1982), strategic management evolved through four phases of development as shown below:

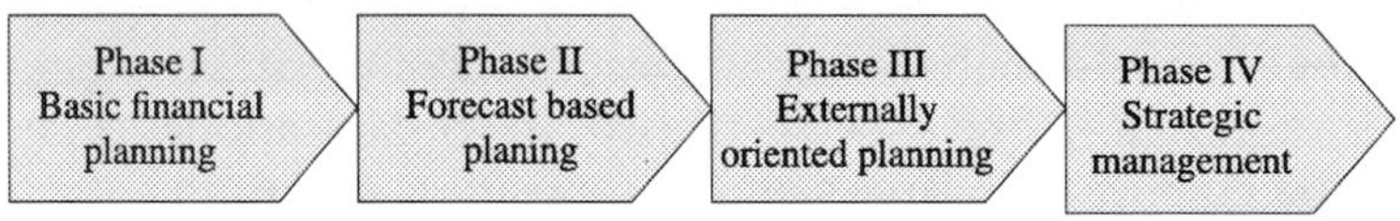

Fig. 1.1 Gluck's four phases of development in strategic management

Phase 1 In phase 1, the evolution of strategic management refers to the traditional formal business planning mode which focused on functional areas. Organisations were more concerned about annual budgets and seek operational control through meeting the annual budgets. The business environment during this phase was stable and there were not many changes occurred in this phase.

Phase 2 In phase 2, as the business environment began to make some changes due to increasing demand for goods and services, there was a concern for organisations to do a forecast to plan. Growth was the major concern in this phase and more effective planning was required to ensure that organisations take the opportunities in the environment. Annual forecast was not sufficient, and multiyear forecasts became necessary. In this phase too, environmental analysis became more evident and important to organisations.

Phase 3 As the business dynamics grew faster, managers realised that it was not adequate to do planning by making business forecasts. Changes in the business environment became more rapid and the level of turbulence became more intense relative to the earlier periods (phase 1 and 2). Thus, in phase 3, businesses had to make immediate response to market changes and competition. This period became intense as business performance showed impressive results (profits) and many players (investors) became more interested to reap part of the potential profits. In this phase, organisations had to make thorough analysis of the environment and competition. The resource allocation process required managers to be more dynamic as they had to make quick decisions to avail the opportunities available at that time. In other words, managers had to make fast changes in financial, human and other resources of the organisation to cope with the changing needs of the business organisation. Phase 3 also showed the emphasis for managerial planning with concerns for the external environment, and the need to react in anticipation of the impending changes in the business environment.

Phase 4 Managers also had to behave or think more 'strategically' at this phase in order to remain competitive. This phase is also known as the 'strategic planning era' in the early 1970's in the USA and Europe. In Malaysia, it became an important phenomenon in the late 1980s and early 1990s. Many public listed organisations and state-owned corporations in Malaysia became interested in this concept in the mid 1990s. Phase 4 is known as the 'strategic management' era. In USA and Europe, this phase gained prominence in the late 1980's. In this phase, the environmental changes were more rapid and the level of turbulence was greater with more uncertainties of the future.

Organisations realised that in order to remain competitive and sustain their competitive edge, there was a need to develop specialised strategic plans relevant for the particular organisation. There was also the need to use the best of all the available resources the organisations had to have a competitive advantage over others in the industry. Consequently, organisations needed to develop flexible organisational processes and systems that could cope with the uncertain business environment. Organisations also had to be more creative and develop supportive cultures and values that can ensure organisational success and superior performance. As such, the focus in management planning had changed from the 'strategic' perspective to that of 'creating the future'.This is the major challenge for managers today as the mode of achieving better organisational performance becomes more demanding and complex. As such, the role of creativity, innovation, research and development (R&D) is more important in today's business environment.

The changes in strategic management has prompted the business policy course to evolve from phase 1 to phase 4 which is more complex and dynamic. The business policy course was concerned with integrating all the functional areas of business and provide experience in solving real-life problems which have multifunctional impact on the organisation. Strategic management, however, was concerned with all that was discussed in the business policy course but also incorporated the external factors that have a major impact on the organisation, and consequently determine the long-term direction of the organisation by formulating and implementing the plans and making evaluation and control of the plans that were set for the organisation. Further, the strategic management area is also concerned about strategic issues, which have long-term impact on the organisation.

1.5 HISTORICAL PERSPECTIVE OF EVALUATION OF STRATEGIC MANAGEMENT

Hofer and others have viewed the evaluation of strategic management in terms of four paradigms shifts, which can also be considered the four overlapping phases in the development of strategic management. These developments have closely followed the demand of real-life business. These paradigm are discussed below.

1.5.1 Ad Hoc Policy Paradigm

The first paradigm was the era of ad hoc policy making. This phase can be traced back to 1900-1930. This was also the era of mass production and maximising output. Normally, the firms commenced operations in a single product line, standardised the product and lowered the cost of production, catering to unique set of customers in a limited geographical area expanded in one or all of the three dimensions of business. Informal control and co-ordination became partially irrelevant as expansion took place and the need to integrate functional areas arose. This integration was brought about by framing policies to guide managerial actions. Coordination was the main concern of the management and there was hardly any element of the strategic management although the strategic planning focused on maximising output.

1.5.2 Integrated Policy Formulation Paradigm

The second paradigm was the era of integrated policy formulation. In the 1930-1940 there were many environmental changes that took place in the US. These changes were in technology, turbulence in political environment, emergence of new industries, demand for novelty products even at higher costs, product differentiation, market segmentation in increasingly competitive and changing markets. All these made investment decisions increasingly difficult. The planned policy formulation replaced the ad hock policy making. This was the era of integrating all functional areas and framing integerated policies to guide managerial actions. That is why it is called integrated policy formulation era.

1.5.3 Strategy Paradigm

The third paradigm was the era of strategy. In the period of 1940-1960, planned policy became irrelevant due to increasingly complex and accelerating changes taking place in the environment and the needs of the business could no longer be served by policy making and functional area integration only. Firms had to anticipate environmental changes. By the 1960s, there was a demand for a critical look at the basic concepts of business and its relationship to the environment. The concept satisfied this requirement and the third paradigm based on strategy emerged in the early sixties.

1.5.4 Strategic Management Paradigm

The fourth paradigm was the strategic management which emerged in 1980 and onwards The initial focus of strategic management was on the interactions of two broad fields of enquiry: the strategic process of business firm and the responsibility of general management. What to produce, where to market, which new business to enter, which one to quit and how to get internally stronger and resourceful are the new stakes. Strategic planning is required to be done to endow the enterprise with certain fundamental competence/distinctive strengths which could take care of eventualities resulting from unexpected environmental changes.

However, the evolution of this fourth phase is still continuing and is yet not formed into a theory of how to manage an enterprise. But strategic management is a very important tool for and way of thinking to resolve strategic issues. The world is substantially compressed and managing the external and internal environment becomes a crucial function.

1.6 THE EVOLUTION OF STRATEGIC MANAGEMENT POST-WORLD WAR II

The evolution of strategic management post-World War II is presented in Table 1.1. Broadly it can be divided into three phases The first phase is known as general management era which comprised the 1950s and 1960s. The second phase is the golden age of strategic planning and comprised the period 1960s-1980s. The third phase is post-modern strategic management era which stared in 1980s and still continuing.

Table 1.1 The post-war evaluation of strategic management.

Phase I 1950s-Late 1960s: The General Management Era
The Importance of Leadership
Universal Managerial Characteristics
The Universal Professional Manager
View the Firm as a Whole
Optimism
Top Management Oriented
Implicit Strategic Management
Phase II Late 1960s-1980s: The Golden Age of Strategic Planning
The Rise of Analysis
Strategic Approaches
Strategic Portfolio
Incorporation of Industrial Organisation and Micro-Economic Approaches
Viewing the Firm as Made Up of Component Business That Have Different Strategic Roles
The Rise of Support Industries and Institutions, e.g., Strategic Consulting Firms, Business Schools, and Strategic Databases
The Emergence of a New Function, Profession and Unit: The Strategic Planning Staff
Formulation Oriented
Staff Oriented
The Centralization and Growth of Power of Strategic Planning
Explicit Strategic Management

Contd...

Contd...

Phase III -1980 onwards Post-Modern Strategic Management
Reaction to Strategic Planning
Renewed Interest in Implementation
Emphasis on the Role of Culture and History in Determining a Firm's Strategy
The Rise of Global Strategy
Targeted and Advanced Analytical Strategy
The Concurrent Use of Multiple Kinds of Strategic Support Systems, Processes, and Structure
The Elevation of Technology to a Strategic Variable
The Use of Inter-organisation Networks and Linkages in Strategy
The Simultaneous Deployment of Multiple Strategic Approaches - Blending Implicit and Explicit Strategy

The first phase was called the general management era of strategic management. This phase dealt with the "implicit" side of strategy, which is informal and instinctual. The general management era focused on leadership qualities, the general role of the CEO and other top managers, interpersonal relationships, the importance of values, and the capacity of informal and formal internal processes, systems, and structure to support strategy.

Based on the works of Chester Barnard, Philip Selznick, Kenneth Andrews, and others, a key assumption underlying the general management era in the early post-war period was that successful top executives are really effective general managers in the broadest sense. They are multifaceted leaders with responsibilities to the shareholders, employees, customers, and members of the larger community. According to the general management heritage, the criteria used for assessing the performance of a CEO and strategy generally are usually broad-based and long term in nature. For example, Barnard emphasised cooperation as a critical function of the executive and he also believed that strategy — the long-term direction of an enterprise — is only possible with an emotional, as well as rational, commitment and with sound and "moral" leadership.

Selznick focused on the process of "institutionalization" — which is to "infuse an organisation with value" beyond the technical requirements for the immediate task at hand. This action can be effectively accomplished only with appropriate strategic leadership. Selznick argued that key tasks for an institutional leader are defining the institutional mission and role, embodying the institution's purpose, defending the institution's integrity, moderating internal conflict, and setting priorities. Kenneth Andrews, a professor at the Harvard Business School, the centre of general management, also presents a broad and complex view of the top manager's job. According to Andrews, the CEO has several simultaneous roles at the personal, administrative, strategic, and even ethical levels. Andrews usefully distinguishes three important kinds of top-level leadership: personal, organisational, and "architect of organisational purpose," with this last category of leadership representing the truly strategic dimension of top management decision making. Going beyond routine and personal attributes, he calls the CEO the "custodian of corporate objectives.

The heritage of the general management tradition has its enduring significance for the corporate strategy field. Strategic decision making cannot be sanitized. The starting point for strategy is a long-term and multifaceted view of corporate objectives. There is also a bias in favour of action, for dealing with the challenges of strategic opportunities and threats. For example, Andrews writes, "Generalizing about how to make an effective strategic match is less rewarding than working at it." These themes – a broad view of the firm, the importance of leadership, and the need for effective implementation – are constantly being rediscovered and are as relevant in the 1980s as they were in the 1960s. This first attribute of strategy, the necessity of broad and committed leadership, provides a permanent link between the earlier general management era of the 1950s and 1960s and the post-modern phase that began in the 1980s.

The second phase, known as the golden age of strategic planning, started in the late 1960s. A new school of strategic management of conceptualization and practice began to surface. It became a strong rival to the general management tradition, and in the 1970s this new stream emerged as the dominant mode of strategic thinking and decision making. This second phase in strategic management, "the golden age of strategic planning", lasted from the late 1960s to about 1980. During this period, strategic planning flowered and gained enormous status. By the 1970s, the formal, systematic, and analytical side of strategy, dominated the entire field. Strategic planning developed into a profession and a management function. A large and influential support and service sector, made up of strategic consulting firms, business information data sources, an increasingly infatuated business press, and business schools, had grown to support and develop strategic planning. Various techniques and approaches also rapidly spread overseas.

Alfred D. Chandler, in his book "Strategy and Structure" exemplified this transition to a focus on professional strategic management. This work dealt with the rise of diversification strategy and the emergence of the multidivisional structure to support this strategy in the post-World War II period in the United States. But, like much historical writing, Chandler also reflected and anticipated the concerns and ideas of his own time, the 1960s. Chandler triggered major conceptualization in strategic management in four critical ways:

(i) Refinement and modification of the general management notions of leadership;
(ii) The identification of a major issue that acted as a stimulus for strategic decision making: diversification;
(iii) Recognition that the various internal support systems – including structure – need to be appropriately designed and in place for effective strategy; and
(iv) The identification of strategic management as something distinct from operational business concerns.

Chandler's insights and uncovering of professional management and systematic managerial techniques and methods matched well with some of the key trends that were occurring in the corporate world in the late 1960s and the 1970s. Corporations continued to grow in size, expanded geographically, and increasingly entered multiple lines of business. The terms "diversification" and "multidivisional structure" were becoming less helpful in accurately describing and assessing the evolution and actions of giant business enterprises. New concepts, techniques, and managerial roles began to emerge to deal with this new complexity and growth of the late 1960s and the 1970s.

Most of this new development can be grouped under the category of strategic planning, and this activity experienced a kind of "golden age" during the late 1960s-1980 period. The development of a rich array of strategic planning methods and viewpoints and structural innovations during the 1970s profoundly influenced strategy making and the practice of management. The new techniques included the statistical analysis of strategic-level databases, such as the PIMS [Profit Impact on Market Strategies] model, the increasing application of strategic portfolios developed by the Boston Consulting Group, Arthur D. Little, McKinsey, and other consulting firms and strategic planning units, and by the end of the 1970s, the incorporation into strategic planning of industrial organisation theory from economics. In addition, new structural innovations were developed, including, first, the SBU [Strategic Business Unit] within the firm and, later, strategic groups within an industry. These achievements enhanced management's capability to run large enterprises while also creating their own set of difficulties.

The third phase, "post-modern strategic management", started in the beginning of the 1980s. The strategic planning in actual practice was undergoing continuous change as it adapted to changing conditions. Strategic planning's golden age was ending by the early 1980s as strategy generally was becoming less monolithic, more pragmatic, more eclectic, and more grounded in specific business operations or industries. The approaches developed during the golden age of the late 1960s and 1970s were not rejected, instead, they were modified and adapted to specific contexts. This new humility and awareness of limits actually improved the usefulness of strategic management process.

The growing reassessment in the 1980s of strategic planning and its trappings was actually well grounded in significant strands of strategy thinking from the previous general management era. In addition, some strategy scholars attempted to broaden and deepen the strategy field and to reconcile and integrate findings from a variety of disciplines. Even more damaging pressures on strategic planning emanated from outside the strategic management field altogether and involved a direct assault on the view that strategy should be developed separately from operations. This critique of strategic planning was best articulated by those who believed that manufacturing and, later, technology had for too long been disregarded as strategic variables and that this neglect was a key factor in the U.S. decline in global competition. According to this line of thinking, manufacturing in the post-war period had become increasingly routine, narrow, and subordinate. Top executives in U.S. firms had become technology averse in making strategic decisions. Instead, there was at the highest level of the firm an infatuation with non-productive concerns, such as strategic planning, finance, and legal issues. In effect, CEOs had lost touch with the true lifeblood of business: technology and operations. It was time to reconnect the fundamentals of business with top management and strategic decision making.

By the beginning of the 1980s, strategic planning came to be known as competitive strategy. Michael Porter in his book "Competitive Strategy", published in 1980, highlights three aspects of competitive strategy: structural analysis of industries, generic strategies, and strategic groups. Clearly, one of the greatest benefits of structural analysis – which included delineating the actions of competitors, buyers, sellers, the threat of substitutes, and new entrants – was that it forced the strategist to view the industry broadly, not just in terms of current competitors.

In identifying three generic strategies for possible use (low-cost leadership, differentiation, and focus) Porter offered alternative avenues to strategic success. He and his colleagues enlarged the discussion of strategic choices and provided strategists with new conceptual degrees of freedom. Similarly, by employing the idea of strategic groups (essentially a cluster of competitors in an industry that are following the same or similar strategies as defined by a designated set of dimensions), diverse generic strategies of firms in an entire industry can be viewed and mapped. The industry can then be usefully reconfigured for strategic planning purposes.Technology and novel structures to promote innovation emerged in the 1980s as important elements of the strategic management.

Post-modern strategy increasingly characterizes the cutting edge of strategic practice today. It blends certain features of general management and strategic planning thinking while also exhibiting new concepts of its own. Moreover, it is both less universal and less elegant than its predecessors. It is more varied, contingent, and complicated in the way its diverse parts have been both disaggregated and reintegrated. It stresses such strategic matters as implementation, the creation of multiple organisational strategic support systems, processes, and pressures, the role of a firm's unique culture and history. In setting and influencing strategy, internal entrepreneurial units, the increasing use of inter-organisation networks and linkages, the growing importance of what is now termed global strategy, advanced and targeted analytical strategic approaches, the relationship between corporate strategy and various functional strategies, and the strategic role of technology.

By the mid-1980s, strategic management's historical evolution, strategy's more complex set of key current dimensions, and the growing concern in strategy over value-intensive objectives in a changing competitive environment all culminated in a new set of dominant strategic actions that tended to characterize much of post-modern strategic behaviour. The first such action is disaggregation the purposeful fragmentation, decentralization, and flattening of an enterprise in order to promote risk taking and innovation. In part, the new emphasis on disaggregation was a somewhat delayed reaction by large corporations to the dramatic and successful experience in the U.S. of small-firm high-technology entrepreneurialism and the continuing vigour of medium size companies, which tended to highlight the benefits of decentralized, small, and flat organisational structures.

The traditional advantages of market power as mass production, mass marketing, and large industrial R&D facilities can lead to significant strategic achievement. Moreover, within post-modern strategy a process of complex reintegration is also occurring, and this new method of assembling a high value critical mass is particularly effective in the current competitive environment. This type of action essentially permits not only the effective mobilization of internal resources but also the selection of external sources for achieving strategic advantage. Complex reintegration allows make-versus-buy of high value resources. An important distinguishing feature of post-modern strategy is a growing use of fluid and network-like inter-organisation structures such as strategic alliances – as well as better and varied use of the traditional hierarchical corporate form. Consequently, post-modern strategy is further modifying the shape of the U.S. corporation by actually promoting the externalizatlon of transactions where appropriate. The implementation of post-modern strategy often requires the kind of action that permits the continuous blending and coexistence of seemingly opposite kinds of behaviour and strategies. This crucial action in post-modern strategy is termed simultaneity, the simultaneous incorporation of diverse and often seemingly contradictory elements in order to achieve a larger set of strategic objectives. The ability to demonstrate simultaneity on an ongoing basis is critical for strategic success today.

1.7 THE INDIAN SCENARIO: EVALUATION OF STRATEGIC MANAGEMENT

Formal management education in India started in the late fifties and gained impetus with the setting up of the Indian Institute of Management (IIMs) and Administrative Staff College of India in early sixties. In the earlier years of the IIMs, the curriculum and philosophy of management education were based on American Model. IIM-Ahmedabad based its teaching methodology on Harvard model of developing and using case studies as the major pedagogical tool. With the spread of IIMs, creation of several university management departments and private management institute , the management education has experienced unparalleled growth. Almost all management education institutes offer the strategic management and business policy course usually in the later part of the degree or diploma programme.

After the opening up of the Indian economy in early 1990s, the All India Council for Technical Education (AICTE), the regulatory body of management education in India, provided proper direction to the growth of management education. The AICTE prescribed business policy, first in 1990 and again in 1995 , as an integrative component in management education curriculum, in the form of a course in corporate policy and strategic policy. The Business Policy and Strategic Management course has gained wider acceptance as an integrative discipline in over 1500 management institutes that have come up in the recent past (1990-2003). A number of doctoral and post-doctoral studies have also been undertaken with a view to enrich the knowledge in the area, especially with a clear focus on Indian companies. Strategic Management Forum of India was formed in 1996 and is exclusively devoted to the development of issues relating to strategic management. A number of publications covering the concepts, techniques and case studies relating to business policy and strategic management have also gone up impressively, especially after 1990s, such as Strategic Marketing, Business Standards strategist, etc.

The Association of Indian Management Schools (AIMS), a representative body of management education and university management departments, has recommended a standard curriculum including "Business Policy and Strategic Management" as a compulsory course. Business Policy is the preferred nomenclature but Strategic Management is being progressively adapted. The All India Management Association (AIMA), a national body for the promotion of the scientific management in India, offers a popular distance education programme in management including a course on strategic management in its curriculum.

Table 1.2 Strategic management in Indian companies.

Till 1980 : Pre-Liberalisation Stage : Strategic Management on Government Fringes
• Subsuming enterprise objectives into the national planning framework.
• Capabilities in generating and grabbing opportunities,
• High diversification, non-competitive scales, and weak technology.
• Secretive & one man Strategic Management Process.
From 1980 to 2000 : Liberalisation Stage: Transitional Euphoria and Reality Check
• 'Foreign complex' governed strategy.
• Strategy of focus through rationalisation and operations improvement.
• Strategy of growth through acquisitions, internationalisation and product market expansion.
• Employing international consulting firms in strategic management process.
From 2000-2010 : Post-Liberalisation Stage
• Acquire a 'global maverick' mindset
• Synergise entrepreneurial flair and acquire professional skills in Strategic Management.
• Portfolio rationalisation, internalisation and entry into emerging sectors.
• Mobilise resources and ensure adequate growth through existing business.
• De-merge businesses as independent companies and improve market capabilities.
• Development of technology capabilities
• Decentralise organisations, develop institutionalised control mechanism.

Strategic planning or corporate planning had its genesis in India sometimes in the sixties when a number of subsidiaries of multinational companies introduced the process in compliance with their parent companies' directives. Since then quite a few companies have introduced formal planning for a variety of reasons. Some introduced it because their top managements felt that it would help them long-term objectives; some introduced it because of a fad, not wanting to be behind by others, and some others because were directed to do so. Many public sector enterprises adopted corporate planning because they were asked to do so by the Bureau of Public Enterprises, the governmental body that regulates all public enterprises. Despite the facts such firms still constitute a small minority.

On the academic side, research in India on strategic planning has not taken off. There are very few studies on corporate planning practices in India. Of late, some leading Indian management education institutions have begun to offer short duration executives development programmes on corporate planning. A quick examination of the teaching materials used in these programmes clearly shows a predominance of materials originally developed in the United States. This is not surprising because strategic planning at the enterprise level had its genesis there. Strategic planning or corporate planning is a management process which enables a firm's management to explore the future impact of change and make current decisions to move towards the envisioned future. The Western economies, characterized by a rapid rate of change and fierce competition became an ideal home for the development of the concept of corporate planning. The Indian economy till recently provided protection to firms from change through a plethora of regulations which did not provide an impetus for the development of planning orientation. However, this scenario is changing rapidly as a result of increasing liberalization effected by the government in its policies towards industry. A number of industries are now characterized by a high degree of competition, e.g., textile, television, passenger car, two-wheeler, commercial vehicles, cable, paint, etc. It is therefore very likely that strategic planning will be adopted by many firms in the near future.

Corporate planning systems vary from organisation to organisation depending on a variety of factors: environmental conditions, organisational size and complexity, age, top management values and styles, initial trigger for the commencement of planning, etc. Variations in the corporate planning systems across organisations may vary depending upon the size of the organisation. These approaches may be any of the four types: top-down approach, bottom-up approach, hybrid between top-down and bottom-up approaches, team approach.

In firms adopting top-down approach, the planning takes place at the top and the various departments are supposed to do what they are told to do by the top management. In the bottom-up approach, the top management asks the departments or divisions to submit their plains , reviewed by the top management and accepted or sent back to the organizing departments or divisions for modification. The consolidated divisional plans in the case of a decentralized company may not add up to the management's targets. Additional plans are then required to be prepared which might necessitate planning for acquisitions or diversification into highly unrelated business areas.

A combination of top-down and bottom-up approaches is the approach which is generally used in decentralized companies. In firms using this approach the top management provides certain guidelines to the divisions or strategic business units (SBUs). The SBUs are distinct businesses with their own set of resources that can be managed in a manner reasonably independently of other businesses within a firm. The top management guidelines are sufficiently broad to permit flexibility to the SBUs in developing their plans. There is a vertical communication between the top management and the divisions or SBUs at different phases of the planning process. Broad objectives, policies and strategies may be arrived at through a dialogue and negotiation between the top management and the divisional or SBUs managers.

In small centralized firms where lateral communication between the top managers is easier than in large decentralized firms, the chief executive may himself, in collaboration with the senior managers, prepare corporate plans. In some very large firms also this practice has been found to exist.

Differences, in the planning systems in organisations may be in terms of the approaches adopted, as noted earlier, and also the dimensions given below:

- Completeness of planning cycle
- Depth of analysis
- Degree of formality
- Use of staff and corporate planning specialists
- Linkage among plans
- Methods of introducing planning
- Degree of documentation
- Participation of people
- Role of the CEO

Strategic planning involves an extended time-frame, the development of a large percentage of the resources of an organisation, a wide spectrum of activities and a major eventual impact. By merging the two models of planning, long-range planning and environmental scanning to form an interrelated model – the Strategic Planning Model – was formed. The Strategic Planning Model is a tool that helps an organisation in setting up goals or objectives; the analysis of the environment and the resources of the organisation; generation of strategic options and their evaluation; and planning, design and implementation of control systems or monitoring mechanisms. Three-dimensional structure of organisation requires strategic planning, operational planning and tactical planning at respective levels. Many organisations develop strategies at three different levels; corporate-level strategic planning, business-level strategic planning and functional-level strategic planning. The adoption of strategic planning in some of the Indian companies are illustrated here.

1.8 CASE STUDY

1.8.1 Bharat Heavy Electricals Limited (BHEL)

Several enterprises in India, both in the private and public sectors, have introduced strategic planning in their organisations. With increasing liberalization of government policies and consequently the enhancement role of competition, corporate planning in India is likely to pick up greater momentum in the future. Bharat Heavy Electricals Limited (BHEL) is one of the earliest enterprises to adopt strategic planning. BHEL is a highly diversified public sector undertaking operating in a number of business sectors: energy, industry, and transportation, the company, with the help of strategic planning, has been able to come to grips with problems of uncertainties created by changing technological and socio-economic environment. Initially, strategic planning in BHEL had short-term orientation, however, in recent times this had changed into a long-term one. Besides, strategic plans are comprehensively prepared. The company views itself as an engineering company with emphasis on marketing. The corporate planning and development division, which is organized around various functions, is responsible for total corporate planning activity in the organisation.

Planning had commenced at BHEL from the very beginning. Till 1969, planning was done with a short-term orientation. The real efforts in the direction of long-term planning were started during 1970-71. Beginning in 1973-74 efforts were made to build systems for comprehensive planning, programming and budgeting. A corporate plan was developed and circulated among executives. Initially, revenue budgets for each division were prepared for two-years so as to achieve linkage between short-term and long-term plans. Frequent discussions were held, functional and cross-functional committees were appointed for achieving integration between head office and the divisions. The organisation's structure was changed to transform the company from manufacturing orientation to an engineering orientation with an increased emphasis on marketing. A Corporate Planning and Development division was created at the corporate level with each division having its own planning and development cell. The Corporate Planning and Development Division was placed under the charge of an Executive Director. The division was organized around the following groups: investment and facilities planning long range planning, operations planning, and optimization and modelling. The investment and facilities planning group was responsible for company-wide investment programmes.

Various activities included project formulation and appraisal, coordination of review committees, project monitoring and preparation of annual capital projects. The long-range planning group was responsible for environmental analysis, review and appraisal of long-term plans, review of integrating devices, transfer of technology, collaboration, subject licensing and training. Operations planning included analysis of performance budgets, coordination of operations, monitoring, project management studies for industrial projects, production coordination and materials management. The optimization and modelling group was responsible for undertaking the development of various models using quantitative techniques and studies relating to optimal utilization and scheduling of machines and facilities, investment analysis and energy modelling.

The Corporate Planning and Development Division was responsible for directing and coordinating the total planning activity in the organisation. But the basic inputs into the plan were generated by the activity in the organisation. But the basic inputs into the plan were generated by the various units. Each division prepared its long-term plans keeping in view its relevant environment. Each division also developed product plans, which included an analysis of technological gaps and action required for bridging the gaps. Based on these technology plans of the units, a corporate technology plan was prepared which provided direction for technology acquisition and/or development. Product plans and divisional plans were reviewed, evaluated coordinated and integrated into sectoral plans.

1.8.2 Development of Strategic Consultancy in India

The Tata Strategic Management Group (TSMG) was founded in 1991, it operated exclusively in the strategy area and worked mostly with Tata group of companies. Today, it is spread over several industries, and has clients from all over India and around the world. It advises clients in the areas of strategy formulation, strategy deployment, performance improvement and business analytics. It works silently, and behind the scenes. But it has been transforming the face of businesses across industries, functions and geographies. According to TSMG chief executive Raju Bhinge, company's vision, "Our goal is to be the leading Indian multinational management consulting firm, with at least 10 lines of business, a presence in 10 countries and over 50 per cent of revenues from outside India." Currently, TSMG is offering management consulting services in West Asia (Dubai, Saudi Arabia and Yemen) and South Asia (Sri Lanka and Bangladesh). This is in addition to India entry studies for clients across the globe (North America, Europe / UK and South East Asia).

TSMG is a Indian-owned management consulting firm. It has created a niche for itself, and enjoys a unique positioning. But the journey has not been an easy one. Though the goodwill enjoyed by the Tata brand did provide the right credentials and helped the company establish its roots, the real challenge has been finding clients outside the group. Competitors of Tata group of companies, for example, were reluctant to work with TSMG, fearing a conflict of interest. And, considering the number of areas the 93-company group has a presence in, this has been an enormous handicap. But TSMG did find a way out, by moving into sectors where the group was not represented. In the final analysis, this limitation has proved to be a blessing in disguise. TSMG put in an extra effort to carve out a foothold and prove its mettle. Of course, being an Indian company with Tata values had its advantages too. As against a McKinsey or a Deloitte, clients were happy to work with a company that delivered quality, was available through the planning and deployment stages of the project, and was affordable too. The other factor that went in its favour was that though it was easy to commission a McKinsey or Deloitte for a project plan, it was very, very expensive to retain their services right through implementation. With TSMG, on the other hand, each project created a kind of symbiosis; the client got a consulting company that would willingly be a partner in implementation, while TSMG gained learning that were much richer than their western counterparts could gather.

One of the first projects that TSMG took up within the group was a strategy study for the Tata Oil Mills (TOMCO), which culminated in its sale to Hindustan Lever. Next came the study for restructuring of Voltas, the strategy study for Lakmé which led to the sale of the cosmetics business to Unilever, the acquisition of Little Woods — a British-owned retail chain in south India — and Trent's entry into apparel retail through Westside and Food & Grocery retail through Star Bazaar. TSMG worked on the acquisition of VSNL, its broadband entry plan and corporate data services growth strategy; it prepared the business plan for the group's entry into consumer electronics retailing, provided JV negotiation and implementation support for the formation of Infiniti Retail. TSMG also worked on the entry plan for theTata Sky satellite television service venture.

From 2005, on the basis of capabilities developed in-house, TSMG began offering some of its services to advanced markets such as the US and the UK. It has three offerings for these markets. One is strategic analysis for understanding country selection, markets, competitors' strategy, etc. The second is financial research, which includes work on valuation, equity, fixed income, etc. Third is statistical optimisation or analytical solutions, which comprises risk modelling and predictive modelling, like fraud in telecom or risk analysis in insurance. With its new business model and internationalisation plans well on track, TSMG has expanded its core competence and is moving into completely new areas of operation. No wonder the company is being ambitious and dreaming big.

A step in this direction was the operational integration of Tata Economic Consultancy Services (TECS) with TSMG in April 2006. TECS's expertise lies in investment advisory, infrastructure and government sectors and perfectly complements the experience TSMG has in strategy. TSMG lacked a focus in infrastructure and government practice, a gap that TECS can fill. Together, their experience could pull in a large number of infrastructure projects.

Infrastructure spends have already seen an upsurge in India and TSMG (along with TECS) has been engaged in six SEZ assignments. While TSMG takes care of positioning and branding, the techno-feasibility aspects – including layout plans and the architecture of the facility – are managed by TECS.

1.8.3 Reliance Industries Ltd

The Reliance Group, founded by Dhirubhai H. Ambani is India's largest private sector enterprise, with businesses in the energy and materials value chain. Group's annual revenues are in excess of US$ 58 billion. The flagship company, Reliance Industries Limited, is a Fortune Global 500 company and is the largest private sector company in India.

Backward vertical integration has been the cornerstone of the evolution and growth of Reliance. Starting with textiles in the late seventies, Reliance pursued a strategy of backward vertical integration – in polyester, fibre intermediates, plastics, petrochemicals, petroleum refining and oil and gas exploration and production – to be fully integrated along the materials and energy value chain. The Group's activities span exploration and production of oil and gas, petroleum refining and marketing, petrochemicals (polyester, fibre intermediates, plastics and chemicals), textiles, retail, infotel and special economic zones. Reliance enjoys global leadership in its businesses, being the largest polyester yarn and fibre producer in the world and among the top five to ten producers in the world in major petrochemical products.

On February 21, 2011, Reliance Industries Ltd and British Petroleum(BP) announced a strategic partnership between the two companies and signed the relationship framework and transactional agreements. The partnership across the full value chain comprises BP taking a 30% stake in 23 oil and gas production sharing contracts that Reliance operates in India, including the producing KG-D6 block. The partnership will aim to combine BP's deep-water exploration and development capabilities with Reliance's project management & operations expertise. The two companies will also form a joint venture (50:50) for sourcing and marketing of gas in India and bid together for incremental opportunities in the deep-water blocks in the east coast of India.

In 2011, Reliance entered into one of the fastest growing opportunities emerging in the U.S. unconventional gas business through three upstream joint ventures. These joint ventures will materially increase Reliance's resources base and provide Reliance with an entirely new platform to grow its exploration and production business while simultaneously enhancing its ability to operate unconventional resource projects in the future.

1.8.4 YES Bank: The Pillar of New Age Banking

YES Bank, India's new age private sector bank, is the outcome of the professional and entrepreneurial commitment of its founder, Rana Kapoor and his top management team. It was established as a state-of-the-art high quality, customer centric, service driven, private Indian bank catering to the future businesses of India. YES Bank has adopted international best practices, the highest standards of service quality and operational excellence, and offers comprehensive banking and financial solutions to all its valued customers. YES Bank has a knowledge driven approach to banking, and a superior customer experience for its retail, corporate and emerging corporate banking clients. YES Bank is steadily evolving as the professionals' bank of India with the long-term mission of "Building the Best Quality Bank of the YES Bank" has exemplified 'creating and sharing value' for all its stakeholders, and has created a differentiated banking paradigm.

Since inception, YES Bank has tried to play a catalytic role in bridging the infrastructure and knowledge gap in various sunrise sectors of the economy. As part of the differentiated strategy, YES Bank has had a strong focus on development banking, as is evident from the cutting-edge work that the bank has done in the area of food & agribusiness, infrastructure, microfinance, and sustainability which in most cases has been first-of-its kind in India. It has focus on governance and good corporate citizenship, actualized through responsible banking approach, stands evidence to YES Bank's strategic vision.

Since inception in 2004, YES BANK has ventured into a '"Full Service Commercial Bank" that has steadily built corporate and institutional banking, financial markets, investment banking, corporate finance, branch banking, business and transaction banking, and wealth management business lines across the country, and is well equipped to offer a range of products and services to corporate and retail customers. YES Bank offers a full-range of client-focused corporate banking services, including working capital finance, specialized corporate finance, trade and transactional services, treasury risk management services, investment banking solutions and liquidity management solutions among others to a highly focused client base. The bank also has a widespread branch network of over 325 branches across 200 cities, with over 312 ATM's and 2 national operating centres in Mumbai and Gurgaon. Since inception, YES Bank has adopted innovative and creative technologies that facilitate robust systems and processes and facilitate in the delivery of world-class banking solutions that significantly improve the business and financial efficiency of their clients.

YES Bank has been recognized amongst the top and the fastest growing bank in various Indian banking league tables by prestigious media houses and global advisory firms, and has received national and international honours for their various businesses including corporate finance, investment banking, treasury, transaction banking, and sustainable practices through responsible banking. The bank has received several recognitions for its world-class IT infrastructure, and payments solutions, as well as excellence in human capital.

1.8.5 YES Bank Brand, Vision and Strategy

YES Bank is pursuing a brand strategy to build one of the finest financial brands in India. YES Bank believes that differentiation begins with its service and trust mark embedded in 'YES', which represents the bank's fundamental goal of being a highly service-oriented financial institution. The endeavour at YES Bank is to provide an unprecedented delightful banking experience to all its customers.

1.8.5.1 Brand cision and commitment

- To be recognised as the "world's best quality bank in India".
- To provide a delightful banking experience to all its customers.
- To be a long-term partner with all stakeholders particularly customers by creating & sharing value.
- To be a solid and trusted financial trust mark backed by two professional promoters and an exceptional management team.

1.8.5.2 Brand pillars

The YES Bank brand is built around 6 key brand pillars, which epitomise the growing strengths of the bank. All communication and advertising has been created around these key brand pillars.

1.8.5.3 Growth

YES Bank's core promise is growth, for it's internal and external stakeholders symbolise in Say YES to Growth.

1.8.5.4 Trust

Promoters, investors and top management team, are all of the highest pedigree with a demonstrated track record, thus inspiring and establishing a Trust Mark - Say YES to Trust.

1.8.5.5 Knowledge driven human capital

It has adopted a knowledge driven entrepreneurial approach to banking and offers financial solutions beyond the traditional realm of banking. The top quality human capital represents the finest talents in Indian banking mobilised from India and abroad.

1.8.5.6 Technology

It is establishing the highest standards in customer service by adopting cutting-edge innovative technology. The only thing constant about its technology is evolution.

1.8.5.7 *Transparency and responsible banking*

It holds transparency and accountability above all else. The bank has established the most stringent corporate governance norms, and is also committed to responsible banking by focusing on sustainability and social responsibility.

1.8.6 YES Bank, enters into strategic partnership with National Collateral Management Services Limited

YES Bank entered into a strategic partnership with National Collateral Management Services Limited (NCMSL), a major agri-infrastructure player in collateral management and warehousing services.The objective of these services will be to assist industries, traders and farmers in financing their capital requirements at all stages of the supply chain, ranging from pre-harvesting to the marketing and export stages. YES Bank will also avail of their premium services such as working capital financing in commodity-based industries, especially agro-based industries. Mr Rana Kapoor, Managing Director & CEO of YES Bank said, "Since inception, YES Bank has adopted a knowledge driven approach with a focus on the emerging sectors of the Indian economy. Food & Agribusiness and Agri Infrastructure have been key focus areas and I truly believe that this partnership with NCMSL will further deliver value to all our stakeholders, and is in accordance with the Bank's Development Banking philosophy. Given the excellent and demonstrated track record of NCMSL, this partnership will enable us to mitigate credit risk for our Commodity Finance product offerings."

YES Bank, through its various initiatives, has consistently highlighted the need to create agri-infrastructure to achieve food security and minimize food wastages by promoting public-private partnership. YES Bank holds a stake in NCMSL, and has also fully underwritten long-term funding requirements of NCMSL to add warehousing capacity across the country.

1.8.7 Hindustan Unilever Limited

Hindustan Unilever Limited (HUL), a subsidiary of Unilever, is India's largest and fast moving consumer goods company. The company offers products in over 20 distinct categories in home, personal care, food and beverages segments. It primarily operates in India. Headquartered in Mumbai, India and employing more than 16,000 people it has acquired a tremendous reputation as one of India's best-managed companies. Despite being the subsidiary of an MNC, HUL was perceived to be more Indian than foreign, in the way it managed its operations. It operated with considerably more autonomy than other subsidiaries in the Unilever system. HUL's origin went back to 1885 when the Lever Brothers set up William Hesketh Lever, in England. In 1888, Lever Brothers entered India by exporting 'Sunlight', its laundry soap. HUL's portfolio of brands included Lux, Lifebuoy, Liril, Surf, Ponds Vaseline, Vim, Clinic All Clear and Axe. Most of these brands had been market leaders for several years in their respective product categories.

In the early 2000s, as HUL struggled to generate growth, brand extension became an important strategic option. HLL extended its popular brands into the premium segment to increase its profits. By early 2003, HUL had launched a number of brand extensions with varying degrees of success. In 2003, in what seemed to be in response to intensifying competition in several segments, HUL decided to strengthen its already overwhelming presence in the talcum powder category where its brand, Ponds Dreamflower, was already the market leader. HUL also extended Lifebuoy, Vaseline and Fair & Lovely to talc category. Over the years, HLL had extended many of its popular brands with varying degrees of success. Some extensions like Clinic All Clear anti-dandruff shampoo to hair oil category had been successful, while others like Ponds Toothpaste had been a dismal failure.

M S Banga, Chairman HUL explained: "I believe that each extension must strengthen the core and the core must remain unchanged. When the core of the equity is in one direction and the product extension is in another and you graft the two, you are unlikely to succeed. The set of peripheral or extended values can be changed over time".

1.8.7.1 Vision of HUL

HUL's vision is to continuously innovate technologies to further reduce water consumption and increase conservation in its operations. Simultaneously, HUL sites will progressively help communities, wherever required, to develop watersheds.

1.8.7.2 Mission of HUL

Unilever's mission is to add vitality to life. We meet everyday needs for nutrition, hygiene, and personal care with brands that help people feel good, look good and get more out of life.

Their deep roots in local cultures and markets around the world give them their strong relationship with consumers and are the foundation for our future growth. We will bring our wealth of knowledge and international expertise to the service of local consumers – a truly multi-local multinational. Our long-term success requires a total commitment to exceptional standards of performance and productivity, to working together effectively, and to a willingness to embrace new ideas and learn continuously.

Exercise

1. Discuss the origin and growth of strategic management.
2. What are the four paradigm shifts which have taken place in the evolution of strategic management? Explain your viewpoint on the relevance of these shifts.
3. The development of strategic management can be traced in four different phases. How have these phases helped in the growth of the discipline. Also explain their importance.
4. Post-Word War II is the period where strategic management has flourished. Explain your viewpoint.
5. The growth of strategic management in India has followed a different route. Explain the significance and importance of the statement.
6. Explain the difficulties encountered in the study of strategic management in India. What were the factors which helped in overcoming these difficulties?

2 Strategic Management Process

2.1 INTRODUCTION

The word "strategy" derive from the Greek word "strateogos"; which means generalship (stratus meaning army) and "ago" (meaning leading/moving). Actually, this word was used in military, here **strategy** refers to the management of troops. Once the enemy has been engaged, attention shifts to schemes and tactics. From here gradually the concept of strategy and the word strategy itself paved its way to the business and management world. In business parlance, there is no definite meaning assigned to it. It is often used to describe the number of things.

Strategy can be seen from different angles be it a perspective, competition, innovation, position, plan, and pattern. Strategy is described as a link between guidelines or goals of higher management on the one hand and plan or actions on the other. A strategy is integrating organisational activities and allocating the scarce resources within the organisational environment so as to meet the present objectives. It should be kept in mind that strategic decisions are not taken in vacuum and that any action undertaken by a firm, will have a reaction from those affected—competitors, customers, employees or suppliers.

Strategy is like the blueprint of decisions an organisation takes in order to achieve its objectives and goals, and plans for achieving these goals, and defines the business the company is likely to persue, the type of economic and human organisation it wants to be, and the contribution it plans to make to its shareholders, customers and society at large.

Understanding strategy is one of the most significant concepts to emerge in the subject of management studies in the recent past. It has come out as a critical input to organisational success and has come in handy as a tool to deal with uncertainties that organisation faces. Strategy has been used as a tool to reduce the ambiguity and provide a solid foundation or theory to conduct a business. Strategy is a convenient way to structure many variables that operarate in organisational context and to understand their interrelationship. It has aided the thinkers and practitioners to formulate their thoughts in an orderly manner and to apply them in practice.

Strategy is a well defined roadmap of an organisation. It defines the overall mission, vision and direction of an organisation. The objective of a strategy is to maximize an organisation's strengths and to minimize the strengths of the competitors. Strategy, in short, bridges the gap between "where we are" and "where we want to be". Strategy, a word of military origin, refers to a plan of action designed to achieve a particular goal. In military usage strategy is distinct from tactics, which are concerned with the conduct of an engagement, while strategy is concerned with how different engagements are linked. How a battle is fought is a matter of tactics: the terms and conditions that it is fought on and whether it should be fought at all is a matter of strategy, which is part of the four levels of warfare: political goals or grand strategy, operations, and tactics. Strategy has been extended beyond its traditional fields, military, business, economics, game theory and other fields.

Different scholars, practioners and consultants have proposed different models and frameworks for analysing strategic choice. It is also important that the organisation has a clear sense of its distinctiveness. According to Michael Porter leading strategy guru, "strategy is about achieving competitive advantage through being different delivering a unique value added to the customer, having a clear and enactable view of how to position yourself uniquely in your industry", for example, in the ways in which Southwest Airlines positions itself in the airline industry and IKEA in furniture retailing, in the way that Marks & Spencer used it. A successful strategy requires that there is fit among a company's activities, that they complement each other, and that they deliver value to the firm and its customers. Strategy is concerned with the match between a company's capabilities and its external environment. Analysts disagree on how this may be done. John Kay argues that strategy is no longer about planning or 'visioning' it is about using careful analysis to understand and influence a company's position in the marketplace. Another leading strategy guru, Gary Hamel, argues that the best strategy is geared towards radical change and creating a new vision of the future in which you are a leader rather than a follower of trends set by others.

2.2 DEFINING THE STRATEGY

Strategy has been defined by different management gurus, practitioners, thinkers and philosophers. Strategy is an action that managers take to attain one or more of the organisation's goals. Strategy is also defined as "general direction set for the company and its various components to achieve a desired state in the future. Strategy results from the detailed strategic planning process." Strategy can also be defined as knowledge of the goals, the uncertainty of events and the need to take into consideration the likely or actual behaviour of others.

Alfred D. Chandler, author of *Strategy and Structure* (1962), in the classic study of the relationship between an organisation's structure and its strategy, defined strategy as "the determination of the basic long-term goals and objectives of an enterprise, and the adoption of courses of action and the allocation of resources for carrying out these goals."

Kenneth Andrews, long-time Harvard professor and editor of the *Harvard Business Review*, published the first edition of *The Concept of Corporate Strategy* in 1971 and updated it in 1980. He defined strategy as "the pattern of decisions in a company that determines and reveals its objectives, purposes or goals, produces the principal policies and plans for achieving those goals, and defines the range of businesses the company is to pursue, the kind of economic and human organisation it is or intends to be, and the nature of the economic and non-economic contribution it intends to make to its shareholders, employees, customers, and communities."

Andrew's definition clearly predicts Mintzberg's attention to outline, preparation, and viewpoint. Andrews also draws a difference between "corporate strategy," which agrees on the businesses in which a company will compete, and "business strategy," which defines the basis of competition for a given business. Thus, he also anticipated "position" as a form of strategy. (Andrews' definition of strategy is rather all-encompassing and is perhaps best viewed as a variation on the military notion of "grand strategy".)

Michael Porter, another Harvard professor, in *Competitive Strategy* (1980) defined competitive strategy as "a broad formula for how a business is going to compete, what its goals should be, and what policies will be needed to carry out those-goals." Porter's competitive strategy is "about being different." He says, "It means deliberately choosing a different set of activities to deliver a unique mix of value." According to Porter strategy is about competitive position, about differentiating yourself from the point of view of the customer, about adding value through a mix of activities different from those used by competitors. In his earlier book, Porter defines competitive strategy as "a combination of the ends (goals) for which the firm is striving and the means (policies) by which it is seeking to get there." Thus, Porter seems to embrace strategy as both plan and position. (In contrast with Andrews' definition, Porter's is much narrower, focusing as it does on the basis of competition.)

Benjamin B. Tregoe and John W. Zimmerman defined strategy as "the framework which guides those choices that determine the nature and direction of an organisation." They also published a book on strategic management "*Top Management Strategy*"in 1980,

In 1994, **Henry Mintzberg**, a professor of management at McGill University, took the entire strategic planning establishment to task in his book, *The Rise and Fall of Strategic Planning*. In effect, Mintzberg declared strategy did indeed have several meanings, all of which were useful. He indicated that strategy is a *plan*, a *pattern*, a *position*, a *perspective* and, he indicated that it can also be a *ploy*, a maneuver intended to outwit a competitor. Henry Mintzberg, points out that people use "strategy" in several different ways, the most common being these four:

1. Strategy is a plan, a "how," a means of getting from here to there.
2. Strategy is a pattern in actions over time; for example, a company that regularly markets very expensive products is using a "high end" strategy.
3. Strategy is position; that is, it reflects decisions to offer particular products or services in particular markets.
4. Strategy is perspective, that is, vision and direction.

Mintzberg argues that strategy emerges over time as intentions collide with and accommodate a changing reality. Thus, one might start with a perspective and conclude that it calls for a certain position, which is to be achieved by way of a carefully crafted plan, with the eventual outcome and strategy reflected in a pattern evident in decisions and actions over time. This pattern in decisions and actions defines what Mintzberg called "realized" or emergent strategy.

John Bryson, professor of planning and public policy at the University of Minnesota published *Strategic Planning for Public and Non profit Organisations* in 1996. Bryson defines strategy as "a pattern of purposes, policies, programs, actions, decisions, or resource allocations that define what an organisation is, what it does, and why it does it."

Robert N. Anthony, author of *Planning and Control Systems* (1965), one of the books that laid the foundation for strategic planning, defines stategy as "the pattern of objectives, purposes or goals and major policies and plans for achieving these goals stated in such a way as to define what business the company is or is to be in and the kind of company it is or is to be."

Igor Ansoff, a well known authority in the field of strategic management , also considered father of strategic management, in his *Corporate Strategy* (1965) explained the concept of strategy as "the common thread among the organisations, activities and product markets, that defines the essential nature of business that the organisation was or planned to be in future". The definition stressed on the commonality of approach that exists in diverse organisational activities including the products and market that define the current and planned nature of business. He gave another definition in 1984 as "Basically a strategy is a set of decision making rules for the guidance of organisational behaviour". This definition has changed drastically what Ansoff had said earlier in 1965.

William Glueck, well known author in strategic management, who was a distinguished Professor of Management at the University of Georgia, defined strategy as "the unified, comprehensive and integrated plan that relates the strategic advantage of the firm to the challenges of the environment and is designed to ensure that basic objectives of the enterprise are achieved through implementation process." The definition lays stress on the following:

- It is a unified, comprehensive and integrated plan.
- Challenges of the environment are seen in the context of strategic advantage.
- Strategy ensures achievement of basic objectives through proper implementation process.

From the definitions discussed above, we may identify the following elements:

- It is a plan or course of action or a set of decision rules.
- It is derived from its policies, objectives and goals.
- It is related to pursue those activities which move an organisation from its current position to a desired future state.
- It is concerned with the requisite resources to implement a plan.

Michael Treacy and Fred Wiersema, authors of *The Discipline of Market Leaders,* in the Harvard Business Review article asserted that companies achieve leadership positions by narrowing, not broadening their business focus. Treacy and Wiersema identify three "value-disciplines" that can serve as the basis for strategy: operational excellence, customer intimacy, and product leadership. As with driving forces, only one of these value disciplines can serve as the basis for strategy. Treacy and Wiersema's three value disciplines are briefly defined below:

(i) Operational Excellence	Strategy is predicated on the production and delivery of products and services. The objective is to lead the industry in terms of price and convenience.
(ii) Customer Intimacy	Strategy is predicated on tailoring and shaping products and services to fit an increasingly fine definition of the customer. The objective is long-term customer loyalty and long-term customer profitability.
(iii) Product Leadership	Strategy is predicated on producing a continuous stream of state-of-the-art products and services. The objective is the quick commercialization of new ideas.

Each of the three value disciplines suggests different requirements. Operational excellence implies world-class marketing, manufacturing, and distribution processes. Customer intimacy suggests staying close to the customer and entails long-term relationships. Product leadership clearly hinges on market-focused R&D as well as organisational nimbleness and agility.

We can summarise strategy as "It is all about integrating organisational activities and utilizing and allocating the scarce resources within the organisational environment so as to meet the present objectives". Strategy can also be defined as knowledge of the goals, the uncertainty of events and the need to take into consideration the likely or actual behaviour of others. Strategy is the blueprint of decisions in an organisation that shows its objectives and goals, reduces the key policies, and plans for achieving these goals, and defines the business the company is to carry on, the type of economic and human organisation it wants to be, and the contribution it plans to make to its shareholders, customers and society at large.

2.3 FEATURES OF STRATEGY

1. Strategy is significant because it is not possible to foresee the future. Without a perfect foresight, the firms must be ready to deal with the uncertain events which constitute the business environment.
2. Strategy deals with long-term developments rather than routine operations, i.e., it deals with probability of innovations or new products, new methods of production, or new markets to be developed in future.
3. Strategy is created to take into account the probable behaviour of customers and competitors. Strategies dealing with employees will predict the employee behaviour.

2.4 STRATEGIC MANAGEMENT – AN INTRODUCTION

Strategic management is all about identification and description of the strategies that managers can carry so as to achieve better performance and a competitive advantage for their organisation. An organisation is said to have competitive advantage if its profitability is higher than the average profitability for all companies in its industry.

Strategic management can also be defined as a bundle of decisions and acts which a manager undertakes and which decides the result of the firm's performance. The manager must have a thorough knowledge and analysis of the general and competitive organisational environment so as to take right decisions. They should conduct a SWOT analysis strengths, weaknesses, Opportunities, and Threats), i.e., they should make best possible utilization of strengths, minimize the organisational weaknesses, make use of arising opportunities from the business environment and shouldn't ignore the threats. Strategic management is nothing but planning for both predictable as well as unfeasible contingencies. It is applicable to both small as well as large organisations as even the smallest organisation faces competition and, by formulating and implementing appropriate strategies, they can attain sustainable competitive advantage.

Strategic management is a way in which strategists set the objectives and proceed about attaining them. It deals with making and implementing decisions about future direction of an organisation. It helps us to identify the direction in which an organisation is moving.

Strategic management is a continuous process that evaluates and controls the business and the industries in which an organisation is involved; evaluates its competitors and sets goals and strategies to meet all existing and potential competitors; and then reevaluates strategies on a regular basis to determine how these have been implemented and whether these were successful or require replacement.

Strategic management gives a broader perspective to the employees of an organisation and they can better understand how their job fits into the entire organisational plan and how it is corelated to other organisational members. It is nothing but the art of managing employees in a manner which maximizes the ability of achieving business objectives. The employees become more trustworthy, more committed and more satisfied as they can correlate themselves well with each organisational task. They can understand the reaction of environmental changes on the organisation and the probable response of the organisation with the help of strategic management. Thus, the employees can judge the impact of such changes on their own job and can effectively face the changes. The managers and employees must do appropriate things in appropriate manner. They need to be both effective as well as efficient.

One major role of strategic management is to incorporate various functional areas of the organisation completely, as well as to ensure these functional areas harmonize and get together well. Another role of strategic management is to keep a continuous eye on the goals and objectives of the organisation.

Strategic management consists of the analysis, decisions, and actions an organisation undertakes in order to create and sustain competitive advantages. This definition captures two main elements that go to the heart of the field of strategic management.

First, the strategic management of an organisation entails three ongoing processes: *analysis, decisions*, and *actions*. That is, strategic management is concerned with the *analysis* of strategic goals (vision, mission, and strategic objectives) along with the analysis of the internal and external environment of the organisation. Next, leaders must make strategic decisions. These *decisions*, broadly speaking, address two basic questions: What industries should we compete in? How should we compete in those industries? These questions also often involve an organisation's domestic as well as its international operations. And last are the *actions* that must be taken. Decisions are of little use, of course, unless they are acted on. Firms must take the necessary actions to implement their strategies. This requires leaders to allocate the necessary resources and to design the organisation to bring the intended strategies to reality. As we will see in the next section, this is an ongoing, evolving process that requires a great deal of interaction among these three processes.

Second, the essence of strategic management is the study of why some firms outperform others. Thus, managers need to determine how a firm is to compete so that it can obtain advantages that are sustainable over a lengthy period of time. That means focusing on two fundamental questions: *How should we compete in order to create competitive advantages in the marketplace?* For example, managers need to determine if the firm should position itself as the low-cost producer, or develop products and services that are unique which will enable the firm to charge premium prices or some combination of both.

Managers must also ask how to make such advantages sustainable, instead of highly temporary, in the marketplace. That is: *How can we create competitive advantages in the marketplace that are not only unique and valuable but also difficult for competitors to copy or substitute?*

Ideas that work are almost always copied by rivals immediately. In the 1980s, American Airlines tried to establish a competitive advantage by introducing the frequent flyer programme. Within weeks, all the airlines did the same thing. Overnight, instead of competitive advantage, frequent flyer programmes became a necessary tool for competitive parity, not competitive advantage. The challenge, therefore, is to create competitive advantage that is sustainable.

Michael Porter argues that sustainable competitive advantage cannot be achieved through operational effectiveness alone. Most of the popular management innovations of the last two decades—total quality management (TQM), just-in-time (JIT), benchmarking, business process reengineering, outsourcing all are about operational effectiveness. Operational effectiveness means performing similar activities better than rivals. Each of these is important, but none leads to sustainable competitive advantage, for the simple reason that everyone is doing them. Strategy is all about being different from everyone else. Sustainable competitive advantage is possible only through performing different activities from rivals or performing similar activities in different ways. Companies such as Wal-Mart, Southwest Airlines, and IKEA have developed unique, internally consistent, and difficult to imitate activity systems that have provided them with sustained competitive advantage. A company with a good strategy must make clear choices about what it wants to accomplish. Trying to do everything that your rivals do eventually leads to mutually destructive price competition, not long-term advantage.

2.5 DEFINING STRATEGIC MANAGEMENT

Strategic management has been defined by various thinkers, philosophers and practitioners. Strategic management can be defined as the formal process for defining company vision & mission, assess internal & external environment, formulate strategies under resource constraints, implement strategies, evaluate the strategies. Strategic management is the art and science of formulating, implementing and evaluating cross function decision that enable the business to achieve its objectives.

Lamb Robert (1984): Strategic management is an ongoing process that evaluates and controls the business and the industries in which the company is involved; assesses its competitors and sets goals and strategies to meet all existing and potential competitors; and then reassesses each strategy annually or quarterly [i.e., regularly] to determine how it has been implemented and whether it has succeeded or needs replacement by a new strategy to meet changed circumstances, new technology, new competitors, a new economic environment, or a new social, financial, or political environment."

Learned (1965): It is the study of the functions and responsibilities of general management and the problems which affect the character and success of the total enterprise.

Schendel and Hofer (1979): Strategic management is a process that deals with the entrepreneurial work of the organisation, with organisational renewal and growth, and, more particularly, with developing and utilizing the strategy which is to guide the organisation's operations.

Bracker (1980): Strategic management entails the analysis of internal and external environments of firms to maximize the utilization of resources in relation to objectives.

Jemison (1981): Strategic management is the process by which general managers of complex organisations develop and use a strategy to co-align their organisation's competence and the opportunities and constraints in the environment.

Van Cauwenbergh and Cool (1982): Strategic management deals with the formulation aspects (policy) and the implementation aspects (organisation) of calculated behaviour in new situations and is the basis for future administration when repetition of circumstances occurs.

Schendel and Cool (1988): Strategic management is essentially work associated with the term entrepreneur and his function of starting (and given the infinite life of corporations) renewing organisations.

Fredrickson (1990): Strategic management is concerned with those issues faced by managers who run entire organisations, or their multifunctional units.

Teece (1990): Strategic management can be defined as the formulation, implementation, and evaluation of managerial actions that enhance the value of a business enterprise.

Rumelt, Schendel, and Teece (1994): Strategic management is about the direction of organisations, most often, business firms. It includes those subjects of primary concern to senior management, or to anyone seeking reasons for success and failure among organisations.

Bowman, Singh, and Thomas (2002): The strategic management field can be conceptualized as one centred on problems relating to the creation and sustainability of competitive advantage, or the pursuit of rents.

Table 2.1 Strategic principle of some companies.

Dell	*Be direct*
eBay	*Focus on trading communities*
General Electric	*Be number one or number two in every industry in which we compete, or get out*
Southwest Airlines	*Meet customers' short-haul travel needs at fares competitive with the cost of automobile travel*
Vanguard	*Unmatchable value for the investor-owner*
Wal-Mart	*Low prices, every day*

Source Arit Gadiesh and James Gilbert, "Frontline Action," *Harvard Business Review*, May 2001, p. 74.

2.6 PHASES OF STRATEGIC MANAGEMENT PROCESS

Strategic management process normally followed in an organisation is presented in Fig. 2.1 above. There are four essential phases of strategic management process. In different companies these phases may have different nomenclatures and the phases may have a different sequence, however, the basic content remains the same. The four phases can be listed as below.

1. Establishing strategic intent
2. Formulation of strategies.
3. Implementation of strategies.
4. Evaluation of strategies.

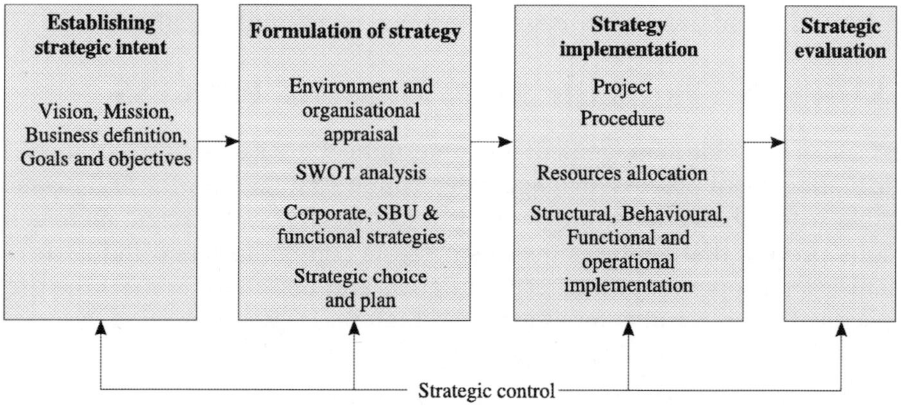

Fig. 2.1 Comprehensive model of strategic management process

Strategic management process starts with the establishment of strategic intent, where- by the firm clearly indicates the position it wants to achieve in future. This is demonstrated by defining its vision, mission goals and objectives. The next phase is related with formulation of strategy. Here the company carries out the environmental and organisational appraisal and SWOT analysis in order to find out the different opportunities and threats as well to ascertain their strength and weaknesses so that they can avail the opportunities and ward off the threats. This analysis gives the companies various strategic analyses and the firms choose their alternative carefully. The internal and external scan helps in selecting the strategic factors. These have to be reviewed and redefined in relation to the mission and objectives. At this stage a set of strategic alternatives are generated. The best strategic alternative is selected and implemented through programmed budgets and procedures.

The strategy implementation requires the company to divide various plans, sub-plans, project implementation, budget formulation, allocation of resources and functional plans. This phase is succeeded by evaluation of strategies. It may not be possible to draw a clear line of difference between each phase, and the change-over from one phase to another is gradual. The next phase in the sequence may gradually evolve and merge into the following phase. An important linkage between the phases is established through a feedback mechanism or corrective action. The feedback mechanism results in a course of action for revising, reformulating, and redefining the previous phase. The process is highly dynamic and compartmentalization of the process is difficult. The changeover is not clear and there is overlap between the boundaries of different phases.

The strategic management formulation and implementation normally vary from company to company, from product to product, many times even with the changing environment within and outside the organisation, and various other factors. Often large firms use detailed strategic management models whereas smaller firms use simpler models. Small businesses concentrate on planning steps compared to larger companies in the same industry. Large firms have diverse products, operations, markets, and technologies and hence they have to essentially use complex systems. Despite that companies have different structures, systems, product profiles, etc. Various components of models used for analysis of strategic management are quite similar.

2.7 STEPS IN STRATEGIC MANAGEMENT PROCESS

The purpose of strategic management is to determine the organisation's strategy. Through strategic management process, managers determine strategies for the organisation which will enable it to achieve its strategic goals and objectives . Strategic management is a continuous process that analyses the business, its competitors and industries in which the organisation is operating, it determines goals and objectives to meet the present and future needs of its own and competitor's and then reassesses each strategy.

Strategic management process has the following four steps:

- Environmental Scanning
- Strategy Formulation
- Strategy Implementation
- Strategy Evaluation

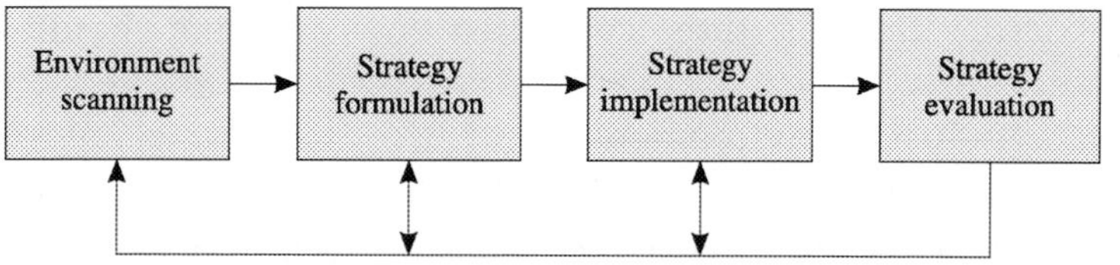

Fig. 2.2 Steps in strategic management process

Step 1 Environmental Scanning

Environmental scanning is the process of collecting, scrutinizing and providing information for strategic purposes. It helps in analysing the internal and external factors influencing an organisation. After the environmental analysis process, the strategist should evaluate it on a continuous basis and devise ways to improve it. Organisational environment consists of both external and internal factors. Environment is scanned to find out the development taking place and forecast the factors that will influence organisational success. Environmental scanning refers to possession and utilization of information about occasions, patterns, trends, and relationships within an organisation's internal and external environment. It helps the managers to decide the future path of the organisation. Environmental scanning helps in identifying the threats and opportunities existing in the environment. While formulating strategy, the organisation must take advantage of the opportunities and minimize the threats. A threat for one organisation may be an opportunity for another.

Internal analysis of the environment: It is the first step of environment scanning. This includes employee interaction with other employees, employee interaction with management, manager interaction with other managers, and management interaction with shareholders, access to natural resources, brand awareness, organisational structure, main staff, operational potential, etc. Also, discussions, interviews, and surveys can be used to assess the internal environment. Analysis of internal environment helps in identifying strengths and weaknesses of an organisation.

External analysis of the environment: External environment of the organisation is dynamic more competitive, and there are rapid changes in the external environment, information from external environment adds crucial elements to the effectiveness of long-term plans. As environment is dynamic, it becomes essential to identify competitors' moves and actions. Organisations have also to update the core competence and internal environment as per external environment. Environmental factors are infinite, hence, organisation should be agile and vigilant to accept and adjust to the environmental changes. For instance, monitoring might indicate that an original forecast of the prices of the raw materials that are involved in the product are no more credible, which could imply the requirement for more focused scanning, forecasting and analysis to create a more trustworthy prediction about the input costs. In a similar manner, there can be changes in factors such as competitor's activities, technology, market tastes and preferences.

While in external analysis, three correlated environments should be studied and analysed:

- immediate/industry environment
- national environment
- broader socio-economic environment/macro-environment

Examining the industry environment needs an appraisal of the competitive structure of the organisation's industry, including the competitive position of a particular organisation and its main rivals. Also, an assessment of the nature, stage, dynamics and history of the industry is essential. It also implies evaluating the effect of globalization on competition within the industry. Analysing the national environment needs an appraisal of whether the national framework helps in achieving competitive advantage in the globalized environment. Analysis of macro-environment includes exploring macro-economic, social, government, legal, technological and international factors that may influence the environment. The analysis of organisation's external environment reveals opportunities and threats for an organisation. Strategic managers must not only recognize the present state of the environment and their industry but also be able to predict its future positions so as to take advantage of the opportunities and ward off the threats likely to occur in future.

Step 2 Strategy Formulation

Strategy formulation is the process of choosing the most appropriate course of action for the realization of organisational goals and objectives and thereby achieving the organisational vision. The process of strategy formulation basically involves six main steps. Though these steps do not follow a rigid chronological order, however they are rational and can be followed in this order. These steps are:

1. **Setting Organisations' Objectives:** The key component of any strategy is to set the long-term objectives of the organisation. The strategy is the medium for achieving organisational objectives. Objectives indicate the position the organisation want to achieve where as strategy indicates the path or the process of reaching there. Strategy includes both, setting of objectives as well the medium to be used to realize those objectives. Thus, strategy is a wider term which believes in the manner of deployment of resources so as to achieve the objectives. While fixing the organisational objectives, it is essential that the factors which influence the selection of objectives must be analysed before the selection of objectives. Once the objectives and the factors influencing strategic decisions have been determined, it is easy to take strategic decisions.
2. **Evaluating the Organisational Environment:** The next step is to evaluate the general economic and industrial environment in which the organisation operates. This includes a review of the organisation's competitive position. It is essential to conduct a qualitative and quantitative review of an organisation's existing product line. The purpose of such a review is to make sure that the factors important for

competitive success in the market can be discovered so that the management can identify their own strengths and weaknesses as well as their competitors' strengths and weaknesses. After identifying its strengths and weaknesses, an organisation must keep a track of competitors' moves and actions so as to discover probable opportunities of threats to its market or supply sources.

3. **Setting Quantitative Targets:** In this step, an organisation must practically fix the quantitative target values for some of the organisational objectives. The idea behind this is to compare with long-term customers, so as to evaluate the contribution that might be made by various product zones or operating departments.
4. **Aiming in Context with the Divisional Plans:** In this step, the contributions made by each department or division or product category within the organisation is identified and accordingly strategic planning is prepared for each sub-unit. This requires a careful analysis of macroeconomic trends.
5. **Performance Analysis:** Performance analysis includes discovering and analyzing the gap between the planned or desired performance. A critical evaluation of the organisation's past performance, present condition and the desired future conditions must be done by the organisation. This critical evaluation identifies the degree of gap that between the actual position and the long-term aspirations of the organisation. The organisation also tries to estimate its probable future condition if the current trends continue.
6. **Choice of Strategy:** This is the ultimate step in strategy formulation. The best course of action is chosen after considering organisational goals, organisational strengths, potential and limitations as well as the external opportunities.

Step 3 Strategy Implementation

Strategy implementation converts the chosen strategy into organisational action so as to achieve strategic goals and objectives. Strategy implementation is the process where organisation develops, utilizes, and amalgamates organisational structure, control systems, and culture to follow strategies that lead to competitive advantage and better performance. Organisational structure allocates special value developing tasks and roles to the employees and states how these tasks and roles can be correlated so as maximize efficiency, quality, and customer satisfaction—the pillars of competitive advantage.

Creating organisational structure for implementing strategy alone is not sufficient to motivate the employees, an efficient organisational control system is also required. The control system gives powers to the managers with motivational incentives for employees as well as feedback on employees and organisational performance.

Following are the main steps in implementing a strategy:

- Creating an appropriate organisation structure for implementing the strategy successfully.
- Allocation of resources to strategy related activities.
- Making policies suitable to strategy implementation.
- Employing best policies and programmes for improvement in the organisation.

- Devising incentives and reward systems according to the accomplishment of results.
- Making use of strategic leadership.

Excellently formulated strategies will fail if they are not properly implemented. Also, it is essential to note that strategy implementation is not possible unless there is stability between strategy and each organisational dimension such as organisational structure, reward structure, resource-allocation process, etc.

Step 4 Strategy Evaluation

Strategic evaluation is the final phase of strategic management. Strategy evaluation is as significant as strategy formulation because it demonstrates the efficiency and effectiveness of the strategic plans in achieving the stated goals and objectives. The strategic managers can also assess the appropriateness of the current strategy in today's dynamic world with socio-economic, political and technological innovations. The significance of strategy evaluation lies in its capacity to coordinate the task performed by managers, groups, departments, etc., through control of performance. Strategic evaluation is significant because of various factors such as developing inputs for new strategic planning, the urge for feedback, appraisal and reward, development of the strategic management process, judging the validity of strategic choice, etc.

2.8 STEPS IN THE PROCESS OF STRATEGY EVALUATION

1. **Fixing benchmark of performance:** The first thing a strategist has to do in strategy evaluation is to set the standards or benchmarks. While determining the benchmark, strategists have to determine: what benchmarks to set, how to set them and how to express them. In order to determine the benchmark performance to be set, it is essential to discover the special requirements for performing the main task. The performance indicator that best identify and express the special requirements might then be determined to be used for evaluation. The organisation can use both quantitative and qualitative criteria for comprehensive assessment of performance. Quantitative criteria includes determination of net profit, ROI, earning per share, cost of production, rate of employee turnover, etc. Among the qualitative factors are subjective evaluation of factors such as skills and competence, risk taking potential, flexibility, etc.
2. **Measurement of performance:** The standard performance is a benchmark with which the actual performance is to be compared. The reporting and communication system help in measuring the performance. If appropriate means are available for measuring the performance and if the standards are set in the right manner, strategy evaluation becomes easier. But various factors such as managers' contribution are difficult to measure. Similarly, divisional performance is sometimes difficult to measure as compared to individual performance. Thus, variable objectives must be created against which measurement of performance can be done. The measurement must be done at the right time else evaluation will not meet its purpose. For measuring the performance, financial statements like balance sheet, profit and loss account must be prepared on an annual basis.

3. **Analysing Variance:** While measuring the actual performance and comparing it with standard performance there may be variance which must be analysed. The strategists must mention the degree of tolerance limits between which the variance between actual and standard performance may be accepted. The positive deviation indicates a better performance but it is quite unusual exceeding the target always. The negative deviation is an issue of concern because it indicates a shortfall in performance. Thus, in this case the strategists must discover the causes of deviation and must take corrective action to overcome it.
4. **Taking Corrective Action:** Once the deviation in performance is identified, it is essential to plan for a corrective action. If the performance is consistently less than the desired performance, the strategists must carry a detailed analysis of the factors responsible for such performance. If the strategists discover that the organisational potential does not match with the performance requirements, then the standards must be lowered. Another rare and drastic corrective action is reformulating the strategy which requires going back to the process of strategic management, reframing of plans according to new resource allocation trend and consequent means going to the beginning point of strategic management process.

2.9 DIFFERENT LEVELS OF STRATEGY

Strategy may operate at different levels of an organisation—corporate level, business level, and functional level.

2.9.1 Corporate Level Strategy

Corporate level strategy occupies the highest level of strategic decision-making and covers actions dealing with the objective of the firm, acquisition and allocation of resources and coordination of strategies of various SBUs for optimal performance. It is believed that strategic decision making is the responsibility of top management. At the corporate level, the board of directors and chief executive officers are involved in strategy making. Corporate planners and consultants may also be involved. Mostly, corporate level strategies are futuristic, innovative and pervasive in nature. Decisions like spreading the range of business interests, acquisitions, diversification, structural redesigning, mergers, takeovers, liquidations come under corporate level strategies. Top management of the organisation makes such decisions. The nature of strategic decisions tends to be value-oriented, conceptual and less concrete than decisions at the business or functional level.

2.9.2 Business-Level Strategy

Business-level strategy is applicable in those organisations, which have different businesses and each business is treated as strategic business unit (SBU). The fundamental concept in SBU is to identify the discrete independent product/market segments served by an organisation. Since each product/market segment has a distinct environment, a SBU is created for each such segment. For example, Reliance Industries Limited operates in textile fabrics, yarns, fibres, and a variety of petrochemical products. For each product group, the nature of market in terms of customers, competition, and marketing channel differs.

Therefore, it requires different strategies for its different product groups. Thus, where SBU concept is applied, each SBU sets its own strategies to make the best use of its resources (its strategic advantages) given the environment it faces. At such a level, strategy is a comprehensive plan providing objectives for SBUs, allocation of resources among functional areas and coordination between them for making optimal contribution to the achievement of corporate-level objectives. Such strategies operate within the overall strategies of the organisation. The corporate strategy sets the long-term objectives of the firm and the broad constraints and policies within which a SBU operates. The corporate level will help the SBU define its scope of operations and also limit or enhance the SBUs operations by the resources the corporate level assigns to it. There is a difference between corporate-level and business-level strategies.

For example, in an organisation corporate strategy usually applies to the whole enterprise, while business strategy, less comprehensive, defines the choice of product or service and market of individual business within the firm. In other words, business strategy relates to the 'how' and corporate strategy to the 'what'. Corporate strategy defines the business in which a company will compete preferably in a way that focuses resources to convert distinctive competence into competitive advantage.

Corporate strategy is not the sum total of business strategies of the corporation but it deals with different subject matter. While the corporation is concerned with and has impact on business strategy, the former is concerned with the shape and balancing of growth and renewal rather than in market execution.

2.9.3 Functional-Level Strategy

Functional strategy, as is suggested by the title, relates to a single functional operation and the activities involved therein. Decisions at this level within the organisation are often described as tactical. Such decisions are guided and constrained by some overall strategic considerations. Functional strategy deals with relatively restricted plan providing objectives for specific function, allocation of resources among different operations within that functional area and coordination between them for optimal contribution to the achievement of the SBU and corporate-level objectives. Below the functional-level strategy, there may be operations-level strategies as each function may be divided into several sub-functions. For example, marketing strategy, a functional strategy, can be subdivided into promotion, sales, distribution, pricing strategies with each sub-function strategy contributing to functional strategy.

Table 2.2 Examples of different strategies.

Level of Strategy	*Definition*	*Example*
Corporate strategy	Market definition	Diversification into new product or geographic markets
Business strategy	Market navigation	Attempts to secure competitive advantage in the existing product or geographic markets

Contd...

Contd...

Functional strategy	Support of corporate strategy and business strategy	Information systems, human resource practices, and production processes that facilitate achievement of corporate and business strategy

Source http://www.enotes.com/management-encyclopedia/strategy-levels

Exercise

1. What do you understand by concept of strategy? Many writers have defined strategy in different ways but there is a common thread in each definition. Explain your viewpoint.
2. There are different levels at which strategy operates. Explain the type of strategy and the levels at which they operate. Explain the relative importance of each level of strategy.
3. The comprehensive model of strategic management process gives the detailed outlook of the strategic management. Explain your viewpoint on the issue and explain the working of the model
4. Each stage/phase of strategic management process is interlinked and it is essential that management takes care of the each stage carefully. Give your viewpoint and explain process by giving suitable examples.
5. Study the strategic management process adopted by any two leading organisations of an industry. What similarities or dissimilarity you find in it. Explain them briefly.

3 Establishment of Hierarchy of Strategic Intent

3.1 INTRODUCTION

Strategic intent refers to the purposes the organisation strives for. These may be expressed in terms of a hierarchy of strategic intent. The framework within which firms operate, adopt a predetermined direction and attempt to achieve their goal is provided by a strategic intent. Strategic intent is a high-level statement of the means by which an organisation will achieve its vision. It is a statement of design for creating a desirable future (stated in present terms). Simply put, a strategic intent is the company's vision of what it wants to achieve in the long term. Any successful business—large or small—didn't achieve success on good ideas alone. Succeeding in the business world requires what professors Gary Hamel and C.K. Prahalad term "strategic intent". Strategic intent, they explain, is a business' long-term, far-reaching goal. In order to determine your business' strategic intent, you must not only consider what you want in the next five or ten years, but what you want to accomplish in a 50-year timeframe.

Gary' Hamel defined strategic intent as "*An ambitious and compelling dream which provides emotional and intellectual energy for the company and defines the journey to the future.*" Strategic intent is the firm's ability to create a clear and compelling statement or vision for itself, and to communicate that vision to its employees, shareholders and most importantly, its customers. When anyone in a firm asks "why are we here", it should be easy to answer. Does your firm have a compelling dream that provides emotional energy and defines its journey to the future? If not, how can you possibly expect to innovate? The firms innovate best when they have a clear strategic intent, the examples are, Apple and Google.

An organisational vision is directional and long-term and a strategic intent is a bridge and a milestone to the strategic vision. Hamel and Prahalad in their book *Competing for the Future defined strategic* intent as "ambitious and compelling". A strategic intent mobilizes the entire organisation effort in the right direction thru the key milestones. A strategic intent is energized thru its strategic architecture. The strategic architecture channelizes all the organisational resources and communications towards the strategic intent. Yet a sense of stretch is needed - as current resources and capabilities are not sufficient for the task. Gaps in technology and the intellectual expertise and skills required to move ahead are identified and acquired speedily (core competence).

In strategic intent, organisations must define what they want to do and why they want to do this. This "why they want to do" underlies the end result that is likely to be achieved through what they want to do. In management literature, this end result is referred to as strategic intent. Strategic intent is defined as "Strategic intent envisions a desired leadership position and establishes the criterion the organisation will use to chart its progress."

A few examples will illustrate how **strategic intent helps move a company towards its vision.**

3.1.1 Coca-Cola

For example, decades ago, Coca-Cola's strategic intent was for there to be a Coke within the reach of every human being on the planet. This seemed like a crazy idea at the time, but think about how prevalent Coke products are these days. By setting a vision of the future and developing long-term goals, Coca-Cola made enormous strides in developing their brand.

3.1.2 NEC versus GTE

NEC (Nippon Electric Company) a much smaller Japanese company overtook and repulsed a much larger American company GTE (now Verizon). NEC set their strategic intent as 'computers and communication' or 'C&C'. They forecasted that five to eight years ahead these two disparate technologies will merge and innovative products would flow out from this fusion such as mobile communication devices that have captured the markets. They developed the appropriate strategic architecture (road map) that guided their strategic moves to acquire appropriate companies and technologies to fill their own gaps.

3.1.3 Komatsu versus Caterpillar

Komatsu announced an aggressive strategic intent – the battle cry of **'Maru-C'** or **'Encircle Caterpillar'**. Rather than face Caterpillar frontally they did a pincer movement by setting up assembly plants in places like Brazil and Mexico. They also established business relationships with multiple countries – thereby encircling Caterpillar. A stunning win over its seemingly invincible American opponent was achieved. The success made Komatsu a world power in earth-moving machinery. An interesting point that surprised many was that Komatsu's strength and energies came from an organisational culture that is known to be **non-aggressive and harmonious** — typical of the Japanese culture and heritage.

3.1.4 Tata's Nano

The leadership at Tata's set a strategic intent to manufacture the world's cheapest car a **'people's car'** within a time-bound schedule – despite all odds.

3.1.5 Tata Consultancy Services

Tata Consultancy Services's strategic intent is ***"flawless execution."*** TCS's clients and the market are increasingly viewing TCS as a superb operator with a well-polished and effective talent management model. Many view TCS as the leading example of how to deliver consistently high quality work at attractive prices. It invests significantly in becoming its clients' strategic delivery partner, including focused initiatives to build relevant IP. TCS has been very thoughtful in segmenting the market and organizing its business by vertical industries.

3.1.6 Infosys

Infosys' strategic intent is being a ***"transformation partner."*** Infosys has invested considerably in building a large and impactful consulting organisation in order to combine consulting with delivery to achieve transformation for its clients. That objective is being bolstered by its 3.0 co-creation strategy, which is a move further down the line of transformation. It is achieving many successes, and is considered a formidable player. The ongoing transition of senior leadership at Infosys seems to be well along its path with clear succession planning underway and significant investment to develop the next generation of management.

Yet, Infosys is taking a challenging strategic intent route as it is squarely emulating Accenture's strategy. The transformation hill is steep to climb because of the difficulties involved in combining consulting with delivery. Accenture has done well, but others have struggled to succeed along this path. Infosys' ability to resolve the key conflicts between consulting and delivery will determine its long-term success.

3.1.7 Cognizant

Cognizant's strategic intent is superb ***"client engagement."*** Cognizant is simply the best at working with clients on business issues. Its secret sauce is the ability to engage with clients on problems and pull through consulting and delivery services. This is different than Accenture's and Infosys' transformation model in that Cognizant focuses on the client relationship and client engagement by working through the suite of problems currently on the client's plate, as compared to game-changing transformation. Cognizant invests significantly in highly empowered onsite teams, and its delivery and consulting organisations are tuned to be responsive to the client engagement team. This overall model and strategy is quite different than any other Indian or multinational firm, and is achieving significant growth and profitability returns.

3.1.8 Canon

Canon rallied its organisation with the war cry **'Beat Xerox'.** It set an objective to manufacture a small home-copier priced reasonably as against Xerox large expensive machines.

3.1.9 DuPont

DuPont asked their scientists to help the corporation "**invent its ways**" out of the company financial malaise.

3.1.10 Texas Instruments

Texas Instruments exhorted their employees to "find new businesses in the white spaces" between existing business units. In other cases, employees were urged to move the firm beyond the constraints of current customers, current business models, and current technologies to explore growth in new directions.

3.1.11 Analog Devices

Analog Devices urged their employees to get into a new industry (the automotive industry).

3.1.12 Otis Elevators

Otis Elevators asked their people to pursue an industry "**Holy Grail**" (to find a way to move people up and down a mile-high building).

3.1.13 ir Product

ir Product urged their employees to lead the next industry **transforming breakthrough** (gas separation technology).

3.1.14 Microsoft

Microsoft stated its strategic intent as "a provider of operating systems to personal computers that weren't made by IBM."

3.1.15 Apple

Apple has a different strategic intent. They are focused on providing a higher-level experience to a much smaller audience with more specific requirements. A PC OEM with a similar intent refers to "skimming the cream" from the market, which I believe Apple does in spades. Apple has done a great job in the past identifying a customer base and satisfying those needs.

3.1.16 Reliance Industries

In 1970s, Dhirubhai Ambani told one of his close colleagues, "do you know who these Tatas and Birlas are? We have to get past them one day. I have inherent desire to become number one industrialist of the country. This intent of Dhirubhai became the strategic intent of RIL. RIL pursued its growth strategy relentlessly. RIL always believed, ***"If you want to become world-class company, you must have world-class technology and world-class people.*** For world-class technology, RIL acquired best-in-class technology.

Exhibit 3.1 Strategic Intent of Dabur India Ltd.

Dabur intends to significantly **accelerate profit table growth**. To achieve their strategic intent, the company will:

- Focus on growing our core brands across categories, reaching out to new geographies, within and outside India, and improve operational efficiencies by leveraging technology.
- Be the preferred company to meet the health and personal grooming needs of our target consumers with safe, efficacious, natural solutions by synthesizing our deep knowledge of ayurveda and herbs with modern science.
- Provide our consumers with innovative products within easy reach.
- Build a platform to enable Dabur to become a global ayurvedic leader.
- Be a professionally managed employer of choice; attracting, developing and retaining quality personnel.
- Be responsible citizens with a commitment to environmental protection.
- Provide superior returns, relative to our peer group, to our shareholders.

Exhibit 3.2 Strategic Intent of Indian Oil Corporation

Indian Oil Corporation (IOC) is the largest Indian company engaged in the business of crude oil refining and offers a variety of products related to oil sector. IOC's strategic intent consists of the following elements in the order given below:

Vision: IOC aims to achieve international standards of excellence in all aspects of energy and diversified business with focus on customer delight through quality products and services.

Mission: Maintaining national leadership in oil refining, marketing, and pipeline transportation.

Objectives: Focusing on cost, quality, customer care, value addition, and risk management.

Exhibit 3.3 Strategic Intent of Tata International

Vision: To be the "Leading International Business Company" of the country and "International Arm" of the Tata Group, with a significant overseas reach, presence and linkages, and with focus on facilitating globalization of Tata Group's core business.

Mission: Promote the Tata Brand Equity internationally. It wants to achieve its vision and mission by undertaking the following activities:

- Promote internationally, products and services from the Tata Group, as also from other utility conscious Indian and overseas companies.
- Source world-class products and services for marketing in India. Promote businesses with strong comparative advantages for the company, and upgrade the company's strengths in the areas of technology, marketing, and finance.

Contd...

- Identify global sources of technology, marketing, and finance and other services to facilitate strategic alliances, joint ventures, and collaborations of Tata Group, in India and overseas.
- Be a market driven company and continually strive to meet stakeholder value and satisfaction through consistent quality in all areas of our operations.
- Nurture and develop human resources, to enable us to undertake the challenges of leadership and innovation, in our areas of activity.

Exhibit 3.4 Strategic Intent of Tata Steel

The Tata Group is known for its ethos of aligning business opportunities with nation building. One of India's most reputed companies from the Tata Group, set up in 1907, Tata Steel is Asia's first and India's largest private sector steel company. Tata Steel is among the lowest cost producers of steel in the world. Its strategic intent is expressed in terms of a hierarchy of vision, mission, strategic goals and strategies.

Vision 2007:

- To seize the opportunities of tomorrow and create a future that will make it an economic value added positive company
- To continue to improve the quality of life of our employees and the communities we serve
- Revitalize the core business for a sustainable future
- Venture into new businesses that will own a share of our future
- Uphold the spirit and values of Tatas towards nation building.

Mission Statement: Consistent with the vision and values of the founder Jamshetji Tata, Tata Steel strives to strengthen India's industrial base through the effective utilization of staff and materials. The means envisaged to achieve this are high technology and productivity, consistent with modern management practices. Tata Steel recognizes that while honesty and integrity are the essential ingredients of a strong and stable enterprise, profitability provides the main spark for economic activity. Overall, the company seeks to scale the heights of excellence in all that it does in an atmosphere free from fear and thereby reaffirms its faith in democratic values.

Strategic Goals:

- Move from commodities to brands
- EVA positive core business
- Continue to be lowest cost producer of steel
- Value creating partnerships with customers and suppliers
- Enthused and happy employees
- Sustainable growth

For people mobilization, RIL adopted the approach, "If you are a big fish, small pond will not suit you. Come and join the best-in-class company". The result is: RIL has a very high percentage of Indian repatriate employees. For mobilizing financial resources, RIL relied on public participation.

3.2 HIERARCHY OF STRATEGIC INTENT

The hierarchy of strategic intent includes the following elements.

- A broad *vision* of what the organisation should be.
- The organisation's *mission*
- The strategic *objectives* and specific goals to be pursued relentlessly
- The *plans* that are developed to accomplish the intentions of management in a concrete way.

The elements of the hierarchy specify the pious intentions, lofty ideals and clear-cut ideas that serve to unify the energy and forces scattered throughout an organisation. They are beginning points for any formal planning process, but they also provide the sense of direction necessary to assure that incremental behaviour culminates in overall progress. Strategic intent is said to have expressed effectively when people believe fervently in their products and industry and when they are focused totally on their firm's ability to outperform its competitors.

The logic, uniqueness and discovery that make the firm's strategic intent come to life are vitally important for their employees. They have to understand, believe and live according to it. Strategy should be a stretch exercise, not a fit exercise. Expression of strategic intent is to help individuals and organisations share the common intention to survive and continue or extend themselves through time and space.

3.3 DEVELOPING A STATEMENT OF STRATEGIC INTENT

Strategic intent takes the form of a number of corporate challenges, specified as short-term projects and opportunities. The strategic intent must convey a significant stretch for your company, a sense of direction, discovery, and opportunity that can be communicated as worthwhile to all employees. It should not focus so much on today's problems, which are normally dealt with by company visions and missions, but rather on tomorrow's opportunities.

The strategic focus is the starting point for developing a statement of strategic intent. A statement of strategy must become then a statement of design through which the principles, processes and practices of an organisation are developed. These statements must represent the whole as seen from any location in the organisation. Strategic intent should specify the competitive factors, the factors critical to success in the future. The end result should lay beyond the present planning period.

Firm's strategic intent should also be accompanied by intermediate goals against which company achievements can be measured. It cannot be developed in a one-day strategy session, it should develop and mature with time. Discovery and detection of opportunity serve as platforms for developing strategic intent. It is based on a vision of how the future will look in 10-15 years. A strategic intent creates a picture of the customer daily life and describes discontinuities and anticipated changes from the world of today. It describes future customer's needs and the success factors required for meeting these needs. "To achieve great things, you need ambitious visions. And it does not matter that vision cannot be laid out in details. It is the direction that counts."

3.4 THE MAIN TENETS OF STRATEGIC INTENT

- **Sense of Direction:** Includes an understanding about the long-term market or competitive position that a firm aims to build over the next decade. Your sense of direction should be a view of the future that conveys a unifying and personalizing sense of direction.
- **Sense of Discovery:** The strategic intent should retain a sense of discovery and excitement about the future. This helps create a competitively unique outlook and gives employees the opportunity to explore new competitive territory.
- **Sense of Destiny:** Strategic intent has an emotional edge to it and it should be a goal that both you and your employees perceive as inherently worthwhile.

3.5 PROCESS OF ESTABLISHING STRATEGIC INTENT

- **Define the Strategic Intent:** In terms of its vision, mission, goals and objectives.
- **Set the Challenges:** Find appropriate challenges and communicate them to the entire workforce. These challenges are the means to get into the Strategic Intent. (For example: Suppose the Strategic Intent of Google is: Allow end users to access all of the information of the Internet with the click of a mouse. A strategic challenge could be: Come up with a search engine capable of producing accurate search results.)
- **Empowerment of the Strategic Intent:** The strategic intent works best when everyone is invested in its goals. Managers and business owners should keep in mind the "wisdom of the anthill" and challenge traditional downward communications styles.

Defining the strategic intent clarifies objectives for both firm and their employees. By setting out their strategic intent, firm makes clear their company's goals and help set the path for future successes.

Hamel and Prahalad indicate in their article titled "Strategic Intent" that few western companies have been able to implement strategic intent in their organisations despite deploying considerable resources for corporate strategic planning. To consider why this might be true it is first necessary to look at the differences in methodologies. Strategic planning determines how to allocate the resources a company has to improve its profitability. Management looks at internal and external opportunities and risks and determines a course for the organisation. Conversely, strategic intent is explained as "Companies that have risen to global leadership over the past 20 years invariably began with ambitions that were out of all proportion to their resources and capabilities.

But they created an obsession with winning at all levels of the organisation and then sustained that obsession over the 10- to 20-year quest for global leadership. They term this obsession "*strategic intent.*"" (Hamel, 2005). Further "... *strategic intent* is more than simply unfettered ambition. (Many companies possess an ambitious *strategic intent* yet fall short of their goals.) The concept also encompasses an active management process that includes focusing the organisation's attention on the essence of winning, motivating people by communicating the value of the target, leaving room for individual and team contributions, sustaining enthusiasm by providing new operational definitions as circumstances change, and using *intent* consistently to guide resource allocations." (Hamel, 2005).

Most managers embrace the concept of winning over time that is one of the basic principles behind strategic intent, but managers of American companies get caught up in the short-term strategic planning of their organisations. Hamel and Prahalad contend that "*Strategic intent* is stable over time. In battles for global leadership, one of the most critical tasks is to lengthen the organisation's attention span. *Strategic intent* provides consistency to short-term action, while leaving room for reinterpretation as new opportunities emerge" (Hamel, 2005). One key to the differences is the time horizon. Most American companies only look at short-term strategic planning, concentrating on the next earnings report or profit statement, unlike international companies that tend to take a long-term approach to business planning.

One possible reason for this difference is the way organisations look at their employees, including management and executive level positions. In America, employees are considered resources to be exploited and discarded when they are not needed. Companies expect employees to work long hours and sacrifice for the company with no job security beyond the next pay check. Companies even go through bankruptcy proceedings to eliminate the pension and health benefits they promised to employees. The employees in turn have no loyalty to the companies and are always working to maximize their bonuses because they have no guarantee of future employment. Employees, who invent new products, or means of improving productivity, often do not want to offer these ideas to their employers for little or no compensation and quit their jobs to start new businesses using their ideas to compete with their former employers.

In contrast many foreign corporations (for example, the Japanese) believe in loyalty to the workers and treat their employees as partners in business rather than as resources. Jobs are guaranteed and retirement benefits are secure. Employees are asked to participate in decision processes and are rewarded for ideas that help the company. Employees are provided training by the company and loyalty is expected in both directions. Profitability is measured for the long term and strategic intent can be implemented. Hamel and Prahalad go further by indicating "Reciprocal responsibility means shared gain and shared pain. In too many companies, the pain of revitalization falls almost exclusively on the employees least responsible for the enterprise's decline. Too often, workers are asked to commit to corporate goals without any matching commitment from the top management — be it employment security, gain sharing, or an ability to influence the direction of the business. This one-sided approach to regaining competitiveness keeps many companies from harnessing the intellectual horsepower of their employees" (Hamel, 2005).

Using the analogy that Hamel and Prahalad present in their article indicating that strategic intent is like a marathon; one could also state that American companies strategic planning is like running a 100-yard dash. They just do it over and over again with each new quarter.

3.6 VISION

Aspirations, expressed as strategic intent, should lead to an end; otherwise they would just be castles in the air. That end is the vision of an organisation or an individual. It is what the firm or a person would ultimately like to become. For instance, some of you, say in 10 years, or maybe even earlier, would like to become general managers managing an SBU in a large, diversified multinational corporation. Or some others among you would like to believe that you will be an entrepreneur in the next 10 years owning your own company dealing with IT services and employing cutting edge technology to serve a global clientele. A firm thinks like that too.

Tata Steel says about its vision: "Tata Steel enters the new millennium with the confidence of a learning, knowledge based and happy organisation. We will establish ourselves as a supplier of choice by delighting our customers with our service and our products. In the coming decade, we will become the most cost competitive steel plant and so serve the community and the nation." A vision, therefore, articulates the position that a firm would like to attain in the distant future. Seen from this perspective, the vision encapsulates the basic strategic intent.

3.6.1 Understanding Vision

A vision is more dreamt of than it is articulated. This is the reason why it is difficult to say what vision an organisation has. Sometimes it is not even evident to the entrepreneur who usually thinks of the vision. By its nature, it could be as hazy and vague as a dream that one experienced the previous night and is not able to recall perfectly in broad daylight. Yet it is a powerful motivator to action. And it is from the actions that a vision could often be derived. Henry Ford wished to democratize the automobile when he visualized that an affordable vehicle could be available for the masses. Walt Disney probably wanted to make people happy.Vision is what keeps the organisation moving forward. Vision is the motivator in an organisation. It needs to be meaningful with a long-term perspective so that it can motivate people even when the organisation is facing discouraging odds.

The world over, backwards and forwards in history, just one thing has fired the imagination of the people: a vision of future that promises to right today's wrongs, a graphic image of a time when injustice, impoverishment will have disappeared. Moses used the vision of a landmark of milk and honey to motivate his people to set off for the promised land. India's freedom fighters used the vision of a country free of its colonial rulers to wrest independence. In the corporate context, vision refers to an inspirational picture of a future that can be created, offering clarity amidst confusion, hope against despair, and unity of purpose amidst diversity of personal causes.

3.6.2 Defining Vision

Vision has been defined in several different ways. Kotter (1990) defines it as a "description of something (an organisation, corporate culture, a business, a technology, an activity) in the future". El Namaki (1992) considers it as a "mental perception of the kind of environment an individual, or an organisation, aspires to create within a broad time horizon and the underlying conditions for the actualization of this perception". Miller and Dess (1996) view it simply as the "category of intentions that are broad, all inclusive, and forward thinking". The common strand of thought evident in these definitions and several others available in strategic management literature relates to 'vision' being future aspirations that lead to an inspiration to be the best in one's field of activity. Burt Nanus, a well-known expert of organisational vision, has defined vision as "a realistic, credible, and attractive future for an organisation." Oren Harari, another expert on organisational vision, defines vision as "A vision describes a set of ideals and priorities, a picture of the future, a sense of what makes the company special and unique, a core set of principles that the company stands for, and a broad set of compelling criteria that will help define organisation success." Robert H. Miles, in an article entitled "Corporate Transformation", states that all successful transformations are Vision led. He defines Vision in the following way: "It requires projection into a dimly outlined future. It requires the creation of goals that stretch the organisation beyond its current comprehension and capabilities".

3.6.3 The Benefits of Having a Vision

Parikh and Neubauer (1993) point out the several benefits accruing to an organisation having a vision. Here is what they say:

- Good visions are inspiring and exhilarating.
- Visions represent a discontinuity, a step function and a jump ahead so that the company knows what it is to be.
- Good visions help in the creation of a common identity and a shared sense of purpose.
- Good visions are competitive, original and unique. They make sense in the marketplace, as they are practical.
- Good visions foster risk taking, experimentation and long-term thinking.
- Good visions represent integrity; they are truly genuine and can be used for the benefit of people.

3.6.4 Characteristics of a Good Vision

- **Realistic:** A vision must be based on reality to be meaningful for an organisation; it should not be merely day-dreaming but a dream to be converted into reality.
- **Credible:** A vision must be believable to be relevant to members of the organisation concerned. One of the purposes of a vision is to aspire those in the organisation to achieve a level of excellence, and to provide direction for their actions.

- **Attractive:** A vision must be attractive so as to inspire and motivate organisational members. People must want to be a part of the future that is envisioned for the organisation.
- **Futuristic:** A vision is not for the present; it is for the future. Simply, a vision is not where an organisation is now but where it will be in future.
- **Idealistic:** A vision should be realistic so that people believe that it is achievable, but idealistic enough so that it cannot be achieved without stretching.

A good vision clarifies direction of the organisation concerned (where the organisation go in future?) A good vision inspires organisational members and encourages commitment from them. A good vision reflects the uniqueness of the organisation, its distinct competence, what it stands for, and what it is able to achieve. A good vision is appropriate for the organisation and for the times. It implies that the vision should be consistent with organisation's values and culture and its place in its environment. A good vision is well articulated and easily understood by those who are responsible to convert it into reality.

3.6.5 Examples of Vision

Reliance Industry Ltd: To achieve global leadership in polymers, fibres and resin businesses through innovative research and technology development in materials, products, and applications through efficient, disciplined, target-oriented, and cost-effective research and development activities.

Infosys: To be a globally respected company that provides best of breed software solutions by best-in-class people.

Dabur: Dedicated to the health and well-being of every household.

Tata Tea: To be India's foremost tea-based beverage company.

Sony: Its vision rests on the values of encouraging individual creativity and its determination to be a pioneer.

Bank of Baroda: Becoming a technology enabled customer centric financial services.

3.6.6 Role of Vision in Strategy Formulation

Vision provides clue about where the organisation is heading for in future. Since various strategies try to ensure that the organisation reaches its destination, these should be in accordance with the vision. Vision of an organisation tries to place it in a unique position which requires unique actions. These actions are defined by various strategies. Since vision is a source of inspiration to organisational members and encourages them for commitment, they tend to give their full contributions in strategy formulation and implementation.

3.6.7 Developing a Vision

Developing a vision is like having a dream to be converted into reality in future. Following steps are relevant for development of a vision:

- Conducting a vision audit – to assess the current direction and momentum of the organisation.
- Targeting the vision – What are the boundaries and constraints to the vision? What must be the vision accomplish? What critical issues must be addressed in the vision?
- Setting the vision context – Identifying what the organisation's future environment might look like.
- Developing the future scenarios
- Generating the alternative visions
- Choosing the final vision

3.6.8 Vision Statement

When you begin the process of strategic planning, visioning comes first. Martin Luther King, Jr. said, "I have a dream," and what followed was a vision that changed a nation. That famous speech is a dramatic example of the power that can be generated by a compelling vision of the future. A vision is a guide to implementing strategy. Visions are about feelings, beliefs, emotions and pictures.

A vision statement answers the question, "What will success look like?" The pursuit of this image of success is what motivates people to work together. It is an important requirement for building a strong foundation. When all the employees are committed to the firm's visions and goals, optimum choices on business decisions are more likely.

The process and outcomes of visioning is to develop an effective basis for business strategy. The foresight of the organisation is to fit the strengths of the organisation with the demands, to make the organisation highly competitive with growth and profits as the rewards.

The vision statement should be built around certain core values. Thus, Sony's vision rests on the values of encouraging individual creativity and its determination to be a pioneer. Such core values reflect how you want your future to look, the timeless principles to be followed while running the show irrespective of what happens in and around the organisation. Values, thus, are the essential glue of vision. Since a company's different business may need to operate with different strategies, it's their shared values that will prevent them from going in different directions. The vision statement should also spell out the core purpose of an organisation very clearly. For example, we know that 3M's purpose is to solve problems innovatively; Nike wants to provide the experience and emotion of competition – winning and crushing competitors; Blue Star wants to provide world class engineering products and services. Unstructured inputs could be taken from everyone developing the corporate vision. Companies like Larsen & Toubro, Crompton Greaves, Gujarat Heavy Chemicals typically follow certain steps in this regard:

1. Elicit ideas from employees as to how their dream organisation should be like in terms of characteristics.
2. Combine these with the company's core values and purpose to build the vision statement.

3.6.9 Creating a Shared Vision

Most managers, nowadays, talk about a shared vision, meaning that individuals from across the organisation have a common mental image and a mutually supported set of aspirations that serve to unite their efforts. People at all levels must share a common inspirational image that compels them to give their best and realize their own dreams. The vision once finalized, must be injected into the veins of the organisation, being shared, owned and lived by every single person in the company.

3.7 MISSION

Organisation, whether it is a business or a social organisation, or university or government organisation, takes resources from the environment and converts the resources into goods and/or services. It supplies the goods and services to the environment at an acceptable price. The organisations which make a net contribution to the society are called 'legitimate.' The organisations should protect this legitimacy over the long run. Thus, every organisation comes into being and exists to accomplish something in the larger environment, and that purpose or mission is clear at the start. As time passes, echnology, consumer preferences and other environmental factors change, the firm's produces new products or renders new services and the interest of the management and employees changes. This results in significant change in the firm. The original mission or purpose may become irrelevant in the long run due to changes in internal environment of the organisation and/or appropriate external environment. When these changes take place, the management must search for new purpose or new state of the mission or restate the original mission.

3.7.1 Understanding Mission

Organisations relate their existence to satisfying a particular need of the society. They do this in terms of their mission. Mission is a statement which defines the role that an organisation plays in a society. It refers to the particular needs of that society for instance, its information needs. A book publisher and a magazine editor are both engaged in satisfying the information needs of society but they do it through different means. A book publisher may aim at producing excellent reading material while a magazine editor may strive to present news analysis in a balanced and unbiased manner. Both have different objectives but an identical mission.

3.7.2 Definitions of Mission

A mission was earlier regarded as the scope of the business activities a firm pursues. The definition of mission has gradually expanded to represent a concept that embodies the purpose behind the existence of an organisation. Whether developing a new business or reformulating direction for an ongoing company, the basic goals, characteristics and philosophies that will shape a firm's strategic posture must be determined. Thus, company's mission will guide future executive action.

Company's mission can be defined as the fundamental, unique purpose that sets a business apart from other firms of its type and identifies the scope of its operations in product and market term. It embodies the business philosophy of strategic decision-makers; implies the image the company seeks to project; reflects the firm's self-concept; indicates the principal product or service areas and primary customer needs the company will attempt to satisfy. In short, the mission describes the product, market and technological areas of emphasis for the business.

- Thompson defines mission as the "essential purpose of the organisation, concerning particularly why it is in existence, the nature of the business it is in, and the customers it seeks to serve and satisfy."
- Hunger and Wheelen say that mission is the "purpose or reason for the organisation's existence".
- According to John Pearce "mission is an enduring statement of purpose that distinguishes one firm from other similar firms".

37.3 Characteristics of a Mission Statement

A mission statement incorporates the basic business purpose and the reason for its existence by rendering some valuable functions for the society. An effective mission statement should possess the following characteristics.

- **Feasible:** The mission should always aim high but it should not be an impossible statement. The mission should be realistic and achievable. Its follwers must find it to be credible. Feasibility depends upon the availability of the resources to achive mission. In the 1960, NASA had a mission to land on the moon. It was a a feasible mission that was ultimately achieved. UTI declared its mission as "to encourage saving and investment habits among common man". By providing tax relief under Sec 88c, the investment upto 1 lakh in UTI is exempted from income tax. Hereby, common man's savings habit is encouraged by UTI.
- **Precise:** A mission statement should not be so narrow as to restrict the organisation's activities nor it should be too broad to make it meaningless. Take the example of mission of Hero Cycle, "Our mission is to achieve synergy between technology, systems and human resources to produce the products and services that meet quality, performance and price aspirations of our customers. While doing so, we maintain the highest standards of ethics and societal responsibilities".
- **Clear:** A mission statement should lead to action. It should not be just a high sounding set of platitude meant for publicity purposes. For example, *India Today* saw it self as "complete news magazine" now visualise its mission as "making sense of India. "BSNL's mission of 'connecting India' leads it to a variety of services with varied tariff structures so as to cater to the preferences of mobile phone users. HUL's mission to "add vitality to life" leading to various strategic actions of being the largest consumers goods company in India.
- **Motivating:** The mission should motivate the employees for action and they should feel it worthwhile working for such an organisation. For example, India Post's mission is to "meet the expectations of the customer' with dedication, devotion and enthusiasm". The mission of the Bank of Baroda, "pursing best

global practices for delivering added value to customers" is an important purpose for its existence and serving its customers.

- **Distinctive:** A mission statement will indicate the major components of the strategy to be adopted. The mission should be unique. When HCL defines its mission as 'to be a world class competitor' it creates a unique place in the minds of Indian personal computer users who across personal computers of MNCs on most of the occasions. Similarly, the mission of Bajaj Auto "value for money for years" is quite distinct from its competitors and now it believes in "inspiring confidence".
- **Indicates major components of strategy:** The mission statement of IOC emphasizes petroleum refining, marketing and transportation with international standards and modern technology. It indicates that IOC is going to adopt diversification strategy in future.

The mission provides direction to insiders and outsiders on what the firm stands for. It is the guiding star for any firm.

3.7.4 Need for an Explicit Mission

The mission contains few specific directives, only broadly outlines or implied objectives and strategies. It is a statement of attitude, outlook and orientation rather than of details and measurable targets. To ensure unanimity of purpose within the organisation it serves as.

- To provide a basis for motivating the use of the organisations' resources;
- To develop a basis, or standard, for allocating organisational resources;
- To establish a general tone or organisational climate;
- To serve as a focal point for those who can identify with the organisation's purpose and direction;
- To facilitate the translation of objectives and goals into a work structure involving the assignment of tasks; and
- To specify organisational purposes and the translation of these purposes into goals.

3.7.5 Formulating a Mission Statement

The process of defining the mission for a specific business can be understood by thinking about a firm at its inception. The sense of mission is usually based on several fundamental elements.

- Belief that the product or service can provide benefits at least equal to its price.
- Belief that the product or service can satisfy customers' needs.
- Belief that the technology to be used will provide a product that its cost- and quality-competitive.
- Belief that hard work and with the support of others, the business will grow and be profitable.

- Belief that the management philosophy of the business will result in a favourable public image.
- Belief that the entrepreneur's self concept can be communicated and adopted by employees and shareholders.

Most organisations derive their mission statements from a particular set of tasks they are called upon to perform in the light of individual, national or global priorities. Mission statements, whether derived from a set priorities or not, could be formulated either formally or informally. Usually, entrepreneurs lay down the corporate philosophy which the organisation follows in its strategic and operational activities. Such a philosophy may not be consciously and formally stated but may gradually evolve due to entrepreneur's actions. Mission statement could be formulated on the basis of the vision that the entrepreneur decides in the intial stages of the organisation's growth.

Major strategist could also contribute to the development of mission statement . They do it informally, by lending a hand in creation of a particular corporate identity or formally, through discussion and by writing down the mission statement. Chief Executive of the organisation plays a major role in formulating a mission statement both formally and informally. They may set up an executive committee to formally discuss and decide on a mission statement. Consultants may also be called upon to make an in depth analysis of the organisation to suggest an appropriate mission statement. Following examples will illustrate how the mission statement was formulated in these companies.

Scientific Instruments Company Ltd took the help of a management consultant in deciding the company's mission and purposes. In the starting point, the company managers, consultants and chief executives spent a lot of time in identifying the mission of the business. After a lot of discussion, the company decided the mission as "to be a vibrant organisation set on contributing to the scientific and technical progress of the country, keeping its customers and employee satisfied in terms of service and work rewards, giving adequate returns on the investment to the shareholders".

In HCL, a core management team assessed the internal strength and designed a customer centric mission statement for team building, mutual trust, internal customer server equations and empowerment.

In Marico Industries, the mission statement was designed in 1990. The CEO outlined the goals and aspirations after hectic consultation with the senior management. A three-day workshop of managers prepared a four-page mission statement. In 1995 it was rewritten in the light of changed circumstances.

Ranbaxy Laboratories realised in 1993 that the competition in pharmaceutical industry is becoming very tough and it cannot survive by selling generic drugs. After a year of deliberation on future direction, strategies involved and past experience, CEO enunciated the mission and communicated extensively thoughout the company, down to the level of its workers.

3.7.6 Mission Statements

Vision is the critical focal point and the beginning to high performance. But obviously a vision alone won't make it happen. Even the most exciting vision will remain only a dream unless it is followed up with striving, building, and improving the organisation through its mission. Why does the organisation exist? What is its value addition? What's its function? How does it want to be positioned in the market and minds of customers? What business is it in? These are all questions of purpose. They deal with the deeper motivations and assumptions underlying the values and purposes and functions.

Mission statements make the organisation different from others. They give meaning to the reason for being, value-add, and define the business of the organisation. As with vision and values, the mission should have clear answer to the above questions. It should arouse a strong sense of organisational identity and business purpose. Through some of these questions often seem deceptively simple, they are not so simple. We need to answer them to prepare a mission statement. For example, the question, "What business are we in?". The implications of making a definitive identification means that the organisation has put boundaries around to give guidance to the strategic direction in which it will move.

Mission Statement of Infosys: "To achieve our objectives in an environment of fairness, honesty, and courtesy towards our clients, employees, vendors and society at large."

Tata Tea: Achieve market and thought leadership for branded tea in India. Be recognized as the foremost innovator in tea and tea based beverage solutions. Drive long-term profitable growth. Co-create enhanced value for all stakeholders. Make Tata Tea a great place to work.

Times of India: "Create & build brands with differentiated content to capture relevant audiences and market the value of these to advertisers to help them sell and strengthen their brands."

3.8 BUSINESS DEFINITION

Understanding business is vital to answering the questions , "What is our Business? Who are our customers? What technology we should use to serve our customers?" Vision and mission statement can use the ideas generated through the process of understanding and defining business.

A business definition is a clear-cut statement of the business or a set of businesses, the organisation engages in presently or wishes to pursue in future. Then it prescribes the arena in which the organisation will play and compete. Business can be defined along three dimensions – product, customer, and technology. However, whatever dimension is chosen for defining business, it must reflect two features: focus and differentiation. Focus of business may be defined in terms of the kind of functions the business performs rather than the broad spectrum of industry in which the organisation operates. Differentiation in business is how an organisation differentiates itself from others so that the business concentrates on achieving superior performance in the market.

The three-dimensional business definition framework, developed by Harvard Professor Derek F. Abell, is a model that can be used for defining the business of a company. The definition of a business is an issue that should not be taken lightly. In

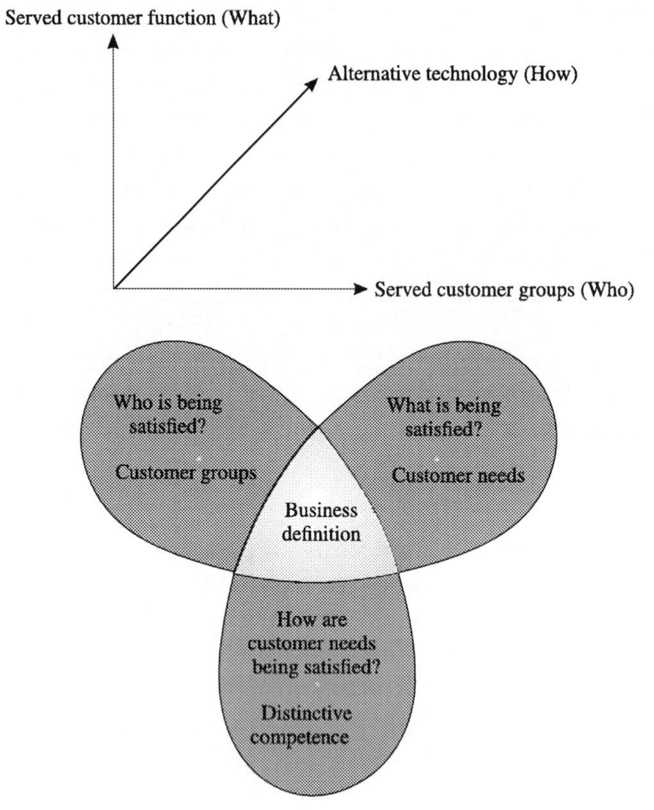

Fig. 3.1 Abell's three-dimensional business definition.

his book *Defining the Business: The Starting Point of Strategic Planning,* Abell says that the standard two-dimensional way of looking at a business (products and markets) has serious flaws. He suggests a three-dimensional model, with the following three axes:

- Served customer groups. Categories of customers. (who)
- Served customer functions. Customer needs. (what)
- Technologies utilized. The way that the needs are being satisfied. (how)

3.8.1 The Context of Defining Business

An organisation must define its business in three contexts:

Customer segment: What is our business is not determined by the producer but by the consumer....by the want the customer satisfies when he buys a product or service Who is the customer? (location, behaviour, how to reach).

Product: Every organisation defines the business it participates in and the product it offers. What does the customer buy?

Technology: Technology consists of equipment, machines, tools and other physical aspects, and sets of activities, methods, and processes used for the production and delivery of product. What does the customer consider value?

Exhibit 3.5 Business Definition of Hero Honda

- **Business definition:** World-class quality auto products that provide the highest level of customer satisfaction.
- **Customer segment:** Individuals who enjoy riding motorcycles with perfection, like speed, style, and fuel economy, located across the country.
- **Product:** It emphasizes world-class quality auto products - presently motorcycles, leaving the scope for adding similar other products in future. Initially, it concentrated on fuel-economy and introduced CD-100 with the slogan "fill it, shut it, forget it". Later additional features have been added.
- **Technology:** The joint venture with Honda of Japan with core competency in automobile engines provided the needed technological edge. Product delivery and after-sales activities have been ensured through a network of dealers armed with service centres backed by qualified technicians trained by the company.

3.9 OBJECTIVES

The accomplishment of purpose or mission of an organisation requires the formulation of a number of objectives. Achievement of the organisational objectives, in turn, requires the formulation and fulfilment of departmental and unit goals. Long-range objectives specify the results that are desired in pursuing the organisation's mission and normally extended beyond the current financial year of the organisation. Long-range objectives are notably speculative for distant years. Short-range objectives are performance targets, normally of less than one-year duration, that are used by the management to achieve the organisation's long-range objectives. The selections of short-range objectives are from an evaluation of priorities relating to long-range objectives. Departmental objectives, both long-range and short-range are formulated based on the respective long-range and short-range objectives of the organisation. Unit objectives are generally specific and are drawn from the departmental objectives.

An objective indicates the result that the organisation expects to achieve in the long run. It is an end result, the end point, something that you aim for and try to reach. It is a desired result towards which behaviour is directed in an organisation. The organisation may or may not reach the desired state, but the chances of doing so are greater if the objectives are framed and understood properly. Objectives are the products of specific concrete thinking. They commit persons and organisations to verifiable accomplishments. Again, objectives determine the scope of future events. They provide the spotlight on the routes over which activities are organized. They serve as reference points to concentrate resources and efforts. They determine what action to take today to obtain results tomorrow. Goals and targets are more precise and expressed in specific terms. They are stated in precise terms as quantitatively as possible. The emphasis in goals is on measurement of progress toward the attainment of objectives. Goals have the following features. They:

- are derived from objectives,
- offer a standard for measuring performance,

- are expressed in concrete terms,
- are time-bound and work-oriented.

3.9.1 Formulating Objectives

The mission and directional course are converted into designated performance outcomes in the process of formulating objectives. Objectives represent a managerial commitment to achieve specified results in a specified period, of time. This clearly spells out the quantity and quality of performance to be achieved, the time period, the process and the person who is responsible for the achievement of the objective.

An organisation's mission statement will be just window-dressing, unless, it is translated into measurable and specific performance targets and managers are pressured to achieve these targets. Thus, objective formulation is a critical step in the strategic management process. It is viewed that, whose managers formulate objectives for each key result area and then actively pursue actions to achieve their performance targets will outperform the companies whose managers operate with hopes and more good intentions. Performance objectives must be stated in quantifiable or measurable terms. They must also contain a deadline for achievement.

3.9.2 Characteristics of Objectives

Objectives have the following features:

- **Objectives Form a Hierarchy:** In many organisations objectives are structured in a hierarchy of importance. There are objectives within objectives. They all require painstaking definitions and close analysis if they are to be useful separately and profitable as a whole. The hierarchy of objectives is a graded series in which an organisation's goals are supported by each succeeding managerial level down to the level of the individual. The objectives of each unit contribute to the objectives of the next higher unit. Each operation has a simple objective which must fit in and add to the final objective. Hence, no work should be undertaken unless it contributes to the overall goal.
- **Objectives Form a Network:** Objectives interlock in a network fashion. They are interrelated and inter-dependent. The concept of network of objectives implies that once objectives are established for every department and every individual in an organisation, these subsidiary objectives should contribute to meet the objectives of the total organisation. If the various objectives in an organisation do not support one another, people may pursue goals that may be good for their own function but may be detrimental to the company as a whole. Managers have to trade off among the conflicting objectives and see that the components of the network fit one another. Because, as rightly pointed out by Koontz, "It is bad enough when goals do not support and interlock with one another. It may be catastrophic."
- **Multiplicity of Objectives:** Organisations pursue multifarious objectives. At every level in the hierarchy, goals are likely to be multiple. For example, the marketing division may have the objective of sale and distribution of products. This objective can be broken down into a group of objectives for the product,

advertising, reach, promotion managers. The advertising manager's goals may include: designing product messages carefully, create a favourable image of the product in the market, etc. Similarly, goals can be set for other marketing managers. To describe a single, specific goal of an organisation is to say very little about it. It turns out that there are several goals involved. This may be due to the fact that the enterprise has to meet internal as well as external challenges effectively. Internal problems may hover around profitability, survival, growth, and so on. External problems may be posed by government, society, stockholders, customers, etc. In order to meet the conflicting various internal and external groups, organisations generally pursue multiple objectives. Moreover, no single objective would place the organisation on a path of prosperity and progress in the long run.

- **Long- and Short-range Objectives:** Organisational objectives are usually related to time. Long-range objectives extending over five or more years are the ultimate or dream objectives for organisations. They are abstractions of the entire hierarchy of objectives of the organisation. For example, planning in India has got objectives like eradication of poverty, checking population growth through birth control, etc. which reflect certain 'ideals' the government wishes to accomplish in the long run. Short-range objectives (one-year goals) and medium-range objectives (two- to five-year period goals), reflect immediate, attainable goals. The short-range and medium-range objectives are the means for achieving long-term goals and the long-term goals supply a framework within which the lower level goals are designed. Thus, all these goals reinforce each other in such a way that the total result is greater than the sum of the efforts taken individually. That is why goal setting is called a "synergistic process". In order to remain viable, every organisation needs to set goals in all three time periods.

3.9.3 Areas of Objectives

Objectives are set for all areas and departments of an organisation. Though the objectives can vary widely from one organisation to another organisation, they can be broadly divided into: profitability, service to customers, employee needs and welfare, and social responsibility. The following are the areas of objectives.

- **Markets:** Objectives are expressed in terms of the market or total rupee sales or total quantity of sales. For example, the objectives of Indian Railways was to increase freight traffic (commercial) to 85% and reduce the freight traffic (military) to 15% in 1997-98 from 60% and 40% respectively.
- **Productivity:** The level of goods and/or services produced by an organisation is relative to the resources used in the production process. Organisations which use fewer resources to produce specified levels of products are said to be more productive than organisations which require more resources to produce at the same level.
- **Innovation:** It is any change made to improve methods of conducting organisational business. Organisational objectives should indicate innovations the organisation desires to implement.

- **Product:** These objectives are expressed in terms of sales and profitability by product line or product, target dates for development of new products and others.
- **Profitability:** Profitability objectives are expressed in terms of profits, return on investment, earning per share, profit to sales, etc. For example, to increase return on investment by 10 % in 1997-98 over 1996-97 financial year.
- **Financial Resources:** These objectives are expressed in terms of the capital structure, new issues of common stock, cash flow, working capital, dividend payments and collection periods.
- **Physical Facilities:** These objectives are expressed in terms of machinery and equipment, square feet, fixed costs, units of production and other measures.
- **Organisation Structure and Activities:** These objectives are stated in terms of changes to be made in the policies of organisation structure or projects to be undertaken.
- **Manager Performance and Development:** These objectives are related to the quality and rate of development of managerial skills, knowledge and performance. Development of managerial performance is very important from the viewpoint of the long-run success of the company and achievement of the other objectives of the company.
- **Employee Performance and Attitude:** These objectives are related to the development of skills, knowledge and performance of non-managerial employees of the company. This area is also related to the development of favourable attitude of the employees towards the organisation. The significance of these considerations should be stressed through the formulation of organisational objectives.
- **Customer Service:** These objectives are related to the quality of the product, pre-sales and post-sales service, delivery times, promptly attending to the customer complaints, price, package and the like.
- **Social Responsibility:** These objectives are related to the obligation of business towards the society with a view to contribute to its welfare. Today, these objectives have become common to all the companies. For example, to contribute to the medical facilities of the community where the company is located.

3.9.4 Importance of Objectives

Why do organisations formulate objectives? And what is their importance? The following four factors explain the need for and importance of objectives.

- **Objectives help to define the organisation in its environment:** The organisations justify their existence to their stakeholders in the environment like customers, government, creditors and society at large.
- **Objectives help in coordinating decisions and decision-maker:** Stated objectives impose some constraints on the employees and modify it towards the desirable direction. It coordinates decision-making process by different employees.

- **Objectives help in formulating strategies:** Mission statements are translated into objectives and objectives are the basis for formulating strategies.
- **Objectives provide standards for assessing organisational performance:** Objectives provide not only the direction to move to the organisation but also provide the ultimate goals and targets that the organisation is expected to achieve. These targets and goals become the standards to judge the organisational performance. Organisations, without clear objectives will not have basis for evaluating their performance or success.

Exhibit 3.6 Case Study of Wal-Mart

In the 1950s, Sam Walton worked in the retail trade for the Chicago based Ben Franklin Stores. It was during this period that he formulated his vision for a discount store. It was a deceptively simple idea: a discount store with wholesale margins on every product, a store that simultaneously offered easy shopping and friendly service. The linchpin, or critical success factor, was that these stores would be situated in small towns. Sam Walton believed that "there was a lot more business in those towns than people ever thought".

At the heart of Walton's vision for Wal-Mart were his personal values of humility, honesty, frugality and trust. Despite his $9 billion family fortune, Sam held onto his Ford truck, casual clothes, modest ranch style house and simple no frills headquarters in out-of-the-way Bentonville.

Walton's personal values were translated into three key business principles:

provide the customer with value and service in a clean and friendly shopping environment,

create a partnership with associates, and

maintain commitment to the community.

The critical and irreplaceable ingredient of Wal-Mart's success were the strengths and virtues of Sam Walton himself — his overriding vision and unwavering values, his courage to take action, and his uncanny ability to motivate and inspire his "associates".

Walton was more than a great leader, he was an astute strategist. He searched with painstaking care for every individual who made up his management team. He sought individuals who believed in the discount concept and were dedicated to working long hours to see the vision become a reality. He created an organisation that thrived on innovation and in an atmosphere where people believed in themselves. He embraced technology as a change agent for innovation and remaining competitive.

The results speak for themselves. Wal-Mart has succeeded in satisfying not only its customers, but its employees, suppliers, investors, and host communities. Wal-Mart outshines the rest of the industry in growth, sales, earnings, margins, and employee and floor productivity.

The paradigm that Sam Walton established has been a winner. The question that remains is, will this paradigm still hold in our rapidly changing world? Or will there come a time when even Wal-Mart will need to break out of its paradigm box?

3.10 SUMMARY

Strategic intent is the leveraging of a firm's internal resources, capabilities and core competence to accomplish the firm's vision, mission and objectives in a competitive environment. The corporate vision has the potential power to focus the collective energy of insiders and to give outsiders a better idea of what an organisation really is. Vision is what keeps the organisation moving forward. The vision statements present the values, philosophies and aspirations. Mission is an enduring statement of purpose that distinguishes one organisation from other similar organisations. Organisation do exist to satisfy a particular need of the society or to fulfill a particular deficiency in the society. A mission statement is a declaration of an organisation's reason of being. Management must take into account three key elements in developing mission statements, viz., history of the organisation, organisation's distinctive competence and the organisation's environment.

The accomplishment of purpose or mission of an organisation requires the formulation of objectives. These objectives are classified into overall organisational objectives, departmental objectives as well as unit level objectives. Based on the time objectives are classified into long-range objectives and short-range objectives. Long-range objectives are notably speculative for distant years. Short-range objectives are performance targets, normally of less than one year duration. Objectives represent a managerial commitment to achieve specified results in a specified period of time.

Exercise

1. Describe the essential characteristics of a mission statement. How is a mission different from a vision?
2. Take the example of any organisation. Define the business of the organisation on three dimensions of business definition. How does it help an organisation to relate with its customers?
3. Objectives are said to be the final frontiers of an organisation. Give your viewpoint and explain the role played by the objectives in an organisation.
4. If you were the CEO of an organisation, how will you define your business, vision and mission of your organisation?
5. Vision is a dream to be solved to stakeholders. Give viewpoint.
6. An organisation has to carefully draft its strategic intent. Do you agree with it? Give your viewpoint.

4 External Environmental Analysis: Tools and Techniques

4.1 INTRODUCTION

Understanding the environment within which the business has to operate, is very important for running a business unit successfully. Because, the environmental factors influence almost every aspect of business, be it its nature, its location, the prices of products, the distribution system, or the personnel policies. Hence, it is important to learn the various components of the business environment, which consists of the economic aspect, the socio-cultural aspects, the political framework, the legal aspects and the technological aspects, etc.

To formulate effective strategies, managers in an organisation need to be aware of realities in the business environment. Strategy formulation thus begins with a scanning of the external as well as internal environment. Analysis of external environment helps to identify the possible threats and opportunities while analysis of internal environment helps to identify strengths, weaknesses and the key people within the organisation. The success of every business depends on adapting itself to the environment within which it functions. For example, when there is a change in the government policies, business has to make the necessary changes to adapt itself to the new policies. Similarly, a change in the technology may render the existing products obsolete, as we have seen that the introduction of computer has replaced the typewriters; colour television has made the black and white television out of fashion. Again a change in the fashion or customers' taste may shift the demand in the market for a particular product, e.g., the demand for jeans reduced the sale of other traditional wear. All these aspects are external factors that are beyond the control of business. So business units have to adapt themselves to changes in order to survive and succeed. Hence, it is necessary to have a clear understanding of the concept of business environment and the nature of its various components.

Environment means the surroundings, external objects, influence or circumstances under which someone or something exists. The environment of any organisation is "the aggregate of all conditions, events and influences the surrounds and affect it". Since the environment influences an organisation in multitudinous ways, its understanding is of crucial importance. The term 'business environment' connotes external forces, factors and institutions that are beyond the control of business and they affect the functioning of a business enterprise.

These include customers, competitors, suppliers, government, and the social, political, legal, technological factors, etc. While some of these factors or forces may have direct influence over the business firm, others may operate indirectly. Thus, business environment may be defined as the total surroundings, which have a direct or indirect bearing on the functioning of business. It may also be defined as the set of external factors, such as economic factors, social factors, political and legal factors, demographic factors, technical factors, etc., which are uncontrollable in nature and affects the business decisions of a firm. The concept of environment can be understood by looking at some of its characteristics.

4.1.1 Characteristics of Business Environment

Business environment shows many characteristics. Some of the important characteristics are briefly described here.

Environment is complex: The environment consists of a number of factors, which are not isolated but interact with each other to create a new set of influence. Hence, it would be complex to comprehend the environment in totality but relatively easier to understand in parts.

Environment is dynamic: The environment is not static, it is constantly changing in nature. Due to many and varied influences operating; there exists a constant dynamism in the environment and there is continuous change as well as its impact on the business.

Environment is multifaceted: The shape and character displayed by the environment depends on the perception of the observer. A similar development in an environment may be viewed as an opportunity by some company and as a threat by some other company.

Environment has far-reaching impact: Environment has far-reaching impact on organisations. The growth and profitability of an organisation depend critically on the environment in which it exists. Any change in environment impacts the organisation in many different ways.

4.1.2 Importance of Business Environment

There is a close and continuous interaction between the business and its environment. This interaction helps in strengthening the business firm and using its resources more effectively. To be more specific, proper understanding of the social, political, legal and economic environment helps in the following ways:

- **Determining Opportunities and Threats:** The interaction between the business and its environment would identify opportunities for and threats to the business. It helps the business enterprises for meeting the challenges successfully.
- **Giving Direction for Growth:** The interaction with the environment leads to opening up new frontiers of growth for the business firms. It enables the business to identify the areas for growth and expansion of its activities.
- **Continuous Learning:** Environmental analysis makes the task of managers easier in dealing with business challenges. The managers are motivated to continuously

update their knowledge, understanding and skills to meet the predicted changes in realm of business.

- **Image Building:** Environmental understanding helps the business organisations in improving their image by showing their sensitivity to the environment within which they are working. For example, in view of the shortage of power, many companies have set up captive power plants (CPP) in their factories to meet their own requirement of power.
- **Meeting Competition:** It helps the firms to analyse competitors' strategies and formulate their own accordingly.
- **Identifying Firm's Strengths and Weakneses:** Business environment helps to identify the individual strengths and weaknesses in view of the technological and global developments.

4.1.3 Importance of Environmental Scanning

The environmental survey is necessary to:

- Learn about events and trends in the environment and project the future position in each factor of environment.
- To identify the favourable and unfavourable factors in the environment from the standpoint of the firm.
- To figure out opportunities and threats hidden in environmental trends and events.
- To assess the scope of various opportunities and shortlist ones which have the potential of becoming promising business
- To formulate strategy in line with opportunities.

4.1.4 Internal and External Environments

The internal environment refers to all factors within an organisation that impact strength or causes weakness of strategic nature. The external environment refers to all factors outside the organisation which provide opportunity or pose threat to the organisation. The environment in which an organisation exists can therefore be described in terms of the strengths and weakneses existing in the internal environment of the organisation and the opportunities and threats in the external environment. These four environmental influences can be described as follows.

- **Strength** is an inherent capacity which an organisation can use to gain strategic advantage. Strengths of a company are its resources and capabilities that can lead to competitive advantage. Examples of strength are: good reputation among customers, resources, assets, people, experience, knowledge, data base, brand image, uniqueness of its products or services, superior technology, capabilities, etc.
- **Weakness** is an inherent limitation or constraint which creates strategic disadvantages. Weaknesses are resources and capabilities that a company does not possess, to the extent that their absence places the firm at a competitive

disadvantage. Examples of weakness are: gaps in capabilities, financial constraints, low morale of employees, overdependence on a single product line.

- **Opportunity** is a favourable condition in the organisation's environment which enables it to consolidate and strengthen its position. Opportunities are conditions in the broad and operating environments that allow a firm to take advantage of organisational strengths, overcome organisational weaknesses, and/or neutralize environmental threats. The examples of opportunities are: economic boom conditions, favourable demographic conditions, arrival of new technology, liberalisation of economy, deregulation, favourable global influence, unfulfilled customers need, etc.
- **Threat** is an unfavourable condition in the organisation's environment which creates a risk or causes damage to the organisation. Threats are conditions in the broad and operating environments that may impede organisational competitiveness or the achievement of stakeholders' satisfaction. The examples of threats are: economic downturn, demographic shifts, unexpected shift in consumer taste and preferences, new regulations, unfavourable political situations, introduction of new technology, product or service by competitors, loss of key personnel, etc.

4.2 SWOT ANALYSIS

SWOT analysis (alternately WOTS -UP or TOWS analysis) is a strategic planning method used to evaluate the **S**trengths, **W**eaknesses/limitations, **O**pportunities, and **T**hreats involved in a business venture. It involves specifying the objective of the business venture or project and identifying the internal and external factors that are favorable and unfavorable to achieve that objective. The technique was developed by Albert Humphrey, who led a convention at Stanford University in the 1960s and 1970s using data from Fortune 500 companies. A SWOT analysis must start with defining a desired end state or objective. A SWOT analysis may be incorporated into the strategic planning model.

Analysing the environment and the company can assist the company in all other tasks of strategic management. For example, a firm's managers should formulate strategic direction and specific strategies based on organisational strengths and weaknesses and in the context of the opportunities and threats found in its environment. A *SWOT analysis* is a tool strategists use to evaluate strengths, weaknesses, opportunities, and threats of the organisation.

Application of SWOT analysis technique involves the following steps:

1. Setting the objectives the organisation or its units
3. Identifying its strengths, weaknesses, opportunities, and threats
2. Asking the questions such as
   (a) How do we maximise our strengths?
   (b) How do we minimise our weaknesses?
   (c) How do we capitalise on the opportunities in our external environment?
   (d) How do we protect ourselves from threat in our external environment?

4. Recommending the strategies which will optimise the answers from these questions.

The SWOT analysis is usually done with the help of a template in the form of a four-cell matrix representing the strengths, weaknesses, opportunities, and threats. The analysis for preparing the SWOT could be done by a group of managers in a workshop session or brainstorming session for generating ideas for SWOT matrix. Exhibit 4.1 shows a typical SWOT analysis of an organisation.

Exhibit 4.1 A Typical SWOT Analysis

Strengths (internal factors)	**Weaknesses (internal factors)**
• Track record (similar successes) • Resource availability • Skill levels • Processes and systems • Good management reputation • Favourable location • ISO -9000 certification • Strong distribution network • Established R& D Centre	• Gaps in knowledge and expertise • Timescale and deadlines • Budget and funding • Competing projects • Processes and systems • Uncertain cash flow • Weak management information system • Absence of strong USP • Low commitment of worker/poor industrial relations
Opportunities (external factors)	**Threats (external factors)**
• Technology and infrastructure development • Changing consumer behaviour • Emerging and developing markets • New innovations • Market demand • Favourable industry trends • Availability of reliable business partners	• Unfavourable political environment • Political influences • Environmental factors • Uncertain competitor intention • Uncertain economical conditions • Seasonal effects • Lack of sustainable financial backing

4.3 ADVANTAGES AND DISADVANTAGES OF USING SWOT ANALYSIS

4.3.1 Advantages of SWOT Analysis

- Simple four-box framework.
- Facilitates an understanding of the strengths and weaknesses of the organisation.
- Encourages the development of strategic thinking.
- Enables a management team to focus on strengths and build opportunities.

- Can enable an organisation to anticipate future business threats and take action to avoid or minimize their impact.
- Can enable an organisation to spot business opportunities and exploit them fully.
- Produces new ideas to help take advantage of an organisation's strengths and defends against threats.
- Awareness of political and environmental threats allows an organisation to have response plans prepared.

4.3.2 Disadvantages of SWOT Analysis

- Some users oversimplify the data used for decisions - it is easy to use scant data.
- To be effective this process needs to be undertaken on a regular basis.
- The best reviews require different people being involved each having a different perspective.
- Access to quality internal data sources, this can be time consuming and politically difficult (especially in more complex organisations - parent company, etc).
- The pace of change makes it increasingly difficult to anticipate developments that may affect an organisation in the future.
- The risk of capturing too much data is that it may make it difficult to see the wood for the trees and lead to 'paralysis by analysis'.
- The data used in the analysis may be based on assumptions that subsequently prove to be unfounded (good and bad).
- Lacks detailed structure - so it may miss key elements.
- May persuade organisations to compile lists rather than think about what is important in achieving objectives.
- Presents lists uncritically and without clear prioritisation so, for example, weak opportunities may appear to balance strong threats.
- Usually a simple list and not critically presented.

4.4 TYPES OF BUSINESS ENVIRONMENT

Business environment may be classified as

(a) Economic environment; and

(b) Non-economic environment.

Economic environment includes economic conditions, economic policies and economic system of the country. Non-economic environment comprises social, political, legal, technological, demographic and natural environment. All these have a bearing on the strategies adopted by the firms and any change in these areas is likely to impact their operations.

4.5 CLASSIFICATION OF ENVIRONMENTAL SECTORS

The classification of the general environment into different sectors helps an organisation to cope up with its complexities, comprehends the different influence operating and relating the environmental changes to its strategic management process. Different bases of classification have been adopted by different authors, but the basis is not an important as the fact that all relevant factors in the environment have to be considered . Depending upon a variety of factors such as the size of the organisation, level and scope of operations, geographical spread of markets, nature of products, type of technology used and managerial philosophy. The environment here has been classified into eight different sectors. These sectors are:

- Economic Environment
- Market Environment
- Political Environment
- Legal/Regulatory Environment
- Socio-cultural Environment
- Technological Environment
- Suppliers' Environment
- International Environment
- Demographic Environment
- Natural Environment

4.5.1 Economic Environment

The economic environment consists of macro-level factors related to the means of production and distribution of wealth that have an impact on the business of the organisation. The survival and success of each and every business enterprise depend fully on its economic environment. The main factors that affect the economic environment are:

(a) **Economic Conditions:** The economic conditions of a nation refer to a set of economic factors that have great influence on business organisations and their operations. These include gross domestic product, per capita income, markets for goods and services, availability of capital, foreign exchange reserve, growth of foreign trade, strength of capital market, etc. All these help in improving the pace of economic growth.

(b) **Economic Policies:** All business activities and operations are directly influenced by the economic policies framed by the government from time to time. Some of the important economic policies are:

(i) Industrial policy
(ii) Fiscal policy
(iii) Monetary policy
(iv) Foreign investment policy
(v) Export-Import policy (EXIM policy)

The government changes policies from time to time in view of the developments in the economic scenario, political expediency and the changing requirements. Every business firm has to function strictly within the policy framework and respond to the changes therein.

(c) **Economic System:** The world economy is primarily governed by three types of economic systems, viz., (i) capitalist economy; (ii) socialist economy; and (iii) mixed economy. India has adopted the mixed economy system which implies co-existence of public sector and private sector.

Some of the economic environment factors to be analysed are:

- General economic conditions, economic conditions of different segments of population.
- Trends in income distribution and consumer spending patterns.
- Rate of growth of each sector of economy.
- Rate of inflation.
- Behaviour of capital market.
- Interest rate/exchange rate/tax rate.
- Prices of materials/energy.
- Labour scene.

Changes in economic environment can have an obvious impact on business activity. For example, an increase in the interest rates translates into fewer sales of major home appliances. Higher increase in interest rates results in higher mortgage rates and higher cost of buying a house. Most of the household goods are bought when people shift their houses. Higher costs of buying the house eat into the budget in appliances.

4.5.2 Market Environment

The market environment consists of the factors related to the groups and other organisation that compete with and have an impact on the organisation's markets and business. Some of the factors and influences operating in the market environment are as follows:

- **Demand related factors:** By monitoring the demand related factors of one's industry a firm gather vital clues on consumption pattern, buying habits, invasion of substitute products, growth potential, attractiveness of the industry, expansion, divestment, etc. The aspects to be considered are: nature of demand, demand potential, current level of demand, changes in demand, consumption pattern, buying habits, etc.

Exhibit 4.2 Important Economic Policies

- **Industrial policy:** The industrial policy of the government covers all those principles, policies, rules, regulations and procedures, which direct and control the industrial enterprises of the country and shape the pattern of industrial development.
- **Fiscal policy:** It includes government policy in respect of public expenditure, taxation and public debt.
- **Monetary policy:** It includes all those activities and interventions that aim at smooth supply of credit to the business and a boost to trade and industry.
- **Foreign investment policy:** This policy aims at regulating the inflow of foreign investment in various sectors for speeding up industrial development and take advantage of the modern technology.
- **Export–Import policy (EXIM policy):** It aims at increasing exports and bridges the gap between expert and import. Through this policy, the government announces various duties/levies. The focus nowadays lies on removing barriers and controls and lowering the custom duties.

- **Consumer related factors:** Monitoring the customer's taste may result in attractive business opportunities. Hence, customer analysis is very important during environmental survey. The factors that have to be monitored in relation to the customers are:
  - Purchasing power
  - Buying motives, attitudes and habits
  - Lifestyle and needs
  - Brand awareness, brand loyalty and brand switching
  - Reasons/motives for customer's patronage of specific brands
- **Product related factors:** Such as image, features, utilities, functions, design, life cycle, price promotion, distribution, differentiation, and the availability of substitutes of product or services.
- **Market intermediary related factors:** Such as level and quality of customer service, middlemen, distribution channels, logistics, cost, delivery and financial intermediaries.
- **Competitor related factors:** Such as different types of competitors, entry and exit of major competitors, nature of competition and the relative strategic position of major competitors.

4.5.3 Technological Environment

The technological environment consists of factors related to technology used in the production of goods and services that have an impact on the business of an organisation. Technological factors to be considered are:

- Source of technology like company, external and foreign sources, cost of technology acquisition, collaboration and transfer of technology.
- Technological development, rate of change of technology and research and development.
- Impact of technology on human beings, the man-machine system and the environmental effects of technology.
- Communication, infrastructure and managerial technology.

For a business firm, technology affects its final products by changing processes in raw material sourcing, production and distribution. Technology, when rightly used can bring about huge changes in the productivity of firms. Computer industry is one example where technology in the industry keeps pushing competition to the brink.

The varying technological environments of different countries affect the designing of products. For example, in USA and many other countries electrical appliances are designed for 110 volts. But when these are made for India, they have to be of 220 volts. In the modern competitive age, the pace of technological changes is very fast. Hence, in order to survive and grow in the market, a business has to adopt the technological changes from time to time. It may be noted that scientific research for improvement and innovation in products and services is a regular feature in most of the big industrial organisations. Nowadays in fact, no firm can afford to persist with the outdated technologies.

4.5.4 Sociocultural Environment

Sociocultural environment regulates the values, morals and customs of society. Important factors to be considered are:

- Demographic characteristics.
- Social concerns, social attitudes.
- Family structure and changes in it.
- Role of women in society, position of children and adolescents in family and society.
- Educational level, awareness and consciousness of rights and work ethics of members of the society.

The social environment primarily affects the strategic management process within the organisation in the areas of mission and objective setting and decision related to products and markets. The social environment of business includes social factors like customs, traditions, values, beliefs, poverty, literacy, life expectancy rate, etc. The social structure and the values that a society cherishes have considerable influence on the functioning of business firms. For example, during festive seasons there is an increase in the demand for new clothes, sweets, fruits, flower, etc. Due to increase in literacy rate the consumers are becoming more conscious of the quality of the products. Due to change in the family composition, more nuclear families with single-child concept have come up. This increases the demand for different types of household goods. It may be noted that the consumption patterns, the dressing and living styles of people belonging to different social strata and culture vary significantly.

4.5.5 Political Environment

Politico-legal forces allocate power and provide laws and regulations that may constrain or protect the business. The factors to be considered are:

- The political system and its features like nature of the political system, ideological forces of the political parties and sentries of power.
- The political structure, its goals and stability.
- Political process like party systems, elections, funding of elections and legislation in economic and industrial matters and regulations.
- Political philosophy, role of government in business and its policy approach towards economic and business development.

With the developments on the political front affecting the economy all the time, the economic environment often becomes a byproduct of the political environment. Legislations regulating the business are the byproducts to of the political configuration. In addition to government and legislative measures, media, social and religious organisations and lobbies of various kinds are also a part of the political environment. They collectively exercise a huge influence on the conduct of business in a country.

The political environment includes the political system, the government policies and attitude towards the business community and the unionism. All these aspects have a bearing on the strategies adopted by the business firms. The stability of the government also influences business and related activities to a great extent. It sends a signal of strength, confidence to various interest groups and investors. Further, ideology of the political party also influences the business organisation and its operations. The Coca-Cola, a cold drink widely used now, had to wind up its operations in India in late seventies. Again the trade union activities also influence the operation of business enterprises. Most of the labour unions in India are affiliated to various political parties. Strikes, lockouts and labour disputes, etc., also adversely affect the business operations. However, with the competitive business environment, trade unions are now showing great maturity and started contributing positively to the success of the business organisation and its operations through workers participation in management.

4.5.6 Legal/Regulatory Environment

Businesses have to operate within the framework of the prevailing legal environment. They have to understand the general legal aspects and those particular to the industry the company is in. Businesses have to understand the implications of such legislations and adapt themselves accordingly.This refers to set of laws, regulations, which influence the business organisations and their operations. The important factors which affect legal/ regulatory environment are:

- The constitutional framework, directive principles, fundamental rights and divisions of legislative power between central and state governments.
- Policies related to licensing, monopolies, foreign investments and financing to industries.
- Policies related to distribution and pricing and their control.
- Policies related to imports and exports.
- Other policies related to PSU, SSI, sick industries, and development of backward areas and control of environmental pollution.

The important legislations that concern the business enterprises in India include:

- Companies Act, 1956
- Foreign Exchange Management Act, 1999
- The Factories Act, 1948
- Industrial Disputes Act, 1972
- Payment of Gratuity Act, 1972
- Industries (Development and Regulation) Act, 1951
- Prevention of Food Adulteration Act, 1954
- Essential Commodities Act, 2002
- The Standards of Weights and Measures Act, 1956
- Monopolies and Restrictive Trade Practices Act, 1969
- Trade Marks Act, 1999
- Bureau of Indian Standards Act, 1986
- Consumer Protection Act, 1986
- Environment Protection Act
- Competition Act, 2002

Besides, the above legislations, the following are also part of the legal environment of business.

(i) **Provisions of the Constitution:** The provisions of the Articles of the Indian Constitution, particularly directive principles, rights and duties of citizens, legislative powers of the central and state governments also influence the operation of business enterprises.

(ii) **Judicial Decisions:** The judiciary has to ensure that the legislature and the government function in the interest of the public and act within the boundaries of the constitution. The various judgments given by the courts in different matters relating to trade and industry also influence the business activities.

4.5.7 Suppliers Environment

Suppliers constitute a major force, shaping competition in any industry with their own bargaining power. They influence the cost of the raw materials and other inputs of the firm. Suppliers adapt changes in their product, process and business practices, and can stay independent of the sourcing firm. Sometimes, suppliers themselves may go for forward integration and could become a real competitor. Some important factors and influences in the suppliers environment are as follows:

- Cost, availability and continuity of supply of raw materials, sub-assemblies, parts and components
- Cost and availability of finance for implementing plans and projects
- Cost, reliability and availability of energy used in the production
- Cost, availability and dependability of human resources
- Cost, availability and existence of means of supply of plants and machinery spare parts and after-sales service
- Infrastructure support and ease of availability of different factors of production, bargaining powers of suppliers, and existence of substitute.

The supplier environment occupies a dominant position in strategic formulation because of the fact that India is a developing country, having scarcity of capital and appropriate raw materials resources. Unlike some of the western nations and Japan, the reliability of supplies is very low, forcing companies to devote a lot of attention and energy in maintaining continuity of supply.

4.5.8 International Environment

The international or global environment consists of all those factors that operate at the transnational, cross-cultural and cross-border levels which have an impact on the business of the organisation. Some important factors and influences in the international or global environment are as follows:

- Globalisation, its process content and direction,
- Global economic forces, organisation, blocks and forums
- Global trade and commerce, its process and trends
- Global financial system, sources of financing and accounting standards

- Geopolitical situations, equations, alliances and strategic interests of nations
- Global demographic patterns and shifts
- Global human resources, availability and quality of skills and expertise, mobility of labourers and other skilled personnel
- Global information systems, communication network and media
- Global technological and quality systems and standards
- Global market and competitiveness
- Global legal systems, adjudication and arbitration mechanism
- Globalisation of management and allied disciplines and diffusion of management techniques in industry
- Resources and raw materials sectors.

The international environment was considered to be of low significance by Indian companies till 1990 but there has been a sea change in the strategic thinking and planning of these companies so as to align them with the emerging global economic order. Evidence is found in global standards adopted by exporting companies, eagerness to adopt global practices, realisation of the impact the international environment likely to have on Indian business and industries. The industry federation such as CII have been drawing attention of the business towards the likely impact it will have on them. Many Indian companies have set up special cells and appointed managers to assess the impact of international business on their business. The establishment of Word Trade Organisation (WTO) in Jan 1995 has provided the right impetus to Indian companies for international trade. Many Indian companies have widened the scope of their business to include their international operations. Ranbaxy, Dr. Reddy Lab, Tata steel , Infosysis, Reliance are some of the shining examples of success in international business .

Exhibit 4.3 International Event Impacting Business Environment

- The North American Free Trade Agreement is spurring many US companies, including small businesses, to move into Canada and Mexico, affecting the market and human resources sectors.
- The European Union (EU) and Association of Southeast Asian Nations (ASEAN) may spawn large, powerful companies that compete easily with US firms. These companies could reshape the industry and market sectors as we now know them.
- Despite recent economic woes, some analysts believe that in the twenty-first century, most of the economic activity in the world will take place in Asia and the Pacific Basin, sharply affecting the economic conditions and financial resources sectors.
- Newly industrialized countries such as Korea, Taiwan, Singapore, and Spain produce huge volumes of low-cost, high-quality commodities that will have an impact on the competitiveness of many industries, markets, and raw materials in North America.
- Eastern Europe, Russia, and China are all shifting toward market economies that also will affect markets, raw materials, industry competition, and worldwide economic conditions.
- Hundreds of partnerships are taking place between North American firms and firms in all parts of the world, facilitating the exchange of technology and production capability, thereby redefining the technology, raw materials, and industry sectors.

Contd...

- Many companies in the United States build twin plants—one in Texas and one in Mexico. The Mexican plants provide component assembly, and that helps combat Mexico's high unemployment called maquiladoras, these plants reshape the human resources and their capabilities.

4.5.9 Demographic Environment

This refers to the size, density, distribution and growth rate of population. All these factors have a direct bearing on the demand for various goods and services. For example, a country where population rate is high and children constitute a large section of population, then there is more demand for baby products. Similarly, the demand of the people of cities and towns are different form the people of rural areas. The high rise of population indicates the easy availability of labour. These encourage the business enterprises to use labour intensive techniques of production. Moreover, availability of skill labour in certain areas motivates the firms to set up their units in such area. For example, the business units from America, Canada, Australia, Germany, UK, are coming to India due to easy availability of skilled manpower. Thus, a firm that keeps a watch on the changes on the demographic front and reads them accurately will find opportunities knocking at its doorsteps.

4.5.10 Natural Environment

The natural environment includes geographical and ecological factors that influence business operations. These factors include the availability of natural resources, weather and climatic condition, location aspect, topographical factors, etc. Business is greatly influenced by the nature of natural environment. For example, sugar factories are set up only at those places where sugarcane can be grown. It is always considered better to establish manufacturing unit near the sources of input. Further, government's policies to maintain ecological balance, conservation of natural resources, etc., put additional responsibility on the business sector.

Exhibit 4.4 Developments in Indian Economy which Affected Business Environment

The economic environment of business in India has been changing at fast rate mainly due to the changes in the economic policies of the government. At the time of independence, the Indian economy was basically agrarian with a weak industrial base. To speed up the industrial growth and solve various economic problems, the government took several steps like state ownership on certain categories of industries, economic planning, reduced role of private sector, etc. The government adopted several control measures on the functioning of private sector enterprises. All these efforts resulted a mixed response. There was growth in net national product, per capita income and development of capital goods sector and infrastructure. But rate of industrial growth was slow, inflation increased and government faced a serious foreign exchange crisis during eighties. As a result, the government of India introduced a radical change in economic policies in 1991. This policy abolished industrial licensing in most of the cases, allowed private participation in most industries, disinvestment was carried out in many public sector industrial enterprises and opened up the economy considerably. Foreign Investment Promotion Board was set up to channelise foreign capital investment in India. These developments can be discussed under three heads, viz., liberalisation, privatisation, and globalisation.

Contd...

Liberalisation: Liberalisation refers to the process of eliminating unnecessary controls and restrictions on the smooth functioning of business enterprises. It includes:

- Abolishing industrial licensing requirement in most of the industries;
- Freedom in deciding the scale of business activities;
- Freedom in fixing prices of goods and services;
- Simplifying the procedure for imports and exports;
- Reduction in tax rates; and
- Simplified policies to attract foreign capital and technology to India.

Through this liberalisation process, Indian economy has opened up and started interacting with the world in a big way. This has resulted in easy entry of foreign business organisations in India. This has further resulted in stiff competition and efficiency. Ultimately, liberalisation has helped us in achieving a high growth rate, easy availability of goods at competitive rates, a healthy and flourishing stock market, high foreign exchange reserve, low inflation rate, strong rupee, good industrial relations, etc.

Privatisation: Privatisation refers to reducing the role of public sector by involving the private sectors in most activities. Due to the policy reforms announced in 1991, the expansion of public sector has literally come to a halt and the private sector registered fast growth in the post-liberalised period. The issues of privatisation include:

- Reduction in the number of industries reserved for the public sector from 17 to 8 in India, (reduced further to 3 later on) and the introduction of selective competition in the reserved area;
- Disinvestment of shares of selected public sector industrial enterprises in order to raise resources and to encourage wider participation of general public and workers in the ownership in business;
- Improvement in performance through an MOU system by which managements are to be granted greater autonomy but held accountable for specified results.

As a result of these steps, the post-liberalisation phase has witnessed a massive expansion of the private sector business in India. The total capital employed in top 500 private sector companies rose from Rs. 1,39,806 crore in 1992-93 to Rs. 2,34,751 crore in 1994-95 (an expansion of 68% in just two years).

Globalisation: Globalisation means 'integrating' the economy of a country with the world economy. This implies free flow of goods and services, capital, technology and labour across national boundaries. To achieve these objectives of globalisation, the government has adopted various measures such as reduction in custom duties, removal of quantitative restrictions or quotas on exports and imports, facilitating foreign investment and encouragement of foreign technology. These measures are expected to achieve a higher rate of growth, enlargement of employment potential, and reduction of regional disparities.

4.6 ENVIRONMENTAL SCANNING

Environmental scanning can be defined as 'the study and interpretation of the political, economic, social and technological events and trends which influence a business, an industry or even a total market'. Environmental scanning can also be defined as the process by which organisations monitor their relevant environment to identify opportunities and threats affecting their business for the purpose of taking strategic decisions. Environmental scanning is the process of gathering information about events and their relationships within an organisation's internal and external environments. The basic purpose of environmental scanning is to help management determine the future direction of the organisation.

Environmental scanning is a research process, in which businesses collect all types of relevant information that helps these businesses in making decisions regarding surviving, expanding or entering new markets. In simple words, it can be described as keeping a close eye on external or internal happenings and analyzing this information to know how it can be detrimental or beneficial for the business.

The information must be collected, arranged and disseminated among the company directors and managers. Mostly, environmental scanning is limited to external factors; however some businesses also carry out internal scanning. Environmental scanning is critical for the management or decision makers, as this information helps in making well informed decisions and that too, at the right time. These decisions include expansion, innovation, entering or leaving a market.

4.7 FACTORS TO BE CONSIDERED FOR ENVIRONMENTAL SCANNING

The factors which need to be considered for environmental scanning are events, trends, issues and expectations of the different interest groups.

- ***Events*** are important and specific occurrences taking place in different environmental sectors
- ***Trends*** are the general tendencies or the course of action along with events that take place. A trend can be defined as an 'environmental phenomenon that has adopted a structural character'. A trend break could be a value shift in society, a technological innovation that might be permanent or a paradigm change.
- ***Issues*** are current concerns that arise in response to events and trends. Issues are often forerunners of trend breaks. Issues are less deep seated and can be 'a temporary short-lived reaction to a social phenomenon'.
- ***Expectations*** are the demands made by interested groups in the light of their concerned issues.

Public issues of shares by Reliance Industries in 1977 was a specific event which led to the trends of wider participation of public in equity participation in private sector companies. The equity participation was earlier limited to an exclusive class of investors and general public was not aware or interested in investing money in shares. The issue that emerged was the development of equity culture in India — that the general public can have the fruits of economic development in the corporate sector would be shared by all sundry.

By monitoring the environment through environmental scanning, an organisation can consider the impact of the different events, trends, issues and expectations on its strategic management process. Since the environment facing any organisation is complex and its scanning is absolutely essential, strategists have to deal cautiously with the process of environmental scanning. They have to make efforts to deal with it in such a manner that unnecessary time and efforts are not expended, while important factors are not ignored. To enable this it is important to devise an approach or a combination of different approaches to environmental scanning.

4.8 APPROACHES TO ENVIRONMENTAL SCANNING

The most widely accepted method for categorizing different approaches of environmental scanning divides into the following three types:

- **Irregular scanning systems or ad hoc approach:** These consist largely of ad hoc environmental studies conducted by organisation such as special survey and studies conducted to deal with specific environmental issues. Examples of such studies for instance, when the organisation has to undertake special projects, evaluating existing strategies or devising new strategies. Changes in the environment or unforseen developments may also be investigated with regards to their impact on the organisations.
- **Regular scanning systems or systematic approach:** These systems revolve around a regular review of the environment or significant environmental components. In this approach information for environmental scanning is collected systematically. Information related to markets and customers, the changes in legislation and regulations which have a direct impact on the organisation's activities, government policy statements directly related to organisation's business and industry and so on could be collected continuously to monitor changes. Continuously updating such information is necessary not only for strategic management but also for operational activities.
- **Processed form approach:** In this approach, an organisation uses the information in the processed form, available from different sources both within and outside the organisation. The organisation uses the information supplied by the government agencies or private institutions, it uses the secondary sources of data which is available in processed form.

Since environmental scanning is absolutely necessary for strategy formulations, organisations use different practical combinations or approaches to monitor their relevant environment. These approaches may range from informal assessment of environmental factors to highly systematic and formal procedures. A highly systematic and formal procedure may be adopted as a proactive measure in anticipation of changes in environmental factors and structured data collection and processing system may be used continuously.

4.9 SOURCES OF INFORMATION FOR ENVIRONMENTAL SCANNING

The various sources of information which can be used for collecting information/data could be classified in different ways. There could be formal or informal, written or verbal and internal or external. Some important sources of information are as follows:

- **Documentary or secondary sources:** These could be newspapers, magazines, journals, books, trade and industry association newsletters, government publications, annual reports of companies. Companies collect information on environmental factors through bulletins of government, banks and their competitors. Many organisations often release periodic internal reports analysing the environment.
- **Mass media:** Mass media like TV, Radio, the Internet, etc., could be used to collect information like the taste, social values, and standard of life of the public.
- **Internal sources:** Like company files and records, databases, management information systems, etc., companies could use internal sources like employees to collect the information about the public and the competitor.
- **External agencies** – Like customers, marketing intermediaries, suppliers, trade associations, government agencies etc., the company could use various external agencies like associations, clubs, etc., also to collect the environmental information. It could also use its own sales force to collect the information.
- **Formal studies** – Companies could do the formal study either themselves or through some research agencies such as marketing research agencies, management consultants and educational institutions to collect the information to re-evaluate their strategies.
- **Spying and surveillance** – Companies could use their own employees, sales agents, and retired employee, etc., to collect the information.

Strategists use information depending upon their needs for environmental scanning. Governmental publications, though rich and comprehensive in nature are usually available after considerable lag of time hence may not be very useful. Private sources though relevant and timely are quite expensive to tap. Therefore, whichever source of information is to be used must be checked for its reliability, time frame, methods of data collection and analysis used and form of presentation used.

Exhibit 4.5 Sources of Information for Environmental Scanning in India

- **International Publications:** International organisations and agencies such as UN, UNESCO. ILO, WHO, UNDP, FAO, World Bank, OECD, provides rich sources for international statistical data. Other sources such as World Developmental Report , World Economic Survey, International Trade Statistics, Year book of UN. There are private data agencies and country credit ratings such as Standard& Poor, Moody which provide ranking of countries with regards to their attractiveness for foreign investment.
- **Government of India Publications:** Many government agencies publish important statistical reports such as Census of India, five year plan reports, annual economic survey ,annual survey of industries, EXIM policy, policies related to specific industries, RBI bulletins, CSO publications are important sources of business and policies having impact on business.
- **Institutional Publications:** Bombay Stock Exchange Directory gives financial information related to public limited companies, the Centre of Monitoring Indian Economy (CMIE) provides comprehensive information on various economic indices, publications of marker research agencies such as National Council for Applied Economic Research, ORG–Marg, publication of trade association such as CII, FICCI, etc.

4.10 FACTORS AFFECTING THE PROCESS OF ENVIRONMENTAL SCANNING

Even if the environmental conditioned are same, the strategists will come out with different strategies to tackle the environment. This is due to many factors which affect the environmental appraisal. Researchers have considered strategic related factors, organisation related factors and environmental related factors which affect the process of environmental scanning.

Strategist-related factors: There are many factors related to the strategist, which affect the process of environmental appraisal. Since strategists play a central role in the formulation of strategies, their characteristics such as age, education, experience, motivation level, cognitive styles, ability to withstand the time pressure and strain, etc., have an impact on the extent to which they are able to appraise their organisation's environment and how well they are able to do it. Apart from these factors, related to strategists as individuals, group characteristics too have an impact on how well environmental appraisal is done. Such group characteristics could be the interpersonal relations between the different strategists involved in appraisal, team spirit, and the power equations operating between them.

Organisation-related Factors: Like those of strategists, many characteristics of the organisation also have an impact on the environmental appraisal process. These characteristics are the nature of business the organisation is in, its age, size and complexity, the nature of its markets, and the product or services that it provides.

Environment-related Factors: The nature of environment facing an organisation determines how its appraisal could be done. The nature of the environment depends on its complexity, volatility or turbulence, hostility, and diversity. Majority of the strategists claim that environment-related factors affect the process of environmental scanning followed by organisation-related and strategist-related factors. Environment-related factors must be given due importance for the environmental scanning. Strategists-related factor as well as organisation-related factors are internal whereas environmental related factor is external area. In sum, how well environmental appraisal is done depends on the strategists, their organisations, and the environment in which their organisations exist.

4.11 IDENTIFYING EXTERNAL ENVIRONMENTAL FACTORS

Environmental scanning results in a mass of information related to different sectors. Without a technique to deal with this information, a strategist would be at loss to comprehend and analyse the environmental factors. These factors are events, trends, issues and expectations of different interested groups. A feasible approach in identifying environmental factors is to study the impact and the probability of impact of such factors on the business organisation.

The following matrix helps to identify the high priority environmental factors.

Exhibit 4.6 Identifying High Priority Environmental Issue

Probability of Impact ↑	*Impact on business* High ←	Medium	Low
High	Critical	High Priority	Low Priority
Medium	High Priority	High Priority	Low Priority
Low	To be watched	Low Priority	Low Priority

The importance of the factors that were identified by the environmental scanning could be judged by the intensity of their impact and their relative probability of impact on the organisation. According to the matrix above the environmental factors could be distributed across nine cells. Issues having high probability of impact and high intensity of impact are critical to which the company has to give more attention, while high priority should be given to issues having medium impact with medium probability. All the other issues having low intensity and low probability of impact are low priority issues, which need to be watched at regular intervals since the environment may keep changing. Thus, the strategists get a clear picture of the environmental factors and their impact and could narrow down the factors that need special attention.

4.12 STRUCTURING ENVIRONMENT APPRAISAL

Structuring environmental factors is complex since the factors cannot be clearly classified into the particular environment. The strategist should use personal experience and judgment to place the various factors under each type of environment so that a clear picture of threat and environment can be obtained. One such technique is environment threat opportunity profile (ETOP). The preparation of ETOP involves dividing the environment into different sectors and then analysing the impact of each sector on the organisation. A comprehensive ETOP requires subdividing each environmental sector into sub-factors and then the impact of each sub-sector on the organisation is described in the form of a statement. An example of the ETOP prepared for a automobile manufacturer is given below (Exhibit 4.7).

Upwards arrows indicate favourable impact, downwards arrows unfavourable impact, while horizontal arrows indicate neutral impact

The preparation of an ETOP provides a clear picture to the organisation to know where it stands with respect to the environment.

4.13 ASSESSING THE IMPACT OF OPPORTUNITIES AND THREATS

The impact of each threat and opportunity could be analysed with the help of opportunity threat matrix. A company after identifying various threats, can use its judgments to place the threats in any of the four cells in the following matrix:

Exhibit 4.7 ETOP for an Automobile Manufacturer Company

Environmental Sectors	*Nature of Impact*	*Impact of each sector*
Social	↑	Customer preference for personal vehicle to public transport
Political	→	No significant change
Economic	↑	Growing affluence among urban consumers
International	↑	High export potential, automobile industry is a thrust area for exports
Regulatory	→	No significant changes in regulations
Market	↑	Industry growth rate is 7 to 8 % per year
Supplier	→	Mostly ancillaries and associated companies supply parts and components; availability is increasing
Technological	↑	Technological upgradation of industry in progress

Similar to the threat matrix we have an opportunity matrix that the opportunities are placed according to their attractiveness as given below:

The matrix helps in prioritization of opportunities and threats that need to be focused by the organisation immediately.

4.14 THE IMPACT MATRIX

The impact of the trend on various strategies could be visualized using an impact matrix. After identifying the emerging trends in mega, micro and relevant environments, the degree of their impact can be assessed with the help of the impact scale. The matrix enables us to have a consolidated view of the impact on different strategies, which a firm may be following. The strategies may relate to various functional areas within a specific business unit or they may relate to overall company for all its business units. To assess the degree and quality of impact of each trend on different strategies a five-point impact scale could be used. The pattern of scoring can be:

+2 extremely favourable impact , +1 moderately favourable impact, 0 no impact

–1 moderately unfavourable impact , –2 extremely unfavourable impact

Exhibit 4.8 SWOT Analysis of India

Strengths	Weaknesses
• Highly educated, skilled, young, capable & dynamic human resources	• Lack of trained & skilled workforce
• English speaking & analytical students	• Small supply of specialized professionals
• World class business, social, spiritual, political leaders, professors, scientists, managers, doctors, engineers, civil servants, etc.	• Lack of spirit of entrepreneurship, patriotism and leadership skills
• Very rich in natural & living resources	• Lack of effective & execution framework
• Biodiversity & traditional knowledge base	• Lack of Indian management models
• Diversity vs. ideas, innovation and integration	• Lack of transparency, trust, responsibility
• Powerful spiritual strength (yoga, ayurvada, healing, therapy services)	• Lack of learning habits & team work spirit
• Geographical location (whole markets are shifting toward Asian nations)	• Fear of sharing knowledge & taking risk
• Strategic position at various platforms	• Thinking win-lose lose-win look-outside
• Big democracy, big market & free media	• Slow absorption of innovation & change
• Range of emerging professional champions	• Lack of Indian management models
• IT & software superpower	• Absence of greater technology impetus
	• Unawareness: Quality, Standardization
	• Lack of emotional, spiritual development
	• Rush of getting high marks not development
	• Blindly respect anything taught by elders
Opportunities	**Threats**
• Big potential market in education sector & emerging new market Segment in services (create it)	• A feeling of unstable government
• General Agreement of Trade on Services	• Self-centred political leadership
• Research & development capability	• Slow & dysfunctional judiciary and corrupt law enforcers
• Generate intellectual property	• Regulation, protection and restriction

Contd...

• Resources building capacity	• Mechanistic, stable, layered-complex system
• Competition cost, quality service	• Corruption, ignorance & Complacency
• Collaboration: win-win thinking	• High competitive & marketing forces To patent Indian intellectual property by outsider (unawareness about own research)
• Hybrid solution, balancing & blending	• Fast change Internet-information technology & new inventions, technology, innovations
• Tourism, health sector, food processing	• Diversity vs. imbalance, clashes
• Rural economy development & social transformation (PURA model)	• Regional, religion, caste, culture conflicts
• Need modernization of infrastructure, library and laboratory	• Migration of all branch to software job
• Internet institute network & e-library	• Job seeking mind sets, not job creator
• Councillors and student advisors	• Unnecessary social pressure on students
	• Excessive rich & powerful mindset

A proper scanning of internal and external environment enables generation of strategic alternatives to utilize the strengths and overcome the weaknesses in the light of the opportunities and threats that operate in the environment.

Exercise

1. Describe the important characteristics of environment and demonstrate how it will be useful for the strategist for understanding it in better ways.
2. How the environmental factors impact business? What will happen if the business does not react to change in environment?
3. What is the importance of SWOT analysis and explain the rationale behind carrying out the SWOT analysis?
4. How does each environmental sector affect the strategist management process in an organisation?
5. How different sources of information help the strategist in carrying out the environmental appraisal?
6. How ETOP is prepared? Does it provide any insight to the strategist in choosing a particular strategy?
7. Choose any industry/company and outline the factors that could create either opportunities or threats and how the organisation should respond to it. Is it possible that same factors could be opportunity for one company and threat to another? How?

5 Organisational Appraisal

5.1 INTRODUCTION

Appraisal of the external environment of a firm helps it to think of what it might choose to do, appraisal of the internal environment, on the other hand, enables a firm to decide about what it can do. The present chapter deals with the internal environment of an organisation. It starts with building a foundation for understanding the internal environment through an explanation of its dynamics. The internal environment of an organisation can also be understood in terms of the organisational resources and behaviour, strengths and weaknesses, synergistic effects, and competence. An organisation uses different types of resources and exhibits a certain type of behaviour. The interplay of these different resources produces synergy or dis-synergy within an organisation, which leads to the development of strengths or weaknesses over a period of time. Some of these strengths make an organisation specially competent in a particular area of its activity causing it to develop competence. Organisational capability rests on an organisation's capacity and ability to use its competence to excel in a particular field.

The resources, behaviour, strengths and weaknesses, synergy, and competence constitute the internal environment of an organisation. All these together determine the organisational capability that leads to strategic advantage. Exhibit 5.1 shows the relationship between these factors and process of development of strategic advantage by an organisation. These terms here been explained here in the specific context of strategic management.

5.1.1 Organisational Resources

According to Barney (1991), who is credited with developing the resource-based view of strategy as a theory, the internal environment of an organisation can be understood as a bundle of resources—tangible and intangible—that include all assets, capabilities, organisational processes, information, knowledge, and so on. These resources could be classified as physical, human, and organisational resources. The physical resources are the technology, plant and equipment, geographic location, access to raw materials, among others. The human resources are training, experience, judgement, intelligence, relationships, and so on, present in an organisation. The organisational resources are the

Exhibit 5.1 Organisational Dynamics and Structuring

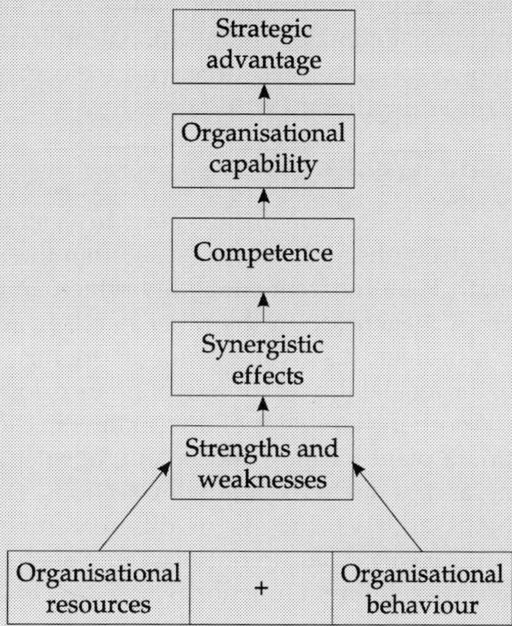

formal systems and structures as well as informal relations among groups. Barney said that the resources of an organisation can ultimately lead to a strategic advantage for it if they possess four characteristics, that is, if these resources are valuable, rare, costly to imitate, and non-substitutable. This theory holds that the firm has resources which are valuable and enable them to achieve strategic advantage. Other resources that cannot be imitated or substituted lead to superior long-term performance and a sustainable strategic advantage. Like individuals, very few organisations are born with a silver spoon in the mouth; most organisations have to acquire resources the hard way. The cost and availability of resources are the most important factors on which the success of an organisation depends. If an organisation is favourably placed with respect to the cost and availability of a particular type of resource, it possesses an enduring strength which may be used as a strategic weapon by it against its competitors. Conversely, the high cost and scarce availability of a resource are handicaps which cause a persistent strategic weakness in an organisation. But the mere possession of resources does not make an organisation capable — much depends on their usage within an organisation.

5.1.2 Organisational Behaviour

Organisational behaviour is the manifestation of the various forces and influences operating in the internal environment of an organisation that create the ability for, or place constraints in the usage of resources. Organisational behaviour is unique in the sense that it leads to the development of a special identity and character of an organisation. Some of the important forces and influences that affect organisational behaviour are: the quality of leadership, management philosophy, shared values and culture, quality of work environment and organisational climate, organisational politics, use of power, among others. The combination of organisation resource with the organisation behaviour, they collectively produce are the strengths and weaknesses.

5.1.3 Strengths and Weaknesses

Organisational resources and behaviour do not exist in isolation. They combine in a complex fashion to create strengths and weaknesses within the internal environment of an organisation. A strength is an inherent capability which an organisation can use to gain strategic advantage. A weakness, on the other hand, is an inherent limitation or constraint which creates a strategic disadvantage for an organisation. Financial strength, for example, is a result of the availability of sources of finance, low cost of capital, efficient use of funds, and so on. Another example is of a weakness in the operations area which results due to inappropriate plant location and layout, obsolete plants and machinery, uneconomical operations, and so on. In the following sections, we will take up a detailed discussion of the strengths and weaknesses in different functional areas within an organisation. Strengths and weaknesses do not exist in isolation but combine within a functional area, and also across different functional areas, to create synergistic effects.

5.1.4 Synergistic Effects

It is the inherent nature of organisations that strengths and weaknesses, like resources and behaviour, do not exist individually but combine in a variety of ways. For instance,two strong points in a particular functional area add up to something more than double the strength. Likewise, two weaknesses acting in tandem result in more than double the damage. In effect, what we have is a situation where attributes do not add mathematically but combine to produce an enhanced or a reduced impact. Such a phenomenon is known as the synergistic effect. Synergy is the idea that the whole is greater or lesser than the sum of its parts. It is also expressed as the two-plus-two-is- equal-to-five-or-three effect'. Within an organisation, synergistic effects occur in a number of ways. For example, within a functional area, say of marketing, the synergistic effect may occur when the product, pricing, distribution, and promotion aspects support each other, resulting in a high level of marketing synergy. At a higher level, the marketing and production areas may support each other leading to operating synergy. On the other hand, marketing inefficiency reduces production efficiency, the overall impact being negative, in which case dis-synergy (or negative synergy) occurs. In this manner, synergistic effects are an important determinant of the quality and type of the internal environment existing within an organisation and may lead to the development of competence.

5.1.5 Competence

On the basis of its resources and behaviour, an organisation develops certain strengths and weaknesses which when combined lead to synergistic effects. Such effects manifest themselves in terms of organisational competence. Competence is a special quality possessed by an organisation that makes them withstand pressures of competition in the marketplace. In other words, the net results of the strategic advantages and disadvantages that exist for an organisation determine its ability to compete with its rivals. Other terms frequently used as being synonymous to competence are unique resources, core capabilities, invisible assets, embedded knowledge, and so on. When an organisation develops its competence over a period of time and hones it into a fine art of competing with its rivals it tends to use the competence exceedingly well. The capability to use the competence exceedingly well turns them into core competence.

When a specific ability is possessed by a particular organisation exclusively, or in a relatively large measure, it is called distinctive competence. Many organisations achieve strategic success by building distinctive competence around the critical success factors (CSFs). CSFs are those factors which are crucial for organisational success. A few examples of distinctive competence are given below:

- Superior product quality in a particular attribute, say, an automobile, which is more fuel-efficient or one which delivers higher power or acceleration is higher than its competing products.
- Creation of a market niche by supplying highly specialised products to a particular market segment like Nano car for entry level segments.
- Differential advantages, based on the superior R&D skills of an organisation not possessed by its competitors, the one possessed by Toyota.
- An organisation's access to a low-cost financial source like equity shareholders, not available to its competitors, such as interest-free loan offered by Gujarat government to Tata Steel for setting up Tata Nano factory in Gujarat.

A distinctive competence is "any advantage a company has over its competitors because it can do something which they cannot or it can do something better than they can". It is not necessary, of course, for all organisations to possess a distinctive competence. Neither do all the organisations, which possess certain distinctive competence, use it for strategic purposes. Nevertheless, the concept of distinctive competence is useful for the purpose of strategy formulation. The importance of distinctive competence in strategy formulation rests with "the unique capability it gives an organisation in capitalising upon a particular opportunity; the competitive edge it may give a firm in the marketplace; and the potential for building a distinctive competence and making it the cornerstone of strategy".

The difference between the three terms: competence, core competence, and distinctive competence, is the degree of uniqueness associated with the net synergistic effects occurring within an organisation. One could think of them as being synonymous so long as they are able to make a distinction among them when necessary. Among the three, it is the term "core competence" that has gained greater currency and popularity. The term "core competence" has been popularised by Prahalad and Hamel as an idea around which strategies could be formulated by an organisation. Several Indian companies have taken to the idea of core competence in right earnest. Examples of companies shedding businesses that are not in line with their perceived core competence and focussing upon those are:

Kumar Mangalam Birla, of the A V Birla group, sees the group's core competence in a wide array of skills related to process industries, project management, operations, raw material sourcing, distribution and logistics, setting up dealer networks, commodity branding, and raising finance at a competitive cost. S Kumar sees its core competence in textile processing, Nandas of Escorts in light engineering, and Reliance Industries in skilful project management and execution.

The idea of core competence seems to be a brilliant way to focus upon the latent strength of an organisation. Yet there are pitfalls of which an organisation has to be aware. Core competence can be developed but also lost. They cannot be taken for granted. The ability of a core competence to provide strategic advantage can diminish over time as they do not exist perpetually. A dilemma associated with core competence is that they have the potential of turning into core rigidities. The external environment is responsible for this sad turn of events. New competitors may figure out a way to serve customers or new technologies may emerge causing the existing company to lose its strategic advantage. Over-reliance on core competence to the extent of becoming prisoners of one's own excellence may result in strategic myopia.

That core competence acts as a double-edged sword is demonstrated by the concept of strategic commitment enunciated by Pankaj Ghemawat in his HBR article 'Distance still matters' (Sep 2001). This means an organisation's commitment to a particular way of doing business, that is, developing a particular set of resources and capabilities. Ghemawat's contention is that once a company has made a strategic commitment it finds it difficult to respond to new competition if doing so requires a break with its commitment. Core or distinctive competence serves a useful purpose if these are used to develop sustained strategic advantages through building up organisational capability.

5.2 ORGANISATIONAL CAPABILITY

Organisational capability is the inherent capacity or potential of an organisation to use its strengths and overcome its weaknesses in order to exploit opportunities and face threats in its external environment. It is also viewed as a skill for coordinating resources and putting them to productive use. Without capability, resources, even though valuable and unique, may be worthless. Since organisational capability is the capacity or potential of an organisation, it means that it is a measurable attribute. And since it can be measured, it follows that organisational capability can be compared. Yet it is very difficult to measure organisational capability as it is, in the ultimate analysis, a subjective attribute. As an attribute, it is the sum total of resources and behaviour, strengths and weaknesses, synergistic effects occurring in and the competence of any organisation. Several thinkers in the field of strategy favour the line that capabilities are the outcome of an organisation's knowledge base, that is, the skills and knowledge of its employees. There is a growing body of opinion that considers organisations as reservoirs of knowledge in which case they are all learning organisations. In fact, the concept of organisational learning has spawned a whole school of strategy thought. It is to be noted that while the concept of a learning organisation is applicable to strategic management in a wider sense at several places, here we are referring to it in the specific context of capability that is seen as an outcome of organisational learning.

Strategists are primarily interested in organisational capability because of two reasons. First, they wish to know what capacity exists within the organisation to exploit opportunities or face threats in its environment. Secondly, they are interested in knowing what potential should be developed within the organisation so that opportunities could be exploited and threats should be faced in future. Organisational capability is measured and compared through the process of organisational appraisal which is the subject matter of this chapter. A feasible approach to appraising the organisation is to start with the factors and influences operating within the organisation. These could be called the organisational capability factors.

5.3 STRATEGIC ADVANTAGE

Strategic advantages are the outcome of organisational capabilities. They are the result of organisational activities leading to rewards in terms of financial parameters, such as, profit or shareholder value, and/or non-financial parameters, such as, market share or reputation. In contrast, strategic disadvantages are penalties in the form of financial loss or damage to market share. Clearly, such advantages or disadvantages are the outcome of the presence or absence of organisational capabilities. Strategic advantages are measurable in absolute terms using the parameters in which they are expressed. So, profitability could be used to measure strategic advantage—the higher the profitability the better the strategic advantage. They are comparable in terms of the historical performance of an organisation or its current performance with respect to its competitors.

Competitive advantage is a special case of strategic advantage where there are one or more identified rivals against whom rewards or penalties could be measured. So, outperforming rivals in profitability or market standing could be a competitive advantage for an organisation. Competitive advantage is relative rather than absolute, and it is to be measured and compared with respect to other rivals in an industry. With rising competitiveness in the industry, mainly owing to liberalisation and the reform process, the usage of the term "competitive advantage" has become more pronounced. The term "competitive advantage" is more popular since it has been used as an important concept by the proponents of the positioning school of thought in strategy. Michael Porter uses competitive advantage as one of the important concepts in his seminal contribution to the area of competitive strategy.

5.4 ORGANISATIONAL CAPABILITY FACTORS

Capabilities are often developed in specific functional areas such as marketing or operations or in a part of a functional areas such as distribution or research and development, etc. It is also feasible to measure and compare capabilities in functional areas. Thus, a company could be considered inherently strong in marketing owing to the competence in distribution skills. Or a company could be competitive in operations owing to superior research and development infrastructure.

Organisation capability factors are the strategic strengths and weaknesses existing in different functional areas within an organisation, which are of crucial importance to strategy formulation and implementation. Organisation capability factors are also called strategic factors, strategic advantage factors, corporate competence factors, etc. Different types of capability factors exist within internal environment of an organisation. Generally accepted and commonly understood functional areas in an organisation are: finance, marketing, operations, human resources, information and general management areas. We will describe these capability factors in all these six functional areas.

5.4.1 Financial Capability Factors

Financial capability factors relate to the availability, usage and management of fund and all allied aspects which have a direct impact on the capacity and capability of the organisation in implementing the strategy. Important factors which influence the financial capability of any organisation are as follows:

(a) Sources of funds: capital structure, procurement of capital, working capital availability, capital and credit availability, reserve and supplies, relationships with lenders, banks and financial institution.

(b) Usage of funds: Capital investment, fixed asset acquisition, current assets, loans and advances, dividend distribution and relationship with shareholders.

(c) Management of funds: Financial, accounting and budgeting system, management control system, state of financial health, return and risk management, cost reduction, tax planning etc.

The following example will illustrate how financial capability factor can have impact on an organisation.

- The superior ability to raise fund, easy access to financial resources and efficient capital budgeting system helped the Reliance Industries to plan for Rs. 61,700 crore expansion plan.
- Mahindra & Mahindra has followed the policy of low asset company, which helped in accumulating surplus more than Rs. 2000 crore.
- Gujrat Ambuja Cement followed a policy of high savings from higher cement cost. This helps them to raise finance whether equity or debt at attractive price globally.

5.4.2 Marketing Capability Factors

Marketing related factors relate to the pricing, promotions and distribution of products or services and all the allied aspects that have a bearing on the capability and capacity to implement its strategies. Some of the factors which influence the marketing capability of any organisation are as follows:

(a) Product-related factors: product variety, differentiations, mix quality, positioning, packaging, etc.

(b) Price-related factors: Pricing objectives, policies, protections, advantages, etc.

(c) Place-related factors: Distribution, transportation and logistics, marketing channels, marketing intermediaries, etc.

(d) Promotion-related factors: Promotional tools, sales promotions, advertising, public relations, etc.

(e) Integrative and systematic factors: Marketing mix, market standing, company image, marketing organisations, marketing management information systems, etc.

The following example will illustrate how marketing capability factor can have impact on an organisation:

- Pfizer India has the distinction of having brands such as Corex and Becosules have achieved top ranks in pharmaceutical industry, it has given Pfizer recognition for its marketing strengths.
- Parle company is recognised for its strong image and consumer appeal. Its products such as Parle-G, Monaco and Krackjack enjoy high market share and are very popular.
- LG India has a very strong and extensive distribution network, it has 43 branches, 150 area offices and more than 10,000 trade partners. Such a network provides LG significant marketing strength in the competitive FMCG industry.

5.4.3 Operations Capability Factors

Operations capability factors relate to the production of products or services, use of materials/resources and all allied aspects that have a bearing on an organisation's capability and capacity to implement its strategies. Some of the factors which influence the operations capability of any organisation are as follows:

(a) Production system factor: Capacity, location, layout, product or service design, work systems, degree of automations, extent of vertical integration, etc.

(b) Operations and control system factor: Aggregate production planning, material supply, inventory, cost and quality control, maintenance systems and procedures, etc.

(c) R&D system factor: Personnel facility, product development, patent rights, level of technology used, technological collaboration and support, etc.

The following example will illustrate how production capability factor can have impact on an organisation:

- Though the JK Tyres pioneered radial tyres in India, but the competitors such Bridgestone who has accessed to latest technology, have outperformed it. JK Tyres faces a strategic disadvantage due to its lower operations capability.
- Mumbai dabhawalas collect and deliver 1,75,000 packages per day and provide door to door quality service to its large and loyal customers.
- Shanti Gears is well known industrial gears company, its operation strengths lie in its modern facility that includes a foundry, forge shops, fabrication and heat treatment equipment. It can produce customised power transmission products for specialised applications making it a market leader offering stiff competition to multinational companies.

5.4.4 Personnel Capability Factors

Personnel capability factors relate to the existence and use of human resources and skills and all allied aspects that have a bearing on an organisation's capability and capacity to implement its strategies. Some of the factors which influence the operations capability of any organisation are as follows:

(a) Personnel system factors: System for manpower planning, selection, development, compensations, communication and appraisal position of the personnel department in the organisation, etc.

(b) Organisational and employee characteristic factors: Corporate image, quality of managers, staff and workers perception about and image of the organisation as an employer, availability of developmental opportunities for employee, working conditions, etc.

(c) Industrial relations factors: Union–management relationship, collective bargaining, safety, welfare and security, employee satisfaction and morale, etc.

The following example will illustrate how personnel capability factor can have impact on an organisation:

- The banking industry in India is highly competitive and it has been increasingly difficult for banks to attract and retain good employees. Attrition rates of staff are very high. HSBC has four Cs plan – communication, customer centricity, competitive benchmarking and collaboration – helps to create a conducive human resources environment.
- Metal Box India Ltd was at once a highly profitable company, but owing to various problems, it had to shut down several plants across the country. It had a high cost structure owing to wage bills and resulted in serious dent in the personnel capability of the company. The company could not overcome its human resources problem.

5.4.5 Information Management Capability Factors

Information management capability factors relate to the design and management of the flow of information from outside and within the organisation for the purpose of the decision making and all allied aspects that have a bearing on an organisation's capability and capacity to implement its strategies. Some of the factors which influence the information capability of any organisation are as follows:

(a) Acquisition and retention of information factors: Sources, quantity, quality and timeliness of information, retention capacity and security of information.

(b) Processing and synthesis of information factors: Database management, computer systems, software capabilities and ability to synthesise the information.

(c) Retrieval and usage of information factors: Availability and appropriateness of information formats, capacity to assimilate and use of information.

(d) Transmission and dissemination of information factors: Speed, scope, width and depth of coverage of the information and willingness to accept information.

(e) Integrative, systemic, and supportive factors: Availability of IT infrastructure, its relevance and compatibility to organisation need, upgradation facility, willingness to invest in state of art systems, availability of computer professionals and top management support.

The following example will illustrate how personnel capability factor can have impact on an organisation:

- Genpact is one of the financial service providers offering a range of financial products. Its strong operations are backed by latest information technology support system. Its successful customer relationship management programme is based on a single database management system having the data base of nearly 2.4 million customers account. This was possible because of latest information technology systems and centralised operations ensuring high standard of customer service.
- NIIT, a major player in IT industry has been able to create a significant information capability for itself by networking its widespread offices in several countries.
- The banking industry has been able to expand globally with the help of IT infrastructure. All modern banking channels such as ATM, Internet banking, Mobile Banking and call centre are made possible with the IT infrastructure. The 24 × 7 banking would not have possible without the support of IT systems.
- The Wal-Mart is known for its efficient supply chain management system, which is based on the efficient transfer of information through electronics means supported by IT system.
- The Hero Motor cops product management is based on its extensive communication system in the form of information chain linking various functions such as marketing, operations, production purchase, materials management and delivery services.

5.4.6 General Management Capability Factors

General management capability factors relate to the integration, coordination and direction of the functional capabilities towards common goals and allied aspects that have a bearing on an organisation's capability and capacity to implement its strategies. Some of the factors which influence the operations capability of any organisation are as follows:

(a) General management system factors: Strategic management systems, process related to strategic intent, strategy formulation and implementation machinery, strategy evaluation system, management information system, corporate planning system, reward and incentives system for top managers

(b) External relations factors: Influence on and rapport with government, regulatory agencies and financial institutions, public relations, corporate social responsibility, public image as corporate citizens, etc.

(c) Organisational climate factors: Organisational/corporate culture, use of power, political process, nature of organisational structure and control, management of change.

(d) General managers factors: Risk propensity, orientation, value, norms, personal goals, competence, track record, balance of functional experience.

The following example will illustrate how personnel capability factor can have impact on an organisation:

- Infosys is one of the leading IT companies in the world, its strategic management system based on the visionary leadership of its founders, wealth sharing philosophy, culture of transparency are the hallmarks of general management, making it the best company to work for.
- The quality and ability of top management was one of strongest general management capability of YesBank, which helped it to enter the highly competitive banking industry and create a niche for itself. In a short span of time it has become one of the leading private banks in India.

5.5 OBJECTIVES OF ORGANISATIONAL APPRAISAL

The analysis of internal resources has five objectives:

- To outline the role that the company's resources and capabilities play in the formulation of its strategy and to pinpoint their crucial importance in establishing competitive advantage.
- To show how the firm can identify, classify, and explore the characteristics of its base of resources and capabilities.
- To develop a set of criteria to analyse the potential of the firm's resources and capabilities to yield long-term profits/returns.
- To identify weaknesses in resources in the context of the external environment and strategy formulated, and to show how strategy is concerned not only with deploying the firm's resources to yield returns over the long term but also with augmenting and strengthening the firm's resources and capabilities.

To develop a framework for resource analysis that integrates the above themes into a practical guide for the formulation of strategies that build competitive advantage.

5.5.1 Structuring Organisational Appraisal

As the environmental appraisal is structured through an environmental threat and opportunity profile, organisational appraisal can also be structured through various techniques. For instance, Glueck proposes a preparation of the strategic advantage profile (SAP) where the results of organisational appraisal are presented in a summarised form. Another approach, suggested by Rowe et al., is to prepare a company capability profile as a means for assessing a company's strengths and weaknesses in dealing with the opportunities and threats in the external environment. Here we propose a similar approach of making an organisational capability profile which can be summarised in the form of a SAP. The SAP is then matched with the environmental threats and opportunity profile, which may have been prepared while structuring the environmental appraisal, in order to look for strategic alternatives and exercise a strategic choice.

5.5.2 Preparing the Organisational Capability Profile

The organisational capability profile (OCP) is prepared in the form of a chart as shown in Exhibit 5.2 which shows a summarised OCP. The strategists are required to systematically assess the various functional areas and subjectively assign values to the different functional capability factors and sub-factors along a scale ranging from the values of –5 to +5. A detailed OCP may run into several pages where each of the sub-factors constituting the different functional capability factors can be assessed.

Exhibit 5.2 Summarised Form of Organisational Capability Profile

Capability factors:	Weakness – 5	Normal 0	Strength + 5
1. Financial capability factors			
(a) Sources of funds			
(b) Usage of funds			
(c) Management of funds			
2. Marketing capability factors			
(a) Product-related			
(b) Price-related			
(c) Promotion-related			
(d) Integrative and systematic			
3. Operations capability factors			
(a) Production system			
(b) Operations and control system			
(c) R&D system			
4. Personnel capability factors			
(a) Personnel system			
(b) Organisational and employee characteristics			
(c) Industrial relations			
5. Information management capability factors			
(a) Acquisition and retention of information			
(b) Processing and synthesis of information			
(c) Retrieval and usage of information			
(d) Transmission and dissemination of information			
(e) Integrative, systemic, and supportive			
6. General management capability factors			
(a) General management system			
(b) External relations			
(c) Organisational climate			
(d) General managers			

After the completion of the chart, the strategists are in a position to assess the relative strengths and weaknesses of an organisation in each of the six functional areas and identify the gaps that need to be filled or the opportunities that could be used. The preparation of an OCP provides a convenient method to determine the relative priorities of an organisation vis-a-vis its competitors, its vulnerability to outside influences, the factors that support or pose a threat to its existence, and its overall capability to compete in a given industry.

5.5.3 Preparing the Strategic Advantages Profile

Based on the detailed information presented in the OCP, it is possible to prepare a concise chart of a strategic advantage profile (SAP). It can also be prepared directly without making a detailed OCP. A SAP provides "a picture of the more critical areas, which can have a relationship to the strategic posture of the firm in the future".

Exhibit 5.3 provides an illustration of an SAP drawn for a hypothetical company in the automobile company. The main business of the company is in the personal car manufacturing for domestic and exports markets. This example relates to a hypothetical company but the illustration is realistic.

Exhibit 5.3 Strategic Advantage Profile (SAP) for an Automobile Company

Capability Factors	*Nature of Impact*	*Competitive strengths or weaknesses*
1. Finance	↓	High cost of capital; reserves and surplus position unsatisfactory
2. Marketing	→	Fierce competition in industry; company's position secure at present
3. Operations	↑	Plant and machinery in excellent condition; captive sources for parts and components available
4. Personnel	→	Quality of managers and workers comparable with that in competitor companies
5. Information	↑	Computerised management information system in the process of development; traditional functions such as payroll and accounting computerized
6. General Management	↑	High quality and experienced top management; generally adopts a proactive stance with regard to decision making

Upward arrow indicates strength, downward arrow indicates weakness, while horizontal arrow indicates a neutral position.

The strategic advantage profile clearly shows the strengths and weaknesses in different functional areas. For instance, the company has to use its strengths in the area of operations and in general management areas. A gap is also indicated in the finance area which has to be overcome if the company has to survive and prosper in a competitive industry like bicycle manufacturing. In marketing, though the competitive position is secure at present, it cannot be said that it will remain so in the future. The SAP indicates that strategists can initiate action to cover the gaps and use the company's strengths in the light of environmental threats and opportunities. The probable line of action to be adopted for covering the gaps and using the company's strengths in the light of environmental threats and opportunities is found through considering strategic alternatives at the corporate-level and the business level and exercising a strategic choice.

5.6 METHODS AND TECHNIQUES OF ORGANISATIONAL APPRAISAL

There are various methods and techniques used for organisational appraisal. These can be broadly categorised in three ways. These are as follows:

1. Internal Analysis
   - (i) VRIO framework
   - (ii) Value Chain Analysis
   - (iii) Quantitative Analysis
     - (a) Financial Analysis
     - (b) Non-Financial Analysis
   - (iv) Qualitative Analysis
2. Comparative Analysis
   - (i) Historical Analysis
   - (ii) Industry Norms
   - (iii) Benchmarking
3. Comprehensive Analysis
   - (i) Key Factor Rating
   - (ii) Business Intelligence System
   - (iii) Balance Score card

These methods and techniques are explained here.

5.6.1 Internal Analysis

5.6.1.1 VRIO framework analysis

VRIO framework is the contribution of Barney, who is credited with the resources based theory (which has been explained earlier in this chapter) VRIO stand for Valuable, Rare, Inimitable and Organised. In order to lead to a sustainable competitive advantage a resource or capability should be valuable, rare, inimitable (including non-substitutable), and organised. This VRIO framework is the foundation for internal analysis. If you ask a business person why their firm does well while others do poorly, a common answer is likely to be "our people." But this is really not an answer, it may be the start of an answer, but one need to probe deeper, what is it about "our people" that are especially valuable? Why don't competitors have similar people? Can't competitors hire our people away? Or is it that there is something special about the organisation that brings out the best in people? These kinds of questions form the basis of VRIO and get to the heart of why some resources help firms more than others.

Valuable: A resource is valuable if it helps the organisation meet an external threat or exploit an opportunity. While it may not help the firm outperform its competitors, it can still be labelled a strength. One good way to think about valuable resources is to ask how they help the company. Common competitive foundations for firms are efficiency, quality, customer responsiveness, and innovation. If a resource helps bring about any one of these four things then it is valuable. Efficiency is simply the amount of output for any unit of input, and is probably the most obvious way a firm can obtain an advantage. If a firm is a more efficient producer of goods or services than its competitors then it has an advantage. Innovation is devising new products or services (product innovation) or new ways of producing/delivering goods or services (process innovation). Product innovation is of direct benefit to the organisation because an organisation can have at least a temporary monopoly on the new product. Process innovation generally influences efficiency rather than having a direct effect.

Quality is the idea that the good does what it is designed for exceptionally well. Customer responsiveness is simply meeting the needs of the customer exceptionally well. It is probably the broadest of the three because it can encompass things like merchandise returns, hours of availability, etc. A resource that isn't even valuable, e.g., tarnished brand name, is best labelled a weakness.

The organisation capabilities possessed by the firm that help it to generate revenue by capitalising on opportunities and/or to reduce costs by neutralising threats. Examples of valuable capabilities are: the abilities to generate an amicable relationship with the government or efficient after-sales service to its customer.

Rare: The organisation capabilities that are possessed by the firm exclusively or just by a few other, or a resource is rare simply if it is not widely possessed by other competitors. Examples of such rare capability are: exclusive location of steel plant close to availability of iron ore and coal, highly motivated workforce such as in the case of Infosys or TCS, Coke's brand name is valuable but most of Coke's competitors (Pepsi, 7 Up, RC) also are widely recognized brand names as well, making it not that rare. Of course, Coke's brand may be the most recognized, but that makes it more valuable but not rare in this case.

Inimitable: A resource is inimitable and non-substitutable if it is difficult for another firm to acquire it or a substitute something else in its place. This is probably the toughest criteria to examine because given enough time and money almost any resource can be imitated. Even patents only last twenty years and can be invented around in even less time. Therefore, one way to think about this is to compare how long you think it will take for competitors to imitate or substitute something else for that resource and compare it to the useful life of the product. Another way to help determine if a resource is inimitable is why/how it came about. Inimitable resources are often a result of historical, ambiguous, or socially complex causes. For example, the U.S. Army paid for Coke to build bottling plants around the world during World War II. Generally, intangible (also called tacit) resources or capabilities, like corporate culture or reputation, are very hard to imitate and therefore inimitable.

Organized: The organisational capabilities possessed by the firm which can be used through appropriate organisational structure, business processes, control system and reward system that are present in the organisation. A resource is organized if the firm is able to actually use it. Generally, organisation is frequently neglected by strategy because it often deals with the inner workings of the management. The good news is that rarely are firms not organized to exploit their valuable resources. The examples of firm organised for uses are: availability of competent R& D personnel and research laboratory to innovate new and improved products or availability of potential business partners, efficient supply chain management system.

If the firm does turn up a valuable, rare, and inimitable resource that the firm is not taking advantage of, then the firm has developed a weakness and nor strengths. Many scholars refer to core competence, a core competence is simply a resource that is VRIO. While VRIO resources are the best, they are quite rare and it is not uncommon for successful firms to simply be combinations of a large number of VRIO or even VRIO resources and capabilities. Recall that even a VRIO resource can be considered a strength under a traditional SWOT analysis. Finally, remember that VRIO analysis is done on each individual resource not on the firm as a whole.

5.6.1.2 Value chain analysis

The term 'value chain' was used by Michael Porter in his book *Competitive Advantage: Creating and Sustaining Superior Performance* (1985). The value chain analysis describes the activities the organisation performs and links them to the organisation's competitive position. Value chain analysis describes the activities within and around an organisation, and relates them to an analysis of the competitive strength of the organisation. Therefore, it evaluates which value each particular activity adds to the organisation's products or services. This idea was built upon the insight that an organisation is more than a random compilation of machinery, equipment, people and money. Only if these things are arranged into systems and systematic activities it will become possible to produce something for which customers are willing to pay a price. Porter argues that the ability to perform particular activities and to manage the linkages between these activities is a source of competitive advantage.

Porter suggested that activities within the organisation add value to the service and products that the organisation produces, and all these activities should be run at optimum level if the organisation is to gain any real competitive advantage. If they are run efficiently the value obtained should exceed the costs of running them, i.e., customers should return to the organisation and transact freely and willingly.

Michael Porter suggested that the organisation is split into 'primary activities' and 'support activities'. Porter distinguishes between primary activities and support activities. Primary activities are directly concerned with the creation or delivery of a product or service. They can be grouped into five main areas: inbound logistics, operations, outbound logistics, marketing and sales, and service. Each of these primary activities is linked to support activities which help to improve their effectiveness or efficiency. There are four main areas of support activities: procurement, technology development (including R&D), human resource management, and infrastructure (systems for planning, finance, quality, information management, etc.).

Primary activities

Inbound logistics: Inbound logistics are the activities concerned with receiving, storing, and distributing inputs to the product/service. This includes materials handling, stock control, transport, etc. It also refers to goods being obtained from the organisation's suppliers ready to be used for producing the end product.

- **Operations:** The raw materials and goods obtained are manufactured into the final product. Value is added to the product at this stage as it moves through the production line. At this stage transformation of various inputs into the final product or service take place. For example, it may include machining, packaging, assembly, and testing.
- **Outbound logistics:** It involves collection, storage, and distribution the product to customers. For tangible products this could be warehousing, materials handling, and transport. In case of services, it may be more concerned with arrangements for bringing customers to the service places if it is a fixed location. Once the products have been manufactured they are ready to be distributed to distribution centres, wholesalers, retailers or customers.
- **Marketing and Sales:** Marketing must make sure that the product is targeted towards the correct customer group. The marketing mix is used to establish an effective strategy, any competitive advantage is clearly communicated to the target group by the use of the promotional mix.
- **Services:** After the product/service has been sold what support services does the organisation have to offer. All the activities that enhance or maintain the value of a product/service such as installation, repair, training, spares, etc. This may come in the form of after sales training, guarantees and warranties.

Support activities

The support activities assist the primary activities in helping the organisation achieve its competitive advantage. They include:

- **Procurement:** This department must source raw materials for the organisation and obtain the best price for doing so. For the price they must obtain the best possible quality.
- **Technology Development:** The use of technology to obtain a competitive advantage within the organisation. This is very important in today's technology driven environment. Technology can be used in production to reduce cost thus add value, or in research and development to develop new products, or via the use of the Internet so customers have access to online facilities.

- **Human resource management:** The organisation will have to recruit, train and develop the people for the organisation if they are to succeed in their objectives. Staff will have to be motivated and paid the 'market rate' if they are to stay with the organisation and add value to it over their duration of employment. Within the service sector, e.g., airlines it is the 'staff' who may offer the competitive advantage that is needed within the field.
- **Firm infrastructure:** Every organisation needs to ensure that its finance, legal and management structures work efficiently and help drive the organisation forward.

The value chain analysis is an useful method for organisational appraisal as it helps in providing clarity about the strengths and weaknesses of the organisation. In general, the activities which provide or create more value to customer at less cost, are strengths. The value chain encompasses the whole organisation and looks at how primary and support activities can work together effectively and efficiently to help gain the organisation a superior competitive advantage. It would seem evident that in searching for the most appropriate means, of differentiating for competitive advantage it is important to look at which activities are the most essential as far as consumers and customers are concerned, and to isolate the key success factors. It is a search for opportunities to be different from competitors in ways that matter, and through this the creation of a superior competitive position. It is perhaps best illustrated by the case of YKK, the Japanese zip manufacturer, the world market leader. The essential components of the strategy are:

- heavily automated plants;
- production of coils in Japan for world supply;
- little dependence on supplies;
- competitive pricing of finished products;
- vertical information design and manufacture of own machinery;
- wide range of colours and sizes

Exhibit 5.4 Porter's Generic Value Chain

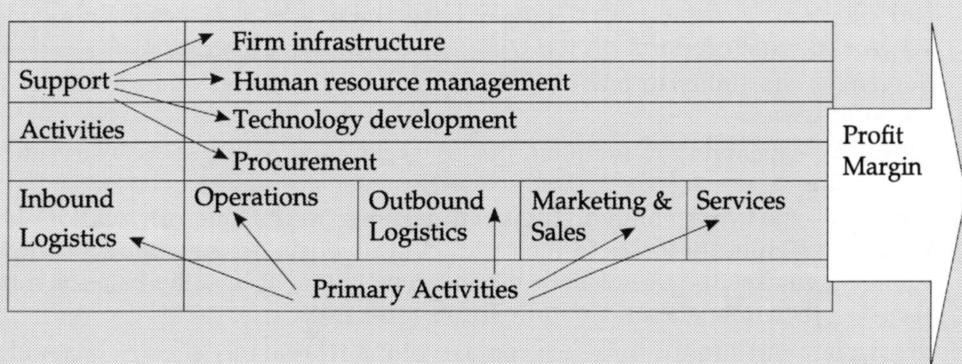

5.6.1.3 *Quantitative analysis*

Quantitative analysis is a process of disseminating financial data in order to make valid projections regarding the future performance of a corporation or market. The primary purpose of quantitative analysis is to employ quantifiable attributes of a particular company in order to determine its security or market value. To do so, quantitative analysis practitioners gather and analyze data such as profit and loss statements, company assets, market share, and earnings records. Quantitative analysis may also involve such characteristics as company liabilities, sales figures, trading trends, and alike. Unlike qualitative analysis, which may consider more uncertain factors like the quality of management, branding, and intrinsic value, quantitative analysis looks only at measurable facets. Thus, technical analysis, which employs mathematical models, would be considered part of quantitative analysis. We will discuss both financial and non-financial analysis.

(i) Financial Analysis: Financial analysis (also referred to as financial statement analysis or accounting analysis) refers to an assessment of the viability, stability and profitability of a business, sub-business or project. It is performed by professionals who prepare reports using ratios that make use of information taken from financial statements and other reports. These reports are usually presented to top management as one of their bases in making business decisions.

- Continue or discontinue its main operation or part of its business.
- Make or purchase certain materials in the manufacture of its product.
- Acquire or rent/lease certain machinery and equipment in the production of its goods.
- Issue stocks or negotiate for a bank loan to increase its working capital.
- Make decisions regarding investing or lending capital.
- Other decisions that allow management to make an informed selection on various alternatives in the conduct of its business.

Financial analysts often assess the firm's:

1. **Profitability** - its ability to earn income and sustain growth in both short term and long term. A company's degree of profitability is usually based on the income statement, which reports on the company's results of operations.
2. **Solvency** - its ability to pay its obligation to creditors and other third parties in the long term.
3. **Liquidity** - its ability to maintain positive cash flow, while satisfying immediate obligations.
4. **Stability** - the firm's ability to remain in business in the long run, without having to sustain significant losses in the conduct of its business. Assessing a company's stability requires the use of both the income statement and the balance sheet, as well as other financial and non-financial indicators.

Both solvency and liquidity are based on the company's balance sheet, which indicates the financial condition of a business as of a given point in time. Financial analysts often compare financial ratios (of solvency, profitability, growth, etc.):

- **Past Performance** – Across time periods for the same firm (the last 5 years for example),
- **Future Performance** – Using past figures and certain mathematical and statistical techniques, including present and future values. This extrapolation method is the main source of errors in financial analysis as past statistics can be poor predictors of future prospects.
- **Comparative Performance** – Comparison between similar firms.

There are many ratios used to analyze financial statements:

- *Liquidity Analysis Ratio*: For example, the net working capital ratio is calculated between net working capital and total assets.
- *Profitability Analysis Ratio*: For example, return on assets ratio is calculated between net income and average total assets. Profit margin ratio is calculated between net income and sales. Earning per share is calculated between net income and number of outstanding shares.
- *Activity Analysis Ratio*: For example, asset turnover ratio is calculated between sales and average total assets. Inventory turnover ratio is calculated between cost of goods sold and average inventories.
- *Capital Structure Analysis Ratio*: The most important ratio is debt to equity ratio, which is calculated between total liabilities and total stockholders' equity.
- *Capital Market Analysis Ratio*: For example, dividend ratio is calculated between annual dividends per common share and market price of common stock per share.

All these ratios are collectively used to carry out the financial analysis of business to assess growth, profitability, and solvency of a business. Remember that ratio analysis is as important as horizontal and vertical analyses and must not be overlooked.

(ii) Non -Financial Analysis: Financial analysis can be expressed in terms of common monetary units such as rupee, pound or dollar. But not everything of the organisations can be expressed in monetary terms and even it may not be desirable. Quantification of intangibles such as good will or employee morale may not be possible. Hence, non financial quantitative analysis can help an organisation in appraisal. Other examples are: employee turnover, absenteeism, market ranking, advertising recall rate, inventory units used per period, etc.

5.6.1.4 Qualitative analysis

Quantitative analysis has its own limitation and it cannot be adopted for all parameters in the organisational appraisal, hence there is need to carry out qualitative analysis, which is based on informed opinion, expert judgement or intuition . Some of the strengths and weaknesses of an organisation cannot be expressed in quantitative terms. For example, corporate culture, ability to absorb and disseminate knowledge or the level of moral of the employee. A systematic qualitative approach using survey methods can be used to find these. Qualitative analysis can also be used to effectively supplement a quantitative analysis or it can also be used to support and reinforce a quantitative assessment. Qualitative assessment is generally considered a soft approach to the hard approach of for quantitative analysis.

5.6.2 Comparative Analysis

The strengths, weaknesses of an organisation and its distinct competence are not absolute but relative. The relativity is based on the uniqueness and exclusivity of the strength and weakness and the distinct competence of an organisation in comparison to the other competitors. To adequately comprehend the strategic capability of an organisation, it is useful to carry out a comparative analysis, with itself in the past to see how the resource basis has shifted over time, with other competitive organisations, and industry norms.

The comparative analysis can be done in three ways: historical analysis, bench marking and industry norms. These have been described here.

5.6.2.1 Historical analysis

Historical analysis looks at the deployment of the resources of a business in comparison with previous years in order to identify any significant changes in the overall levels of resources. Typically, measures like sales-capital ratio, sales-employees ratio are used as well as identification of any significant variations in the proportions of resources devoted to different activities. Such analysis appears straightforward, but in a tabulated form often discloses drifts normally not visible. Thus a company, basically in manufacturing and retailing its own products, finding the retail market relatively favourable may gradually emphasise on retailing to such a degree as to drift away from the traditional base of manufacturing. It is only when resource utilisation is compared across the years that the drift becomes apparent. It is now for the company to reassess where its major thrust of business should lie in the future. In other words, the company has gradually redefined the boundaries of its value chain over time.

Historical analysis has some limitations. First, it only indicates the area of bad performance where the organisation is lacking. The analysis does not indicate the reason of bad performance so the corrective action cannot be taken on the basis of historic analysis alone. Secondly, if the measurement of past performance is on the smaller base area, it may show either dramatic improvement of fall in the performance that may turn out to be very illusory. Lastly, it is only meant to show the improvement of fall in performance with regards to one's own past performance, while the organisation should be more concerned with the performance in comparison to their competitors.

Comparison with Industry Norms: The historical analysis discussed above is upgraded considerably by additional comparison with the industry as a whole. It helps to put the company's resources and performance in perspective and provides the company with a broad idea about its competitive position in relation to the industry. The industry to which a business belongs is the most obvious choice for comparison with regards to a wide range of parameters. The company may crosscheck its cost structure with that of its competitors. The company may set the advertising budget equal to its nearest competitors. It is assumed that the business in the industry operates in the similar relevant environment and a comparison can give significant information on the basis of which to assess where one stands in comparison to its competitors.

The dangers of such comparison with the industry as a whole are, however, several. It may overlook the fact that the industry as a whole is doing badly and is losing out competitively to other industries and other countries with better resources and with the capability to satisfy customer needs better. The industry norms, averaging out companies with different strategies, often average out different things and in the process hide more than they reveal. Thus, for instance, comparing labour costs; for companies with cost competitiveness as the critical strategy, labour cost should necessarily be low, whereas for companies with differentiation as the critical strategy, labour cost, is no longer critical and can easily be somewhat higher, so long as it is more than compensated by the added value gained by differentiation, duly reflected in higher price. What is more important, therefore, is to compare similar value activities between organisations if the strategic context is not forgotten. This would, however, mean keeping detailed profiles of competitors' resources, and may prove very difficult and expensive.

5.6.2.2 Benchmarking

Benchmarking is the process of comparing one's business processes and performance metrics to industry's bests and/or best practices from other industries. Dimensions typically measured are quality, time and cost. In the process of benchmarking, management identifies the best firms in their industry, or in another industry where similar processes exist, and compare the results and processes of those studied (the "targets") to one's own results and processes. In this way, they learn how well the targets perform and, more importantly, the business processes that explain why these firms are successful.

The term benchmarking was first used by cobblers to measure people's feet for shoes. They would place someone's foot on a "bench" and mark it out to make the pattern for the shoes. Benchmarking is used to measure performance using a specific indicator (cost per unit of measure, productivity per unit of measure, cycle time of x per unit of measure or defects per unit of measure) resulting in a metrics of performance that is then compared to others.

Benchmarking is of three types: performance, process and strategic benchmarking. Process benchmarking or best practice benchmarking is used in management and particularly strategic management, in which organisations evaluate various aspects of their processes in relation to best practice companies' processes, usually within a peer group defined for the purposes of comparison. Performance benchmarking is comparing one's own with that of some other organisation for the purpose to determine how good one's own organisation is. Strategic benchmarking is comparing the long term, significant decision and action undertaken by the organisation with other organisations to achive their strategic goals and objectives.

This comparison allows organisations to develop plans on how to make improvements or adapt specific best practices, usually with the aim of increasing some aspect of performance. Benchmarking may be a one-off event, but is often treated as a continuous process in which organisations continually seek to improve their practices. There is no single benchmarking process that has been universally adopted. The wide appeal and acceptance of benchmarking has led to the emergence of various benchmarking methodologies. One seminal book on benchmarking is Boxwell's *Benchmarking for Competitive Advantage* (1994). Robert Camp (who wrote one of the earliest books on benchmarking in 1989) developed a 12-stage approach to benchmarking. The 12-stage methodology consists of:

- Select subject
- Define the process
- Identify potential partners
- Identify data sources
- Collect data and select partners
- Determine the gap
- Establish process differences
- Target future performance
- Communicate
- Adjust goal
- Implement
- Review and recalibrate

The following is an example of a typical benchmarking methodology.

- **Identify your problem areas** – Because benchmarking can be applied to any business process or function, a range of research techniques may be required. They include: informal conversations with customers, employees, or suppliers; exploratory research techniques such as focus groups; or in-depth marketing research, quantitative research, surveys, questionnaires, re-engineering analysis, process mapping, quality control variance reports, or financial ratio analysis. Before embarking on comparison with other organisations it is essential that you know your own organisation's functions, processes; base lining performance provides a point against which improvement effort can be measured.
- **Identify other industries that have similar processes** – For instance, if one were interested in improving hands offs in addiction treatment he/she would try to identify other fields that also have hands off challenges. These could include air traffic control, cell phone switching between towers, transfer of patients from surgery to recovery rooms.
- **Identify organisations that are leaders in these areas** – Look for the very best in any industry and in any country. Consult customers, suppliers, financial analysts, trade associations, and magazines to determine which companies are worthy of study.
- **Survey companies for measures and practices** – Companies target specific business processes using detailed surveys of measures and practices used to identify business process alternatives and leading companies. Surveys are typically masked to protect confidential data by neutral associations and consultants.
- **Visit the "best practice" companies to identify leading edge practices** – Companies typically agree to mutually exchange information beneficial to all parties in a benchmarking group and share the results within the group.

- **Implement new and improved business practices** – Take the leading edge practices and develop implementation plans which include identification of specific opportunities, funding the project and selling the ideas to the organisation for the purpose of gaining demonstrated value from the process.

Despite its popularity, benchmarking has some limitations. These limitations are :

- It is tough process to use, time consuming, expensive and require a high level of commitment.
- It will serve little purpose if it is done selectively, it needs to be done on continuous basis for effective results.
- Financial statement of many companies are available, which indicates the previous years figure, which may not be rally useful.
- It may not be possible to find comparable benchmarking in all types and area of activities and the organisation may have to rely on the second or third best available choice.

5.6.3 Comprehensive Analysis

A comprehensive analysis help in helps to deal with the limitation of various analytical techniques, already discussed in previous sections. There are three popular methods and technique of key factor ratings, business intelligence system and balance score card used for performing comprehensive analysis. These techniques have been explained here.

5.6.3.1 Key factor rating

This method takes into account the key factors affecting organisational functioning. Information regarding the key factors is generally collected after a series of meetings, discussions and surveys. Answers in each functional area are being closely examined with a view to rate the key factors. The relative impact of each factor (favourable or unfavourable) on a particular result is also examined using mathematical models. Key factors or strategic internal factors are a firm's basic capabilities, limitations, and characteristics.

Exhibit 5.5 lists typical factors, broken along functional lines, some of which would be the focus of internal analysis in most business firms. To develop or revise a strategy, managers would identify the few factors on which success will most likely depend. These factors are the *key strategic factors.* Strategists examine past performance to isolate key internal contributors to favourable (or unfavourable) results. The same examination and questions can be applied to a firm's current situation, with particular emphasis on changes in the importance of key dimensions over time. Analysis of past trends of sales, costs and profitability is also of major importance in identifying strategic internal factors. Identification of strategic factors also requires an external focus. When a strategist isolates key internal factors through analysis of past and present performance, industry conditions/trends and comparison with competitors also provide insights. Changing industry conditions can lead to the need to re-examine internal strengths and weaknesses in the light of newly emerging determinants of success in the industry. Furthermore, strategic internal factors are offer chosen for in-depth evaluation because firms are contemplating expansion of products or markets, diversification, and so forth. Clearly scrutinizing the industry under consideration and current competitors is a key means of identifying strategic factors if a firm is evaluating a move into unfamiliar markets.

Key factor rating is quite a comprehensive method as it covers a range of issues concerning different areas of the organisation. But it also has some limitation these are:

Exhibit 5.5 Key Internal Factors

Key Marketing Factors

Firm's products/services: breadth of product line.
Concentration of sales in a few products or to a few customers.
Ability to gather needed information about markets.
Market share or sub-market shares.
Product/service mix and expansion potential: life cycle of key products
Services: profit/sales balance in product/service.
Channels of distribution: number, coverage and control.
Effective sales organisation: knowledge of customer needs.
Product/service image, reputation, and quality.
Pricing strategy and pricing flexibility.
Procedures for digesting market feedback and developing new products, services, or markets.
After-sales service and follow-up.
Goodwill/brand loyalty.

Key Finance and Accounting Factors

Ability to raise short-term capital.
Ability to raise long-term capital: debt/equity.
Corporate level resources (multi-business firm).
Cost of capital in relation to industry and competitors.
Tax considerations.
Relations with owners, investors, and stockholders.
Leverage position: capacity to utilize alternative financial strategies such as lease, or sale and lease back.
Cost of entry and barriers to entry.
Price-earnings ratio.
Working capital: flexibility of capital structure.
Effective cost control: ability to reduce cost.
Financial size.
Efficient and effective accounting system for cost, budget and profit planning.

Contd...

Key Production/Operation/Technical Factors

Raw material cost and availability; supplier relationship.
Inventory control systems; inventory turnover.
Location of facilities; layout and utilization of facilities.
Economies of scale.
Technical efficiency of facilities and utilization of capacity.
Effective use of subcontracting.
Degree of vertical integration; value added and profit margin.
Efficiency and cost-benefit of equipment.
Effective operation control procedures design, scheduling, purchasing, quality control and efficiency.
Costs and technological competence in relation to industry and competitors.
Research and development/technology/innovation.
Patents, trademarks, and similar legal protection.
Key personnel/human resources factors
Management personnel.
Employees skill and morale.
Labour relations costs in comparison to industry and competition.
Efficient and effective personnel policies.
Effective use of incentives to motivate performance.
Ability to level peaks and valleys of employment.
Employee turnover and absenteeism.
Specialized skills.
Experience.

Key Organisation of General Management Factors

Organisational structure.
Firm's image and prestige.
Firm's record of achieving objectives.
Organisation of communication system.
Overall organisational control system (effectiveness and utilization).
Organisational climate: culture.
Use of systematic procedures and techniques in decision-making.
Top management skills, capabilities, and interest.
Strategic planning system
Inter-organisational synergy (multi-business firm).

- Its comprehensiveness makes it an unwieldy method to use. It will require a variety of information from different parts of organisation, making it a slow and inefficient method.
- This method is a subjective method as managers have to assign the rating on the basis of their judgement. Subjectivity has its limitations and would require improvements based on reference to objective factors as one set of factors after the other are considered.
- Key factors rating methods needs to be supplemented with the audit, otherwise there is a possibility of evaluation efforts being duplicated.

5.6.3.2 Balanced scorecard

The balanced scorecard (BSC) is the most widely applied performance management system today. The balanced scorecard was originally developed as a performance measurement system in 1992 by Dr. Robert Kaplan and Dr. David Norton at the Harvard Business School. Unlike earlier performance measurement systems, the balanced scorecard measures performance across a number of different perspectives—a financial perspective, a customer perspective, an internal business process perspective, and an innovation and learning perspective. Through the use of the various perspectives, the balanced scorecard captures both leading and lagging performance measures, thereby providing a more "balanced" view of company performance. Leading indicators include measures, such as customer satisfaction, new product development, on-time delivery, employee competence development, etc. Traditional lagging indicators include financial measures, such as revenue growth and profitability. The balanced scorecard performance management systems have been widely adopted globally, in part, because this approach enables organisations to align all levels of staff around a single strategy so that it can be executed more successfully.

The balance scorecard identifies four perspectives or key performance indicators as given below:

- **The Innovation, Learning & Growth Perspective:** This perspective encourages the identification of measures that answer the question: "Can we continue to improve and create value?". It includes employee training and corporate cultural attitudes related to both individual and corporate self-improvement. In a knowledge-worker organisation, people – the only repository of knowledge – are the main resource. In the current climate of rapid technological change, it is becoming necessary for knowledge workers to be in a continuous learning mode. Metrics can be put into place to guide managers in focusing training funds where they can help the most. In any case, learning and growth constitute the essential foundation for success of any knowledge-worker organisation. Kaplan and Norton emphasize that 'learning' is more than 'training'; it also includes things like mentors and tutors within the organisation, as well as that ease of communication among workers that allows them to readily get help on a problem when it is needed. It also includes technological tools; what the Baldrige criteria call "high performance work systems."

- **The Internal Business Process Perspective:** This perspective refers to internal business processes. It encourages the identification of measures that answer the question "What must we excel at?" Metrics based on this perspective allow the managers to know how well their business is running, and whether its products and services conform to customer requirements (the mission). These metrics have to be carefully designed by those who know these processes most intimately; with our unique missions these are not something that can be developed by outside consultants.
- **The Customer Perspective:** This perspective encourages the identification of measures that answer the question "How do customers see us?"Recent management philosophy has shown an increasing realization of the importance of customer focus and customer satisfaction in any business. These are leading indicators: if customers are not satisfied, they will eventually find other suppliers that will meet their needs. Poor performance from this perspective is thus a leading indicator of future decline, even though the current financial picture may look good. In developing metrics for satisfaction, customers should be analyzed in terms of kinds of customers and the kinds of processes for which we are providing a product or service to those customer groups.
- **The Financial Perspective:** This perspective encourages the identification of a few relevant high-level financial measures. In particular, designers were encouraged to choose measures that helped inform the answer to the question "How do we look to shareholders?" Timely and accurate funding data will always be a priority, and managers will do whatever necessary to provide it. In fact, often there is more than enough handling and processing of financial data. With the implementation of a corporate database, it is hoped that more of the processing can be centralized and automated. But the point is that the current emphasis on financials leads to the "unbalanced" situation with regard to other perspectives. There is perhaps a need to include additional financial-related data, such as risk assessment and cost-benefit data, in this category.

Each of these perspectives can be used individually, but using them in combination provides deeper insights and a balanced approach to strategy formulation. One perspective is not allowed to outweigh other when the strength and weakness of an organisation are assessed. Hence, the balanced score card provides a balanced and comprehensive framework for internal assessment of an organisation.

Exhibit 5.6 An Example of a Balance Scorecard

Financial Perspective: Return on Capital Employed, Cash Flow, Project Profitability, Profit Forecast Reliability, Sales Backlog.

Innovation and Learning Perspective: Percentage of Revenue from New Services, Rate of Improvement Index, Staff Attitude Survey, Employee Suggestions, Revenue per Employee.

Customer Perspective: Pricing Index, Customer Ranking Survey, Customer Satisfaction Index, Market Share, Business Segment Tier I Customers, Key Accounts.

Internal Business Perspective: Hours with Customers, Tender Success Rate, Rework, Safety Incident Index, Project Performance Index, Project Closeout Cycle.

Organisations have adapted the balanced scorecard to their particular external and internal circumstances. Both commercial and not-for-profit organisations have successfully used the BSC framework. Since 1992, Drs. Kaplan and Norton have studied the success of various applications of the BSC in different types of organisations. Companies have used as few as four measures and as many as several hundred measures when designing a BSC performance measurement system. Based on this research, it has been found that a BSC framework using about 20–25 measures is the usual recommended best practice. Smaller organisations might use fewer measures, but it is generally not advisable to go beyond a total of 25 measures for any single organisation, holding company, or conglomerate group of holding companies.

5.6.3.3 Business intelligence systems

Business intelligence is a general term used to refer to a number of activities a company may undertake to gather information about their market or their competitors. Some areas often included under the blanket heading of business intelligence are: competition analysis, better understanding of organisational data and provide the information organisations need to make enlightened decisions. Moreover, business intelligence systems are primarily focused on reporting, querying, and analysis of data residing in an enterprise data warehouse (EDW), and both dependent and independent data marts.

In most cases, a company will either hire an outside agency or create their own dedicated business intelligence group. This group will then gather information from inside the company about how well the company has been performing and where improvements may be made. The group then looks to outside sources, which may include public records of other businesses in the same sector, market analysis by third parties, and customer survey information. The group may then delve further into specific competitors; both by examining their public information and business model, and in some cases by using an industrial spy to covertly gather information.

The main goal of a business intelligence system (BIS) is to assist in making good business decisions. These computer-based systems identify and analyze business data such as sales revenue and buying trends to provide perspective on business operations that supports the decision-making process.

Business intelligence systems are contrasted to more classic forms of information gathering by their interdepartmental focus and their general overview towards business performance. They are also unique in their use of advanced technology and techniques to mine for data and to crunch that data in the most optimal manner. While a group in charge of market analysis might have a strong understanding of the particular sector of the market in which the business operates, their lack of the same detailed understanding about specific competitors and the inner management of the company make their information less useful. In a business intelligence model, all these various forms of business improvement are tied together so that communication is quick and easy, and each segment helps inform the other segments so their insights are even more valuable than they would be on their own.

Once a business intelligence system is in a place, the company can expect to find improved turnaround times on data collection, ideas for new business initiatives, more targeted marketing campaigns, a much more precise picture of customer needs and desires, and a strong understanding of how best to compete with top competitors. The improvement in business agility that comes with business intelligence is substantial in most cases, and allows a company to take better advantage of constantly evolving market conditions.

The use of industrial espionage in business intelligence is widely considered something of a grey area. Some businesses choose not to engage in covert information gathering, while others consider it a core part of a healthy business intelligence programme. Many areas commonly referred to as industrial espionage are fully legal, such as careful tracking of patent filings and corporate newsletters to predict where a competitor is moving in the marketplace.

Business Intelligence System can have very productive and effective improvement in the organisation's performance:

Corporate performance management

Optimising customer relations, monitoring business activities, and traditional support system.

Specific stand-alone application for specific applications or strategies.

Management reporting for business intelligence.

5.6.3.4 Applications of business intelligence system

- Operational Reports: Displays data with rich presentation and within a structured layout (i.e., rows and columns).
- Query and Analysis: Interactive methods to query data, present data in an ad-hoc manner, and to find information on an as-needed basis.
- Dashboard Management: Graphical interfaces and real-time methods to provide guided analysis and to intuitively monitor organisational metrics.
- On-line Analytical Processing (OLAP): The capability of manipulating and analysing data from multiple perspectives in a rapid fashion.
- Data Mining & Predictive Analytics: Utilizing statistics, algorithms, and sophisticated data search capabilities to discover hidden patterns and relationships in data and project future results.

Exercise

1. How do organisations determine strength and weakness? What step they can take to overcome their weaknesses.
2. How VIRO framework can help the organisations to identify their strength and over come their weaknesses.
3. Although the balance scorecard is a very comprehensive method but it is difficult to comprehend and implement it. Express your viewpoint.

4. Historical analysis indicates the past performance of the company, it may not give the current or future perspective. In this context how useful this technique may be for the organisational appraisal.
5. Balance scorecard provides a balanced view of the different perspectives of the organisation, yet it may not be able bring the true picture of organisation's strengths and weaknesses. Justify your answer with suitable examples.
6. How do we prepare the strategic advantage profiles of a company? Select a company and prepare SAP for it.
7. Organisational capability profile (OCP) provides the true picture of the capability of the organisation. How organisation can benefit from it? How one should prepare OCP?
8. What pitfalls one should avoid while using a financial analysis for organisational appraisal?
9. How we can use industry norms and benchmarking for organisational appraisal.
10. What is the importance of value chain analysis in assessing the weakness and strength of the organisation.
11. How does the key factor rating method work for organisational appraisal?

6 Corporate Level Strategies: Stability and Retrenchment Strategies

6.1 INTRODUCTION

The overall **corporate level strategy** is concerned with the broad scope of an organisation's strategic activities and the matching of these to the organisation's environment, its resources, capabilities and the values and expectations of its various stakeholders. It looks at the whole strategic scope of the enterprise. This is the "large picture" view of the organisation and includes deciding in which service or products markets to compete and in which geographic regions to operate. For multi-business firms, the resource allocation process—how equipment, funds, human and other resources are distributed—is typically established at the corporate level.

Corporate level strategies address the entire strategic scope of the enterprise. This is the "big picture" view of the organisation and includes deciding in which product or service markets to compete and in which geographic regions to operate. For multi-business firms, the resource allocation process—how cash, staffing, equipment and other resources are distributed—is typically established at the corporate level. In addition, because market definition is the domain of corporate-level strategists, the responsibility for diversification, or the addition of new products or services to the existing product/service line-up, also falls within the realm of corporate-level strategy. Similarly, whether to compete directly with other firms or to selectively establish cooperative relationships—strategic alliances—falls within the purview corporate-level strategy, while requiring ongoing input from business-level managers. Critical questions answered by corporate-level strategists thus include:

1. What should be the scope of operations; i.e., what businesses should the firm be in?
2. How should the firm allocate its resources among the existing businesses?
3. What level of diversification should the firm pursue, i.e., which businesses represent the company's future? Are there additional businesses the firm should enter or are there businesses that should be targeted for termination or divestment?
4. How diversified should the corporation's business be? Should we pursue related diversification, i.e., similar products and service markets, or is unrelated diversification, i.e., dissimilar product and service markets, a more suitable

approach given current and projected industry conditions? If we pursue related diversification, how will the firm leverage potential cross-business synergies? In other words, how will adding new product or service businesses benefit the existing product/service line-up?

5. How should the firm be structured? Where should the boundaries of the firm be drawn and how will these boundaries affect relationships across businesses, with suppliers, customers and other constituents? Do the organisational components such as research and development, finance, marketing, customer service, etc., fit together? Are the responsibilities or each business unit clearly identified and is accountability established?
6. Should the firm enter into strategic alliances—cooperative, mutually beneficial relationships with other firms? If so, for what reasons? If not, what impact might this have on future profitability?

As the previous questions illustrate, corporate strategies represent the long-term direction for the organisation. Issues addressed as part of corporate strategy include those concerning diversification, acquisition, divestment, strategic alliances, and formulation of new business ventures. Corporate strategies deal with plans for the entire organisation and change as industry and specific market conditions warrant.

Top management has primary decision making responsibility in developing corporate strategies and these managers are directly responsible to shareholders. The role of the board of directors is to ensure that top managers actually represent these shareholder interests. With information from the corporation's multiple businesses and a view of the entire scope of operations and markets, corporate-level strategists have the most advantageous perspective for assessing organisation-wide competitive strengths and weaknesses, although as a subsequent section notes, corporate strategists are paralyzed without accurate and up-to-date information from managers at the business-level.

In addition, because market definition is within the scope of corporate-level strategists, the responsibility for diversification, or the addition of new products or services to the existing product/service line-up, also falls within the realm of corporate-level strategy. Likewise, whether to compete directly with other firms or to selectively establish cooperative relationships—strategic alliances—falls within the realm of corporate-level strategy, while needing ongoing input from business-level managers.

6.1.1 Functions of Corporate Strategy

Corporate strategy performs the following functions:

(i) It provides a dual approach to problem solving. Firstly, it exploits the most effective means to overcome difficulties and face competition. Secondly, it assists in the deployment of scarce resources among critical activities.

(ii) It focuses attention upon changes in the organisational set up, administration of organisational process affecting behaviour and the development of effective leadership.

(iii) It offers a technique to manage changes. The management is totally prepared to anticipate, respond and influence to look at changes. It also offers a different way of thinking.

(iv) It furnishes the management with a perspective whereby, the latter gives equal importance to present and future opportunities.

(v) It provides the management with a mechanism to cope with highly complex environment characterized by diversity of cultural, social, political and competitive forces.

6.1.2 Significance of Corporate Strategy

In the present-day competitive environment, no business organisation can dream of survival without formulating appropriate corporate strategy. As the environment is continuously changing, the need for corporate strategic framework is more specific. The following areas clearly show the importance of corporate strategy:

(i) Corporate strategy rationalises allocation of scarce resources.

(ii) Corporate strategy motivates employees examples to shape their work in the context of shared corporate goals.

(iii) Strategy assists the management to meet unanticipated future changes.

(iv) Organisational effectiveness is ensured through implementing and evaluating the strategy.

(v) Corporate strategy is a powerful tool to management to deal with the future which is uncertain and hazy in all respects.

(vi) Corporate strategy improves the capability of management in coping with the volatile external environmental forces.

(vii) Corporate strategy encourages the management to choose the best course of action to realize the objectives.

(viii) Strategy planning system provides an objective basis for measuring performance.

6.1.3 Limitations of Corporate Strategy

The corporate strategy has the following specific limitations:

(i) The process of strategy formulation is not an easy one. The process of forming corporate strategy is complex, cumbersome and complicated.

(ii) Corporate strategies are useful for long range problems. They are not effective to overcome current exigencies.

(iii) The corporate strategy formulation process calls for considerable time, money and effort. Developing appropriate corporate strategy is not a simple and economical proposition. For financially weak companies, cost becomes a great hindrance.

(iv) As future is uncertain and cannot be predicted accurately, the strategic planning system based on hazy and uncertain estimates is not exact.

(v) Implementation of corporate strategy is influenced by organisational factors, behavioural factors and motivational factors. The gap between formulation and implementation of corporate strategy does not give desired results to the organisation.

6.1.4 Levels of Corporate Strategy

Corporate strategy may exist at three levels in an organisation. They may be at corporate level, business level and operating level. In this section, a brief description of these three levels of strategy is given:

- **Corporate Level Strategy:** It is believed that strategic decision making is the responsibility of top management. At the corporate level, the board of directors and chief executive officers are involved in strategy making. Corporate planners and consultants may also be involved. Mostly, corporate level strategies are futuristic, innovative and pervasive in nature. Decision like spreading the range of business interests, acquisitions, diversification, structural redesigning, mergers, takeovers, liquidations come under corporate level strategies.
- **Business Level Strategy:** Strategic business unit (SBU) managers are involved at this level in taking strategic decisions. These strategies relate to a unit within an organisation. At business level, the objectives are formulated for SBUs and resources are allocated among functional areas. These strategies operate under the defined scope of corporate level strategy. Business level strategy is more specific and action oriented. It relates mainly with the "how" aspect. The corporate level strategy is related to the "what" aspect of corporate strategy.
- **Operating Level Strategy:** This level of strategy is at the operating end of the organisation. It is also known as functional level strategy. These decisions relate to training, investment in plant, advertising, sales promotion, total quality management, market segmentation, etc. This decision is almost tactical. They deal with a relatively restricted plan providing objectives for specific function, allocation of resources among different operations within the functional area and coordination between them.

Exhibit 6.1 shows distinctive characteristics of the three levels of strategy.

6.1.5 Types of Corporate Strategies/Grand Strategies

Corporate-level strategists have a tremendous amount of both latitude and responsibility. The myriad decisions required of these managers can be overwhelming considering the potential consequences of incorrect decisions. One way to deal with this complexity is through categorization; one categorization scheme is to classify corporate-level strategy decisions into three different types, or grand strategies. These grand strategies involve efforts to expand business operations (expansion/ growth strategies), decrease the scope of business operations (retrenchment strategies), or maintain the status quo (stability strategies). There are four corporate strategic alternatives. These strategies are as follows:

- Stability Strategy
- Expansion or Growth Strategy
- Retrenchment Strategy
- Combination Strategies

Exhibit 6.1 Strategic Decisions at Different Levels of Corporate Strategy

Dimensions	*Levels*		
	Corporate	*Business*	*Operating Functional*
Time Horizon	Long	Medium	Short
Type of Decision	Philosophical	Mixed	Operational
Risk Involved	High	Medium	Low
Impact	Significant	Major	Insignificant
Profit Potential	High	Medium	Low
Flexibility	High	Medium	Low
Adaptability	Poor	Medium	Significant
Innovations	Innovative	Mixed	Routine
Levels of Decision Making	Highest	Middle	Lowest

6.1.6 Major Reasons for Adopting Different Corporate Strategies

- **Stability Strategy:** When firms are satisfied with their current rate of growth and profits, they may decide to use a stability strategy. This strategy is essentially a continuation of existing strategies. Such strategies are typically found in industries having relatively stable environments. The firm is often making a comfortable income operating a business that they know, and see no need to make the psychological and financial investment that would be required to undertake a growth strategy.

  The following examples will show how organisation could aim at stability in its businesses:

  - A photocopier company such as Zerox or Canon provides better after sales services to its customer to improve product image and increase the sales of accessories and other consumables.
  - A energy producing company such as NTPC may modernise its power plants to increase the efficiency and productivity.
  - A packed tea company such as Tata Tetley or Lipton Tea may provide special service of bulk supply to its institutional buyers directly from its own warehouses instead of supplying through marketing intermediaries thus improving its marketing efficiency.

- **Expansion or Growth Strategy:** Expansion strategy is followed when an organisation aims at high growth by substantially broadening the scope of its existing businesses in terms of its respective customer functions, customer groups or alternative technologies either singly or jointly in order to improve its overall performances. Expansion strategies are mainly adopted when the environment demands in increase in the pace of activities, the increase in size may lead to more control over the market, namely, competitors. Growth strategies are designed to expand an organisation's performance, usually as measured by sales, profits, product mix, market coverage, market share, or other accounting and market-based variables.

The expansion or growth strategies are further classified as:

(i) Concentration
(ii) Integration
(iii) Diversification
(iv) Cooperation
(v) Internationalization

Mergers, takeovers, joint ventures and strategic alliances come under expansion through cooperation. International strategies are further classified into global strategy, transnational strategy, international strategy and multidomestic strategy.

Typical growth strategies involve one or more of the following:

- With a concentration strategy the firm attempts to achieve greater market penetration by becoming more efficient at servicing its market with a limited product line (e.g., McDonalds in fast foods).
- By using a vertical integration strategy, the firm attempts to expand the scope of its current operations by undertaking business activities formerly performed by one of its suppliers (backward integration) or by undertaking business activities performed by a business in its channel of distribution (forward integration).
- A diversification strategy entails moving into different markets or adding different products to its mix. If the products or markets are related to existing the product or service offerings, the strategy is called concentric diversification. If expansion is into products or services unrelated to the firm's existing business, the diversification is called conglomerate diversification.
- Cadbury, a chocolate manufacturer expands its customer groups by including middle-aged and old age persons to its existing customers comprising children and adolescents.
- A stockbroker's firm offered personalised financial services to its investors apart from dealing in shares and debentures, in order to increase the scope of its business and its risk
- Relance India Ltd has diversified its business to different sectors such as energy, telecom, infrastructure, retails in order to expand its business.

- **Retrenchment Strategy:** These are followed when an organisation aims at contraction of its activities. Retrenchment strategies involve a reduction or elimination of the scope of a corporation's activities, which also generally necessitates a reduction in number of employees, sale of assets associated with discontinued product or service lines, possible restructuring of debt through bankruptcy proceedings, and in the most extreme cases, liquidation of the firm. The common strategies adopted in retrenchment are:

(i) Turn around strategy
(ii) Divestment strategy
(iii) Liquidation strategy

- Firms pursue a turnaround strategy by undertaking a temporary reduction in operations in an effort to make the business stronger and more viable in the future. These moves are popularly called downsizing or rightsizing. The hope is that going through a temporary belt-tightening will allow the firm to pursue a growth strategy at some future point.
- A divestment decision occurs when a firm decides to sell one or more of the businesses in its corporate portfolio. Typically, a poorly performing unit is sold to another company and the money is reinvested in another business within the portfolio that has greater potential.
- Bankruptcy involves legal protection against creditors or others allowing the firm to restructure its debt obligations or other payments, typically in a way that temporarily increases cash flow. Such restructuring allows the firm to attempt a turnaround strategy. For example, since the airline hijackings and the subsequent tragic events of September 11, 2001, many of the airlines based in the U.S. have filed for bankruptcy to avoid liquidation as a result of stymied demand for air travel and rising fuel prices. At least one airline has asked the courts to allow it to permanently suspend payments to its employee pension plan to free up positive cash flow.
- Liquidation is the most extreme form of retrenchment. Liquidation involves the selling or closing of the entire operation. There is no future for the firm; employees are released, buildings and equipment are sold, and customers no longer have access to the product or service. This is a strategy of last resort and one that most managers work hard to avoid.

- **Combination Strategies:** These are followed when an organisation adopts a combination of stability, expansion and retrenchment either at the same time in different businesses or at different times in the same business. Any combination strategy is the result of a serious attempt on the part of the strategist to take into account the variety of environmental and organisational factors that affect the strategic formulations. Complicated situations generally require complex solutions. Combination strategies are the complex solutions that strategist have to offer when faced with the challenges of real-life situations. The following examples will show how the companies have used this strategy.
  - A paints company augmented its offering of decorative paints to provide a wider variety to its customers (stability strategy), and expands its product range to include industrial and automotive paints (expansion strategy). Simultaneously, it closed down its division which used to undertake large-scale painting contract jobs (retrenchment strategy).
  - The well known companies of the TTK group, based in Southern India, adopted a restructuring plan in the late 1980s involving following various strategies such as merger of TTK chemicals with TTK pharma (cooperation strategy), joint venture of TT industries & Textiles Ltd.(expansion through

joint venture strategy), TTK Ltd. diversified into the field of non-stick cooking utensils (diversification strategy) and TTK maps & publications expanded into the general publishing business after a turnaround (expansion strategy).

- The Tube Investments of India (TI), a Murugappa group company, has created strategic alliances in its three major businesses: tubes, cycles, and strips. In cycles, it has entered into regional outsourcing arrangements with the UP-based Avon (which we could term competition, as Avon is TI's competitor in the cycle industry) and Hamilton Cycles in the western region. In steel strips, TI has entered into a manufacturing contract with Steel Tubes of India, Steel Authority of India, and the Jindals.
- Adoption of combination strategy may apply the combination either simultaneously (across the different businesses) or sequentially. For instance, Tata Iron & Steel Company (TISCO) had first consolidated its position in the core steel business, then divested some of its non-core businesses.
- Reliance Industries, while consolidating its position in the existing businesses such as textile and petrochemicals, aggressively entered new areas such as Information Technology.

Exhibit 6.2 Types of Corporate/Grand Strategy at a Glance

1. **Stability Strategy**
   - (i) No change strategy
   - (ii) Profit strategy
   - (iii) Pause/Proceed with caution strategy
2. **Expansion or Growth Strategy**
   - (i) Concentration
   - (ii) Integration
   - (iii) Diversification
   - (iv) Cooperation : Mergers, takeovers, joint ventures and strategic alliances
   - (v) Internationalization: Global, transnational, international and multidomestic strategy
   - (vi) Digitalisation
3. **Retrenchment Strategy**
   - (i) Turnaround strategy
   - (ii) Divestment strategy
   - (iii) Liquidation strategy
4. **Combination Strategies**
   - (i) Simultaneous combination
   - (ii) Sequential combination
   - (iii) Combination of simultaneous and sequential

6.2 THE STABILITY STRATEGIES

Stability strategy implies continuing the current activities of the firm without any significant change in direction. A firm is said to be following a stability strategy if it is satisfied with the same consumer groups and maintaining the same market share, satisfied with incremental improvements of functional performance and the management does not want to take any risks that might be associated with expansion or growth. Stability strategies are adopted by an organisation when it attempts at incremental gains to improve functional performance by marginally changing one or more of its businesses in terms of their respective customers functions, customer groups or alternative technologies. Normally, this strategy is adopted when the environment is relatively unstable; expansion may be perceived as threatening. It is less risky, involves less changes and people feel comfortable with things and generally adopted when a company or firms are looking for consolidation through stability after a period of rapid expansion. When firms are satisfied with their current rate of growth and profits, they may decide to use a stability strategy. This strategy is essentially a continuation of existing strategies. Such strategies are typically found in industries having relatively stable environments. The firm often makes a comfortable income operating a business that they know, and see no need to make the psychological and financial investment that would be required to undertake a growth strategy.

Stability strategy is most likely to be pursued by small and medium sized businesses or firms in a mature stage of development, stability strategies can be useful in short run when such organisation are satisfied with their current performance. Stability strategies are implemented by 'steady as it goes' approaches to decisions. No major functional changes are made in the product line, markets or functions. However, stability strategy is not a 'do nothing' approach nor does it mean that goals such as profit growth are abandoned. The stability strategy can be designed to increase profits through such approaches as improving efficiency in current operations.

6.2.1 Why do Companies Pursue a Stability Strategy?

A stability strategy refers to a strategy by a company where the company stops the expenditure on expansion, in other words it refers to situations where companies do not venture into new markets or introduce new products. Stability strategy is adopted by company due to the following reasons:

- The firm is doing well or perceives itself as successful in their present strategies and it plans to consolidate its position in the industry in which the company is operating.
- When the economy is in recession or there is a slowdown in the economy then the companies want to have more cash in their balance sheet rather than investing that cash for expansion or other such expenses.
- When the company has too much debt in the balance sheet then also the company stops or postpones its expansion plans because if it takes more debt for expansion than it would not able to pay interest on such debt and it may create liquidity crunch for the company.

- When the company is operating in an industry which has reached maturity phase and there is no further scope for growth then also the company adopts stability strategy.
- When the gains from expansion plans are less than the costs involved for such expansion then the company follows the stability strategy.
- It is less risky, it is easier and more comfortable to continue with the same strategies instead of introducing new ones.
- The environment is relatively unstable and firms do not want to take risk of expansion.
- The firms believe that too much expansion can lead to inefficiencies and may result into substantial loss and they do not have the capacity to bear such losses.

An organisation's strategists might choose stability when

- The industry or the economy is in turmoil or the environment is volatile.
- Uncertain conditions might convince strategists to be conservative until they are more certain.
- Environmental turbulence is minimal and the firm does not foresee any major threat to itself and the industry concerned as a whole.
- The organisation just finished a period of rapid growth and needs to consolidate its gains before pursuing more growth.
- The firm's growth ambitions are very modest and it is content with incremental growth.
- The industry is in a mature stage with few or no growth prospects and the firm is currently in a comfortable position in the industry.

Situations where a stability strategy is more advisable than the growth strategy

- If the external environment is highly dynamic and unpredictable, it is advisable to continue with the present strategies instead of embarking upon the growth strategy.
- Strategic managers may feel that the cost of growth may be higher than the potential benefits hence, stability is preferred over the expansion.
- Excessive expansion may result in violation of MRTP act.

6.2.2 Nature of Stability Strategy

A firm following stability strategy maintains its current business and product portfolios; the existing level of effort; and is satisfied with incremental growth. It focuses on fine-tuning its business operations and improving functional efficiencies through better deployment of resources. In other words, a firm is said to follow stability/consolidation strategy, if:

- It decides to serve the same markets with the same products.
- It continues to pursue the same objectives with a strategic thrust on incremental improvement of functional performances.
- It concentrates its resources in a narrow product market sphere for developing a meaningful competitive advantage.

- If a firm lacks concern for business and it growth targets are modest and wishes to maintain a status quo.

Since products, markets and functions remain unchanged, stability strategy is basically a defensive strategy. It is ideal in stable business environments where an organisation can devote its efforts to improving its efficiency while not being threatened with external changes. In some cases, organisations are constrained by regulations or the expectations of key stakeholders and hence they have no option except to follow stability strategy. Generally, large firms with a sizeable portfolio of businesses do not usually depend on the stability strategy as a main route, though they may use it under certain special circumstances. They normally use it in combination with the other generic strategies, adopting stability for some businesses while pursuing expansion for the others. However, small firms find this a very useful approach since they can reduce their risk and defend their position by adopting this strategy. Niche players also prefer this strategy for the same reasons.

Stability strategy does entail changing the way the business is run, however, the range of products offered and the markets served remain unchanged or narrowly focused. Hence, stability strategy is perceived as a non-growth strategy. As a matter of fact, this strategy does provide room for growth, though to a limited extent, in the existing product-market area to achieve current business objectives. Implementing stability strategy does not imply stagnation since the basic thrust is on maintaining the current level of performance with incremental growth in ensuing periods.

6.2.3 Rationale for Using Stability Strategy

There are a number of circumstances in which the most appropriate growth stance for a company is stability rather than growth. Stability strategy is normally followed for a brief period to consolidate the gains of its expansion and needs a breathing spell before embarking on the next round of expansion. Organisations need to 'cool off' for a while after an aggressive phase of expansion and must stabilize for a while or they will become inefficient and unmanageable. India Cements went through a rapid expansion by acquiring other cement companies before stabilizing and consolidating its operations. Videocon and BPL had first diversified into new businesses and then started consolidating once faced with stiff competition.

Managers pursue stability strategy when they feel that the enterprise has been performing well and wish to maintain the same trend in subsequent years. They would prefer to adopt the existing product-market posture and avoid departing from it. Sometimes, the management is content with the status quo because the company enjoys a distinct competitive advantage and hence does not perceive an immediate threat.

Stability strategy is also adopted in a number of organisations because the management is not interested in taking risks by venturing into unknown terrain. In fact they do not consider any other option as long as the pursuit of existing business activity produces the desired results. Conservative managers believe product development, market development or new ways of doing business entail great risk and therefore, avoid taking decisions, which can endanger the company. A number of managers also pursue consolidation strategy involuntarily. In fact, they do not react to environmental changes and avoid drastic changes in the current strategy unless warranted by extraordinary circumstances.

Sometimes environmental forces compel an organisation to follow the strategy of status quo. This is particularly true for bigger organisations, which have acquired dominant market share. Such organisations are usually not permitted by the government to expand because it may lead to monopolistic and restrictive trade practices detrimental to public interest.

6.3 TYPES OF STABILITY STRATEGIES

6.3.1 Pause/Process with Caution Strategy

Pause/proceed with caution stability strategy is a tactic, sometimes employed by the firm that wishes to test the ground before moving ahead with a full-fledged expansion strategy, or by firms that have an intense pace of expansion and wish to rest for a while before moving ahead. Some organisations pursue stability strategy for a temporary period of time until the particular environmental situation changes, especially if they have been growing too fast in the recent past. Stability strategies enable a company to consolidate its resources after prolonged rapid growth. The purpose is to allow all the people in the organisation to adapt to the changes. It is a deliberate and conscious attempt to postpone strategic changes to a more opportune time. This strategy is sometimes essential in several cases where an intervening phase of consolidation is necessary before an organisation could embark upon further expansion strategies. The pause/proceed with caution strategy is a temporary time out and a deliberate and conscious attempt to adjourn majour strategic move to more apprtune time or when organisation is ready to move on with rapid stride again.

The Dell computer company had phenomenal growth followed by internal chaos within the firm. They put their growth on hold, took care of their infrastructure and is booming again with mail order distribution.

The Indian shoe market dominated by Bata and Liberty, with increasing presence of global brands such as Adidas, Nike or Reebok, not many may be aware of that Hindustan Unilevers better known for soaps and detergents, produced substantial quantity of shoes and shoe uppers for the export market. In late 2000, it started selling a few thousand pairs in the cities to find out the market reaction. This is a pause/proceed with caution strategy before it went full steam to focus on export market and into another FMCG sector that has a lot of potential.

6.3.2 No-Change Strategy

A no-change strategy is a decision to do nothing new, i.e., continue current operations and policies for the foreseeable future. When faced with a predictable and certain external environment and the firm has a stable internal environment, the firm will continue with its present strategy. This is so because the organisation does not find it worthwhile to alter the present situation by changing its strategy. When there are no significant opportunities or threats operating in the environment, or if there are no major new strengths and weaknesses within the organisation or if there are no new competitors or threat of substitutes, the firm may decide not to do anything new. Taking into account the external and internal environmental situation the firm decides to maintain its strategy and do not undertake any new strategy.

Several small and medium sized firms operating in a familiar market, more often a niche market, that is limited in scope and offering products or services through a time tested technology rely on the no-change strategy. Such a strategy serves the organisation well until it is time to wake up in the face of threat emerging in the environment or some upset occurring which threatens the existence of the organisation.

6.3.3 Profit Strategy

The no-change strategy is a short-term measure and no organisation can indefinitely continue with the no-change strategy for long. Sometimes things do change and the firm is faced with the situation where it has to do something. A firm may assess the situation and assume that its problem are short-lived and will go away with time. Till then a firm tries to sustain its profitability by adopting a profit strategy. The profit strategy is an attempt to artificially maintain profits by reducing investments and short-term expenditures. Rather than announcing the company's poor position to shareholders and other investors at large, top management may be tempted to follow this strategy. Obviously, the profit strategy is useful to get over a temporary difficulty, but if continued for long, it will lead deteriorate the company's position. The profit strategy is thus usually the top management's short-term and often self-serving response to the situation.

For instance, in a situation when the profit is becoming lower, the firm takes measures to reduce investments, cut costs, raise prices, increase productivity and adopt other measures to solve temporary difficulties. The problem arises due to unfavourable situation like economic recession, government attitude, and industry downturn, competitive pressures and like. During this kind of situation that the firm assumes to be temporary it would adopt profit strategies. Some firms to overcome these difficulties would sell off assets such as prime land in a commercial area and move to suburbs. Others remove some of its non-core business to raise money, while others decided to provide outsourcing service to other organisations.

In general, stability strategies can be very useful in the short run, but they can be dangerous if followed for too long. Steel Authority of India adopted stability strategy because of over capacity in steel sector. Instead it has concentrated on increasing operational efficiency of its various plants rather than going for expansion. Other industries are heavy commercial vehicle, coal industry. Apart from overcapacity, regulatory restrictions in some industries have forced companies to adopt stability strategy. Cigarette and liquor industries fall in this category because of strict control over capacity expansion. Both these industries require licences under the provisions of Industries (Development and regulations) Act, 1951.

Many companies in public sector have been forced to adopt stability strategy because of government's policy of cutting the role of public sector and budgetary support for expansion of these companies has been withdrawn.

6.3.4 Approaches to Stability Strategy

There are various approaches to developing stability/consolidation strategy. The management has to select the one that best suits the corporate objective. Some of these approaches are discussed below. In all these approaches, the fundamental course of action remains the same, but the circumstances in which the firms choose various options differ.

Holding Strategy: This alternative may be appropriate in two situations:

(a) the need for an opportunity to rest, digest, and consolidate after growth or some turbulent events - before continuing a growth strategy, or

(b) an uncertain or hostile environment in which it is prudent to stay in a "holding pattern" until there is change in or more clarity about the future in the environment.

With a holding strategy the company continues at its present rate of development. The aim is to retain current market share. Although growth is not pursued as such, this will occur if the size of the market grows. The current level of resource input and managerial effort will not be increased, which means that the functional strategies will continue at previous levels. This approach suits a firm, which does not have requisite resources to pursue increased growth for a longer period of time. At times, environmental changes prohibit a continuation in growth.

Stable Growth: This alternative essentially involves avoiding change, representing indecision or timidity in making a choice for change. Alternatively, it may be a comfortable, even long-term strategy in a mature, rather stable environment, e.g., a small business in a small town with few competitors. It simply means that the firm's strategy does not include any bold initiatives. It will just seek to do what it already does, but a little better. In this approach, the firm concentrates on one product or service line. It grows slowly but surely, increasingly its market penetration by steadily adding new products or services and carefully expanding its market.

Harvesting Strategy: Where a firm has the dominant market share, it may seek to take advantage of this position and generate cash for future business expansion. This is termed harvesting strategy and is usually associated, with cost cutting and price increases to generate extra profits. This approach is most suitable to a firm whose main objective is to generate cash. Even market share may be sacrificed to earn profits and generate funds. A number of ways can be used to accomplish the objective of making profits and generating funds. Some of these are selective price increases and reducing costs without reducing price. In this approach, selected products are milked rather than nourished and defended. Hindustan Lever's Lifebuoy soap is an example in point. It yielded large profits under careful management.

Profit or Endgame Strategy: A profit strategy is one that capitalizes on a situation in which old and obsolete product or technology is being replaced by a new one. This type of strategy does not require new investment, so it is not a growth strategy. Firms adopting this strategy decide to follow the same technology, at least partially, while transiting into new technological domains. Strategists in these firms reason that the huge number of products based on older technologies on the market would create an aftermarket for spare parts that would last for years. Sylvania, RCA, and GE are among the firms that followed this strategy. They decided to stay in the vacuum tube market until the "end of the game." As with most business decisions, timing is critical. All competitors eventually must shelve the old assets at some point of time and move to the new product or technology. The critical question is, "Can we make more money by using these assets or by selling them?" The answer to that question changes as time passes.

6.4 RETRENCHMENT STRATEGIES

Retrenchment is a corporate-level strategy that seeks to reduce the size or diversity of an organisation's operations. Retrenchment is also a reduction of expenditures in order to become financially stable. Retrenchment occurs when an organisation regroups through cost and asset reduction to reverse declining sales and profits. This strategy is designed to fortify an organisation's basic distinctive competence. A retrenchment strategy is followed when an organisation aims at a contraction of its activities through substantial reduction or the elimination of the scope of one or more of its businesses in terms of their respective customer groups, customer functions, or alternative technologies either singly or jointly in order to improve its overall performance. A corporate hospital decides to focus only on special treatment and realize higher revenues by reducing its commitment to general cases which are less profitable.

Retrenchment revolves around cutting sales. Retrenchment seeks to reduce the size or diversity of an organisation's operations. Retrenchment is also a reduction of expenditures in order to become financially stable. Retrenchment is a pullback or a withdrawal from offering some current products or serving some markets. In a military situation a retrenchment provides a second line of defence. Retrenchment is often a strategy employed prior to or as part of a turnaround strategy.

Many firms experience deteriorating financial performance resulting from market erosion and wrong decisions by management. Managers respond by selecting corporate strategies that redirect their attempt to turnaround the company by improving their firm's competitive position or divest or wind up the business if a turnaround is not possible. Turnaround strategy is a form of retrenchment strategy, which focuses on operational improvement when the state of decline is not severe.

The growth of industries and markets are threatened by various external developments (government policies, demand saturation, emergence of substitute products, or changing customer needs) and internal developments (poor management, wrong strategies, poor quality of functional management, and so on.) In these situations the industries

Exhibit 6.3 Strategies for Stability

What makes stability an issue? Under what conditions would we pay any attention at all to stability? When we care about something that may be threatened by a force acting on it. If we care about a thing, and there are no forces acting to change it, we don't need to worry about stability. And there is little point maintaining the stability of something we don't care about. Stability is an issue only when we care about something that is threatened. How can we maintain stability? There are three general strategies: **adapt, isolate, and absorb.**

The first strategy is to *adapt* — **the thing you want to stabilize, to modify so that it now benifts from the forces that previously threatened it.** For example, when the United States experienced oil crises in 1973 and 1979, US automobile manufacturers began making smaller and lighter cars with more fuel efficient engines. And when Japanese companies began to export inexpensive, high quality cars to the United States, US manufacturers began to sell foreign-made automobiles under American company's brand names.

The second strategy is to *isolate* — **the thing, to separate it from the forces that threaten it.** For example, the paint on your car separates the metal from the wind, rain, and salt that can corrode it.

The third strategy is to *absorb* — **the threatening forces, to convert them into a form that is either less harmful or more useful.** Then either incorporate the new form or dissipate it. Absorbing is a combination of adapting and isolating. You adapt to the environment so as to better convert or direct the threatening force. And you direct or convert the force so as to separate it from the thing you are trying to stabilize. For example, the shock absorbers and the tyres on your car absorb mechanical motion. They convert mechanical motion into heat, a more readily disposable form, then dissipate the heat. Another example, your automobile insurance converts sudden, large expenses that could threaten your financial stability into smaller, more predictable expenses.

Note that each strategy for maintaining stability requires change. In order to keep the important thing stable, we must be willing to change something else, something that is less important. When you buy automobile insurance, you give up something less important, your available funds, in order to maintain something more important, your overall financial stability.

Here's a question that now intrigues me: **How do we decide which strategy or combination of strategies to employ to keep some precious things stable?** Do we adapt to changes when we can, and isolate ourselves only from forces to which we cannot adapt? Or are there some forces that we will try first to isolate ourselves from, and adapt only if isolation fails? What about the nature or value of the thing we're trying to keep stable? How does that influence our choice of strategy?

Source http://cwd.dhemery.com/2004/01/strategies_for_stability/

and markets and consequently the companies face the danger of decline and will go for adopting retrenchment strategies. For example, fountain pens, manual typewriters, teleprinters, steam engines, jute and jute products, slide rules, calculators and wooden toys are some products that have either disappeared or are facing decline.

Retrenchment strategies involve a reduction in the scope of a corporation's activities, which also generally necessitates a reduction in number of employees, sale of assets associated with discontinued product or service lines, possible restructuring of debt through bankruptcy proceedings, and in the most extreme cases, liquidation of the firm.

There are five activities that characterize retrenchment:

- *Captive Company:* Essentially, a captive company's destiny is tied to a larger company. For some companies, the only way to stay viable is to act as an exclusive supplier to a giant company. A company may also be taken captive if their competitive position is irreparably weak.
- *Turnaround:* If your company is steadily losing profit or market share, a turnaround strategy may be needed. There are two forms of turnarounds: First, one may choose contractions (cutting labour costs, PP&E and marketing). Second, they may decide to consolidate.
- *Bankruptcy:* This may also be a viable legal protective strategy. Bankruptcy without a customer base is truly a bad place. However, if one declares bankruptcy with loyal customers, there is at least a possibility of a turnaround.
- *Divestment:* This is a form of retrenchment strategy used by businesses when they downsize choose their business activities. Divestment usually involves eliminating a portion of a business. Firms may to sell, close, or spin-off a strategic business unit, major operating division, or product line. This move often is the final decision to eliminate unrelated, unprofitable, or unmanageable operations.
- *Liquidation:* This is very simple. Take the book value of assets, subtract depreciation and sell the business. This may be hard for some companies to do because there may be untapped potential in the assets.

6.5 TYPES OF RETRENCHMENT STRATEGIES

- Turnaround strategies,
- Divestment strategies
- Liquidation strategies.

Turnaround Strategies: Turnaround strategies derives their name from the action involved that is reversing a negative trend. There are certain conditions or indicators which point out that a turnaround is needed for an organisation to survive. They are:

- Persistent negative cash flows
- Negative profits
- Declining market share
- Deterioration in physical facilities
- Over manning, high turnover of employees, and low morale
- Uncompetitive products or services
- Mismanagement

An organisation which faces one or more of these issues is referred to as a 'sick' company.

There are three ways in which turnarounds can be managed:

- The existing chief executive and management team handles the entire turnaround strategy with the advisory support of a specialist consultant. This method can be successful if the chief executive has a reasonable amount of credibility left with the banks and financial institutions. This type of turnaround is rarely attempted by companies.

- In the second method, the existing team withdraws temporarily and an executive consultant or turnaround specialist is employed to do the job. The consultant is normally deputed by the banks and financial institutions and the person revert the company to the team of chief executive once the job of turnaround is completed. This method is rarely adopted by Indian companies, though it is more common in western companies.
- The last method involves the replacement of the existing team specially the chief executive, or merging the sick organisation with a healthy one. This method is more common in the Indian companies.

When a chief executive officer (CEO) is replaced by the another, the new CEO can follow two types of approaches : surgical and non-surgical. The surgical approach to turn around involves the tough attitude and pattern of action followed is same everywhere. The new CEO quickly asserts the authority by issuing orders and direction for change, centralise functions, fire employees, close down plants and divisions. Then the product mix may be changes, obsolete machinery is replaced with new one, R&D, marketing and financial controls are strengthened, accountability is fixed. This continues till the business shows sign of turnaround. The second approach - non-surgical is a humane approach which involves understanding of problem of the organisation, eliciting options, adopting conciliatory attitude and coming to negotiated settlement among different fictions. In this approach, the emphasis is on behavioural change and improving the work culture and morale of the employee. Both the approaches may succeed, depending upon the circumstances and conditions prevailing, the second approach has higher potential of success in the long run.

Before a turnaround can be formulated for an Indian company, it has to be first declared as a sick company. The declaration is done on the basis of the Sick Industrial Companies (Special Provision) Repeal Act (SICA) 2003, which has replaced Sick Industrial Companies Act (SICA) 1985. The act provides for a quasi judicial body called the Board of Industrial and Financial Reconstruction (BIFR) and the Appellate Authority for Industrial and Financial Reconstruction (AAIFR) which acts as the corporate doctor whenever companies fall sick.

It is the responsibility of the company to report its sickness whenever the accumulated losses at the end of financial years exceed 50% of the peak net worth attended during the preceding five years. BIFR prepares a rehabilitation scheme for the revival of sick units, decides on the need for a change of management or amalgamation with other companies and undertake the sale or lease of the undertaking and other appropriate measures. Apart from BIFR, banks and financial institutions also play an active role in the turnaround strategy. The RBI also coordinates with activities between commercial banks and lending institutions. The government provides tax benefits under Section-72A of the Income Tax Act to companies which amalgamate sick unit for revival.

Metal Box India Ltd. a reputed company in the packaging industry, turned sick due to its wrong strategic move of diversifying into bearings manufacture in the early eighties. Eight of its nine units closed down as results of which the BIFR and the ICICI formulated a rehabilitation package for the turnaround of the company.

6.5.1 Divestment Strategies

A divestment strategy involves the sale or liquidation of a portion of business, or a major division, profit centre or SBU. Divestment is usually a part of rehabilitation or restructuring plan and is adopted when a turnaround has been attempted but has proved to be unsuccessful. Harvesting strategy is a variant of the divestment strategies, involves a process of gradually letting the company business wither away in a carefully controlled manner. Another term common in Indian context is disinvestment. Disinvestment involves the sale of government equity in public sector enterprise to another enterprise, institutional investors, mutual funds or to the general public, thereby diluting the government shareholding. Many government companies such as ITC hotels, Maruti Udyog, BALCO, Videsh Sanchar Nigam Ltd (VSNL) have been disinvested.

Reasons for divestment:

- The business that has been acquired proves to be a mismatch and cannot be integrated within the company. Similarly, a project that proves to be unviable in the long term is divested.
- Persistent negative cash flows from a particular business create financial problems for the whole company, creating a need for the divestment of that business.
- Severity of competition and the inability of a firm to cope with it may cause it to divest.
- Technological upgradation is required if the business is to survive but where it is not possible for the firm to invest in it. A preferable option would be to divest.

Exhibit 6.4 The Ten Elements of Turnaround Strategies

These elements have been compiled after a study of ten Indian companies where turnaround strategies were successful. These elements are:

- Changes in the top management
- Initial credit building actions
- Neutralising external pressure
- Initial control
- Identifying quick paying activities
- Quick cost reduction
- Revenue generation
- Assets liquidation for generating cash
- Mobilisation of the organisation
- Better internal coordination

Source Pardip N Khandwalla "10 elements in turnarounds" Business World , June 7-14,1989, p 18-19

- Divestment may be done because by selling off a part of a business the company may be in a position to survive
- A better alternative may be available for investment, causing a firm to divest a part of its unprofitable business.
- Divestment by one firm may be a part of merger plan executed with another firm, where mutual exchange of unprofitable divisions may take place.
- Lastly, a firm may divest in order to attract the provisions of the MRTP Act or owing to oversize and the resultant inability to manage a large business.

There are many examples of how companies have attempted divestment strategies.

TATA group is a highly diversified entity with a range of businesses under its fold. They identified their non-core businesses for divestment. TOMCO was divested and sold to Hindustan Levers as soaps and detergents were not considered a core business for the Tatas. Similarly, the pharmaceuticals companies of the Tatas, Merind and Tata Pharma, were divested to Wockhardt. The cosmetics company Lakme was divested and sold to Hindustan Levers, as besides being a non-core business, it was found to be a non-competitive and would have required substantial investment to be sustained.

Asian Paints undertook an international divestment when it decided to divest its stack in its Australian operations. It offloaded its stack in Asian Paints Queensland Ltd to its international subsidiary Asian Paints (International), Mauritius.

Hindustan Unilever Ltd divested its marine food business to Mumbai based Temptation Foods which is a fruit and vegetables export company. Hence, it decided to get out of its non-core businesses. It also sold its seafood processing plant in Andhra Pradesh and shut down its operations in Gujarat.

Indian Organic Chemicals was set up by Ghai Group in 1960. It diversified into food processing in 1986 from its main business of organic chemicals. But by 1989 its food division "Future Food" reached a position where they had to divested. The reason for failure were; unfair competition from unorganised sectors, technological problems, mismatch between marketing orientation and manufacturing orientation.

VST Natural products, the food business company of VST, the tobacco company was divested to Global Green Company of Thapar groups. The reason of divestment were: non-availability of raw materials, inadequate working capital, etc.

It is clear that normally divestment is attempted when the business is not running successful or as a result of failures. It may be result of companies focusing on their core business and divesting the non-core business. When divestment does not work, liquidation is the only strategic alternative left.

6.5.2 Liquidation Strategies

A retrenchment strategy which is considered the most extreme and unattractive is the liquidation strategy, which involves closing down a firm and selling its assets. It is considered the last resort because it leads to serious consequences such as loss of employment for workers and other employees, termination of opportunities where a firm could pursue any future activities and the stigma of failure. The psychological implications of liquidation are as follows:

- The prospects of liquidation create a bad impact on the company's reputation.
- For many executives who are closely associated firms, liquidation may be a traumatic experience.

Many small sized units and proprietorship and partnership firms liquidate frequently, but medium and large sized firms rarely liquidate in India owning to a number of reasons. The company management, government, banks and financial institutions, trade unions, suppliers and creditors are extremely reluctant in taking a decision or ask for liquidation. While the management may hesitate to liquidate due to fear of failure or stigma, the government may not easily allow liquidation due to political and other risks involved. Trade unions would resist due to loss of employment of workers. Ceasing operations does not mean organisation is freed from its contractual obligations to the creditors and suppliers, unless of course it is declared insolvent or bankrupt.

6.5.3 Legal Aspects of Liquidation

Under the Companies Act (1956), liquidation is known as winding up. The Act defines winding up of a company as the process whereby its life is ended and its property administered for the benefit of its creditors and members. The Act provides for a liquidator who takes control of the company, collects its assets, pays it debts, and finally distributes any surplus among the members according to their rights. At the end of winding, the company will not have any assets or liabilities. On dissolution of the firm's name is struck off from register of companies and its legal personality as a corporation comes to an end. Liquidation or winding off in accordance with the Company Act (1956), may be done in three ways:

- Compulsory winding up under an order of the court
- Voluntary winding up
- Voluntary winding up under the supervision of the court.

Liquidation strategies are not popular anywhere in the world, much less in Indian context, still there have been instances where there was no alternative but to liquidate the company. Here are some examples from Indian context:

- The cooperative banking sector in the various states of India had faced massive liquidation owning to rampant mismanagement and corruption. More than 100 banks have been ordered to be liquidated under the orders of the various courts in India.
- Digital Publishing Solution Private Ltd. went in for a voluntary liquidation.
- Alpic Finance, a non-banking financial company was ordered to be liquidated by the Bombay High Court on the petition of Small Industrial Devolvement Bank of India, when it defaulted on the payment to the investors. These investors got the first charge on the asset of the company but the depositors lost their money.
- Punjab Wireless System was liquidated on the order of the Punjab and Haryana High Court on a private petition, due to the inability of the company to discharge its debts and liabilities.

- On May 14, 1986, the Bombay High Court appointed a provisional liquidator in the petition for the voluntary liquidation of Empress Mills at Nagpur. Empress Mills was a 113-years-old mill owned by the Tatas. Behind the liquidation petition lay a host of reasons. The major strategic cause for liquidation lies in the fact that for nearly 50 years, Empress Mills did not invest in modernization or keep pace with competition. In the wider context, the government policies did not prove favourable for the cotton textile industry. The management of the mill carried the blame for neglect and delayed action.

Exercise

1. What do you understand by "Corporate Strategy". What is the importance of these strategies and how does it affect the future of the organisation?
2. Select a high profile industry such as IT or automobiles. Identify the major corporate strategies adopted by them. Were these strategies succussful?
3. Why a firm would like to adopt stability strategy? What are conditions when stability strategies are adopted.
4. How does an organisation find out that it needs a turnaround strategy? What actions are undertaken in this strategy.
5. Under what conditions an organisation decides to adopt the divestment strategy. Give examples of the organisation who have adopted these strategies and what was the impact of these strategies.
6. Some organisations are forced to adopt liquidation strategy. What are conditions when it is adopted and procedures of liquidation in Indian context?
7. Is it necessary for an organisation to adopt only one strategy or it can have many strategies adopted simultaneously? Give your viewpoint.

7 Corporate Level Strategy: Expansion or Growth Strategy

7.1 INTRODUCTION

Every enterprise seeks growth as its long-term goal to avoid annihilation in a relentless and ruthless competitive environment. Growth offers ample opportunities to everyone in the organisation and is crucial for the survival of the enterprise. However, this is possible only when fundamental conditions of expansion have been met. Expansion strategies are designed to allow enterprises to maintain their competitive position in rapidly growing national and international markets. Hence, to successfully compete, survive and flourish, an enterprise has to pursue an expansion strategy. Expansion strategy is an important strategic option, which enterprises follow to fulfil their long-term growth objectives. They pursue it to gain significant growth as opposed to incremental growth envisaged in stability strategy. Expansion strategy is adopted to accelerate the rate of growth of sales, profits and market share faster by entering new markets, acquiring new resources, developing new technologies and creating new managerial capabilities.

A growth strategy is one that an enterprise pursues when it increases its level of objectives upward, much higher than an exploration of its past achievement level. The most frequent increase indicating a growth strategy is to raise the market share and or sales objectives upward significantly. If we look at the corporate performance in the recent years, we find how various organisations have grown both in terms of sales and profit as well as assets. For example: Reliance Industries Limited, Nirma Limited. Organisations may select a growth strategy to increase their profits, sales and/or market share. They also pursue growth strategy to reduce cost of production per unit. Growth strategies involve a significant increase in performance objectives. These strategies are adopted when firms remarkably broaden the scope of their customer groups, customer functions and alternative technologies either singly or in combination with each other.

Expansion strategy provides a blueprint for business enterprises to achieve their long term growth objectives. It allows them to maintain their competitive advantage even in the advanced stages of product and market evolution. Growth offers economies of scale and scope to an organisation, which reduce operating costs and improve earnings. Apart from these advantages the organisation gains a greater control over the immediate environment because of its size. This influence is crucial for survival in mature markets where competitors aggressively defend their market shares.

Conditions/Reasons for Adopting for Expansion /Growth Strategies

In the long run, growth is necessary for the very survival of the organisations themselves, particularly when the environment is quite volatile. Growth offers many economies because of large scale operations. Growth strategy is taken up because of managerial motivation to do so. Managers with high degree of achievement and recognition always prefer to grow. There are certain intangible advantages of growth. These may be in the form of increased prestige of the organisation, satisfaction to employees and social benefits. Example: Growing companies have high level of prestige in the corporate world, e.g., Reliance, Infosys, Hindustan Unilever, etc. Firms opt for expansion strategy under the following circumstances:

- When the firm has lofty growth objectives and desires fast and continuous growth in assets, income and profits. Expansion through diversification would be especially useful to firms that are eager to achieve large and rapid growth since it involves exploiting new opportunities outside the domain of current operations.
- When enormous new opportunities are emerging in the environment and the firm is ready and willing to expand its business scope.
- Firms find expansion irresistible since sheer size translates into superior clout.
- When a firm is a leader in its industry and wants to protect its dominant position.
- Expansion strategy is opted in volatile situations. Substantive growth would act as a cushion in such conditions.
- When the firm has surplus resources, it may find it sensible to grow by levering on its strengths and resources.
- When the environment, especially the regulatory scenario, blocks the growth of the firm in its existing businesses, it may resort to diversification to meet its growth objectives.
- When the firm enjoys synergy that ensues by tapping certain opportunities in the environment, it opts for expansion strategies.
- Economies of scale and scope and competitive advantage may accrue through such synergistic operations. Over the last decade, in response to economic liberalisation, some companies in India expanded the scale of existing businesses as well as diversified into many new businesses.

Growth of a business enterprise entails realignment of its strategies in product market environment. This is achieved through the basic growth approaches of intensive expansion, integration (horizontal and vertical integration), diversification and international operations. Firms following intensification strategy concentrate on their primary line of business and look for ways to meet their growth objectives by increasing their size of operations in this primary business. A company may expand externally by integrating with other companies. An organisation expands its operations by moving into a different industry by pursuing diversification strategies. An organisation can grow by "going international", i.e., by crossing domestic borders by employing any of the expansion strategies discussed so far.

7.2 TYPES OF GROWTH/EXPANSION STRATEGIES

The expansion or growth strategies are further classified as:

(i) Concentration Expansion Strategy
(ii) Integration Expansion Strategy
(iii) Diversification Expansion Strategy
(iv) Cooperation Expansion Strategy
(v) Internationalization Expansion Strategy

7.2.1 Expansion Through Concenration

Concentration involves expansion within the existing line of business. Concentration expansion strategy involves safeguarding the present position and expanding in the current product-market space to achieve growth targets. Such an approach is very useful for enterprises that have not fully exploited the opportunities existing in their current products-market domain. A firm selecting an intensification strategy, concentrates on its primary line of business and looks for ways to meet its growth objectives by increasing its size of operations in its primary business. Intensive expansion of a firm can be accomplished in three ways, namely, market penetration, market development and product development is first suggested in Ansoff's model. Concentration strategy is followed when adequate growth opportunities exist in the firm's current products-market space. However, while going in for internal expansion, the management should consider the following factors:

- While there are a number of expansion options, the one with the highest net present value should be the first choice.
- Competitive behaviour should be predicted in order to determine how and when the competitors would respond to the firm's actions. The firm must also assess its strengths and weaknesses against its competitors to ascertain its competitive advantages.
- The conditions prevailing in the environment should be carefully examined to determine the demand for the product and the price customers are willing to pay.
- The firm must have adequate financial, technological and managerial capabilities to expand the way it chooses.
- Technological, social and demographic trends should be carefully monitored before implementing product or market development strategies. This is very crucial, especially, in a volatile business environment.

The product/market grid first presented by Igor Ansoff (1968), shown in Exhibit 7.1, has proven to be very useful in discovering growth opportunities. This grid best illustrates the various intensification options available to a firm. The product/market grid has two dimensions, namely, products and markets. Combinations of these two dimensions result in four growth strategies. According to Ansoff's Grid, three distinct strategies are possible for achieving growth through the concentration route. These are:

Exhibit 7.1 Ansoff's Product-market Expansion Grid

Product → / Market ↓	Present	New
Present	Market Penetration	Product Development
New	Market Development	Diversification

Source H I Ansoff "Strategies for Diversification" *Harvard Business Review* 1957.5 pp. 113-124

Market Penetration: The firm seeks to achieve growth with existing products in their current market segments, aiming to increase its market share. When a firm believes that there exist ample opportunities by aggressively exploiting its current products and current markets, it pursues market penetration approach. Market penetration involves achieving growth through the existing products in the existing markets and a firm can achieve this by:

- Motivating the existing customers to buy its product more frequently and in larger quantities. Market penetration strategy generally focuses on changing the infrequent users of the firm's products or services to frequent users and frequent users to heavy users. Typical schemes used for this purpose are volume discounts, bonus cards, price promotion, heavy advertising, regular publicity, wider distribution and obviously through retention of customers by means of an effective customer relationship management.
- Increasing its efforts to attract its competitors' customers. For this purpose, the firm must develop significant competitive advantages. Attractive product design, high product quality, attractive prices, stronger advertising, and wider distribution can assist an enterprise in gaining lead over its competitors. All these require heavy investment, which only firms with substantial resources can afford. Firms less endowed may search for niche segments. Many small manufacturers, for instance, survive by seeking out and cultivating profitable niches in the market. They may also grow by developing highly specialized and unique skills to cater to a small segment of exclusive customers with special requirements.
- Targeting new customers in its current markets. Price concessions, better customer service, increasing publicity and other techniques can be useful in this effort.

In a growing market, simply maintaining market share will result in growth, and there may exist opportunities to increase market share if competitors reach capacity limits. While following market penetration strategy, the firm continues to operate in the same markets offering the same products. Growth is achieved by increasing its market share with the existing products. However, market penetration has limits, and once the market approaches saturation another strategy must be pursued if the firm is to continue to grow. Unless there is an intrinsic growth in its current market, this strategy necessarily entails snatching business away from competitors. The market penetration strategy is the least risky since it leverages many of the firm's existing resources and capabilities. Another advantage of this strategy is that it does not require additional investment for developing new products.

Reliance has captured substantial market share in textile yarn and intermediaries where as ITC has captured substantial market share in cigarettes by following market penetration strategy.

Market Development: Market development strategy tries to achieve growth by introducing existing products in new markets. Market development options include the pursuit of additional market segments or geographical regions. The development of new markets for the product may be a good strategy if the firm's core competence are related more to the specific product than to its experience with a specific market segment or when new markets offer better growth prospects compared to the existing ones. Because the firm is expanding into a new market, a market development strategy typically has more risk than a market penetration strategy. This is because managers do not have normally sound knowledge of new markets, which may result in inaccurate market assessment and wrong marketing decisions. In market development approach, a firm seeks to increase its sales by taking its product into new markets. The two possible methods of implementing market development strategy are:

- The firm can move its present product into new geographical areas. This is done by increasing its sales force, appointing new channel partners, sales agents or manufacturing representatives and by franchising its operation.
- The firm can expand sales by attracting new market segments. Making minor modifications in the existing products that appeal to new segments can do the trick.

Many companies which find that the urban market is saturated and there is little scope for expansion, opt for developing new market in rural areas. Some of the companies which have made keen attempt to develop rural market are HUL (personal products), Colgate (oral care products), LG (TV), Videocon (consumer durables), etc.

Product Development: Expansion through product development involves development of new or improved products for its current markets. The firm remains in its present markets but develops new products for these markets. Growth will accrue if the new products yield additional sales and market share. This strategy is likely to succeed for products that have low brand loyalty and/or short product life cycles. A product development strategy may also be appropriate if the firm's strengths are related to its specific customers rather than to the specific product itself. In this situation, it can leverage its strengths by developing a new product targeted to its existing customers. Although the firm operates in familiar markets, product development strategy carries more risk than simply attempting to increase market share since there are inherent risks normally associated with new product development. Samsung Electronics for example (TV) may offer slim line TV, Plasma TV, etc., as its product development strategy. The three possible ways of implementing the product development strategy are:

- The company can expand sales through developing new products.
- The company can create different or improved versions of the current products.
- The company can make necessary changes in its existing products to suit the different likes and dislikes of the customers.

Combination Strategy: Combination strategy combines the concentration strategy variants, i.e., market penetration, market development and product development to grow. In the market development and market penetration strategy, the firm continues with its current product portfolio, while the product development strategy involves developing new or improved products, which will satisfy the current markets.

Diversification: The firm grows by diversifying into new businesses by developing new products for new markets.

7.2.1.1 Benefits of concentric expansion strategy

A firm that is familiar with an industry would naturally like to invest more in known business rather than unknown ones, the managers of the firms are more comfortable in dealing with the present business. It involves minimal organisational changes. It enables the firm to master one or a few businesses and enable it to specialize by gaining an in depth knowledge of these businesses. Managers face fewer problems when dealing with known situations. Intensive focusing of resources on a few businesses may also create conditions for the firm to develop a competitive advantage. System and processes within a firm are developed in such a way that people are familiar with them . The decision making process is under less strains as there is high level of predictability. Past experience is valuable as it is replicable.

7.2.1.2 Limitations of concentric expansion strategy

"Putting all one's eggs in one basket has its own problems". Concentration strategies are heavily dependent on the industry. Adverse condition in an industry affect the firm if they are intensely concentrated. If the industry goes into recession, the concentrated firm will find it too difficult to withdraw from it. Factors like product obsolescence, fickleness of markets, and emergence of newer technologies are threats to concentrated firms. Concentration strategies may result in doing too much of a known thing. This may create an organisational inertia; managers may not be able to sustain interest and find the work less challenging and less stimulating. Concentration strategies may lead to cash flow problems that may pose a dilemma before a firm. Large cash inflows are required for building up assets while the businesses are growing. But when these businesses mature, firms often face a cash surplus with little scope for investing in the present businesses.

Bajaj Auto has consistently concentrated on two- and three-wheeler automobiles since its inception as it finds it to be a high growth and attractive industry to invest in it. It has tried various means to sustain its market share in a competitive market. At different times, it has adopted variations of concentrated strategies of market penetration, e.g., selling more in urban areas, and product development, e.g., state of art motorcycle and ungeared scooters. For its rivals it has remain a formidable competitors with proven products manufactured through tried and tested technology and sold in familiar markets. Of late Bajaj Auto has started diversifying in four wheeler and developing a small car in collaboration with Nissan.

Xerox India (formerly Modi Xerox) is the Indian subsidiary of Xerox Corporation, the well known American printer, photocopier and office supplier company. In a bid to expand its share in small and medium size businesses segment in India, it adopted a concentration strategy through market penetration, market development and product development. For market penetration, it offered print jobs service through laser printers and multifunctional devices, increasing its product range to over 20 products and services. Market development activities included educating the small business entrepreneurs to create new markets for its products.

7.2.2 Expansion through Integration

When firms use their existing base to expand in the direction of their raw materials or the ultimate consumers, or, alternatively they acquire complimentary or adjacent businesses, integration takes place. Integration basically means combining activities related to the present activity of a firm. In contrast to the intensive growth, integration strategy involves expanding externally by combining with other firms. Combination involves association and integration among different firms and is essentially driven by need for survival and also for growth by building synergies. Combination of firms may take the merger or consolidation route. Merger implies a combination of two or more concerns into one final entity. The merged concerns go out of existence and their assets and liabilities are taken over by the acquiring company. A consolidation is a combination of two or more business units to form an entirely new company. All the original business entities cease to exist after the combination. Since mergers and consolidations involve the combination of two or more companies into a single company, the term merger is commonly used to refer to both forms of external growth. As is the case in all the strategies, acquisition is a choice a firm has made regarding how it intends to compete . Firms use integration to:

- increase market share,
- avoid the costs of developing new products internally and bringing them to the market,
- reduce the risk of entering new business,
- speed up the process of entering the market,
- become more diversified and
- quite possibly to reduce the intensity of competition by taking over the competitor's business.

The costs of integration include reduced flexibility as the organisation is locked into specific products and technology, financial costs of acquiring another company and difficulties in integrating various operations. There are many forms of integration, but the two major integrating strategies are:

7.2.2.1 Types of integration strategy

Vertical Integration: Vertical integration refers to the integration of firms involved in different stages of the supply chain. Thus, a vertically integrated firm has units operating in different stages of supply chain starting from raw material to delivery of final product to the end customer. The vertical integration may take place in two types:

- **Backward Integration:** In backward integration the firm moves towards the source of raw materials.
- **Forward Integration:** In forward integration, the firm moves closer to the ultimate customers.

An organisation tries to gain control of its inputs (backward integration) or its outputs (forward integration) or both. Vertical integration may take the form of backward or forward integration or both. The concept of vertical integration can be visualized using the value chain. Consider a firm whose products are made via an assembly process. Such a firm may consider backward integrating into intermediate manufacturing or forward integrating into distribution. Backward integration sometimes is referred to as upstream integration and forward integration as downstream integration. For instance, Nirma undertook backward integration by setting up plant to manufacture soda ash and linear alkyl benzene, both important inputs for detergents and washing soaps, to strengthen its hold in the lower-end detergents market. Reliance started its business with textiles and went for backward integration to produce PFY and PSF, critical raw materials for textiles, PTA and MEG-raw materials for PSF and PFY, paraxylene-raw materials for PTA and MEG, and finally naphtha for producing paraxylene.

Forward integration refers to moving closer to the ultimate customer by increasing control over distribution activities. For example, a personal computer assembler could own a chain of retail stores from which it sells its machines (forward integration). Many firms in India such as DCM, Mafatlal and National Textile Corporation have set up their own retail distribution network to have better control over their distribution activities. Some companies expand vertically backwards and forward. Reliance Petrochemicals grew by leveraging backward and forward integration: it began with manufacturing of textiles and fibres, moved to polymers and other intermediates then went into the manufacture of fibres, then to petrochemicals and oil refining. In power, Reliance Energy wants to do the same thing and the catch phrase that for this vertical integration is ' from well-head to wall-socket'. Reliance Energy's strategy is to straddle the entire value chain in the power business. It plans to generate power by using the group's production of gas, transmit and distribute it to the domestic and industrial consumers, reaping the returns of not just generating power using its own gas but selling what it generates not as a bulk supplier but to the end user. In essence, a firm seeks to grow through vertical integration by taking control of the business operations at various stages of the supply chain to gain advantage over its rivals. The record of vertical integration is mixed and hence, decisions should be taken after a comprehensive and careful consideration of all aspects of this form of integration. In most cases the initial investments may be very high and exiting an arrangement that does not prove beneficial may be hard. Vertical integration also requires an organisation to develop additional product market and technology capabilities, which it may not currently possess.

Modern Group, involved in the vertical integration. Forward integration took place at Modern Suitings when it diversified into worsted suitings. With an investment of Rs.7 crore, it acquired sulzer looms, sophisticated fabric processing facilities and other sophisticated equipment to manufacture a premium terrywool suiting with the brand name 'Amadeus'. Backward integration at Modern Woollens involved collaboration with Schild of Switzerland for wool processing, combing, and woollen tops which are necessary for the production of woollen textiles. In this manner, a number of backward and forward linkages were being attempted within the Modern Group:

Factors conducive for vertical integration include:

- Taxes and regulations on market transactions.
- Obstacles to the formulation and monitoring of contracts.
- Similarity between the vertically-related activities.
- Sufficient large production quantities so that the firm can benefit from economies of scale.
- Reluctance of other firms to make investments specific to the transaction.

Vertical integration may not yield the desired benefit if,

- The quantity required from a supplier is much less than the minimum efficient scale for producing the product.
- The product is a widely available commodity and its production cost decreases significantly as cumulative quantity increases.
- The core competence between the activities are very different.
- The vertically adjacent activities are in very different types of industries (for example, manufacturing is very different from retailing).
- The addition of the new activity places the firm in competition with another player with which it needs to cooperate. The firm then may be viewed as a competitor rather than a partner.

Why firms integrate vertically? There are number of factors and benefits associated with the vertical integration. These are listed below:

- It reduces transportation costs if common ownership results in closer geographic proximity:
- It improves supply chain coordination.
- It helps in capturing upstream or downstream profit margins.
- It increases entry barriers to potential competitors, for example, if the firm can gain sole access to scarce resource.
- It allows the firm to gain access to downstream distribution channels that otherwise would be inaccessible.
- It facilitates investment in highly specialized assets in which upstream or downstream players may be reluctant to invest.

- It facilitates investment in highly specialized assets in which upstream or downstream players may be reluctant to invest.

The downside risks of an integration strategy to a company include:

- Difficulty of effectively integrating the firms involved.
- Incorrect evaluation of target firm's value.
- Overestimating the potential for synergy between the companies involved.
- Creating a combination too large to control.
- The huge financial burden that acquisition entails.
- Capacity balancing issues. (For instance, the firm may need to build excess upstream capacity to ensure that its downstream operations have sufficient supply under all demand conditions).
- Potentially higher costs due to low efficiencies resulting from lack of supplier competition.
- Decreased flexibility due to previous upstream or downstream investments, (however, that flexibility to coordinate vertically-related activities may increase.).
- Decreased ability of increased product variety if significant in-house development is required.
- Developing new core competence may compromise the existing competence.

There are alternatives to vertical integration that may provide some of the same benefits with fewer drawbacks. The following are a few of these alternatives for relationships between vertically related organisations.

- Long-term explicit contracts and implicit contracts (relying on firm's reputation)
- Franchise agreements
- Joint ventures
- Co-location of facilities

Horizontal Integration: The acquisition of additional business in the same line of business or at the same level of the value chain (combining with competitors) is referred to as horizontal integration. Horizontal growth can be achieved by internal expansion or by external expansion through mergers and acquisitions of firms offering similar products and services. A firm may diversify by growing horizontally into unrelated business. Integration of oil companies, Exxon and Mobil, Indian Oil Corporation and Burma Petroleum is an example of horizontal integration. Aditya Birla Group's acquisition of L&T Cements from Reliance to increase its market dominance is an example of horizontal integration. This sort of integration is sought to reduce intensity of competition and also to build synergies.

Solidaire India Ltd. is a prominent manufacturer of TVs and has a sizeable presence in the market in southern India. It started with the name of Hi Beam Electronics Ltd. in 1974. Subsequently, this unit was merged with two other units to form a consortium called TriStar Electronics. In 1978, the brand name Solidaire was adopted. In this manner the growth strategy of the company started with horizontal integration.

Exhibit 7.2 Digital Giants to Accelerate Vertical Integration

Samsung Electronics and LG Electronics plan to streamline production lines in cooperation with their affiliates to reduce factors of uncertainty in the procurement of components. The two South Korean giants seek to manufacture top-of-the-line products like cell phones and digital TVs in a self-sufficient fashion. LG Group will invest 30 trillion won by 2010 to develop certain electronic components that include system integrated chips, plasma displays and camera modules. Samsung Electronics already retains a strong portfolio, comprising Samsung Corning (display-specific glass), Samsung SDI (displays) and Samsung Electro-Mechanics (camera modules), and aims to further hone its push for vertical integration. So-called vertical integration refers to the degree to which a company owns or controls its upstream suppliers, sub-contractors or affiliates and its downstream buyers. The advantage of the strategy is the expansion of core competencies by reducing risks in the supply of components as well as the slashing of transportation costs. Some experts have said vertical integration is vital to the improvement of these two giant digital firms' competitiveness despite criticism that such expansion would increase the entry barriers for industry newcomers.

Another example of horizontal integration is takeover of Neyveli Ceramics and Refractories Ltd. (Neycer) by Spartek Ceramics India Ltd. in the early 1990s. Both the companies were in sanitary ware and tile production. By acquiring Neycer, Spartek became the largest ceramic tile manufacturer in the country.

7.2.2.2 Benefits of horizontal integration

The following are the benefits of horizontal integration:

- **Economies of scale** – It leads to lower cost structure by spreading the fixed cost of operation over a large base of products, thereby reducing the cost of production per unit. It can also be achieved by selling more of the same product, for example, by geographic expansion.
- **Economies of scope** – It allows sharing of common resources base to a variety of products. It is commonly referred to as 'synergies'.
- **Increased market power** – Bigger size of operations allows the organisation exerting market power of bargaining over suppliers and downstream channel members.
- **Reduction in industry rivalry** – After horizontal integration, there are few competitors left in the market, thereby reducing the intensity of the rivalry in the industry.
- **Increased product differentiation** – Horizontal integration allows the organisation to offer a wide range of products which can be bundled together. Through product bundling, the customer gets a complete range of products at a single combined price, providing the advantage of product differentiation.
- **Synergy** – It is achieved by using the same brand name to promote multiple products as well as lower cost of global operations made possible by operating plants in foreign markets.

7.2.2.3 Risk of horizontal integration

Horizontal integration by acquisition of a competitor will increase a firm's market share. However, if the industry concentration increases significantly then anti-trust issues may arise. Aside from legal issues, another concern is whether the anticipated economic gains will materialize. Before expanding the scope of the firm through horizontal integration, the management should be sure that the imagined benefits are real. Many blunders have been made by firms that broadened their horizontal scope to achieve synergies that did not exist, for example, computer hardware manufacturers who entered the software business on the premise that there were synergies between hardware and software. However, a connection between two products does not necessarily imply realizable economies of scope. Finally, even when the potential benefits of horizontal integration exist, they do not materialize spontaneously. There must be an explicit horizontal strategy in place. Such strategies generally do not arise from the bottom–up, but rather, must be formulated by corporate management.

7.2.3 Expansion Through International Strategy

International strategy is a type of expansion strategy that requires firms to market their products or services beyond the domestic or national market. Firm would have to assess the international environment, evaluate its own capabilities, and devise appropriate international strategy. An organisation can "go international" by crossing domestic borders international expansion involves establishing significant market interests and operations outside a company's home country.

Foreign markets provide additional sales opportunities for a firm that may be constrained by the relatively small size of its domestic market and also reduces the firm's dependence on a single national market. Firms expand globally to seek opportunity to earn a return on large investments such as plant and capital equipment or research and development, or enhance market share and achieve scale economies, and also to enjoy advantages of locations. Other motives for international expansion include extending the product life cycle, securing key resources and using low-cost labour. However, to mould their firms into truly global companies, managers must develop global mind-sets. Traditional means of operating with little cultural diversity and without global competition are no longer effective firms.

International expansion is fraught with various risks such as, political risks (e.g., instability of host nations) and economic risks (e.g., fluctuations in the value of the country's currency). International expansions increases coordination and distribution costs, and managing a global enterprise entails problems of overcoming trade barriers, logistics costs, cultural diversity, etc. There are several methods for going international. Each method of entering an overseas market has its own advantages and disadvantages that must be carefully assessed. Different international entry modes involve a trade-offs between level of risk and the amount of foreign control the organisation's managers are willing to allow. It is common for a firm to begin with exporting, progress to licensing, then to franchising finally leading to direct investment. As the firm achieves success at each stage, it moves to the next. If it experiences problems at any of these stages, it may not progress further. If adverse conditions prevail or if operations do not yield the desired returns in a reasonable time period, the firm may withdraw from the foreign market. The decision to enter a foreign market can have a significant impact on a firm.

Expansion into foreign markets can be achieved through: exporting, licensing, joint venture strategic alliance or direct investment. These terms are briefly explained here.

Exporting: Exporting is marketing of domestically produced goods in a foreign country and is a traditional and well-established method of entering foreign markets. It does not entail new investment since exporting does not require separate production facilities in the target country. Most of the costs incurred for exporting products are marketing expenses.

Licensing: Licensing permits a company in the target country to use the property of the licensor. Such property usually is intangible, such as trademarks, patents, and production techniques. The licensee pays a fee in exchange for the rights to use the intangible property and possible for technical assistance. Licensing has the potential to provide a large ROI since this mode of foreign entry also does require additional investments. However, since the licensee produces and markets the product, potential returns from manufacturing and marketing activities may be lost.

Direct Investment: Direct investment is the ownership of facilities in the target country. It involves the transfer of resources including capital, technology, and personnel. Direct investment may be made through the acquisition of an existing entity or the establishment of a new enterprise. Direct ownership provides a high degree of control in the operations and the ability to better know the consumers and competitive environment. However, it requires a high degree of commitment and substantial resources.

Joint Venture Strategy: Joint ventures are partnerships in which two or more firms carry out a specific project or corporate in a selected area of business. Actually, corporate partnerships are formed for specific and time bound objectives which, once achieved, leave little reason for the alliance to be continued. Joint ventures that last longer do so because their objectives have been redesigned" Examples of joint ventures are:

- IBM, World Trade Corporation and Tata Industries Ltd. created joint venture to form Tata Information Systems Ltd. The stated purpose was to make it India's top information technology company
- Cummins Engine Company and TELCO formed a joint venture to manufacture Telco Engines
- Reliance Industries and Nynex Corporation
- Tata Industries and Bell Canada
- Ashok Leyland and Singapore Telecom

There are five common objectives in a joint venture: market entry, risk/reward sharing, technology sharing and joint product development, and conforming to government regulations. Other benefits include political connections and distribution channel access that may depend on relationships. Joint ventures are favoured when:

- The partners' strategic goals converge while their competitive goals diverge.
- The partners' size, market power, and resources are small compared to the industry leaders.
- Partners' are able to learn from one another while limiting access to their own proprietary skills.

The critical issues to consider in a joint venture are ownership, control, length of agreement, pricing, technology transfer, local firm capabilities and resources, and government intentions. Potential problems include, conflict over asymmetric investments, mistrust over proprietary knowledge, performance ambiguity – how to share the profits and losses, lack of parent firm support, cultural conflicts, and finally, when and how when to terminate the relationship. Joint ventures have conflicting pressures to cooperate and compete:

- Strategic imperative; the partners want to maximize the advantage gained for the joint venture, but they also want to maximize their own competitive positions.
- The joint venture attempts to develop shared resources, but each firm wants to develop and protect its own proprietary resources.
- The joint venture is controlled through negotiations and coordination processes, while each firm would like to have hierarchical control.

Strategic Alliances: Strategic alliance is a combination of the efforts of two or more organisations to develop competitive advantage In strategic alliance, two or more partners join hands together for certain specified objectives, generally, for certain specific period. when these objectives are achieved, partners terminate their alliance. Examples: Oberoi Group of Hotels has entered into strategic alliance with Lufthansa Airlines, Hong Kong Bank, and Mercury Travels. All these four organisations undertake promotional activities jointly. Any person who stays in Oberoi Hotels gets bonus point. His bonus point increases if he travels by Lufthansa, uses Hong Kong Bank facilities, and engages Mercury Travel's services. On the basis of his accumulated bonus points, he gets various prizes including free air ticket to New York.

7.2.3.1 Types of international strategies

International Strategy: Firms adopt international strategy when they create value by transferring products and services to foreign markets where these products and services are not available. International firm, by maintaining a tight control over its overseas operations, offers standardized products and services in different countries with little or no differentiation. Like IBM, Kellogg, Proctor & Gamble, Microsoft, etc., adopt this strategy for the different countries they operate in.

Multidomestic Strategy: The organisation decentralizes operational decisions and activities to each country in which it is operating and customizes its products and services to each market. Firm adopts a multidomestic strategy when they try to achieve a high level of local responsiveness by matching their products and services offerings to the national conditions operating in the countries they operate in. Multidomestic firm attempts to

Exibit 7.3 Four Types of International Strategies

Pressure for cost Reduction ↑		
	Global Strategy	**Transnational Strategy**
	International Strategy	**Multidomestic Strategy**

→ Pressure for local reponsiveness →

Source Bartlett CA, & Ghoshal, Managing Across Borders, Boston, M A, Harvard Business School Press, 1989.

extensively customize their products and services according to the local conditions operating in the different countries. U.S. auto manufacturers maintained decentralized overseas units that produced cars adapted to different countries and regions. General Motors produced Opel in Germany and Vauxhall in Great Britain while Chrysler produced the Simca in France and Ford offered a Canadian Ford. Other examples are Coca Cola, McDonald, Pizza Hut, etc.

Global strategy: The global firms try to focus intensively on a low cost structure by leveraging their expertise in providing certain products and services, and concentrating the production of these standardized products and services at a few favourable locations around the world. These products and services are offered in an undifferentiated manner in all countries the global firm operates in, usually at competitive prices. For example, Ford is treating its Contour as a car for all world markets—one that can be produced and sold in any industrialized nation.

Transnational Strategy: Firms adopt a transnational strategy when they adopt a combined approach of low-cost and high local responsiveness simultaneously for their products and services. The organisation seeks the best of both the multidomestic and global strategies by globally integrating operations while tailoring products and services to the local market. In other words a company 'thinks globally but acts locally'. Many authors refer to this concept as 'Glocalization'. Global electronic communications and connectivity can help integrate operations while flexible manufacturing enables firms to produce multiple versions of products from the same assembly line, tailoring them to different markets. This gives more choice in locating facilities to take advantage of cheaper labour or to get the best of other factors of production.

7.2.4 Expansion Through Diversification

Diversification is defined as the entry of a firm into new lines of activity, through internal or external modes. Diversification is the process of entry into a business which is new to an organisation either market-wise or technology-wise or both. In diversification, firm acquires ownership or control over another firm against the wishes of the latter's management. But in practice it can be both, hostile or friendly. The primary reasons a firm pursues increased diversification are value creation through economies of scale

Exhibit 7.4 Managing Global Supply Chains to Enhance Competitiveness

Logistics capabilities (the movement of supplies and goods) make or mar global operations. Global operations involve highly coordinated international flow of goods, information, cash, and work processes. Setting up a global supply chain to support producing and selling products in many countries at the right cost and service levels is a very difficult task. However, the benefits of managing this difficult task many are, which include rationalization of global operations by setting up right the number of factories and distribution centres and integration of far-flung operations under a unified command to better manage inventory and order filling activities. Optimizing global supply chain operations can cut the delivery time and cost drastically and improve global competitiveness. Smart supply chain planning may result in locating facilities where they make the most logistical sense, while saving on taxes. This is better than simply locating where labour is cheapest, but where taxes and other cost may not be most favourable.

and scope, or market dominance. In some cases firms choose diversification because of government policy, performance problems and uncertainty about future cash flow. In one sense, diversification is a risk management tool, in that its successful use reduces a firm's vulnerability to the consequences of competing in a single market or industry. Risk plays a very vital role in selecting a strategy and hence, continuous evaluation of risk is linked with a firm's ability to achieve strategic advantage . Internal development can take the form of investments in new products, services, customer segments, or geographic markets including international expansion. Diversification is accomplished through external modes through acquisitions and joint ventures.

Firms choose expansion strategy when their perceptions of resource availability and past financial performance are both high. The most common growth strategies are diversification at the corporate level and concentration at the business level. Reliance Industry, a vertically integrated company covering the complete textile value chain has been repositioning itself to be a diversified conglomerate by entering into a range of businesses such as power generation and distribution, insurance, telecommunication, and information and communication technology services. Tata Tea's takeover of Consolidated Coffee (a grower of coffee beans) and Asian Coffee (a processor) are the examples of related diversification.

Why firm Adopts Diversification Strategy?

Diversification is a strategy that takes a company into new markets with new products or services. Companies may choose a diversification strategy for different reasons.

(i) **Economies of scope:** Companies might wish to create and exploit economies of scope, in which the company tries to utilize its exciting resources and capabilities in other markets. This can oftentimes be the case if companies have underutilized resources or capabilities that cannot be easily disposed or closed. Using a diversification strategy, companies may therefore be able to utilize all its capabilities or resources, and able to attract new business from market segments not catered to earlier.

(ii) **Utilisation of managerial skills:** Managerial skills found within the company may be successfully used in other markets, where the dominant logic and managerial procedures of management can be successfully transferred to other markets.

(iii) **Cross-subsidizing business:** Companies pursuing a diversification strategy may be able to cross-subsidize one product with the surplus of another. This way, companies with a very diverse portfolio of products catering to different markets may potentially grow in power, and be able to withstand a prolonged period of price competition, etc. When having subsidized one product for a substantial period of time, the company might possibly be able to win a monopoly, making it the only supplier in the respective market.

(iv) **Spread financial risks:** Companies may also want to use a diversification strategy to spread financial risk over different markets and products, so that the entire success of the company is not reliant on one market or product only.

(v) **To Grow:** Growth is an implicit objective in nearly all organisations. Stock markets tend to reward growing companies. Managers find growth extremely attractive because it hold out the prospects of increased earnings for the firm leading to increased compensations for themselves. They also see the acquisition of new knowledge as instrumental in improving their self-actualisation prospects.

(vi) **Fuller utilisation of Resources and Capabilities:** Firms find that they have unutilised or underutilised capacities sometimes in manufacturing some times in other fields . Alternatively a firm could find that it can perform a business activity at a lower cost and with better timeliness than if it utilised its internal capabilities. For example, in Timex Watches it was decided that share dept functions could be performed at much lower cost than if they were done by an outside agency. It also provided a better level of service to shareholders.

(vii) **To escape from an unattractive or undesirable industry:** The best example of this type of diversification is the Tobacco industry where the giants including Phillip Morris, R.J. Reynolds and British American Tobacco have all diversified because of the severe regulatory pressures applied to their industry. It is interesting to note that whereas BAT's diversification into financial services has been highly successful, similar attempts to diversify by their Indian subsidiary ITC were unsuccessful and it had to exit this business after a few years.

(viii) **To make use of surplus cash flows:** There are many examples of this type found in Indian industry. Bajaj Auto and Bombay Dyeing have consistently over the last few years invested surplus cash from their core businesses in two-wheelers and textiles respectively into treasury operations mostly short term lending to other cash strapped corporates. At times a firm might use surpluses from one of its cash-rich businesses to cross fund other businesses.

There may however be other reasons for companies to use a diversification strategy than the those listed above, and companies may very well benefit from a diversification strategy for other reasons. However, it is important for companies to realize the possible danger of diversifying its scope of operations to much. Companies might risk neglecting its core capabilities and become too diversified, where too many different products supplied to different markets might have negative effects on products and services, where product quality or uniqueness might suffer due to the shift in focus on different products and markets.

Diversification strategy can be split into two different types:

- Related diversification or concentric diversification
- Unrelated diversification or conglomerate diversification

7.2.4.1 Related diversification or concentric diversification

Related or concentric diversification occurs when a firm adds related products or markets. The goal of such diversification is to achieve strategic fit. Strategic fit allows an organisation to achieve synergy. In essence, synergy is the ability of two or more parts of an organisation to achieve greater total effectiveness together than would be experienced if the efforts of the independent parts were summed. Synergy may be achieved by combining firms with complementary marketing, financial, operating, or management efforts. Financial synergy may be obtained by combining a firm with strong financial resources but limited growth opportunities with a company having great market potential but weak financial resources. For example, debt-ridden companies may seek to acquire firms that are relatively debt-free to increase the lever-aged firm's borrowing capacity. Similarly, firms sometimes attempt to stabilize earnings by diversifying into businesses with different seasonal or cyclical sales patterns.

Strategic fit in operations could result in synergy by the combination of operating units to improve overall efficiency. Combining two units so that duplicate equipment or research and development are eliminated would improve overall efficiency. Quantity discounts through combined ordering would be another possible way to achieve operating synergy. Yet another way to improve efficiency is to diversify into an area that can use by-products from the existing operations. For example, breweries have been able to convert grain, a by-product of the fermentation process, into feed for livestock. Also breweries have been able to achieve marketing synergy through national advertising and distribution. By combining a number of regional breweries into a national network, beer producers have been able to produce and sell more beer than independent regional breweries.

Management synergy can be achieved when management experience and expertise is applied to different situations. Perhaps a manager's experience in working with unions in one company could be applied to labour management problems in another company. Caution must be the exercised, however, in assuming that management experience is universally transferable. Situations that appear similar may require significantly different management strategies. Personality clashes and other situational differences may make management synergy difficult to achieve. Although managerial skills and experience can be transferred, individual managers may not be able to make the transfer effectively.

When expanding into different products or markets using existing capabilities, companies can create related diversification by using its capabilities and resources in other settings. A car manufacturer might for instance expand its operations into manufacturing of motorcycles or trucks, and use its capabilities and resources to become successful in these markets. Likewise, a company might create related diversification by integrating into the existing value network. For instance, companies producing steel might go into the mining business, where it might control the supplies, etc., for its main operations. Likewise, clothes manufacturers might create their own brand shops, in which they sell their clothes.

Maruti used to initially only assemble cars. It progressively introduced engine and transmission manufacture into its operations. On the other hand a firm might decide to move up the value chain. Reliance, in its textile operation only manufactured the cloth. Later on it opened exclusive retail outlets which addressed not only the sales and distribution aspects of its business, but also contributed to brand building. Sometimes a firm may reverse the direction of its vertical integration. Telco which in its early years had embarked on a massive programme of backward integration which resulted in its producing most of the parts for its trucks and buses, in recent years has consciously moved out of component manufacture and sought to concentrate on final assembly of its products.

Hindustan Lever, the FMCG major, used to be largely in the soaps and detergents business. In the last ten years, it has diversified into the foods and beverages business largely through the acquisition of first Lipton Tea and later the acquisition of Brooke Bond. IBM has entered the Infotech consultancy business another example of related diversification.

Larsen and Toubro (L&T) has diversified over the past three decades around its core competence in construction engineering. Originally, the firm only made parts and machinery for construction. Later the firm diversified into excavating and earth moving equipment and still later into the cement industry thus taking a stake in one of the vital inputs to its industry. Each of these diversifications addressed the "scope" opportunity for a firm which had a clear definition and understanding of its competitive space. Escorts, another prominent engineering company has a widely diversified product portfolio which includes tractors, two-wheelers and several critical automobile components for auto engines. The company's diversification was developed around its core competence in automobile engineering . It is another matter that this firm has recently diversified into unrelated areas including electronics and telecommunications without much success.

7.2.4.2 Unrelated diversification or conglomerate diversification

Conglomerate diversification occurs when a firm diversifies into areas that are unrelated to its current line of business. In this case companies expand their operations into markets or products beyond current resources and capabilities. Synergy may result through the application of management expertise or financial resources, but the primary purpose of conglomerate diversification is improved profitability of the acquiring firm. Little, if any, concern is given to achieving marketing or production synergy with conglomerate diversification.

The unrelated diversification seems to be applicable and meaningful in at least two cases:

- Firstly, if the parent company is able to provide different businesses with managerial knowledge and expertise that strengthens the individual business, it will be very feasible to diverse into different markets that will potentially increase parent company profits.

- Secondly, unrelated diversification might give a company the opportunity of increasing the strength of the economy of different markets, and to develop competence that can be shared between different markets and products.

One of the most common reasons for pursuing a conglomerate growth strategy is that opportunities in a firm's current line of business are limited. Finding an attractive investment opportunity requires the firm to consider alternatives in other types of business. Philip Morris's acquisition of Miller Brewing was a conglomerate move. Products, markets, and production technologies of the brewery were quite different from those required to produce cigarettes. Firms may also pursue a conglomerate diversification strategy as a means of increasing the firm's growth rate. As discussed earlier, growth in sales may make the company more attractive to investors. Growth may also increase the power and prestige of the firm's executives. Conglomerate growth may be effective if the new area has growth opportunities greater than those available in the existing line of business.

The American tobacco firms Phillip Morris and R.J. Reynolds entered the FMCG arena specifically in food and beverages, BAT's major and extremely successful diversification was into financial services. General Electric is the ultimate example of a firm which has pursued unrelated diversification with dizzying success for several years. However, how much that has to do with the dynamism of its legendary leader Jack Welch will only be clear after the firm has been under new leadership for a few years. The 1970s it must be mentioned witnessed a surge of conglomeratism. Many of the firms that pursued the strategy of unrelated diversification went bankrupt leading to revulsion for this form of diversification. However, the other successful instance of conglomeratism—Asea Brown Boveri—shows that if pursued properly, unrelated or to put it more accurately seemingly unrelated diversification can be extremely advantageous.

Probably the biggest disadvantage of a conglomerate diversification strategy is the increase in administrative problems associated with operating unrelated businesses. Managers from different divisions may have different backgrounds and may be unable to work together effectively. Competition between strategic business units for resources may entail shifting resources away from one division to another. Such a move may create rivalry and administrative problems between the units. Caution must also be exercised in entering businesses with seemingly promising opportunities, especially if the management team lacks experience or skill in the new line of business.

Without some knowledge of the new industry, a firm may be unable to accurately evaluate the industry's potential. Even if the new business is initially successful, problems will eventually occur. Executives from the conglomerate will have to become involved in the operations of the new enterprise at some point. Without adequate experience or skills (management synergy) the new business may become a poor performer.Without some form of strategic fit, the combined performance of the individual units will probably not exceed the performance of the units operating independently. In fact, combined performance may deteriorate because of controls placed on the individual units by the parent conglomerate. Decision-making may become slower due to longer review periods and complicated reporting systems.

7.2.5 Cooperation Expansion Strategy

A cooperative strategy is a strategy in which firms work together to achieve a shared objective. Cooperative strategies are used to gain competitive advantage by joining with one or two competitors against other competitors of the industry. Cooperative strategy is the third major alternative (internal growth and mergers and acquisitions are the other two) firms use to grow, develop value-creating competitive advantages, and create differences between them and competitors. Thus, cooperating with other firms is another strategy that is used to create value for a customer that exceeds the cost of creating that value and to create a favourable position in the marketplace relative to the five forces of competition. Increasingly, cooperative strategies are formed by firms competing against one another, as shown by the fact that more than half of the strategic alliances (a type of cooperative strategy) established within a recent two-year period were between competitors such as FedEx and the U.S. Postal Service. The two general types of cooperative strategies are collusion and strategic alliance.

7.2.5.1 Collusion

Collusion is the strategy by which the firms join together to reduce the output and hence results in the increase of prices by the normal economic law of supply and demand. It could be either explicit in which the companies cooperate through direct communication or negotiation or tacit in which the firms cooperate through informal signals. Both the types of the collusive strategies are illegal in most of the countries.

According to Barney, tacit collusion in the industries is most likely to be successful if:

(i) there is a small number of identifiable competitors
(ii) costs are similar among firms
(iii) one firm tends to act as the price leader
(iv) common industry culture that accepts cooperation
(v) sales are characterized by high frequency of small orders
(vi) large inventories and backlog are the normal patterns to be followed at the time of demand.
(vii) there are high entry barriers to keep out the new competitors.

7.2.5.2 Strategic alliances

A strategic alliance is the cooperation between one or two companies to achieve the mutually beneficial strategic objectives. A strategic alliance is a partnership between firms whereby firms' resources, and capabilities are combined to pursue mutual interests to develop, manufacture, or distribute goods or services. The reasons for the formation of strategic alliance are:

(i) To obtain technology or manufacturing capabilities: A company having competitive advantage in one field could forge alliance with another company of different competitive advantage to gain over the other competitors.

(ii) To obtain access to specific markets: Instead of buying or building its own companies the firm could give rights to companies in other countries to market its product.

(iii) To reduce the financial risk: By means of strategic alliance the company could reduce the loss that may happen if the new project fails.

(vi) To reduce political risk: The company could get rid of the political disturbance by forming the partnership with the company that is having good relation with the political parties of the particular country

(v) To achieve or ensure competitive advantage: By forming the strategic alliance the company would be able to achieve new or increase its existing competitive advantage.

7.2.5.3 *Various types of strategic alliances*

- **Mutual service consortia:** A mutual service consortium is a partnership of similar companies in similar industries who pool their resources to gain a benefit that are too expensive to develop alone such as access to advance technology. It is fairly weak and distant alliance due to very little interaction between the players.
- **Joint venture:** A joint venture is a "cooperative business activity, formed by two or more separate organisations for strategic purposes, that creates an independent business entity and allocated ownership, operational responsibilities, financial risks and rewards to each member while preserving their separate identity". Disadvantages of joint ventures include loss of control, decrease in the profitability, transfer of technology to the partners and probability of conflict between the partners. However, research shows that the joint ventures tend to be more successful if both the partners are having equal stake in the partnership and are dependent on each other for the success.
- **Franchising:** It is a cooperative strategy used to spread risk and use resources and capabilities. In other words, a *franchise* refers to a contract between two legally independent companies that allows the franchisee to sell the franchisor's product or do business under its trademarks over a given time and location. Franchising is a particularly attractive strategy to use in fragmented industries where no firm or small set of firms has a dominant share in the industry, making it possible for a company to gain a large market share by consolidating independent companies through contractual relationships.
- **Equity strategic alliance:** It is an alliance where partner firms own unequal shares of equity in a venture formed by combining some of their resources and capabilities to create a competitive advantage. Ford Motor Company and Mazda Motor Corporation formed a long-standing equity strategic alliance.
- **Non-equity strategic alliance:** It is an alliance where a contract is given to supply, produce, or distribute a firm's products without any equity sharing. It

requires less formal and demand fewer partner commitments. It is unsuitable for complex projects that require effective transfers of tacit knowledge between partners.

- **Licensing arrangement:** A licensing arrangement is the strategic alliance by which the firm in one country grants licence to a firm in other country to produce and/ or sell its product.

The licensee pays the compensation to the licensing firm in exchange of the technology. This is more useful where a company could not enter due the investment restriction in the particular country.

Other types of strategic alliances include distribution agreements, supply contracts, and marketing agreements (such as code-sharing agreements among airlines). Typically taking the form of a non-equity strategic alliance, outsourcing is the purchase of a value-creating primary or support activity from another firm.

Exercise

1. What is the need for adopting growth strategies? What are the conditions where growth strategy is more suitable? Briefly explain different types of growth strategies.
2. Discuss the advantages and disadvantages of adopted concentration growth strategy. Give the examples of firm who have used concentration strategy. How successful was the strategy?
3. Describe the reason for adopting related or unrelated diversification. What are the risks associated with diversification strategy. Give examples from Indian and global context.
4. Why does a firm adopt integration strategy? What are different types of integration strategy a firm can adopt? Under what condition firm adopt integration in India?
5. Why does a domestic firm adopt international strategy? Discuss the four types of international strategies and their advantages and risks.
6. In your opinion which strategies Indian company should adopt to compete globally. Give examples of Indian companies turning global and their success in world market.
7. How strategic alliance can help an Indian firm to enter in a foreign country? What are the different types of strategic alliances a company can adopt. Discuss their advantages and risks.

8 Business-Level Strategies

8.1 INTRODUCTION

Business-level strategies are similar to corporate strategies in that they focus on overall performance. In contrast to corporate-level strategy, however, they focus on only one business rather than a portfolio of businesses. Business units represent individual entities oriented towards a particular industry, product, or market. In large multi-product or multi-industry organisations, individual business units may be combined to form strategic business units (SBUs). An SBU represents a group of related business divisions, each responsible to corporate headquarters for its own profits and losses. Each strategic business unit likes to have its own competitors and its own unique strategy. A common focus of business-level strategies is sometimes on a particular product or service line and business-level strategies commonly involve decisions regarding individual products within this product or service line. There are also strategies regarding relationships between products. One product may contribute to corporate-level strategy by generating a large positive cash flow for new product development, while another product uses the cash to increase sales and expand market share of existing businesses. Given this potential for business-level strategies to impact other business-level strategies, business-level managers must provide ongoing, intensive information to corporate-level managers. Without such crucial information, corporate-level managers are prevented from best managing overall organisational direction. Business-level strategies are thus primarily concerned with:

- Coordinating and integrating unit activities so they conform to organisational strategies (achieving synergy).
- Developing distinctive competence and competitive advantage in each unit.
- Identifying product or service-market niches and developing strategies for competition.
- Monitoring product or service markets so that strategies conform to the needs of the markets at the current stage of evolution.

In a single-product company, corporate-level and business-level strategies are the same. For example, a furniture manufacturer producing only one line of furniture has its corporate strategy chosen by its market definition, wholesale furniture, but its business is still the same, wholesale furniture. Thus, in single-business organisations, corporate and business-level strategies overlap to the point that they should be treated as one united strategy. The product made by a unit of a diversified company would face many of the same challenges and opportunities faced by a one-product company. However, for most organisations, business-unit strategies are designed to support corporate strategies. Business-level strategies look at the product's life cycle, competitive environment, and competitive advantage much like corporate-level strategies, except the focus for business-level strategies is on the product or service, not on the corporate portfolio.

Business-level strategies thus support corporate-level strategies. Corporate-level strategies attempt to maximize the wealth of shareholders through profitability of the overall corporate portfolio, but business-level strategies are concerned with (1) matching their activities with the overall goals of corporate-level strategy while simultaneously, (2) navigating the markets in which they compete in such a way that they have a financial or market edge—a competitive advantage—relative to the other businesses in their industry.

8.2 PORTER'S GENERIC STRATEGIES

Porter's generic strategies framework constitutes a major contribution to the development of the strategic management literature. Generic strategies were first presented in two books by Professor Michael Porter of the Harvard Business School in 1980 and 1985. Porter suggested that some of the most basic choices faced by companies are essentially the scope of the markets that the company would serve and how the company would compete in the selected markets. Competitive strategies focus on ways in which a company can achieve the most advantageous position that it possibly can in its industry. The profit of a company is essentially the difference between its revenues and costs. Therefore, high profitability can be achieved through achieving the lowest costs or the highest prices vis-à-vis the competition. Porter used the terms 'cost leadership' and 'differentiation', wherein the latter is the way in which companies can earn a price premium.

8.2.1 Main Aspects of Porter's Generic Strategies Analysis

Companies can achieve competitive advantages essentially by differentiating their products and services from those of competitors and through low costs. Firms can target their products by a broad target, thereby covering most of the marketplace, or they can focus on a narrow target in the market. According to Porter, there are three generic strategies that a company can undertake to attain competitive advantage. These strategies are:

(1) Cost leadership,
(2) Differentiation,
(3) Focus on a particular market niche.

The generic strategies provide direction for business units in designing incentive systems, control procedures, operations, and interactions with suppliers and buyers, and with making other product decisions. These three generic strategies are defined along two dimensions: strategic scope and strategic strength. *Strategic scope* is a demand-side dimension and looks at the size and composition of the market you intend to target. *Strategic strength* is a supply-side dimension and looks at the strength or core competency of the firm. In particular he identified two aspects that he felt were most important: product differentiation and product cost efficiency or product cost leadership.

Competitive/target/ strategic scope	Strategic strength/competitive advantage →	
	Low cost products/services	Differentiated product/services
Broad target	Cost leadership	Differentiation
Narrow target ↓	Focussed cost leadership	Focussed Differentiation

Fig. 8.1 Porter's generic business strategies

Source Michael Porter (1985), *Competitive Advantage: Creating and Sustaining Superior Performance*, New York Free Press, pp. 15.

8.2.2 Cost-Leadership Strategy

This strategy involves the firm winning market share by appealing to cost-conscious or price-sensitive customers. This is achieved by having the lowest prices in the target market segment, or at least the lowest price to value ratio (price compared to what customers receive). To succeed at offering the lowest price while still achieving profitability and a high return on investment, the firm must be able to operate at a lower cost than its rivals. There are three main ways to achieve this.

The first approach is achieving a high asset turnover. In service industries, this may mean, for example, a restaurant that turns tables around very quickly, or an airline that turns around flights very fast. In manufacturing, it will involve production of high volumes of output. Products can be designed to simplify manufacturing. A large market share combined with concentrating selling efforts on large customers may contribute to reduced costs. Extensive investment in state-of-the-art facilities may also lead to long run cost reductions These approaches mean that fixed costs are spread over a larger number of units of the product or service, resulting in a lower unit cost, i.e., the firm hopes to take advantage of economies of scale and experience curve effects. For industrial firms, mass production becomes both a strategy and an end in itself. Higher levels of output both require and result in high market share, and create an entry barrier to potential competitors, who may be unable to achieve the scale necessary to match the firm's low costs and prices. Companies that successfully use this strategy tend to be highly centralized in their structures. They place heavy emphasis on quantitative standards and measuring performance towards goal accomplishment.

The second dimension is achieving low direct and indirect operating costs. This is achieved by offering high volumes of standardized products, offering basic no-frills products and limiting customization and personalization of service. Production costs are kept low by using fewer components, using standard components, and limiting the number of models produced to ensure larger production runs. Overheads are kept low by paying low wages, locating premises in low rent areas, establishing a cost-conscious culture, etc. Maintaining this strategy requires a continuous search for cost reductions in all aspects of the business. This will include outsourcing, controlling production costs, increasing asset capacity utilization, and minimizing other costs including distribution, R&D and advertising. The associated distribution strategy is to obtain the most extensive distribution possible. Promotional strategy often involves trying to make a virtue out of low cost product features.

The third dimension is control over the supply/procurement chain to ensure low costs. This could be achieved by bulk buying to enjoy quantity discounts, squeezing suppliers on price, instituting competitive bidding for contracts, working with vendors to keep inventories low, using methods such as Just-in-Time purchasing or Vendor-Managed Inventory. Wal-Mart is famous for squeezing its suppliers to ensure low prices for its goods. Dell Computer initially achieved market share by keeping inventories low and only building computers on order. Other procurement advantages could come from preferential access to raw materials, or backward integration.

Some writers posit that cost leadership strategies are only viable for large firms with the opportunity to enjoy economies of scale and large production volumes. However, this takes a limited industrial view of strategy. Small businesses can also be cost leaders if they enjoy any advantages conducive to low costs. For example, a local restaurant in a low rent location can attract price-sensitive customers if it offers a limited menu, rapid table turnover and employs staff on minimum wages. Innovation of products or processes may also enable a start up or small company to offer a cheaper product or service where incumbents' costs and prices have become too high. An example is the success of low-cost budget airlines who despite having fewer planes than the major airlines, were able to achieve market share growth by offering cheap, no-frills services at prices much cheaper than those of the larger incumbents.

The companies that attempt to become the lowest-cost producers in an industry are generally referred as those following a cost leadership strategy. The company with the lowest costs would earn the highest profits in the event when the competing products are essentially undifferentiated, and selling at a standard market price. Companies following this strategy place emphasis on cost reduction in every activity in the value chain. It is important to note that a company might be a cost leader but that does not necessarily imply that the company's products would have a low price. In certain instances, the company can for instance charge an average price while following the low cost leadership strategy and reinvest the extra profits into the business . Examples of companies following a cost leadership strategy include Ryan Air, and EasyJet, in airlines, and Tesco, in superstores.

This strategy requires firms to develop policies aimed at becoming and remaining the lowest cost producer and/or distributor in the industry. Note here that the focus is on cost leadership, not price leadership. This may at first appear to be only a semantic difference, but consider how this fine-grained definition places emphases on controlling costs while giving firms alternatives when it comes to pricing (thus ultimately influencing total revenues). A firm with a cost advantage may price at or near competitors prices, but with a lower cost of production and sales, more of the price contributes to the firm's gross profit margin. A second alternative is to price lower than competitors and accept slimmer gross profit margins, with the goal of gaining market share and thus increasing sales volume to offset the decrease in gross margin. Such strategies concentrate on construction of efficient-scale facilities, tight cost and overhead control, avoidance of marginal customer accounts that cost more to maintain than they offer in profits, minimization of operating expenses, reduction of input costs, tight control of labour costs, and lower distribution costs. The low-cost leader gains competitive advantage by getting its costs of production or distribution lower than the costs of the other firms in its relevant market. This strategy is especially important for firms selling unbranded products viewed as commodities, such as steel.

Cost leadership provides firms above-average returns even with strong competitive pressures. Lower costs allow the firm to earn profits even after competitors have reduced their profit margin to zero. Low-cost production further limits pressures from customers to lower price, as the customers are unable to purchase cheaper product from a competitor.

The risk of following the cost leadership strategy is that the company's focus on reducing costs, even sometimes at the expense of other vital factors, may become so dominant that the company loses vision of why it embarked on one such strategy in the first place. A cost leadership strategy may have the disadvantage of lower customer loyalty, as price-sensitive customers will switch once a lower-priced substitute is available. A reputation as a cost leader may also result in a reputation for low quality, which may make it difficult for a firm to rebrand itself or its products if it chooses to shift to a differentiation strategy in future. The greatest risk of pursuing a cost strategy is that it is fairly easy for direct competitors to follow suit as the ways outlined above to achieve cost reduction are not unique and are readily available given the same level of investment in driving down costs. One way to stay ahead of the competition in a relatively levelled playing field is to introduce continuous optimization of the production and value chain by introducing lean manufacturing techniques like Six-Sigma or Kaizen.

Conditions when cost leadership strategy work best:

- When the market for the product or service is such that price competition among rivals is a dominant competitive force.
- When the industry's product is a standard, commodity-type item readily available from a variety of sellers.
- When there are not many ways to achieve product differentiation that have value to the buyer.
- When most buyers use the product in the same ways and have much the same needs/requirements.
- When there is lesser customer loyalty and buyers incur low switching costs in changing from one seller to another and are prone to shop for the best price.
- When buyers are price sensitive and bases their purchase decision primarily on price.
- When there are large number of buyers and have significant bargaining power.

8.2.3 Differentiation Strategies

When a company differentiates its products, it is often able to charge a premium price for its products or services in the market. Some general examples of differentiation include better service levels to customers, better product performance, etc., in comparison with the existing competitors. Porter has argued that for a company employing a differentiation strategy, there would be extra costs that the company would have to incur. Such extra costs may include high advertising spending to promote a differentiated brand image for the product, which in fact can be considered a cost and an investment. McDonalds , for example, is differentiated by its very brand name and brand images of Big Mac and Ronald McDonald.

Differentiation has many advantages for the firm which makes use of the strategy. Some problematic areas include the difficulty on part of the firm to estimate if the extra costs entailed in differentiation can actually be recovered from the customer through premium pricing. Moreover, successful differentiation strategy of a firm may attract competitors to enter the company's market segment and copy the differentiated product .

Differentiation strategies require a firm to create something about its product that is perceived as unique within its market. Whether the features are real, or just in the mind of the customer, customers must perceive the product as having desirable features not commonly found in competing products. The customers also must be relatively price-insensitive. Adding product features means that the production or distribution costs of a differentiated product will be somewhat higher than the price of a generic, non-differentiated product. Customers must be willing to pay more than the marginal cost of adding the differentiating feature if a differentiation strategy is to succeed.

Differentiation may be attained through many features that make the product or service appear unique. Possible strategies for achieving differentiation may include warranty (Sears tools have lifetime guarantee against breakage), brand image (Coach handbags, Tommy Hilfiger sportswear), technology (Hewlett-Packard laser printers), features (Jenn-Air ranges, Whirlpool appliances), service (Makita hand tools), and dealer network (Caterpillar construction equipment), among other dimensions. Differentiation does not allow a firm to ignore costs; it makes a firm's products less susceptible to cost pressures from competitors because customers see the product as unique and are willing to pay extra to have the product with the desirable features.

Differentiation often forces a firm to accept higher costs in order to make a product or service appear unique. The uniqueness can be achieved through real product features or advertising that causes the customer to perceive that the product is unique. Whether the difference is achieved through adding more vegetables to the soup or effective advertising, costs for the differentiated product will be higher than for non-differentiated products. Thus, firms must remain sensitive to cost differences. They must carefully monitor the incremental costs of differentiating their product and make certain the difference is reflected in the price.

8.2.4 Focus Strategy

Porter initially presented focus as one of the three generic strategies, but later identified focus as a moderator of the two strategies. Companies employ this strategy by focusing on the areas in a market where there is the least amount of competition. Organisations can make use of the focus strategy by focusing on a specific niche in the market and offering specialised products for that niche. This is why the focus strategy is also sometimes referred to as the niche strategy. Therefore, competitive advantage can be achieved only in the company's target segments by employing the focus strategy. The company can make use of the cost leadership or differentiation approach with regard to the focus strategy. In that, a company using the cost focus approach would aim for a cost advantage in its target segment only. If a company is using the differentiation focus approach, it would aim for differentiation in its target segment only, and not the overall market.

This strategy provides the company the possibility to charge a premium price for superior quality (differentiation focus) or by offering a low price product to a small and specialised group of buyers (cost focus). Ferrari and Rolls-Royce are classic examples of niche players in the automobile industry. Both these companies have a niche of premium products available at a premium price. Moreover, they have a small percentage of the worldwide market, which is a trait characteristic of niche players. The downside of the focus strategy, however, is that the niche characteristically is small and may not be significant or large enough to justify a company's attention. The focus on costs can be difficult in industries where economies of scale play an important role. There is the evident danger that the niche may disappear over time, as the business environment and customer preferences change over time.

Focus, the third generic strategy, involves concentrating on a particular customer, product line, geographical area, channel of distribution, stage in the production process, or market niche. The underlying premise of the focus strategy is that the firm is better able to serve its limited segment than competitors serving a broader range of customers. Firms using a focus strategy simply apply a cost-leader or differentiation strategy to a segment of the larger market. Firms may thus be able to differentiate themselves based on meeting customer needs through differentiation or through low costs and competitive pricing for specialty goods.

A focus strategy is often appropriate for small, aggressive businesses that do not have the ability or resources to engage in a nationwide marketing effort. Such a strategy may also be appropriate if the target market is too small to support a large-scale operation. Many firms start small and expand into a national organisations. Wal-Mart started in small towns in the South and Midwest. As the firm gained in market knowledge and acceptance, it was able to expand throughout the South, then nationally, and now internationally. The company started with a focused cost-leader strategy in its limited market and was able to expand beyond its initial market segment.

Firms utilizing the focus strategy may also be better able to tailor advertising and promotional efforts to a particular market niche. Many automobile dealers advertise that they are the largest-volume dealer for a specific geographic area. Other dealers advertise that they have the highest customer-satisfaction scores or the most awards for their service department of any dealer within their defined market. Similarly, firms may be able to design products specifically for a customer. Customization may range from individually designing a product for a customer to allowing the customer input into the finished product. Tailor-made clothing and custom-built houses include the customer in all aspects of production from product design to final acceptance. Key decisions are made with customer input. Providing such individualized attention to customers may not be feasible for firms with an industry-wide orientation.

8.3 ANALYSIS OF PORTER'S GENERIC STRATEGIES

Firms can choose from one of the three generic strategies to compete in the marketplace, regardless of the context of industry. The companies that are successful at making use of the cost leadership strategy are often positioned to capitalize on a value proposition which emerges from their low cost emphasis, like the success story of Tesco , in the UK. These companies typically focus their efforts on value-oriented customers in the market. Value products are focused on providing value-oriented customers with products that are indeed value-for-money, relative to competitive offerings. Interestingly, an emphasis on cost leadership in this sense can act as a form of differentiation. Successful implementation of a cost leadership strategy would benefit from process engineering skills, products designed for ease of manufacture, access to inexpensive capital, tight cost control and incentives based largely on quantitative targets. McDonalds, restaurants, for example, achieve low costs through standardised products, and centralised buying of supplies, etc. Despite the benefits that the cost leadership strategy entails, there is limited empirical evidence that supports successful implementation of cost leadership strategies.

Contrary to the cost leadership strategy, there is empirical evidence to support the differentiation strategy. Pearson and Hall investigated sixty-four American companies and the findings of the study revealed that companies following a differentiation strategy had superior performance compared to those companies that were not following the same. It is important for analysts to note that there is more than one way in which a company can make use of differentiation. Differentiation can be achieved through a differentiated product, superior quality, and customer services, etc. A key question to ask is whether the customers of the company perceive the point of difference as one that is worth a price premium.

The focal point for the company pursuing a differentiation strategy should be the customer, and not the competitors. Differentiation strategy can be successful if the point of differentiation perceived by customers as valuable should coincide with the distinctive competence of the company. For example, Orange succeeded by providing the most basic requirements for mobile phone communication, better than the competition, and it created a differentiation in the minds of the consumers. Orange provided the customers with mobile phone communication requirements like better network coverage, network reliability, and charging customers for only what they use, instead of features like free phone calls, which even have a higher cost for provider. Therefore, a customer-focused differentiation strategy when implemented with a clear vision benefits the company in many ways including price premium, brand loyalty and sometimes even reduced costs, like the case of Orange. In order to effectively maintain a differentiation strategy, the firm should have strong skills in R&D, product engineering, change management, marketing, advertising, and HRM. Continuous innovation plays a vital role in case of differentiation, as is exemplified by companies like IBM, also referred to as the IT blue hood of the corporate world. IBM was awarded more US patents in 2003 than any other company, for the eleventh year running, which qualifies IBM as one of the most innovative and successful companies in its industry.

Notably, a number of small and medium sized companies have found that the niche strategy is the most useful strategic area to explore for them. While most companies employ cost leadership strategy, differentiation, or a mix of these two strategies, there are relatively fewer companies that adopt a niche strategy. Perhaps one of the most important elements to consider in case of a niche strategy is whether the size of the market is appropriate from the revenue potential aspect, and if the company has the capability to provide the specialised products that the consumers in the niche market need and want.

It has been noted that a shortcoming of the low-cost-differentiation dichotomy is that the two strategies are not opposite in entirety, and are neither always mutually exclusive. Most successful firms exhibit one or more forms of differentiation, along with forms that are directly associated with cost leadership and even the focus orientation. This is one of the trickiest areas in the analysis of generic strategies that reality can be different and more subtle than the stark contrasts that are highlighted by Porter. It is important to conduct the analysis with an open mind, and to explore the relative advantages, disadvantages, and risks that the various strategies may offer to a company vis-à-vis the competition and overall business environment.

Information technology and the advent of the Internet have caused major changes in the business environment and have accelerated the speed of change. Porter's generic strategies of differentiation and cost leadership will be applicable to e-business firms in a broad sense, while the focus/niche strategy will not be as viable for e-business firms, compared to their traditional counterparts. They suggest that an integration of cost leadership and differentiation strategies would be most promising in the e-business context, but individually differentiation will show superior performance compared to cost leadership. As more and more companies are transforming their bricks-and-mortar existences to brick-and-click, it is vital for analysts to understand the role that generic strategies are playing in the digital era.

8.3.1 Sources of information for Porter's Generic Strategies Analysis

Analysts can explore various sources to find information necessary for conducting the generic strategies analysis. Possible sources of information include company and competitor websites in order to view the existing portfolio of products or services that are being offered to customers. The annual reports of the company can be used to analyse the relationships between costs and profitability, and how a particular strategy is affecting the firm's overall performance. Marketing communications tools used by the company and competitors may also reflect the generic strategies. Advertisements can be a useful source of information to analyse the strategy that is being pursued by the company, and how that differs from that of the competition. Journal articles, trade publications and reputed magazine articles are useful sources of information to analyse industry trends, customer preferences in a given market, and the strategies that are being pursued by the companies in a particular industry.

8.3.2 Relationship Between Porter's Generic Strategies Analysis & Industry Forces

The three generic strategies suggested by Porter can be effectively utilised to defend against competitive forces in the business environment. The industry forces take the form of competitive rivalry, barriers to entry, threat of substitutes, buyer power, and supplier power.

- **Competitive rivalry:** If the competition in the industry in which the company operates is fierce, the advantage of a cost leadership strategy would be that the firm would be able to compete on price. However, cost leadership strategy is not the most desirable strategy in this event, as competitors may put intense price pressures, such that all companies would end up reducing their prices drastically. Differentiation would be a viable strategy in this case as there is a likelihood that the loyal customers would stay with the company. It would also be hard for competitors to cope with the specialised needs of customers who are part of a niche segment in the market.
- **Barriers to Entry:** A company employing any one of the three strategies would find it easy to create barriers for new entrants. The learning curve of cost leaders in an industry, along with the economies of scale through experience curve effects, would often make it impossible for potential entrants to compete on price, as the more mature firm can further lower prices without compromising its profitability. High customer loyalty towards a company's brands, which is true for the differentiation strategy, can play a vital role in discouraging potential entrants. Customers often choose to be with a niche player because of a certain core competence that only that particular player is providing in the market. Also companies that make use of the focus strategy over time often develop a thorough understanding of their customers' needs, which is a difficult task for a potential entrant. In this way, focus can act as an entry barrier also.
- **Threat of substitutes:** It is the differentiation and differentiation-focused strategies that effectively reduce the threat of substitutes. Threat of substitutes is reduced in case of the differentiation strategy due to customer loyalty to the unique aspects of a particular product or service, which no substitute product can offer in the

customer's mind. In case of the later strategy, the very nature of the company's products and core competence of the firm reduce the threat of substitutes.

- **Buyer Power:** The power of buyers changes in accordance with the three generic strategies. Cost leaders have the unique ability to offer lower price options to large and powerful buyers. However, the scenario differs for companies making use of the differentiation and focus strategies. Buyers in case of these two strategies would have less power as there are few alternatives available to them.
- **Supplier Power:** Suppliers can exercise their power primarily in case of differentiation and focus/niche strategies. Companies making use of these strategies have the ability to pass the price increases of suppliers to their final customers, through the premium pricing strategy.

8.3.2.1 Limitations of Porter's generic strategies analysis

During the 1980s, the generic strategies were regarded as fundamental to strategy and the ideas suggested by Porter were used extensively. It became clear over time that in reality there were some shades of grey in the distinction between differentiation and cost, compared to the black and white that is projected in theory. It is very difficult for most companies to completely ignore cost, no matter how different their product offering is. Similarly, most companies will not admit that their product is essentially the same as that of others.

It is important for analysts to bear in mind that Porter's generic strategies should be considered a part of a broader strategic analysis. The generic strategies only provide a good starting point for exploring the concepts of cost leadership and differentiation. Perhaps a major limitation of the generic strategies is that they may not provide relevant strategic routes in the case of fast growing markets. It is important to conduct other analyses like PESTEL analysis to analyse how the generic strategy being employed by a company should change in accordance with external factors. Other useful analyses would include SWOT analysis, analysis of the key success factors, etc.

Porter's generic strategies framework suggests that a company can maximize performance by striving to be the cost leader in an industry, by differentiating its products or services from those of other companies, and by focusing on a narrow target in the market. A company that attempts to combine cost leadership and differentiation strategies would invariably be stuck in the middle, which according to Porter is not a desirable notion. It is seen that each of the generic strategies has advantages and inherent risks that should be analysed carefully with respect to the company and its competitors. It is noted that in practice, most successful companies make use of a combination of low cost and differentiation strategies, which is true even in the context of online business.

8.4 TACTICS FOR BUSINESS STRATEGIES

Business tactics are specific moves, manoeuvres and actions taken in isolation or in a series by the managers in order to move from one milepost to another in the pursuit of operationalizing strategy. Tactics are short-term, linear, and single, with localized focus and having fairly limited impact on business performance. Tactics are by nature short-term affairs that function in consonance with all-inclusive strategic policy, but tweak it each time a business faces an issue or snag.

Tactics are ploys, patterns or manoeuvres the companies develop and implement to drive and support the strategy, and to get you closer to your objective. *In business, tactics are manoeuvres and techniques that help the company to reach target market and acquire customers. It can also be stop customers from going to competitors.* In business, getting a customer can be likened to scoring points against the opposition in a sporting contest. The more points you score, the better it is for you. The way in which you score points is through your tactics. Specifically, business tactics include product, marketing, promotional, branding, channel/distribution and pricing initiatives and campaigns you create and then execute in the market place. These initiatives are the specific plays or moves you develop and execute to help you build brand awareness, and convert that brand awareness into customers.

In business there is one function that drives the maximum numbers of tactics and that function is marketing. Put another way, your marketing function - and everyone involved in it - is the business equivalent of a championship-winning sports team or a Navy Seals unit. The marketing function drives success in the business. And the purpose of every other function in business - administration, operations, accounting etc - is to support the marketing function. Peter Drucker put it more definitively when he stated that: "Because it is its purpose to create a customer, any business enterprise has two - and only these two - basic functions: marketing and innovation. They are the entrepreneurial functions."

8.4.1 Characteristics of Tactical Strategies

Tactical strategies are those that pertain to everyday moves a company makes to improve its market share, competitive pricing, customer service or other aspects that can give it an advantage. Tactics tend to be short-term considerations about how to deploy resources to win a battle. Tactics are most meaningful in the service of long-term goals and values. It has the following characteristics:

- **Tactics Involve Timing:** Businesses employ a variety of tactics for short-term gain. A sale on an item that a competitor carries can work to the advantage of a company by winning over new customers. A decision to centralize staff to save money on clerical support can be a tactic to reduce costs so that more money can be put into an advertising campaign. These examples show the day-to-day nature of tactics. They are calculated to have a quick effect.
- **Tactics Relate to Local Conditions:** Tactics are adjustments a company makes to local conditions. When sudden demand springs up in an area, a nimble company may employ a tactic to meet that demand, such as an advertising campaign and attractive short-term pricing. If a competitor goes out of business, the company can use a tactic of welcoming a competitor's expired coupons and offering to meet its prices.

- **Tactics Change Often:** The rate of change for tactics is much faster than for long-term goals. Tactics that don't work can be abandoned almost immediately. Tactics that are effective may only last as long as conditions permit. While the company sticks to its long-term goals, the tactics it uses may be discarded often.
- **Tactics Are Ruled by Doctrine:** A company must establish guidelines to govern the use of tactics. Unethical moves can easily be eliminated by a sound doctrine and so can actions that can harm the public. It is easy in the heat of the moment to move to take advantage of a developing situation, but company policy and doctrine must limit the tactical options management will consider.

8.5 TYPES OF TACTICS

Business tactics are specific operating plans which are part of and fit into the larger strategic plan. In warfare, tactics are plans made to fight and win battles. Strategy is the larger set of plans to win wars. Similarly, **business tactics** can be viewed as short-term plans to achieve smaller goals, also called targets, and are part of a larger strategic plan to achieve long term goals. A useful way of viewing tactics is to consider them as linking elements between strategy formulation and strategy implementation. There are two types of primary tactics, viz.

(i) Timing Tactics and

(ii) Market Location Tactics.

8.5.1 Timing Tactics

Timing tactics refer to the order in which a firm makes market moves in relation to its competitors. A firm may choose to be first in the market with a product or new features to an existing product. This is known as a first mover tactic. Usually, a firm that employs this tactic is a market leader with an established acceptance of its brand. However, a notable exception to this has been Microsoft who has launched its P.C. related software products much after the initiator companies and still managed to gain leadership position with its products. We may recall the success of Excel which became the leader in the spreadsheet category and MS Word which gained the number one slot in Word Processor software. Most leading Indian firms be they in the automobile sector like Telco or in the FMCG sector like Nestle have been able to employ first mover tactics because of their undisputed position as market leaders.

There are two basic timing strategies that you can use when moving into a new market. The first timing tactic is to be a pioneer or a first mover. Pioneers into a market have the advantage of launching a novel product or idea, they have the advantage of a larger market share and they have the advantage of curiosity purchases. On the other hand, pioneers shoulder the brunt of the risk involved with entering a new market or launching a new type of product. If the idea flops then the pioneers are faced with huge losses.

The second timing strategy that you can use is a late mover tactic. This tactic lets the pioneers break in the market, develop the technology and develop the demand for the products. Then they launch their own line. This strategy's advantages include preexisting demand for products and services, mature technology and established product recognition. On the other side of the coin, however, are a few drawbacks including more competition and market domination by the established brand.

Take the example of Parle which is the first mover in the mineral water industry in India which has attracted companies, such as, Coca Cole (with the Kinley brand) and Pepsi (with the Aquafina brand). Parle has dominated a major share of the mineral water market leading to its Bisleri brand becoming generic to the product category. A case of a late-mover in this industry is nestle which planned to introduce its brand Pure Life by the end of 2000. Likewise, in the mutual funds industry, Unit Trust of India (UTI), set up in 1964, is the first-mover with a clear lead of several years over other mutual funds in the public and private sectors. IIM Ahmedabad is the first-mover in the autonomous institutions segment in the management education industry.

Being the first mover does not always constitute an advantage. UTI might be the first mover but there are many late-movers, such as, the Kotak Mahindra group, which have posed a stiff challenge to it. Similarly, the Indian School of Business at Hyderabad is likely to challenge the dominant position of the IIMs. Late-movers such as ICICI-Prudential Life Insurance, HDFC Standard Life Insurance, and Max New Life Insurance are likely to make life difficult for the first-mover Life Insurance Corporation (LIC) of India.

There are advantages and disadvantages associated with being the first-mover or late-mover. Often the advantages of one type are the disadvantages for the other. This means that the advantages enjoyed by the late-movers can be disadvantages for the first-mover firms.

8.5.1.1 First mover advantage

First mover advantage (FMA) is the advantage gained by the initial occupant of a market segment. This advantage may stem from the fact that the first entrant can gain control of resources that followers may not be able to match. FMA is sometimes the advantage gained by the initial or "first-moving" significant occupant of a new market segment. This advantage may stem from the fact that the first entrant can gain control of resources that followers may not be able to match. It is important to note that the first-mover advantage refers to the first significant company to move into a market, not merely the first company. In order for a company to try and become a first-mover that company needs to figure out if the overall rewards outweigh the beginning/underlying risks. Sometimes first-movers are rewarded with huge profit margins and a monopoly-like status. Other times the first-mover is not able to capitalize on its advantage, leaving the opportunity for other firms to compete effectively and efficiently versus their earlier entrants. Following are advantages which might occur to the first movers:

- They can establish a position as the market leaders. They can establish business models and gain valuable experiences that can enable them to reap the benefits of a learning curve that can help them in assuming cost leadership.
- Moving first in an industry results in forming early commitments to suppliers of raw materials, new technology, and distribution channels creating cost advantages over late-movers.

- They develop an image of being pioneers which helps to build reputation. First-movers create standards in different areas for all subsequent products and services in the industry.
- Moving first constitutes a pre-emptive strike and creates lead for the first-movers. For the late-movers, imitation may be difficult and risky.
- First-time customers are likely to remain loyal.

First-mover advantages can arise from three primary sources.

- **Technological Leadership:** A firm can gain FMA when it has had some sort of upper hand in its research and development (R&D) resulting from a direct breakthrough in technology. R&D expenditures can also provide technological leadership. The technological pioneers can retain their advantage if they protect their R&D through patents or if they successfully keep them as trade secrets. The diffusion of innovation can diminish the first-mover advantages over time, and can be triggered via workforce mobility, publication of research, informal technical communication, reverse engineering, plant tours, etc. With their short life-cycles patent-races can actually prove to be the downfall of a slower moving first-mover firm. Technology leadership helped Procter & Gamble propel their disposable diapers into the US market. They used a learning-based preemption to help invest in low-priced European synthetic fibre which helped create the diapers at a cheaper, more profitable price.
- **Pre-emption of scarce assets:** Pre-emption of input factors, if the first-mover firm has superior information, it may be able to purchase assets at market prices below those that will prevail later in the evolution of the market. Pre-emption of locations in geographic and product characteristics space, in many markets there is room for only a limited number of profitable firms; the first-mover can often select the most attractive niches and may be able to take strategic actions that limit the amount of space available for subsequent entrants. First-mover can establish positions in geographic or product space such that latecomers find it unprofitable to occupy the interstices. Entry is repelled through the threat of price warfare, which is more intense when firms are positioned more closely.
- **Switching costs and buyer choice under uncertainty:** Switching costs are extra resources that late entrants must invest to attract customers away from the first-mover firm. Buyer choice under uncertainty refers to the concept that buyers may rationally stick with the first brand they encounter that performs the job satisfactorily. For individual customers benefits of finding a superior brand are seldom great enough to justify the additional search costs that must be incurred. It can pay off for corporate buyers since they purchase in large amounts. If the pioneer is able to achieve significant consumer trial, it can define the attributes that are perceived as important within a product category. For instance in airline frequent-flyer miles many consumers find it important that an airline provides this service and are willing to actually pay more for an airfare ticket if it means they will get points towards their next flight.

8.51.2 First-mover disadvantages

Although in some cases being a first-mover can create an overwhelming advantage, in some cases products that are first to market do not succeed. These products are victims of first-mover disadvantages. These are:

- Being a pioneer is often costlier than being a follower. Pioneering firms have to spend resources on creating customer awareness and education regarding the products, especially if these are new products. Late-movers face lesser risks when the markets are already developed.
- Late-movers can imitate technological advances, skills, know-how and marketing approaches easily negating the advantages that first-movers are likely to have.
- Technological change is often rapid creating obsolescence for the first-movers.
- Late-movers can jump the technological thresholds and use the latest technology available.
- Customer loyalty is not guaranteed and can often prove to be ephemeral. Late movers can snatch the market share from the first-mover. If the first-movers have to retain market share and customer loyalty then additional efforts have to be put in.

First-mover advantages can arise from three primary sources.

- **Free-rider effects:** Secondary or late-movers to an industry or market, have the ability to study the first movers and their techniques and strategies. "Late movers may be able to 'free-ride' on a pioneering firms investments in a number of areas including R&D, buyer education, and infrastructure development". The basic principle of this effect is that competition is allowed to benefit and not incur the costs which the first-mover has to sustain. These "imitation costs" are much lower than the "innovation costs" the first mover had to spend, and also can cut into the profits which the pioneering firm would otherwise be enjoying.
- **Resolution of technological or market uncertainty:** First-movers must deal with the entire risk associated with creating a new market, as well as the technological uncertainties which will follow. Late-movers are given the advantage of not sustaining the risks, mostly monetary, with creating a new market. While the first movers have nothing to draw upon when deciding potential revenues and firm sizes, late-movers are able to follow industry standards and adjust accordingly . The first-mover must take on all the risk as these standards are set, and in some cases they do not last long enough to operate under these standards.
- **Shifts in technology or customer needs:** "New entrants exploit technological discontinuities to displace existing incumbents". In this case of first mover disadvantages, the late entrants are able to assess a market need that will replace what is currently being offered. This takes place when the first mover does not adapt or see the change in the customer needs, but also when competitor develops a better, more efficient, and sometimes less expensive product. Often this new technology is introduced while the older technology is still growing, and in this case the new technology may not be seen as an immediate threat. An example of this is the steam locomotive industry not responding to the invention and commercialization of diesel fuel. This disadvantage is closely related to the

incumbent inertia, and occur if the firm is unable to recognize a change in the market, or if a ground breaking technology is introduced. In either case, the first movers are at a disadvantage, in that although they created the market, they have to sustain it and can miss on opportunities.

- **Incumbent inertia:** As firms enjoy the success of being the first entrant into the market, they can also become complacent and not fully capitalize on their opportunity. Firms that have severe fixed assets cannot adjust to the new challenges of the market as they have no room to change. Firms that simply do not wish to change their strategy or products and incur sunk costs from "cannibalizing" or changing the core of their business, fall victim to this inertia. Some firms simply will not change as it will not maximize their short-term profits to do so. Although these numbers will be higher in the long run, the organisation will fail. These firms are sometimes unable to be sustained in a changing and competitive environment. They may pour too many of their early assets into what works in the beginning, and not project to what will need to work in the long run. "Vulnerability of the first-mover is often enhanced by 'incumbent inertia'. Such inertia can have several root causes:
  1. The firm may be locked into a specific set of fixed assets.
  2. The firm may be reluctant to cannibalize existing product lines.
  3. The firm may become organisationally inflexible.

The advantages and disadvantages for a first-mover show that good timing is important. But advantages cannot just flow to the first-movers. In case conditions are conducive to being a first-mover, then what matters are the strategies, positioning, and entry barriers that the first-mover firm is able to create. It is not always that a firm has to be a first-mover even if it has the opportunity. Smart late-movers can overturn the apple-cart and beat the first-movers at their own game. Sometimes fence-sitting still some other firm has tested the waters in an industry may be a prudent business strategy than jumping straightaway in order to be the first-mover. Late-movers can succeed if they have the staying power, can learn from the mistakes of the first movers and fine-tune their business tactics accordingly.

When Should You Move In?

Determining whether to be a pioneer or a late-mover is not always an easy choice. Some companies make the choice based on the stage of development that their product is in. If they are the first to master the technology and are ready to launch their product when their competition is still six to twelve months out from launching theirs, then it is a good idea to be the market pioneer. On the other hand, if there are several companies ready to launch a similar product or a controversial product, then waiting for three to six months to enter the market can be a good idea. This waiting period will allow the pioneers to field test the products, identify technology products and to find market niches that have not been filled by the pioneers. If you don't know when to enter a market you can use your SWOT matrix to determine if your strengths, weaknesses, opportunities and threats are pointing you towards and early or late entry into the market.

8.6 MARKET LOCATION TACTICS

Market location is an important business tactics that encourage us to know where to compete. It can be said that, the target market the firm aims at when the business strategies are applied. In business operation, it is a normal situation that we can find several companies who offer the same products or services. Consequently, there is unequal status of the companies in the market regarding market share. There are firms that operate only on the fringes and not in the mainstream markets while a few others have a small market share, some other firms have relatively larger market share, and one firm has the largest market share There are four types of market locations on the basis of the role that firms plays in the target including:

- Market Leader
- Market Challenger
- Market Follower
- Market Niches.

8.6.1 Market Leaders

These are the organisations that have the largest market share in the relevant product market and usually lead the industry in factors such as technological development, product and market attributes, price benchmark or distribution channel design. The market leaders can retain their position, they can adopt the following approaches:

- Expanding the market through new user, new use and more usage.
- Defending their position through offensive and defensive tactics.
- Expanding the market share through enhancement of operational effectiveness through new product development, manufacturing efficiency, improving product quality, superior support services, etc.

8.6.2 Market Challengers

These are the organisations that have second or lower ranking in the industry. These organisations can either challenge the leader or follow them. When they seek to challenge the leader, they hope to gain the market share. The tactics adopted by the the market challenger have several components. The challenger has to define the objectives and the opponent, choose a general attack strategy and then choose a specific attack strategy. The most common objectives of the challenger is increasing the market share and drive out the leader from the industry. They generally adopt the attack tactics which could include frontal attack, flank attack, or encirclement attack. They can also adopt guerrilla or by pass attack.

8.6.3 Market Follower

These are the organisations that imitate the market leader but do not upset the balance of the competitive power of the industry. They refer to avoid the direct attack, keep out of way of the other organisation and reap the benefits of the innovations of the market leaders through imitation. They generally adopt the cloner, counterfeiter, imitator or adopter strategy to remain in the business.

8.6.4 Market Niches

In this case the organisations carve out a distinct niche, normally left uncovered by the leader of the followers or a niche which is of little interest or no interest to others. It is similar to focus strategy as they target a market position which is small, unique and requires special competency in order to be served. This can be achieved by providing a special product or service attributes, serving in distinct geographical region, offering a customised product to slect group of customers. Market niches can adopt three approaches:

- Creating niches, involving ways or means to identify or create a niche in the industry.
- Expanding niches by enhancing the coverage to include similar or new market niches.
- Protecting niches through shielding the niches from attack by other organisations in the industry.

8.7 DIFFERENT TYPES OF TACTICS A FIRM CAN ADOPT

- **Offensive Tactic:** A notable market location tactics is the *offensive tactic* where a competitor's initiating tactic is an advertising campaign or a price promotion is met by an overwhelming response in sales or marketing. A fine example can be found in Honda's response to Suzuki's attempts through massive advertising and aggressive selling to gain the number one position in the Japanese motor cycle market. Honda's response was to declare a war on Suzuki with the rallying slogan to all its marketing and sales people "Annihilate Suzuki" Honda spent billions of yens over a three-month period and significantly reduced its profits for that year but had the satisfaction of obtaining Suzuki's public apology for their recklessness in trying to unseat the premier firm in the motor cycle business and to acknowledge Honda's supremacy in the market.
- **Flanking Tactics:** Sometimes firms employ 'flanking tactics" by introducing new products that do not directly contest the with their competitor's product, but offer an interesting alternative. Cyrix the U.S. semiconductor manufacturer faced with Intel's blockbuster 386 microprocessor chip introduced a Mathematics Co-processor chip that offered an additional facility to the segment of P.C. users who favoured heavy computational capability and thereby created a unique selling proposition (U.S.P) through which it gained considerable market share. Timex Watches in India faced with the absolutely dominant position of Titan Watches in the Indian watch market, launched a complete range of plastic watches that offered a refreshing product alternative to the market particularly to the youth market (18 to 35 age group) and was able to achieve a staggering sales volume of 2 million watches in just two years, a figure that the market leader took more than five years to reach in considerably less competitive conditions.
- **Encirclement tactics:** E*ncirclement tactics is where* the firm launches a huge variety of products to minimize the impact of a single extremely strong competitor product. Frito Lay has done just that in India by launching a huge variety of salted and flavoured potato chips against the sole potato chip product of its major rival Uncle Chips.

- ***Bypass* Tactics:** It consists of introducing an improved product to gain advantage over one's rivals. Motorola introduced an electronic ballast (choke) to contest the vacuum tube lamp market with its rivals in the U.S. Hindustan Lever and Procter and Gamble introduced improved detergents Surf Excel and Ariel Plus to bypass the mass market leader Nirma.
- **Guerilla Tactics**: Using a "hit and run" attack on a competitor, with small, intermittent assaults on different market segments. This offers the possibility for even a small firm to make some gains without seriously threatening a large, established competitor and evoking some form of retaliation.These tactics are employed by two strongly positioned players who employ hit-and-run manoeuvres to disconcert their opponents in the market place. Coke and Pepsi in India steal each other's cases (the containers that hold the bottles} quite often to gain a temporary advantage in the marketplace. The Indian watch marked is punctuated by the tactical promotions and discount schemes that major players resort to in order to affect increase in unit sales.
- **Defensive Tactics:** These tactics are employed by firms as a response to their competitors move or as pre-emptive in nature. Examples of these are exclusive agreements with distributors and dealers to handle a firm's products. Another example would be keeping prices low or even reducing them from previous levels to discourage aggressive entry of new competitors or new products from existing competitors. An exhaustive list of defensive tactics would include ***foreclosing on technologies*** through patenting and licensing favoured by pharmaceutical companies and software companies, ***limiting outside access*** to facilities and personnel favoured by aircraft manufacturers and semiconductor companies, ***boycotting*** suppliers who deal with competitors – a practice which existed for a long time in the auto industry, *and* ***lobbying*** with government to prevent entry or to restrict growth of competitors, a practice universally followed in India by incumbent industry players during the long years of the license permit raj. Two examples of firms that employed several of these tactics simultaneously are Titan in India and Microsoft worldwide. Sadly these tactics provide short-term advantage , usually build a lot of resentment throughout the industry and invariably draw vehement responses which tend to neutralise the initial gains.

8.8 COMPARING STRATEGY AND TACTICS

It is also worth discussing the difference between strategic choices (those which occur at the 'strategy stage') and tactical choices (which occur in the 'tactics stage').

The essential element of strategy is the set of 'committed choices' (of policies, assets and of their governance structures) made by management in setting the business model up, which often are not easily reversible. Tactical choices such as prices, the intensity of advertising or of R&D, minor product medications and so on, on the other hand, are relatively easy to change.

Strategic policy choices identify the particular way a firm intends to focus a particular activity or function. Thus, while Wal-Mart's price policy is described by the motto 'Every Day Low Prices', the actual implementation of this policy, in terms of particular pricing decisions, is tactical: each store sets its prices in a particular way depending on local market conditions, but coherent with the established policy. Asset choices concern how the firm intends to invest and, therefore involve key organisational commitments. For instance, Wal-Mart is committed to large investments into information technologies and distribution centres. The particular timing of these investments, how each will be financed, etc., are tactical aspects to be decided later on in the game. Governance choices are the third category of business model choices: giving powerful incentives to store managers, for example, is a Wal-Mart strategy choice, whereas specific contracts for particular store managers are tactical decisions.

In the case of Metro Newspaper, its strategic choices include being ad-sponsored and charging zero price for the newspaper, whether to own paper print facilities or to outsource this function, and general policies about how many ads Metro newspapers will carry and at what rates, the balance between news and opinion pieces, etc. Precise choices about advertising rates, numbers of pages and ads in each edition, the balance between news and opinion pieces, etc., are all tactical choices, which can be adjusted (within the limits imposed by Metro's business model), depending on local market conditions. Strategic choices set up the business model, which then places constraints on the tactics available to Metro to compete in the marketplace.

In the automobile industry, strategy is about changing features of the automobile such as shape, engine power, wheels, seats, etc... Tactics, however, are about what one does with the automobile, such as driving it fast or slow, or with the windows down. Reconfigurations to the car are possible, but costly, but tactical changes are usually (comparatively) easy to implement in the short term.

Exercise

1. Business-level strategies give the competitive edge to the company. Give your viewpoint.
2. Discuss the generic strategies given by Porter. How relevant these strategies are in the present competitive environment?
3. Select a market leader from the industry and identify the business level strategies adopted by him.
4. Discuss the condition under which an organisation can attain the cost leadership. How is it achieved?
5. What are the different market location tactics that can be adopted by a firm? Which tactic is more suitable for market leader, challenger, follower and market niche.
6. Timing tactics can make or mar the success of an organisation. Explain.
7. First-mover advantages tactics must be selected carefully. Explain the condition when such tactics should be adopted.
8. Discuss the different business level strategies Indian firm can adopt to compete globally.

9 Strategy Analysis and Choice

9.1 INTRODUCTION

Organisations continually face the challenges of exercising the choice among the alternatives. Strategies analysis and choice largely involves making subjective decisions based on objective information. This is chapter introduces important concepts that can help strategists generate feasible alternatives, evaluate those alternatives, and choose a specific course of action. This chapter focuses on establishing long-term objectives, generating alternative strategies, and selecting strategies to pursue. Strategy analysis and choice seeks to determine alternative course of action that could best enable the firm to achieve its mission and objectives. The firm's present strategies, objectives, and mission, coupled with the external and internal audit information, provide a basis for generating and evaluating feasible alternative strategies.Unless a desperate situation faces the firm, alternative strategies will likely represent incremental steps to move the firm from its present position to a desired future position.

9.2 PROCESS OF STRATEGIC CHOICE

Strategic choices concerns the "decisions about an organisation's future and the way in which it needs to respond to pressures and influences". Strategic choice is a part of the strategic process and involves elements like the identification and evaluation of alternatives which then leads to a choice. Once you have conducted the external and internal analyses the different alternatives available to you should be clear. Identifying them is however not always easy, and asking yourself questions like what the future focus is and what the expansion plans are might facilitate the identification process of these alternatives. There are three aspects that you should consider when you choose a strategy. Porter's generic strategies help you identify the grounds you stand on, then the possible directions that should be considered, and possible methods. Strategic choices also occur at different levels, at the business level, at the corporate and at the international level. The available options can develop into different directions and different methods can be of relevance when evaluating them. A great challenge is to get choices on different levels to be consistent with each other.

There are four steps in the process of strategic choice as given below:

- Focusing on the strategic alternatives
- Analysing the strategic alternatives
- Evaluating the strategic alternatives
- Choosing the strategic alternatives
- Focusing on the Strategic Alternatives

9.2.1 Focusing on the Strategic Alternatives

The aim of focusing on a few strategic alternatives is to narrow down the choice to a manageable numbers of the feasible strategies. The strategists can never consider all feasible alternatives that could benefit the firm, because there are an infinite number of possible actions and an infinite number of ways to implement those actions. Therefore, a manageable set of the most attractive alternative strategies must be developed. The advantages, disadvantages, trade-offs, costs, and benefits to these strategies should be determined. Focusing on the alternatives can be done by visualizing the future state and working backwards to identify gaps in the situation. This can be done through gap analysis. Here the company sets the objectives for next three to five year time period and identify the gaps in the desired future state and the present state.

Depending upon how wide or narrow the gap is, different alternatives can be thought of. At corporate level the strategic alternative can be four: expansion, stability, retrenchment and combination. If the gap is narrow, stability will be a good option but if the gap is wide expansion strategies will be the ideal option. However, all these will also depend on the expected environmental opportunities and threat. In a complex situation where multiple options are, the combination strategies will work better. At the business level the firm has to decide between positioning the firm as a cost leader, differentiator or to focused. Organisation need to understand the conditions in the industry weigh carefully and calculate the associated risk and benefits of each competitive positioning before making a choice. There are several choices at business level that a manager has to make in order to attain competitive advantage. A company is usually made up of a number of business units where each unit is responsible for its own competitive strategy since they often compete in different markets under different conditions. A competitive strategy can be viewed in different ways and there are usually several options available. The strategy clock can be used to evaluate the different options available to differentiate your firm and what kinds of strategies that are likely to fail. The strategies in the strategy clock have different focuses; there are strategies based on price, on product differentiation, a mixture of the two, or more focused strategies, and some strategies that are just doomed to fail. Regardless of what strategy you have, the competitive advantage that a company might have in the hypercompetitive markets today is only temporary, which requires more options and more choices that have to be acted on more rapidly than before. Choices you make are also likely to have an effect on the available options for others. Game theory is a theory about competitive moves in a market where every choice made affects the choices for the others. Similarly, at functional levels also the different alternative may be carefully considered before making a decision.

9.2.2 Analysing the Strategic Alternatives

All the identified alternatives should be subjected to a though analysis based on certain factors. These factors can be called as selection factors. Selection factors can be divided in to two groups: objective and subjective factors. Objectives factors are based on the analytical techniques and the real facts or data used to determine/facilitate a strategic choice. They can be the market share, ROI, annual turnover, profits etc. Subjective factors on the other hand are based on the person judgment or the descriptive factors such as perception of the top management regarding the business prospect of company for next three to five years or the company image in the mind of the customers or industry perception of the company. The identified alternative should be subjected to analysis based on the selection factors.

All participants in the strategy analysis and choice activity should have the firm's external and internal audit information by their side. This information, coupled with the firm's mission statement, will help participants crystallize in their own minds particular strategies that they believe could benefit the firm most. Creativity should be encourages in this through process.

9.2.3 Evaluating the Strategic Alternatives

Evaluation of strategic alternatives basically involves bringing together the analysis done on the basis of the objectives and subjective factors. Based upon both the factors, subjective and objective, the merits and demerits of alternatives have to be examined in view of the strength and the weakness of the organisation. It can also be viewed on the basis of the capabilities of the organisation to undertake the particular alternatives. There is no set procedure for this analysis; the strategist may use any approach which suits the circumstances. Alternative strategies proposed by participants should be considered and discussed in a meeting or series of meetings. Proposed strategies should be listed in writing. When all feasible strategies identified by participants are given and understood, the strategies should be ranked in order of attractiveness by all participants, with 1 = should not be implemented, 2 = should possibly be implemented, 3 = should probably be implemented, and 4 = should definitely be implemented. This process will result in a prioritized list of best strategies that reflect the collective wisdom of the group. Long-term objectives represent the results expected from pursuing certain strategies. Strategies represent the actions to be taken to accomplish long-term objectives. The time frame for objectives and strategies should be consistent, usually from 2 to 5 years.

Identifying and evaluating alternative strategies can involve many managers who earlier prepared the organisational mission statement, performed the external audit, and conducted the internal audit. Representatives from each department and division of the firm should be included in this process, as was the case in previous strategy-formulation activities.

9.2.4 Choosing from Among the Strategic Alternatives

The evaluation of strategic choice should lead to a clear assessment of which alternative is the most suitable for the organisation under the existing condition. The final step is therefore, of making strategic choice. One or more strategies have to be chosen for implementation. A blueprint will describe the condition under which the strategy would operate. This blueprint is the strategic plan which will contain the details, procedure and activities to be performed for implementing the chosen strategy.

An increasing number of firms recognize that establishing long-term objectives and strategies must be a give-and-take process. In practice, organisations generally establish objectives and strategies concurrently. Objectives become crystallized as feasible strategies are formulated and selected. Objectives should be quantitative, measurable, realistic, understandable, challenging, hierarchical, obtainable, and congruent among organisational units. Each objective should also be associated with a time line. Objectives are commonly stated in terms such as growth in assets, growth in sales, profitability, market share, degree and nature of diversification, degree and nature of vertical integration, earnings per share, and social responsibility. Clearly established objectives offer many benefits. They provide direction, allow synergy, aid in evaluation, establish priorities, reduce uncertainty, minimize conflicts, stimulate exertion, and aid in both the allocation of resources and the design of jobs. Long-term objectives are needed at the corporate, divisional, and functional levels in an organisation. They are an important measure of managerial performance. Many practitioners and academicians attribute a significant part of American industry's competitive decline to the short-term, rather than long-term strategy orientation of American managers.

9.3 TOOLS AND TECHNIQUE FOR STRATEGIC ANALYSIS

Strategic planning may be characterized as a systematic effort to produce fundamental decisions and actions that shape and guide what a business organisation is, what it does, and why it does it. The objective of strategic planning is to develop a map by which to manage an organisation's positioning. Although some would suggest that strategic planning has lost some of its effectiveness, most managers continue to recognize the need for effective strategic planning and implementation. While strategic planning requires a significant amount of time and can be quite frustrating, if done properly, it can enable a firm to recognize its most effective position within its industry.

There are a variety of perspectives, models and approaches used in strategic planning. The development and implementation of these different tools depend on a large number of factors, such as size of the organisation, nature and complexity of the organisation's environment, and the organisation's leadership and culture. Five strategic planning tools are presented below: the Boston Consulting Group Matrix; the GE Market Growth/ Market Share Matrix; SWOT Analysis; TOWS Analysis; Porter's Generic Competitive Strategies; and Porter's Five Forces Model.

9.3.1 Boston Consulting Group (BCG) Matrix

In the late 1960s the Boston Consulting Group, a leading management consulting company, designed a four-cell matrix known as BCG Growth/Share Matrix. This tool was developed to aid companies in the measurement of all their company businesses according to relative market share and market growth. The BCG Matrix made a significant contribution to strategic management and continues to be an important strategic tool used by companies today. The matrix provides a composite picture of the strategic position of each separate business within a company so that the management can determine the strengths and the needs of all sectors of the firm. The development of the matrix requires the assessment of a business portfolio, which includes an organisation's autonomous divisions (activities, or profit centres).

Exhibit 9.1 BCG Market Growth/Share Matrix

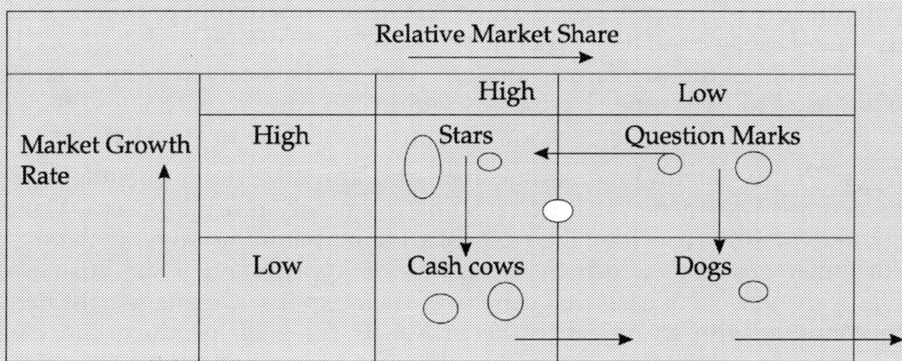

The BCG Matrix presents graphically the differences among these business units in terms of relative market share and industry growth rate. The vertical axis represents in a linear scale the growth rate of the market in which the business exists (see exhibit) which a particular business competes. The values of the vertical axis are the relevant market growth rates (i.e., 5 per cent, 10 per cent, 15 per cent, 20 per cent, etc.). Usually, a 10 percent cut-off level is selected in order to distinguish high from low market growth rate. The horizontal axis represents in a logarithmic scale the market share of a business within a firm relative to the market share of the largest competitor in the market. Relative market share is an indicator of organisation's competitive position within the industry, and underlies the concept of experience curve. Thus, business organisations with high relative market share tend to have a cost leadership position.

Each of a company's products or business units is plotted on the matrix and classified as one of four types: question marks, stars, cash cows, and dogs.

- ***Stars:*** Products which enjoy a high market share and a high growth rate are referred to as stars. These businesses are very important to the company because they generate a high level of sales and are quite profitable. However, because they are in a high growth market, which is very attractive to competitors, they require a lot of resources and investments to maintain a high market share. Often the cash generated by stars must be reinvested in the products in order to maintain market share. Though they earn high profits, they require additional commitment of funds because of the need to make further investments for expanding their production and sales. Eventually, as growth declines and additional investment needs diminish, stars become cash cows.

- ***Question marks:*** Products with high growth potential but low present market share are called question marks. Additional resources are required to improve their market share and potentially convert them into stars. If relative market share cannot be increased, the question mark becomes a dog. Of course, there is no guarantee that this would happen, that is why they are called question marks.
- ***Cash cows:*** Products which enjoy a relatively high market share but low growth potential are called cash cows. These businesses are highly profitable and leaders in their industries. They generate substantial profits and cash flows but their investment requirements are modest. The funds received from cash cows are often used to help other businesses within the company, to allow the company to purchase other businesses, or to return dividends to stockholders.
- ***Dogs:*** Products with low market share and limited growth potential are referred to as dogs. They generate little cash and frequently result in losses. Management should carefully consider their reasons for maintaining dogs. If there is a loyal consumer group to which these businesses appeal, and if the businesses yield relatively consistent cash that can cover their expenses, management may choose to continue with them. Since the prospects for such products are bleak, it is advisable to phase them out rather than continue with them.

Strategic business units, which are often used to describe the products grouping or activities, are represented with a circle in the BCG Matrix. The size of the circle indicates the relative significance of each business unit to the organisation in terms of revenue generated (or assets used). The direction of arrow indicates where the business can go from the present position. Although the BCG Matrix is not used as often as it was in past years, one big advantage of the matrix is its ability to provide a comprehensive snapshot of the positions of a company's various business concerns. Furthermore, an important benefit of the BCG Matrix is that it draws attention to the cash flow, investment characteristics, and needs of an organisation's business units, helping organisations to maintain a balanced portfolio.

General Electric Nine-Cell Matrix / Stop Light Strategy Matrix

In the 1980s General Electric, along with the McKinsey and Company Consulting group, developed a more involved method for analyzing a company's portfolio of businesses or product lines. This nine-cell matrix considers the attractiveness of the market situation and the strength of the particular business of interest. These two dimensions allow a company to use much more data in determining each business unit's position.

The key to the successful implementation of this strategic tool is the identification and measurement of the appropriate factors that define market attractiveness and business strength. Those individuals involved in strategic planning are responsible for determining the factors. The attractiveness of the market may be based on such factors as market growth rate, barriers to entry, barriers to exit, industry profitability, power of the suppliers and customers, availability of substitutes, negotiating power of both customers and members of the channel of distribution, as well as other opportunities and threats.

The strength of a particular business may be based on such factors as market-share position, cost placement in the industry, brand equity, technological position, and other possible strengths and weaknesses. The development of General Electric (GE) Matrix requires assessing the criteria to evaluate both industry attractiveness and business strength. The calculation of scores for these dimensions is frequently based on a simple weighted sum formula.

To consider this approach as a matrix analysis, market attractiveness is placed on the vertical axis with the possible values of low, medium, and high (see exhibit). Business strength is placed on the horizontal axis with the possible values of weak, average, and strong. A circle on the matrix represents each business unit (or product line). The size (area) of each circle represents the size of the relevant market in terms of sales. Three zones of three cells each are made, denoting different combinations represented by green, yellow and red colours. For this reason, this matrix is also known as "Stop Light Strategy Matrix".

The nine cells of this matrix define three general zones of consideration for the strategic manager. According to this approach, the first zone or green zone contains businesses that are the best investments. These are units in high market attractiveness and strong in business strength, followed by those that are strong in business strength and medium in market attractiveness, and those that are medium in business strength and high in market attractiveness. Management should pursue investment and growth strategies for these

Exhibit 9.2 GE Business Strength/Market Attractiveness

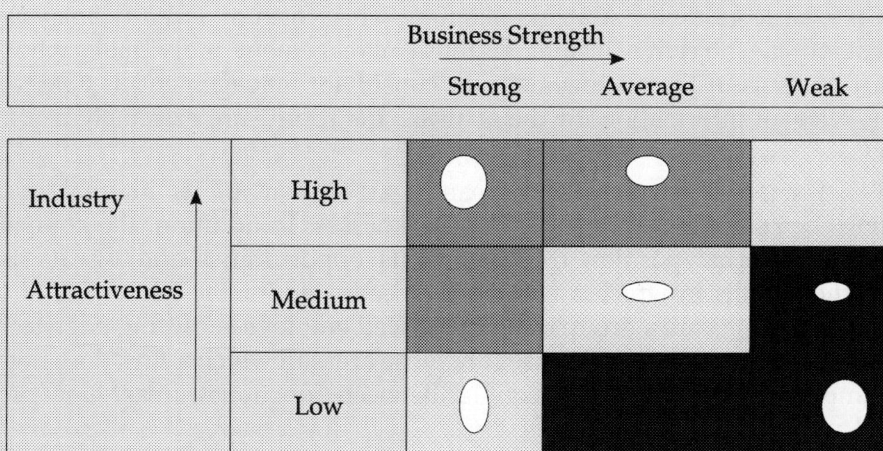

units. The management should be careful in determining the appropriate strategy for those business units located in any of the three cells in the diagonal of this matrix.

The second zone or yellow zone includes those business units that have moderate overall attractiveness, have medium business strength and market attractiveness, weak business strength and high market attractiveness, and strong business strength and low market attractiveness. These businesses should be managed according to their relative strengths and the company's ability to build on those strengths. Moreover, possible changes in market attractiveness should be carefully considered.

Those businesses that fall in the last zone or red zone are low in overall attractiveness; these are a good investment only if additional resources can move the business from a low overall attractiveness position to a moderate or strong overall attractiveness position. If not, these businesses should be considered for divestment or harvesting.

The GE Matrix may be considered an improvement over the BCG Matrix. The major advantage of using this matrix design is that both a business' strength and an industry's attractiveness are considered in the company's decision. Generally, it considers much more information than BCG Matrix, it involves the judgments of the strategic decision-makers, and it focuses on competitive position.

A major disadvantage, however, is the difficulty in appropriately defining business strength and market attractiveness. Also, the estimation of these dimensions is a subjective judgment that may become quite complicated. Another disadvantage lies in the lack of objective measures available to position a company; managers making these strategic decisions may have difficulty determining their unit's proper placement. Some argue that the GE Matrix cannot effectively depict the positions of new products or business units in developing industries.

9.3.2 SWOT Analysis Matrix

One of the most widely used strategic planning tools is a SWOT (strengths, weaknesses, opportunities, threats) analysis. Most companies use, in one form or another, SWOT analysis as a basic guide for strategic planning. The worth of a SWOT analysis is often dependent on the objective insight of those management individuals who conduct the SWOT analysis. If the management (or consultant management) is able to provide objective, relevant information for the analysis, the results are extremely useful for the company.

A SWOT analysis involves a company's assessment of its internal position by identifying the company's strengths and weaknesses. In addition, the company must determine its external position by defining its opportunities and threats. Strengths represent those skills in which a company exceeds and/or the key assets of the firm. Examples of strengths are a group of highly skilled employees, cutting-edge technology, and high-quality products. Weaknesses are those areas in which a firm does not perform well; examples include continued conflict between functional areas, high production costs, and a poor financial position.

Opportunities are those current or future circumstances in the environment that might provide favourable conditions for the firm. Examples of opportunities include an increase in the market population, a decrease in competition and a legislation that is favourable to the industry. Threats are those current or future circumstances in the environment, which might provide unfavourable conditions for the firm. Examples of threats include increased supplier costs, a competitor's new product-development process, and a legislation that is unfavourable to the industry.

Careful determination and classification of a company's strengths, weaknesses, opportunities, and threats provide an excellent way for a company to analyze its current and future situation. It is not necessary for a company to take advantage of all opportunities, nor is it necessary for a company to develop methods to deal with all threats. Additionally, a company need not strengthen all of its weaknesses or be too smug about all its strengths. All of these factors should be evaluated in the context of each other in order to provide the company with the most useful planning information.

9.3.3 TOWS Matrix

The Threats-Opportunities-Weaknesses-Strengths (TOWS) Matrix is an important tool that helps managers develop four types of strategies:

- SO : Strengths - Opportunities Strategies,
- WO : Weaknesses - Opportunities Strategies,
- ST : Strengths Threats - Strategies, and
- WT : Weaknesses - Threats Strategies.

Matching key external and internal factors is the most difficult part of developing a TOWS Matrix and requires good judgment, and there is no one best set of matches. Note in Table 6.2 that the first, second, third, and fourth strategies are SO, WO, ST, and WT strategies respectively.

- ***SO strategies*** use a firm's internal strengths to take advantage of external opportunities. All managers would like their organisations to be in a position where internal strengths can be used to take advantage of trends and events in the environment. For example,Mercedes Benz, with its technical know-how and reputation for quality (internal strengths), could take advantage of the increasing demand for luxury cars (external opportunity) by building a new manufacturing plant (SO strategy). Organisations generally will pursue WO, ST, or WT strategies in order to get into a situation where they can apply SO strategies. When a firm has major weaknesses, it will strive to overcome them, making them strengths. When an organisation faces major threats, it will seek to avoid them in order to concentrate on opportunities.
- ***WO strategies*** aim at improving internal weaknesses by taking advantage of external opportunities. Sometimes key external opportunities exist, but a firm has internal weaknesses that prevent it from exploiting those opportunities. For example, there may be a high demand for electronic devices to control the

amount and timing of fuel injection in automobile engines (opportunity), but a certain auto parts manufacturer may lack the technology required for producing these devices (weakness). One possible WO Strategy would be to acquire this technology by forming a joint venture with a firm having competence in this area. An alternative WO strategy would be to hire and train people with the required technical capabilities.

- ***ST strategies*** use a firm's strengths to avoid or reduce the impact of external threats. This does not mean that a strong organisation should always meet threats in the external environment head-on. General Motors found this out in the 1960s when Ralph Nader (an external threat) exposed safety hazards of the Corvair automobile. GM used its strength (size and influence) to ridicule Nader, and the direct confrontation caused more problems than expected. In retrospect, this ST strategy was probably inappropriate for GM at the time.
- ***WT strategies*** are defensive tactics directed at reducing internal weaknesses and avoiding environmental threats. An organisation faced with numerous external threats and internal weaknesses may indeed be in a precarious position. In fact, such a firm may have to fight for its survival, merge, retrench, declare bankruptcy, or choose liquidation. A schematic representation of the TOWS matrix is provided in Exhibit 9.3.

Exhibit 9.3 TOWS Matrix

	Strengths- S List the internal strengths of the firm	**Weaknesses-W** List the internal weaknesses of the firm
Opportunities-O List opportunities available for the firm	**SO Strategies** Use strengths to take advantage of opportunities	**WO Strategies** Overcome weaknesses by taking advantage of opportunities
Threats-T List threats faced by the firm	**ST Strategies** Use strengths to avoid threats	**WT Strategies** Minimize weaknesses and avoid threats

A TOWS Matrix is composed of nine cells. As shown, there are four key factor cells, four strategy cells, and one cell that is always left blank (the upper left cell). The four strategy cells, labeled SO, WO, ST, and WT, are developed after completing four key factor cells, labelled S, W, O, and T. There are eight steps involved in constructing a TOWS Matrix:

1. List the firm's key external opportunities.
2. List the firm's key external threats.
3. List the firm's key internal strengths
4. List the firm's key internal weaknesses.

5. Match internal strengths with external opportunities and record the resultant SO strategies in the appropriate cell.
6. Match internal weaknesses with external opportunities and record the resultant WO strategies.
7. Match internal strengths with external threats and record the resultant ST strategies.
8. Match internal weaknesses with external threats and record the resultant WT strategies.

Some examples of SO, WO, ST, and WT Strategies:

1. A strong financial position (internal strength) coupled with unsaturated foreign markets (external opportunities) could suggest market development to be an appropriate SO strategy.
2. A lack of technical expertise (internal weakness) coupled with a strong demand for computer services (external opportunity) could suggest the WO strategy of acquiring a high-tech computer company.
3. A strong distribution system (internal strength) coupled with intense government deregulation (external threat) could suggest concentric diversification to be a desirable ST strategy.
4. Poor product quality (internal weakness) coupled with unreliable suppliers (external threat) could suggest backward integration to be a feasible WT strategy.

The purpose of each Stage 2 matching tool is to generate feasible alternative strategies, not to select or determine which strategies are best! Not all of the strategies developed in the TOWS Matrix therefore will be selected for implementation. The strategy-formulation guidelines can enhance the process of matching key external and internal factors. For example, when an organisation has both the capital and human resources needed to distribute its own products (internal strength) and distributors are unreliable, costly, or incapable of meeting the firm's needs (external threat), then forward integration can be an attractive ST Strategy. When a firm has excess production capacity (internal weakness) and its basic industry is experiencing declining annual sales and profits (external threat), then concentric diversification can be an effective WT strategy. It is important to use specific, rather than generic, strategy terms when developing a TOWS Matrix.

9.3.4 Porter's Five-Force Model

Before a company enters a market or market segment, the competitive nature of the market or segment is evaluated. Michael E Porter suggests that five forces collectively determine the intensity of competition in an industry: threat of potential entrants, threat of potential substitutes, bargaining power of suppliers, bargaining power of buyers, and rivalry of existing firms in the industry. By using the model shown in exhibit a firm can identify the existence and importance of the five competitive forces, as well as the effect of each force on the firm's success.

The threat of new entrants deals with the ease or difficulty with which new companies can enter an industry. When a new company enters an industry, the competitive climate changes; there is new capacity, more competition for market share, and the addition of new resources. Entry barriers and exit barriers affect the entrance of new companies into a marketplace. If entry barriers (capital requirements, economies of scale, product differentiation, switching costs, access to distribution channels, cost of promotion and advertising, etc.) are high, a company is less likely to enter a market. The same holds true for exit barriers.

The threat of substitutes affects competition in an industry by placing an artificial ceiling on the prices companies within an industry can charge. A substitute product is one that can satisfy consumer needs also targeted by another product; for example, lemonade can be substituted for a soft drink. Generally, competitive pressures arising from substitute products increase as the relative price of substitute products declines and as consumer's switching costs decrease.

Exhibit 9.4 Porter's Five Forces Model

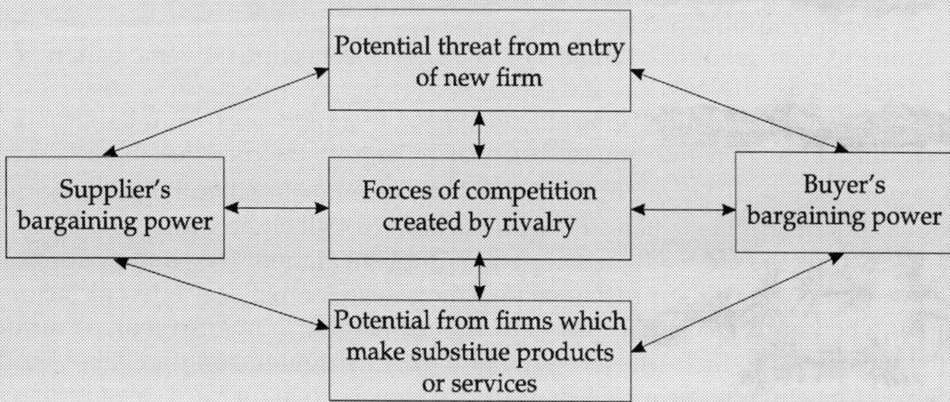

The bargaining power of buyers is affected by the concentration and number of consumers, the differentiation of products, the potential switching costs, and the potential of buyers to integrate backwards. If buyers have strong bargaining power in the exchange relationship, competition can be affected in several ways. Powerful buyers can bargain for lower prices, better product distribution, higher-quality products, as well as other factors that can create greater competition among companies.

Similarly, the bargaining power of suppliers affects the intensity of competition in an industry, especially when there is a large number of suppliers, limited substitute raw materials, or increased switching costs. The bargaining power of suppliers is important to industry competition because suppliers can also affect the quality of exchange relationships. Competition may become more intense as powerful suppliers raise prices, reduce services, or reduce the quality of goods or services.

Competition is also affected by the rivalry among the existing firms, which is usually considered the most powerful of the five competitive forces. In most industries, business organisations are mutually dependent. A competitive move by one firm can be expected to have a noticeable effect on its competitors, and thus, may cause retaliation or counter-efforts (e.g., lowering prices, enhancing quality, adding features, providing services, extending warranties, and increasing advertising).

The nature of competition is often affected by a variety of factors, such as the size and number of competitors, demand changes for the industry's products, the specificity of assets within the industry, the presence of strong exit barriers, and the variety of competitors.

Recently, several researchers have proposed a sixth force that should be added to Porter's list in order to include a variety of stakeholder groups from the task environment that wield over industry activities. These groups include governments, local communities, creditors, trade associations, special interest groups, and shareholders.

The implementation of strategic planning tools serves a variety of purposes in firms, including the clear definition of an organisation's purpose and mission, and the establishment of a standard base from which progress can be measured and future actions planned. Furthermore, the strategic planning tools should communicate those goals and objectives to the organisation's constituents. Thus, the worth of these tools, as well as others, is often dependent on the objective insight of those who participate in the planning process. It is also important for those individuals who will implement the strategies to play a role in the strategic-planning process; this often requires a team effort that should allow a variety of inputs and should result in a better overall understanding of the company's current and future industry position.

9.4 STRATEGIC POSITION AND ACTION EVALUATION (SPACE)

SPACE is an approach to hammer out an appropriate strategic posture for a firm and its individual business. An extension of the two-dimensional portfolio analysis, SPACE involves consideration of four dimensions:

- Company's competitive advantage
- Company's financial strength
- Industry strength
- Environmental stability

The factors determining competitive advantage, financial strength, industry strength, and environmental stability are shown as below.

To apply the SPACE approach to a firm, the following procedure may be followed:

1. Numerically assess the firm on the factors which have a bearing on the four dimensions. The scale of assessment for the factors relating to the dimensions of company's financial strength and industry strength may be 0 to 7, with 0 reflecting the most unfavourable assessment and 7 the most favourable. However, the scale of assessment for the factors relating to the dimensions of environmental stability and company's competitive advantage may be 0 to –7, with 0 reflecting the most favourable assessment and –7 the most unfavourable.

Company's Competitive Advantage	Company's Functional Strength
Market share Product quality Product life cycle Product replacement cycle Customer loyalty Competition's capacity utilisation Technological know-how Vertical integration	Return on investment Leverage Liquidity Capital required/capital available Cash flow Ease of exit from market Risk involved in the business
Industry strength	**Environmental stability**
Growth potential Profit potential Financial stability Technological know-how Resource utilisation Capacity intensity Ease of entry into market Productivity, capacity utilisation	Technological changes Rate of inflation Demand variability Price range of competing products Barriers to entry into market Competitive pressure Price elasticity of demand

2. Average the numerical values assigned for various factors relating to a given dimension to get the numerical score for the dimension.
3. Plot the scores for the four dimensions on the axes of the SPACE chart.
4. Connect the scores to plotted to get a four-sided polygon, reflecting the size and direction of the assessment.

9.4.1 Strategic Postures

The basic strategic postures associated with the SPACE approach are as follows:

Aggressive Posture: This is appropriate for a company which:

(i) enjoys a competitive advantage and considerable financial strength and
(ii) belongs to an attractive industry that operates in a relatively stable environment.

An aggressive posture means that the firm must fully exploit opportunities available to it, seriously look for acquisition possibilities in its own or related industries, concentrate resources to maintain its competitive edge, and enhance its market share. The aggressive posture is similar to the generic strategy of *overall cost leadership* suggested by Michael Porter

Competitive Posture: This is suitable for a company witch:

(i) enjoys a competitive advantage but has limited financial strength, and
(ii) belongs to an attractive industry operating in a relatively unstable environment.

The key planks of the competitive posture are as follows: maintain and enhance competitive advantage by product improvement and differentiation, widen the product line, improve marketing effectiveness, and augment financial resources. There is a great deal of *product differentiation* suggested by Michael Porter.

Conservation Posture: This is appropriate for a company which:

(i) enjoys financial strength but has limited competitive advantage, and

(ii) belong to a not-so-attractive industry operating in a relatively stable environment.

A conservative posture call for the following action: prune non-performing products, reduce costs, improve productivity, develop new products, and access more profitable markets. The conservation posture described here is somewhat similar to the generic strategy of *focus* suggested by Michael Porter.

Defensive Posture: This is suitable for a company which:

(i) lacks competitive advantage as well as financial strength, and

(ii) belong to a not-so-attractive industry operating in an unstable environment.

A defensive posture involves the following actions: discontinue unviable products, control costs aggressively, monitor cash flows strictly, reduce capacity, and postpone or limit investment. The defensive posture so defined may be likened to gamesmanship which calls for employing maneuvers to keep the company afloat, check the onslaught of competition, and eventually facilitate withdrawal or exit.

9.5 DIRECTIONAL POLICY MATRIX (DPM)

The Directional Policy Matrix (DPM) is a method of business portfolio analysis formulated by Shell International Chemical Company. DPM analysis is aimed at determining the appropriate strategic planning goals and the right strategies to achieve those goals across the portfolio of products, strategic business units (SBUs) and markets. The Directional Policy Matrix (DPM) is a tool for helping you determine what your preferred segments are. In completing a DPM the organisation can understand where you should invest in and the direction the organisation should take. The directional policy matrix helps you determine whether decisions made in the day-to-day running of the organisation are in its best interest.

In broad terms, the DPM is a framework and process to review the performance and relative potential of each product/SBU/market and to decide which products/SBUs/markets to:

- Build/develop further/increase market share
- Maintain/resource to keep the status quo or current market share
- Harvest/sell off or withdraw from having squeezed the last potential sales
- Divest/drop or exit immediately.

The DPM is a method of business portfolio analysis is shown in Exhibit 9.5. It has nine cells in which businesses are located depending upon their scores on each of the two axes: expected market profitability and competitive positions. The horizontal axis, labelled "business sector prospects" or "prospects for market sector profitability," is a measure similar to industry attractiveness used in the GE planning grid. A firm is rated on a scale from "unattractive," through "average," to "attractive" depending upon an evaluation of its industry's market growth, market quality, and environmental aspects. Similarly, its location on a scale that runs from a "weak," through "average," to "strong" competitive position is determined by answering questions about its market share position, production capabilities, and R&D strengths.

The cell labels represent possible strategic choices or types of resource deployments most appropriate for the firm, given its score on each of the two axes. More specifically these cell labels have the following implications:

Exhibit 9.5 The DPM Method of Business Portfolio Analysis

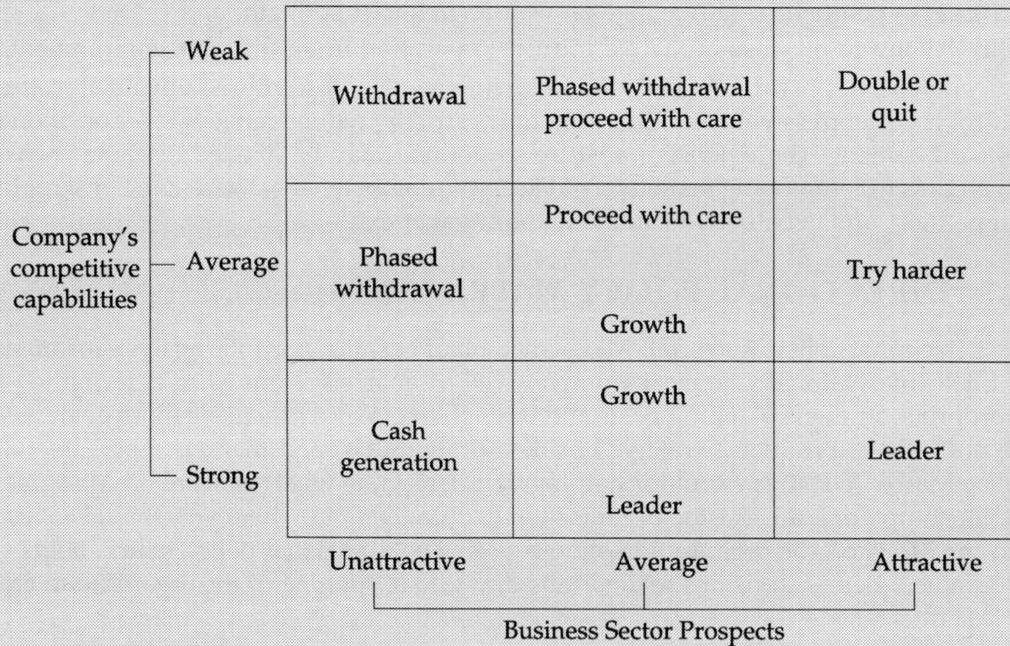

1. **Disinvest:** Likely already losing money; net cash flow negative over time. Losses may be minimized by divestiture or even liquidation.
2. **Phased Withdrawal:** Probably not generating sufficient cash to justify continuation; assets can be redeployed.
3. **Cash Generator:** Equivalent to a "cash cow" in the GE planning grid. This cell would be occupied by a firm or product in later stages of the life cycle that does not warrant heavy investment, but can be "milked" of cash due to its strong competitive position.

4. **Proceed with Care:** Similar to a "question mark;" firms falling in this sector may require some investment support but heavy investment would be extremely risky.
5. **Growth:** Similar to a GE planning grid "green-light" strategy. A firm, product, or SBU in these sectors would call for investment support to allow growth with the market. It should generate sufficient cash on its own.
6. **Double or Quit:** Units in this sector should become "high fliers" in the not too distant future. Consequently those in the upper rightmost corner of cell (1, 3) should be singled out for full support. Others should be abandoned.
7. **Try Harder:** External financing may be justified to push a unit in this sector to a leadership position. However, such a move will require judicious application of funds.
8. **Leader:** The strategy for this segment is to protect this position by external investment (funds beyond those generated by the unit itself, occasionally); earnings should be quite strong and a major focus may be maintaining sufficient capacity to capitalize on strong demand.

The DPM can thus be used to identify strategies for single businesses as well as for plotting combinations of units in multibusiness or multiproduct firms. Locating competitors on the DPM can provide useful insights into the nature of corporate-level strategic configurations. However, there is room for error in the positioning of a firm or product on the two axes, and thus DPM location should be interpreted with an open mind and not in isolation.

The Directional Policy Matrix measures the attractiveness of a segment and the capability of the organisation to support that segment.

9.5.1 Attractiveness of a Market Segment

Evaluating the attractiveness of a segment should include these variables:

- Size of the segment (number of customers, units or sales)
- Growth rate of the segment (a very important variable)
- Profit margins of the segment to the sales organisation
- Ongoing purchasing power of the segment
- Attainable market share given promotional budget, fragmentation of the market and competitors' promotional expenditures
- Required market share to break even.

9.5.2 Capability of the Organisation

Evaluating the capability of the organisation to meet the needs of the segments should include these variables analyzed against the competition:

- Competitive capability of the organisation against the marketing mix (product/service, place, price and promotion)
- Access to distribution channels
- Capital and human resource investment required to serve the segment

- Brand association of the organisation in the eyes of the segment
- Current market share/likely future market share.

9.6 LIFE CYCLE ANALYSIS

Life cycle analysis relies on the belief that there are predictable relationships among the stages in product or business unit life cycles on one hand, and certain elements of strategy on the other.

The typical product life cycle curve is analogous to the life cycle of biological organisms as shown in the Exhibit. Note the relationship between unit profit margin and sales revenues at the different stages. During pre-introduction and introduction, the firm is investing heavily to build sales growth through product awareness and refinement, with emphasis on the latter. Thus, profit margin is negative until growth begins to occur. If sales growth precedes at a high enough rates, then unit profit margin will swing positive during the growth phase. Typically the firm's emphasis is shifted from product refinement to building market share, thus increasing the length and slope of the curve during this phase.

As more and more competitors enter the market, however, share is whittled away. Consequently the product's growth rate begins to level off and the product enters the maturity stage. During growth ever-increasing sales volume can drive unit profit margin higher and higher. As competitive pressures mount, though, profit margin is eaten away. Emphasis shifts to production efficiency as management attempts to maintain profit margin during the maturity phase.

Finally, as sales decline sets in, attention is concentrated on maintaining cash flow. Often a policy is in place that makes product discontinuance a function of the magnitude of net cash flow.

In multiproduct firms attention is focused on the net effect on sales, profit margins, and cash generation of the performance of the firm's stable products. Overall sales performance is a function of the balance of separate products' performance. Multi-business firms, that is, conglomerates or holding companies, can be viewed as a collection of multiproduct firms. The life cycle curves of the separate SBUs would not line up as neatly as they do in the diagram, but rather would be superimposed on each other in a complex network of curves.

9.6.1 Strategic Implications of Life Cycle Curves

Life cycle curves can be useful devices for explaining the relationships among sales and profit attributes of separate products, collections of products in a business, and collections of businesses in a conglomerate or holding company. Life cycle analysis has been suggested by some of its advocates as a basis for selecting appropriate strategy characteristics at all levels. It also may be viewed as a guide for business-level strategy implementation since it helps in selection of functional-level strategies, as discussed below.

Exhibit 9.6 Typical Product Life Cycle Curve

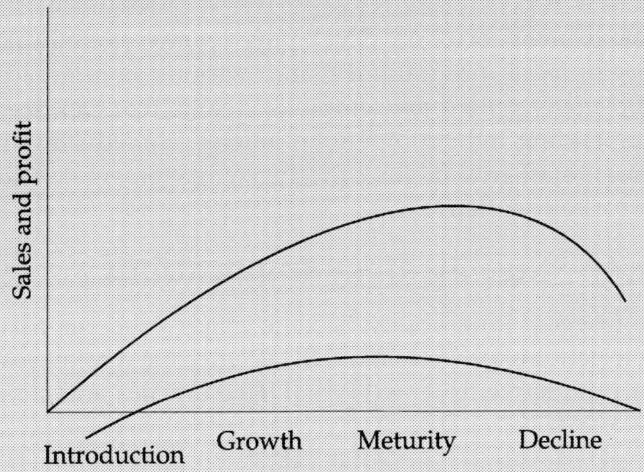

9.6.2 Pre-introduction and Introduction Strategic Implications

During the early stages of the life cycle, marketing strategy should focus on correcting product problems in design, features, and positioning so as to establish a competitive advantage and develop product awareness through advertising, promotion, and personal sales techniques. At the same time, personnel strategy could focus on planning and recruiting for new product human resource needs and dealing with union requirements. Also, one would expect the nature of research and development strategy to shift from a technical research orientation during preintroduction to more of a development orientation during actual introduction.

Financial strategy would be likely to address primarily sources of funds needed to fuel R&D and marketing efforts as well as the capital requirements of later production facilities. Capital budgeting decisions would be outlined during these early stages so that capacity would be adequate to serve growth needs when sales volume began to accelerate.

9.6.3 Growth Stage Strategy Implications

During the growth stage, strategic emphases change relative to introduction. Marketing strategy is concerned with quickly carving out a niche for the product or firm and for its distribution capabilities, even when doing so might involve taking risks with overcapacity. Too often, firms have unadvisedly accepted quality shortfalls as a necessary cost of rapid growth. Widening profit margins during growth may even permit certain functional inefficiencies and risk taking. Communication strategy is directed toward establishing brand preference through heavy media use, sampling programmes, and promotion programs, and strategy should emphasize (1) resource acquisition to maintain strength and (2) development of ways to continue growth when it begins to slow.

Personnel strategy may focus on developing loyalty, commitment, and expertise. Training and development programmes and various communication systems are established to build management and employee teams that can deal successfully with the demands of impending tight competition among firms during the maturity phase. General Electric tries to staff growth-stage product management positions with "growers" who have an entrepreneurial flair.

9.6.4 Maturity-Stage Strategy Implications

Efficiency and profit-generating ability become major concerns as products enter the maturity stage. Competition grows as more firms enter the market and the implication is that only the most productive firms with established niches and competent people will survive.

Marketing efforts concentrate on maintaining customer loyalty and in strengthening this with distributors personally selling to dealers, sales promotions, and publicity.

Production strategy concentrates on efficiency and, at the same time, sharpens the ability to meet delivery schedules and minimize defective products. Cost control systems are often put in place.

Personnel strategy may focus on various incentive systems to produce manufacturing efficiency. Advancements and transfers are used and some firms try to fit management positions to managers who have personalities more attuned to the belt-tightening needs of products and SBUs at the maturity stage. Chase Manhattan Bank, for example, shifted a manager with recognized cost-cutting abilities so that he could streamline its European operations.At Corning Glass Company, when its television-tube business seemed to have reached maturity, a manager with cost-cutting skills was appointed as its manager.

9.6.5 Decline-Stage Strategy Implications

When a product reaches the point where its markets are saturated, an effort is often made to modify it so that its life cycle is either started anew or its maturity stage extended. When falling sales of a product cannot be reversed and it enters the decline stage, management's emphasis may switch to milking it dry of all profit. Advertising and promotion expenditures are reduced to a minimum. People are transferred to new positions where their experience can be brought to bear on products in earlier growth stages (if management was skilful enough to have created such products).

Various strategies have been suggested for products that have entered the decline stage. Hofer and Schendel suggest four choices when sales are less than 5 per cent of those of the industry leaders: (1) concentration on a small market segment and reduction of the firm's asset base to the minimum levels needed for survival; (2) acquisition of several similar firms so as to raise sales to 15 per cent of the leaders' sales; (3) selling out to a buyer with sufficient cash resources and the willingness to use them to effect a turnaround; and (4) liquidation. Other variations of these are described by various authors at both the product and business levels.

9.7 HOFER'S PRODUCT MARKET EVOLUTION MATRIX

Developed by Charles W. Hofer and based on the product life cycle, the 15-cell product/market evolution matrix (shown in Exhibit 9.7) depicts the types of developing products that cannot be easily shown on other portfolio matrixes. Products are plotted in terms of their competitive positions and their stages of product/market evolution. As on the GE Business Screen the circles represent the sizes of the industries involved, and the pie wedges represent the market shares of the firm's business product lines. Present and future matrixes can be developed to identify strategic issues. In response to Exhibit 9.7, for example, we could ask why product B does not have a greater share of the market, given its strong competitive position. We could also ask why the company has only one product in the developmental stage. A limitation of this matrix is that the product life cycle does not always hold for every product. Many products, for example, do not inevitably fall into decline but (like Tide detergent and Colgate toothpaste) are revitalized. He proposed a new assessment matrix of business portfolio of the company, organized into 15 quadrants known as "Hofer Matrix" or "Product/Market Evolution Matrix" and is quite similar to the Arthur D. Little matrix. Exhibits 9.7 displays the present matrix where strategic business units are graphically represented according to two basic indicators: competitive position on the market and the stage corresponding to the product/market evolution. As in the case of the other approaches, Hofer matrix implies the division of the company into strategic business units. The next step resides in assessing the competitive position of business units, by using techniques similar to those used by the McKinsey matrix. The position occupied by each strategic business unit is graphically represented by using the two axes of the matrix. Thus, on the horizontal axis the competitive position of strategic business units is set in terms of strong , average and weak , on the vertical axis the stage of the life cycle specific to the market where these operate is set.

Exhibit 9.7 Product/Market Evolution Portfolio Matrix

Development	A B		
Growth			
Shake out			C
Maturity/Saturation	D	E F	
Decline G			
Stages of Product Development ↑	Strong	Average	Weak

Competitive positive →

Further on, strategic business units are outlined, from a graphical point of view, under the form of circles. The size of each circle is proportional to the size of the market where the strategic business unit carries out its activity (measured on the basis of total income resulted on the mentioned markets), while the hatched areas, inside the circle, represent the market shares held by the strategic business units. The power of the Hofer matrix resides in the fact that it may outline the distribution of strategic business units during stages specific to life cycle of the market (industry). Similar to the McKinsey matrix, the present matrix offers the company the possibility to make a diagnosis regarding the portfolio, in order to establish if it exhibits a balanced or unbalanced structure. A balanced portfolio should be composed of strategic business units of the type corresponding to "stars" and to "cash cows" and to a few "question marks", which have recently penetrated the market or which are about to become "stars". Of course, in practice, most of the companies will have portfolios whole salient feature will be the unbalanced put back on a growth track.

9.7.1 Strategic Consequences

The strategic consequences of this analysis focus on the various stages of life cycle when strategic business units are not covered. Thus, similar to the other methods of business portfolio analysis, the Hofer matrix also suggests that each position held by a strategic business unit indicates the selection of a strategic alternative. Hofer, suggested following strategies:

1. Strategic business unit "A" seems to be a potential "star". It holds a large market share, it is in the stage of life cycle development and has a strong competitive position on the market. As such, unit "A" represents a potential candidate in the competition for corporate resource competition.
2. Unit "B" is very similar to unit "A". Nevertheless, investments in unit "B" must take into account the fact that although it has a strong market position, its market share is quite small. Consequently, the cause for which market share has such a small value must be identified. Furthermore, a strategy that may contribute to the increase of market share must be developed, thus accounting for the future necessary investment.
3. Unit "C" has a small market share, its salient feature resides in the fact that it holds a competitively weak position and it entered a small market whose development is underway. A strategy that may increase the market share and develop the competitive position must be elaborated so that the future investments be accounted for. For the unit "C" a strategy residing in the elimination from the market must be applied, so that the investment for the first two units may be favourised.
4. Unit "D" is characterized by a strong competitive position on the market and it holds a large market share. In this case, it is recommended that investments be made with a view to maintaining the current position on the market. On the lung run, it will become a "cash cow".
5. Unit "E" together with unit "F" are included into the "cash cow" category and they should be capitalized on because of great cash flows that they generate.

6. Unit "G" is included into the "dogs" category and the management thereof is recommended, with a view to generating short-term cash flows in as much as it is possible. Nevertheless, on the long term the strategy of limitation or liquidation on the market must be selected. Taking into account that the structure of business portfolio varies from company to company and that they may take multiple forms of graphic expression, Hofer suggested that the majority of business portfolio strategies specific to companies represent variations of one of the three characteristic situations of an ideal portfolio.

Picture 2 exhibits the three ideal situations and by means thereof several distinct objectives are outlined, objectives that a company may set with a view to meeting them by means of strategic earmarking of financial resources.

9.7.2 Strengths and Weaknesses of the Hofer Method

The main strengths of the matrix resides in the fact that it provides an image regarding the manner of distribution of the businesses undertaken by a company during specific stages of a life cycle. The company may predict how the present portfolio will develop in the future and it may also act in real time in order to guarantee that his portfolio is in a balanced condition. Another advantage of the present matrix is that it manages to divert the management's attention from the corporate level and focus on potential strategies specific to the strategic business unit. According to specialty literature, the market life cycle represents one of the main factors that contribute to the adoption of strategic decisions at the level of the strategic business unit. Therefore, following the use of the Hofer matrix, the corporate management may identify strategic procedures that must be integrated and implemented at the level of strategic business units.

The **disadvantage** of the matrix resides in the fact that it does not focus on all the relevant factors that influence the level of attractiveness of a market. According to the McKinsey matrix, the present model illustrates as well the fact that the stage of the market life cycle is very important, but this element must not be deemed as being the only and the main influence factor of the level of market attractiveness. Therefore, there are other significant factors that may exert influence over the company's portfolio, without being dependent on the stage in which the market evolution is found. Taking into consideration the above mentioned, we must emphasize the fact that the restriction of the portfolio analysis to a single method, is not a wise decision. Each method presents a series of advantages and disadvantages and each of them tries to offer, at one time, a diagnostic of the business portfolio specific to a company.

9.8 PROFIT IMPACT OF MARKET STRATEGY (PIMS)

PIMS is a statistical model that investigates the relationship between strategic variables and profitability of companies. It was the result of the initiative taken at General Electric in the 1960's under the leadership of Sidney Schoeffler. This model relies on empirical data across various industries to study the impact of various strategic variables on profit volumes of organisations. It was a major breakthrough in the field of marketing studies in that it relied on a verifiable method of empirical analysis using regression techniques as opposed to bald conceptual frameworks not supported by hard data from the industry. The model is an endeavour to generalize the strategic determinants of profitability without disregarding the peculiarities of a given market terrain.

The **PIMS study** lends predictability to strategic decision making. It relies on ROI as a key criterion of strategy choices. The most important aspect of the model is the variables it uses in analyzing the impact on profitability of strategic decisions. The nature and number of variables used in the analysis is an on-going development. They can be broadly divided into 2 types:

- Market related variables
- Non-market related variables.

Market related variables include aspects such as market share, relative market share, pricing, product quality, etc. Non-market variables include factors such as R&D expenditures, investment intensity, technological development and labour productivity.

Some of the key findings of PIMS are that high market share leads to high profitability. This has been the most studied finding of the PIMS project and has been confirmed in subsequent studies. The model also reports a positive correlation between product quality and profitability as also between employee productivity and profitability. As regards, capital intensive initiatives, it finds that capital intensive strategies are characterized by low return on investments. A normative implication of this finding is that labour productivity ought to be the focal point for strategic decisions as opposed to heavy investment in machinery or technology.

While the generalization afforded by the vast database of the PIMS project is attractive and indeed useful, it must be taken with a pinch of salt. One general criticism of the PIMS model is that the model fails to make any clear distinction between causal relation and co-incidence. However, this criticism seems to disregard the essential nature of empirical analysis on which the model relies. However, there is some merit to the apprehension that confusion between causal relation and mere coincidence can be misleading. Another important criticism is the multi-colliniarity of the variables. It means that the variables used may affect each other and hence are not independent. This problem is widely acknowledged to be implicit in the model. However, notwithstanding the limitations, the robust database on which the model rests is certainly of great value in strategic decision-making. The model coupled with sharp awareness of market peculiarities is still a critical source of input for managers.

9.9 GRAND STRATEGY MATRIX

In addition to the TOWS Matrix, SPACE Matrix, and BCG Matrix, the Grand Strategy Matrix has become a popular tool for formulating alternative strategies. All organisations can be positioned in one of the grand strategy matrix's four strategy quadrants. A firm's divisions could likewise be positioned. As illustrated in Exhibit 9.8 the grand strategy matrix is based on two evaluative dimensions: competitive position and market growth.

Appropriate strategies for an organisation to consider are listed in sequential order of attractiveness in each quadrant of the matrix.

Firms located in Quadrant 1 of the grand strategy matrix are in an excellent strategic position. For these firms, continued concentration on current markets (market penetration and market development) and products (product development) are appropriate strategies. It is unwise for a Quadrant 1 firm to shift notably from its established competitive advantages. When a Quadrant I organisation has excessive resources, then backward forward, or horizontal integration may be effective strategies. When a Quadrant 1 firm is too heavily committed to a single product, then concentric diversification may reduce the risks associated with a narrow product line. Quadrant 1 firms can afford to take advantage of external opportunities in many areas; they can aggressively take risks when necessary.

Exhibit 9.8 Grand Strategy Matrix

	Rapid Market Growth		
Weak Competitive Position	**Quadrant II** 1. Market development 2. Market penetration 3. Product development 4. Horizontal integration 5. Divestiture 6. Liquidation	**Quadrant I** 1. Market develop 2. Market penetration 3. Product development 4. Forward integration 5. Backward integration 6. Horizontal integration 7. Concentric diversification	**Storng Compitive Position**
	Quadrant III 1. Retrenchment 2. Concentric diversification 3. Horizontal diversification 4. Conglomerate diversification 5. Divestiture 6. liquidation	**Quadrant IV** 1. Concentric diversification 2. Horizontal diversification 3. Conglomerate diversification 4. Joint ventures	
	Slow market growth		

Firms positioned in Quadrant II need to evaluate their present approach to the marketplace seriously. Although their industry is growing, they are unable to compete effectively, and they need to determine why the firm's current approach is ineffectual and how the company can best change to improve its competitiveness. Since Quadrant II firms are in a rapid-market-growth industry, an intensive strategy (as opposed to integrative or diversification) is usually the first option that should be considered. However, if the firm is lacking a distinctive competence or competitive advantage, then horizontal integration is often a desirable alternative. As a last result, divestiture or liquidation should be considered. Divestiture can provide funds needed to acquire other businesses or buy back shares of stock.

Quadrant III organisations compete in slow-growth industries and have weak competitive positions. These firms must make some drastic changes quickly to avoid further demise and possible liquidation. Extensive cost and asset reduction (retrenchment) should be pursued first. An alternative strategy is to shift resources away from the current business into divestiture or liquidation. Finally, Quadrant IV businesses have a strong competitive position but are in a slow growth industry. These firms have the strength to launch diversified programmes into more promising growth areas. Quadrant IV firms have characteristically high cash flow levels and limited internal growth needs and can often pursue concentric, horizontal, or conglomerate diversification successfully. Quadrant IV firms may also pursue joint ventures.

9.10 QUANTITATIVE STRATEGIC PLANNING MATRIX (QSPM)

Other than ranking strategies to achieve the prioritized list, there is only one analytical technique in the literature designed to determine the relative attractiveness of feasible alternative actions. This technique is the *Quantitative Strategic Planning Matrix (QSPM),* which comprises Stage 3 of the strategy formulations analytical framework. This technique objectively indicates which alternative strategies are best. The QSPM uses input from Stage I analyses and matching results from Stage 2 analyses to decide objectively among alternative strategies. That is, the EFE Matrix, IFE Matrix, and Competitive Profile Matrix that make up Stage 1, coupled with the TOWS Matrix, SPACE Analysis, BCG Matrix, IE Matrix, and Grand Strategy Matrix that make up Stage 2, provide the needed information for setting up the QSPM (Stage 3). The QSPM is a tool that allows strategists to evaluate alternative strategies objectively, based on previously identified external and internal critical success factors. Like other strategyformulation analytical tools, the QSPM requires good intuitive judgment.

The basic format of the QSPM is illustrated in Exhibit 9.9. Note that the left column of a QSPM consists of key external and internal factors (from Stage 1), and the top row consists of feasible alternative strategies, (from Stage 2). Specifically, the left column of a QSPM consists of information obtained directly from the EFE Matrix and IFE Matrix. In a column adjacent to the critical success factors, the respective weights received by each factor in the EFE Matrix and the IFE Matrix are recorded.

The top row of a QSPM consists of alternative strategies derived from the TOWS Matrix, SPACE Matrix, BCG Matrix, IE Matrix, and Grand Strategy Matrix. These matching tools usually generate similar feasible alternatives. However, not every strategy

Exhibit 9.9 The Quantitative Strategic Planning Matrix

Key Factors	*Weight*	Strategic Alternatives *Strategy 1*	*Strategy 2*	*Strategy 3*
Key External Factors				
Economy				
Political/Legal/Governmental				
Social/Cultural/Demographic/Environmental				
Technological				
Competitive				
Key Internal Factors				
Management				
Marketing				
Finance/Accounting				
Production/Operations				
Research and Development				
Computer Information Systems				

suggested by the matching techniques has to be evaluated in a QSPM. Strategists should use good intuitive judgment in selecting strategies to include in a QSPM.

Conceptually, the QSPM determines the relative attractiveness of various strategies based on the extent to which key external and internal critical success factors are capitalized upon or improved. The relative attractiveness of each strategy within a set of alternatives is computed by determining the cumulative impact of each external and internal critical success factor. Any number of sets of alternative strategies can be included in the QSPM, and any number of strategies can make up a given set, but only strategies within a given set are evaluated relative to each other. For example, one set of strategies may include concentric, horizontal, and conglomerate diversification, whereas another set may include issuing stock and selling a division to raise needed capital. These two sets of strategies are totally different, and the QSPM evaluates strategies only within sets. Note in Table 66 that three strategies are included and they make up just one set.

A QSPM for a food company is provided in Table 66. This example illustrates all the components of the QSPM: Key Factors, Strategic Alternatives, Weights, Attractiveness Scores, Total Attractiveness Scores, and the Sum Total Attractiveness Score. The three new terms just introduced: (1) Attractiveness Scores, (2) Total Attractiveness Scores, and (3) Sum Total Attractiveness Score are defined and explained below as the six steps required to develop a QSPM are discussed.

Step 1: Make a list of the firm's key external opportunities/threats and internal strengths/weaknesses in the left column of the QSPM. This information should be taken directly from the EFE Matrix and IFE Matrix. A minimum of 10 external critical success factors and 10 internal critical success factors should be included in the QSPM.

Exhibit 9.10 A QSPM for Campbell Soup Company

	Strategic Alternatives				
	Joint Venture in Europe		*Joint Venture in Asia*		
Key Factors	*Weight*	*AS*	*TAS*	*AS*	*TAS*
Opportunities					
1. One European currency-Euro	.10	4	.40	2	.20
2. Rising health consciousness in selecting foods	.15	4	.60	3	.45
3. Free market economies arising in Asia	.1.0	2	.20	4	.40
4. Demand for soups increasing 10 per cent annually	.15	3	.45	4	.60
5. NAFTA	.OS	–	–	–	–
Threats					
1. Food revenues increasing only 1 per cent annually	.10	3	.30	4	.40
2. ConAgra's Banquet TV Dinners lead market with 27.4 per cent share	.05	–	–	–	–
3. Unstable economies in Asia	.10	4	.40	1	.10
4. Tin cans are not biodegradable	.1.5	–	–	–	–
5. Low value of the dollar	1.0	4	.60	2	.30
Strengths					
1. Profits rose, 30 per cent	.10	4	.40	2	.20
2. New North American division	.10	–	–	–	–
3. New health-conscious soups are successful	.10	4	.40	2	.20
4. Swanson TV dinners' market share has increased to 25.1 per cent	.05	4	.20	3	.1.5
5. One-fifth of all managers' bonuses is based on overall corporate performance .05	–	–	–	–	–
6. Capacity utilization increased from 60 per cent to 80 per cent	.15	3	.45	4	.60
Weaknesses					
1. Pepperidge Farm sales have declined 7 per cent	.05	–	–	–	–
2. Restructuring cost $302 million	.05	–	–	–	–

Contd...

3. The company's European operation is losing money	1.5	2	.30	4	.60
4. The company is slow in globalizing	.15	4	.60	3	.45
5. Pretax profit margin of 8.4 per cent is only one-half industry average	.05	–	–	–	–
Sum Total Attractiveness Score	1.0		5.30		4.65

AS = Attractiveness Score; TAS = Total Attractiveness Score

Attractiveness Score: 1 = not acceptable; 2 = possibly acceptable; 3 = probably acceptable; 4 = most acceptable.

Step 2: Assign weights to each key external and internal factor. These weights are identical to those in the EFE Matrix and the IFE Matrix. The weights are presented in a straight column just to the right of the external and internal critical success factors.

Step 3: Examine the Stage 2 (matching) matrices and identify alternative strategies that the organisation should consider implementing. Record these strategies in the top row of the QSPM. Group the strategies into mutually exclusive sets if possible.

Step 4: Determine the attractiveness scores (AS), defined as numerical values that indicate the relative attractiveness of each strategy in a given set of alternatives. *Attractiveness scores* are determined by examining each key external or internal factor, one at a time, and asking the question, "Does this factor affect the choice of strategies being made?" If the answer to this question is *yes,* then the strategies should be compared relative to that key factor. Specifically, attractiveness scores should be assigned to each strategy to indicate the relative attractiveness of one strategy over others, considering the particular factor. The range for attractiveness scores is 1 = *not attractive,* 2 = *somewhat attractive,* 3 = *reasonably attractive,* and 4 = *highly attractive.* If the answer to the above question is no, indicating that the respective key factor has no effect upon the specific choice being made, then do not assign attractiveness scores to the strategies in that set. Use a dash to indicate that the key factor does not affect the choice being made. Note: If you assign an AS score to one strategy, then assign AS score(s) to the other. In other words, if one strategy receives a dash, then all others must receive a dash in a given row.

Step 5: Compute the total attractiveness scores. *Total attractiveness scores* are defined as the product of multiplying the weights (Step 2) by the attractiveness scores (Step 4) in each row. The total attractiveness scores indicate the relative attractiveness of each alternative strategy, considering only the impact of the adjacent external or internal critical success factor. The higher the total attractiveness score, the more attractive the strategic alternative (considering only the adjacent critical success factor).

Step 6: Compute the sum total attractiveness score. Add total attractiveness scores in each strategy column of the QSPM. The sum *total attractiveness scores* reveal which strategy is most attractive in each set of alternatives. Higher scores indicate more attractive strategies, considering all the relevant external and internal factors that could affect the strategic decisions. The magnitude of the difference between the sum total attractiveness scores in a given set of strategic alternatives indicates the relative desirability of one strategy over another.

In Exhibit 9.10, two alternative strategies establishing a joint venture in Europe and establishing a joint venture in Asia are being considered by Campbell Soup.

Note that NAFTA has no impact on the choice being made between the two strategies, so a dash – appears several times across that row. Several other factors also have no effect on the choice being made, so dashes are recorded in those rows as well. If a particular factor affects one strategy but not the other, it affects the choice being made, so attractiveness scores should be recorded. The sum total attractiveness score of 5.30 in Table 66 indicates that the joint venture in Europe is a more attractive strategy when compared to the joint venture in Asia.

You should have a rationale for each AS score assigned. In Table 66, the rationale for the AS scores in the first row is that the unification of Western Europe creates more stable business conditions in Europe than in Asia. The AS score of 4 for the joint venture in Europe and 2 for the joint venture in Asia indicates that the European venture is most acceptable and the Asian venture is possibly acceptable, considering only the first critical success factor. AS scores, therefore, are not mere guesses; they should be rational, defensible, and reasonable. Avoid giving each strategy the same AS score. Note in Table 6.6 that dashes are inserted all the way across the row when used. Also note that never are double 4's, or double 3's, or double 2's, or double 1's in a given row. These are important guidelines to follow in constructing a QSPM

9.11 STRATEGIC PLAN

A strategic plan (also called a corporate, group, or perspective plan), is a document which provides information regarding the different elements of strategic management and the manner in which an organisation and its strategists propose to put the strategies into action. A comprehensive strategic plan document could contain the following information:

1. A clear statement of strategic intent covering the vision, mission, business definition, goals and objectives.
2. Results of environmental appraisal, major opportunities and threats, and critical success factors.
3. Results of organisational appraisal, major strengths and weaknesses, and core competence.
4. Strategies chosen and the assumptions under which the strategies would be relevant. Contingent strategies to be used under different conditions.
5. Strategic budget for the purpose of resource allocation for implementing strategies and the schedule for implementation.
6. Proposal organisational structure and the major organisational systems for strategy implementation, including the top functionaries and their role and responsibility.

7. Functional strategies and the mode of their implementation.
8. Measures to be used to evaluate performance and assess the success of strategy implementation.

Typically, a strategic plan document could run into several pages and be treated as a formal report. Another possibility is that a brief document of three to five pages could briefly cover the points mentioned above. Much would depend on the nature and size of the company and the management policies regarding the preparation of the strategic plan document. It must be remembered, however, that when approved and accepted, a strategic plan document has to be communicated down the line to middle-level managers who will be responsible for its implementation.

Most large-size companies in India formulate strategic plans. Medium-sized and small-scale companies also perform the exercise though not necessarily in a formal and structured manner. The AIMA commissioned a nationwide study to find out what management techniques and tools companies are likely to employ. *Business Today* reported that 56 per cent of the total 160 companies surveyed had a published business strategy. Among these, 77 per cent were giant companies, 69 per cent were large, 53 per cent were medium sized, and 45 per cent were small companies. The time period covered in the strategic plan was less than three years for 44 per cent of the companies; 40 per cent planned for three to five years time horizon, while 16 per cent did it for a period of more than five years. In terms of company size, 45 per cent of the giant companies planned for more than five years, while 70 per cent of the small companies planned for a period of less than three years.

A special feature of strategic plans is that many companies consciously formulated their plans keeping in view the timeframe adopted for national-level planning. Thus, companies normally have a five-year planning period which is synchronized with that of the national five-year plans. In fact, core public enterprises have to link their corporate plans with the national five-year plans. Many public sector enterprises such as SAIL, BHEL, HMT and others have formulated corporate plans of varying duration. SAIL had drawn up an ambitious 15-year corporate plan, while planning at BHEL has taken shape in the form of the first corporate plan which started in 1974.

Like public sector enterprises, private sector companies too formulate strategic plans. Multinational company (MNC) subsidiaries often have to prepare and plan the documents to be submitted to their parent companies for approval. Often, the MNC subsidiaries draw their strategic plans on the basis of guidelines provided by their parent institutions. Professional private sector companies may have executive committees consisting of senior level managers who formulate strategic plans. Family groups often draft group strategic plans to provide strategic directions to the different companies in the group.

The formulation of a strategic plan document provides a means not only to formalize the effort that goes into strategic planning but also for communicating to insiders and outsiders what the company stands for, and what it plans to do in a given future time period. A strategic plan is not always publicised. Rather, companies prefer to treat is as confidential, primarily for protecting their competitive interests. But the main features of the plan are often spelt out for communication to outsiders and for public relations purposes.

The methods of analysis of the business portfolio facilitate the debate and outline of the competitive positions of the company and also contribute to the generation of a series of questions related to the way in which the allotment of its actual resources contribute to the achievement of success and vitality on long term. At the same time, these methods, besides the fact that they help the managers to control the allotment of resources and suggest realistic objectives for every strategic business unit, also offer the possibility to use the strategic units as indispensable resources in the process of achievement of the objectives established at a corporate level.

In conclusion, it is recommended the combined use of a large variety of methods of analysis of the business portfolio, by the managers from a corporate level, because, in this way they will understand much better the whole market mix included in the custody account analysis, the strategic position held by every strategic business unit, within a market, the performance potential of the portfolio as well as the financial aspects related to the process of allotment of resources, for the business units within the portfolio. It should also be mentioned that the methods of analysis of the business portfolio are not instruments, which offer accurate answers, in spite of the appearances created by the stage of analysis, in which the strategic business units are represented graphically and with austerity. Nevertheless, their main virtue is simplicity, since these underlie the need to further research.

Exercise

1. How does a large business group wish to identify strategies for its different business in its portfolio? How it can do it?
2. What are advantages of using BCG matrix as a portfolio tool? How does it help in identifying the strategies for business organisation.
3. Describe the GE nine-cell matrix for analysing corporate portfolio. Does it have any advantage over the BCG matrix?
4. Describe the contents of a good working strategic plan for a large business group or a public sector enterprise in India.
5. Discuss the relevance of industry, strategic group and competitor analysis to the strategic choice process.
6. Carry out the SAP and ETOP of any real firm.
7. How fire forces model can help the business group to identify its strategies. Take the example of business group from India and how this model helps them?
8. There can be many subjective factors that might affect strategic choice. How a business leader can take care of these factors while identifying strategic choice?
9. What is the process of strategic choice? Explain the four steps with relevant examples.
10. Briefly explain the various tools and techniques a firm can adopt for strategic analysis. What relevant factors you will consider before selecting a particular tool?

10 Strategy Implementation

10.1 INTRODUCTION

The task of strategic management is far from complete after strategies have been formulated and a concrete strategies plan has been prepared. Then it is the job of strategists to put the plan into action. It is important to consider the interrelationship between the formulation and implementation of strategies. It is to be noted that the division of strategic management into different phases is only for the purpose of orderly study. In real life, the formulation and implementation processes are intertwined. Two types of linkages exist between these two phases of strategic management. The forward linkages deal with the impact of the formulation on implementation while the backward linkages are concerned with the impact in the opposite direction.

10.1.1 Forward Linkages

The different elements in strategy starting with the various constituents of strategic intent through environmental and organisational appraisal, strategic alternatives, strategic analysis and choice and ending with the strategic plan, determine the course that an organisation adopts for itself. With the formulation of new strategies, or reformulation leading to modified strategies, many changes have to be effected within the organisation. For instance, the organisational structure has to undergo a change in light of the requirements of a modified or new strategy. The style of leadership has to be adapted to the formulation of strategies. A whole lot of changes have to be undertaken in operationalising the formulated strategies. Clearly, the strategies formulated provide the direction to implementation. In this way, the formulation of strategies has forward linkages with their implementation.

10.1.2 Backward Linkages

Just as implementation is determined by the formulation of strategies, the formulation process is also affected by factors related with implementation. Recall that in the previous chapter, while dealing with strategic choice we observed that past strategic actions also determine the choice of strategy. Organisations tend to adopt those strategies which can be implemented with the help of the present structure of resources combined with some additional efforts. Such incremental changes, over a period of time, take the organisation from where it is to where it wishes to be.

It is to be noted that while strategy formulation is primarily an entrepreneurial activity, based on strategic decision-making, the implementation of strategy is mainly an administrative task based on strategic as well as operational decision-making. Looked at from another angle, formulation is a managerial task requiring analysis and thinking, implementation primarily rests on action and doing. The next section focuses on the various issues involved in the implementation of strategies.

10.2 ASPECTS OF STRATEGY IMPLEMENTATION

The different aspects involved in strategy implementation cover practically everything that is included in the discipline of management studies. A strategist, therefore, has to bring to his or her task a wide range of knowledge, skills, attitudes, and abilities. The implementation tasks put to test the strategists'. abilities to allocate resources, design structures and systems, formulate functional policies, take into account the leadership style required, and plan for operational effectiveness, besides, dealing with various other issues.

The strategic plan devised by the organisation proposes the manner in which the strategies could be put into action. Strategies, by themselves, do not lead to action. There are, in a sense, statements of intent: implementation tasks are meant to realise the intent. Strategies, therefore, have to be activated through implementation. Strategies lead to several plans, each plan leads to several programmers. Each programme results in several projects. Projects are supported by funds through budgets. The administrative mechanisms of policies, procedures, rules and regulations support the working of the organisation while it implements the projects, programmes, plans, and strategies. In this manner, strategy sits at the top of a pyramid that has projects as its base as shown in Exhibit 10.1. First of all, strategies should lead to plans. For instance, if stability strategies have been formulated, they may lead to the formulation of various plans. One such plan could be a modernization plan. If expansion strategies have been adopted, various types of expansion plans will have to be formulated. An expansion plan could be designed to set up an additional plant to manufacture the same products. Similarly, diversification strategies could lead to new product development plans. Plans result in different kinds of programmes. A programmes is a broad term which includes goals, policies, procedures, rules and steps to be taken in putting a plan into action. Programmes are usually supported by funds allocated for plan implementation.

Programmes lead to the formulation of projects. A project is a highly specific programme for which the time schedule and costs are predetermined. It requires the allocation of funds based on capital budgeting by organisation. Thus, R & D programmes may consists of several projects, each of which is intended to achieve specific and limited objective, requires separate allocation of funds, and is to be completed within a set time schedule.

Project creates the needed infrastructure for the day-to-day operations in an organisation. They may be used for setting up new or additional plans, modernizing the existing facilities, installation of newer systems, and for several other activities that

Exhibit 10.1 Stages of Strategy Implementation

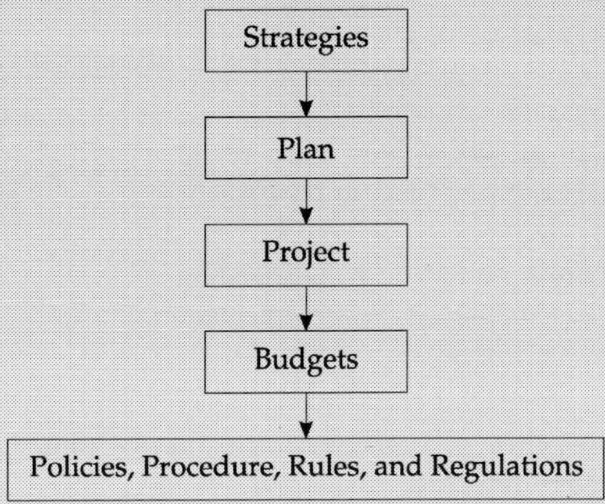

are needed for the implementation strategies. In practice companies may not make such a fine distinction among plans, programmes, and projects as we have done here. But as students of management we have to understand the difference and learn to distinguish between the different terms used in strategic management. Implementation of strategies is not limited to the formulation of plans, programmes, and projects.

10.2.1 A Model of Strategy Implementation

Exhibit 10.2 presents a model of strategy implementation that attempts to capture the major themes in strategy implementation and activities that make up each theme. The forward linkage from strategic plan guides the implementation process and connects it to the proceeding phase of strategy formulation. The feedback flowing in reverse form the following steps of strategy evaluation and control moves through the implementation phase and go back to strategy formulation establishing the backward linkages.

10.2.2 Major Themes in Strategy Implementation

The model of the strategic management shows three major themes:

- **Activating Strategies:** In order to activate the strategies, there are three set of activities every organisation has to perform. These activities are; project implementation, procedural implementation and resource allocation.
- **Managing Change:** The next theme is the core of strategy implementation and deals with the managing change in complex situations. There are three set of activities under this theme. These are structural implementation, leadership implementation and behavioural implementation.

- **Achieving Effectiveness:** The last theme is the outcome of the process. This theme will cover two sets of activities, namely functional and operational implementation.

Exhibit 10.2 Model of Strategy Implementation

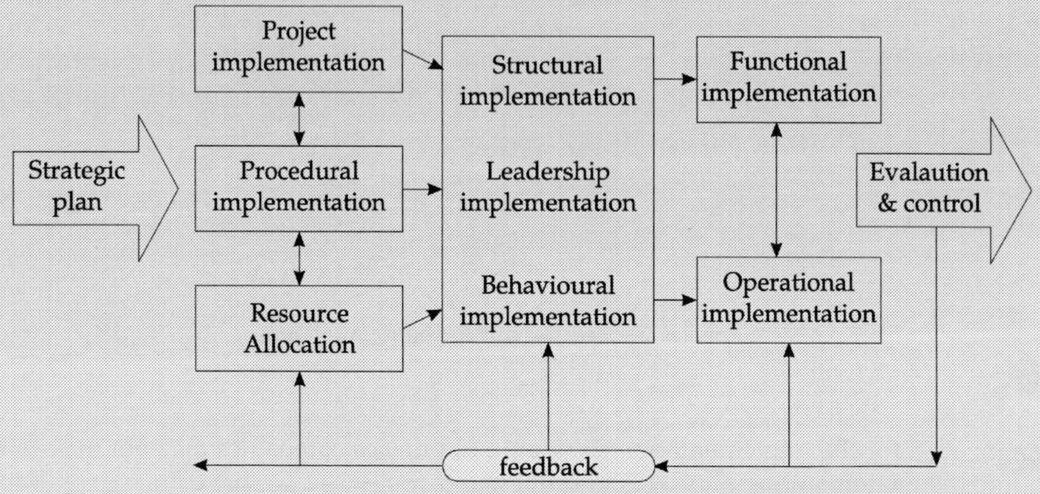

For the purpose of discussion and orderly presentation, we deal with the different aspects of implementation in the sequence indicated below. But it should be noted that the sequence does not mean that activities under each of the aspects are necessarily performed one after another. Many activities can be performed simultaneously, certain other activities may be repeated over time, and then there are activities which are performed only once.

1. Project implementation
2. Procedural implementation
3. Resource allocation
4. Structural implementation
5. Behavioral implementation
6. Functional and operational implementation

While dealing with the several aspects given above, we have to cover a lot of ground in terms of concepts, methods, techniques and approaches. In practice a strategist would have to draw upon diverse specializations available within the organisation. Experts from different areas such as project management, corporate management, legal affairs finance, marketing, operations, and personnel, and economists, planners, technologists and others contribute in some or the other way in the implementation of strategies. Here, emphasis will be laid on how strategy affects the different implementation aspects and how they are adapted to suit the needs of a particular strategy. We move ahead on the assumption that a strategy creates its own requirements of the various aspects of implementation. As the strategy is modified or replaced with a new one, each of the aspects of implementation has to undergo a change. No wonder, strategy implementation is also, and rightly so-called by some as change management.

Management issues central to strategy implementation include establishing annual objectives, devising policies, allocating resources, altering an existing organisational structure, revising reward and incentive plans, minimizing resistance to change, matching managers with strategy, developing a strategy-supportive culture, adapting production/ operations processes, and developing an effective human resource function. Management changes are necessarily more extensive when strategies to be implemented move a firm in a major new direction. Managers and employees throughout an organisation should participate early and directly in strategy-implementation decisions. Their role in strategy implementation should build upon prior involvement in strategy-formulation activities. Strategist's genuine personal commitment to implementation is a necessary and powerful motivational force for managers and employees. Too often, strategists are too busy to actively support strategy-implementation efforts, and their lack of interest can be detrimental to organisational success. The rationale for objectives and strategies should be understood and clearly communicated throughout an organisation. Major competitor's accomplishments, products, plans, actions, and performance should be apparent to all organisational members. Major external opportunities and threats should be clear, and managers and employees questions should be answered. Top-down flow of communication is essential for developing bottom-up support.

Hamel and Prahalad emphasize the need for firms to develop a competitor focus at all hierarchical levels by gathering and widely distributing competitive intelligence; every employee should be able to benchmark her to his efforts against best-in-class competitors so that the challenge becomes personal. This is a challenge for strategies of the firm. Firms should provide training for both managers and employees to insure they have and maintain the skills necessary to be world-class performers. Even after the grand strategies are determined and long-term objectives tentatively set, the strategic management process is far from complete. The tasks of operationalising, institutionalizing, and controlling the strategy still remain. These tasks signal a critical new phase in the strategic management process: translating strategic thought into strategic action. Shifting from formulation to implementation gives rise to three interrelated concerns:

1. Identification of measurable, mutually determined annual objectives.
2. Development of specific functional strategies.
3. Communication of concise policies to guide decisions.

Annual objectives translate long-range aspirations into this year's budget. If annual objectives are well developed, they provide clarity, which is a powerful, motivating facilitator of effective strategy implementation.

Functional Strategies translate grand strategy at the business level into action plans for subunits of the company. Operating managers assist in developing these strategies, which, in turn, helps clarify what the manager's units are expected to do in implementing the grand strategy.

Policies are specific guides for operating managers and their subordinates. Policies, often misunderstood and misused, can provide a powerful tool for strategy implementation if they are clearly linked to operating strategies and long-term objectives.

Such measures as market share, ROI, return on equity (ROE), stock price, and new market penetration provide guidance in assessing the ultimate effectiveness of a chosen strategy. While such objectives clarify the long-range purpose of a grand strategy and the basis for judging its success, they are less useful in guiding the operating strategies and immediate actions necessary to implement a grand strategy.

A critical step in successful implementation of grand strategy is the identification and communication of annual operating objectives that relate logically to the strategy's long-term objectives. Accomplishment of these annual objectives adds up to successful execution of the business's overall long-term plan. A comprehensive set of annual objectives also provides a specific basis for monitoring and controlling organisational performance. Such objectives can aid in the development of trigger points that alert top management for variations in key performance areas that might have serious ramifications for the ultimate success of a strategy.

Annual objectives are specific, measurable statements of what an organisation subunit is expected to achieve in contributing to the accomplishment of the business's grand strategy. Although this seems rather obvious, problems in strategy implementation often stem from poorly conceived or stated annual objectives. To maximize these objectives contribution, certain basic qualities must be incorporated in developing and communicating them. An annual objective must be clearly linked to one or more long-term objectives of the business's grand strategy. However, to accomplish this, it is essential to understand how the two types of objectives differ. Four basic dimensions distinguish annual and long-term objectives:

1. ***Time frame***: Long-term objectives are focused usually five years or more into the future. Annual objectives are more immediate, usually involving one year.
2. ***Focus***: Long-term objectives focus on the future position of the firm in its competitive environment. Annual objectives identify specific accomplishments for the company, functional areas, or other subunits over the next year.
3. ***Specificity***: Long-term objectives are broadly stated. Annual objectives are very specific and directly linked to the company, a functional area, or other subunit.
4. ***Measurement***: While both long-term and annual objectives are quantifiable, long term objectives are measured in broad, relative terms; for example, 20 per cent market share. Annual objectives are stated in absolute terms, such as a 15 per cent increase in sales in the next year.

Annual objectives add breadth and specificity in identifying what must be accomplished in order to achieve the long-term objective. For example, the long-term objective to obtain 20 per cent market shares in five years. Clarifies where the business wants to be. But achieving that objective can be greatly enhanced if a series of specific annual objectives identify what must be accomplished each year to achieve that objective. If market share is now 10 per cent, then one likely annual objective would be to achieve a minimum 2 per cent increase in relative market share in the next year. Specific annual objectives should provide targets for performance of operating areas if the long-term objective is to be achieved. The link between short-term and long-term objectives should resemble cascades through the business from basic long-term objectives to numerous specific annual objectives in key operating areas. Thus, long-term objectives are segmented and reduced to short-term (annual) objectives. The cascading effect has the added advantage of providing a clear reference for vertical communication and negotiation, which may be necessary to ensure integrated objectives and plans at the operating level.

10.3 PROJECT IMPLEMENTATION

Strategies lead to plans, programmes, and projects. Knowledge related to project formulation and implementation is covered under the discipline of project management. The Project Management Institute of the US defines a project as .a one-shot, time limited, goal-directed, major undertaking, requiring the commitment of varied skills and resources. The goals or objectives for a project are derived from the plans and programmes, which are based on the strategies adopted. A project passes through various phases before a set of tasks can be accomplished.

10.3.1 Phases of Project

A project through different phases, not necessarily in the order is listed below.

1. ***Conception phase***: This phase is an extension of the strategy formulation phase of strategic management. Ideas generated during the process of strategic alternatives and choice consideration from the core of the future projects that may be undertaken by the organisation. The project ideas that are conceived have to be allocated priorities on the basis of which they will be chosen for further development.
2. ***Definition phase***: After a set of projects has been identified and arranged according to the priority, it should be subjected to a preliminary project analysis which examines the marketing, technical, financial, economic and ecological aspects. This analysis is done to find out whether it would stand the scrutiny of the financial institutions, banks and investors. After this screening, the viable projects are taken up and feasibility studies conducted. Feasibility studies are done for in-depth, detailed project analysis and result in an adequately formulated project. The results are documented in the form of a project feasibility report. After the project definition phase, the project is cleared for implementation. But before being implemented, the project has to be further planned.
3. ***Planning and organizing phase***: Detailed planning, related to different aspects of the projects, such as, infrastructure, engineering designs, schedules and budgets, finance, and so on, has to be completed. A project structure which would deal with the organisation and manpower, systems and procedures, and so on, has also to be created which would enable the project manager to implement the project.

Exhibit 10.3 Contents of a Typical Feasibility Report

Project reports are prepared for internal as well as external purposes. Internally, the reports may be presented to the top management committees or Board of Directors for approval and sanction.

Externally, the reports are submitted to financial institutions which evaluate the project proposals for the purpose of granting financial assistance. Currently, the central financial institutions (IDBI, ICICI, IFCI, etc.) seek the following information for the purpose of financial assistance.

1. General information, such as, name, form of organisation, location, nature of project (new, expansion, modernization, diversification), nature of industry and products, and so on.
2. Information regarding project promoters.
3. Particulars of the industrial concern seeking financial assistance.
4. Particulars of the project (details regarding capacity, process, technical arrangements, management, location and land, buildings, plants and machinery, raw materials, utilities, effluents, labour, housing for labour, schedule of implementation, etc.
5. Cost of the project including land and site development, buildings, plant and machinery, technical know-how fee, and so on.
6. Means of financing (share capital, rupee loans, foreign currency loans, debentures, internal cash accruals, etc.)
7. Marketing and selling arrangements.
8. Profitability and cash flow.
9. Economic considerations (prices of competing products, economic benefits to the country and region, development of industrially backward areas, development of ancillary industries, etc.).
10. Environment considerations (water and air pollution, effluent disposal, and energy conservation).
11. Government consents including letter of intent, industrial licence, capital goods clearance, import licence, foreign exchange permission, approval of technical/financial collaboration, clearance by regulatory authorities, and so on.

4. ***Implementation phase***: The detailed engineering, order placement for equipment and material awarding contracts, civil and other types of construction, and so on, have to be undertaken during the implementation phase leading to the testing, trial, and commissioning of the plant.
5. ***Clean-up-phase***: The final phase in project implementation deals with disbanding the project infrastructure and handing over the plant to the operating personnel. It is to be noted that the above phases in projects are more relevant to new plants that are being set up to implement expansion and diversification strategies. But for other minor projects like a relocation of facilities, modernization and upgradation of technology and so on, a similar, though less detailed process, may be followed.

10.4 PROCEDURAL IMPLEMENTATION

Any organisation which is planning to implement strategies must be aware of the procedural framework within which the plans, programmes, and projects have to be approved by the government at the central, state and local levels. The procedural framework consists of a number of legislative enactments and administrative orders, besides the policy guidelines issued by the Government of India from time to time. The regulatory mechanisms for trade, commerce, and India span the whole range of legal structure from the Constitution of India, the Directive Principles, Central laws, State laws, general laws, sector-specific laws, industry-specific laws and the rules and procedures imposed by the implementing authorities at the local level. The laws lay down elaborate rules and procedures to be followed.

Following the procedures laid down for project implementation constitutes an important component of strategy implementation in the Indian context. The Government has an elaborate set of procedures depending on the type of project to be implemented. Government agencies at the central and state levels ply a major role while some procedures require the involvement of the local governmental agencies. All the subjects having a bearing on industrial development are handled by different ministries and departments at the central government level. There are apex level committees such as the Cabinet Committee on Economic Affairs. Apart from these agencies, the regulatory agencies, such as, Central Electricity Regulatory Commission (CERC), Telecom Regulatory Authority of India (TRAI), Insurance Regulatory and Development Authority (IRDA), also play a significant role. At the State level, the Directorate of Industries is the pivot around which the entire industrial activity in the State revolves. Government policies, laws, rules and regulations and procedures are constantly under change especially under conditions where India is fast adapting to the international environment and incorporating liberalization and globalization measures in its policies. Our purpose here is to only briefly refer to the procedural aspects of strategy implementation. The matter here is not meant to be a presentation of a comprehensive manual or guidelines for setting up projects in India. For that to take place, readers would have to refer to specialized subjects such as business and law, and the entrepreneurs would have to take resource to specialized advise from chartered accountants, company secretaries, industry experts and consultants. You are advised to find out the latest available position regarding these regulatory mechanisms and procedures from the business press.

The regulatory elements to be reviewed are as below.

- Formation of a company
- Licensing procedures
- Securities and Exchange Board of India (SEBI) requirements
- Foreign collaboration procedures
- Foreign Exchange Management Act (FEMA) requirements
- Import and export requirements
- Patenting and trademarks requirements
- Labour legislation requirements

- Environmental protection and pollution control requirements
- Consumer protection requirements
- Incentives and facilities benefits

10.4.1 Formation of a Company

The formation of a company is governed by the provisions of the Companies Act, 1956 and consists of promotion registration, and flotation. Promotion denotes the preliminary steps taken for the purpose of registration and flotation. Registration involves registering the memorandum of the company, articles of association, and the agreements with the Registrar of Companies, who issues a certificate of incorporation. Flotation means raising the capital to commence business.

10.4.2 Licensing Procedures

They system of planning (or planned development) rests on three policy documents consisting of Industrial Policy Resolution, 1956, Industries (Development and Regulation) Act (IDRI), 1951, and the statements of 1978, 1980, 1982, and 1991. The Policy Resolutions classify the industries into three categories. The first category industries are those that are directly under the government. The second category consists of industries which are promoted by the government and where the private sector supplements the efforts. The third category industries are left for the private sector. The IDRA, 1951 provided for a licensing system for the development and regulation of scheduled industries listed in the Schedule of the Act. A licence is a written permission from the government an industrial undertaking to manufacture specified articles included in the Schedule. If the licence is to be given subject to the fulfilment of certain conditions (say, foreign collaborations or capital goods import) then a letter of intent conveying the intention of the government to grant a licence, subject to the fulfilment of those conditions, is issued. Section 30 of the IDRA deals with the Registration and Licensing of Industrial Undertaking Rules. Under this Act, a licence was necessary for establishing a new unit, manufacturing a new article. (Any item related to a scheduled industry other than those specified in the license), substantial expansion of capacity in an existing business, and changing location.

One of the significant liberalization measures in the post-1991 period has been to abolish industrial licensing, irrespective of the level of investment, for all industries except a few. These industries relate to security, defence, or environmental concerns and certain items of conspicuous consumption that have a high proportion of important inputs. The licensing procedure requires the applicant to approach the Secretariat for Industrial Assistance (SIA), which is a common secretariat for receiving and processing all types of applications related to industrial project.

10.4.3 SEBI Requirements

The SEBI Act, 1992, replaced the Capital Issues Control Act, 1956, to deal with the capital markets. It had already been in existence since 1988 and became a statutory body in 1992.

According to the SEBI Act, the SEBI has three objectives:

- to protect the interests of investors in securities;
- to promote the development of the securities market; and
- to regulate the securities market.

It is a quasi-judicial body, under the Securities Laws Ordinance, 1995, to deal with issue of capital, transfer of shares, and other related aspects. Its jurisdiction covers the primary market, secondary market, mutual funds, foreign institutional investors, and foreign brokers. Though certain provisions of the Companies Act, 1956 cover the issue of capital control, the SEBI enjoys comprehensive power of the significant aspects of the Indian capital market. It issues guidelines from time to time to oversee matters under its control. These guidelines are of relevance to companies accessing the capital market for funds for projects emanating as offshoot of their corporate and business strategies. For the purpose of strategy implementation, this Act is relevant so far as the provision of financial resources is concerned. Apart from this, this Act also affects mergers and amalgamations as they regulate the capital reorganisation plans for mergers.

10.4.4 Foreign Collaboration Procedures

Many strategic alternatives (for instance, expansion/diversification into high technology industries) call for foreign collaboration and investment. The government policy, in general, allows foreign investment and collaboration in a selective basis in priority areas, export oriented or high-technology industries, and permitting existing foreign investment in non-priority areas.

All proposals to set up projects with foreign collaboration require prior government approval. The regulatory framework deals with the need for foreign technology, royalty payments, terms and conditions for collaboration agreements, and foreign investment.

Foreign investments are of two types: foreign direct investment (FDI), and foreign institutional investment (FII) or portfolio investment. FDI can take place through wholly owned subsidiaries, joint ventures, or acquisition. Portfolio investment takes place through investment by the foreign institutional investors and investments in instruments such as global depository receipts (GDRs) and foreign currency convertible bonds (FCCBs). Special treatment is accorded to non-resident Indians. (NRIs) and overseas corporate bodies (OCBs), predominantly owned by NRIs, in matters of foreign investments.

Joint ventures have been considered an important route for channelizing foreign investments into and outside India. Apart from regulations concerning joint ventures in India, government policy is encouraging the setting up of joint ventures abroad. The RBI, Foreign Investment Promotion Board (FIPB), and Project Approval Board are the major regulatory agencies for joint ventures abroad. The procedural aspects of foreign collaboration include preliminary evaluation by the promoter, obtaining industrial licence (if necessary), applying for foreign collaboration to the concerned agency, applying for import of capital goods (if required), finalization of agreement, and clearance from the RBI.

10.4.5 Foreign Exchange Management Act (FEMA) Requirements

The Foreign Exchange Management Act (FEMA) replaced the Foreign Exchange Regulation Act (FERA), 1973 in June 2000. The FEMA, 2000 has substantially liberalized provisions and rules related to the maintenance of dollar accounts by exporters, remittance of foreign exchange for visits abroad, agency commission, export claims reduction in export value, reimbursement of expenses incurred on dishonored export bills, consular fee, and so on. Foreign exchange transaction are classified as current account and capital account transactions. Several sets of rules have been made to facilitate foreign exchange transactions for the purpose of augmenting export activities from India. Exports of goods and services are governed under the Foreign Exchange Management (Export of Goods and Services) Regulations, 2000. The opening, holding, and maintaining of foreign currency accounts is governed by the Foreign Exchange Management Regulations, 2000 (Foreign Currency Account by a Person Resident in India). In keeping with the imperatives of globalization, foreign exchange remittances for maintaining overseas branches and offices by Indian companies have been considerably liberalized.

10.5 IMPORT AND EXPORT REQUIREMENTS

Strategy implementation in areas such as modernisation, expansion, and diversification requires the consideration of import and export requirements. Imports are vital for capital goods and raw materials provision for new and existing projects. The high priority is accorded to import substitution by the government. Often it offers a viable alternative to companies for setting up new projects or for introducing new products or services. Export considerations by the companies usually arise in the form of statutory stipulation in lieu of foreign collaboration and investments, and imports. In certain cases, exports offer an expansion opportunity for companies which operate in markets which are highly competitive or saturated. Thus, imports and exports requirements constitute an important part of any strategy implementation scheme.

The Export-Import Policy (Exim Policy) enunciates the foreign trade policy of the country. It is generally announced for a period of five years corresponding to the five-year planning period. The policy implementation and the legal framework for imports and exports in India is largely based on the Foreign Trade Development and Regulation Act (FTDRA), 1992, that replaced the Import and Export (Control) Act, 1947. The objective of the Act is to provide for the development and regulation of foreign trade by facilitating imports, and augmenting exports from India.

The Department of Commerce in Ministry of Commerce is responsible for the country's external trade and all matters connected with commercial trade relations with other countries. There are several autonomous bodies, such as, commodity boards, export inspection council, export promotion councils, public sector undertakings such as the State Trading Corporation of India, among others under the administrative control of the Ministry of Commerce. The FTDR Act provides for the appointment of the Director

General of Foreign Trade(DGFT) who is responsible for advising on the formulation and implementation of the Exim Policy. Besides the Directorate General of Foreign Trade, there is Directorate General of Commercial Intelligence and Statistics for collection, analysis, and dissemination of commercial information related to foreign trade.

It is important for strategists to understand the rationale for the development and regulation of imports and exports. The government is interested in imports regulation because its apportions the available foreign exchange among different types of users, aim at import substitution progressively so that the balance of payments (bop) position is not affected adversely, and for the protection of domestic industries. Exports are considered obligatory in many cases, including those of FEMA companies. Fiscal measures are adopted by the government to discourage imports and exports of certain products. The matter of exports and imports has a substantial number of procedural aspects and associated documentation work. Other important matters are related to customs, financing of imports, foreign exchange, and incentives and support for export activities. The supportive measures for exports will be referred to in a later section which deals with incentives and other facilities. Most companies have to rely on exports and imports in the course of their strategy implementation. Specialized knowledge and advice is required to follow the procedures which are quite detailed and comprehensive.

10.5.1 Patenting and Trademarks Requirements

Patents, trademarks, copyrights, designs, and so on, are assuming greater significance in the Indian industry owing to international environmental changes. The major impact on these issues is of the WTO requirements related to the trade related aspects of Intellectual Property Rights (TRIPs). The increasing competitiveness means that it is necessary to know the rights and privileges, and the legal procedures for protecting products and ideas. Familiarity with the law related to these is essential for strategy implementation. These laws are of special significance to industries, such as, chemicals, computer software, entertainment, food, and pharmaceuticals, where patents are a major competitive tool.

India is in the process of adapting its law related to patents and trademarks in line with the international requirements. Indian Patents Act, 1970 governs patenting in India, and it has been amended in the form of Indian Patents (Amendment) Act, 1995 to incorporate the intellectual property rights requirements. The Trade and Merchandise Marks Act, 1958 provides for the registration and better protection of trademarks and for the prevention of the use of fraudulent marks on merchandise. The Copyrights Act, 1957 relates to copyrights. These Acts define the terms, prescribe the procedures for registration, and mention the rights and duties of the entities holding the patents, trademarks, and copyrights.

10.5.2 Labour Legislation Requirements

An essential part of procedural implementation in any project as well as in a going concern is that of labour legislation. For the companies, labour constitutes a significant resource for the purposes of strategy implementation. For the government, the protection of labour interest has long been held to be a major responsibility of the State. Labour legislation consists of several laws related to different aspects. A classification of these laws is as below:

- Labour laws related to the weaker sections such as women and children.
- Labour laws related to specific industries such as mines and minerals, plantation, transport, construction, contact labour, and others.
- Labour laws related to specific matters such as wages, social security, bonus, etc.
- Labour laws related to trade unions, industrial relations and worker's participation in management

According to the Indian Constitution, labour is a common subject among the Central and the State governments. While the Central government enacts, amends and repeals most of the legislations, the major administrative authority to adopt and implement the laws rests with the state governments. Besides the Central and State ministries of labour, there are a host of commissions, standing committees, statutory agencies, labour courts and tribunals, boards, and so on, to implement the labour legislation.

An aspect related to labour is the issue of exit policy. It refers to the policy concerned with the action to be taken regarding surplus manpower in companies, owing to a variety of reasons, such as, restructuring, retrenchment, closure, or technological developments. Voluntary retirement schemes and golden handshake schemes are quite popular in the Indian industry, particularly, in the public sector enterprises, banks, large private companies, and other overmanned organisations. There is no specific policy or law dealing with the exit, and the actions are governed under the existing laws and regulations as and where they are applicable. However, the exit policy is gradually coming under formation and informed opinion is that a time may come when there will be adequate political will to enact and implement it. Exit policy, and the resultant rules and procedures have relevance to strategy implementation in cases of retrenchment grand strategies and the formulation and implementation of functional strategies related to human resource management.

The matter of procedural implementation regarding labour legislation has a significant bearing on the implementation of strategies in the areas of objective-setting, strategic choice, social responsibility, formulation and implementation of human resource management, and operational strategies.

10.5.3 Environmental Protection and Pollution Control Requirements

The issue of physical environment has attained global and national importance owing to a variety of reasons. Overuse and misuse of the basic life support systems and natural resources like air, land, water, flora and fauna, and non-renewable sources, such as, oil and natural gas, are citied as major factors leading to environmental and ecological degradation. The Indian public's awareness has also heightened considerably with controversies regarding disasters, such as, the Bhopal Gas Tragedy of 1984 and, more recently, the Sardar Sarovar and Narmada Sagar dam projects, and the relocation of polluting industrial units outside the urban periphery occupying the headlines. Environmental aspects of nuclear power, the disappearance of plant and animal genetic resources, the limitations of existing pollution control technologies in industry, the destruction of wetlands and other special habitats and other issues. Industrial activity contributes to environmental degradation in the form of air, water, land, and noise pollution affecting the biodiversity of a region.

There are a host of Central and State laws dealing with the prevention and control of pollution and environmental protection. Some of these are: The Environment (Protection) Act, 1986; The Water (Prevention and Control of Pollution) Act, 1974; The Air (Prevention and Control of Pollution) Act, 1981; The Wildlife (Protection) Act, 1972; and The Forest (Conservation) Act, 1980. Besides there are elaborate procedures laid down under rules such as the Hazardous Wastes (Management and Handling) Rules, 1989 and the Manufacture, Storage and Import of Hazardous Chemicals Rules, 1989. The major responsibility to deal with environmental issues lies with the State Pollution Control Boards. The boards implement the pollution control laws. Any new project has to seek a no-objection certificate from the board, which then regulates and monitors the emission and discharge of hazardous wastes. Such monitoring takes place on the basis of standards, including ambient air quality standards for discharge of effluents and emission of smoke and vapour, and noise. Project implementation, particularly in the case of process-based and chemical industries, requires adherence to the procedures laid down for environmental protection and pollution control boards.

10.5.4 Consumer Protection Requirements

In the course of strategy implementation, companies are increasingly required to conform to legislative measures to protect the consumers. There is apprehension that consumers may be subjected to unethical and unfair acts of companies and they need to be protected through the law. The growth of consumerism and consumer awareness, coupled with growing competition, makes it imperative that companies conform to the procedures laid down in the law regarding consumer protection. Besides the law, there is also the social requirement of being perceived as a consumer-friendly organisation.

In India, consumer protection is ensured through a plethora of legislations. Some of these are: Essential Commodities Act, Trademarks and Merchandise Act, Sale of Goods Act, Standard Weights and Measures Act, and the IDR Act. However, the central legislation is the Consumer Protection Act, 1986, amended through the Consumer Protection (Amendment) Ordinance, 1993. This Act provides for the protection of consumer rights and the redressal of consumer disputes.

The Consumer Protection Act provides for the establishment of a Central Consumer Protection Council and State Consumer Protection Council in each State. The Department of Food and Civil Supplies is the nodal ministerial agency for the enforcement of the Act. The Act also provides for a three-tier consumer disputes redressal system at the

District, State, and Central levels. At the district level, there is a District Forum, a State Commission at the State level, and a National Commission at the central level. These forums are primarily for the purposes of consumer disputes redressal and remedial action by the companies.

According to the Competition Act, consumer courts will be the sole guardians of consumer interests since the Competition Commission of India shall not deal with these matters. The issue of consumer protection is highlighted in the procedural implementation at the level of business and operational strategies, and in the implementation of functional policies related to operations, quality, and marketing.

10.5.5 Procedures for Availing Benefits, Incentives and Facilities

Project implementation requires a consideration of various incentives, subsidies, and facilities. It is beneficial for entrepreneurs to be aware of these and take the benefits from them. In providing incentives, and so on, the government does not play a regulatory but a promotional role. This role is manifested in various forms. In line with the objectives laid out in the Industrial Policy resolution, the government attempts to achieve employment generation, correction of regional imbalances, promotion of export-oriented industries and utilisation of installed capacity through higher production levels and productivity.

Though the primary instrument for achieving national plan objectives is regulation, promotional activities also play an important role. The fiscal, monetary, and budgetary policies of the government are aimed at the stimulation of activity in the priority industrial sectors. Government has discretionary control over money supply, banks, financial institutions and lending rates. Budget pronouncements may result in the reduction of excise duties, corporate and personal taxation rates, and so on, which increase the availability of finance for expansion activities. The government also plays a promotional role in terms of purchasing, pricing, distribution, ensuring availability of raw materials, and provision of infrastructural facilities. A number of industries are critically dependent on government purchases. The Directorate General of Supplies and Disposal is the largest purchasing agency in the country. The system of administered pricing has a far-reaching impact on many industries, such as, steel, cement, fertilizers, and others. The distribution of many goods, such as, steel, cement, fuel (commonly known as essential commodities) affects industries, such as, sugar, vanaspati, edible oils, common cloth, and several oters. The government also undertakes the supply of essential raw materials or scarce imported raw materials (e.g., newsprint) which affects the supplier environment in many industries. In many industries, the critical success factors (CSFs) include the regular availability of vital raw materials in sufficient quantities. Through the provision of infrastructural facilities, such as, power, water, skilled manpower, banking and financial services, health services, public utilities like transportation, and industrial sites and sheds, the government seeks to ensure balanced regional development through a dispersal of industries.

Various state governments and Union Territory administrations offer additional schemes. The schemes are administered through the central and state level ministries and departments by involving financial institutions. Expansion strategies can be implemented profitably if the various incentives can be availed of under the different government schemes. In the special case of small-scale industries wishing to implement their strategies, many benefits can be availed of under small-scale industries and its numerous agencies situated at various places in India. Export promotion efforts by the government take the form of several incentives like liberal import facilities, priority in financing and transportation, and so on. 100 per cent export-oriented units and units in free-trade zones enjoy special incentives and facilities. From the point of view of strategic management, all the above measures undertaken by the government are highly relevant for business organisations. Strategic decision-making has to take these factors into account in objective-setting, strategic choice, and strategy implementation.

10.5.6 Overview of Procedural Implementation

In the preceding section, an attempt has been made to provide information related to a broad range of elements in the regulatory framework within which Indian organisations have to operate. It is to be observed that the role of the government is quite comprehensive and affects practically each and every aspect of an organisation's management, especially activities related to strategic management. While there are differing viewpoints regarding the extent the manner in which the regulatory framework should operate, an existentialist view for strategists is to continually look for opportunities within the business environment, as such an environment is primarily the creation of government plans, priorities, policies and actions. Strategy formulation and implementation within organisations have to follow the ground rules laid by the government closely. We have indicated the major regulatory and promotional aspects that have to be considered by strategists.

Many areas remain, for instance, the matter of direct and indirect taxation to be dealt with the relevant laws and procedures, or industrial sickness to be dealt with under the Sick Industrial Companies (Special Provisions) Act, 1985. These are areas that deal with special situations. Strategists would have to be aware of the details of procedural implementation relevant to the industry to which their companies belong. Several organisations, usually large ones and public enterprises have to maintain a close liaison with various governmental agencies in order to get approvals, sanctions, permissions, and statutory benefits. This liaison is usually exercised through formal as well as informal means. Formally, companies maintain liaison offices in New Delhi and the state capitals, or employ advisors and consultants who assist and guide the organisations regarding procedural matters. Companies going in for expansion strategies, particularly diversification, usually look for industry experts and consultants who can advise them on all the aspects of the establishment of a project and guide them through the maze of governmental regulations. Most companies retain, commission or contract out the services of chartered accountants, company secretaries, legal experts and lawyers to advise them on procedural and legal matters. Informally, organisations seek to coordinate the influence governmental action through unconventional means, such as, political donations and lobbying.

Project and procedural implementation result in the necessary infrastructure and the required permission for an organisation to proceed with other aspects of strategy implementation.

10.6 RESOURCE ALLOCATION

Strategists have the power to decide which divisions, departments, or SBUs are to receive how much money, which facilities, and which executives. This is what we mean by resource allocation. The resource allocation decisions are very similar in that they set the operative strategy or the firm. Assume, for example, that resources are allocated to the existing units on some formula basis (e.g., 10 per cent above last year's budget). The implicit operative strategy is expansion. If the official strategy is expansion in some lines of business and stability in others, then greater resource flows to areas targeted for expansion are necessary to give force to the strategy. The formula approach (such as 10 per cent above last year's budget for all lines of business) would not reinforce such a strategy. What is important to understand is that once the strategic choice is made, resources must follow the strategy, or we haven't put our money where our mouth is. If a firm's strategists describe a strategy in words but do allocate money and executive talent and other resources to support it, the strategy will be considered a paper strategy. So resource allocation decisions about how much to invest in which areas of the business reinforce strategy and commit the organisation to its chosen strategy.

Let us consider how resource allocation is important to several strategic options. If new product development is seen as the key to an active offensive strategy, more funds and personnel will be needed in research and development, with the possibility of long-term capital expenditures for a new plant or new equipment. If the strategy calls for expansion in new markets, greater flows of funds for advertising, sales personnel, and or market research will be required. If retrenchment is under way, resource allocation is of particular significance. Care must be taken to protect units which provide long-term competitive advantages. Unfortunately, the easy way out is often used. Everyone is cut back equally, or resource flows are reduced for units which have a longer-term payout but are short-term users of resources without commensurate revenue generation. The usual example is to cut R & D or maintenance where long-term developments may be most critical for future competitive advantage. Thus, shortsighted resource allocation decisions may come at the expense of the ability to pursue a long-term strategy.

Of course, resource allocation decisions are linked to objectives through the strategies being implemented. Decisions about dividend policies, for instance, are important in relation to objectives and the long-term ability to attract sources of capital. Thus, how to share expected profits among investors, management, the labour and whether to reinvest in the business are important resource allocation choices with long-term strategy implications. External parties play a major role. For instance, government regulations may require a firm to invest large amounts of capital in nonproductive assets such as pollution-control equipment. Influential stockholders may force the firm to make greater dividend payouts. Thus, the strategic agenda is partially set by the factors influencing the setting of objectives, since they will limit the resources available for implementing strategy as expressed in the allocation decisions. Finally, resource allocation is linked to the development of competitive advantage.

It is presumed that those approaches were considered during strategy formulation. They key here is to make sure that preferential distribution of capital goes to the most critical units, the units where the strategy is directed at creating competitive advantages. This is one tool that strategists can use to link resource allocation decisions to choice of strategy. If you recall, several prescriptions for investment and cash flow decisions can be made by using BCG Matrix depending on the type of SBU identified in the matrix. Thus, "cash cows" are SBUs from which resources can be obtained for allocation to "question marks" or to "stars". Of course, there are several problems with this approach for strategic choice, and they apply here as well. For instance, resource allocation for new SBUs with initially low market shares might be overlooked. But for multiple SBUs this is one tool to aid thinking about how to allocate resources.

The primary approach to resource allocation in the implementation process is through the budgeting system. One system for budgeting resources within one firm is the product life cycle budgeting system used by Lear Siegler. This firm believes that the product life cycle of the product lines should influence its budgeting of resources. It believes that cash flow, departmental expenses, revenues, and capital expenditures should vary during the cycle. Therefore, the balance sheets and income statements should look different at different stages of the cycle. The firm suggests adjusting resources accordingly. Thus, to the extent that the product life cycle influences strategy, budgets tied to such a cycle will affect the product strategy. Others agree with this approach and suggest that zero based budgeting is particularly useful when retrenchment strategies are being used. From a long-term perspective, the capital budget is very critical. Here, plans for securing and distributing capital for large-scale investments are needed to accomplish strategy.

Mergers, introduction of major new product lines, an increase in plant capacity and vertical integrations are key mission changes which will require long-term capital investment decisions.

The more routine year-to-year allocation decisions are made within this context. But they are also important for making sure that the strategic direction of the firm is being followed, and they serve as a guide to future strategy. So let's look at this budget process in more detail. Remember that resource allocation as expressed in the budget needs to be carefully linked to strategy. Exhibit 10.4 shows how these can be linked in a multiple-SBU firm. Note that the process will involve planning at various levels in a back-and-forth fashion over time. In a series of negotiations among managers at the SBU and corporate levels, the strategy and plans to implement it are worked out. The final output is a set of budgets which give force to the overall plan. Let's look at these stages of the budgeting process in a bit more detail.

Step 1: Top management initiates the budgeting process. It communicates the objectives of the firm for the period. Of the various internal planning premises and assumptions

Exhibit 10.4 Framework for the Strategic Budgeting Process

	Step 1	*Step 2*	*Step 3*	*Step 4*	*Step 5*
Corporate Level	State corporate objectives & strategy and identification of assumptions	Approve or alter goals and strategy	Make tentative resource allocations and call for budgets	Review and approve requests	Prepare summary budgets
	↓	↓	↓	↓	↓
SBU Level	Define SBU's objectives and strategy	Prepare premises and forecast	Prepare preliminary budget	Propose resource requirement changes	Receive approved budgets and make final plans

which must be formulated, the sales forecast is clearly the most fundamental. Indeed, since anticipated product demand must be determined before budgets and plans for resource inputs are made, the sales forecast is typically cited as the key basis for all internal planning. Among other things, the sales forecast is the basis for production planning, materials planning, capital planning. Moreover, projected sales indicates output for a company constitute the revenue side of an organisation's income statement. Thus, on the basis of forecasted sales, an organisation is able to project production requirements, establish what materials need to be purchased, determine the number of personnel to be recruited, estimate the level and timing of required financial resources, and decide what it can afford in the way of operating expenses (such as those for advertising and sales promotion) for the purpose of exacting a certain profit level.

Step 2: The budget department (in large firms) or administrator communicates information and offers advice to the units preparing the budgets. This unit prepares the forms and procedures for developing a budget. It helps those preparing budgets with technical problems and in the actual preparation. If there are budget specialists at the division level, it trains these persons and coordinates their work.

Step 3: Each unit prepares a preliminary budget for the next period. Normally, the unit begins with the previous period's budget and performance against this budget. Next the unit states how the next period will differ from the current period. So the next year's budget that the unit proposes is based on the past budget plus or minus expected changes.

This shows how the units management expects to achieve its objectives. This is a critical stage if strategic change is taking place. The unit must specify what resources it will need to accomplish the strategy.

Step 4: The preliminary budgets developed in step 3 are reviewed and approved. The budget department analyzes and reviews each unit's past performance and determines whether its projections are realistic given the likely future conditions. After comparing the budgets of the various units, the budget department submits them to top the management along with recommendations for approval or adjustment. Top management examines the budgets and approves it if they are consistent with past performance, anticipated revenues, and the firm's strategy.

This is the stage at which the resource allocation choice will be made. Who gets the money to hire more people, buy new furniture or machinery, or build a new building? In most enterprises resources are scarce, and not every unit can be given what it wants (and says it needs). The allocation of funds can be crucial to the success of a unit (and to the career of its manager). Loss of marketing funds for TV spots at a strategic time, for example, can wreak a unit's results. Because the decisions involved are so difficult, they are often made by a budget committee or a number of managers.

Step 5: At this stage summary budgets are usually prepared. Projected receipts and expenses are put together, and subsidiary budgets are developed, for example, the operating budget, financial budgets, the capital budget, and expense budgets. The operating budget specifies materials, labour, overheads, and other costs. Financial budgets project cash receipts and disbursements; the capital budget project major additions or new construction. The expense budgets project expenses not covered in other budgets, such as marketing costs. Finally, in the summary budget (profit and loss or income statement), the total obtained by combining the subsidiary budgets is subtracted from the projected receipts.The remainder is a profit or loss. If the budgets meet objectives, approvals are made, and the budgets are enacted. If changes are needed, negotiations will take place.

The mechanics of preparing capital and operating budgets are beyond our purview. But this process is important, as it relates to the formation and implementation of strategy. Through the entire process, a variety of real problems of relevance to strategists often emerge. Estimating both revenues and costs is difficult. In the case of an automaker, for example, how many new cars will the company sell? This depends on a number of factors, such as the economy, competitor's products, and how consumers evaluate its product in comparison with competing products. The company's pricing policy and marketing image affect this estimate, as do product quality, engineering, and the aggressiveness and reliability of dealers.

Moreover, the question of who gets the most money from the budget has a major effect on the work environment as well as on the careers of managers. If, as a manager, you lose the budget battle, your employees will have to do more work with fewer helpers and less desirable equipment. They will feel that you have failed them, and they will treat you accordingly. This is one of the problems with using the product portfolio approach. Few managers want to have their units known as "dogs" or "question marks". It is also a problem affecting retrenchment strategies. Negotiations to protect a unit in the budget battle may come at the expense of pursuing a strategy in the best interests of the overall organisation. Indeed, gamesmanship, overstatement of real budget needs, and even secrecy can lead to highly political budget battles across departments.

Another problem is that the usual budget process tends to be designed for allocating resources to existing departments or various investment proposals. These may or may not be tied to strategic changes desired by the organisation; if they are not, then the budget process reinforces existing resource allocation patterns.

The budget process itself can lead to problems if it is not tied to the strategic direction of the firm. In fact, the process sets the operative strategy as we suggested earlier. So if lower levels are unaware of shifts in strategic direction and if top managers fail to communicate strategic change or are weak negotiators, any intended strategy change is unlikely to take place. Finally, you should note that the budget process is tied to the way units and divisions are arranged organisationally. New SBUs can be at a disadvantage if they are unaware of the "ins and outs" of the budget procedures used in their organisation. And if truly major strategic shifts are occurring, the structure is likely to change along with the way resources are allocated.

The major difficulty arises due to a scarcity of resources. Financial, physical, and human resources are hard to find. Firms usually face difficulties in procuring finance. Even if finance is available, the cost of capital is a constraint. Those firms that enjoy investor confidence and high creditworthiness possess a competitive advantage as it increases their resource-generation capability. Physical resources would consist of assets, such as, land, machinery, and equipment. In a developing country like India, many capital goods have to be imported. The government may no longer impose many conditions but it does place a burden on the firm's finances and this places a restriction on firms wishing to procure physical resources. Human resources are seemingly in abundance in India but the problem arises due to the non-availability of skills that area specially required. Information technology and computer professionals, advertising personnel, and telecom, power and insurance experts are scarce in India. This places severe restrictions on firms wishing to attract and retain personnel. In sum, the availability of scarce resources is a real problem faced in resource allocation.

Within organisations, there are several difficulties encountered in resource allocation. The usual budgeting for existing SBUs, divisions, and departments places restrictions on generating resources for newer units and those with a greater potential for growth. Overstatement of needs is another frequent problem in a bottom-up approach to resource allocation. The budgeting and corporate planning departments may have to face the ire of those executives who do not get resources according to their expectations. Such negative reactions may hamper the process of strategic planning itself. When strategic budgeting is used for resource allocation, powerful units may be divested of resources for reallocation to potential units. Budget battles may ensue if resource allocation affects vested interests. It must be pointed out, however, that the CEO has a major role to play in managing the process of resource allocation. Strategic management, based on a participative mode, and the communication of the strategic plan to all executives creates a congenial environment where the resource allocation decisions may be taken amicably.

Exercise

1. Describe the characteristics of strategy implementation by using strategy implementation model. Explain the steps with examples.
2. Describe the major barriers to strategy implementation and discuss the means available to overcome such issues.
3. What are different themes of strategy implementation and discuss the interrelationship between them.
4. Explain the different phases of project implementation. Are these phases interrelated or can be taken up simultaneously?
5. Explain the role of regulatory framework applicable in India if a company is to be formed.
6. SEBI role is to deal with capital market. How does it affect the companies?
7. How a foreign collaborator can have alliance with Indian companies? Is there any government agency involved in approving such collaboration.
8. Requirements such as patent rights, IPR, labour legislation, etc. create difficulty in project implementation. What are difficulties faced by company and how to overcome these?
9. What are the major issues involved in resources allocations? How important is resources allocation to achieve the objectives of the company?
10. Consider any Indian company. What steps it should take for resources allocation for implementing strategies?

11 Strategy Implementation: Structures, Design and Change

11.1 INTRODUCTION

We usually conceive of organisation structure as a chart consisting of boxes in which the names of positions or designations of personnel (and sometimes the name of the person occupying the position) are written in a hierarchical order along with the relationship that exists between various positions. To a strategist, an organisation structure is not only a chart but much more. An organisation structure is the way in which the tasks and subtasks required to implement a strategy are arranged. The diagrammatic representation of structure could be an organisation chart but a chart shows only the skeleton. The "flesh and blood" that bring life to an organisation are the several mechanisms that support the structure. All these cannot be depicted on a chart. But a strategist has to grapple with the complexities of creating the structure, making it work, redesigning when required, and implementing changes that will keep the structure relevant to the needs of the strategies that have to be implemented.

To find out what the structural mechanisms are, it is useful to consider the case of a new organisation which has decided to achieve a set of objectives through implementation of certain strategies. The implementation of strategies would require the performance of tasks. Some of these tasks are related to the formulation and implementation of programmes and projects.

We dealt with these tasks in the previous chapter which was on activating strategies. Having laid the foundations of an organisation, the strategists now have to devote their attention to the tasks, that would have to be performed on a continuing basis for the implementation of strategies. It would be practically impossible to list all such tasks, so the strategists would attempt to enumerate the major tasks. These major tasks would have to be grouped on the basis of the commonality of the skills required to perform them. Having grouped the major tasks, each category of such tasks will have to be again segregated on the basis of the ability of an individual to perform a unit of tasks. This is the process by which organisational units, such as, departments, are created and hierarchies defined.

The total responsibility to implement strategies has to be subdivided and distributed to different organisational units. The authority to discharge the responsibilities will also have to be delegated if the tasks have to be performed. To ensure that different organisational units do not work at cross-purpose, coordination will have to be ensured through communication. The performance will have to be appraised and controlled so that the tasks are performed in a sequence and according to a schedule. Desirable behaviour to perform these tasks will have to be encouraged and undesirables behaviour curbed. For this, rewards and penalties will have to be used. Since the performance of tasks cannot be left to chance, the creation of motivation will have to be facilitated so that organisational effort is directed towards a common purpose. Further, individuals will have to be trained so that objective-achieving capability is created and sustained.

The new organisation that has been exemplified will come into being and start functioning in the manner described above. All the activities mentioned will now have to be performed on a continuing basis. We cannot derive the different mechanisms on the basis of the above example. These are summarised as follows:

1. Defining the major tasks required to implement a strategy
2. Grouping tasks on the basis of common skill requirements
3. Subdivision of responsibilties and delegation of authority to perform tasks
4. Coordination of divided responsibility
5. Design and administration of the inforamtion system
6. Design and administration of the control system
7. Design and administration of the appraisal system
8. Design and administration of the motivation system
9. Design and administration of the development system
10. Design and administration of the planning system

The first four of these mechanisms will lead to the creation of the structure. The other six mechanisms are devised to hold and sustain the structure. Collectively, we could refer to the last six mechanisms as organisational systems. Note that structural mechanism alone will not fulfill the requirements of strategy implementation. Structure is the "hardware" while the other aspects constitute the software of structure implementation. The other major aspects of implementation relate to the leadership styles, corporate culture, and other related issues. Here, we focus our attention on the structural mechanism required for the implementation of strategies.

The prescription for consciously matching an organisation's structure to the particular needs and requirements of strategy has arisen out of research done by Chandler. Chandler has further extended the thinking to include environment and effectiveness in the sequence to pinpoint the nature of choices that strategists make. He says that managerial choice occurs at the interface of environment and strategy, which then determines the structure. Though Chandler's thesis that strategy changes require structural changes to achieve economic efficiency is logically powerful, subsequent researches have not conclusively proved the relationship that structure follows strategy.

But often, structural consideration also affect if not determine strategy, which is a case of backward linkage. Theorists in Business Policy, therefore, are more concerned with the match that should exist between strategy and structure. In other words, a particular strategy creates special requirements that should be fulfilled by the structure. If it does not, then the structure will have to be redesigned. What shape the structure should take if a particular strategy is to be implemented successfully is difficult to answer. But here again, theory offers alternatives. One such alternative is to link structure to the stage of development that an organisation exists in at a given point of time.

Besides Chander, Salter, Thain, and Scott have contributed to the thinking that any organisation, as it grows in size and diversity, moves from a simple to a complex organisational form. This concept is analogous to that of the product. life cycle. Organisations too follow a life cycle consisting of the introduction, growth, maturity, and decline phases. The life cycle of organisations could be divided into four states that are not distinct and may overlap.

Stage I: These organisations are small-scale enterprises usually managed by a single person who is the entrepreneur-owner-manager. These organisations are characterized by the simplicity of objectives, operations, and management. The form of the organisation is also simple and could be termed entrepreneurial. The strategies adopted are generally of the expansion type.

Stage II: These organisations are bigger than Stage I organisations in terms of size and have a wider scope of operations. They are characterized by functional specialization or process orientation. The organisational form is simple functional (typically divided into the finance, marketing, operations, and personnel departments) or process-oriented (divided into process-based departments arranged in a particular sequence according to the technology employed). The strategies adopted may range from stability to expansion.

Stage III: These organisations are large and widely scattered organisations generally having units or plants at different places. Each division is semi-autonomous and linked to the headquarters but functionally independent. The divisions may have a simple functional form depending on their particular needs. The strategies adopted may be either stability or expansion.

Stage IV: These organisations are the most complex. They are generally large multi-plant, multiproduct organisations that result from the adoption of related and unrelated diversification strategies. The organisational form is divisional. The corporate headquarters assume the responsibility of providing strategic direction and policy guidelines through the formulation of corporate-level strategies. The divisions (which may be companies, profit centres or SBUs) formulate their business-level strategies and may adopt Stage I, II or III types of structures.

The stage of development theories presents a convenient way to understand the way the structure may evolve as the organisation moves from one stage to the next. But, in practice, many variations may occur. It is not necessary that all organisations should pass through every stage of development. Nor does every organisation exhibit the characteristics of exclusively one stage.

A look at different organisations will show that they do seem to follow the different stages mentioned above. Most companies have started as one- or two-person units in an entrepreneurial mode, through expansion and in time, the companies have become bigger, creating the need for a subdivision of task which usually takes place along functional lines. Further, expansion creates the need for setting up additional plants, and if diversification strategies are adopted, then the organisational forms may ultimately become divisional. Exhibit 11.1 presents an interesting analysis of how organisational structures have evolved in the Indian context.

Business Today makes an interesting analysis of the chronological evolution of the organisational structure within Indian firms. The structures analyzed show the firms responding to the environmental situation prevailing during a particular time period. Here is an account of how structures have evolved from the pre-1940s to the post 1990s.

Exhibit 11.1 The Evolution of the Organisation Structure in Corporate India

- One-man organisation (Pre-1940): The CEO is the hub around which there are workers.
- The classic triangle (1940–50): The functions of sales, finance, and production are designed below the direct control of the CEO.
- The managing agency (1950–60): The foreign company provides the licence to the local partner who acts as the managing agent. The functional areas are directly looked after by the managing agent who acts as the CEO.
- The functional structure (1960–70): The traditional and popular structure of various functional areas directly under the control of the CEO.
- The cross-holding structure (1970–80) The promoter (most often a family group or a powerful industrialist) has equity holding in several companies and exercises organisational control in the same proportion.
- The conglomerate (1980–90): The business/family group emerges as the focal point managing a clutch of business interests vested in different companies. Each company manages one or more businesses.
- The streamlined group (Post-1990): The group emerges as the focal point of structure with businesses vested in subsidiaries, joint ventures, and equity alliances. The organisational control is exercised through a flagship company.

11.2 STRUCTURES FOR STRATEGIES

Implementation is necessary to spell out more precisely how the strategic choice will come to be. Structural and administrative mechanisms which are compatible and workable need to be established to reinforce the strategic direction chosen and provide guides for action. A good strategy without effective implementation is not likely to succeed. Closing the gap between ideal and expected outcomes requires more than making a strategic choice. Exhibit 11.2 is one consulting group's representation of the fact that strategy formation is but one component of a network of organisation activities which must be integrated to accomplish objectives. The McKinsey 7S framework suggests that the following components must fit together to make a strategy work effectively.

Exhibit 11.2 McKinsey 7S Framework

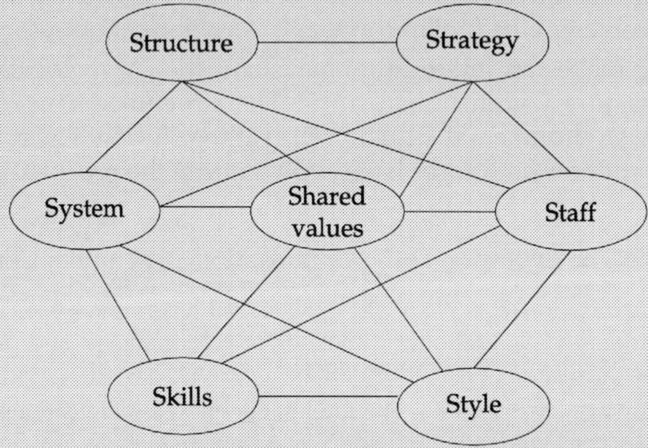

1. ***Strategy:*** A coherent set of actions aimed at gaining a sustainable advantage over competition, improving position vis-a-vis customers, or allocating resources.
2. ***Structure*** The organisation chart and accompanying baggage that show who reports to whom and how task are both divided up and integrated.
3. ***Systems:*** The process and flows that show how an organisation gets things done from day to day (information system, capital budgeting systems, manufacturing process, quality control systems, and performance measurement systems all would be good examples.
4. ***Style:*** Tangible evidence of what management considers important by the way it collectively spends time and attention and uses symbolic behaviour. It is not what management says is important; it is the way management behaves.
5. ***Staff:*** The people in an organisation. Here it is very useful to think not about individual personalities but about corporate demographics.
6. ***Shared Values (or superordinate goals):*** The values that go beyond, but might well include, simple, goal statements in determining corporate destiny. To fit the concept, these values must be shared by most people in an organisation.
7. ***Skills:*** A derivate of the rest skills are those capabilities that are possessed by an organisation as a whole as opposed to the people in it.

An organisation is necessary if strategic purpose is to be accomplished. Thus, organisational structure is a major priority in implementing a carefully formulated strategy. If activities, responsibilities, and interrelationships are not organized in a manner that is consistent with the strategy chosen, the structure is left to evolve on its own. If structure and strategy are not coordinated, the result will probably be inefficiencies, misdirection, and fragmented efforts.

The need for structure becomes apparent as the business evolves. In a small firm where one person manages current operations and plans for the future, organisational structure is relatively simple. Owner-managers have no organisational problem until their hurried trips to the plant, late-night sessions assimilating financial information for their CPA, and pressed calls on potential customers are inadequate to meet the demands of a business's increasing volume. As the magnitude of business activity increases, the need to subdivide activities, assign responsibilities, and provide for the integration and coordination of the new organisational parts becomes imperative. Thus, how to structure the organisation to effectively execute the business's strategy has become a major concern.

What is structure? A basically simple concept: the division of tasks for efficiency and clarity of purpose, and coordination between the interdependent parts of the organisation to ensure organisational effectiveness. Structure balances the need for specialization with the need for integration. It provides a formal means of decentralizing and centralizing consistent with the organisational and control needs of the strategy. Structure is not the only means for getting organized to implement the strategy. Reward systems, planning procedures, and information and budgetary systems are other examples that should be employed. In the day-to-day implementation of strategy, these elements operate interdependently with the formal organisational structure to shape how things are done. These other means may also be important, but it is through structure that strategists attempt to balance internal efficiency and overall effectiveness within a broader environment.

11.3 STRUCTURAL CHOICES

There are five basic types are currently used by most business firms:

1. Simple
2. Functional
3. Divisional
4. Strategic business unit
5. Matrix.

Diversity and size create unique structural needs for each firm, but these five structural choices involve basic underlying features common to most business organisations. Structure is not an end in itself but rather a means to an end. It is a tool for managing the size and diversity of a business to enhance the success of its strategy. This section identifies structural options and examines the role of structure in strategy implementation

11.3.1 Simple and Functional Organisation Structures

Exhibit 11.3 shows a model of simple and functional organisational structures. In the smallest business enterprise, the simple structure prevails. All strategic and operating decisions are centralized in the owner-manager's domain. With the strategic concern primarily survival, and the likelihood that one bad decision could seriously threaten continued existence, this structure maximizes that owner's control. It also allows rapid response to product market shifts and the ability to accommodate unique customer demands without coordination difficulties. Simple structures encourage employee involvement in more than one activity and are efficacious in businesses that serve a localized, simple product/market. This structure can be very demanding on the owner-manager and, as volume increases, can pressure the owner-manager to give increased attention to day-to-day concerns at the expense of time invested in strategic management activities.

Exhibit 11.3 Simple and Functional Organisation Structures

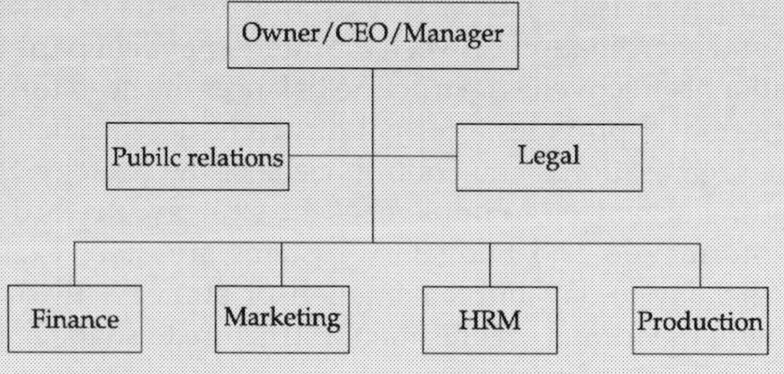

Functional structure predominates in firms that concentrate on one or a few related products/markets. Functional structures group similar tasks and activities (usually, production/operations, marketing, finance/accounting, research and development, personnel) as separate functional units within the organisation. This specialization encourages greater efficiency and refinement of particular expertise and allows the firm to seek and foster distinct competence in one or more functional areas. Expertise is critical to single-product/market companies and to firms that are vertically integrated.

The strategic challenge in the functional structures is effective coordination of the separate functional units. The narrow technical expertise sought through specialization can lead to limited perspectives and different priorities across different functional units. Specialists may not understand problems in other functional areas and may begin to see the firm's strategic issues primarily as "marketing" problems or "production" problems. This potential conflict makes the coordinating role of the chief executive critical if a strategy is to be effectively implemented using the functional structure. Integrating devices (such as project team or planning committees) are frequently used in functionally organized businesses to enhance coordination and to facilitate understanding across functional areas.

11.3.2 Divisional Structure

When a firm diversifies its products/service lines, covers broad geographic areas, utilizes unrelated market channels, or begins to serve distinctly different customer groups, a functional structure rapidly becomes inadequate. For example, functional managers may wind up overseeing the production or marketing or numerous and different products or services. And coordination demands on top management are beyond the capacity of a functional structure. Some form of divisional structure is necessary to meet the coordination and decision-making requirements resulting from increased diversity and size. Such a structure is illustrated in Exhibit 11.4 A divisional structure allows corporate management to delegate authority for the strategic management of a distant business entity. This can expedite critical decision making within each division in response to varied competitive environments, and it forces corporate management to concentrate on corporate level strategic decisions. The semi-autonomous divisions are usually given profit responsibility. The divisional structure thus seeks to facilitate accurate assessment of profit and loss.

Exhibit 11.4 Divisional Organization Structure

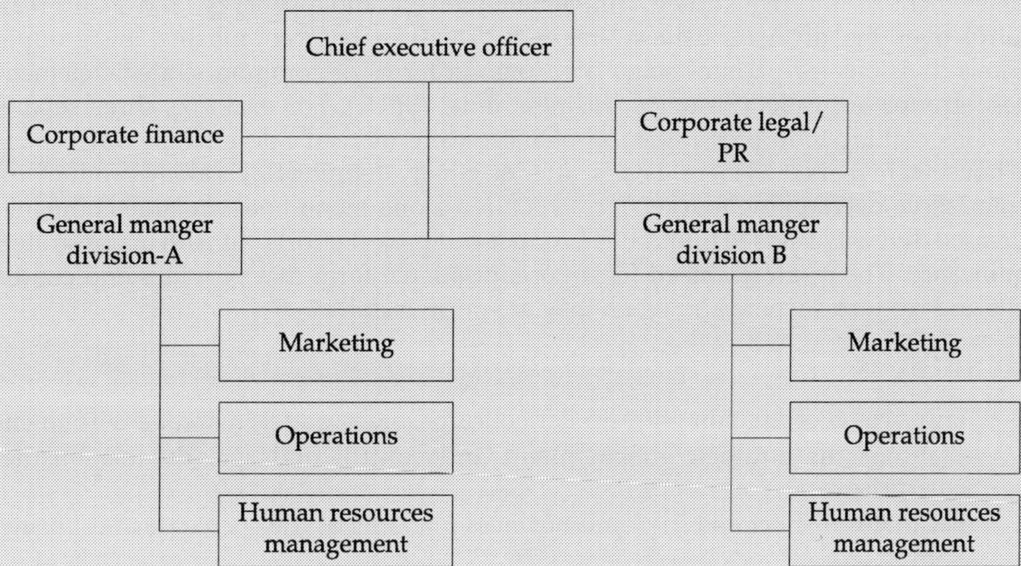

Advantages

- Forces coordination and necessary authority down to the appropriate level for rapid response.
- Places strategy development and implementation in closer proximity to the division's unique environment.
- Frees chief executive officer for strategic decision making.
- Sharply focuses accountability for managers with profit responsibility.
- Retains functional specialization within each division.
- Good training ground for strategic managers.

Disadvantages

- Fosters potentially dysfunctional competition for corporate-level resources.
- Problem with the extent of authority given to division managers.
- Potenital for policy inconsistencies between divisions.
- Potential of arriving at a method to broader distribute corporate overhead costs that is acceptable to different division performance.

11.3.3 Strategic Business Units (SBU) Structure

Some firms encounter difficulty in controlling their divisional operations as the diversity, size, and number of these units continues to increase. And corporate management may encounter difficulty in evaluating and controlling its numerous, often multi-industry divisions. Under these conditions, it may become necessary to add another layer of management to improve strategy implementation, promote synergy, and gain greater control over the diverse business interests. This can be accomplished by grouping various divisions (or parts of some divisions) in terms of common strategic elements. These groups are called Strategic Business units (SBUs). For example, three separate divisions making food preparation appliances were merged into a single SBU serving the houseware market. General Foods, after originally defining SBUs along product lines (which serve overlapping markets), restructured along menu lines. In large companies, increased diversity leads to numerous product and project efforts, all with major strategic significance. The result is a need for an organisational form that provides and controls skills and resources where and when they are most useful.

Advantages

- Improves coordination with similar concerns and product/market environments.
- Tightens the strategic management and control of large, diverse business enterprises.
- Facilitates distinct and in-depth business planning at the corporate and business levels.
- Channels accountability to distinct business units

Disadvantages

- Places another layer of management divisions strategic between the divisions and corporate management.
- Dysfunctional competition for corporate resources may increase.
- The role of the group's vice-president can be difficult to define.
- Difficulty in defining the degree of autonomy for the group's vice-presidents and division managers.

Exhibit 11.5 Strategic Business Unit Organisational Structure

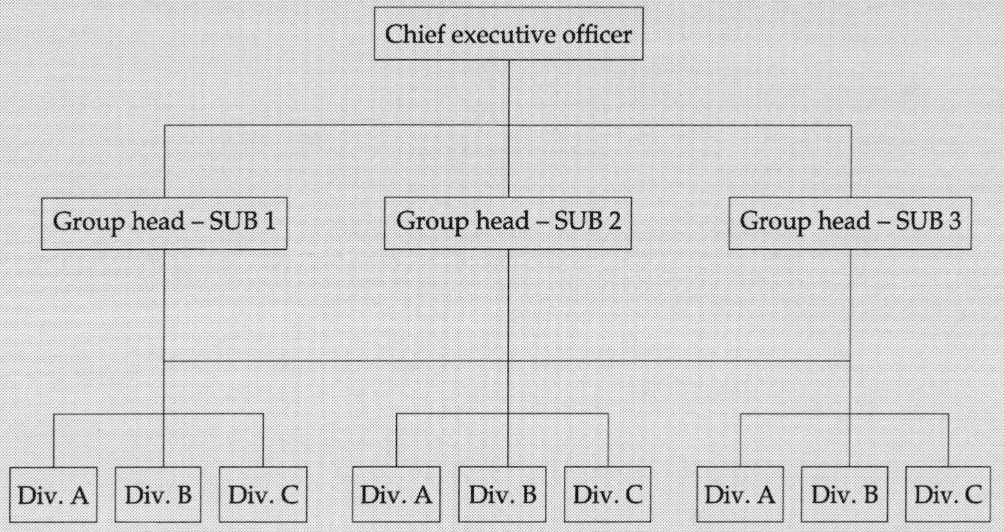

11.3.4 Matrix Organisation

The matrix organisation provides for dual channels of authority, performance responsibility, evaluation and control, as shown in Exhibit 11.6. Essentially, subordinates are assigned to both a basic functional area and a project or product manager. The matrix from is included to combine the advantages of functional specialization and product/project specialization. In theory, the matrix is a conflict resolution system through which strategic and operating priorities are negotiated, power is shared, and resources are allocated internally on a strongest case for what is best overall for the unit basis. The matrix organisation, pioneered by firms like defense contractors, construction companies has increasingly been used to meet this need. The list of companies now using some form of matrix organisation includes Citicorp, Digital Equipment, General Electric, Shell Oil, Dow Chemical, and Texas Instruments.

The matrix organisation provides for dual channels of authority, performance responsibility, evaluation and control, as shown in Exhibit 11.6. Essentially, subordinates are assigned to both a basic functional area and a project or product manager. The matrix from is included to combine the advantages of functional specialization and product/project specialization. In theory, the matrix is a conflict resolution system through which strategic and operating priorities are negotiated, power is shared, and resources are allocated internally on a strongest case for what is best overall for the unit basis.

Exhibit 11.6 Strategic Business Unit Organisational Structure

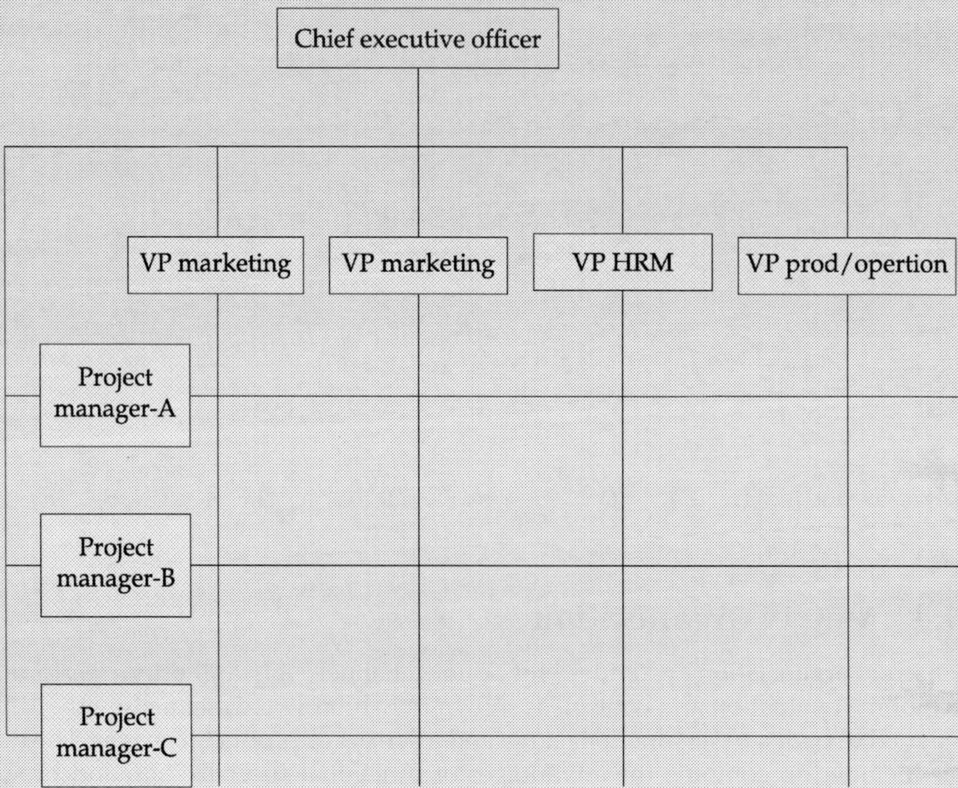

Advantages

- Accommodates a wide variety of project oriented business activities.
- Good training ground for strategic managers.
- Maximizes efficient use of functional managers.
- Fosters creativity and multiple sources of diversity.
- Broader middle-management exposure to strategic issues for the business.

Disadvantages

- Dual accountability can create confusion and contradictory policies.
- Necessitates tremendous horizontal and vertical coordination.
- The matrix structure increases the number of middle managers exercising general management responsibilities and broadens their exposure to organisation wide strategic concerns. Thus, it can accommodate a varied and changing project, product/market, or technology focus and can increase the efficient use of functional specialists who otherwise might be idle.

Citicorp used the matrix organisation to implement an international expansion strategy focusing on both geographically different financial service requirements and at the same time targeting the multinational corporation market segment. The change was designed to increase the priority given to large, international organisations. The strategy ultimately gave Citicorp a better understanding of the worldwide financial officers of these corporation. Matrix structure was a strategic tool that allowed Citicorp to gain a competitive advantage with this important segment.

While the matrix structure is easy to design, it is difficult to implement. Dual chains of command challenge fundamental organisational orientations. Negotiating shared responsibilities, use of resources, and priorities can create misunderstanding or confusion among subordinates. To overcome the deficiencies that might be associated with a permanent matrix structure some firms are using a temporary or flexible structure to accomplish a particular strategic task. This approach, used recently by firm like General Motors, IBM, and Texas Instruments, is meant to take temporary advantage of a matrix-type team while preserving the shape and spirit of the underlying divisional structure. Thus, the basic idea of the matrix structure, to simplify and amplify the focus of resources on a narrow but strategically important product, project, or market, appears to be an important structural alternative within large, diverse organisations.

11.3.5 Which Structure is Best?

Considerable research has been done on this question, and the collective answer is that it depends on the strategy of the firm. The structural design ties together key activities and resources of the firm. Therefore, it must be closely aligned with the needs/demands of the firm's strategy. Alfred Chandler provided a landmark study in understanding the choice of structure as a function of strategy. Chandler studied 70 large corporations over an extended time period and found a common strategy-structure sequence:

1. Choice of a new strategy.
2. Emergence of administrative problems; decline in performance.
3. A shift to an organisational structure more in line with the strategy's needs.
4. Improved profitability and strategy execution.

General Electric's recent history supports Chandler's thesis. Operating with a simple divisional structure in the late 1950s, GE embarked on a broad diversification strategy. In the 1960s, GE experienced impressive sales growth. However, GE also experienced administrative difficulties in trying to control and improve the corresponding lack of increase in profitability. In the early 1970s, GE executives redesigned its organisational structure to accommodate the administrative needs of strategy (ultimately choosing the strategic business unit structure), subsequently improving profitability of and control over the diversification strategy.

Chandler's research and the GE example allow us to make four important observations. First, all forms of organisational structure are not equally effective in implementing a strategy. Second, structures seem to have a life of their own, particularly in larger organisations. As a result, the need for immediate and radical changes in structure is not immediately perceived. Once the need is perceived, lagging performance may be necessary before politically sensitive structure is changed or organisational power redistributed. Third, sheer growth can make restructuring necessary. Finally, as firms diversify into numerous related or unrelated products and markets, structural change appears to be essential if the firm is to perform effectively. Research on corporate stages of development provides further understanding of the structures-strategy relationship. After studying numerous business firms, these researchers concluded that companies move through several stages as size and diversity increase.

Exhibit 11.7 is a synthesis of these stage-of-development theories. The figure shows that a firm moves through each stage, size, diversity, and competitive environment change. To complete effectively at different stages requires, among other things, different structures. Again, the choice of structure appears contingent on the strategy of the firm in terms of size, diversity of the product / services offered, and markets served. Firms in the metal container industry can help to illustrate this point. Continental Can, employs a divisional structure. This is used to implement a diversification strategy intended to serve virtually every user of metal containers, as well as to compete in unrelated markets like forest products. Crown, Cork and Seal, the industry's fourth largest company, employs a modified functional structure to serve a limited domestic and international market of users with specialized container needs. Both firms are successful. Both derive their greatest revenues from the same industry. But each employs a different organisational structure because their strategies (narrow versus broad product/ market scope) are different.

Exhibit 11.7 Corporate Stages of Development

Stage	*Characteristics of the Firm*	*Typical Structure*
I	Simple, small business. Offering one product/service or one line of products/services to small, distinct local or regionalized market.	Simple to functional
II	Singular or closely related line of products services but to a larger and sometimes more diverse market. (Geography, channels, or customers).	Functional to divisional
III	Expanded but related lines of product/services to diverse, large markets.	Divisional to matrix
IV	Diverse, unrelated lines of products/services to large, diverse markets.	Divisional to SBUs

The choice of structure must be determined by the firm's strategy. And the structure must segment key activities and/or strategic operating units to improve efficiency through specialization, response to a competitive environment, and freedom to act. At the same time, the structure must effectively integrate and coordinate these activities and units to accommodate interdependence of activities and overall control. The choice of structure reflects strategy in terms of the firm's:

(1) Size
(2) Product/service diversity
(3) Competitive environment and volatility
(4) Internal political considerations
(5) Information/coordination needs for each component.

Even a change in strategy, with its accompanying alteration of administrative needs, does not lead to an immediate change in structure. The research of Chandler and others suggests that commitment to a structure lingers even when it becomes inappropriate for a current strategy. Whether this is due to inertia, organisational politics, or a realistic assessment of the relative costs of immediate structural change, historical evidence suggests that the existing structure will be maintained and not radically redesigned until a strategy's profitability is increasingly disproportionate with increasing sales.

11.4 ORGANISATIONAL DESIGN AND CHANGE

It is an extremely difficult proposition to decide which type of structure would satisfy the requirements of a particular strategy. In general; strategists have to ask themselves: "What is required to implement the strategic plan and how best can be done?" This entails what we indicated in organisation structure has to be based on those functions and activities that are critical from the viewpoint of strategy.

There is no clear answer to the question: "Which structure is best suited to a particular Strategy?" Frequently, structures evolve as the organisation moves from one stage of growth to the next. The external and the internal environments affect structural design in different ways. For instance, an organisation which faces a stable environment may use a functional structure since there is less need for interdepartmental coordination and communication, and innovation, On the other hand, a volatile environment demands a rapid-response capability, flexibility and quick decision-making. Such demands can be better met by the creation of a divisional or a matrix type of structure. The internal environment may also affect the structure in a similar fashion. A bureaucratic, slow moving organisation may work better with a functional structure. In sum, it could be said that there is no one absolutely correct way to organize and the organisational design has to be based on the particular needs of the organisation at a given time.

The needs of an organisation can be derived from its mission and objectives. These needs are the key activities which have to be performed to achieve objectives and realise the mission. Organisational design, therefore, starts with the identification of such key activities. The sequence of steps followed in organisational design could be described as below.

1. Identification of key activities necessary to be performed for the achievement of objectives and the realization of the mission through the formulated strategy.
2. Grouping of activities that are similar in nature and which need a common set of skills to be performed.
3. Choice of structure that could accommodate the different groups of activities.

4. Creation of departments, divisions, and so on to which the groups of activities could be assigned.
5. Establishing an interrelationship between different departments for the purpose of coordination and communication.

These five steps lead to the development of an organisational design but the process of organisation is not complete yet. There are various other issues to be talked to see that the organisation becomes an effective medium for the implementation of strategy. For instance, it was mentioned in the previous sections that the basic units for structuring are the departments, based on functional specializations. But this thinking is changing as organisations are attempting to create a more responsive structure in terms of processes based on cross-functional teams. Strategists have to grapple with a number of issues before the task of orgnisational design is over. The major issues are the span of management control, basic departmentation, line and staff relationships, and the use of committees and group decision-making.

The span of management control refers to the ways in which activities can be grouped. The different structures, as described in the previous section, consist of various departments, each of which deals with a distinct group of activities. The activities could also be organized on the basis of the processes leading to the manufacture of a product or provision of a service. These structures form the core of basic departmentation. Line and staff relationship describe the way in which authority is dispersed within the organisation structure. Where a higher-level manager exercise direct supervision over a subordinate, authority is delegated in a direct line or steps. Staff positions are advisory in nature. Within the staff departments, however, authority may again be delegated on the basis of line relationships.

The use of committees and group decision-making is often done as an organisational device though it is not per se a part of the organisational structure. Still, committees are considered an inseparable part of structure. When they are constituted formally on a permanent basis, the committees work on the basis of specially delegated authority and responsibility. Other similar forms of group decision-marking as well as group functioning are the teams, task forces, project units, liaison groups, etc.

It is to be pointed out those significant changes in thought related to organisation structural design has been taking place worldwide and is impacting Indian companies too. The major ideas in this context are: restructuring, reorganisation, reengineering, de-layering, flat structures, and so on. Restructuring and reorganisation refer to changing the organisation structure in line with the changes in the environment and strategies. Reengineering (or business process reengineering) is the fundamental rethinking and radical redesign of business processes to achieve dramatic gains in areas such as cost, quality, service, and speed. De-layering is reducing the number of levels in the organisational hierarchy with a view to facilitate better control and communication within the organisation. Flat structures result due to de-layering. In this manner, organisations attempt to adapt their organisational structures. Some of the changing structural characteristics of organisations are shown in Exhibit 11.8.

Exhibit 11.8 Changes in Contemporary Organisation

Traditional Organisation Design Characteristics	*Emerging Organisation Design Characteristics*
One large firm patterns	Small business units having cooperative relationships
Vertical communication	Horizontal communication patterns
Centralized top-down decision making	Decentralized participative decision making
Vertical integration	Outsourcing and virtual organizations
Work/quality-based teams	Autonomous work teams
Functional work teams	Cross-functional work teams
Minimum training	Extensive training
Individual-focused specialized job design	Value-chain team-focused job design

The above description of the five essential steps, four related issues, and the emerging thought in organisational design are, in fact, a theoretical basis for the creation of structure. It is up to the strategists to use this theoretical foundation and the emerging thought to design an organisational structure that would suit the requirements of a particular strategy. The skills of strategists are put to test when they design an appropriate organisational structure. Again, a more rigorous test is faced when the existing structure has to be changed to suit the requirements of a modified or new strategy. Right at the outset, it must be pointed out that organisation change takes place along two broad dimensions:

- the structural changes; and
- the accompanying behavioural changes.

The first type of change is related to modifications in structural relationships and may entail the creation or disbandment of departments or managerial positions. The second type of change relates to the concomitant behavioural modifications that are essential to absorb the impact of organisation changes. Students of management are quite familiar with the concepts of formal and informal organisations. What we are referring to then in the first and second cases are the formal and informal organisations respectively. While formal organisational changes are mainly administrative in nature and can be brought about by the means of organisational planning and implementation the informal organisation changes are more complex and evolve as a response to formal organisational changes.

An example will serve to illustrate the nature of structural and behavioural changes. An organisation which follows a corporate-level strategy of stability has a simple functional structure in existence. This firm now plans to diversify into a related area and this strategic shift is to be reflected in organisational changes. The choice of structure leads to divisional form of structure where a new division with a few departments is created to support the related product lines. Some of the functions like personnel and finance are retained at the corporate level as centralized departments.

Again, for instance, taking the case of business strategies it can be seen that a firm pursuing a low-cost strategy in a mature, stable business can do with a simple functional structure. If there are some changes required then these can be planned in advance. But if a firm operates in a volatile environment and decides to adopt a differentiation business strategy then a divisional structure could serve its needs better. Like this, the firm can hope to cater to changing customer needs more effectively. Keeping in mind the type of environment faced by a firm at a given time and the strategy that it adopts at the corporate- and business-level, the structural change can be envisaged. But organisational changes go beyond mere structural modifications and encompass the issues of how people would react to the changed situation, how the new relationships would be managed and in what manner would the cohesiveness of the organisation be maintained.

Organisational change is the movement of an organisation away from its present state and towards some desired future state to increase its effectiveness. Even in most stable organisations, change is necessary just to keep the level of given stability. The economic, social and technological environment is so dynamic that without the change that would be adaptive to the changed environment, even the most successful organisations will be left behind, unable to survive in the changed environment. Rapid change is not confined to high technology industries such as computers, software, biotechnology, robotics and so on. Many organisations which were once considered stable such as publishing, retailing, and even hospitals now face the need to adapt to change quickly. Accordingly, management must continuously monitor the outside environment and be sufficiently innovative and creative to find new and better utilisation of organisational resources so that the organisation always maintains its competitive edge. Whether the change involves creativity and innovation within the organisation or simply a response to outside forces which may require organisational realignment, management must be aware of the forces and the need for change. Typically, organisations have little choice but to change. According to Barney and Griffin, the primary reason cited for organisational problems is the failure by managers to properly anticipate or respond to forces for change.

Recent surveys of some major organisations around the world have shown that all successful organisations continuously interact with the environment and make necessary changes in their structural design or philosophy or policies or strategies as the need be. The survey found that 44 per cent of Japanese firms, 59 per cent of American firms, 60 per cent of German firms and 71 per cent of South Korean firms so surveyed had significantly changed their organisational structure between 1989 to 1991.

Adapting to change would mean that the organisations have to learn new technologies, new markets and new ways of managing. In the future, the only truly sustainable source of competitive advantage will be the organisation's ability to change and learn new skills.

Learning organisations are firms that view change as a positive opportunity to learn and create new sources of competitive advantage. Bringing about organisational change that facilitates learning is not an easy task. Since, man follows the path of least resistance, it is easier to employ known methods than to change to new methods where the outcomes may not be as certain. Hence, a change will be easier to make and adjust to, if the potential rewards after the change are sufficiently attractive. Accordingly, senior managers must be sensitive to any such resistance to change from the subordinates and take steps to encourage all constituencies of the organisation to join in and facilitate the needed changes. It must be noted, however, that what the employees resist is not the technical changes which they are generally willing to adopt, but the social changes which are the changes in the human relationships that most often accompany technical changes.As a result, the emphasis must be on reducing the strain that might develop due to changes in these relationships.

11.4.1 Characteristics Enhancing Capabilities to Adaptation to Rapid Change

Some organisations possess characteristics that greatly enhance their capabilities to adapt to rapid change Pitts and Lei have listed six such characteristics as shown in Exhibit 11.9.

1. Frequent Rotation of Managers

Managers usually become emotionally attached to their jobs, especially when they have been on the job for a long time. They become familiar with their work and their environment and they feel comfortable with their strategies and the way they do things. Over time, they develop a tendency to become less accepting of changes such as new strategies, approaches and way of doing things. One way to overcome this hesitation to change on the part of managers is their periodic rotation throughout the firm. This would give them exposure to various activities and experiences and they can appreciate the need for keeping an open mind and not be overly attached to just one activity. Such rotation also promotes the building of interrelationships across divisional and possibly functional lines.

Exhibit 11.9 Characteristics Enhancing Capabilities to Adaptation to Rapid Change

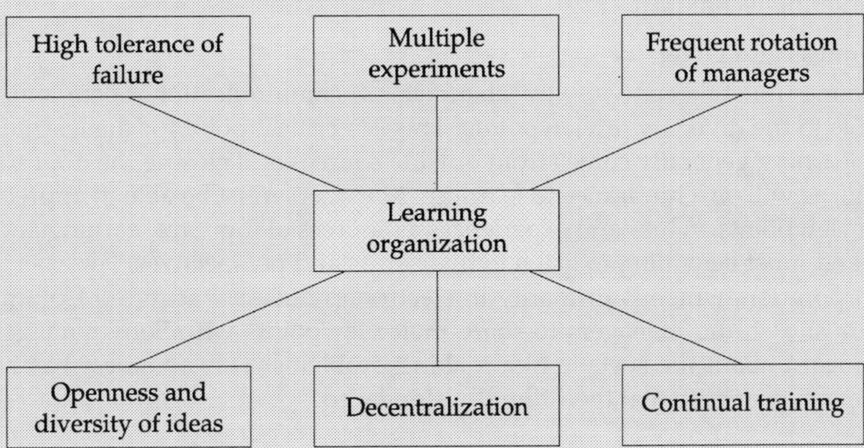

General Motors practices such managerial rotation at their Saturn automobile manufacturing operations. Even employees are rotated through various activities so that not only do they acquire new and different skills in this process, but they also contribute towards an environment of informality and harmony. This results in improvements in the quality of the output.

2. Continual Learning

One reason why employees resist changes is the level of their comfort with their own skills and fear about the outcome of any change. If the organisations have in-house facilities for regular and continuous training and development through which managers and their subordinates can learn new skills, then such resistance to change can be eliminated. Japanese companies put a high premium on internal training programmes and they encourage all employees to learn new skills and technologies. Sony, for example, views these training and development programmes as an ongoing investment for overall continuous improvement in all operations and functions.

3. Decentralization

Decentralization requires that the decision making authority be dispersed by extension and delegation through all levels of management. It tends to create a climate where by taking additional responsibilities and challenges, the organisational members receive executive training for growth and development. This freedom to make decisions gives the workers a feeling of status and recognition and this results in a feeling of dedication, commitment and belonging. This decentralization of authority is also practical because the lower level subordinates are much closer to the points of operations and are in a position to know the problems more quickly and more accurately and hence are more likely to make the right decisions. Such authority encourages innovation, learning and creativity. For example, Johnson and Johnson, a conglomerate of 50 operating divisions, has decentralized all divisions so that each division has the authority to do whatever is needed to succeed in its market. This high degree of decentralization has enabled all business units to become some of the most successful innovators in their products and in their marketing techniques.

4. Openness and Diversity

Management must keep two-way channels of communication open and must be responsive to the diversity of viewpoints. This is a critical point for the learning process because learning generally comes from outside sources and closing the door to new and diverse ideas will be a hindrance to learning. Managers must be able to appreciate other people's viewpoints, values and experiences as sources of input for learning and decision making and must be willing to listen to their ideas and perspectives. For example, when Sony Corporation, which is primarily in electronics business acquired Columbia's film producers and studio managers to share their viewpoints with Sony managers so that they can learn about the specific film making problems. This openness has resulted in solving many problems that their film division faced.

5. High Tolerance of Failure

If managers are punished for their failures, then they will shy away from some good but risky adventures, even if the rewards of success are very high. All innovative projects have always some chances of failure. Fear of failure should not keep innovation under check. Accordingly, the senior management must encourage their subordinates if their projects and efforts are meaningful and reasonable. In successful companies, failures are defined as experiments to learn from and an acceptable part of the learning process and personal growth. A case in point is Sony's development of digital cameras during the 1980s. The buying public was not ready for it and the project failed. Sony did not penalize their managers who were responsible for developing this product, but instead encouraged them to learn from this experience and apply their expertise in designing new products and technologies. Even with this failed product, Sony gained many insights into digital technology which was used into the new versions of many electronic devices such as CDs, VCRs and so on.

6. Multiple Experiments

The dynamics of technological advancements has made the development of new products, in keeping up with technology, much more complex task and process. Sometimes, a number of alternatives need to be pursued simultaneously to determine which one is better. It also makes it unlikely that a superior approach will be overlooked. The cost of running multiple projects should also be taken into consideration. The potential benefits must outweigh any costs involved. Looking at a problem from different angles and viewpoints might result in better solutions. Multiple approaches also encourage people to look at situations differently and expose them to different ways of thinking about and doing things. Sony Company's success with Walkman was a result of experimentation by several project teams which looked into the type of format which would be most desirable by consumers and would also be relatively easy to manufacture.

Many organisations have fully incorporated the characteristics discussed above. These organsiations can adapt quickly to environmental changes and continuously create new sources of competitive advantage.

11.4.2 Learning Organisations

The learning process is undertaken at two different levels. These are lower level learning and higher level learning. The lower level learning is characterized by refinements in the existing beliefs, understandings and organisational processes. On the other hand, the higher level learning involves developing new beliefs, understandings and organisational processes. Both types of learnings are critical to organisational success. Lower level learning is described by one management scholar as exploitation of the known and higher level learning as exploration of the new. Without lower level learning, it will be difficult for organisations to maintain a competitive edge in the existing market. Without higher level learning, the organisations will be so set with their routines that they become vulnerable to competitive forces created by new technologies and new products and services.

Research conducted by Cohen and Leviathan suggests two factors which contribute to the extent of higher level learning. First is the result of "problematic search". In other words, if the established procedures and methodologies fail to deal with problems or crisis effectively, then managers search for new ways to solve such problems and this leads to higher level learning. Similarly, if the activities and operations are not consistent with the aspirations and vision of upper level managers, then they will initiate a problematic search to look for areas which can be further improved.

The second factor that influences higher level learning is known as "absorptive capacity", which has been defined as the ability of the organisations to recognize and understand the value of new developments and absorb these developments in their system and use it for organisational benefit. Thus, organisations monitor their external environments for any developments in emerging technologies and adopt these technologies in the organisation's internal environment.

Some changes are deliberate, initiated by central management, carefully planned and goals oriented. The objectives of the planned change are twofold. First, it seeks to improve the ability of the organisation to adapt to changes in its environment. Second, it seeks to change employee behaviour. Once the need for change and the targets for change have been identified, the following general steps can be taken to implement such changes.

- ***Develop New Goals and Objectives:*** The managers must identify as to what new outcomes they wish to achieve. This may be a modification of previous goals due to change in internal and external environment or it may be a new set of goals and objectives.
- ***Select an Agent for Change:*** The management must decide as to how this change will be brought about. The decision may include inviting outside consultants and specialists who could suggest the various methods to bring in the change and monitor the change process.
- ***Diagnose the Problem:*** It is important to gather all pertinent data regarding the area where change is needed. This data should be critically analyzed to pinpoint the key issues. Then the solutions can be focused on those key issues.
- ***Select Methodology:*** Because of natural resistance to change, it is very important to chart out a methodology for change which would be correct and acceptable to all. Member's emotions must be taken into consideration when devising such methodology.
- ***Develop a Plan:*** This step involves putting together a plan as to what is to be done. For example, if a company wants to develop and implement flextime policy, as to making the hours of work flexible to workers, it must decide as to what type of workers will be affected by it or whether flextime should be given to all members or only to some designated members.
- ***Select a Strategy for Implementation of the Plan:*** In this stage, the management must decide on the "when", "where" and "how" of the plan. This includes the right timing of putting the plan to work, how the plan will be communicated to the workers in order to have the least resistance and how the implementation will be monitored.

- ***Implement the Plan:*** Once the right timing and the right channels of communication have been established, the plan is put into action. It may require briefing sessions or in-house seminars so as to gain acceptance of all the members and specially those who are going to be directly affected by the change.
- ***Receive and Evaluate Feedback:*** Evaluation consists of comparing actual results to the set goals. Feedback will confirm if these goals are being met so that if there is any deviation between the goals and the actual performance outcomes, the corrective measures can be taken.

11.4.3 Developing a Philosophy Towards Change

According to Plunkett and Attner, managers can help create a climate that could be more conducive to change. The following three elements can be taken into account when developing a philosophy towards change.

- **Mutual Trust:** Research studies have shown that trust is the most important factor in creating a in effective and successful organisation. Mutual trust is a strong bond in friendship, in marriage as well as in organisational relationships. It gives great security in times of adversity and in an atmosphere of trust, employees will feel comfortable as the organisation moves through change.
- **Organisational Change:** Organisational learning refers to the ability of the management to integrate new ideas into established systems so that a change for the better can be continuously in effect. There are many ways of doing things, and as such ways are adopted that encourage employees to share ideas and participate as change agents, all members learn to find the best ideas and put these ideas to work.
- **Adaptability:** Adaptability means flexibility rather than rigidity. It means being open to new and different ways of doing things. If the managers are open-minded, responsive to any feasible ideas and recognize that change is beneficial and not threatening, then the organisation can be moulded to accept and promote change.

11.4.4 Change Agents

Change agents are those elements which are responsible for bringing about the change, especially in the individual behaviour patterns. This is the most important type of change since other types of changes such as in strategy, structure or process can always be introduced simply be the management. However, behaviour patterns may have to be modified so that such management induced changes are accepted by the workers. Also, because behaviour is a highly complex phenomenon, it may require a number of strategies to make desirable changes in human behaviour. These change agents may either be the initiators of change or serve as catalysts for such change. Four types of change agents have been identified.

- **Outside Pressures:** These are pressures from te external environment and are directed towards change in the entire organisation. These pressures may be in the form of government intervention, if there are serious quality or safety defects. The government may also get involved if there are labour strikes for long periods of time or mass demonstrations against the organisation. For example, in America, the government has ordered a recall of many types of automobiles when some safety defects have been discovered. Similarly, health inspectors have closed down many restaurants where health and safety violations were discovered in food and cleanliness.

- **Internal Organisational Development:** This can come slowly through and within the organisation itself. This may include redefining of goals as well as participative goal setting. Such development can be achieved through management by objectives (MBO), work redesign, team development and so on.
- **Individual Change:** This change is the modification of behaviour within the individual where personal goals may be better served in the changed environment of the organisation. For example, in a government job, a person who is habitually late coming to work without any obvious repercussions or reprimands, might change his behaviour if the organisation starts taking notice of such tardiness in a negative way.
- **Changes from Central Management:** The organisational changes may come from the top management, who may be convinced about its necessity and may direct structural, strategic or technological changes that would be beneficial to the organisation and its members.

There have been a number of change agents that have been at work in changing the organisational processes and structures in response to environmental challenges. In America, for example, Ralph Nader, a consumer advocate, has been responsible for many changes in the areas of quality and safety of many products and especially in the automobile industry. In addition, such forces as women's liberation movement, strong labour unions and specific federal and state laws and regulations have brought about numerous changes that have affected the work ethics of the organisations and work roles of their members.

Similarly, in India, where the bureaucratic structure is deeply embedded in the organisational system, pressures to give more freedom to the workers, to bring about equal opportunity for employment for all, irrespective of religion or gender and to keep pace with the changing world in technological development and processes.

11.4.5 Managing Resistance to Change

If the changes are to be implemented successfully, they need full acceptance from the employees. The easiest way to get this accepted is the participation of employees in the change effort. Research conducted by Coch and French in a clothing factory indicated that the total participation in the change process resulted in increased productivity. Some of the specific strategies employed in reducing resistance to change are as follows:

- **Shape Political Dynamics:** Accepting and implementing change becomes easier if the management can win the support of the most powerful and influential individuals in the organisation. Doing so builds a critical internal mass of support for change. These influential people could be informal leaders who can influence their followers and these can also be formal leaders such as managers and supervisors. Such endorsement for change by the leaders is an effective way to get others to go along.

- **Participation and Involvement:** A person who is involved in the process of change from the very beginning is more strongly committed to the change than someone who did not participate. The management must recognize this fact. The participation of employees in the process of change should be genuinely wanted by the employers so that they are enthusiastic about it. It should not simply be a mechanical act of calling upon many employees to participate. Participation should be a part of and a result of total treatment of the employees. Thus, once they understand the need for change, they would be less likely to resist it.
- **Communication and Education:** If the employees do not have adequate information or if the information they have is inaccurate, then it is necessary to educate them about the change, its process, its working and its results. This education can be carried out through training classes, meetings and conferences. The reasons for the change must be communicated very clearly and without ambiguity at these meetings and the top management must show considerable emotional sensitivity towards workers. This will help persuade employees about the necessity for change and once persuaded they may even actively seek the change.
- **Reward Constructive Behaviours:** Once successful mechanism to facilitate organisational change is rewarding people for behaving in the desired fashion. This is especially critical during the transition period. For example, employees who are required to learn new skills due to technological changes and learn them well should be praised for their successful efforts and they may also be offered financial incentives.
- **Leadership:** The greater the prestige and the credibility of the manager who is acting as a change agent, the greater will be his influence upon the employees who will be involved in the change process. Accordingly, it is important for the manager to win the confidence of the employees so that they become enthusiastic partners in the process of change.
- **Negotiation and Agreement:** Negotiation and agreement technique is used when costs and benefits must be balanced for the benefit of all concerned parties. This is often used in bargaining with labour unions. It is especially important in situations where the individuals or groups will end up as losers as a result of the change and where such individuals or groups have considerable power to resist.
- **Willingness for the Sake of the Group:** Some individuals may be willing to accept change, even if they are not totally satisfied with it, if the group that they belong to is willing to accept such change. This is especially true about the individuals who have a continuous psychological relationship with the group so that there is sufficient group cohesiveness or group togetherness. Accordingly, management must isolate such groups who have considerable influence upon it members and try to induce the group to involve itself in the change process and accept the necessary change.

These measures can assist considerably in reducing resistance to change. The management must understand that while unilateral use of authority and the power vested with them can sometimes bring change, and it may be necessary to use this power under certain situations, such a change would be highly resented and may be short-lived. For long-term stability of the change process, the management must invite active and willing participation from the employees and share with them the benefits derived from the change.

11.4.6 Change Process

Once the resistance to change has been overcome and the need for change and the objective of such change are established and accepted, the management must introduce the change process in such a manner that such change is more or less permanent and the management does not shift back to the original and more familiar ways of doing things. To make the change more lasting, Kurt Lewin proposed three phases of the change process for moving the organisation from the present to the future. These stages are: unfreezing, changing and refreezing.

1. Unfreezing the Situation

The process of unfreezing simply makes the individuals or organisations aware of the necessity for change and prepares them for such a change. Lewin proposes that the change should not come as a surprise to the members of the organisation. Sudden and unannounced change would be socially destructive and morale lowering. The management must pave the way for the change by first "unfreezing the situation", so that members would be willing and ready to accept the change. This way, if there is any resistance to change, it can be neutralized. According to Schein, unfreezing is the process of breaking down the old attitudes and behaviours, customs and traditions so that they start with a clean slate. This can be achieved by making announcements, holding meetings and promoting the ideas throughout the organisation via bulletin boards, personal contacts and group conferences. One type of message to the members of the organisation, suggested by Kreitner is as follows: We can all improve the effectiveness of our organisation while increasing our personal satisfaction, if we all cooperate in a comprehensive program of finding out where we are, where we want to go and how we can get there.The unfreezing process basically cleans the slate so that it can accept new writings on it which can then become the operational style.

2. Changing to New Situation

Once the unfreezing process has been completed and the members of the organisation recognize the need for change and have been fully prepared to accept such change, their behaviour patterns need to be redefined. H.C.Kellman has proposed three methods for reassigning new patterns of behaviour. These are:

- **Compliance**: Compliance is achieved by strictly enforcing the reward and punishment strategy for good or bad behaviour. Fear of punishment, actual punishment or actual reward seems to change behaviour for the better. For example, many people have stopped smoking because of the warning given by the doctors that smoking causes cancer of the lungs.

- **Identification:** Identification occurs when members are psychologically impressed upon to identify themselves with some given role models whose behaviour they would like to adopt and try to become like them. Many public organisations use celebrities as role models in advising young people not to use drugs.
- **Internalization:** It involves some internal changing of the individual's thought processes in order to adjust to a new environment. Members are left alone to look within themselves and they are given freedom to learn and adopt new behaviour in order to succeed in the new set of circumstances. Sometimes, such soul searching brings about a new dimension to the philosophy of existence and thus brings about changes in such behavioural patterns that are not considered socially, morally or professionally redeeming.

3. Refreezing

Refreezing occurs when the new behaviour becomes a normal way of life. The new behaviour must replace the former behaviour completely for successful and permanent change to take place. Accordingly, in order for the new behaviour to become permanent, it must be continuously reinforced so that this new acquired behaviour does not diminish or extinguish. This must be clearly understood that the change process is not a one-time application but a continuous process due to dynamism and ever changing environment. Accordingly, the process of unfreezing, changing and refreezing is a cyclical one and remains continuously in action.

The implementation of this three-step change model can be seen in the case of kidnapping victims or prisoners of war or deprogramming of some religious cultists. The prisoners of war, for example, may be brainwashed into believing that they are fighting a losing and immoral war and that their perceived enemy is really their friend. This can be done by certain shock treatments which involve these three steps of unfreezing, changing and refreezing process as explained earlier. If these prisoners return back to their own country, the process can be repeated to bring them back to their original behaviour. Another methodology to induce, implement and manage change was also proposed by Kurt Lewin, who named it "force-field analysis" This analysis is based upon the assumption that we are in a state of equilibrium where there is a balance between forces that induce change and forces that resist change. To achieve change we must overcome this status quo. The change forces are known as 'driving forces' and the forces that resist change are known as 'restraining forces' as shown below:

Managers who are trying to implement changes must analyze this balance of driving and restraining forces and then strengthen the driving forces or weaken the restraining forces sufficiently so that the change can take place.

Some of the other strategies pursued by strategic managers to bring about changes are:

Reengineering, Restructuring and *Innovation*. In order to achieve the goal of competitive edge, the organisations may adopt one or more of these strategies.

(i) **Reengineering:** Reengineering is the fundamental and radical redesign of business processes to achieve dramatic improvements in critical, contemporary measures of performance such as cost, quality, service and speed. Reengineering involves complete overhaul of the organisation and strategic managers must completely rethink about the operations and activities of the organisation and focus on business processes rather than on business functions. A business process is any activity that promotes efficiency. It is not the responsibility of any one function but cuts across functions. The primary emphasis of reengineering is on customer satisfaction. The question that strategic managers always keep in focus is "how can we reorganize the way we do our work and our business processes in order to provide the best quality and the lowest-cost goods and services to the customer?" The proper response to this question results in fundamental changes in the business processes. The next question that requires attention is, "how can we now continue to improve our processes and find better ways of managing task and role relationships?

(ii) **Restructuring:** Restructuring involves making changes in the structure of the organisation so that some relationships in the organisation can be combined to make a flat structure and this should improve communication and thus efficiency. This requires eliminating unproductive division as well as some layers of corporate hierarchy. The process of making a flat organisation by reducing the number of managerial levels and divisions is known as downsizing. There are a number of reasons why downsizing becomes necessary. It is possible that the company has grown to be too tall over the years so that the human resources are not optimally utilized. Also a change in economic environment may reduce business activity thus necessitating structural changes. When Jack Smith became the Chief Executive Officer (CEO) of General Motors (GM) in 1992, the company had 22 levels in hierarchy and more than 20,000 corporate managers. Smith quickly moved to restructure the company so that it resulted in 12 hierarchical levels and 10,000 corporate managers.

(iii) **Innovation:** Innovation is a process by which organisations use their skills and resources to create new innovative technologies or new products or new services so that they can better serve the needs of the customers. Without such innovation, organisations will be left behind. The new more powerful laptop computers are the result of technological innovation. Innovation can result in spectacular success for an organisation. For example, Apple Computer brought in a revolution in computer industry when it introduced a personal computer (PC). Similarly, Honda made inroads in American economy by introducing a 50-cc motor cycle and at one time it controlled 80 per cent of the market. Mary Kay Cosmetics developed a new way of serving customers by going to customers rather than customers coming to the cosmetic outlets. Of all the strategies employed by strategic managers to bring about change, innovation is the most involved, and has the prospects for the greatest long-term success. Not all innovations are successful and hence, and cost and benefit study should be conducted before commercializing the innovation.

Resistance to change can be considered the single greatest threat to successful strategy implementation. Resistance in the form of sabotaging production machines, absenteeism, filing unfounded grievances, and an unwillingness to cooperate regularly occurs in organisations. People often resist strategy implementation because they do not understand what is happening or why changes are taking place. In that case employees may simply need accurate information. Successful strategy implementation hinges upon managers ability to develop an organisational climate conducive to change. Change must be viewed as an opportunity rather as a threat by managers and employees.

Resistance to change can emerge at any stage or level of the strategy-implementation process. Although there are various approaches for implementing changes, three commonly used strategies are:

- **Force change strategy:** A force change strategy involves giving orders and enforcing those order; this strategy has the advantage of being fast, but it is plagued by low commitment and high resistance.
- **Educative change strategy:** The educative change strategy is one that presents information to convince people of the need for change; the disadvantage of an educative change strategy is that implementation becomes slow and difficult. However, this type of strategy evokes greater commitment and less resistance than does the force strategy.
- **Rational or self-interest change strategy:** Finally, a rational or self-interest change strategy is one that attempts to convince individuals that the change is to their personal advantage. When this appeal is successful, strategy implementation can be relatively easy. However, implementation changes are seldom to everyone's advantage.

The rational change strategy is the most desirable, so this approach is examined a bit further. Managers can improve the likelihood of successfully implementing change by carefully designing change efforts. Jack Duncan describe a rational or self-interest change strategy as consisting of four steps.

- First, employees are invited to participate in the process of change and the details of transition; participation allows everyone to give opinions, to feel a part of the change process, and to identify their own self-interests regarding the recommended change.
- Second, some motivation or incentive to change is required; self-interest can be the most important motivator.
- Third, communication is needed so that people can understand the purpose for the changes.
- Fourth, giving and receiving feedback is that; everyone enjoys knowing how things are going and how much progress is being made.

Igor Ansoff summarizes the need for strategists to manage resistance to change as follows:

Observation of the historical transitions from one orientation to another shows that, if left unmanaged, the process becomes conflict-laden, prolonged, and costly in both human and financial terms. Management of resistance involves anticipating the focus of resistance and its intensity. Second, it involves eliminating unnecessary resistance caused by misperceptions and insecurities. Third, it involves planning the process of change. Finally, it involves monitoring and controlling resistance during the process of change. Due to diverse external and internal forces, change is a fact of life in organisations.

The rate, speed, magnitude, and direction of changes vary over time by industry and organisation. Strategists should strive to create a work environment in which change is recognized as necessary and beneficial so that individuals can adapt to change more easily. Adapting a strategic-management approach to decision making can itself require major changes in the philosophy and operations of a firm.

Strategists can take a number of positive actions to minimize managers and employees resistance to change. For example, individuals who will be affected by a change should be involved in the decision to make the change and in decisions about how to implement change. Strategists should anticipate changes and develop and offer training and development workshops so managers and employees can adapt to those changes. They also need to communicate the need for changes effectively. The strategic-management process can be described as a process of managing change. Robert Waterman describes how successful (renewal) organisations involve individuals to facilitate change. Implementation starts with, not after, the decision. When Ford Motor Company embarked on the programme to build the highly successful Taurus, management gave up the usual, sequential design process. Instead they showed the tentative design to the workforce and asked their help in devising a car that would be easy to build. Team Taurus came up with no less than 1401 items suggested by Ford employees. What a contrast from the secrecy that characterized the industry before! When people are treated as the main engine rather than interchangeable parts, motivation, creativity, quality, and commitment to implementation go up.

Exercise

1. Discuss the major structure that could be used in creating an organisational structure. Write the advantages and disadvantages of each type of structure from the strategy implementation viewpoint.
2. What are the emerging forms of organisational structures. How are they suitable for the competitive nature of business environment?
3. The purpose of organisation structure is to fit the requirements of strategies implementation. Comment.
4. Explain the importance of the McKinsey 7S framework for effective strategy implementation.
5. Which organisation structure is suitable for an organisation? What factors must be considered for choosing a particular organisation structure?
6. What are important characteristic enhancing capabilities which help in adapting to change in an organisation? Explain their importance.
7. Learning organisations are those which adapts to change and remain competitive. Explain the concept of learning organisation and how is it suitable to the competitive environment.
8. What are the change agents? How do they help in adapting the organisation to changes?
9. How organisation can manage resistance to change?
10. Explain the change process and its elements and how they are interlinked with each other.

12 Behavioural Implementation

12.1 INTRODUCTION

It is important to emphasize that culture, values, and leadership, jointly and severally, significantly influence the shaping of corporate strategies. The culture of an organisation is reflected in the way that people in the organisation perform tasks, set objectives, and administer resources to achieve them, and is in its turn strongly influenced, if not moulded by the values originating largely from national history, tradition, and ethos. It is universally recognized that the more successful organisations are those that are well led rather than those that are only well managed. Perhaps the most essential quality of a leader is his vision reflected in the mission of the organisation. A successful leader is however, endowed with the capacity to convert that vision into the mission and goal of the organisation and lead the organisation to the achievement of its goals. For sustained success of the organisation, however, this vision needs to be transmitted to become the abiding core values and culture of organisation.

Objectives tend to emerge as the wishes of the most dominant coalition, usually the management of the organisation, although there are notable exceptions. However, in pursuing these objectives the dominant group is very strongly influenced by its reading of the political situation (i.e., the perception of the power structure). For example, they are likely to set aside some of the expectations in order to improve the opportunities of achieving others. Special reference must be made to the power of shareholders. Some of them have a short-term viewpoint being basically interested in quick return. Others have a long-term view and also look for growth in the value of the shares. With the evolution and development of a professional managerial class the direct intervention of shareholders has become much less frequent. They tend to remain quiescent so long as their expectations are at least moderately met. If, however, they perceive or are made to perceive any threat to these prospects or are reasonably convinced of a better return under an alternative management, their intervention is immediate and decisive.

12.2 GENERAL INFLUENCE ON INDIVIDUALS AND GROUPS

These are perhaps best encapsulated as in Exhibit 12.1. When analyzing the significance of these factors on the strategic development of any organisation, it is useful to ask the following questions:

- Which factors within and outside the organisation have the most influence on the expectations of groups and individuals within it?
- To what extent do the current strategies reflect the influence of any one of a combination of these factors?
- How far would these factors help or hinder changes that would be necessary to pursue new strategic?

Exhibit 12.1 Influence on Individuals and Groups

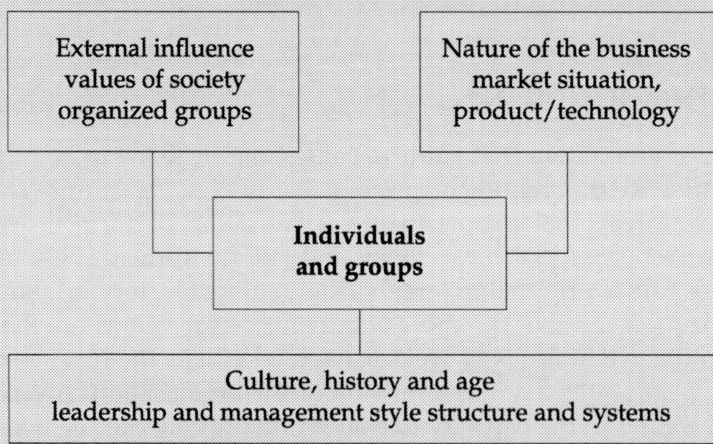

12.2.1 Values of Society

Attitudes to work, authority, equality, and a whole range of other important issues are constantly shaped and changed by society at large. From the point of view of corporate strategy it is important to understand this process for two reasons:

- The values of society change over time and corporate strategies need to be adapted accordingly.
- Companies that operate internationally would have the added problem of having to cope with very different standards and expectations across countries.

We can quote two examples to strengthen this viewpoint:

Hofstede has undertaken extensive research into how national culture influences employee motivation, management styles, and organisational structures. He concludes that individual countries are markedly different from one another.

Terry, in his study of influence of British culture on the performance of managers concludes that the biggest single advantage of the British is that they do not palm when things get rough. On the other hand, their identifiable traits are insularity, chauvinism, and a low regard for professionalism in business.

12.2.2 Organized Groups

Individuals often owe allegiance to other groups such as trade association and professional bodies, which greatly influence their attitudes. Consequently, very often this professional staff has a strong "professional view" of its role which may not be in accordance with the managerial view of how it can best be used as a resource. At the corporate level, the entire organisational ethos of the company may be influenced by its membership of a trade association or similar body. These bodies may exert influence informally, but often seek to impose norms of behaviour on member companies through the development of "codes of conduct". At the international level, the Organisation of Petroleum Exporting Countries (OPEC) is an example. In India we have AIMA, CII, ASSOCHAM and Chambers of Commerce of different states/area who have developed their own "codes of conduct" for their members.

12.2.3 Nature of the Business

In the case of business, issues such as market situation and the nature of product/ technology within the company influence attitudes to company policy.

12.2.4 Market Situation

Different companies face quite different market conditions and any one company will face different conditions over time. Consequently, the attitude of people within the company will also change, often quite markedly, as external conditions change. Policy decisions that can be made in companies facing a highly competitive and depressed market will meet with considerable resistance in other companies facing less stringent conditions.

People are also influenced by the position of the company in relation to the life cycle of its products and market. People who have only known a company during a period of rapid growth may have developed expectations that are inappropriate when its product enters the stage of maturity.

12.3 LEADERSHIP IMPLEMENTATION

The role of appropriate leadership in strategic success is highly significant. It has repeatedly been observed that leadership plays a critical role in the success and failure of an enterprise and it has been considered one of the most important elements affecting organisational performance. For the manager, leadership is the focus of activity through which the goals and objectives of the organisation are accomplished. While dealing with the role of strategists we learnt about the roles that different strategists play in strategic management. In particular, the role of chief executives as organisational leaders was discussed with a view to highlight the importance that is accorded to them since they are the most important of all strategists. Here, we discuss the leadership role that is assigned to strategists in general. We start with a review of the leadership theories and what lessons can be drawn from them for the purpose of strategy implementation.

12.3.1 Theoretical Understanding of Leadership

Leadership has been studied and researched for a number of years, resulting in numerous theories and models. No universally accepted theoretical framework has as yet been developed. However, enough is already known to be able to understand the various factors that affect the content and process of leadership. Exhibit 12.2 presents an overview of leadership's theory through the different evolutionary eras and the emphasis placed on it in each era. It should, however, be noted that the eras are not chronological but have been set in terms of the similarity of approach adopted by several theorists. Thus, an era represents a group of leadership theories all of which adopt a similar approach. King points out that the future development of leadership theory may be based on an integrated approach. Alber S King traces the historical development of leadership theories and identifies nine evolutionary eras, each focusing on a specific theme of leadership.

Exhibit 12.2 Theory and Practice of Leadership

Era	*Focus on*
1. Personality	Traits and qualities, and great personalities
2. Influence	Relationship between individuals
3. Behaviour	Actions of leaders
4. Situation	Situations in which the leader operates
5. Contingency	Dependence on behaviour, personality influence exerted by the leader on subordinates, and situations
6. Transactional	Role-differentiation and social interaction between the leader and subordinates
7. Anti-leadership	Absence of a real concept of leadership
8. Culture	Culture of the entire organisation
9. Transformational	Use of influence to create intrinsic motivation

The tenth era, which King terms as the integrative era, may probably focus on an integration of the different approaches. The evolutionary eras, as classified by King, bring into clear focus the changing emphasis of different theories of leadership. A greater understanding of the phenomenon of leadership may come through the integration of the different approaches in future.

Sziglayi and Wallace have proposed an integrative model of leadership based on three different theoretical approaches of leadership: trait (or personality), behavioural, and situational theories. Their integrative model of leadership includes four factors on the basis of which behavioural scientists and prastising managers can attempt to understand the phenomenon of leadership. These four factors are:

- The leader (individual characteristics, leadership style, dimension and reinforcing power).
- The subordinate (individual characteristics, and perception).
- The situation (nature of task, nature of group, organisational factors, sources of influence other than the leader).
- The performance outcomes.

From the above, it can be seen that leadership has proved to be an elusive concept. Yet, the different attempts at explaining the phenomenon of leadership have increased our understanding of the issue and provided significant insights into its complexities. Several conclusions can be drawn from theory regarding the manner in which leadership could be implemented by strategists. On the basis of its present state of knowledge, it can be said that the leader must:

- Develop new qualities to perform effectively.
- Be a visionary, willing to take risks, and be highly adaptable to change.
- Exemplify the values, goals, and culture of the organisation, and be aware of the environmental factors affecting the organisation.
- Pay attention to strategic thinking and intellectual activities.
- Adopt a collective view of leadership in which the leaders influence is dispersed across all levels of the organisation.
- Lead by empowering others and place an increasing emphasis on statesmanship.
- Adopt a new perspective on power to build subordinates' skills and confidence to make them agents of change.
- Create leadership at lower levels and facilitate the transformation of followers into leaders.
- Delegate authority and place emphasis on innovation.

12.3.2 Qualities and Skills for Effective Leadership

- A vision, articulated through the culture and value systems.
- The ability to build and control an effective team of managers.
- The ability to recognize and synthesize important developments, both within and outside the organisation. Requires strategic awareness, the ability to judge the significance of an observed event, and conceptualization skills.
- Effective decentralization, delegation and motivation.
- Credibility and competence: knowing what you are doing and having this recognized. Requires the ability to exercise power and influence and to create change.
- Implementation skills: getting things done, requires drive, decisiveness, and dynamism.
- Perseverance and persistence in pursuing the mission or vision, plus mental and physical stamina.

The leader should have some entrepreneurial qualities which takes the form of:

i. Expansion of the concept of vision.
ii. Differentiation between leadership and management.
iii. Expansion on certain other requirements of leadership.

12.3.3 Vision

The leader's vision which gives point to the work of others should have the following attributes. The vision must be different. A plan or a strategy which is a projection of the present or a replica of what everyone else is doing is not vision. A vision should:

- Reform the known scene.
- Reconceptualize the obvious,
- Connect previously unconnected dreams.
- He or she must only believe in it but must be seen to believe in it. The leader must remember that the vision remains a dream without the work of others.

12.3.4 Difference Between Leadership and Management

- Management is all about coping with complexity. Its practices and procedures are largely a response to the emergence of large organisations. Without good management, complex enterprises tend to become chaotic in ways that threaten their very existence. Leadership, by contrast, is about coping with change and determining directions.
- Companies manage complexity first by planning and budgeting: setting targets or goals for the (near) future (typically for the next month or year), establishing detailed steps for achieving these targets, and then allocating resources to accomplish them. By contrast, leading an organisation to constructive change begins by setting a direction: developing a vision of the future (often the distant future) along with strategies to initiate the changes needed to achieve that vision.
- Management develops the capacity to achieve its plan by organizing and staffing, and in effect aligning people. Management ensures plan accomplishment by controlling and problem solving.
- Monitoring results in relation to the plan in some detail, both formally and informally, by means of reports, meetings, and other tools; identifying deviations. For leadership, however, achieving a vision involves motivation and inspiration, and thereby keeping people moving in the right direction, despite major obstacles to change, by appealing to basic but often untapped human needs, values and emotions.

One of the major attributes of leadership is an attitude biased in favour of risk taking when oriented towards growth and success. This is particularly important as it implies a clear distinction between a first generation entrepreneurial strategic leader and a professional manager as chief executive. A first generation entrepreneurial strategic leader usually has personal values biased towards growth-oriented risk taking, and an ability to imprint his personal values and motivations on the organisation. As the company grows older, its strategic leadership is taken over by professional managers whose culture and values are oriented towards managerial bureaucracy and its characteristic, comparatively negative attitude towards risk and innovation. This is amply evident in the recent history of Ford and General Motors. Chrysler, in comparison, demonstrates entrepreneurship and dynamism as it was reborn and, in consequence, has a 'younger top management'.

As a company grows older and takes on the role of a historical firm rather than an emerging one, however, the role of providing strategic leadership shifts to the general management and shareholders and, the founder entrepreneur often finds his personal vision and goals at variance with those of the organisation and finds himself pushed by the wayside.

This also marks a clear distinction between Japanese strategic leadership and that of the West, in particular the USA. Most Japanese industrial organisations still have their first generation entrepreneurs as CEOs who have successfully imprinted their personal values and attitudes on the organisations concerned and been able to impart sustained dynamism to them. The significant difference between Japanese and Western leadership is, however, elsewhere. Generally speaking, Japanese firms do not have individual leadership but group leadership. What is important is how individual followership is transformed into group leadership and through this organisational process individual passiveness is transformed into collective dynamism. We cannot induce a dynamic and innovative set of organisational decision sets from a simple aggregation of a set of non-innovative and reserved individual decision codes. What is required is some form of quality transformation process, in turn, requiring an organisational device to effect it, so that the passive decision codes of individual members can be changed into active codes of the firm.

Exhibit 12.3 The Transformation of Decision Codes

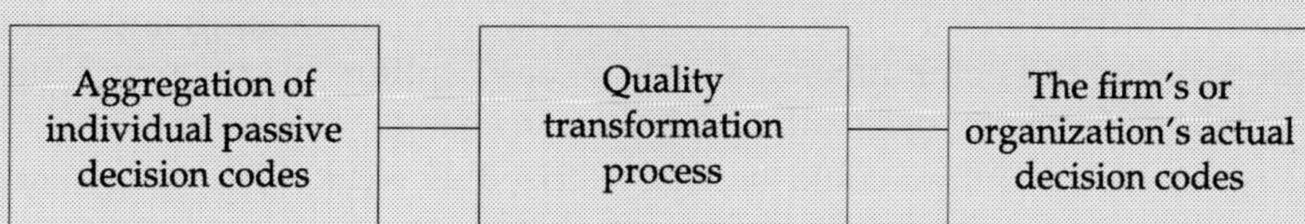

The most significant aspect of Japanese strategic leadership is the development and use of this transformation device. This is reflected in a chain of leadership based on merit in apparent contradiction to the concept of seniority embedded in the Japanese management system. The Japanese reward system has two distinct characteristic. While respect for seniority remains undisturbed as does lifetime employment as the backdrop, there is a bifurcation at senior levels. Those with requisite merit are promoted within the organisation and those lacking it are diverted out of the organisation into subsidiaries or supplier organisations under the firm's umbrella. It is only a transient phenomenon and is likely to go the Western way.

12.4 CORPORATE CULTURE

The phenomenon which often distinguishes good organisations from bad ones is the "corporate culture". The well-managed organisations apparently have distinctive cultures that are, in some way, responsible for their ability to successfully implement strategies. Every organisation has a culture (which may include several subcultures) that exerts powerful influences on the behaviour of managers. Corporate or organisational culture is the set of important assumptions – often unstated that members of an organisation share in common. There are two major assumptions in common: beliefs and values. Beliefs are assumptions about reality, derived and reinforced by experience. Values are assumptions about ideals that are derived and worth striving for. When beliefs and values are shared in an organisation, they create a corporate culture.

The manifestation of corporate culture in an organisation is evident in:

- shared things (e.g., the way people dress)
- shared sayings (e.g., lets get down to work)
- shared actions (e.g., a service-oriented approach)
- shared feelings (e.g., hard work is not rewarded here)

These shared assumptions can help to decipher the composition of the corporate culture of any organisation.

12.4.1 Impact of Culture on Corporate Life

The fact that organisations may have a strong or weak culture affects their ability to perform strategic management. Culture affects not only the way managers behave within an organisation but also the decisions they make about the organisation's relationships with its environment and its strategy. Culture can be a strength as well as a weakness. As strength, culture can facilitate communication, decision-making and control, and create cooperation and commitment. As a weakness, culture may obstruct the smooth implementation of strategy by creating resistance to change.

An organisation's culture could be characterized as weak when many subcultures exist, few values and behavioural norms are shared, and traditions are rare. In such organisations, employees do not have a sense of commitment, loyalty, and a sense of identity. Rather than being members of organisation these are wage-earners. There are several traits exhibited by organisations that have a weak or unhealthy culture. Some of these are: politicized organisational environment, hostility to change, promoting bureaucracy in preference to creativity and entrepreneurship, and unwillingness to look outside the organisation for best practices.

An organisation's culture could be strong and cohesive when it conducts its business according to a clear and explicit set of principles and values, which the management devotes considerable time to communicating to employees, and which values are shared widely across the organisation. There are three factors that seem to contribute to the building up of a strong culture. These are:

- a founder or an influential leader who established desirable values;
- a sincere and dedicated commitment to operate the business of the organisation according to these desirable values; and
- a genuine concern for the well-being of the organisation's stakeholders.

Exhibit 12.4 illustrates how corporate culture in two different groups – multinational subsidiaries and professionally-managed companies versus family businesses and non-resident Indian's companies may create a different impact on an organisation. While the views expressed in this exhibit are decidedly in favour of family business and non-resident Indian's companies, there is no doubt that in each sector of industry, the management style and corporate culture is distinctive. What is more appropriate to say is that Indian organisations, particularly family businesses, seem to be in a ferment now, and that companies known for their conservatism and traditional orientation have to now shift over to a more open and participative corporate culture if they have to maintain progress.

S K Bhattacharya has analyzed the major difference in multinational subsidiaries and professionally managed companies on the one hand, compared to family business and non-resident Indian's companies on the other, with regard to corporate culture.

Having discussed that constitutes corporate culture and how it affects corporate life, it is important to understand its relationship with strategy. Since each strategy creates its own unique set of managerial tasks, strategy implementation has to consider the behavioural aspects and ensure that these tasks are performed in an efficient and effective manner. Managerial behaviour arising out of corporate culture can either facilitate or obstruct the smooth implementation of strategy. The basic question before strategists, therefore, is how to create a strategy-supportive corporate culture. In other words a major role of the leadership within an organisation is to create an appropriate strategy-culture fit.

12.4.2 Approaches to Create a Strategy Supportive Culture

1. **To ignore corporate culture:** The first approach may be followed when it is nearly impossible to change culture. This is advisable because it is really difficult to change a nebulous phenomenon such as corporate culture. Besides, cultural changes, when enforced in a short duration, may be traumatic for members of an organisation.
2. **To adapt strategy implementation to suit corporate culture:** It is easier to change implementation to suit the requirements of corporate culture. This is possible because the behavioural aspects of implementation offer a range of flexible alternatives to strategists in terms of structure, systems of corporate culture. However, each situation in the organisation would call for an innovative solution and would test the capabilities of managers as strategists.
3. **To change the corporate culture to suit strategic requirements:** As said earlier, it is extremely difficult to change corporate culture. But in some cases it may be imperative. For instance, the post-liberalization spate of takeovers and acquisitions in the Indian industry led to a situation where many erstwhile multinational subsidiaries were taken over by family business groups. This led to a process

Exhibit 12.4 Impact of Culture on Two Different Groups of Organisations

Dimensions of Corporate Culture	*Multinational subsidiaries and professionally managed companies*	*Family business and NRI's companies*
1. Nature of desired managerial skills and capabilities	Emphasis on professional qualifications and rank	Emphasis on demonstrated skills, depth, and quality of knowledge
2. Actual performance or results achieved	Emphasis on seniority, conformity to organisational values, loyalty, and a relative fit between desired managerial behaviour and position in hierarchy	Emphasis on originality of action and thinking, innovation, and upgradation of knowledge and skills by personal efforts
3. Managerial style of planning and decision making	Emphasis on information gathering, bureaucratic mode of functioning, risk-aversion, and non-entrepreneurial decision making	Emphasis on selective information usage, and intuitive and qualitative decision making of an entrepreneurial nature
4. Management systems adopted	Emphasis on the use of elegant, sophisticated and rational systems which degenerate due to low usage	Emphasis on reliance on business sense and no-frills systems geared to quick action
5. Nature of management control	Emphasis on comprehensive, formal, and written reporting, and rationalization of failures rather than resolution of problems	Emphasis on primary use of verbal reporting and remedial action

often prolonged and painful of cultural transition. But such a transition may be brought about by a careful understanding of the existing culture, making strategic tasks explicit, assessing risks of cultural change, enhancing managerial capability to imbibe changes, and, most importantly, exhibiting a strong, assertive leadership.

4. **To change the strategy to fit the corporate culture:** Rather than changing culture to suit strategy, it is better and more economical to consider the cultural dimension while formulating strategy in the first place. One of the important factors is commitment to past strategic actions which should take care that strategic changes are not drastic but incremental, allowing the cultural ripple

effects to settle down to create a more conducive environment for strategy implementation. However, if an impregnable cultural barrier is faced after strategy implementation, it may be better to abandon the strategy or use a combination of the above three approaches.

It is important to realize that an understanding of the process of policy-making in an organisation cannot be achieved without paying attention to the issue of organisational culture. It is equally important when analyzing the strategic position of an organisation to assess how this culture has influenced the development of the organisation and the strategies it has pursued. A useful analysis of culture can be achieved by examining the cultural web of factors within an organisation that preserve and sustain commonly held core beliefs. An examination of the recipe is important for two reasons:

- It provides a background against which an assessment of future strategic choices can be made, both in relation to options that may be open within the current recipe and for those requiring more significant change.
- Where the recipe would need to be changed to provide a background against which to assess how change might be achieved.

While different facets of the cultural web will be discussed in order to build up an analysis of the influence of culture on strategy, it must be remembered that it is the subtle interrelationship between these various facets that is of greatest importance. The impact of the cultural web on an organisation can be analyzed by looking at the issues depicted in Exhibit 12.5.

Stories, rituals, and symbolic behaviour in organisations provide valuable insight into the organisation's core beliefs. These factors are a product of the history and age of the organisation since they come into being and develop over time through the experiences of individuals and groups undertaking the day-to-day tasks. The stories and myths distil the essence of the company's past strategies, legitimize the behavioural pattern of individuals and groups currently within the organisation and the attitude of outsiders towards it.

It is an oft-repeated and confirmed observation that the way companies are organized and managed has a strong relationship with the era in which that particular industry had its origins. History and tradition can be a considerable problem where culture has developed in a way that threatens the survival of the organisation in the light of a changing environment-such as new technologies or competitors. This is of particular significance to India and other developing countries.

12.4.3 Strategy Formulation as a Cultural Process

In the context of the role of the cultural web, it is perhaps useful and necessary to discuss strategy formulation as a cultural process in some detail. It is too simplistic to think of strategy as a response to the environment, for it is evident that faced with similar environments, organisations will respond differently. This response is likely to be influenced by the past experience of managers and by the wider social and political processes in the organisation. It is this social and cultural process that needs to be clearly

Exhibit 12.5 Analysing the Impact of the Cultural Web on Strategy

Aspects of the cultural web	*Some useful questions*
Stories and myths	1. What core beliefs do the stories reflect? 2. How strongly held are these beliefs with power holders? 3. How pervasive are the beliefs (through the levels)? 4. How do beliefs relate to strengths and weaknesses? 5. How are the heroes? 6. Do the heroes conform to, or challenge the beliefs?
Rituals and symbols	1. What behaviour is expected and rewarded (e.g., risk taking)? 2. What language is used to describe the organization and its activities? 3. What is the dominant attitude towards each stakeholder group?
Leadership and management style	1. What are the core beliefs of the leadership? 2. Which aspects are stressed in public (e.g., annual reports)? 3. How do they regard structures (e.g., centralists or devolutionists)? 4. What type of strategy is favoured (e.g., defensive or speculative)? 5. What attributes are sought in new recruits?
Structure and systems	1. Do structures/systems encourage collaboration or competition? 2. Which aspects of strategy are most closely monitored and controlled?

understood and appreciated. By "organisational culture" we mean the deeper level of basic assumptions and beliefs, that are shared by members of an organisation. Often it manifests itself through organisational symbols, such as logos, organisation charts, status symbols, policies, rewards and incentive, and the like, in short, "the way we do things here".

12.4.4 The Recipe and the Cultural Web

The set of beliefs and assumptions which forms part of the culture of an organisation has variously been called interpretative schemes, paradigms, and recipes. The recipe is a set of beliefs and assumptions held relatively commonly throughout the organisation that is taken for granted within, that is, organisation but is discernible to the external observer. The recipe makes sense of the situation in which managers find themselves and provides a basis for formulation of strategy. This process is shown in Exhibit 12.6.

Exhibit 12.6 The Role of the Recipe in Strategy Formulation

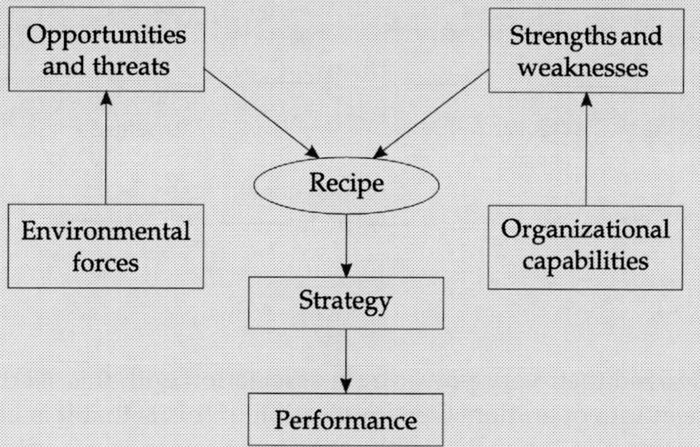

The relationship and distinction between the recipe and organisational strategy need to be clarified. Environmental forces and organisational capabilities do not in themselves create organisational strategy, it is people who create strategy. The mechanism by which this is done is the recipe. The forces at work in the environment, and the organisation's capabilities in coping with these, are made sense of through the assumptions and beliefs called the recipe and on the basis of this strategy is formulated. The strategies that managers advocate and those that emerge through the social and political processes are then typically configured within the bounds of this recipe. However, environmental forces and organisational capabilities, whilst having this direct influence on strategy formulations, nevertheless do impact much more directly on organisational performance. It is, however, necessary to distinguish between actual influence and managerial perception of influence on the organisation. Lack of attention to this difference can give rise to significant problems.

The recipe may, thus be a very conservative influence or strategy, and particularly since the links between the recipe itself and the way things are done in the organisation are likely to be close. This is illustrated Exhibit. 12.7.

Thus, for example, the links between the power structure in the organisation and the core set of beliefs held by mangers in that organisation are likely to be strong. The recipe represents the "formula for success" which is taken for granted in the business and likely to have grown up over years. The most powerful groupings within the business are

Exhibit 12.7 The Cultural Web of an Organisation

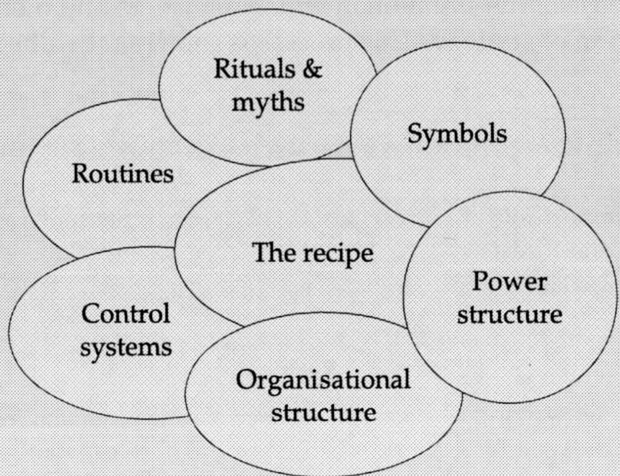

likely to have derived their very power from association with this set of beliefs and their ability to put them into operation. One implication of this is that it is likely that a purely analytical questioning of the recipe will not only be taken as evidence of the analyst's lack of understanding of the problems of the business but may actually be perceived as a political threat, rather than objective analysis, for it will very likely be perceived as an attack on those most associated with such core beliefs, even if the managers, may be more influenced by the recipe and its cultural underpinnings in formulating, persisting with, and adjusting strategy. The recipe is also likely to be associated with control systems, routines, and rituals of the organisation that will tend to preserve the status quo. The point is that the recipe is not just a set of beliefs and assumptions, rather it is embedded in a organisation's specific cultural web that legitimizes and preserves the assumptions and beliefs in the organisation.

12.4.5 A Cultural View of Patterns of Strategic Change

Faced with pressures for change, consequent upon buffeting through environmental changes, managers are likely to deal with the situation in ways that protect the recipe from challenge. This raises difficulties when managing strategic change, particularly when the action required falls outside the ambit of the current recipe and the constraints of the cultural web, that is, managers would have to change their core beliefs substantially. When necessary, such drastic changes may be desirable, but do not occur easily. Managers are more likely to attempt to deal with the situation by searching for what they understand and deal with in terms of the existing recipe. Faced with stimulus for action, say declining performance, managers first seek for means of improving the implementation of existing strategy. This could be through a tightening of controls. If this is not effective, then a change of strategy may occur, but still a change which is in line with the existing recipe. Thus, for instance, managers may seek to extend the market for their product but retain the same views about the range of products, the principal virtues of the product, the nature of what remains as their main markets, and how they should go about operating in these markets. There is still no change in recipe and such changes are unlikely until this attempt at reconstructing the strategy of keeping the recipe intact also fails. Change of recipe is usually the last resort and perhaps is automatically accompanied by changes in strategy and methods of control.

This is but an alternative picture of instrumentalism and an almost certain conseq-uence is the strategic drift occurring where strategy lags environmental change to lesser or greater degree. Under usual conditions of evolutionary strategic change, this drift may not be disastrous and can usually be made up. In cases of environmental discontinuity, however, as has been already discussed and we appear to be currently facing such drift may be akin to disaster and incrementalism is simply inadequate. This chapter argues that managers would have to accept the need for urgent change in recipe if necessary, entailing a tremendous cultural shift. This is perhaps the greatest challenge facing the management today.

12.4.6 Personal Values and Business Ethics

Only personal values and a sense of business ethics can help a strategist to distinguish between moral and amoral use of politics and power as a means to attain organisational goals. What are personal values and business ethics? Why and how are they important? What is the relation of values and ethics to strategy?

Personal values refer to a conception of what an individual or groups regard as desirable. A value is a view of life and a judgment of what is desirable which very much a part is of a person's personality and a group's morale. Thus, attitude to labour welfare is a value which may prompt an industrialist to do much more for workers than the labour laws stipulate. Service-mindedness is a value, which when cherished in an organisation, manifests in better customer satisfaction. Personal values are imbibed from parents, teachers, and elders, and as an individual grows, values are adapted and refined in the light of new knowledge and experiences. Within organisations, values are imparted by the founder-entrepreneur or a dominant chief executive, and these remain in some form a long time after that person is not there. J. R. D Tata, the previous chairman of the Tata group, when asked to define the House of Tata and what links the different Tata companies together said "I would call it a group of individually-managed companies united by two factors. First, a feeling that they are part of a larger group which carries the name and prestige of Tatas, and public recognition of honesty, reliability and trustworthiness. The other reason is more metaphysical. There is an innate loyalty, a sharing of certain beliefs. We all feel a certain pride that we are somewhat different from others". The several values that J R D Tata refers to have been derived from the ideals of J N Tata, the founder of the Tata group.

Business ethics is the study of how personal moral norms apply to activities and goals of a commercial enterprise. It is not a separate moral standard, but the study of how the business context poses its own unique problems for the moral person who acts as the agent of this system. Practically, business ethics operates as a system of values and is concerned primarily with the relationship of business goals and techniques to specifically human ends. Specifically, human ends means viewing the needs and aspirations of individuals not merely as individuals but as a part of society. It also means realization of the personal dignity of human beings.

A major task of leadership is to inculcate personal values and impart a sense of business ethics to the organisational members. At one end, values and ethics shape the corporate culture and dictate the way how politics and power will be used and, at the other end, clarify the social responsibility of the organisation. The twin issues of personal values and business ethics have come to occupy centre stage in management. There is an increasing awareness around the world about ethical practices in business. International organisations such as the World Bank and IMF are concerned about whether the aid provided by them is used for the intended purposes and not frittered away by corrupt government officials. "Transparency International" brings out an annual rating of countries on an index of corruption that serves as a guideline for foreign investors and international donor agencies. Within India, there are significant social, cultural, political, technological, and economic factors affecting personal values and business ethics within industry.

Corporate governance has attracted worldwide attention as a means to induce ethical behaviour in business. A typical dilemma faced by strategists is to somehow reconcile the pragmatic demands of work (which often degenerate to a distortion of values and unethical business practices to the call of the "inner voice" which somehow prevents them from using unethical means for achieving organisational goals. This dilemma stems from the fact that apparently the value system of the organisation has already been contaminated beyond redemption. Some analysts attribute this to the acceptable transition of a developing society where social mechanisms have become obsolete.

Corruption in industry, which is a major by-product of the degradation of value and ethics, is also related to the inability of industry to stand up to the discretionary powers of a regulatory system designed and administered by an unholy alliance of bureaucrats and politicians. But repeated observations have shown that organisations that have an explicit belief in, and recognition of, besides other values — the importance of economic growth and profits are driven by values rather than avarice. It has been possible for Indian companies such as Asian Paints, Bajaj Auto, ICICI, Infosys, and Amul to excel on the basis of superordinate goals, i.e., a set of values and aspirations and corporate culture. Strategists, therefore, have to provide the right values and ethical sense to the organisations they manage. Exhibit 12.8 provides material on which to determine the "rightness" of values and ethics based on Indian psycho-philosophical thought.

Personal values and ethics are important for all human beings. They are specially important for strategists as they are custodians of immense economic power vested in

Exhibit 12.8 Values and Ethics in the Context of Indian Psycho-Philosophical

With regard to values and ethics rooted in Indian thought, several ideas have been proposed:

1. The concept of self in man has to embrace the spiritual dimension beyond the physical, social and economic dimensions.
2. The creative energies of human beings are derived from and rooted in the Supreme Creative Intelligence.
3. Managerial decision making requires the interplay of both analytic and holistic faculties.
4. The final resolution of managerial conflicts lies in the de-egoisation of the self.
5. The key to cooperation and teamwork lies in realizing that the same "atman" dwells in all.
6. The quality of managerial decision making and skills can be improved through an understanding and internalization of the doctrine of karma.
7. Motivational strategies need to be based on a giving model rather than a needing model of man.
8. Ability for developing effective leadership style requires an understanding of three qualities of man: sattwa (righteousness), rajas (selfishness), and tamas (laziness).
9. All managerial decisions are subjective in the ultimate analysis and the effectiveness of such decisions depends critically on the purity of the mind of the decision maker.

business organisations by society. The possession of personal values by strategists is good, but the important issue is whether it is right to let them affect the considerations for strategy formulation and implementation. Rather a more relevant question could be:"Can strategists prevent their personal values from affecting strategy formulation and implementation?" To answer this Christensen and others say: "Executives in charge of company destinies do not look exclusively to what a company might do or can do". In apparent disregard of the second of these considerations, they sometimes seem heavily influenced by what they personally want to do. If we now look at the last proposition in Exhibit 12.8, we find that it is indeed true. The intentions of individuals, that is, their purity of mind as decision-makers within an organisation matter a lot in strategic management. There has to be a right connection between values, ethics, and strategy. It is imperative that strategists take strategic decisions not only on the basis of purely economic reasons but also consider values and ethics.

Prof S. K. Chakraborty of IIM, Calcutta has done extensive pioneering work on Indian psycho-philosophical thought, contained in ancient texts, to derive insights for the purpose of developing managerial effectiveness. His basic idea is to rely on education versus training, values versus skills, principles versus policies, and wisdom versus knowledge to develop managerial effectiveness. His model of managerial effectiveness is based on seven Indian thoughts: the concept of self and reality, dis-identification, theory of Gunas, theory of Samskaras, the doctrine of Karma, theory and method of work.

Business ethics has traditionally been considered to integrate core values, such as, honesty, trust, respect, and fairness into strategic management, policy-making, practising management, and decision-making. It has been perceived as a set of legally driven codes, in the form of a list of do's and don'ts for the company executives, that have to be complied with. A significant change is occurring in considering business ethics as central to managing organisations. Companies are formulating value-based, globally consistent codes for ethical understanding and appropriate decision-making at all levels even as they face immense external challenges.

Business ethics is being identified as a major source of competitive advantage. In 1999 a study by the DePaul University of 300 companies found that firms making an explicit commitment to follow an ethics code provided more than twice the shareholder value than those that did not. An earlier study of 1997 had found that companies with a defined commitment to ethical principles outperformed others. What this means is good ethics is also good business. Companies recognized as ethical organisations are able to attract investment and human capital, retain talent, differentiate themselves in the markets, and create a perception of being customer-friendly. A chairman of a successful company in India says: "Value-based organisations have demonstrated that even so called soft concepts can be extremely powerful. Money can't buy reputation and integrity; both have to be earned. Organisations based on strongly-held shared values amongst their customers and employees (and in that order) have been able to professionalize and develop their market potential through strong brand loyalty and relationship building with their constituents."

Recognizing the immense significance of business values and ethics in the context of good business, there have been attempts at describing how ethics can be imbibed as a part of managerial activities through the adoption of a practical framework. At this point, it is necessary to differentiate between values and ethics. Values are personal in nature (e.g., a belief in providing customer satisfaction and being a good paymaster) while ethics is a generalized value system (e.g., avoiding discrimination in recruitment and adopting fair business practices). Business ethics can provide the general guidelines within which strategic management can operate. Values, however, offer alternatives to choose form. For example, philanthropy as a business policy is optional. A strategist may or may not possess this value and still remain within the limits of business ethics. It is values, therefore, that vary among the strategists in an organisation, and such a variance may be a source of conflict at the time of strategy formulation and implementation. A major set of tasks in strategy implementation is to create consistency among the business values and ethics and the proposed strategy. This is done through inculcating the right set of values, reconciling divergent values, and modifying values that are not consistent with the strategy.

Organisations derive values and ethics from their corporate culture. Corporate culture, as we have seen earlier, is the outcome of the shared assumptions that individual members of the organisation have. The right set of values and a code of ethics have to be formulated by an organisation on the basis of its founding philosophy, cherished traditions, norms of ethical behaviour, and social requirements. Several organisations have formulated such codes for their members.

Inculcating values and ethics: Once the values and ethical codes are formulated, strategists have to set about inculcating them. Several actions could be taken for this to be accomplished. A representative list of such actions is given below.

- Considering values and ethics in recruitment and selection to ensure compatibility of the character traits of potential employees to the ethical system of the organisation.
- Incorporating the statement of values and code of ethics into employee training and educational programmes.
- Example-setting by top management in terms of actions and behaviour that reinforce the values.
- Communication of the value and code of ethics through wide publicity and explanation of compliance procedures.
- Constant monitoring of compliance by superior staff and top management.
- Consistent nurturing of values within the organisation through their integration into policies practices, and actions.
- Paying special attention to those parts of the organisation that are susceptible to ethically sensitive activities, such as, purchase and procurement, dealing with government and other external agencies.

Reconciling divergent values: Strategists have to reconcile divergent values and modify values, if necessary. A typical situation of value divergence may arise while setting objectives and determining the precedence of different objectives. One group of strategists (may be, a coalition) is interested in production-oriented objectives such as standardization and mass production while another group may stress marketing related objectives, like product quality and variety, and small-lot production. These interests may be legitimate in the sense that they arise from their functional bias. It is for the chief executive now to reconcile the divergent values. Obviously, this can be done best in the light of strategic requirements and environmental considerations.

Modifying values to create consistency: Modification of values is frequently required for strategy implementation. A particular strategy, say of expansion, may be suboptimal if existing values do not conform to these requirements. In such cases, modification of values is necessary. But what was said of corporate culture is true for values too, they are difficult, if not impossible, to change. A judicious use of politics and power, redesigning of corporate culture, and making systematic changes in organisation can help to modify values gradually.

Of late this absence of a uniform national ethos and sense of value based on ethical considerations is being increasingly noticed by management philosophers and sundry models are being advanced that will, hopefully lead to the development of value-based ethical standards in Indian industries.

12.4.7 Chakraborty Model

Chakraborty bases his model on Vedantic principles and considers them as the long lived national ethos of India. His model of ethical morality is briefly structured on the following:

- The basic concept is to harness secular complexity to the guiding hand of sacred simplicity. This is achieved by referring to the four goals of the human system:
  - *Dharma* (rectitude and righteousness)
  - *Artha* (money and wealth)
  - *Kama* (desires and needs)
  - *Moksha* (liberation of the spiritual core).

The secular goals of *artha* and *karma* are integrated into the model within the bounds of *dharma* or ethic moral propriety and *moksha* or liberation of the inner spirit core. To make Vedantic spirinomics a reality, the following correctives may be sought from sacred simplicity.

- To aim and strive for a "pure-mind", meaning emotions, feelings, impulses; the matter of the heart, so to say, should take precedence over intellect/sharpening.
- Emphatically follow the law, "the subject is the cause, the object is the effect" Indeed, in any management system, the crux lies in human beings, not in the system or its structural dimensions.
- Work must be done without personal claims to egocentric results (i.e., rewards) as the primary driving force. This in effect means desireless work (*nishkam karma*).
- Transition from this concept of "egoless work to the ethico-moral concept of ego-led" work as enshrined in the doctrine of karma, as explained in essence by Toynbee.

The ethical level of a society at a particular moment depends on the state of *karma* – account of each of the participants in society. The most important objective for a human being, both for its own sake and for the sake of society is to improve his *karma*.

Human personality comprises (a) an outer active, involved in all dynamic self called *prakriti*, and (b) an inner, quiescent witness and silent self called *purusha*. Even when one works in the midst of turbulent or hectic external circumstances, the inner *purusha* exists all the time as a permanent background of stillness. The practice of this depth awareness is a crucial process for effective self management.

The exchange theory of generating the means of human sustenance and economic wealth is obtained through a systemic framework linking the human and the cosmic. This is expressed by the concept of *yagnartha karma*, i.e., work done is a sacrifice. In consequence, care and concern flow in this theory not merely from an awakened moral conscience, but from a more all-embracing cosmic and spiritual conscience.

Creativity in future must, on the whole, be directed towards serving the simple living high thinking goal for humanity in conformity with the Vedantic transformational goal of unfolding the higher self or core self within which is *poorna* or that which is autonomously whole and self-sufficient. The credibility of a leader rests ultimately on the attribute of impersonal love springing from the higher self.

These ethical considerations lead to the concept of a business *ashram* as a credible Indian concept of an ethical view of business. Some possible tangible outcomes of widespread adoption of this business *ashram* vision would be the following.

- There should be a growing tendency towards products with longer life cycles as against the ever shorter ones today.
- Organisations should tend to contract rather than expand, as is the current tendency.
- Localized, decentralized economic activities should increase faster than centralized ones. Production and distribution should be more space-specific.
- The need for high speed, long distance, continuous travel should gradually decline. Bicycles should once again come into their own at the expense of cars and airplanes.
- Employee relations are likely to become more cooperative and less adversarial, as a consequence of greater identification with smaller sized enterprises and the spirit of trusteeship implied amongst owners/top managers.
- Competitive advertising, preying upon gullible customers, is likely to decline.
- Business growth fuelled by greed and achieved through manipulation, financial mergers, and heavy debt financing are likely to be less and less favoured.
- Local resources for local markets to meet local needs being once again the principal thrust, the frenzied search for strategic advantage, strategic intent, strategic response, and so on for global markets should slow down.
- Mental illnesses due to overconsumption outside and undernourishment within should fall.
- Living in society is likely to become simpler and less energy intensive. Change for the sake of change will appear to be less justifiable.
- Loyalty and gratitude to organisations and colleagues may once again become important features of professionalism.
- Reduction in greed and interpersonal rivalry should give basic human values like sharing and humility a better chance of coming into their own.
- Networking, interpersonal on inter-organisational, may rest on something more dignified and genuine than the self-centred instrumental motives of the present.
- More and more decisions are likely to be subjected to the test of whether their effects are likely to be spiritually, ethically, and ecologically positive or negative.

12.5 ETHICS, VALUES, CULTURE, AND LEADERSHIP

A significant change has become evident in corporate attitude to business ethics since the eighties. Prior to the eighties business ethics tended to be reflected in the desire to do good work, i.e., showing benevolent intentions cost effectively. This form of corporate paternalism was no longer considered sufficient in the eighties. Rather, the attitude on business ethics centred on the personal behaviour of the individual rather than just the image of the organisation. It implied not only that relationship between organisations are governed by implicit or explicit codes of behaviour but that the constituents of business extend beyond customers and shareholders to encompass all those who work for the organisations, communities and, in effect, everyone directly affected by the organisation's activities. But what would these codes of ethics, that in effect are a quantification of business ethics, contain? This is where differences arise. The cause for this difference is not difficult to locate. To quote Michael Hoffman, professor of philosophy and business ethics: "Our present century has been weaned away on relativism (denial of ethical absolutes), on pragmatism (the belief that some things is right if it works), on positivism (equating knowledge with observable experience), and on behaviorism (interpreting human actions as totally determined and predictable). The unifying thread of all this is the reduction of everything considered true and meaningful to material reality or physical experience. Science and materialism have flourished and ethics and values have been relegated to matters of emotion, attitude and feeling.

Such ideology permits no significant development of the non-material non-measurable aspects of our lives, such as freedom, morality and divinity. However, there is something about the human spirit which resists this sterile picture and cries out for a different ideology, which will preserve our humanity and provide our life with a value system. The trouble is that too many businesses leaders proclaim simplistically that they are in business "to make money". You cannot tack on "ethics or social responsibility" to business behaviour like an unrelated musical cadenza. They must be inherent in all that a business does.

A survey of a large number of businesses evinces surprising unanimity in the identification of issues that all involve ethical considerations for business. These problems generally fall into four basic categories and are shown in Exhibit. 12.9.

- **Equity** is generally used to mean basic fairness, apart from any established legal or human right. For example, executive salary scales are sometimes the subject of controversy when critics say that it is inequitable for certain employees to receive annually thirty or forty times more than the lowest paid worker in the firm. Some arguments for comparable worth are also rooted in an ethical appeal to greater fairness in determining the material rewards for work. Equity issues are, however, not limited to salary and pay considerations. They can also arise in the pricing discretion companies are permitted under the applicable law. As in the case of compensation practices, ethical questions can be raised with regard to either results or the means used to attain them.
- **Rights** are treatments to which a person has just claim. The origin of the claim may be legislation, legal precedent or community notions of dignity. Modern views or rights are generally protective in nature. They seeks to defend individual autonomy from encroachment by powerful institutions or the community at large. Societies accept the concept of rights to varying degrees. The Japanese, for example, rely heavily on their traditional concept of reciprocal obligation, which mandates discussion, conciliation, and adjustment of differences instead of an appeal to abstract concepts of justification. Rather than filing lawsuits, Japanese who allege discrimination usually form a victim group that negotiates with company representatives. The resulting accommodation does not set a precedent,

Exhibit 12.9 Ethical Categories of Current Corporate Issues

Equity	*Rights*	*Honesty*	*Exercise of corporate power*
Executive salaries Comparable worth Product pricing.	Corporate due process, Employer health screening, Employee privacy, Sexual harassment, Affirmative action, Equal employment opportunity, Shareholders interest, Employment at will, Whistle blowing.	Employee conflict of interest, Security of company records, Inappropriate gifts, Unauthorized payments to foreign officials, Advertising content, Government contract issues, Financial and cash management procedures, Conflict between corporation's ethical system and business practices in foreign countries.	Political action committees, workplace safety, Environmental issues, Disinvestment, Corporate contribution, Social issues raised by religious organizations, Plant/Facility closures and downsizing.

but establishes a basis for ongoing dialogue. Dignity is a subcategory of rights, where protection is rooted in the community's sense of elemental decency rather than regulated by specific constitutional, judicial or legislative mandates. For example, employee privacy and sexual harassment are issue subject to increasing legislative and judicial activity, but the legislative and judicial systems have yet to find an absolute formula for extending these rights to employees.

- **Honesty** in corporate ethics relates to the integrity and truthfulness of a company's actions or politics. Issues of honesty arise both in connection with corporate behaviour and with employees acting under the company's nominal supervision. Misleading advertising, questionable financial and cash management procedures, gifts for foreign officials and waste or fraud in the performance of government contracts are examples of corporate behaviour that may be labelled as dishonest. Other honesty issues arise in connection with the company's responsibility for supervision of those who act in its name, and the reciprocal obligation of employees to observe company and community standards in their business dealings. The misappropriation of proprietary information for personal enrichment, or to help a competitor, is an abuse of trust. Acceptance of inappropriate gifts can corrupt the purchasing process. Conflicts of interest between employee activities outside the workplace and company interests can create situations of divided loyalty. In all these circumstances it is the employee who has an ethical responsibility, but a company cannot escape the consequences of lack of proper supervision.

- **Exercise of corporate power** corporations recognize a responsibility to contribute to community enterprises that are consistent with their mission and with their commitments to the various constituencies they serve. Corporate financial and executive assistance and efforts to generate public support for programmes are believed to be an important element of the company's ethical profit. Business organisations also acknowledge the ethical component of adhering to standards for workplace, product, and environmental safety. Beyond generally accepted responsibilities, more controversial positions advocated by religious or political groups may raise ethical questions that have an impact on corporate policy and practices. For instance, in past several years companies faced external pressures to disinvest from South Africa. In consequence, while some companies withdrew from South Africa, several others argued that the ethical position was to remain in South Africa, because they believed foreign investment was a critical level for social change in that country.

12.6 ETHICS AND LEADERSHIP OF THE FUTURE

Certain common and distinct features portend the future quite decisively. Among these are the following:

- Emergence of the information society resulting from developments in microelectronics, making information across the would easily and readily available to every citizen, leading gradually but inexorably to the emergence of a borderless world.
- Geostrategic changes resulting in the emergence of three gigantic trading and industrial economic groups, NAFTA, the EEC, and Japan and ASEAN, and the consequent serious concern on the part of other regions of the world finding themselves hemmed in and buffeted.
- The awakening of minorities, nationalism, and regionalism
- Development, growth, and cultural awakening of the developing countries of the world, with the consequent impact on their national ethos.
  - The population explosion.
  - The environment, with global warming as an immediate, visible source of anxiety.
  - The advance of high technology
  - The loss of values: a general loss loosening the bonds that had previously ensured the coherence of society and confined individuals to its norms.
- Exponential growth in sundry categories of crime, violence, and coercion, organized for monetary gain or political power. Some such manifestations are:
  - The mafia
  - The drug network
  - Likely limitation of energy resources

- Increasing impact of the globalization of industrial and business activities with MNCs expanding and proliferating, pushing the world and various countries towards increasing liberalization and withdrawal or easing of restrictions and border controls.

In the context of the above and the need for multinationals to be able to avoid loss of face and likely nationalistic backlash in the developing countries around the world, it would be necessary for these international companies to develop new codes of ethics. In short, it is necessary to carefully distinguish between values at the individual and the collective level. In many cases they are compatible. The fight against pollution provides a good example of this. Indeed, the interdependence of nationals and the globalization of a number of problems entail an increase in universal awareness and need for a new international code of ethics at the collective level. A number of new ethics dictated by the pressure of new ethics dictated by the pressure of new facts are:

- ***The ethics of nature:*** Imposed by global environmental issues.
- ***The ethics of life:*** Discussed increasingly because of the controversy about genetic engineering.
- ***The ethics of development:*** Resulting from the increasingly unbearable gap between the rich and the poor.
- ***The ethics of money:*** Because it is divorced from economic realities and dominates the ambitions of too many individuals.
- ***The ethics of images:*** Who should rule over the media and modulate the excessive dramatization of the image on television?
- ***The ethics of solidarity:*** Dictated by the fact that the dimension of the problems posed to humanity today requires cooperation between human beings as a condition of their survival.

It is necessary for multinationals if they are to survive and thrive that the personal ethical convictions of their employees and the company's culture are compatible with the code of ethics described above.

12.6.1 Leadership of the Future

In considering this question we again sharply underline two major aspects of development in the future:

- The proliferation and growth of MNCs (or, rather, internationalization of companies) consequent to the increasing trend towards globalization.
- Development, growth, and cultural awakening of the developing countries of the world with the consequent impact on their national ethos.

Against this backdrop, a typical leader of the future would be the CEO of an international company. Certain requirements of such a leader perhaps merit consideration, but before that the nature of the likely developments may be shortlisted.

- The pace of change will be felt in several areas. Globalization will no longer be an objective but an imperative, as markets open and geographic barriers become increasingly blurred and perhaps even irrelevant. Corporate alliances, joint ventures, and acquisition will increasingly be driven by competitive pressures and strategic rather than financial structuring. Technological innovation and the translation of that innovation into market place advantage will accelerate further.

- There are going to be increasing demands for sensitivity to the environment. Only total commitment of everyone in the company will provide the level of responsibility that will be acceptable to employees, governments, and customers.

This change in environment must bring in a change in the culture of successful companies. The essence of business in the present century is going to be tapping talent. What really matters is not so much where to locate the plants, it is how to locate the best people and motivate them. In all this, the keyword is partnership. Partnership will be of all kinds: increasingly strategic interdependence between companies, governments and people. Setting up in new countries will be different from what it used to be. Once, you dropped an American off in Venezuela or Thailand with a boatload of toothpaste and had him build a business. Now it will be necessary to establish a partnership with local business people or local government. Simultaneously, the top down approach to decision-making, previously in practice, will no longer be valid. The fundamental difficulty will be how to execute a global strategy and still allow those leading the local entity to feel that they are controlling their own destiny. They need to be encouraged to be entrepreneurial so that they can feel responsible for the results.

As already mentioned, this involves a shift in culture. To move towards a winning culture it will be necessary to create what might be called a "boundaryless company". The barriers between functions such as engineering and marketing, between people based on salaries, and geographic barriers between locations must disappear. The lines between the company and its vendors and customers must be blurred into a smooth, fluid process, and with no objective other than satisfying the customer and winning in the marketplace.

When it comes to managing people, business will need to move away from the authoritarian approach towards a shared decision-making approach. The radical change in employee involvement will give workers responsibility in the total business process, and a consequence will be a flattening of the organisational pyramid. Global companies simply cannot prosper in a diverse, multicultural world unless they reflect the diversity to some degree. It is like the Darwinian ideal that diversity in the gene pool creates strength in and survivability of the species. A corporation that successfully draws on the talents and abilities of all its employees as individuals will be best positioned for success.

As companies reflect more cultural diversity, they will become more tolerant, more willing to use differences, rather than similarities, as criteria for individual success within the organisation. Any business climate in which broadly different individuals may succeed will be one in which the organisation as a whole prospers. In this context, the general features of a future leader may be outlined :

(a) **Areas of Expertise:** Strategy formulation, human resource management, marketing/sales, negotiation/conflict resolution and foreign languages and computer literacy.

(b) **Personal Characteristics:** Creative, enthusiastic, open-minded, intelligent, inspiring, energetic, encouraging.

(c) **Desirable Characteristics but Rated Somewhat Lower:** Analytic, loyal, physically fit, organised, risk-taking, diplomatic, intuitive, collaborative

(d) **Desirable Characteristic, Rated Lowest:** Tough, personable, patient, dignified, conservative

(e) **Management Style**

- visionary,
- delegate authority; readily reassign or terminate individuals not meeting targets,
- maintain a lean staff and set a personal example of cost consciousness, and
- superb communicator,

12.6.2 Power

Another, widely pervasive element, influencing the decision-making process in an organisation is the exercise of power. For the purpose of strategic analysis, power is best understood as the extent to which individuals or groups are able to persuade, induce or coerce others into following certain courses of action. This is the mechanism by which one set of expectations will dominate policy-making or seek compromise with others.

12.6.3 Sources of Power within Organisations

The normally recognized sources of power are summarized in Exhibit 12.10.

- **Hierarchy** provides people with formal power over others and is one method by which senior managers influence policy. It is, however, important to remember that this type of power has very limited effect if used in isolation.
- **Influence** can be an important source of power and may arise from personal qualities (the charismatic leader) or because a high level of consensus exists

Exhibit 12.10 Sources of Power

Within Organization	*For External Stakeholders*
1. Hierarchy (formal power), e.g., autocratic decision making.	1. Control of strategic resources, e.g., materials, labour, money.
2. Influence (informal power), e.g., charismatic leadership.	2. Involvement in strategic implementation, e.g., distribution outlets, agents.
3. Control of strategic resources, e.g., strategic products (steel, oil).	3. Possession of knowledge (skills), e.g., subcontractors.
4. Possession of knowledge/skills, e.g., computer specialists.	4. Through internal links, e.g., informal influences.
5. Control of environments, e.g., negotiating skills.	
6. Involvement in strategic implementation, e.g., by exercising discretion.	

within the group or company (i.e., people are willing to support the prevailing viewpoint). Indeed, there is strong support for the view that the most important task of managers is to shape the culture of the organisation to suit its strategy. However, the extent to which an individual or group can use his/its influence is determined by a number of other factors. In many situations, prior commitments to principles may be quite central to the organisation's mission. Thus, a no redundancy policy may be interpreted to counter actions proposed by senior management (such as productivity levels).

- **Control of strategic resources** is a major source of power within companies. However, the relative importance of different resources will change over time and power derived in this way can show dramatic changes. Within any one company, the extent to which various departments are seen as powerful will vary with the company's circumstances. Design or R&D departments may be powerful in companies developing new products or processes. Whereas marketing people may dominate those that are primarily concerned with developing new markets.
- **Knowledge/skills** Individuals can derive power from their specialist knowledge or skills. Certain individuals may be viewed as irreplaceable to the company, and some would jealously guard this privileged position by creating a mystique around their jobs. This can be a risky personal strategy, since others within the organisation may be either spurred to acquire the skills or to devise methods of bypassing them. The powers of many organisation's computer specialists were threatened by the advent of minicomputers which provided others the means of bypassing those specialists.
- **Control of the environment** It is well known that events in the company's environment are likely to influence its performance. Hence, the more uncertain the environment, the more likely the company to be dependent upon individuals within the organisation with specialist knowledge of that aspect of the environment. This is particularly true when the environment is hostile. That is probably why more than anything else, financial and marketing managers are seen as dominant in the policy determination of a company.
- **Exercising discretion** is the most significant source of power within an organisation and is often overlooked. Whatever the strategic decision taken, its execution cannot be controlled in all its minutest details, and even the dynamics of the situation change between the time a decision is taken and its implementation. It is therefore up to the implementers to interpret and execute the particular parts of that policy, and in doing so, use their own personal discretion. This is a major source of power for middle management in organisations.

12.6.4 Sources of Power for External Stakeholders

Resource dependence is the most common source of power. Thus major suppliers, banks, and shareholders all derive power from this source. Involvement in implementation through linkages between value chains can be an important source of power for supplier channels, and buyers. One of the major changes since the sixties in many industries has been the extent to which power shifted from the manufacturing sector to the distribution sector. The greater the knowledge distribution companies have of trends in consumer tastes the greater their ability to dictate terms to manufacturers rather than simply function as outlets for goods designed and planned by manufacturing companies.

Knowledge and skills critical to the success of the company may be a source of power . This is the source of power for many subcontractors. Internal links can provide a route for external stakeholders to influence company strategy. This, of course, is highly influenced by the nature of the organisation. Thus a highly authoritarian organisation is likely to be hostile to any attempts by outside stakeholders to formally involve themselves in formulation of strategy and any influence on policy by an external stakeholder must be derived in other ways. In contrast, organisations believing in industrial democracy would actively seek to involve a wide variety to stakeholders in strategic decision-making.

12.6.5 Methods of Assessing Power

It is useful to analyze and arrive at some simple guidelines on how to assess power in an organisation. It is suggested that the best way to cope with this complex situation is to step back from the details and look for the indicators of power. There are four major indicators each for the internal and the external sources of power.

Internal Sources

- The status of the individual or group, as indicated by position within the hierarchy, individual salaries, and job grades of the group, reputation of the individual or group.
- The claim on resources as measured by the department's budget, or the number of employees within the group, in particular, tends in the proportion of resources claimed by the group. The less powerful group would invariably find its resources eroded by the more powerful.
- Representation in a powerful position, such as on the Board of Directors or the various decision-making committees.
- Symbols of power, such as size and location of individual's office, whether s/he has a secretary, carpets, and a private telephone.

External Sources

- The status of an external party, such as a supplier, this is often indicated by the way such a party is discussed among company employees and whether they respond quickly to its demands.
- Resource dependence can be measured directly. For example, the proportion of the company's business tied up with any one customer or supplier and the ease with which the supplier, financier, or customer can be replaced at short notice.
- Negotiating arrangements: Whether external parties are dealt with at arm's length or are actively involved in negotiations with the company. Thus a customer who is invited to negotiate over the price of a contract is in a more powerful position than a similar party that is given a fixed price on a take-it or leave-it basis.

- Symbols are equally valuable clues, i.e., whether the management team wines and dines with some customer or supplier, or the level of person in the company who deals with the particular supplier. The care and attention paid to correspondence with outsiders will tend to differ from one party to another.

12.7 SOCIAL RESPONSIBILITY

In the past twenty-five years or so there has been increasing awareness and acceptance by management of the diversity of stakeholder interests and expectations to be accommodated. This has given rise to the notion of social responsibility, by which is meant the acceptance by management of organisation responsibilities of a social nature, wider than the legal minimum that it is bound to fulfill. There are a wide variety of issues that can be considered to fall under this broad heading. These are summarized in Exhibit. 12.11.

Exhibit 12.11 Some Questions of Social Responsibility

Internal Aspects	*External Aspects*
Employee welfare: Providing medical care, assistance with mortgages, extended sick-ness leave, assistance for dependent, etc.	***Pollution control:*** Reducing pollution below legal standards even if competitors are not doing so, etc.
Working conditions: Enhanced working surroundings, social and sporting clubs, above minimum safety standards, etc.	***Product safety:*** Danger arising from the careless use of products by consumers, etc.
Job design: Designing jobs to the increased satisfaction of workers rather than efficiency etc.	***Marketing practices:*** Curtailing advertis-ing that promotes products which harm health (e.g. tobacco and sweets), etc.
	Employment: Positive discrimination in favour of minorities
	Community activity: Sponsoring local events and supporting local good causes etc.

How organisations respond to these issues varies considerably as has been summarized in Exhibit 12.12.

Within the categories listed in (Exhibit 12.12) four groups of responses may be discussed. Each of them may give rise to conflicts of objective and policy. We briefly discuss these.

(i) The first group is at one extreme, and its only business is the business. Its only social responsibility is to increase profit. It would, in consequence, treat the legal requirements regarding social responsibilities as unavoidable hindrances. The first three categories fall in this group.

(ii) The next group is categories 4 to 7. Here social responsibility is exercised in a carefully selective way, usually justified in terms of economic common sense. Sponsorship or welfare provision would be rationalized as sensible expenditure akin to any other form of investment or promotion expenditure, being considered to be in the long-term interest of the company. The companies falling in this group would argue that management ignores social influences at its peril and the smarter companies are those that recognize and cope with these issues in policy-making. The conflicts of responsibility that arise here are for example, between pollution control and job position control and job provision. Extra costs in pollution control mean uncompetitive costs and thus threaten plant closure and job loss.

(iii) The next group would be in category 8. It considers a wide variety of social responsibility issues as important influences on policy-making. The companies falling in this group would retain uneconomic units to preserve jobs, avoid manufacture of anti-social products, and would be prepared to bear reduction in profitability for the social good. Conflict will naturally come when this reduced profitability threatens survival.

(iv) Lastly, there would be organisations in categories 9 to 10 that are run specifically in response to community needs. Here societal needs are paramount and profit is secondary – often a constraint. Conflict would arise in keeping the organisation efficient and commercial, thus minimizing the subsidy requirements.

Exhibit 12.12 Social Responsibility: Roles of the Firm

	Behaviour and Attitude		
Role	*Economic*	*Social*	*Political*
Profit maximizer	Profit dominates	Regarded as an impediment to profit	Actively avoids involvement with political system
Profit satisfier	Growth business	Reacts against societal and social pressures as incursions	Avoids interaction with political system
Defender of the enterprise	The business of business is business	Reacts against the societal component as not being within the first's proper ambit	Stands up for free enterprise
The lone wolf	Prime emphasis on profit	Voluntarily but unilaterally assumes responsibility	Avoids involvement unless cornered
Socially engaged	Prime emphasis on profit	Interactively engaged	Engaged only in negotiation of the rules of the game

Contd...

Socially progressive	Prime emphasis on profit	Interactively engaged	Positively involved in formulation of national industrial policies
Global actor	Prime emphasis on profit	Interactively engaged	Assumes a responsibility to foster a balance between national and international economic policies
Developer of society	Financial self-sufficiency	Produces changes in the lives of mankind through innovation.	Positively involved with emphasis on planned development of social infrastructures
Social servant	Secondary to social obligations	Provides essential but non-economic goods and services	Positively involved in formation of national industrial policies with emphasis on social matters
Employment provider	Subsidized operation	Provides jobs	Subsidized and supported by government

Exercise

1. Leadership implementation plays a significant role in the success of the organisation. What quality and skills are required in effective leadership?
2. How can the strategic leader match their leadership style to the requirements of the strategy being implemented?
3. What is the impact of culture on "corporate culture"? How an organisation can create a strategy supportive culture.
4. How can we make strategy formulation and implementation as a part of cultural process?
5. What is the impact of personal value and ethics on the leadership implementation in the organisation?
6. The development of leadership in the organisation depends on the society culture, value and ethics. Does this help in the effective leadership implementation?
7. What are the sources of power within the organisation and outside the organisation?
8. Corporate social responsibility is assuming an important role in business organisations. How is it linked to leadership and can impact the organisation and society?

13 Functional Implementation: Plans and Policies

13.1 INTRODUCTION

A functional strategy is the short-term game plan for a key functional area within a company. Such strategies clarify grand strategy by providing more specific details about how key functional areas are to be managed in the near future. Functional strategies must be developed in the key areas of marketing, finance, production/operations, R&D, and personnel. They must be consistent with long-term objectives and grand strategy. Functional strategies help in implementation of grand strategy by organizing and activating specific subunits of the company (marketing, finance, production, etc.) to pursue the business strategy in daily activities. In a sense, functional strategies translate thought (grand strategy) into action designed to accomplish specific annual objectives. For every major subunit of a company, functional strategies identify and coordinate actions that support the grand strategy and improve the likelihood of accomplishing annual objectives.

To better understand the role of functional strategies within the strategic management process, they must be differentiated from grand strategies. Three basic characteristics differentiate functional and grand strategies:

1. Time horizon covered.
2. Specificity.
3. Participation in the development.

13.1.1 Time Horizon

The time horizon of a functional strategy is usually comparatively short. Functional strategies identify and coordinate short-term actions, usually undertaken in a year or less. Sears, for example, might implement a marketing strategy of increasing price discounts and sales bonuses in its appliance division to reduce excess appliance inventory over the next year. This functional strategy would be designed to achieve a short-range (annual) objective that ultimately contributes to the goal of Sears' grand strategy in its retail division over the next five years. This shorter time horizon is critical to successfully implementing a grand strategy for two reasons. First, it focuses functional manager's attention on what needs to be done now to make the grand strategy work. Second, the short-time horizon allows functional managers to recognize current conditions and adjust to changing conditions in developing functional strategies.

13.1.2 Specificity

A functional strategy is more specific than a grand strategy. Functional strategies guide functional actions taken in key parts of the company to implement the grand strategy. The grand strategy provides general direction. Functional strategies give specific guidance to managers responsible for accomplishing annual objectives. Such strategies are meant to ensure that managers know how to meet annual objectives. It is not enough to identify a general grand strategy at the business level. There must also be strategies outlining what should be done in each functional area if the annual (and ultimately long term) objectives of the company are to be achieved. Specific functional strategies improve the willingness (and ability) of operating managers to implement strategic decisions, particularly when those decisions represent major changes in the current strategy of the firm.

Specificity in functional strategies contributes to successful implementation for several reasons. First, it adds substance, completeness, and meaning to what a specific subunit of the business must do. The existence of numerous functional strategies helps ensure that managers know what needs to be done and can focus on accomplishing results.

Second, specific functional strategies clarify for top management how functional managers intend to accomplish the grand strategy. This increases top management's confidence in and sense of control over the grand strategy. Third, specific functional strategies facilitate coordination between operating units within the company by clarifying areas of interdependence and potential conflict.

13.1.3 Participation in the Development

Different people participate in strategy development at the functional and business levels. Business strategy is the responsibility of the general manager of a business unit. Development of functional strategy is typically delegated by the business-level manager to principal subordinates charged with running the operating areas of the business. The business manager must establish long-term objectives and a strategy that corporate management feels contributes to corporate-level goals. Key operating managers similarly establish annual objectives and operating strategies that help accomplish business objectives and strategies. Just as business strategies and objectives are approved through negotiation between corporate managers and business managers, the business manager typically ratifies the annual objectives and functional strategies developed by operating managers. The involvement of operating managers in developing functional strategies contributes to successful implementation because understanding of what needs to be done to achieve annual objectives is thereby improved. And perhaps most critical, active involvement increases commitment to the strategies developed.

It is difficult to generalize the development of strategies across functional areas. For example, key variables in marketing, finance, and production are different.

Furthermore, within each functional area, the importance of key variables varies across business situations. A key task of strategy implementation is to align or fit the activities and capabilities of an organisation with its strategies. Strategies operate at different levels and there has to be congruence and coordination among these strategies. Such a congruence is the vertical fit. Then, there has to be congruence and coordination among the different activities taking place at the same level. This is horizontal fit.

When a lower-level strategy, such as a functional strategy, is aligned with a higher level strategy, in this case the business strategy, then a vertical fit takes place. The vertical fit alone is not sufficient to integrate the strategic network. It is also essential to create horizontal fit at the level of individual functional strategies. What this means is that the different functional areas of marketing, finance, operations, personnel, and information management and all the operation activities performed in these areas should not work at cross-purpose. There has to be an alignment among them which is the horizontal fit. In this manner, the vertical fit leads to functional strategies and their implementation, and the horizontal fit leads to operational implementation.

The consideration of vertical fit leads us to define functional strategies in terms of their capability to contribute to the creation of a strategic advantage for the organisation. Looked at this way, we have primarily a function of the R & D department, but an organisation may structure it in such a way, we have the following types of functional strategies.

- **Strategic marketing management** means focusing on the alignment of marketing management within an organisation with its corporate and business strategies to gain a strategic advantage.
- **Strategic financial management** means focusing on the alignments of financial management within the organisation with its corporate and business strategies to a gain a strategic advantage.
- **Strategic operations management** implies focusing on the alignment of operations management within the organisation with its corporate and business strategies to gain a strategic advantage.
- **Strategic human resource** management means focusing on the alignment of human resource management within an organisation with its corporate and business strategies to gain a strategic advantage.
- **Strategic information management** means focusing on the alignment of information management within an organisation with its corporate and business strategies to gain a strategic advantage.

It should be noted that these are emergent areas in the discipline of management. The literature and texts in each of these functional areas assign a definite meaning to these terms. You might have noted that managers in the industry and business magazines and newspapers frequently use terms, such as, marketing strategy, advertising strategy or purchasing strategy. Several terms are also prefixed with the term "strategic", for instance, strategic procurement or strategic recruitment. You should be cautious while using these two terms since the terms "strategy and strategic" are often used without much discretion. In strategic management there is a definite meaning conveyed by these terms, but in practice the usage tends to trivialize the real meaning. So, when you wish to prefix a term such as "strategic" before, say, procurement, then make sure that strategic procurement is carried out while keeping in view the objectives and strategies of an organisation, and it is seen as something which has a vital long-term significance to the future of the organisation. Horizontal fit means that there has to be an integration of the operational activities undertaken to provide a product or service to a customer. These have to take place in the course of operational implementation.

Operational implementation is the approach adopted by an organisation to achieve operational effectiveness. When an organisation performs value-creating activities optimally and in a way which is better than its competitors, it results in operational effectiveness. A value chain is a set of interlinked value-creating activities performed by an organisation. These activities may begin with the activity of procurement of basic raw materials and include the act of processing in its various stages, right up to the obtainment of end products which may be marketed to the ultimate consumer.

To reiterate this, the value chain of a manufacturing organisation is divided into primary and support activities. Primary activities are directly related to the flow of products to the customer and include five sub-activities: inbound logistics (receiving, storing, etc.), operations (transformation of raw materials to finished products), and outbound logistics (order processing, physical distribution, etc.), marketing and sales (pricing, promotion, etc.), and service (installation, repairs, etc.). Support activities are provided to sustain the primary activities. These consist of the firm's infrastructure (including, finance, accounting, general management, etc.), human resource management, technology development, and procurement.

In most organisations, the value-chain activities are dispersed among the different functional areas to be performed by organisational units one of which is a department. For instance, a marketing department is typically responsible for three of the five primary value-chain activities, namely, outbound activities logistics, marketing and sales, and service. The operations department usually performs two more activities: inbound logistics and operations. The support value-chain activities involve several other departments. For example, procurement is generally placed with the operations department, but all the departments may also be procuring items regularly. Technology development may primarily be a function of the R&D department, but an organisation may structure it in such a way that it may be placed under the operations department. All departments deal with the finance and human resource management functions, but specialized departments of finance, accounting and human resource management usually exist to deal with these activities. So, a value-chain classification and departmental segregation do match to an extent.

The considerations of vertical fit and horizontal fit help to explain why integration is necessary for the different subsets of functional activities. Functional strategies are not implemented directly. They have to be defined in terms of plans and policies. So, functional implementation takes place through functional plans and policies.

13.2 FUNCTIONAL PLANS AND POLICIES

For effective implementation, strategists have to provide directions to functional managers regarding the plans and policies to be adopted. In fact, the effectiveness of strategic management depends critically on the manner in which strategies are implemented. In this section, we look at the nature of functional plans and policies, why they are needed, and how they are developed.

As we already know that functional strategies operate on a level below the business strategies. There might be several sub-functional areas within functional strategies. For instance, a company might have a textile division among its several business areas. Within the textile division there might be functional areas, such as, marketing, operations, R & D, and so on. Further and functional area of marketing may have sub-functions such as, product development, advertising and sales promotion, market research and so on.

Functional strategies, defined in terms of functional plans and policies, plans or tactics to implement business strategies, are made within the guidelines which have been set at higher levels. Plans are formulated to select a course of action, while policies are required to act as guidelines to those actions. Functional plans and policies, are therefore, in the nature of the tactics which make a strategy work. Functional managers need guidance from the corporate and business strategies in order to make decisions. In simple terms, functional plans tell the functional managers what has to be done, while functional policies state how the plans are to be implemented.

Glueck has suggested five reasons to show why functional plans and policies are needed. Functional plans and policies are developed to ensure that:

1. The strategic decisions are implemented by all the parts of an organisation.
2. There is a basis available for controlling activities in the different functional areas of a business.
3. The time spent by functional managers on decision-making may be reduced as the plans lay down clearly what has to be done and the policies provide the discretion framework within which decisions need to be taken.
4. Similar situations occurring in different functional areas are handled by the functional mangers in a consistent manner.
5. Coordination across the different functions takes place where necessary.

The development of functional plans and policies is aimed at making the strategies formulated at the top management level practically feasible at the functional level. Strategies need to be segregated into viable functional plans and policies that are compatible with each other, thereby augmenting the horizontal fit. In this way, strategies can be implemented by the functional managers.

The process of development of functional plans and policies may range from the formal to the informal. Larger and more complex organisations may have several hundred policies related to every major aspect. Many of these policies could have been formulated through a formal process and published in many manuals and documents. Smaller organisations with simpler businesses may operate with fewer policies, most of which could be informal and understood rather than written down.

The process of developing functional plans and policies, formal or informal, is similar to that of strategy formulation. Environmental factors relevant to each functional area will have an impact on the choice of plans and policies. Organisational plans and policies shall affect the choice of functional plans and policies. Finally, the actual process of choice will be influenced by objective as well as subjective factors. Then functional plans and policies will affect, and are affected by, the resource allocation decisions.

But before we move on to the next section, two points have to be noted. First, functional areas have been traditionally segregated into finance, marketing, production and personnel. Information management has emerged as a significant function within organisations. But not all organisations divide functional areas traditionally. They do it on the basis of what they actually need. For instance, service organisations will have a different functional areas. Second, the discussion of functional plans and policies that follows is only indicative and not exhaustive. This is understandable because functional managers in each area would formulate plans and policies in much greater detail than we can possibly do here. Creating plans and policies leads to conditions where subordinate managers will know what they are supposed to do and willingly implement the decision.

Managers create plans and policies to make the strategies work. Policies provide the means for carrying out plans and strategic decisions. The critical element is the ability to factor the grand strategy into plans and policies that are compatible, workable, and not just theoretically sound. It is not enough for managers to decide to change the strategy. What comes next is at least as important. How do we get there? When and how efficiently? A manager answers these questions by preparing plans and policies to implement the grand strategy. For example, let us say that the strategic choice was to diversify. Now the executive must decide what to diversify into, where to diversify, how much money will be needed, where the money will come from, and what changes are needed in marketing, production, and other functions to make diversification work.

The amount of planning and policy-making in the formal sense will vary with the size and complexity of the firm. If the firm is small, or if it is a simple business, a few policies and plans will suffice. The plans and policies are generally understood and verbal. Larger and more complex firms find that policies and plans on every major aspect of the firm: marketing, finance production and operations, personnel, and so forth are necessary, for the competitive advantage of the large firm is its power, not its speed. That is where the smaller firm or decentralized division excels.

The processes involved in establishing plans and policies are quite similar to those influencing strategy formation and choice. That is, environmental factors can influence the choices : internal polices and the power of subunits jockeying for position play a role etc. Hence, resistance to change, conflict resolution techniques, and coalition building will all be at play in the development of plans and policies. Without good plans and policies managers would make the same decisions over and over again. And different managers might choose different directions, and this could create problems. On the other hand, plans and policies should never be so inflexible as to prevent exceptions for good reasons. So criteria for judging the adequacy of plans and policies developed would include the following:

- Do they reflect present or desired company practices and behaviour?
- Are they practical, given existing or expected situations?
- Do they exist in areas critical to the firm's success?
- Are they consistent with one another, and do they reflect the timing needed to accomplish goals?

As a result, policies and plans will:

- Specify more precisely how the strategic choice will come to be, what is to be done, who is to do it, how it is to be done, and when it should be finished.
- Establish a follow-up mechanism to make sure the strategic choice, plans, and policy decisions will take place.
- Lead to new strengths which can be used for strategy in the future.

One example of a set of plans for several strategies is given in Exhibit 13.1. For each of these plans, a set of policies will have to be established for the appropriate area of the business. The policies will ensure that the plans are carried out as intended and that the different areas are working toward the same ends. Companies have plans and policies that cover nearly every major aspect of the firm. The example in Exhibit 13.1 illustrates only a few areas. The minimal plans and policies which must be developed are the key functional decisions for each area of the business.

Then we will return to some questions about how these are to be integrated, since our criteria suggest that plans and policies need to be consistent, provide for coordination, and deal with timing issues.

Specialists in each area develop plans and policies in much more breadth and depth than we can cover here. But the list indicates the types of major questions which need to be addressed if strategy is to be implemented effectively.

13.3 FUNCTIONAL STRATEGIES IN MARKETING AREA

The role of the marketing function is to profitably bring about the role of products/ service in target markets for the purpose of achieving the business goals. Functional strategies in the marketing area should guide this endeavour in a manner consistent with the grand strategy and other functional strategies. Effective marketing strategies guide marketing managers in determining who will sell what, where, when, to whom, in what quantity, and how. Marketing strategies must therefore entail four components: product, price, place and promotion. Exhibit 13.2 illustrates the types of questions that operating strategies must address in terms of these four components.

A functional strategy for the product component of the marketing function should clearly identify the customer needs the firm seeks to meet with its product and/or service. An effective functional strategy for this component should guide marketing managers in decisions regarding features, product lines, packaging, accessories, warranty, quality, and new product development. This strategy should provide a comprehensive statement of the product/service concept and the target market(s) the firm is seeking to serve. This, in turn, fosters consistency and continuity in the daily activity of the marketing area.

Exhibit 13.1 Alternative Business Strategies and Plans

Strategy	*Marketing Product Line Plans*	*Manufacturing Plans*	*Human Resource Plans*	*Financial Plans*	*Timing*
Retrenchment	Identify product lines for divestment of those with low sales or margins.	Identify plants to close on the basis of capacity utilisation.	Reduce personnel on the basis of skills needed in the future and seniority.	Eliminate or reduce dividends, and manage cash flows.	Sell plants and reduce personnel in one year; cut dividends now.
Stability	Push the high margin products in the line.	Defer plant and equipment investments over $ 200,000.	Invest in training programmes to improve management skills.	Develop good bank relations, maintain steady dividends, and strengthen the balance sheet.	Continue for three years unless trends show high opportunity.
Expansion	Extend and improve product lines; volume is more critical than margins.	Expand plant capacity to support new products as necessary.	Hire additional sales, R&D, and production workers and managers.	Increase the debt-equity ratio by one-third. Consider the impact of dividend policy on cash flow needs.	Evaluate market share position and financial condition after two years.

A product or service is not good to a customer if it is not available when and where it is wanted. So, the functional strategy for the place component identifies where, when, and by whom the product/services are to be offered for sale. The primary concern here is the channel(s) of distribution, the combination of marketing institutions through which the products/services flow to the final user. This component of marketing strategy guides decisions regarding channels (for example, single versus multiple channels) to ensure consistency with the total marketing effort.

The promotion component of marketing strategy defines how the firm will communicate with the target market. Functional strategy for the promotion component should provide marketing managers with basic guides for the use and mix of advertising, personal selling, sales promotion, and media selection. It must be consistent with other marketing strategy components and, due to cost requirements, closely integrated with financial strategy.

Exhibit 13.2 Functional Strategies in Marketing

Key functional strategies	*Typical questions that should be answered by the functional strategy*
Products (or services)	Which products do we emphasize? Which products/services contribute most to profitability? What is the product/service image we seek to project? What changes should be influencing our customer orientation?
Price	Are we primarily competing on price? Can we offer discounts or other pricing modifications? Are pricing policies standard nationally or is there regional control? What price segment are we targeting (high, medium, low, etc.)? What is the gross profit margin? Do we emphasize cost/demand or competition oriented pricing?
Place	What level of market coverage is necessary? Are there priority geographic areas? What channels of distribution are key? What are the channel objectives, structure, and management? Should the marketing managers change their degree of reliance on distributors, sales reps, and direct selling? What sales organization do we want? Is the sales force organized around territory, market or product?
Promotion	What are key promotion priorities and approaches? Which advertising/communication priorities and approaches are linked to different products, markets and territories? Which media would be most consistent with the total marketing strategy

Functional strategy regarding the price component is perhaps the single most important consideration in marketing. It directly influences demand and supply, profitability, consumer perception, and regulatory response. The approach to pricing strategy may be cost oriented, market oriented, or competition (industry) oriented. With a cost oriented approach, pricing decisions focus on total cost and usually involve an acceptable markup or target price ranges. Pricing is based on consumer demand (e.g., gasoline pricing in a deregulated oil industry) when the approach is market oriented. With the third approach, pricing decisions focus around those of the firm's competitors.

Pricing and other marketing policies become particularly critical at various stages of product development and the firm's strategy. Price has become a primary weapon in tactical battles to secure a market share. For example, if rapid expansion is desired early in the development of a product, pricing may be below cost. (Of course, a desire to attract customers through loss leaders may be another reason for selling below cost.) Being a price leader or follower is a policy which managers need to address.

Here in particular you can see how the development of plans can be affected by managerial values. Offensive versus defensive strategists will view a particular pricing question differently. During periods of stable demand we would expect prices to remain relatively fixed (perhaps adjusted for inflation). If the strategy is retrenchment, price increases and a reduction in promotion and distribution costs would be expected if not outright abandonment. If the firm is retrenching out of certain areas as opposed to liquidating, an orderly withdrawal through various de-marketing mechanisms would be necessary.

Packaging can be an alternative competitive weapon in the strategy of the firm. If product stability is the strategy, packing changes (e.g., toothpaste in a pump, or shaving cream in a brush) can help expand the pace of market penetration.

Policies and plans must be made which interrelate several aspects of the strategy. For instance, a policy of different prices for different customers (or a one-price policy) is one which can have an impact on the product and market strategy. As you will see later, plans and policies must also be set in relation to other aspects of the business- for instance, price is particularly critical in relation to volume-cost-profit conditions, which affect production and the financial condition.

13.4 FUNCTIONAL STRATEGIES IN FINANCE/ACCOUNTING

While most operating strategies guide implementation in the immediate future, the time frame for financial functional strategies varies because strategies in this area direct the use of financial resource in support of the business strategy, long-term goals, and annual objectives. Financial operating strategies with longer time perspectives guide financial managers in long-term capital. Investment, use of debt financing, dividend allocation, and the firm's leveraging posture. Operating strategies designed to manage working capital and short-term assets have a more immediate focus. Exhibit 13.3 highlights some key questions financial strategies must answer for successful implementation.

Long-term financial strategies usually guide capital acquisition in the sense that priorities change infrequently over time. The desired level of debt versus equity versus internal long-term financing of business activities is a common issue in capital acquisition strategy. For example, Delta Airline has a long standing operating strategy that seeks to minimize the level of debt in proportion to equity and internal funding of capital needs. General Cinema Corporation has a long-standing strategy of long-term leasing to expand its theatre and soft-drink bottling facilities. The debt-to-equity ratios for these two firms are approximately 0.50 to 2.0, respectively. Both have similar records of steady profitable growth over the last 20 years and represent two different yet equally effective operating strategies for capital acquisition.

Exhibit 13.3 Functional Strategies in Finance

Key Functional Strategies	*Typical Questions that Should be Answered by the Functional Strategy*
Capital Acquisition	What is an acceptable cost of capital? What is the desired proportion of short- and long-term debt; preferred and common equity? What balance is between internal and external funding? What risk and ownership restrictions are appropriate? What level and forms of leasing should be used in providing assets?
Capital Allocation	What are the priorities for capital allocation projects? On what basis is final selection of projects to be made? What level of capital allocation can be made by operating managers without higher approval?
Dividend and Working Capital Management	What portion of earnings should be paid out as dividends? How important is dividend stability? Are things other than cash appropriate as dividends? What are the cash flow requirements; minimum and maximum cash balances? How liberal/conservative should credit policies be? What limits, payment terms, and collection procedures are necessary? What payment timing and procedure should be followed?

Another financial strategy of major importance is capital allocation. Growth-oriented grand strategies generally require numerous major investments in facilities, projects, acquisitions, and/or people. These investments cannot generally be made immediately, nor are they desired to be. Rather, a capital allocation strategy sets priorities and timing for these investments. This also helps manage conflicting priorities among operating managers competing for capital resources.

Retrenchment or stability often require a financial strategy that focuses on the reallocation of existing capital resources. This could necessitate pruning product lines, production facilities, or personnel to be reallocated elsewhere in the firm. The overlapping careers and aspirations of key operating managers clearly create an emotional setting. Even with retrenchment (perhaps even more so!), a clear operating strategy that delineates capital allocation priorities is important for effective implementation in a politically charged organisational setting.

Capital allocation strategy frequently includes one additional dimension, i.e., level of capital expenditure delegated to operating managers. If a business is pursuing rapid growth, flexibility in making capital expenditures at the operating level may enable timely resources to an evolving market. On the other hand, capital expenditures may be carefully controlled if retrenchment is the strategy.

Dividend management is an integral part of a firm's internal financing. Because dividends are paid on earnings, lower dividends increase the internal funds available for growth, and internal financing reduces the need for external, often debt, financing. However, stability of earnings and dividends often makes a positive contribution to the market price of a firm's stock. Therefore, a strategy guiding dividend management must support the business's posture toward equity markets.

Working capital is critical to the daily operation of the firm, and capital requirements are directly influenced by seasonal and cyclical fluctuations, firm size, and the pattern of receipts and disbursements. The working capital component of financial strategy is built on an accurate projection of cash flow and must provide cash management guidelines for conserving and rebuilding the cash balances required for daily operation.

Sources of capital are related to uses of capital. A prime example is leasing versus buying fixed assets. A policy to lease classes of assets will change the nature of the need for funds over time and the nature of the balance sheet. Thus owning a building (say, the Pan Am building in Manhattan) versus leasing such space has an impact on working capital needs and the ability to finance other types of activities. Hence, a strategy of rapid expansion, if funds are limited in the short term, might be accomplished through leasing rather than buying. Sale- and-leaseback arrangements became quite popular in the early 1980s because of the favourable tax benefits associated with such policies.

Other financial policies concern the evaluation of proposals for investing in certain projects. For instance, a "hurdle rate of return" may be specified as a policy guide before some strategic option will be considered. Hurdle rates may differ, depending on how risk is assessed. Another method for assessing potential investment alternatives includes a risk-adjusted discount rate in the net present value approach. A policy of a mix of investment risks is as useful as marketing-mix policies or planning a mix of basic and applied research. The investment risk mix is related to strategic choice, of course. If expansion is the desired strategy, greater risks are acceptable. A mix of low-risk projects only may be an indication that retrenchment is on the horizon. In the Mid-1980s, corporate treasures made increasing use of "swap transactions" which allowed firms to trade interest rate payments and limit some exposure to risk of interest rate fluctuation. In addition, more and more firms sought to hedge foreign currencies as part of their financial plans.

The other area in which risk plans are needed is in the area of insurance. Corporate liability insurance in the mid-1980s was becoming very expensive, and in some instances difficult to get at all. Some firms were forced out of business because they did not believe they could expose themselves to the risk of doing business without insurance.

Other firms chose a plan of in-house protection, but such plans require a large resource base. Still others joined consortia to pool resources as an alternative to traditional insurers.

Another possibility is to change the nature of coverage for catastrophic risks and at the same time reduce or eliminate coverage for more common risks. Choices here can affect the strategy in terms of costs of doing business, or even lead to ultimate retrenchment (liquidation or sale). Specific targets for current assets and cash flows are also needed for items such as inventories (finished goods and raw materials) and accounts receivable and payable.

Policies for the desired proportion of funds tied up in these accounts and the accounting treatment (e.g., LIFO or FIFO, or book or market value) are relevant here, as are rules for financial disclosure based on historical or inflation-related reporting. Some of these policies are mandated by SEBI or other government bodies, but managers should decide which approach provides them with the most useful information for decision making (as opposed to which treatment makes the books look better). Alternative treatments of accounting data can lead to significant differences in the data upon which managers base their decisions.

Policies governing asset use have a direct impact on other components of strategy and cannot be made in isolation. For example, a policy with respect to maintaining a particular monetary value of safety stock of finished goods relates to marketing policy regarding customer relations and the ability to deliver outputs, as well as to production policy regarding lead times and the size of production runs. Or if an airline is trying to enhance relations with travel agents in a new territory, then extending the time for accounts receivable on the payment for tickets may be an important decision affecting marketing and finance.

Financial plans also become important in particular strategic actions such as mergers or liquidations or bankruptcies. In some cases, legal factors restrain choices. But there are usually several options which require a financial decision as to how to best implement the strategy. Such an option would require a policy decision or would be made in relation to other plans associated with the desired financial structure of the business.

If a firm is divesting or liquidating, financial policies as well as other plans will need to be specified. For instance : How urgent is it? What will the cash flow look like? What will creditors get? Who are the potential buyers? What will be the price? How will we lay offs people? In the early 1980s, many firms began to alter their plans to focus on debt reduction and increasing the cash flow due to stability strategies taken in response to disinflation.

Finally, some financial policies can have an indirect effect on strategy through the executive compensation system. For instance, firms which use stock options as a form of competition may ultimately change the nature of control of the business or influence risk choices made by the executives involved. The implications could be positive or negative, and so such outcomes should be considered as these plans and policies are established. Hence, some of the crucial financial questions needing implementation include:

- Where will get additional funds to expand, either internally or externally?
- If external expansion is desired, how and where will it be accomplished?
- What will be strategy do to our cash flow?

- What accounting systems and policies do we use (for example, LIFO and FIFO)?
- What capital structure policy do we pursue? No debt or a heavily leveraged structure?
- How much should we pay out in dividends.
- How much cash and how many other assets do we keep on hand?
- Should we hedge our foreign currency exchange risk?

It is crucial that financial plans and policies are such that the funds needed are available at the right time and at the lowest cost.

13.5 FUNCTIONAL STRATEGIES IN RESEARCH AND DEVELOPMENT

With the increasing rate of technological change in most competitive industries, research and development (R&D) has assumed a key functional role in many organisations. In the technology-intensive computer and pharmaceutical industries, for example, firms typically spend between 4 and 6 per cent of their sales on R&D. In other industries, such as the hotel/motel and construction industries, R&D spending is less than 1 per cent of sales. Thus, R&D may be a vital function — a key instrument of business strategy — although in stable, less innovative industries, R&D is less critical as a functional strategy than is marketing or finance.

Exhibit 13.4. illustrates the types of questions addressed by an R&D operating strategy. First, R&D strategy should clarify whether basic research or product development research will be emphasized. Several major oil companies now have solar energy subsidiaries with R&D strategy emphasises on basic research, while smaller competitors emphasize product development research.

Directly related to the choice of emphasis between basic research and product development is the time orientation for these efforts mandated by R&D strategy. Should efforts be focused on the near or the long term? The solar subsidiaries of the major oil companies have long-term perspectives, while their smaller competitors appear to be focusing on the immediate future. These orientations are consistent with each business strategy if the major oil companies want to ensure their long-term position in the energy field, while the smaller companies want to establish a competitive niche in the growing solar industry.

R&D strategy should also guide organisation of the R&D function. For example, should R&D efforts be conducted solely within the firm or should portions of the work be contracted outside? A closely related issue is whether R&D should be a centralized or decentralized function. The basic R&D posture of the firm influences each of these decisions because strategy in this area can be offensive, defensive, or a combination of these. If the R&D strategy is offensive, technological innovation and new product development are emphasized as the basis for the firm's future success, as is true for small, high-technology firms. However, his orientation entails high risk (and high payoff)

Exhibit 13.4 Functional Strategies in R&D

R&D Decision Area	*Typical questions that should be answered by the functional strategy*
Basic Research versus Commercial Development	To what extent should innovation and breakthrough research be emphasized in relation to the emphasis on product development, refinement, and modification? What new projects are necessary to support growth?
Time Horizon	Is the emphasis on short term or long term? Which orientation best supports the business strategy? Marketing and production strategy?
Organizational Fit	Should R&D be done in-house or contracted out? Should it be centralized or decentralized? What should be the relationship between the R&D unit(s) and product managers? marketing managers? production managers?
Basic R&D Posture	Should the firm maintain an offensive posture, seeking to lead innovation and development in the industry? Should the firm adapt a defensive posture, responding quickly to competitors' developments?

and demands considerable technological skill, forecasting expertise, and the ability to quickly transform basic innovations into commercial products. Guidelines are needed to encourage the types of R&D efforts required for the strategy. For example, if new product development is the basic strategic direction of the firm, then the research effort will be geared to focus on this activity. Of course, stability strategies which may call for product improvements would require a greater emphasis on modification to the existing line. If a turnaround strategy is desirable, R&D efforts may be focused on improving production processes to reduce costs. Unfortunately, retrenchment strategies often are implemented by cutting R&D activities which may be needed for long-term improvements in the business. Such short-sighted policies provide an example of how the implementation of the current strategy may limit long-term strategy development.

The strategy of vertical integration (e.g., backward or forward expansion in function) is another area where R&D policy becomes particularly relevant. The technologies involved in providing inputs or subsequent processing of outputs associated with changing functions would normally require policies to provide for resources and expertise in the new areas of activity. Another area would include the relative focus of effort on performing basic or applied research. Few companies will authorize the research department to study anything its scientists may be interested in. But the extent of concern with short-term commercialization versus theoretical knowledge which may lead to major breakthrough is an issue of some importance. If a firm is going to undertake basic research, it must be prepared to accept certain financial outcomes and commitments: longer-term risk with potentially no payout or long payback periods, and enough capital to exploit discoveries if and when they are made. Of course, the firm may need to engage in some basic research if the nature of its business requires it (e.g., most pharmaceutical firms depend on basic research).

Some R&D options are available which reflect whether the strategy is offensive or defensive. That is, as with policies such as pricing, strategists can choose to be leaders or followers. If leadership is endorsed, greater emphasis will be placed on R&D in order to be "first to market" Of course, the costs and risk can be high. Others prefer to be fast seconds or followers who take basic research done by others and pursue product modification. In the follower approach, another option is to buy the R&D efforts of others (such as university, government, or independent research labs). Buying patents or paying licence or royalty fees may be another option for firms which do not have strengths in the R&D area or for firms which do not wish to make a commitment to or take the risks of building technological leadership. Another option is the joint venture strategy, which combines internal and external approaches. Such strategies require polices for negotiating contracts and agreements using outputs from research efforts, and deciding how the firm's own R&D departments will be involved in the joint efforts.

Policies as to the amount of financial commitment in R&D can be based on the following guidelines:

- Maximum range 0.5 to 2 per cent gross profit, depending on the industry
- Minimum range-competitor actions.

However, these figures provide a potentially wide range of discretion within which managers must subjectively determine how the R&D activity fits as a component of overall strategy. Perhaps more importantly, questions of how these funds will be used need to be addressed. Exhibit 13.4 suggests that changing policies on how R&D personnel use their resources can impact a firm's strategy.

13.6 FUNCTIONAL STRATEGIES IN PRODUCTION/ OPERATIONS MANAGEMENT

Production/operations management (POM) is the core function in a business firm. POM is the process of converting input (raw material, supplies, people, and machines) into value-enhanced output. This function is most easily associated with manufacturing firms. However, it applies equally to all other types of business (including service and retail firms, for example). Functional strategies in POM must guide decisions regarding the basic nature of the firm's POM system, seeking an optimum balance between investment input and production/operations out put and location, facilities design, and process planning on a short-term basis.

Exhibit 13.5 illustrates these concerns by highlighting key decision areas in which the POM strategies should provide guidance. The facilities and equipment component of

Exhibit 13.5 Functional Strategies in POM

Key Operating Strategies	*Typical Questions that Should be Answered by the Functional Strategy*
Facilities and Equipment	How centralized should the facilities be? (One big facility or several small facilities?) How integrated should the separate processes be? To what extent will further mechanization or automation be pursued? Should size and capacity be oriented towards peak or normal operating levels?
Purchasing	How many sources are needed? How do we select suppliers and manage relationships over time? What level of forward buying (hedging) is appropriate?
Operations Planning and Control	Should work be scheduled to order or to stock? What level of inventory is appropriate? How should inventory be used (FIFO/LIFO), controlled, and replenished? What are the key foci for control efforts (quality, labour cost, downtime, product usage, other)? Should maintenance efforts be preventive or breakdown oriented? What emphasis should be placed on job specialization? Plant safety? Use of standards?

POM strategy involves decisions regarding plant location, size, equipment replacement, and facilities utilization that should be consistent with grand strategy and other operating strategies. The purchasing function is another area that should be addressed in the POM strategy. From a cost perspective area a new suppliers is an advantage or risky? What criteria (for example, payment requirements) should be used in selection of vendors? How should purchases be made in terms of volume and delivery requirements to support operations? If such questions are critical to the success of a grand strategy, functional strategy guidelines improve implementation.

Functional strategies for the planning and control component of POM provide guidelines for ongoing production operations. They are meant to encourage efficient organisation of production/operations resources to match long-range, overall demand.

Often this component dictates whether production/operations will be demand oriented, inventory oriented, or subcontracting oriented. If demand is cyclical or seasonal, then POM strategy must ensure that production/operations processes are efficiently geared to this pattern. A bathing suit manufacturer would prefer inventories to be at their highest in the early spring, for example, not the early fall. If demand is less cyclical, a firm might emphasize producing to inventory, wanting a steady level of production and inventories. When demand fluctuations are less predictable, many firms subcontract to handle sudden increases in demand while avoiding idle capacity and excess capital investment.

Plans must be made for the levels of production or operations desired to fit the strategy. If rapid expansion is desired through internal means, does the firm have sufficient capacity to accommodate such expansion? Is the plant being used on overtime, double, or triple shifts? If retrenchment is under way, do we want to cut back production volume or keep the plant going and build inventories? These questions may call for a plant for long-term production vis-à-vis marketing plans.

Generally, three options exist for scheduling capacity usage: demand matching, operations smoothing, and subcontracting. If demand is seasonal, for example, demand matching calls for producing output with the season. Operations smoothing calls for continuous production to meet average demand levels. Subcontracting allows a firm to maintain steady minimal levels of output while meeting peak periods with output from subcontractors. Each of these approaches, of course, implies some tradeoffs with respect to the costs of equipment, overtime, inventories, labour, maintenance, and subcontracting. When demand downturns occur, a plan to build inventory instead of retrenching becomes a major strategic decision.

As the plan is determined, there may remain a need or desire for longer term capacity build-up. Here the options may include adding capacity, merging with another producer, or joint ventures. In any case, questions concerning the types of equipment, the amount of capacity, and the interface with existing units need to be addressed. Naturally, the overall size of a plant is of importance here and involves questions of economies of scale. This is partly determined by the technology employed but is also influenced by production scheduling and the basic marketing strategy. A large, efficient plant may not be effective if it is not producing the kinds of outputs called for by the strategy.

Capacity planning is also related to the policy question regarding scheduling. If demand matching is used, then plant size is geared to the production of peak output; otherwise, capacity can be smaller. Assuming that a strategy of expansion is under way, another question of importance is where to locate plants of operations facilities. For instance, a major component in airline operations is the location of facilities for aircraft maintenance. Of course, the critical elements of the firm's marketing and financial plans are relevant to the location decision. For instance, if new distribution approaches are a part of the strategy, locating plants near potential markets may outweigh factors such as the availability or cost of raw material inputs. The financial trade-offs of locating facilities near sources of labor or energy versus customers also need to be examined. Naturally, the type of product and logistics costs of inputs versus outputs becomes relevant considerations. Another factor of some importance is the degree of certainty associated with a new strategy. For instance, in the selection of a site for a new plant, the availability of land for further expansion later may be important if the decision is to plan for anticipated sales increases in the long run. And if the decision involves a move to foreign countries, social stability and tax conditions may play a role.

Finally, plants may be located near existing facilities to take advantage of economies of organisation, purchasing, and the like. In some cases, the decision is to replace existing facilities (or equipment) with new ones to take advantage of new technologies that are replacing obsolete ones. In other cases, the decision is to add on to an existing plant or build nearby. In still others, the firm seeks to take advantage of lower-cost foreign labour by locating plants outside its home country. Again, factors such as labour, transportation, market location, and technologies play key roles in these determinations. The types of processes to use are largely determined by the technology needed to produce given outputs. Still, some discretion or options may exist, particularly with respect to issues like the quality of processing equipment and allowable tolerances.

Many Japanese firms have gained significant competitive advantages by pursuing a policy of high-quality statistical control for their processing systems. Policies regarding investment to maintain or replace a plant and equipment can be important to the long-term ability of a firm to compete successfully and achieve objectives such as profits. Of course, the need for the maintenance of facilities varies from firm to firm. Maintenance at nuclear power plants or of aircraft is an absolute necessity. But there are often choices about whether to follow routine schedules (e.g., preventive maintenance) or whether to defer maintenance until there is a breakdown or replacement becomes necessary. Of course, keeping up-to-date, cost-effective equipment is a question of importance in creating a competitive advantage.

The overall quality component of a firm's strategy may determine the type of policy established for maintenance. But the criticality of prompt delivery of outputs may also play a role, and once again trade-offs with regard to inventory policies, the use of overtime, production schedules, and the like, become relevant.

Another key area in the operations of the firm involves sources of inputs or services important to the strategy. Choices about whom to purchase from involve more than a simple question of cost or availability. For instance, options may exist for shipping outputs by various forms of transportation (e.g., rail, airplane, ship). The speed of delivery versus costs may be important in the selection of the mode as well as the vendor. Further, whether to use one or more vendors or several sources for inputs and services is a question of some significance. Increasing dependence on one or a few sources may increase favourable treatment and cost savings but could come at the expense of flexibility.

Perhaps the key strategic issue involving sourcing is the make or buy question. In many instances, the decision is made by purchasing departments largely on the basis of the price to buy versus the cost to make. Yet such a policy is, in effect, a strategic decision regarding the development of competitive advantages. For instance, different financial needs are involved in making versus buying, and these can affect the capital structure.

If quick delivery is important to the strategy, consideration must be given to the varying reliability of suppliers versus the control over components or supplies made in-house. If expansion strategies for new products are desired, a firm may opt for buying specialty products to round out a line or making these itself. Of course, plant capacity, personnel skills, and the financial condition all play a role in such a decision.

Similarly, if retrenchment is the strategic choice, cost trade-offs of making versus buying can play a role here. Network firms have gone to extreme vertical *disintegration* by choosing to eliminate control over internal production. Many use foreign suppliers as sources. In essence, the question of vertical integration as a strategy is implicit in make or buy decisions. Hence, internal and external factors as well as objectives involved in strategy formulation should guide the establishment of policies in this area : strategic choice should not be left to the purchasing department by default.

Here, policies such as relying on supplies within 60 miles of a plant, or shipping finished goods immediately (instead of producing for inventory) can implement a just-in-time approach to accomplishing aggregate manufacturing flexibility. Similarly, personnel policies allowing the hiring of temporary or part-time workers for operations as necessary increase flexibility and can reduce costs. Allen-Bredley Company found that its highly automated assembly line increased flexibility, albeit at a cost of lower output. Yet the flexibility was seen as a higher-order priority than output, one that was essential to Allen-Bradley's future competitive ability.

POM is a crucial functional area in implementing strategies. Traditionally, marketing and POM have been rivals. But they must coexist and work together, and their tasks must be coordinated through appropriate policies and plans, if any strategy is to work. POM operating strategies must be coordinated with marketing strategy if the firm is to succeed. Careful integration with financial strategy components (such as capital budgeting and investment decisions) and the personnel function are also necessary. Exhibit 13.6 illustrate the importance of such coordination by showing the different POM concerns that arise when different marketing/financial/personnel strategies are required as elements of the grand strategy.

13.6.1 Functional Strategies in Human Resources Management

The strategic importance of functional strategies in the Human Resources area has become more widely accepted in recent years Human Resources Management aids in accomplishing grand strategy by ensuring the development of managerial talent, the presence of systems to manage compensation and regulatory concerns, and the development of competent, well-motivated employees. Functional strategies in Human Resources should guide the effective utilization of human resources to achieve both the annual objectives of the firm and the satisfaction and development of employees. These strategies involve the following areas:

- Employee recruitment, selection, and orientation.
- Career development and counselling, performance evaluation, and training and development.

Exhibit 13.6 Operations Management Concerns Associated with Different Elements of a Strategy

Possible elements of strategy	*Concomitant Conditions That may Affect or Place Demands on the Operations Function*
1. Compete as low-cost provider of goods or services	Broadens market. Requires longer production runs and fewer product changes. Requires special purpose, equipment and facilities.
2. Compete as high-quality provider	Often possible to obtain more profit per unit, and perhaps more total profit from a smaller volume of sales. Requires more quality-assurance effort and higher operating cost. Requires more precise equipment, which is more expensive. Requires highly skilled workers, necessitating higher wages and greater training efforts.
3. Stress customer service	Requires broader development of service people, service parts and equipment. Requires rapid response to customer needs or changes in customer tastes, rapid and accurate information system, careful coordination. Requires a higher inventory investment.
4. Provide rapid and frequent introduction of new products	Requires versatile equipment and people. Has higher research and development costs. Has high retraining costs and high tooling and changeover in manufacturing. Provides lower volumes for each product and fewer opportunities for improvements due to the learning curve.
5. Strive for absolute growth	Requires accepting some projects or products with lower marginal value, which reduces ROI Diverts talents to areas of weakness instead of concentrating on strengths.
6. Seek vertical integration	Enables company to control more of the process. May not have economies of scale at some stages of process. May require high capital investment as well as technology and skills beyond those currently available within the organisation.

Contd...

7. Maintain reserve capacity for flexibility	Provides ability to meet peak demands and quickly implement some contingency plans if forecasts are too low. Requires capital investment in idle capacity. Provides capability to grow during the lead time, normally required for expansion.
8. Consolidate processing (centralize)	Can result in economies of scale. Can locate near one major customer or supplier. Vulnerability: one strike, fire, or flood can stall the entire operation.
9. Disperse processing of service (decentralize)	Can be near several market territories. Requires more complex coordination network: perhaps expensive data transmission and duplication of some personnel and equipment at each location. If each location produces one product in the line, then other products still must be transported to be available at all locations. If each location specializes in a type of component for all products, the company is vulnerable to strike, fire flood, etc. If each location provides total product line, then economies of scale may not be realized.
10. Stress the use of mechanization, automation, robots	Requires high capital investment. Reduces flexibility. May affect labour relations. Makes maintenance more crucial.
11. Stress stability of employment	Serves the security needs of employees and may develop employee loyalty. Helps to attract and retain highly skilled employees. May require revision of make-or-buy decisions, use of ideal time, inventory, and subcontractors as demand fluctuates.

- Compensation.
- Labor/union relations.
- Equal employment opportunity requirements.
- Discipline, control, and evaluation.

Operating strategy for recruitment, selection, and orientation guides Human Resources Management decisions for attracting and retaining motivated, productive employees. This involves such questions as:

- What are the key human resource needs to support a chosen strategy?
- How do we recruit for these needs?
- How sophisticated should the selection process be?
- How should new employees be introduced to the organisation?

The recruitment, selection, and orientation component of personnel strategy should provide basic parameters for answering these questions. The development and training component should guide personnel actions taken to meet future human resource needs of the grand strategy. Merrill Lynch, a major brokerage firm, has a long-term corporate strategy of becoming a diversified financial service institution. In addition to handling stock transactions, Merrill Lynch is actively moving into such areas as investment banking, consumer credit, and venture capital. In support of these far-reaching, long-term objectives, Merrill Lynch has incorporated extensive early-career training and ongoing career development programmes to meet its expanding need for personnel with multiple competence.

Functional strategies in the Human Resources area are needed to guide decisions regarding compensation, labour relations, EEOC requirements, discipline, and control to enhance the productivity and motivation of the workforce. Involved are such concerns as;

- What are the standards for promotion?
- How should payment, incentive plans benefits, and seniority policies be interpreted?
- Should there be hiring preference?
- What are appropriate disciplinary steps?

These are specific personnel decisions that operating managers frequently encounter. Functional strategies in the Human Resources should guide such decisions in a way that is compatible with business strategy, strategies for other functional areas, and the achievement of annual objectives.

Perhaps one of the most difficult decisions regarding personnel occurs when a firm is pursuing a retrenchment strategy. At these times, questions usually include whether or not to lay off or terminate employees, how many, and who. Again, union contracts may establish some kind of policy here (resulting from earlier negotiations where a previous policy was laid down). But a firm may also attempt to protect labour and seek a shortened workweek or maintain the level of production for a time. Such policies relate to those in production and finance. A related matter is the relative proportion of managers and workers in the line and staff functions. Several writers have suggested that the policies of many firms have stressed placing the brightest and best people in staff functions at the expense of the line, which does the basic work. This has been blamed for declining productivity, inadequate plant investment, marginal quality standards, and the like. As a result, many firms have begun a streamlining programme by cutting the corporate level and other staff levels. Their goal is to pare overhead costs and gain some control over unwieldy, top-heavy structures. Of course, such trade-offs must be made with other objectives and considerations in mind.

Some firms incorporate a long-term human resource plan as an integral component of the strategic plan. Human resource managers have become an integral component in the strategic management activity, particularly as firms engage in mergers or major retrenchments requiring significant changes in the workforce. Thus requires forecasts of human resource needs (labour and management) in conjunction with other changes going on in the planning effort. Human Resource Managers need to foster more effective balancing of professional and private lives. A corporate objective to become more "lean and mean" must include consideration for the fact that a good home life contributes immensely to a good work life.

The work/family issue is no longer just a women's problem. Some specific measures that firms are taking to address this issue are providing spouse relocation assistance as an employee benefit, providing company resources for family recreational and educational use, establishing employee country clubs, such as those at IBM and Bethlehem Steel, and creating family/work interaction opportunities. Some organisations have developed "*family days*", when family members are invited to the workplace, taken on plant or office tours, dine by management, and given a chance to see exactly what other family members do each day. "Family days" are inexpensive and increase the employee's pride in working for the organisation. *Flexible working hours* during the week is another human resource response to the need for individuals to balance work life and home life. The work/family topic is being made part of the agenda at meetings and thus is being discussed in many organisations.

Policies and plans with respect to all the functions of a firm normally involve some questions of legality. For instance, a merger strategy to be implemented through the purchase of a competitor involves legal question. A marketing policy to give exclusive territories to distributors may involve legal issues. Securing favourable price breaks on large purchases of materials or hiring certain classes of employees for the executive ranks also involves legal issues, and so on. Some firms may pursue a policy for the purpose of testing a legal issue, as Sears did when it challenged the Equal Employment Opportunity Commission. Other executives may delay implementing plans unit advice of counsel is sought as to the legal ramifications of pursuing a given strategy in a certain way. Of course, implementing a strategy by moving into international territories compounds the difficulties and introduces the question of whether policies need to be established that are common to all SBUs or whether autonomy is to be granted to suit local conditions. The legal ramifications may have a great deal to do with a firm's policy on organizing such units. More firms appear to be increasing the size of in-house legal departments as problems connected with product liability, employee health and safety, employment practices, pollution problems, etc are cropping up.

Somewhat related to policies concerning legal issues is the whole area of social responsibility. Policies in this area remain quite nebulous. A whole variety of issues can be involved, including advertising ethics, bribing government officials (foreign or domestic), and corporate philanthropy. Like legal policies relations policies can cut across all the functional areas. There may be ethical questions in developing certain areas of research (such as research on DNA) or in selling products that are unsafe to certain types of consumers (such as infant formula in Africa). Of course, some production processes may be designed to use state-of-the-art technology to prevent pollution, or there may be an option to continue the legal dumping of dangerous chemical wastes. The list of issues seems to be endless. As a result, the public affairs government relations function has grown increasingly important, more staff members and resources are being allocated to this office, and more authority to make policies had been granted.

Policies here have an impact on the image the organisation wishes to present. But some can also be seen as necessary to protect long-term economic interests. For example, many firms operating in South Africa under conditions of apartheid face critical policy questions. Thus some firms may choose to encourage employee participation in community activities, involve themselves in political action committees (PACs), or provide financial support for community development projects. In many instances, these policies may be a way to "manage the environment". Remember, strategies can be active or passive. More firms these days appear to exercise active approaches to influencing their environment to create opportunity or avert threat. In addition to involvement with PACs the public relations staff or high-level executives will monitor the progress of pieces of legislation in central or state capitals. This involves watching committee assignments for bills, noting hearing schedules for bills of interest, and determining the action to be taken on each bill (testimony at hearings, speaking with committee members, attending the hearing, briefing key legislators regarding the issues, etc.).

As we discussed each area earlier, you may have noted that effective decisions cannot be made without regard to their impact on other areas of the business. Otherwise, sub-optimization is likely to result. Trade-offs is generally required in this process. A policy of minimizing the inventory may come at the expense of satisfying customers. Exhibit 13.7 shows some of the common trade-offs occur across areas as well.

Hence, top executives must be involved with negotiations and policy formulation to assure that the plans that are developed are working together to accomplish the key tasks needed to carry out a given strategy. The extent of involvement needed relates to the strategy itself. Consider, for instance, the need to link R& D, production, and marketing departments. If the strategy is to develop and produce products for specific customer needs, there will be a greater need to coordinate the activities of the three departments than if a "push strategy" in marketing is in use (selling whatever products are developed and produced). An example of this is Ford's "Team Taurus" normally, the 5-years process of creating a new automobile is sequential product planners define a concept, the design team takes over, and then engineering develops specifications that are passed on to manufacturing and suppliers. Such an approach was creating problems at Ford. The Team Taurus approach put together a group from planning, design, engineering, and manufacturing at the beginning of the process. The group asked assembly-line workers

Exhibit 13.7 Some Important Trade-off Decisions in Various Policy Areas

Policy Area	*Decision*	*Alternatives*
Plant and Equipment	Span of process	Make or buy
	Plant size	One big plant or several smaller ones
	Plant location	Locate near markets or locate near materials
	Investment decisions	Invest mainly in buildings or equipment or inventories or research
	Choice of equipment	General-purpose or special-purpose equipment
	Kind of tooling	Temporary, minimum tooling or "production tooling".
Production Planning and Control	Frequency of inventory taking	Few or many breaks in production for buffer stocks
	Inventory size	High inventory or a lower inventory
	Degree of inventory control	Control in great detail or in lesser detail
	What to control	Controls designed to minimize machine downtime or labour cost or time in process, or to maximize output of particular products or material usage
	Quality control	High reliability and quality or low costs
	Use of standards	Formal or informal or none at all
Labour and Staffing	Job specialization	Highly specialized or not highly specialized
	Supervision	Technically trained first-line supervisors on non-technically trained supervisors
	Wage system	Many job grades or few job grades; incentive wages or hourly wages
	Supervision style	Close supervision or lenient supervision
	Industrial engineers	Many or few

Contd...

Product Design/ Engineering	Size of product line	Many customer specials or few specials or none at all
	Design stability	Frozen design or many engineering change orders
	Technological risk	Use of new processes unproved by competitors or follow-the-leader policy
	Engineering, use of manufacturing engineering	Complete packaged design or design-as you-go approach Few or many manufacturing engineers
Organisation and Management	Kind of organization	Functional or product focus or geographical or other
	Executive use of time	High involvement in investment or production planning or cost control or quality control or other activities
	Degree of risk assumed	Decision based on much or little information
	Use of staff	Large or small staff group
	Executive style	Much or little involvement in detail; authoritarian or non-directive style, much or little contract with organisation

and suppliers for their ideas, at the same time doing extensive market research and back engineering on competitors' products to identify customer-desired features. Such integration was seen as necessary if Ford was to compete with foreign automakers.

If the business is highly capital-intensive with high manufacturing costs, then a stronger linkage between R& D and manufacturing is likely to be helpful for developing cost saving process improvements. The idea is that policies can be developed to encourage the organisation to maintain a desired liaison across units to effect the communication and coordination needed. In some instances, specialized formal units (e.g., expediters) may be set up in the organisation to facilitate this coordination. The management information system may be used here for coordination and control.

The timing of these plans and policies must be designed so that they mesh correctly. For instance, a number of computer companies attempted to rush into new products with marketing programmes promising more than could be delivered. Customers were anxiously awaiting the arrival of their new machines before production was capable of providing the necessary output. So lead times within each area of the business need to be considered in relation to one another before plans are implemented. Further, some policy decisions can be made and implemented immediately (e.g., change from LIFO to FIFO, hire unskilled workers). Others take long lead times to come to fruition (e.g., research and development, building new plants). For example, Genentech had a plant whereby it would hire sales force personnel contingent on approval of a new drug by the FDA, which takes some time. Thus, in effect, firms create a cascade of plans and policies, with the long-range choices affecting medium- and short-range decisions.

Policies also vary over time, shifting with strategic needs. One interesting perspective sheds some light on what may be one way to determine how plans need to change with certain strategies. Fox has shown how implementation will vary depending on where the firm's main product or service is in the product-service life cycle. Exhibit 13.8 presents his framework.

Exhibit 13.8 Strategic Choice Framework

	Strategic choice
	↓
Longer than 3 years:	Long-range policies, plans, programmes
	↓
1 to 3 years:	Medium-range policies, plans, programmes
	↓
Less than 1 year:	Short-range policies, plans, programmes

Of course, a multiple-SBU firm may have a number of products, each of which is in a different stage of development. Hence specific guidelines are subject to some question as to their overall usefulness. Nonetheless, the exhibit does illustrate how policies can be meshed with different demands imposed by a strategy change.

Finally, it should be remembered that if contingency planning or second-generation planning is being used, alternative functional policies for each contingency plan must be developed. These and many other functional plans and policies are needed to implement the grand strategy. Your ability to formulate these will be a good indication of your practical ability to make the strategy work. Research suggests that the success of a firm's strategy depends on proper implementation and balancing of resources, plans, and policies.

13.7 OPERATIONAL IMPLEMENTATION

Operation implementation is the approach adopted by an organisation to achieve operational effectiveness. This is the final aspect of strategy implementation. Operation implementation deals with the nitty-gritty of strategy. This is time for action as this is the stage at which the most tangible work gets done. Obviously, the scope of operation implementation would be very wide. It would cover practically everything that is done in an organisation. It is the major task of line managers. Just like a war is won ultimately on the basis of ammunition and supplies rather than grand strategies alone, the success of corporate and business strategies crucially depends on how operational implementation is done and in what way operational effectiveness is achieved.

Porter considers operational effectiveness as necessary but not sufficient to the success of strategy. He explains the term as "performing similar activities better than rivals perform them". Operational effectiveness includes but is not limited to efficiency. It refers to any number of practices that allows a company to better utilize its inputs by, for example, reducing defects in products or developing better products faster.

On the fundamental objects of the discipline of management has been to show organisations ways to improve their operational effectiveness. While doing so, a number of practices have developed over a period of time. These practices or techniques or methods are derived from concepts, theories, and models, which, in turn, have been sourced from management thoughts and philosophies. There has been a virtual explosion of management philosophies, theories, and practices in the second half of the twentieth century, and the trend continues in the twenty-first century. A majority of these developments relate to the basic issue of improving operational effectiveness. Managers have desperately looked for new philosophies, theories, and practices that can help them in improving operational effectiveness. Often this search has led them to tangible results. Sometimes, though, it has resulted in disappointment.

The scope of operational implementation and operational effectiveness is very wide. You have learnt about several management practices in the area of strategic management, and in other courses as well. The functional area courses such as, marketing or finance; and core courses like, economics or quantitative methods; deal primarily with the techniques, methods, and practices meant to help organisations improve operational effectiveness. All these come to the fore during the course of operational implementation. This section would, therefore, not attempt to achieve the impossible, that is, to discuss all the practices in operational implementation. Rather it would attempt to draw your attention to the critical areas of operational implementation and point out some representative practices. For discussing operational implementation, we propose to deal with operational effectiveness in terms of 4-P's: productivity, processes, people, and pace.

- **Productivity** is the measure of the relative amount of input needed to secure a given amount of output. It is frequently expressed mathematically as the ratio of the quantity of output to the quantity of input. Inputs are resources (such as finance, raw materials, machinery and equipment, information, time or management). Outputs are the products and services.

Exhibit 13.9 Relationship of Implementation to the Product Life Cycle

Stage of PLC	*Functional focus*	*R&D*	*Production*	*Marketing*	*Physical* ***Distribution***
Pre-commercialization	Coordination of R&D and other functions	Reliability tests; release blueprints	Production design; process planning; purchasing; department lines up vendors and subcontractors	Test marketing Detailed marketing paln	Plan shipping schedules, mixed carloads; rent warehouse space, trucks
Introduction	Engineering: debugging in R&D production, and field	Technical corrections (engineering changes)	Subcontracting; centralize pilot plants; test various processes; develop standards	Induce trial; fill pipelines; sales agents or commissioned salespeople; publicity	Plan a logistics system
Growth	Production	Start successor product	Centralize production; phase out subcontractors; Expedite vendors' output; long runs	Channel commitment; brand emphasis Salaried sales force; reduce price if necessary	Expedite deliveries; shift to owned facilities
Maturity	Marketing and logistics	Develop minor; variants; reduce costs through value analysis; originate major adaptations to start new cycle	Many short runs; decentralize; import parts, low-priced models; routinization; cost reduction	Short-term promotions; salaried salespeople; cooperative advertising; forward integration routine marketing research; panels, audits	Reduce costs and raise customer service level; control finished goods inventory

Contd...

Decline	Finance	Withdraw all R&D from initial version	Revert to subcontracting; simplify production line careful inventory control; buy foreign or competitive goods; stock spare parts	Revert to commission basis; withdraw most promotional support; raise price, selective distribution; careful phase out, considering entire channel	
HRM	*Finance*	*Management Accounting*	*Other*	*Customers*	*Competition*
Recruit for new activities; negotiate operational changes with unions	Life cycle plan for cash flows profits, investments, subsidiaries	Payout planning full costs/ revenues; determine optimum lengths of lifecycle stages through present value method	Final legal clearances (regulatory hurdles, patents); appoint life-cycle coordinator	Panels and other test respondents	Neglects opportunity or is working on similar idea
Staff and train middle management; stock options for executives	Accounting deficit; high net cash outflow; authorize large production facilities	Help develop production and distribution standards; prepare sales aids, sales management portfolio		Innovators and some early adopters	Monopoly disparagement of innovation Legal and extralegal interference
Add suitable personnel for plants, many grievances; heavy overtime	Very high profits, net cash outflow still rising, sell equities	Short-term analyses based on return per scarce resource		Early adopters and early majority	Oligopoly; a few imitate, improve, or cut prices

Contd...

Contd...

Transfers, advancements; incentives for efficiency, safety, and soon	Declining profit rate but increasing net cash inflow	Analyze different costs/ revenue; spearhead cost reduction, value analysis, and efficiency drives	Pressure for resale; price maintenance; price cuts bring price wars: possible price collusion	Early adopters, early and late majority, some laggards; first discontinued by late majority	Monopoly competition first shakeout, yet many rivals
Find new slots; encourage early retirement	Administer system; retrenchment; sell unneeded equipment; export the machinery	Analyze escapable costs; pinpoint remaining outlays	Accurate sales forecast very important	Mainly laggards	Oligopoly, after second shakeout, only few rivals

- **Processes** are courses of action used for operational implementation. Processes are often implemented through methods. These methods are systematic and orderly procedures, and consist of sequential steps implemented in a chronological order. The purpose of all processes is to achieve optimum utilization of resources.
- **People** are the stakeholders in the organisation. The significant people are the investors, employees, suppliers, customers. Among these, employees play a direct and central role in operational implementation.
- **Pace** is the speed of operational implementation and is measured in terms of time. Efficiency is the parameter often used to express the pace of operational implementation. Efficiency is the amount of work done (or performance) per unit time.

The areas of operational effectiveness are not mutually exclusive. A practice that is chosen to achieve productivity adopts a process that is followed by people and is executed at defined pace. What is important is the overall effects achieved, that is, operational effectiveness. This is the reason why horizontal fits is so important to operational implementation. Next, we shall take up the four areas of operational effectiveness for discussion. But let us clarify two points before we discuss these four areas.

First, we said above that by taking up these four areas we hope to cover the major aspects of operational implementation. Yet the scope of operational implementation is so wide that other aspects may have to be included in practice. For instance, profitability may be an aspect that matter at the level of operational implementation. The several small activities that make up operational implementation contribute to profitability. So some of you might feel that profitability should also be included as an area of operational implementation.

Secondly, within one area we include practices that primarily relate to that area. To some of you it may seem that practice we place in one area should really belong to another area. This is understandable since the integrated nature of operational implementation makes it possible that one practice contributes to more than one area. For instance, a productivity practice may also contribute to better process and it usually leads to faster pace.

The discussion that follows will primarily be in terms of the practices, techniques, and methods used in a particular area. These practices have been proposed from time to time by management theories, practitioners, and consultants. Each practice is based on a set of concepts, theories and models. And these, in turn, are derived from management thoughts and philosophies. Different thoughts and philosophies have dominated the practice of managements' at different times. Environmental factors, to a large extent, have been the stimuli for these practices. So, if scientific management held sway over managements practice in the beginning of the twentieth century then the application of information technology assumed greater importance by the close of the millennium. Along the way, we have seen the rise and fall of management practices. We will close this section by referring to this issue. But before we do that let us have an overview of the management practices in the four areas of operational effectiveness. More emphasis shall be laid on the modern practices so that you are able to relate to the role that they play in operational implementation.

13.7.1 Productivity

One of the earliest practices to be adopted for operational effectiveness was that of scientific management, propounded by Frederick Taylor in the beginning of the twentieth century. It focused on the optimum utilisation of resources such as workers, machine, and time. It led to the development of work-study techniques of time and motion study that are still used extensively in industrial engineering. Operations research techniques came to be used during and after the Second World War. Linear and non-linear programming helped in the development of techniques aimed at optimum utilisation of resources. The 1970s saw computer applications in manufacturing substantially enhancing the productivity of operations. Computer-aided design (CAD) and computer-aided manufacturing (CAM) permitted the resolution of problems that would otherwise not be possible owing to the vast amount of computations involved. The 1980s witnessed the spread of quality and productivity techniques popularized by Japanese firms. The 1990s saw a virtual explosion in terms of techniques and method for productivity improvement. In a large measure, these were motivated by the pressure of Japanese competitive superiority in manufacturing and quality over the American and European firms.

The modern practices of productivity enhancement are an amalgam of the traditional methods, variations made upon the traditional methods, and new methods. Automated assembly lines, for instance, can be seen as an extension of the scientific management philosophy, aided by computerized manufacturing by computerized numerical control (CNC) machines, and implemented through flexible manufacturing system incorporating cellular manufacturing layout and robotics technology.

The significant modern practices observed here are of just- in- time (JIT) manufacturing, cycle time reduction, group technology, mass customization, concurrent engineering and processing, optimized production technology, flexible manufacturing systems, cellular manufacturing, total productive maintenance, and lean manufacturing.

- **Just-in-time manufacturing** (1970s) is a Japanese productivity technique designed to tackle cost reduction from a system-wide perspective. It is a comprehensive approach and includes simpler product designs, fewer parts requirements, streamlining of process flows, fewer changes, and reduction of production set-up times. Such a production system requires fewer suppliers who supply small quantities in a perfectly-timed arrangement, resulting in practically no inventory.
- **Cycle time reduction** (1980s) though the concept of cycle time is much older this technique aims at minimizing the time taken for the allocated work to be done at each workstation on an assembly line.
- **Group technology** (1980s) is a way of organizing and using data for components that make up a number of products that have similar properties and manufacturing requirements. Assimilation of data helps in avoiding duplication of design and manufacturing a variety of products.
- **Mass customization** (early 1990s) attempts to blend the desirable attributes of mass production and customized production.
- **Concurrent engineering and processing** (early 1990s) involves integrated, simultaneous design of products or services and their related processes, including manufacturing and support. It is intended to involve designer and engineers from the time the customer requirements and product concept are defined.
- **Optimized production technology** (1980s) is a computer-based system for planning production, materials requirements, and resource utilisation through focusing on the bottleneck work centres and careful management of materials and resources related to those centres, so that the output is maximized and inventories are reduced.
- **Flexible manufacturing system** (1980s) is a computer-controlled process technology suitable for producing batches of a variety of high quality products quickly. It falls between the traditional high-volume mass production and job-shop type of production systems and retains the advantages of both.
- **Cellular manufacturing** (1980s) is a system where the arrangement of production facility is done in such a manner that the equipment used to make similar parts, or families of parts, are grouped together. This idea seems to be quite close to the traditional concept of process layout-based production system.
- **Total productive maintenance** of Seiichi Nakajima (1984) challenged the traditional concept of maintenance as reactive problem-fixing by a comprehensive system of managing productivity through organisation-wide autonomous maintenance done by everyone rather than a department alone.
- **Lean manufacturing** (1990) is based on the thinking that all the stages of manufacturing between sourcing to marketing should be so integrated that a variety of products are produced with minimum resources and at the exact time that they are required.

As a practice for operational implementation, productivity is significant for all types of strategies but is especially relevant for business strategies of cost-leadership, differentiation, and focus. Productivity improvements have a tremendous potential for exercising cost control and effecting cost reduction, resulting in the implementation of cost-leadership strategies. The disaggregation of process, possible through say, flexible manufacturing systems, makes it possible to reap the advantages of mass production, and batch manufacturing makes it possible for the firms to implement differentiation strategies. Similarly, focus, based either on low-cost or differentiation, is also possible.

As you must have noted, most modern productivity improvement techniques attempt to retain the advantages of mass production, that is low cost, with customized production, that is necessary for differentiation to be created.

13.7.2 Processes

Processes have an overwhelming presence in management. The term "management" is defined in terms of the managerial processes of planning, organizing, leading, and controlling. Decision-making in management and strategic management are processes too. The functional areas of marketing, finance, operations, human resource management, and information management operate on the basic of well-established processes. These functional areas have myriad processes, such as, selling, marketing research, budgeting, inventory control, maintenance management, staffing, management development, and informing processing.

The history of management is replete with examples of processes designed to make human work systematic and meaningful. From Henri Fayal's (1916) processing of managerial activities of planning, organizing, command, coordination, and control, through Peter Ducker's (1973) enunciation of the practices of management, to be process of knowledge management formalized by Tom Davenport (1998), the quest for processes has been rewarding though tortuous at times.

The modern practices related to processes are several. Among these the major comprehensive processes are business process reengineering, enterprise-wide resources planning, quality management processes, benchmarking, value chain, and supply-chain management.

Quality Management Systems (such as total quality management, based on W E Deming's [1986] theory, and total quality control, an empirical Japanese administrative system) aid in the operational implementation of quality management processes. Motorola's **Six-Sigma System** of measuring, analyzing, improving, and controlling quality rigorously in processes and sub-processes so that the defect rate is just 3.4 per million units.

Michael Porter's (1980) **value-chain analysis** deals with the set of interlinked value-creating activities performed by an organisation and helps in examining all the activities that a firm performs and how they interact. This could result in process improvements. The concept of value-chain led to the development of several concepts in the 1980s and 1990s.

Business Process Reengineering, propounded by the Michael Hammer and James Champy (1993), aims at transforming or reinventing organisation for greater efficiency and deals with the fundamental rethinking and redesigning of business processes to achieve dramatic improvements in cost, quality, service, and speed.

Enterprise Resource Planning (ERP of the early 1990s) are software packages that link the isolated information centres into an integrated enterprise-wide structure of functional and activity database. These systems are successors to the material requirement planning (MRP-I) and manufacturing resources planning (MRP-II) systems, long used for planning and scheduling the time-phased material requirements for operations.

Benchmarking (1990s) is the process aimed at finding the best practices within and outside the industry to which an organisation belongs. The purpose of benchmarking is to find the best performance in an area so that one could match one's own performance with them, and even surpass them.

Supply-Chain Management (1990s) traverses the whole value-chain to manage the procurement of a whole range of inputs that are required to produce a product or service so that the process can be performed in an integrated and optimum manner. Vendors, transporters, and buyers become a part of the firm's value-chain, and the benefits of process improvements and operational effectiveness are shared by all.

Outsourcing (1990s) is a variation of the traditional make-or-buy concept where portions of value-chain activities are commissioned to external suppliers on the basis of economic analysis, so that the firm's own focus remains on its core competence. A related concept is of the modular organisation where the value-stream, down to its components, is broken down and a decision taken to focus on core activities and to outsource rest of the activities to outside agencies who can perform them more efficiently. Here too, the vendors and suppliers are a part of the firm's processing system and the benefits from optimization and operational effectiveness are shared by all.

Processes, as practices for operational implementation, are significant for all types of strategies. Since process improvement is the basic purpose of all new processes, there are several benefits of lower cost, better quality, lesser wastage, lesser production time, and higher productivity. So processes are relevant for operational implementation of all types of business strategies. For instance, strategic advantage results from the ability of a company to manage its value-chain in a way that enables it to offer better customer value, thereby making it more competitive. Also, deconstructing value-chains by using supply-chain management and outsourcing makes it possible to offer higher differentiation, as the firm's own facilities are not tied down to mass manufacturing.

13.7.3 People

Nineteenth century management considered people as just a unit of productive labour within and a member of the buying community outside. Operational implementation was all about taking maximum work out of wage-earners and paying them as little as possible. The worker management relation was the master-servant type or, at best, a paternalistic "mai-baap" connection. The emergence of human relations, industrial sociology, industrial psychology, and the ideas of human behaviour and motivation during the period 1930 through 1960 caused a drastic change in the perception of people as a critical resource. The transformation of labour relations to personnel management and then to human resource management and strategic human resource management is an indication of the change that has taken place with regard to people management.

Operational implementation with regard to people management assumes a wider scope when strategies have to address, i.e., an extended body of stakeholders. The coverage includes not only the people the employees, within but also outside, such as, the customer, suppliers, and the society at large. The content of optional implementation, therefore, must take into account activities related to all these stakeholders. That people factor becomes a critical contributor to operational effectiveness is indicated by a plethora of terms such as job-enrichment, empowerment, team-building, multi-skilling, knowledge-worker, human capital, intellectual capital, organisational learning, and knowledge management related to employees. The focus of competitive strategies and marketing has decidedly shifted in the favour of the customers. Integrative processes, such, as supply-chain management, include suppliers as a part of the organisational system. And issues, such as, corporate governance, ethics and values, and social responsibility, widen the concerns of people management to adopt operational measures to address a wider audience of stakeholders.

Here we focus on some of the major practices related to people management in the contemporary context. Strategic recruitment and selection encompasses manpower planning aligned with strategic, scientific selection processes designed on the basics of psychometric to have the right match between employee and job requirements, campus recruitment and the Internet-based recruitment through job and career websites.

Performance management includes aspects, such as, psychometric testing for placement, carefully designed orientation programmes, flexibility in working hours, application of behavioural sciences in designing motivational systems, building up self-directed teams, empowerment through flatter structures, decentralization and involvement, effective communication skills, negotiation techniques, and career planning and development. Training and development is done through an increasing emphasis on creativity and innovation, multi-skilling, cross-cultural training, and using the principles of organisational learning and knowledge management processes.

Performance appraisal and retention management is done through design and application of formal performance appraisal, pay-for-performance systems that clearly link performance with rewards, feedback systems, non-monetary incentives, and employee stock option schemes. Separation management is no longer considered just as retrenchment and paying the dues stipulated under the law. Exit interviews, early retirement schemes, sabbaticals, voluntary retirement schemes, and outplacement services are becoming the norm as many companies are downsizing.

Besides the people within, companies are also focusing on customers through customer survey and feedback, market research, relationship marketing, and customer relationship management. Investors are provided with better information through transparent disclosures and aesthetically-designed corporate annual reports. They are also treated to special discount schemes for the company's product and services. Companies are becoming more socially responsive to the ultimate stakeholder, i.e., the society, by engaging in innovative social development programmes. Emphasis is placed on building up reputation and there is more openness and transparency in providing better service and more information. As can be seen, people management offers a wide scope for enhancing operational effectiveness.

13.7.4 Pace

The final area that we take up for discussion is the pace. By this is meant the speed of operational implementation. The area is important since time is now recognized as being of essence to strategy implementation. In terms of value-chain, pace can be seen as performing every activity faster than the rivals so that strategic advantage results.

Operational implementation makes it possible to speed up activities. Time study was proposed by Taylor and his associates as early as 1900 in order to analyze the sequence of production work to identify wastage and to build up more efficient process. For most part of the early twentieth century, the traditional techniques prevailed and several of them are still in use. The nature of managerial work was studied by Mintzberg (1973). While researching on how managers actually spend their time he found that they engage in bursts of activities interspersed by interruptions. This led to a greater understanding of how suboptimal utilisation of time takes place within organisations.

Network analysis and activity charts (1970s), successors to Gantt charts of 1901, have been popular techniques to optimize time and resource allocation by focusing on the functional critical path. Timely project execution is seen as a source of saving on cost overruns.

Time-based management (late 1980s), including time-based competition (1990s), are ideas that have been advanced to illustrate the point that time can be used as a strategic weapon. First-movers in competitive markets are assumed to gain advantages not available to late-movers. Time management (1980s) has emerged as a significant practice to increase productivity and efficiency. Most productivity and process related practices also result in time saving.

Organisational mechanisms such as delegation are preferred as they enable managers to focus on critical activities through "**management by exception** "or "**the 80-20 principle**". Technology support has made it possible to use time-saving devices. But, by far, the most significant technology that quickens the pace of operational implementation is IT. What is remarkable about computers and IT is that almost all the developments have taken place in the second half of the twentieth century prompting some people to call this period as the information age and the economy as the knowledge economy. Workers are now knowledge-workers, since most people within an organisation are involved in some aspect of information management.

Information management is the branch of management that deals with the collection, processing, storing, and disseminating of information for the purpose of managerial decision making. Information system is a system in which data flow takes place between people and organisational unit, such as, departments and functions. From simple transaction processing system, the developments in information system have led to management reporting system, decision support system, group support system, executive support system, and export support system.

Information technology constitutes the hardware and software that is used in information systems. Embedded information technology is IT that is integrated with the other components, such as, products and services. Knowledge based products or services are called such because their function and performance and embedded within them.

The first-order information systems are the single-user systems in applications, such as, electronic spreadsheets for automation and analysis of record-keeping, database management systems for managing data productivity, multimedia presentation for integration of data formats of text, sound, image, animation, and video. The second order information systems are the multiuser and network systems that use telecommunications technology with IT resulting in applications such as electronic mail (e-mail), voice mail, video-conferencing, work-group conferencing, electronic bulletin boards, electronic funds transfer, electronic data interchange and electronic commerce.

The potential of convergence of IT, telecommunication, and consumer electronics technology is being realized in the form of greater interactivity. The implications of the developments in information management are mind-boggling and exciting for operational implementation. IT is augmenting immensely the capability or organisations to enhance their operational effectiveness. The most significant benefit is in terms of the speed of processing and dissemination of data, an aspect of what we refer to as pace here. Several of practices that we refer to in this section — such as, flexible manufacturing systems, ERP or knowledge management — have been possible through the application of IT. It is obvious; therefore, that pace is of immense practical value for all types of strategies.

Given such a wide array of practices, methods, and techniques for enhancing operational effectiveness in the areas of productivity, processes, people, and pace, the managers have a difficulty in choosing which of these to pick up to use in operational implementation. The choice is made even more difficult owing to factors, like the credibility of the originators of these practices, who are often high-profile management consultancy firms or respected academician-consultants. And many of these are global consultancy firms and global management gurus. They make presentations so effectively in conjunction with a blitzkrieg of publicity in the business media that the power of their technique seems to be overwhelming. Managers in firms often fall for techniques and choose them indiscriminately. Disappointment results and soon the technique is termed a fad not worth using.

Several management techniques have risen like a phoenix and then have bitten the dust. Managers, possibly in their desperate search for a panacea for organisational ills, opt for the latest technique and then find that it does not work. This is not a correct approach. The malady often does not lie with the technique but in the way it is chosen and applied. Managers need to derive the areas of improvements from the requirements of the strategy that they are implementing. Organisational analysis can serve as a starting point for identifying the areas where functioning needs to be improved. Having done that, the technique can then be chosen and applied. After all, continuous improvement is the ultimate goal of all implementation as encapsulated in the Japanese concept of kaizen.

It is important to remember that any technique has a history, background, context, and requirements. A technique cannot be applied blindly. There are essential prerequisites to applying a technique and then there are the consequences. A proper understanding of all these aspects is necessary in applying a technique. For instance, supply-chain management cannot be applied if the supplier-company relationship is not congenial, the cost of implementation is prohibitive, the quality of products needs improvement, the speed of work within the organisation is suboptimal, and there is no flexibility of operations. Then support systems, such as, an information system with adequate inputs of IT, are required for the application of supply-chain management to be feasible.

There is enough information available regarding the management principles, theory, concepts, and models working behind a technique. On the one hand, managers need to be aware of these to enhance their understanding and gain a comprehensive assessment of the usage of a technique. On the other hand, managers need to have an in-depth understanding of their organisation. A match of what the organisation needs and what the technique has to offer has to be made.

The application of techniques is facilitated with the help of books and journals, manuals, in-house experts, and consultants related to the management techniques. A dedicated and patient approach can help managers in applying the practices, methods, and techniques for enhancing operational effectiveness and effective operational implementation.

Exercise

1. What factors do the marketing plans and policies deal with? Why are they important for strategy implementation?
2. What are the concerns of operations plans and policies? Why are these plans and policies significant for strategy implementation?
3. What difficulty do managers face in choosing operational implementation practices? How can this difficulty be minimized?
4. Take the example of any Indian business organisation. Suggest the major elements of the marketing plans and policies the organisation should consider implementing.

5. What are the different mechanisms used for the integration of functional plans and policies?
6. What are the latest operational effectiveness techniques in the areas of productivity, process, people and place?
7. Why is there need for integration of functional plans and policies?
8. Explain the different functional strategies an organisation can use in R&D, finance, production, operations management & HRM.
9. What is the relationship of product life cycle with different functional areas?
10. How can an organisation improve the productivity and what new techniques and tools an can be adopted to increase the productivity?

14 Strategic Evaluation and Control

14.1 INTRODUCTION

There are three primary types of organisational control: strategic control, management control, and the operational control. Strategic controls, the process of evaluating strategy, is practised both after strategy is formulated and implementation. The organisation's strategists evaluate strategy once it has been formulated to ascertain whether it is appropriate to mission accomplishment and again once it has been implemented to determine if the strategy is accomplishing its objectives.

Management control is the process of assuring that major subsystems progress towards the accomplishment of strategic objectives is satisfactory. For example, is SBU/Product Division's ROI performance acceptable? Or, is the production department meeting its quality control objectives? Whereas operational control is the process of ascertaining whether individual and work group role behaviours (performance) are congruent with individual and work group role prescriptions. For example, is Rama reaching his sales quota? Like the phase of planning, the types of control are not distinct entities. Rather, in various organisations, one type of control may be almost indistinguishable from another. Furthermore, the devices used in one type of control may also be employed in another. For example, management control devices such as ROI may be used to measure not only the performance of organisational components but the total organisation as well.

While most operational and many management control systems may possess automatic correction activities, the evaluation of strategy requires executive judgment. Strategic, management, and operational control systems perform an important integrative function. The measurement of performance as related to objective accomplishment coordinates activity. Experience and research have revealed that any number of variables may cause performance to be incongruent with strategy. For example, the assumptions under which strategy was formulated may change. Or, strategy, plans, and policies may not be adhered to. Deviations from either assumptions or guidance lead to unsatisfactory results. Therefore, the successful strategy must have control as one of its dimensions.

What is controlled varies from level to level in the organisation. The organisation strategists are responsible for strategic control, as are the stockholders, theoretically. Management control is principally the function of top management, especially the CEO.

Operational control is primarily the concern lower-level managers. Strategic control and management control are concerned with perspectives broader than the details dealt with in operational control. Note, however, that strategic information systems allow top management to view the details of operations if necessary. While much of what follows is related to formal control systems, informal control systems may suffice in the smaller organisation, especially for operational control where personal observation is possible.

14.2 STEPS OF STRATEGIC CONTROL

Strategic control may be depicted as a **six**-step feedback model as follow:

1. ***The establishment of standards of performing:*** Standards are specific points against which actual performance will be judged. As such they are more detailed expressions of strategic objectives and are the bases of role prescriptions. Establishing standards for organisational subcomponents is the first step in management control, and establishing them for individuals is the first step in operational control.
2. ***The statement of acceptable tolerances:*** The standard is a single point on a continuum of possible behaviours, but it is not always necessary to perform exactly to that point. Normally, deviation from standards will be tolerated within certain control limits.
3. ***Measurement of actual performance***: Measurement is the third step in management or operational control. It involves the identification of role behaviour either for components of individuals. Measurement techniques vary from situation to situation and are often imprecise.
4. ***Comparison of standards and performance:*** While comparing standards and performance might appear to be a simple task, it is quite complex in the more qualitative performance areas because of the inability to quantify either standards or performance.
5. ***Action:*** Where performance is satisfactory, that is, congruent with standards no action is necessary. But where it is not, corrective action must be taken.
6. ***Preventive action:*** As Bill Greenwood has observed, it is insufficient simply to correct problems. Rather, action must be taken to assure these problems do not occur again.

This model focuses on results (output). In fact, most control systems – strategic, management, or operational – focus on results. Often, the consequence of utilizing these feedback control systems is that the unsatisfactory performance continues until the malfunctioning is discovered. One technique for reducing the problems associated with feedback control system is "feed forward control". First suggested by Harold Koontz and Robert W. Bradspies, feedforward control focuses on the inputs to the system and attempts to anticipate problems with outputs (see Exhibit 14.1) With respect to strategy and planning, feed forward control has wide applicability. For example, the feed forward principle underlies the concept of simulation modeling. What if, questions are, after all, examinations of hypothesized inputs to determine resultant effects on system outputs. Simulations of performance can be made in any number of strategic situations to test for changes in basic assumptions. In fact, any situation with identifiable inputs which can be modeled can and should utilize the feed forward approach.

Exhibit 14.1 The Organisation as a Processing System

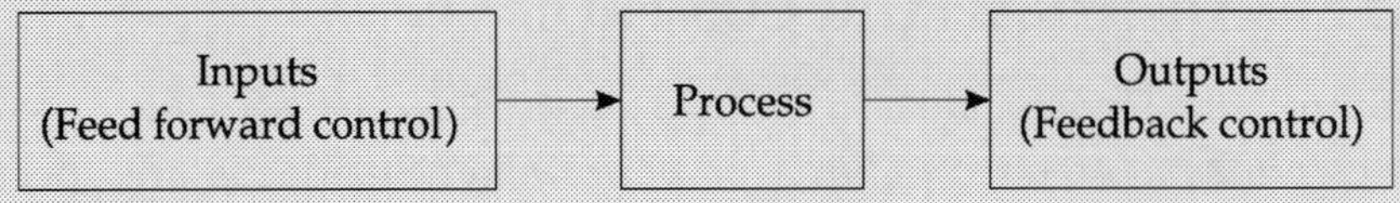

Once strategy has been formulated, it should be evaluated. Several criteria for evaluation have been suggested. The best known of these, the Tilles model, can be summarized as follows:

- Is the strategy internally consistent, for example, is it consistent with mission and consistent among its own plans?
- Is it consistent with the environment?
- Is it consistent with internal resources?
- Does it have an appropriate amount of risk?
- Does it have a proper time horizon?
- Is it workable?

E.P. Learned and others, building on the Tilles model, suggest that the following are proper evaluative questions:

- Is it identifiable? Has it been clearly and consistently identified and are people aware of it?
- Is it appropriate to the personal values and aspirations of key managers?
- Does it constitute a clear stimulus to organisational efforts and commitment?
- Is it socially responsible?
- Are there early indications of the responsiveness of market segments to the strategy?
- Does it rely on weaknesses or do anything to reduce them?
- Does it exploit major opportunities?
- Does it avoid, reduce, or mitigate the major threats? If not, are there adequate contingency plans?

These questions relate directly to the strategic management process model. In fact, these questions, when considered in total, comprise a checklist to determine if the strategic management process model has been properly followed. All these questions can be applied as the strategy progresses through its various stages, including implementation. Progress and changes can thus be observed. Specific standards of performance are established by the strategic objectives of the master strategy and subsequent component objectives.

Once implement occurs, measurements will be taken to determine if the objectives have been reached. The tolerances established in Step 2 of the six-step feedback model vary from firm to firm. Tolerances are primarily judgmental. They tell how much deviation from the standard management can live with. Corrective and preventive action may require that strategy be changed. Management control becomes a distinct concern when decentralization occurs. Where management control is imposed, it functions within the framework established by the strategy. Management control focuses on the accomplishment of the objectives of the various sub-strategies comprising the master strategy and the accomplishment of the objectives of the intermediate plans. Normally, these objectives (standards) are established for major subsystems within the organisation. Such as SBUs, projects, products, functions, and responsibility centres. Allowable tolerances vary from organisation to organisation. Typical management control measures include ROI, residual income, cost, product quality, efficiency measures, and so forth. These control measures are essentially summations of operational control measures. When corrective or preventive action is taken, it may involve minor or very major changes in the strategy. Often, top management strategists may be removed from their positions as a consequence of poor performing as indicated by these control measures. One large firm has a policy for its European operating division managers: "Two consecutive quarters of declining ROI and you are fired!" Often, critical decisions for a company's future result from rather imperfect control information.

Operational control systems are designed to ensure that day-to-day actions are consistent with established plans and objectives. Operational control is concerned with individual and group role performance as compared with the individual and group role prescriptions required by organisational plans. Such control systems are normally concerned with the past (unless feed forward systems are being utilized). Operational control focuses on events in a recent period. Operations control systems are derived from the requirements of the management control system. Specific standards for performance are derived from the objectives of the operating plans, which are based on intermediate plans, which are based on strategy. Performance is compared against objectives at the individual and group levels. Corrective or preventive action is taken where performance does not meet standards. This action may involve training, motivation, leadership, discipline, or termination.

It is important to know who the participants are and what role they will play in strategic evaluation and control. This will answer the question: who evaluates the strategy and how do they do it? Going beyond the role of evaluators, we are also interested in knowing who the appraisers are and how they help in strategic evaluation. The various participants in strategic evaluation and control and their respective roles are described below:

- **Shareholders-Lenders:** Theoretically, every organisation is ultimately responsible to its shareholders-lenders and the public in the case of private companies, and the government in the public sector companies. The role of shareholders, in practice, however, is limited. This is specially true of the general public where the individual holding is too small to be of any effective value in strategic evaluation.

Lenders such as financial institutions and banks which have an equity stake are typically concerned about the security and returns on their shareholding rather than in the long-term assessment of strategic success. The government, through its different agencies, does play a significant role in the strategic evaluation and control of public sector companies.

- **The Board of Directors:** The Board of Directors enacts the formal role of reviewing and screening executive decision in the light of their environmental, business and organisational implications. In this way, the board is required to perform the functions of strategic evaluation in more generalized terms. But there is a lot of variation among Indian companies in the way in which the Board may perform its control functions. In some companies, the Board may have the real authority to oversee strategic evaluation, while in other companies its authority may be usurped by other like chief executive or a higher de facto authority, such as the family council, in the case of family-owned companies, the headquarters in the case of MNC subsidiaries, or the controlling ministry in the case of public sector companies.
- **Chief Executives:** Chief Executives are ultimately responsible for all the administrative aspects of strategic evaluation and control. Ideally, a chief executive should not sit in judgment over the performance of the organisation under his or her control. Rather, the chief executive should be evaluated on the basis of his/her performance. This leads to the question that who should evaluate the chief executive. Normally, the evaluation of a person should be done by an individual or a group to whom he reports. In cases where the chief executive is accountable to no one in particular (this is possible in the case of an entrepreneurial organisation), it is difficult to allocate this responsibility apart from relying on self-evaluation. But in the other cases, the ownership pattern can determine who should evaluate the chief executive. Thus, the family council in family-owned companies and majority shareholders in other cases could evaluate a chief executive's performance.
- **The SBU or Profit-Centre Heads:** The SBU or profit-centre heads may be involved in performance evaluation at their levels and may facilitate evaluation by corporate-level executives.
- **Middle-level managers:** Middle-level managers may participate in strategic evaluations and control as providers of information and feedback, and as the recipients of directions from above, to take corrective actions. While evaluating organisational units one cannot avoid relying on the performance evaluation of individuals.

Financial controllers, company secretaries, and external and internal auditors form the group of persons who are primarily responsible for operational control based on financial analysis, budgeting, and reporting. Audit and executive committees, setup by the Board of the chief executive, may be charged with responsibility of continuous screening of performance. The corporate planning staff or department may also be involved in strategic evaluation.

14.2.1 Types of Barriers in Evaluation

There are five major types of barriers in evaluation, these are the limits of control, difficulties in measurement, resistance to evaluation, tendency to rely on short-term assessment, and relying on efficiency versus effectiveness.

- **Limits of control:** By its very nature, any control mechanism presents the dilemma of too much versus too little control. It is never an easy task for strategists to decide the limits of control. Too much control may impair the ability of managers, adversely affect initiative and creativity, and create unnecessary impediments to efficient performance. On the other hand, too less control may make the strategic evaluation process ineffective and redundant.
- **Difficulties in measurement:** The process of evaluation is fraught with the danger of difficulties in measurement. These mainly relate to the reliability and validity of the measurement techniques used for evaluation, lack of quantifiable objectives or performance standards, and the inability of the information system to provide timely and valid information. The control system may be distorted and may not evaluate uniformly or may measure attributes which are not intended to be evaluated.
- **Resistance to evaluation:** The evaluation process involves controlling the behaviour of individuals and, like any other similar organisational mechanism, is likely to be resisted by managers.
- **Short-termism:** Managers often tend to rely on short-term implications of activities and try to measure the immediate results. Often, the long-term impact of performance on strategy and the extended effects of strategy on performance is ignored. This is so as immediate assessment seems to be the easy way out and taking the long-term implications into account may be seen as too tedious.
- **Relying on efficiency versus effectiveness:** It is instructive to remember that efficiency is doing the things right. while effectiveness is doing the right things. There is often a genuine confusion among managers as to what constitutes effective performance. Measuring the wrong parameters may lead to a situation where the right type of performance does not get rewarded. In fact, sometimes performance that does not really contribute to the achievements of objectives may be rewarded if assessed on the basis of efficiency alone.

How can these barriers be avoided? The true function of measurement (or evaluation) is to increase perceptions of the problems limiting achievement. This is indeed a profound statement. It is the attitude towards evaluation that is more important than the process of evaluation itself. For instance, bureaucratic control often ends up being control just for the sake of control and not for the real purpose of finding out what is obstructing effective performance. The real worth of evaluation lies in its ability to throw up the problems that are constraining achievement and then doing something about them so that performance can be made effective. The basic issue in all evaluation should be that control should be dictated by strategy. There needs to be a vertical fit between the strategy requirements, and the evaluation and control exercised over the performance. The guidelines below are suggested in order to make controls effective.

- Control should involve only the minimum amount of information as too much information tends to clutter up the control system and creates confusion.
- Control should monitor only managerial activities and results even if the evaluation is difficult to perform.
- Controls should be timely so that corrective action can be taken quickly.
- Long-term and short-term controls should be used so that a balanced approach to evaluation can be adopted.
- Controls should aim at pinpointing exceptions as nitpicking does not result in effective evaluation. The 80:20 principle, where 20 percent of the activities result in 80 percent of achievement, needs to be emphasized. Getting bogged down with the activities that do not really count for achievement makes the evaluation ineffective.
- Reward for meeting or exceeding standards should be emphasized so that managers are motivated to perform. Unnecessary emphasis on penalties tend to pressurize the managers to rely on efficiency rather than effectiveness.

14.3 STRATEGIC CONTROLS

Ordinarily, a significant time span occurs between initial implementation of a strategy and achievements of its intended results. During that time, numerous projects are undertaken, investments are made, and actions are undertaken to implement the new strategy. Also during that time, both the environmental situation and the firm's internal situation are developing and evolving. Strategic controls are necessary to steer the firm through these events. They must provide the basis for correcting the actions and directions of the firm in implementing its strategy as developments and changes in its environmental and internal situations take place.

Prudential Insurance Company provides a useful example of the proactive, steering nature of strategic control. Several years ago, Prudential committed to a long-term market development strategy wherein it would seek to attain the top position in the life insurance industry by differentiating its level of service from other competitors in the industry. Prudential decided to establish regional home offices, thus achieving a differential service advantages. Exercising strategic control, prudential managers used the experience at the first regional offices to re-project overall expenses and income associated with this strategy. In fact, the predicted expenses were so high that the location and original schedule for converting other regions had to be modified. Conversion of corporate headquarters was sharply revised on the basis of the other early feedback. Thus, the steering control (strategic control) exercised by Prudential managers significantly altered the strategy long before the total plan was in place. In this case, major objectives remained in place while changes were made in the strategy; in other cases, strategic controls may initiate changes in objectives as well.

The four basic types of strategic controls are:

1. Premise control
2. Implementation control

3. Strategic surveillance
4. Special alert control.

14.3.1 Premise Control

Every strategy is based on assumed or predicted conditions. These assumptions or predictions are planning premises. A firm's strategy is designed around these predicted conditions. Premise control is designed to check systematically and continuously whether or not the premises set during the planning and implementation process are still valid. If a vital premise is no longer valid, then the strategy may have to be changed. The sooner an invalid premise can be recognized and revised, the better the chances that an acceptable shift in the strategy can be devised. Premises are primarily concerned with two types of factors: environmental and industry.

They are described below.

- **Environmental Factors:** A company has little or no control over environmental factors, but these factors exercised considerable influence over the success of the strategy. Inflation, technology, interest rates, regulation, and demographic/social changes are examples of such factors. Strategies are usually based on key premises about these factors.
- **Industry Factors**: These factors affect the performance of companies in a given industry. They differ among industries, and a company should be aware of the factors that influence success in its particular industry. Competitors, suppliers, substitutes, and barriers to entry are a few such factors about which strategies assumptions are made.

Premises, some major and some minor, are often made about numerous environmental and industry variables. To attempt to track every premise may be unnecessarily expensive and time-consuming. Therefore, managers must select those premises and variables that (a) are likely to change and (b) would have a major impact on the company and its strategy if they did.

The key premises should be identified during the planning process. The premises should be recorded, and responsibility for monitoring them should be assigned to the persons or departments who are qualified sources of information. For example, the sales force may be a valuable source for monitoring the expected price policy of major competitors, while the finance department might monitor interest rate trends. All premises should be placed on key success premise so as to avoid information overload. Premises should be update (new predictions) based on update information. Finally, key areas within the company or key aspects of the strategy that the predicted changes may significantly impact should be pre-identified so that adjustments necessitated by a revised premise can be determined and initiated. For example, senior marketing executives should be alerted about changes in competitors' pricing policies in order to determine if revised pricing, product repositioning or other strategy adjustments are necessary.

Exhibit 14.2 Four Types of Strategic Control

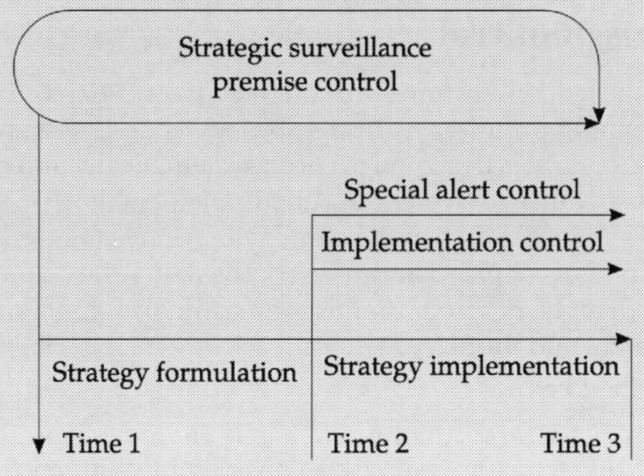

14.3.2 Implementation Control

The action phase of strategic management is located in the series of steps, programmes, investments, and moves undertaken over a period of time to implement the strategy. Special programmes are undertaken. Functional areas initiate several strategy-related activities. Key people are added or reassigned. Resources are mobilized. In other words, managers convert broad strategic plans into concrete actions and results for specific units and individuals as they go about implementing strategy. And these actions take place incrementally over an extended period of time designed ultimately to enact the planned strategy and achieve long-term objectives. Strategic control can be undertaken within this context. We refer to this type of strategic control as implementation control. Implementation control is designed to assess whether the overall strategy should be changed in light of unfolding events and results associated with incremental steps and actions that implement the overall strategy. The earlier example of Prudential Insurance Company updating cost and revenue projections based on early experiences with regional home offices is an illustration of an implementation control. The two basic types of implementation control are:

(1) Monitoring strategic thrusts (new or key strategic programs) and
(2) Milestone reviews.

Monitoring Strategic Thrusts: Implementing broad strategies often involves undertaking several new strategic projects specific narrow undertakings that represent part of what needs to be done if the overall strategy is to be accomplished. These projects or thrusts provide a source of information from which managers can obtain feedback that helps determine whether the overall strategy is progressing as planned and whether it needs to be adjusted or changed.

While strategic thrusts seem a readily apparent type of control, using them as control sources is not always easy to do. Early experience may be difficult to interpret. Clearly identifying and measuring early steps and promptly evaluating the overall strategy in light of this early, isolated experience can be difficult. Two approaches are useful in enacting implementation controls focused on monitoring strategic thrusts. One way is to agree early in the planning process on which thrusts, or phases of those thrusts, *are critical factors in the success of the strategy or of the thrust.* Managers responsible for these implementation controls single these out from other activities and observe them frequently.

Milestone Reviews: The second approach for monitoring strategic thrusts is to use stop/go assessments linked to a series of meaningful thresholds (time, costs, research and development, success, etc.) associated with particular thrusts. Days Inn's nationwide market development strategy in the early 1980s included a strategic thrust of regional development via company-owned inns in the Rocky Mountain area. Time problems in meeting development targets led company executives to reconsider the overall strategy, ultimately deciding to totally change it and sell the company. Managers often attempt to identify critical milestones that will occur the time period the strategy is being implemented. These milestones may be critical events, major resource allocations, or simply the passage of a certain amount of time. In each case, a milestone review usually involves a full-scale reassessment of the strategy and the advisability of continuing or refocusing the direction of the company.

A useful example of strategic implementation control based on milestone review can be found in Boeing's product development strategy to enter the supersonic transport (SST) airplane market. Competition from the joint British/French Concord effort was intense. Boeing had invested millions of dollars and years of scarce engineering talent through phase I of its SST venture. The market was believed large, but the next phase represented a billion-dollar decision for Boeing. This phase was established as a milestone review by Boeing's management. Cost estimates were greatly increased; relatively few passengers and predictions of rising fuel costs raised estimated operating costs; the Concord had massive government subsidy, while Boeing did not. All factors led Boeing management to withdraw, in spite of high sunk costs, pride, and patriotism. Only an objective, full-scale strategy reassessment could have led to such a decision. In this example, a major resource allocation decision point provided the appropriate point for a milestone review. Milestone reviews might also occur concurrent with the timing of a new major step in the strategy's implementation or when a key uncertainty is resolved. Sometimes managers may even set an arbitrary time period, say, two years, as a milestone review point. Whatever the basis for selecting the milestone point, the critical purpose of a milestone review is to undertake a thorough review of the firm's strategy so as to control the company's future.

14.3.3 Strategic Surveillance

By their nature, premise control and implementation control are focused control. The third type of strategic control, strategic surveillance, is designed to monitor a broad range of events inside and outside the company that are likely to threaten the course or the firm's strategy. The basic idea behind strategic surveillance is that some form of general monitoring of multiple information sources should be encouraged, with the specific intent being the opportunity to uncover important yet unanticipated information.

Strategic surveillance must be kept unfocused as much as possible and should be designed as a loose "environmental-scanning activity" Trade magazines, *The Wall Street Journal*, trade conferences, conversations, and intended and unintended observations are all sources of strategic surveillance. While strategic surveillance is loose, its important purpose is to provide an ongoing, broad-based vigilance in all daily operations so as to uncover information that may prove relevant to firm's strategy.

14.3.4 Special Alert Control

Another type of strategic control, really a subset of the other three, is special alert control. A special alert control is the need to thoroughly, and often rapidly, reconsiders the firm's basic strategy based on a sudden, unexpected event. A political coup in the Middle East, an outside firm suddenly acquiring a leading competitor, an unexpected product difficulty like Tylenol's experience with poisoned capsules — all of these represent sudden changes that can drastically alter the company's strategy. Such an occurrence should trigger an immediate and intense reassessment of the company's strategy and its current strategic situation. Many firms have developed crisis teams to handle initial response and coordination when faced with unforeseen occurrences that may have an immediate effect on the firm's strategy. Increasingly, companies are developing contingency plans along with crisis teams to respond to such circumstances. Exhibit 14.3 summarizes the major characteristics of the four types of strategic controls. While each type of strategic control is different, they share a common purpose: to assess whether the strategic direction should be altered in light of unfolding events. Unlike operational control, strategic controls are designed to continuously and proactively question the basic direction of the strategy.

Operations controls are concerned with providing action control. Strategic controls are concerned with steering the company's future direction; both are needed to manage the strategic process effectively. Strategic controls are useful to top management in monitoring and steering the basic strategic direction of the company. But operating managers also need control methods appropriate to their level of strategy implementation. The primary concern at the operating level is allocation of the company's resources.

14.4 EVALUATION TECHNIQUES FOR STRATEGIC CONTROL

The essence of strategic control is to continually assess the changing environment to uncover events that may significantly affect the course of an organisation's strategy. Techniques for strategic control could be classified into two groups on the basis of the type of environment faced by the organisations. The organisations that operate in a relatively stable environment may use strategic momentum control, while those which face a relatively turbulent environment may find strategic leap control more appropriate.

Exhibit 14.3 Summary Characteristics of the Four Types of Strategic Control

	Types of Strategic Control			
Basic Characteristics	*Premise Control*	*Implementation Control*	*Strategic Surveillance*	*Special Alerts*
Objects of control	Planning premises and projections	Key strategic thrusts and milestones	Potential threats and opportunities related to the strategy	Occurrence of recognizable but unlikely events
Degree of focusing, data acquisition	High	High	Low	Low
Formalization	Medium	High	Low	High
Centralization	Low	Medium	Low	High
Used with environmental factors	Yes	Seldom	Yes	Yes
Industry factors	Yes	Seldom	Yes	Yes
Strategy-specific factors	No	Yes	Seldom	Yes
Company-specific factors	No	Yes	Seldom	Seldom

Strategic Momentum Control: These types of evaluation techniques are aimed at assuring that the assumptions on whose basis strategies were formulated are still valid, and finding out what needs to be done in order to allow the organisation to maintain its existing strategic momentum. There are three techniques which could be used to achieve these aims: responsibility control centres, underlying success factors, and generic strategies.

- Responsibility control centres form the core of management control systems and are of four types: revenue, expense, profit, and investment centres. Each of these centres is designed on the basis of the measurement of inputs and outputs. The study and application of responsibility centre is done under the discipline of management control systems.
- The underlying success factors enable organisations to focus on the CSFs in order to examine the factors that contribute to the success of strategies. By managing on the basis of the CSFs, the strategists can continually evaluate the strategies to assess whether or not these are helping the organisation to achieve its objectives.
- The generic strategies approach to strategic control is based on the assumption that the strategies adopted by a firm similar to another firm are comparable.

Based on such a comparison, a firm can study why and how other firms are implementing strategies and assess whether or not its own strategy is following a similar path. In this context, the concept of strategic group is also relevant. A strategic group is a group or firms that adopt similar strategies with similar resources. Firms within a strategic group, often within the same industry, and sometimes in other industries too, tend to adopt similar strategies.

Strategic Leap Control: Where the environment is relatively unstable, organisations are required to make strategic leaps in order to make significant changes. Strategic leap control can assist such organisations by helping to define the new strategic requirements and to cope with emerging environmental realities. There are four techniques or evaluation used to exercise strategic leap control: strategic issue management, strategic field analysis, systems modeling and scenarios.

1. **Strategic Issue Management** is aimed at identifying one or more strategic issues and assessing their impact on the organisation. A strategic issue is a forthcoming development, either inside or the organisation, which is likely to have an important impact on the ability of the enterprise to meet its objectives. By managing the basis of strategic issues, the strategists can avoid being overtaken by surprising environmental changes and design contingency plans to shift strategies whenever required.
2. **Strategic Field Analysis** is a way of examining the nature and extent of synergies that exist or are lacking between the components of an organisation. Whenever synergies exist the strategists can assess the ability of the firm to take advantage of those. Alternatively, the strategists can evaluate the firm's ability to generate synergies where they do not exist.
3. **Systems Modeling** are based on computer-based models that simulate the essential features of the organisation and its environment. Through systems modeling, organisations may exercise pre-action control by assessing the impact of the environment on organisation because of the adoption of a particular strategy.
4. **Scenarios** are perceptions about the likely environment a firm would face in the future. Its use could be extended to evaluation by enabling organisations to focus strategies on the basis of forthcoming developments in the environment.

Several of the above techniques for strategic control, with the possible exception of responsibility centre are or a relatively recent origin. The development of these techniques is an evidence of the expanding body of knowledge in strategic management. As the use and application of strategic management gains approval, it is quite likely that organisations would start using such techniques. Operational control, however, uses more familiar techniques which have traditionally been used by strategists. In the next part of this section, we look at techniques for operational control.

14.5 EVALUATION TECHNIQUES FOR OPERATIONAL CONTROL

The evaluation techniques can be classified in three parts:

- Internal analysis
- Comparative *analysis*
- Comprehensive analysis.

Internal Analysis: Internal analysis, which consists of value-chain analysis, quantitative (financial and non-financial) analysis, and qualitative analysis, deals with the identification of the strengths and weaknesses of a firm in absolute terms.

- ***Value chain analysis*** focuses on a set of interrelated activities performed in a value-chain analysis for the purpose of operational evaluation lies in its ability to segregate the total tasks of a firm into identifiable activities which can then be evaluated for effectiveness.
- ***Quantitative analysis*** takes up the financial parameters and the non-financial quantitative parameters, such as, physical units or time, in order to assess performance. The obvious benefit of using quantitative factors (either financial or physical parameters) is the ease of evaluation and the verifiability of the assessment done. These are probably the most used methods for evaluation of operational control. Among the scores of financial techniques described in all standard texts in the area of finance are traditional techniques, such as, ratio analysis, or newer techniques, such as, economic value-added (EVA) and its variations, and activity based costing (ABC). These are proven methods so far as their efficacy for evaluating operational effectiveness is concerned. Apart from the financial quantitative techniques, there are several non-financial quantitative techniques available for the evaluation for operational control, such as: computation of absenteeism, market ranking, rate of advertising recall, total cycle time of production, service call rate, or number of patents registered per period. Many more techniques can be evolved by firms to suit their specific requirement.
- ***Qualitative analysis*** supplements the quantitative analysis by including those aspects which are not feasible to measure on the basis of figures and numbers. The methods that could be used for qualitative analysis are based on intuition, judgment, and informed opinion. Techniques like surveys and experimentation can be used for the evaluation of performance for exercising operational control.

Comparative analysis: This consists of historical analysis, industry norms, and benchmarking. It compares the performance of a firm with its own past performance, or with other firms.

- ***Historical analysis*** is a frequently used method for comparing the performance of a firm over a given period of time. This method has the added benefit of enabling a firm to note how the performance has taken place over a period of time and to analyze the trend or pattern. Such an analysis can offer the firm a better perception of its performance as compared to an absolute assessment.
- ***Industry norms*** is a comparative method for analyzing performance that has the advantage of making a firm competitive in comparison to its peers in the same industry. Being a comparative assessment, evaluation on the basis of industry norms enables a firm to bring its performance at least up to the level of other firms and then attempt to surpass it.
- ***Benchmarking*** is a comparative method where a firm first finds best practices in an area and then attempts to bring its own performance in that area in line with the best practice. Best practices are the benchmarks that should be adopted

by a firm as the standards to exercise operational control. Through this method, performance can be evaluated continually till it reaches the best practice level. In order to excel, a firm shall have to exceed the benchmarks. In this manner, benchmarking offers firms a tangible method to evaluate performance.

Comprehensive analysis: This includes balanced scorecard and key factor rating. This analysis adopts a total approach rather than focusing on one area of activity, or a function or department.

- ***Balanced scorecard*** method is based on the identification of four key performance measures of customer perspective, internal business perspective, innovation and learning perspective, and the financial perspective. This method is a balanced approach for performance measurement as a range of parameters are taken into account for evaluation.
- ***Key factor rating*** is a method that takes into account the key factors in several areas and then sets out to evaluate performance on the basis of these. This is quite a comprehensive method as it takes a holistic view of the performance areas in an organisation.

Besides the several techniques referred to above, we mention below four other techniques that are used by some companies to assess performance. These are the network techniques, parta system, management by objectives, and the memorandum of understanding.

- ***Network techniques*** such as program evaluation and review technique (PERT), critical path method (CPM), and their variants, are used extensively for the operational controls of scheduling and resource allocation in projects. When network techniques are modified for use as a cost accounting system, they become highly effective operational controls for project costs and performance.
- ***The parta system*** is an indigenous system adopted usually by *Marwari* firms to keep track of daily cash generation. Parta is the pre-determined budget of the net cash inflows before tax and dividend. The parta is decided in between the family group and company head, and actual performance is compared to this budgeted parta on a daily basis, thus making parta an effective operational control device.
- ***Management by Objectives (MBO)*** is a system, proposed by Peter Drucker, which is based on a regular evaluation of performance against objectives which are decided upon mutually by the superior and the subordinate. By the process of consultation, objective-setting leads to the establishment of a control system that operates on the basis of commitment and self-control. Thus, the scope of MBO to be used as an operational control is quite extensive.
- ***Memorandum of understanding:*** Just like MBO is a commitment to objectives between individuals, a memorandum of understanding (MoU) is an agreement between a public enterprise and the government, represented by the administrative ministry in which both parties clearly specify their commitments and responsibilities. Having done that, the enterprises are evaluated on the basis of the MoU. Though an MoU is usually thought of as a technique used solely in the context of public enterprises, its use can be extended to any situation

where an external agency is required to evaluate a firm's performance. Thus, a multinational company can set an MoU with its subsidiary and a family business group council can use an MoU to evaluate its constituent companies. With the greater professionalization of private firms, especially in the family business sector, the use of MoUs can be helpful. But in India the usage of MoU is traditionally confined to the evaluation of performance in a public enterprise.

Operational control systems guide, monitor, and evaluate progress in meeting annual objectives. While strategic controls attempt to steer the company over an extended time period (usually five years or more), operational controls provide post-action evaluation and control over short time periods usually from one month to one year. To be effective, operational control systems must take four steps common to all post-action controls:

1. Set standards of performance.
2. Measure actual performance.
3. Identify deviations from standards.
4. Initiate corrective action or adjustment.

14.6 BUDGETARY CONTROL SYSTEMS

The budgetary process was the forerunner of strategic planning. Capital budgeting in particular provided the means for strategic resource allocations. With the growing use of strategic management, such allocations are now based on strategic assessment and priorities, not solely on capital budgeting. Yet capital and expenditure budgeting, as well as sales budgeting, remain important control mechanisms in strategy implementation.

A budget is simply a resource allocation plan that helps managers coordinate operations and facilitates managerial control of performance. Budgets themselves do not control anything. Rather, they set standards against which action can be measured. They also provide a basis for negotiating short-term resource requirements to implement strategy at the operating level. Most firms employ a budgeting system, not a singular budget, in controlling strategy implementation. Exhibit 14.4 represents a typical budgeting system for a manufacturing business. A budgeting system incorporates a series of different budgets fitting the organisation's unique characteristics. Because organisations differ, so do their budgets. Yet most firms include three general types of budgets—revenue, capital, and expenditure in their budgetary control system.

- **Revenue Budgets:** Most firms employ some form of revenue budget to monitor their sales projections (or expectations), because this reflects a key objective of the chosen strategy. The revenue budget provides important information for the daily management of financial resources and key feedback as to whether the strategy is working. For evaluative purposes, the revenue budget may be derived from revenue forecasts arrived at in the planning process, or it may be linked to past revenue patterns. For example, most hotel/motel operators emphasize daily revenue compared to revenue for the same day in the previous year as a monitor of sales effectiveness. A revenue budget is particularly important as a tool for control of strategy implementation. Revenue budgets provide an early warning system about the effectiveness of the firm's strategy. And if the deviation is considerably below or above expectations, this budgetary tool should initiate managerial action to reevaluate and possibly adjust the firm's operational or strategic posture.

- **Capital Budgets:** Capital budgets outline specific expenditures for plant, equipment, machinery, inventories, and other capital items needed during the budget period. To support their strategies, many firms require capital investment or divestiture. A firm committed to a strong growth strategy may need additional capacity or facilities to support increased sales. On the other hand, a firm intent on retrenchment may have to divest major parts of its current operations to generate additional resources. In both cases, the firm is concerned with management of significant financial resources, probably over an extended time period. For effective control, a capital budget that carefully plans the acquisition and expenditure of funds, as well as the timing, is essential. Two additional budgets are often developed to control the use of capital resources. A *cash budget* forecasts receipts and disbursements of cash flow during the budget period. And a *balance sheet budget* is usually developed to forecast the status of assets, liabilities, and net worth at the end of the budget period.
- **Expenditure Budgets:** Numerous expense/cost budgets are necessary for budgetary control in implementation of strategy in various operating units of the firm. An expenditure budget for each functional unit and for sub-functional activities can guide and control unit/individual execution of strategy, thus increasing the likelihood of profitable performance. For example, a firm might have an expenditure budget for the marketing department and another for advertising activities. In such budgets, Rs. variables will be the predominant measure, although non-Rs. measures of physical activity levels may occasionally be used as a supplement. For example, a production budget might include standards for expenditures as well as standards for output level or productivity. These non-Rs. variables might also include targets or milestones that provide evidence of necessary progress in particular strategic programmes. An expenditure or operating budget is meant to provide concrete standards against which operational costs and activities can be measured and, if necessary, adjusted to maintain effective strategy execution. The expenditure budget is perhaps the most common budgetary tool in strategy implementation. If its standards are soundly linked to strategic objectives, then it can provide an effective communication link between top management and operating managers about what is necessary for a strategy to succeed. It provides another warning system alerting management to problems in the implementation of the firm's strategy.

The budgeting system Exhibit 14.4 provides an integrated picture of the firm's operation as a whole. The effect on overall performance of a production decision to alter the level of work-in-process inventories or of a marketing decision to change sales organisation procedures can be traced through the entire budget system. Thus, coordinating these decisions becomes an important consideration for the control of strategy implementation.

Exhibit 14.4 provides and illustration of how budgets can be coordinated to aid in coordinating operations. In this chart, production, raw material purchases, and direct labour requirements are coordinated with anticipated sales. In more comprehensive systems, other budgets may be included : manufacturing expense, inventories, building services, advertising, maintenance, cash flow administrative overhead, and so on.

Exhibit 14.4 A Typical Budgeting System for Controlling Strategy Implementation

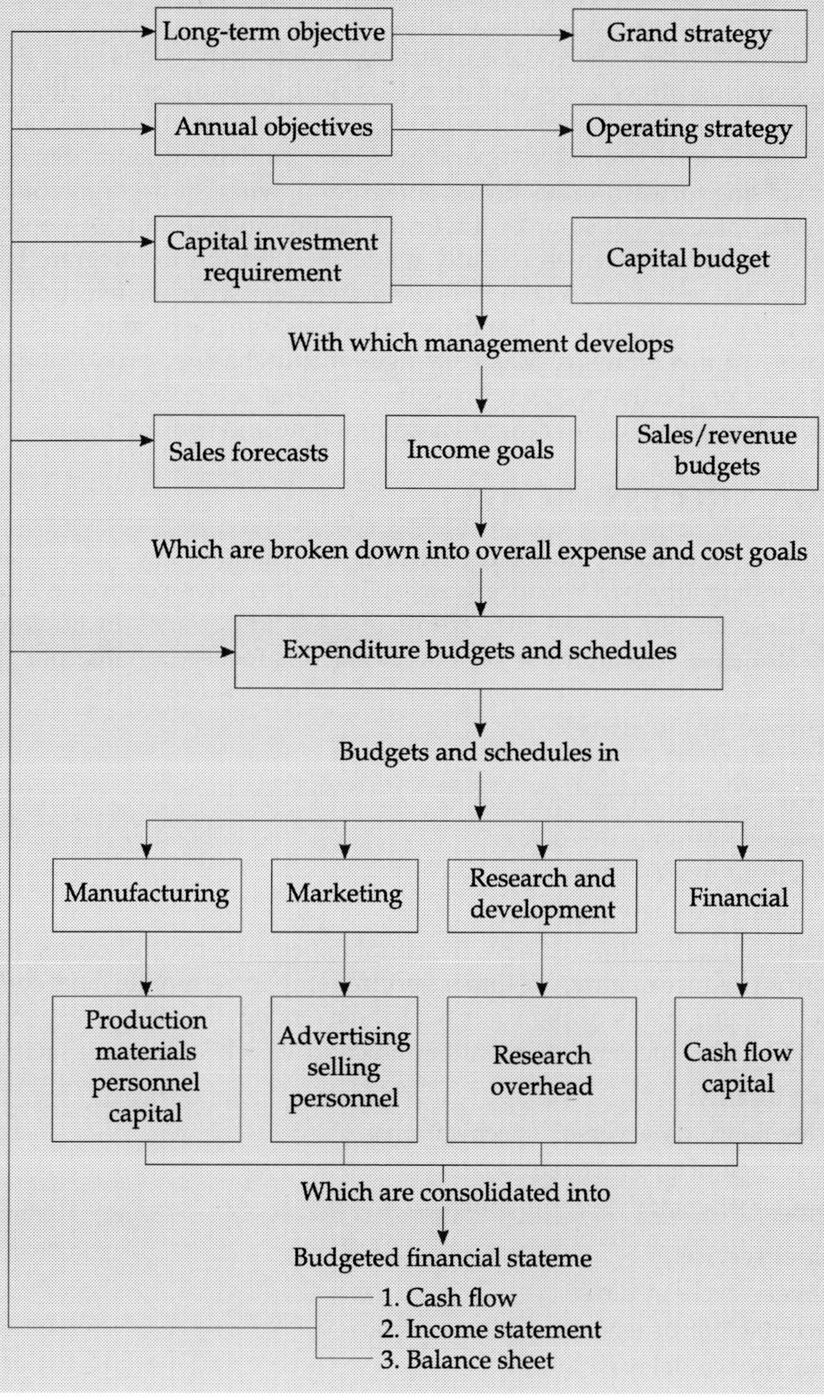

14.7 SCHEDULING

Timing is often a key factor in the success of a strategy. Schedule is simply a planning tool for allocating the use of a time-constrained resource or arranging the sequence of interdependent activities. The success of strategy implementation is quite dependent on both. So scheduling offers a mechanism with which to plan for, monitor, and control these dependencies. For example, a firm committed to a vertical integration strategy must carefully absorb expanded operations into its existing core. Such expansion, whether involving forward or backward integration, will require numerous changes in the operational practices of some of the firm's organisational units. A good illustration of this is Coors Brewery, which recently made the decision to integrate backward by producing its own beer cans. A comprehensive two-year schedule of actions and targets for incorporating manufacture of beer cans and bottles into the product chain contributed to the success of this strategy. Major changes in purchasing, production scheduling, machinery, and production systems were but a few of the critical operating areas that Coor's scheduling efforts were meant to accommodate and control.

14.8 KEY SUCCESS FACTORS

One useful way to effect operational control is to focus on "key success factors". Key success factors identify performance areas that must receive continuous management attention. These are the factors that are of greatest importance in implementing the company's strategies. Examples of key success factors focused on internal performance include:

(1) Improved productivity,
(2) High employee morale,
(3) Improved product/service quality,
(4) Increased earnings per share,
(5) Growth in market share, and
(6) Completion of new facilities.

Each key success factor must have measurable performance indicators. Management must identify product quality, customer service, employee morale, and competition as the four key determinants of the success of their strategy to rapidly expand. They can further identify three measures to monitor and control each key success factor as follows:

For product quality:

- Performance data versus specifications.
- Percentage of product returns.
- Number of customer complaints.

For customer service:

- Delivery cycle in days.
- Percentage of orders shipped complete.
- Field service delays

For employee morale:

- Trends in employee attitude survey.
- Absenteeism versus plan.
- Employee turnover trends.

For competition:

- Number of firms competing directly.
- Number of new products introduced.
- Percentage of bids awarded versus standard.

Key success factors succinctly communicate the critical elements for which operational managers must be responsible in making the strategy successful. Because their achievement requires the successful performance of several key individuals, these factors can be a foundation for teamwork among managers in meeting the company's strategic objectives.

Budgeting, scheduling, and monitoring *key success factors* are important means to control the implementation of strategy at the operational level of the company. Common to each operational control system is the need to establish measurable standards and to monitor performance against these standards.

14.8.1 Monitoring Performance and Evaluating Deviations

Operating control system requires the establishment of performance standards. In addition, progress must be monitored and deviations from standards evaluated as the strategy is implemented. Timely information must be obtained so that deviations can be identified, the underlying causes determined, and actions taken to correct or exploit them.

Exhibit 14.5 illustrates a simplified report on the current status of key performance indicators linked to the firm's strategy. These performance indicators represent progress after two years of a five-years plan intended to differentiate the firm as a customer service oriented provider of high-quality products.

Management's concern is comparing *progress* to date with expected progress at this point in the plan. Of particular interest is the current deviation because it provides a basis for examining suggested actions (usually from subordinate managers) and for finalizing decisions on any necessary changes or adjustments in the company's operations.

In Exhibit 14.5, the company appears to be maintaining control of its cost structure. Indeed, it is ahead of schedule on reducing overhead. The company is well ahead of its delivery cycle target, while slightly below its service/sales personnel ratio objective. Product returns look OK, although product performance against specification is below standard. Sales per employee and expansion of the product line are ahead of schedule. Absenteeism in the service area is meeting projections, but turnover is higher than planned. Competitors appear to be introducing products more rapidly than expected.

After deviations and the underlying reasons for them are identified, the implications of these deviations for the ultimate success of the strategy must be seriously considered. For example, the rapid product line expansion indicated in exhibit 14.5 may be in response to competitors' increased rate of product expansion. At the same time, product performance is still low and, while the installation cycle is slightly above standard (improving customer service), the ratio of service to sales personnel is below its target. Contributing to this substandard ratio (and perhaps reflecting a lack of organisational commitment to customer service) is the exceptionally high turnover in customer service personnel. The rapid reduction in indirect overhead costs might mean that administrative integration of customer service and product development requirements had been reduced too quickly.

As a result of this information, operations managers face several options. The deviations observed may be attributed primarily to internal factors or discrepancies. In this case, priorities can be scaled up or down. For example, greater emphasis might be placed on retaining customer service personnel while de-emphasizing overhead reduction and new product development. On the other hand, the management team could decide to continue as planned in the face of increasing competition and decide to accept or gradually improve the customer service situation. Another possibility is reformulating the strategy or a component of the strategy in the face of rapidly increasing competition. For example, the firm might decide to shift emphasis toward more standardized or lower priced products to overcome customer service problems and take advantage of an apparently ambitious sales force.

This interpretation of Exhibit 14.5 is but one of many possible explanations. The important point is the critical need to monitor progress against standards and give serious, in-depth attention to both the reasons underlying observed deviations and the most appropriate responses to them. Evaluations such as these are appropriate for organisational subunits, product groups, and operating units in a firm. Budgets, schedules, and other operating control systems with performance targets and standards linked to the strategic plan deserve this type of attention in detecting and evaluating deviations. The time frame is more compressed usually quarterly or even monthly during the budgeted year. The operating manager typically reviews year-to-date progress against budgeted figures. After deviations are evaluated, slight adjustments may be necessary to keep progress, expenditures, or other factors in line with programmed needs of the strategy. In the unusual event that deviations are extreme, usually because of unforeseen change, management is alerted to the possible need for revising the budget, reconsidering certain functional plans related to budgeted expenditures, or examining the units and effectiveness of the managers responsible.

An acceptable level of deviation should be allowed before action is taken; if not, the control process will become an administrative overload. Standards should not be regarded as absolute because the estimates used to formulate them are typically based on historical data, which, by definition, are "after the fact" Furthermore, absolute standards (keep equipment busy 100 per cent of the time, or meet 100 per cent of quota) are often used with no provision for variability. Standards are also often derived from averages, which, by definition, ignore variability. These difficulties suggest the need for definition acceptable *ranges* of deviation in budgetary figures or key indicators of strategic success. This approach helps in avoiding administrative difficulties, recognizing measurement variability, delegating more realistic authority to operating managers in making short-term decisions, and hopeful improves motivation.

Exhibit 14.5 Monitoring and Evaluating Performance Deviations

Key Success Factors	*Objective, Assumption or Budget*	*Forecast Performance at This Time*	*Current Performance*	*Current Deviation*	*Analysis*
Cost control: Ratio of indirect overhead to direct field and labour costs	10%	12%	15%	+3 (ahead)	Are we moving too fast or is there more unnecessary overhead than originally thought?
Gross profit	39%	40%	40%	0%	
Customer service: Installation cycle in days	2.5 days	3.2 days	2.7 days	0.5 (ahead)	Can this progress be maintained?
Ratio of service to sales personnel	3.2	2.7	2.1	– 0.6 (behind)	Why are we behind here? How can we maintain the installation cycle progress?
Product quality: Percentage of products returned	1.0% ă 0.1%	2.0%	2.1%	(behind)	Why are we behind here? Ramifications for other operations?
Product performance versus specification	100%	92%	80%	– 12% (behind)	
Marketing: Sales per employee monthly	Rs. 12,500	Rs. 12,100	Rs. 12,700	+ Rs 600 (ahead)	Good progress. Is it creating any problems to support?
Expansion of product line	6	3	5	+2 product (ahead)	Are the products ready? Are the perfect standards met?

Contd...

Contd...

Employee morale in service area: Absenteeism rate	2.5%	3.0%	3.0%	(on target)	
Employee Turnover rate	5%	7%	15%	– 8% (behind)	Looks like a problem! Why are we so far behind?
Competition: New product introductions (average number)	6	6	3	– 3 (behind)	Did we underestimate timing, implications for our basic assumptions?

Some companies use trigger point for clarification of standards, particularly in monitoring key success factors. A ***trigger point*** is a level of deviation of a key indicator or figure (such as a competitor's actions or a critical cost category) that management identifies in the planning process as representing either a major threat or an unusual opportunity. When that point is "hit", management is immediately alerted (triggered) to consider necessary adjustments in the firm's strategy. Some companies take this idea a major step forward and develop one or more *contingency plans* to be implemented once predetermined trigger points are reached. These contingency plans redirect priorities and actions rapidly so that valuable reaction time is not wasted on administrative assessment and deliberation of the extreme deviation.

Correcting deviations in performance brings the entire management task into focus. Managers can correct performance by changing measures. Perhaps deviations can be resolved by changing plans. Management can eliminate poor performance by changing how things are done, by hiring new people, by retaining present workers, by changing job assignments, and so on. Correcting deviations from plans, therefore, can involve all of the functions, tasks, and responsibilities of operations managers. Operational control systems are intended to provide essential feedback so that company managers can make the necessary decisions and adjustments to implement the current strategy.

14.8.2 Ratio Analysis

Ratios of financial statement items (here, balance sheets and income statements) are widely used to measure strategic and management performance. With the exception of the current and quick ratios, few generally acceptable and appropriate ratio values exist. The exact number of ratios to use the circumstances in which to use them, their components, and their exact meanings are often not agreed upon. Every financial analyst seems to have a preferred system.

The major problem with using these sources is finding the exact industry or group of firms against which to compare the subject firm. While data on large organisation is abundant, the multiplicity and diversity of products among firms makes comparisons suspect. Data on intermediate-sized firms is virtually nonexistent. Even where comparative ratios are available, they must be used with caution. Financial statement information is subject to varying accounting practices which hamper comparisons. Footnotes to these statements often make significant differences as to the true value of certain items.

14.8.3 Return on Investment (ROI)

As a result of the positive aspects of decentralization, it has become a popular organisational design technique. The need arises to control the resulting subsystems. Two primary types of control systems exist to exert financial control over these decentralized units: those that control projects and those that control responsibility centres. There are five types of responsibility centres:

1. Standard cost centres are those for which standard costs can be computed. By multiplying this cost times units, an output measure is devised.

2. Revenue centres are those for which revenues can be determined.
3. Discretionary expense centres are organisational units, normally staff units, whose output is not commonly measured in financial terms.
4. Profit centres are subsystems for which both costs and revenues can be measured and where responsibility for the difference, i.e., profit has been assigned.
5. Investment centres are profit centres for which the assets employed in obtaining profit are identified. (These are SBUs or major project divisions.)

ROI is the performance measure most frequently used for the last of these responsibility centres, i.e., the investment centre. ROI is a critical issue in large organisations. Inappropriate division control systems reduce executive motivation. This can and usually does result in reduced profits. Indeed, while ROI analysis has several advantages, it also has several limitations. Advantages of ROI analysis include the following:

1. ROI is a single comprehensive figure influenced by everything that happens.
2. It measures how well the division manager uses the property of the company to generate profits. It is also a good way to check on accuracy of capital investment proposals.
3. It is a common denominator which can be used to compare many entities.
4. It provides an incentive to use existing assets efficiently.
5. It provides an incentive to acquire new assets only when such acquisition would increase the return.

Limitations of ROI analysis include the following:

1. ROI is very sensitive to depreciation policy. Depreciation write-off variances among divisions affect ROI performance. Accelerated depreciation techniques reduce ROI, conflicting with capital budgeting discounted cash flow analysis.
2. ROI is sensitive to book value. Older plants with more depreciated assets and lower initial costs have relatively lower investment bases than newer plants (note also the effect of inflation on raising costs of newer plants and on the distortion of replacement costs), thus causing ROI to be increased. Asset investment may be held down or assets disposed of in order to increase ROI performance.
3. In many firms that use ROI, one division sells to another. As a result, transfer pricing must occur. Expenses incurred affect profit. Since in theory the transfer price should be based on total impact on firm profit, some investment centre managers are bound to suffer, equitable transfer prices are difficult to determine.
4. If one division operates in an industry with favourable conditions and another in an industry with unfavourable conditions, one will automatically look better than the other.
5. The time span of concern is short range. The performance of division managers should be measured in the long run. This is top management's time span capacity how long it takes for their performance to realize results.
6. The business cycle strongly affects ROI performance, often despite managerial performance.

Despite these criticisms, ROI will likely continue as the leading index of management performance if for no other reason than its simplicity. Importantly, though, ROI must be supplemented with other decision information. ROI is an important concept in terms of both total organisational control and subsystem control. As noted, it is the most widely used measure of a firm's operating efficiency. While ROI represents net income as a percentage of total assets, it is a function of many variables ROI results from two key factors, profit margin on sales and assets turnover.

14.9 MANAGEMENT AUDITS

One of the major questions confronting organisations today is how to evaluate the performance of the top management team. In order for this end to be achieved, several factors must be considered:

- Did top management accomplish the objectives it established?
- How good were the objectives it established? How good were the strategies it employed to accomplish these objectives?
- What factors beyond the control of top management affected its performance?
- How well has it responded to and how well has it anticipated these factors?

These questions are operational control criteria for top management. Note, it is strategy that is at issue. Several systems have attempted to measure top management's performance. One more promising is the management audit which examines all facets of organisational activity.

The audit has been widely used in many or the largest corporations and in smaller firms as well. Importantly, the audit can be adapted to organisations with missions other than profit, such as commonweal, service, and mutual benefit organisations.

Although management audit activity has seemed to decline in recent years, several additional approaches to the management audit have been suggested. Of interest is Greenwood's management audit. He suggests that a management audit should examine:

- Strategy and strategy determinants, especially environmental factors.
- The major functional activities of firm-marketing, operations (production), personnel, and accounting and finance.
- Whether managers are performing the major functions of management, i.e., planning, organizing, staffing, directing, and controlling.

Management audits may also follow a format parallel to the content of the master strategy. Such an analysis is divided into four major parts: those for enterprise, corporate, business, and functional strategies. This approach includes recognition of product divisions but examines strategy on the basis of functional activities within divisions if they exist. In observing any technique, it is important to note its weaknesses. While the strength of the management audit is that it often has been able to successfully predict corporate performance, it is not always accurate. Such audits have predicted success for some companies that failed miserably. Why? First, and probably most important at this time, the environment may change drastically. Regardless of its weaknesses, the audit serves an important function in its comprehensive examination of the organisation. While examination of the "bottom line" indicates problems, the auditing of other areas is vital in explaining the causes of these problems. The audit is primarily effective because it looks beyond financial information and systematically appraises the performance of top management.

14.9.1 Human Resource Accounting (HRA)

The evaluation of human assets offers great promise, but to date this promise has been largely unfulfilled. The relevance of human resource accounting to strategic management is connected principally to evaluating the worth of the abilities, skills, knowledge, aspirations, and so forth of the strategic decision makers. But, in addition, the evaluation of corporate strengths and weaknesses requires an assessment of all employees and their potential related to threats and opportunities.

To date, much of the implementation of HRA has involved calculations of the historical cost of human assets to the organisation. A typical cost model observes the cost of recruiting and acquisition, formal training, orientation, development, familiarization, and related human resource expenses. Other HRA cost models exist. One might calculate opportunity cost, for example, and replacement cost based on historical cost with operation costs added. In addition to cost models of HRA, one other major model, the economic value approach, exists in aggregate or on an individual basis. Ultimately, this latter is the information sought, but the difficulties, and even impossibilities of estimation, in this author's opinion, severely limit the applicability of the approach. The main problem with the economic value approach is one of validity. Such approaches require estimation of the worth of individuals to the organisation. The question is, how can one be sure that these estimations are meaningful?

14.9.2 The Social Audit

In recent years, business's critics have demanded that social audits of corporations be conducted. The term ***social audit*** refers to any device which attempts to evaluate an organisation's social performance. Areas which might be audited include environmental protection, equal employment opportunity, consumer satisfaction, governmental relationships, energy usage, and employee job satisfaction. Ultimately, the aim is to determine the social impact of the firm on its stakeholders. While some social areas are readily definable, a quantitative measure of both requirements and performance for many of these areas is extremely difficult, if not impossible, to obtain. Furthermore, it is difficult to obtain agreement as to exactly what business should accomplish. Each pressure group seems to have its own set of demands.

Obviously, business cannot respond to all of them. Many corporations have audited their activities in several of the social responsibility areas, and the scoring systems which have been used are becoming more quantitatively oriented. The process of strategic evaluation and control does into operate in isolation; it works on the basis of the different organisational systems that are used to implement strategies. Here, we shall briefly review the role of organisational systems in evaluation.

- **Information System:** Evaluation is done by comparing actual performance with standards. The measurement of performance is done on the basis of reports generated through the information system. In fact that purpose of information management system is to enable managers to keep track of performance through control reports. Several of the techniques described in the previous section, whether for strategic surveillance of financial analysis, are based on the use of an information system to provide relevant and timely data to managers to allow them to evaluate performance and strategy, and initiate corrective action. In fact, with the increasing sophistication of the information management systems and the use of IT, it is possible to devise elaborate methods for evaluation. Techniques such as data warehousing and data mining enable organisations to delve deeper into their internal systems and come up with information that can be useful for evaluation and control purposes.

- **Control System:** The control system, of course, is at the heart of the any evaluation process, and is used for setting standards, measuring performance, analysing variances, and taking corrective action.
- **Appraisal System:** The appraisal system actually evaluates performance and so is a part of the wide control system. However, its significant role in evaluation is yet to be acknowledged. When the performance of managers is appraised, it is their contribution to the organisational objectives which is sought to be measured. In practice, it is difficult to differentiate strictly between the performance of individuals and that of the organisational units they belong to. Thus, the achievement of a department or a profit centre is the sum total, or even more, synergistically, of the individual performance of managers and employees in the department or profit centre. The evaluation process, through the appraisal system, measures the actual performance and provides the basis for the control system to work.
- **Motivation System:** The central role of the motivation system is to induce strategically desirable behaviour so that managers are encouraged to work towards the achievement of organisational objectives. Now, if we look at the way the evaluation process works, we will observe that its efficacy depends on the extent to which it is able to bring actual performance to the level of the standards. In other words, the lesser the deviation of actual performance from standards, the higher is the efficacy of the evaluation process. The motivation system plays a significant role in ensuring that deviations do not occur, or if they do, then they are corrected by the means of rewards and penalties. Incentive systems are directly related to the amount of deviation. Performance checks, which are a feedback in the evaluation process are done through the motivation system.
- **Development System:** The development system prepares the managers for performing strategic and operational tasks. Among the several aims of development, the most important is to match a person with the job to be performed. This, in other words, is matching actual performance with standards. This matching can be done provided it is known what a manager is required to do, and what is deficient in terms of knowledge, skills, and attitude. Such a deficiency is located through the appraisal system. In reality, what we term corrective action in the evaluation process is, in reality, the taking of steps that would lead to the development of individuals who are enabled to perform required. The role of the development system in evaluation is, therefore, to help strategists to initiate and implement corrective action.

- **Planning System:** In the planning system (which is more concerned with the formulation of strategies), we deal with the issue of planning for evaluation. Since the evaluation process is a part of strategic management it has to be planned for. Questions such as these are to be dealt with: who will perform evaluation? How will the information generated be used? How much resource will be required? To what extent will control be exercised so that it is cost-effective? And what administrative systems will be required to support the evaluation system? Further, the evaluation processes also provides feedback to the planning system for the reformulation of strategies, plans, and objectives. Thus, the planning system closely interacts with the evaluation process on a continual basis. Several additional factors should be considered with respect to control.
- **Control Policies:** Just as organisations establish strategic and implementation policies, they must also establish policies which guide control of the organisation. Control policies naturally evolve from the objectives and standards established for performance. The organisation must simply indicate to its mangers and other employees, what the specific objectives are, how performance against these will be measured, what comparisons will ensure, and how differences between expectations and performance will be handled. Rewards must naturally be tied to results. The organisation needs policies establishing total performance measurements, intermediate organisational level performance measurements, and work group and individual performance measurements. Of principal concern is that the "what and how" of control is sufficiently definitive to motivate employees to perform.

14.9.3 Role of Information in Control

A decision can be only as good as the information upon which it is based. In strategic control, management control, and operational control situations, for both feed forward and feedback control systems, comparison and adjustment occur as information is received. The absence of information, such as is the rule in management-by-exception control systems, is also important. There are differences in the characteristics of the information required in strategic control, management control, and operational control. These differences are portrayed in Exhibit 14.6. Mass of information at operational levels must be meaningfully reduced before top management reports are prepared.

Exhibit 14.6 Information Requirements in Different Control Systems

Characteristics of Information	*Operational Control*	*Management Control*	*Strategic Control*
Source	Largely internal	Internal, partly environmental	Internal and environmental
Scope	Well defined, narrow	Moderately broad	Broad in scope
Level of aggregation	Detailed	Aggregated	Aggregated
Time horizon	Historical	Historical	Future and historical
Frequency of use	Very frequent, continuous	Periodic	Occasional, but with increasing frequency

14.9.4 Integrated Planning and Control Systems

In a previous text, the importance of integrated planning and control was stressed from a planning perspective – objectives provide direction and motivation. Objectives are anticipated results. As such, for control purposes, they provide standards against which to compare performance. PERT , CPM, MBO, budgets, and other planning and control systems can and should be applied to ensure successful mission accomplishment. It is essential that implementation be controlled if it is to be effective.

Execution and control of strategy ultimately depend on individual organisational members, particularly key managers. And motivating and rewarding good performance by individuals and organisational units are key ingredients in effective strategy implementation. While positive reinforcements are given primary emphasis, sanctions or negative reinforcements are important tools for controlling and adjusting poor performance. Motivating and controlling individuals efforts, particularly those of managerial personnel, in execution of strategy is accomplished through a firm's reward sanction mechanisms – compensation, raises, bonuses, stock option, incentives, benefits, promotions, demotions, recognition, praise, criticism, more (or less) responsibility, group norms, performance appraisal, tension, and fear. These mechanisms are positive and negative, short run and long run.

Control mechanisms align personal and subunit actions and objectives with the objectives and needs of the firm's strategy. This is not easy, and reward-sanction structures controlling strategy execution vary greatly across different firms. For example, Harold Geneen, former CEO of ITT, purportedly used an interesting combination of money (compensation and incentives), tension (strict accountability for results), and fear to control individual manager's efforts toward strategy implementation. Geneen provides his managers with enough incentives to make them tolerate the system.

Financial incentives are important reward mechanisms. They are particularly useful in controlling performance when they are directly linked to specific activities and results. Intrinsic, non-financial rewards, such as flexibility and autonomy in the job and visible control over performance, are important managerial motivators. And negative sanctions, such as withholding financial and intrinsic rewards or the tensions emanating from possible consequences of substandard performance, are necessary ingredients in directing and controlling managers' efforts.

The time horizon on which rewards are based is a major consideration in linking rewards and sanctions to strategically important activities and results. Numerous authors and business leaders have expressed concern with incentive systems based on short-term (typically annual) performance. They fear short-term reward structures can result in actions and decisions that undermine the long-term position of a firm. A marketing director who is rewarded based on the cost effectiveness and sales generated by the marketing staff might place significantly greater emphasis on established distribution channels than on "inefficient" nurturing and development of channels that the firm has not previously used.

A reward system based on maximizing current profitability can potentially shortchange the future in terms of current investments (time, people, and money) from which the primary return will be in the future. If the firm's grand strategy is growth through, among other means, horizontal integration of current products into new channels and markets, the reward structure could be directing the manager's efforts in a way that penalizes the ultimate success of the strategy. And the marketing director, having performed notably within the current reward structure, may have moved on to other responsibilities before the shortcomings emerge.

Short-term executive incentive schemes typically focus on last year's (or last quarter's) profits. This exclusive concentration on the bottom line has four weaknesses in terms of promoting a new strategy:

- It is backward looking. Reported results reflect past events and, to some extent, past strategy.
- The focus is short term, even though many of the recorded transactions have effects over longer periods.
- Strategic gains or losses are not considered due to, among other things, basic accounting methods.
- Investment of time and money in future strategy can have a negative impact.

Since such outlays and efforts are usually intermingled with other expenses, a manager can improve his or her bonus by not preparing for the future. While there are clear dangers in incentive systems that encourage decidedly short-run thinking and neglect the longer term, there is real danger in hastily condemning short-term measures. Arguing that managers must be concerned with long-run performance is easy; it also may be too easy to make the mistake of concluding that short-term concerns are not important or that they are necessarily counterproductive to the strategic needs of the organisation. Such a simplistic and quick conclusion can be dangerous. In an effectively implemented strategy, short-term objectives or aims support, and are critical to, the achievement of long-term strategic goals. The real problem is not the short- versus long-term concerns of management; it is the lack of integration of and consistency between long- and short-term plans and objectives in the control system that is vital to the successful implementation of strategy. The critical ingredients for the achievement of this consistency are appropriate rewards and incentives.

To integrate long- and short-term concerns, reward systems must be based on the assessment and control of both the short-run and long-run (strategic) contributions of key managers. An effective reward system should provide payoffs that control and evaluate the creation of *potential* future performances as well as last year's results. Exhibit 14.7 illustrates a management reward system tied to a five-year cycle of strategy implementation. Review and evaluation in a specific year include both an assessment of performance during that year and an evaluation of progress toward the five-year strategic objectives. The annual objectives and incentives in each year can reflect adjustments necessary for successful implementation of the strategy. This helps integrate short- and long-term considerations in strategy implementation by linking adjustments necessary in supporting revised, long-term considerations to next year's reward structure.

Exhibit 14.7 Annual Incentive System with Long-term Perspective

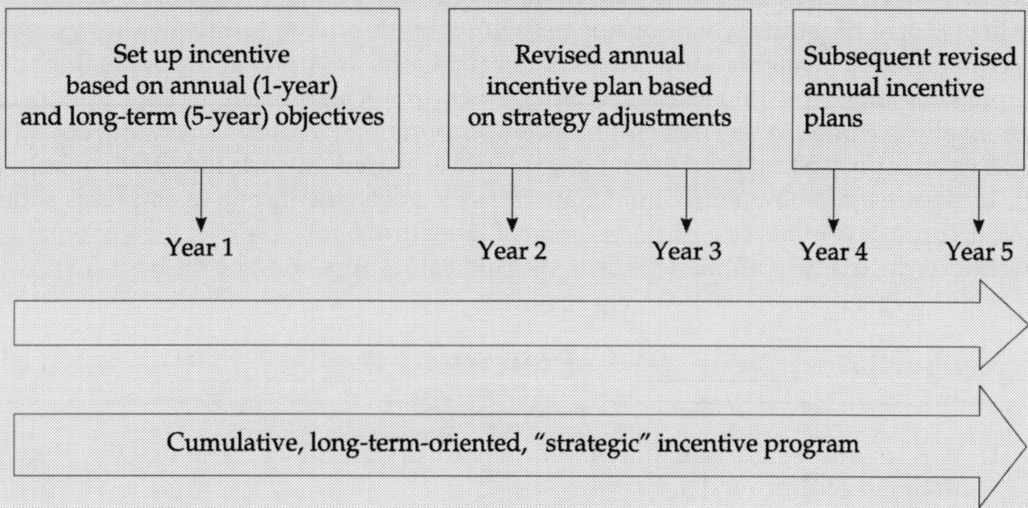

The second component in the management reward system in Exhibit 14.7 is an incentive based on cumulative progress towards strategic objectives. It is shown as increasing in size or amount over time, which reinforces a long-term, strategic perspective. Incentives based such as stock option, deferred bonuses, or cumulative compensation indexed to future performance indicators are ways this reward component could be structured. The key ingredient is an incentive system linked to longer-term progress toward strategic goals. This approach reinforces the interdependence or performance over the five-year period rather than the importance of any one year.

These incentive priorities (long-term versus short-term) should vary depending on the basic nature of the strategy. Another refinement suggested in constructing incentive systems that reward long-term (strategic) as well as short-term thinking is the use of strategic budgets. In this approach, strategic budgets are employed simultaneously with operating budgets, but the objectives and plans associated with each budget vary a great deal. The focus of the operating budget is control and evaluation of business as usual. The strategic budget specifies resources (and targets) for key programmes or activities linked to major initiatives that are integral to the long-term strategy. Concerned that executive incentive plans can and should give more explicit weight to strategic activities, proponents of a strategic budget approach suggest three basic steps:

1. Measure progress toward strategic targets separately from results of established operations.
2. Determine incentive awards separately for established operations and for progress towards strategic targets.
3. Devise a long-term, stock option equivalent to encourage revisions of strategy and entrepreneurial risk taking.

Common to each of these reward and sanction approaches is growing recognition of the need for a two-tiered incentive system linked to short-run and long-term considerations. The relative emphasis in terms of reward linkages should be determined by the focus of the strategy. For businesses with growth-oriented strategies, for example, incentive systems weighted towards long-term payoffs are more appropriate. Incentive emphasizes long-term value based on either stock appreciation, length of the option, or a combination of both. While this emphasis is appropriate, short-term operating objectives deserve attention so that short-term performance is geared towards long term objectives. For businesses pursuing more immediate strategic goals, the incentive emphasis should shift accordingly. In harvest business units of large firms, for example, greater emphasis on short-term, easily quantified performance indicators appears to be the basis for reward systems designed to evaluate strategic results.

Exercise

1. Why is strategic evaluation important to organisations? Discuss the steps of strategic control model.
2. What types of barriers are commonly faced during evaluation? How can these be avoided?
3. What is the role of different stakeholders in strategic evaluation and control? Explain them with examples.
4. What is strategic control? Discuss the different types of strategic control and explain their impact with the help of suitable examples.
5. How is strategic surveillance done?
6. Explain the importance of different evaluation techniques for strategic control.
7. What are different evaluation techniques for operational control. How do these help the organisation to achieve operational efficiency?
8. Budgetary control is the most effective means of strategic control. Give your viewpoint and explain the different budgetary control techniques.
9. Explain the role of information system in strategic evaluation and control.
10. Key success factor determines the success or failure of the organisation. Give your viewpoint.
11. How can the performance of top management team be evaluated? Explain the following techniques and their role in it.
    - HR accounting
    - Social audit

Case Studies

1 Air Deccan: Revolutionising the Indian Skies

Civil aviation in India, since its inception, has been a mode of transport mainly for the elite, and it implies that it is within the means of affordability of less than 1% of the population only. The launch of Air Deccan in the last two years has changed this paradigm forever. The singular driving force behind this audacious venture is Captain Gopinath, whose dream is to make 'flying : affordable for every Indian. Over the years, there have been many low-cost airlines in service in the advanced countries. Many of them have succeeded despite the general downtown in the aviation industry post-9/11. Equally tenacious entrepreneurs, who saw the potential for a low-cost and 'no frills' airline, have launched many of these ventures. In what is peculiar to India, Captain Gopinath saw the market not in terms of those who were flying, who would want a low-cost airline, but instead as the more than one billion Indians, who had no possibility of flying ever in their lives in the legacy airlines, simply because there was no way they could ever afford the price. That Air Deccan could even think of launching a regular airline, given their very modest means, and more importantly, strong political support of the existing players, is a feat by itself. Its continued growth, month after month, is a saga of fortitude and tenacity. This case study describes the story of the launch of Air Deccan and the challenges ahead of it.

Air Deccan has implemented several measures that are unique in the Indian context. This has resulted in steady increase in the market share of the airline, much to the consternation of the established players, viz., Jet Airways, Air Sahara and Indian Airlines. Consequently, it has resulted in fierce competition and price wars in the Indian skies, with the net result that the passenger has benefited significantly. There are a number of challenges that Air Deccan has to contend with. It has set for itself a mission to enable every Indian to fly. Passenger fares for long haul flights such as Bangalore to Delhi, covering over 2000 km, can now be purchased for as low as Rs. 500 (about US$10), if purchased early. It perceives the market as practically unlimited, and sees itself as the largest airline in India five years hence. The case discussion in the class can focus on the challenges that the company has to face to reach this very ambitious goal.

With daily sales in excess of Rs. 15 million , and growing steadily, Air Deccan has redefined the paradigm of air travel in India. Until the launch of Air Deccan, air travel was essentially meant for the affluent sections of the society, due to the high pricing structures. Air Deccan has transformed the aviation landscape in the country. Today, air travel, if planned well in advance, is often cheaper than travel by second-class train.

While there are many low cost airlines the world over, especially in the USA, Europe, Far East and Australia, the challenges of replicating this in India were not trivial. Three powerful established players (Indian Airlines, Jet Airways and Sahara) were not amused with this upstart airline and with their deep connections in the political and bureaucratic system of the country, wanted to scuttle the start-up airline. In the initial stages of the company, many of the established players (Indian Airlines, Jet Airways and Sahara) would have trivialized the company and not expected it to reach the level it has reached now. Suddenly, the company has appeared as a big dot on the radar screen of these well established players. The existing paradigm is that running an airline requires large funding, something that Captain Gopinath lacked. Hence, the existing players would have concluded that this venture was bound to fail. However, there was a lot of entrepreneurial creativity manifested by Captain Gopi that helped him make his dream a reality, and today Air Deccan is a force to reckon with. Besides, many other 'me too' low cost airlines are already on the anvil.

Capt. Gopinath, despite heavy odds, including lack of finance, he and his team came up with creative solutions at every step, to overcome the hurdles. His entrepreneurial style warrants close study to draw out useful lessons for any aspiring entrepreneur. Captain Gopinath crafted the company from scratch. He went on a 'boot strapping' mode, which is the hallmark of a successful entrepreneur. The constancy of purpose, focus and humility are evident. His ability to sense opportunities from chance encounters (such as a visit to the USA or the Southeast Asian countries) are out of the ordinary experience. These and many other qualities are a 'must have' list of qualities of a successful entrepreneur However, it is fair to say that while the progress has been spectacular, challenges abound. Issues relating to the continued growth and success of Air Deccan require a clear strategy.

The company, as of June 2005, is growing from strength to strength. Captain Gopinath and Air Deccan are regularly featured in the various media in India as having ushered in the democratization of air travel in India. The company is bullish about the future. Several companies are seeking to emulate the Air Deccan model. The three established airlines were under constant price pressure from these low cost operators. The overall scenario is fairly dynamic as of now and experts expect considerable churn to take place in the coming years.

QUESTIONS

1. What lessons you can pick up from the launch of the entrepreneurial venture by Captain Gopinath?
2. While low cost airlines are not new to the world, Air Deccan was clearly the torchbearer of this concept in India. What additional challenges did Captain Gopinath have to contend with vis-à-vis a low cost operator in the advanced countries?
3. Develop a business model for Air Deccan.
4. Going forward, what are the challenges that the company has to grapple with?
5. What should be the strategy of the company?

2 Strategic Vendor Management: Cisco IT

With more than 35,000 employees and hundreds of locations, Cisco Systems has an enormous IT infrastructure budget. Each Cisco office has many complex IT requirements, including: high-speed connections; voice, data, and video networking equipment; computers, servers, and storage; and, security and support. Cisco uses its own products and services wherever possible, but still spends US$ 500 million a year globally on other IT products and services.

The Cisco global network is one of the most innovative enterprise environments in the world, and is an important contributor to the company's high productivity ratings. This can increase pressure to introduce new services or equip new offices quickly. In the past, Cisco had no consistent process for new products and services. Every time Cisco opened a new location or an implemented a new service in an existing location, one of several scenarios ensued:

- The fastest path involved local managers calling up local suppliers and ordering whatever was needed. This represented the most expensive solution for Cisco. A lack of formal contracts often led to disagreements over prices, warranties, and support.
- Another approach involved regional IT offices negotiating contracts with local suppliers. Each contract was negotiated individually, so past lessons and economies of scale were not referenced.
- Sometimes, the IT group would call for requests for proposals or quotes (RFPs or RFQs), and award the business based on responses. While this resulted in better prices, the proposal process was not consistent, resulting in little or no emphasis on establishing strategic vendors or planning for the future.

This lack of consistent process meant that Cisco could receive 20 different agreements for the same service with the same vendor. Agreements in different countries would have different prices, lengths, terms, and service levels. This was an inefficient and complex process for both the vendor and Cisco to manage. In addition, the number of vendors calling on Cisco was dramatically increasing in the last few years; without a standard and consistent method for dealing with these contacts, more Cisco employees were required to spend more time responding to these contacts.

In addition to the complexity of these agreements, the lack of strategic planning began to cost Cisco significant amounts of money. Cisco discovered that it had signed multiyear contracts for products or circuits that became obsolete as they moved to larger offices or new technologies. Furthermore, with so many small agreements, Cisco missed the opportunity to negotiate for better terms or prices based on its total sales volume. This resulted in Cisco paying more than necessary for products or services. A benchmarking survey in EMEA showed that Cisco typically paid more than other enterprises for similar services.

This lack of consistency was negatively affecting the relationships between Cisco and its vendors. Informal contracts do not properly set expectations for either the seller or the buyer. It was also not always clear to vendors what Cisco deemed its criteria for awarding business. There was no standard process for weighting bids, vendor communication, and oversight. Disagreements escalated to both Cisco and vendor senior management. This was particularly serious because many Cisco vendors are also significant Cisco customers. Sales teams began to complain that the situation was affecting their customer relationships.

SOLUTION

The impetus for change began in Europe, where the vast number of service providers started choosing suppliers for WAN infrastructure, particularly complex. In 2001, the Europe, Middle East and Africa (EMEA) theatre of Cisco IT Infrastructure formed a vendor management office (VMO). Its primary goal was to develop a strategic, consistent approach to selecting WAN infrastructure vendors in EMEA that would reduce both cost and risk for Cisco. It chose to work only with vendors strategic to the needs, marketplace, and business of Cisco. Within a short period of time they had successfully renegotiated contracts and repaired relationships, which attracted attention within Cisco.

The VMO became a global IT group in May 2002. Its mandate has expanded to include managing strategic vendors that supply hardware infrastructure, software, storage, telecom services, and outsourced infrastructure services. In addition, the VMO provides value and expertise in process and business development, asset management, and vendor engagement. The VMO has defined seven phases of Cisco vendor management that result in successful outcomes for all parties . This process helps organize and standardize the various functions of the VMO, while encouraging change and continuous improvement.

- **Engage:** When changing business climates or technologies generate the need for products or services within Cisco, the VMO leads the engagement of vendors to help ensure consistency and fairness of communications. New vendors might call Cisco hoping for new business opportunities, or Cisco might receive sales referrals from other business partners or from Cisco sales groups. At other times the VMO might actively seek out a vendor, when internal Cisco client groups require new service, or bankruptcies or other business problems affect a current vendor's ability to deliver service, or when new technologies emerge that the VMO would like to explore to help improve client services.
- **Investigate:** To evaluate competing products and services, the VMO works with client groups within Cisco IT Infrastructure Operations to investigate industry trends in technology, pricing, and standards. The VMO also works with sales,

marketing, development, business units, finance, and procurement to identify potential vendors, and investigate possible solutions. This requires the VMO staff to be familiar with a wide variety of industry technologies and trends, and select VMO staff are organized into technology sector specialization. These sector specialists monitor the technology trends and pricing trends, and engage external technology consultants to learn more. The VMO also meets with vendor management groups in other companies and participates in customer forums and panels to share and gain information.

- **Evaluate:** If warranted, the VMO initiates a bid process, which results in a shortlist of quality candidates that meet all Cisco client and IT criteria. "We try and communicate all the business issues that exist and make business decisions that are strategic to Cisco accordingly," says Wallace Chan, IT program manager, VMO. This process helps to educate vendors about Cisco needs and expectations, and to engage in clear communication about what the vendor can deliver, in a consistent, open, and fair manner. The VMO will issue a Request for Information (RFI) to gain more information from vendors if needed; or a more detailed RFP if a firm and competitive bid from multiple vendors is desired. The primary goal of the VMO is to avoid competitive RFPs whenever possible, and to select and develop the best strategic vendor to meet each new client's need.
- **Negotiate:** Once a vendor has been selected, the VMO manages the negotiation. This negotiation includes balancing the internal client needs for reliable and high-performance service (articulated in clear service-level agreements [SLAs]), low prices, and strong strategic partnerships, and the vendor's needs for clear deliverables and a fair price for the services delivered. This negotiation process is the most successful when both Cisco and the strategic vendor act as partners that desire a winning relationship for both parties.
- **Contract:** Following the negotiation phase, the Cisco purchasing group confirms the contract, working closely with the Cisco legal department to resolve any contract issues. The VMO remains engaged through this process, but allows the purchasing group to manage the contracting process. To help streamline this process, the VMO has established several guidelines, for example, keeping the contract length to no more than 24 to 36 months, and avoiding any minimum annual revenue commitments (MARCs) or minimum term revenue commitments (MTRCs) that are more than 50 per cent of the total expected cost over the year (for the MARC) or over the life of the contract (for the MTRC). Lengthy contracts and contract revenue commitments can result in lost flexibility or additional costs for Cisco when unexpected technology, service, or client changes take place. Making use of current master sales agreements with each strategic vendor can also help to simplify the contracting process.
- **Compliance:** Once the contract is signed, the VMO generates quarterly reviews that compare commitments and performance with established criteria. This process continues to set expectations between Cisco and the strategic vendor, and improves communications, while still holding the vendor accountable for the quality of their service. Within the VMO, Cisco assigns a primary contact for each strategic vendor. This VMO contact manages the overall relationship, serves as the primary vendor contact, and helps ensure vendor information is communicated to appropriate stakeholders globally within Cisco. Throughout the

life of the contract, the VMO manages all aspects of the vendor relationship. This continual performance monitoring requires support from the Cisco IT operations groups, and also improves IT operations' insight into the vendor relationship.

- **Renew:** When it is time to renew the contract, the VMO proactively reengages with vendors and Cisco client groups to restart the process. It is important to begin this process with ample time before the contract expires, to help ensure that there is time to investigate options. The VMO must determine if it is best to renew the contract (while renegotiating terms based on the current situation) or repeat the 7-step process. This decision process should include a discussion of the implications of the end of the contract with the appropriate internal Cisco clients, and obtaining their new requirements. The VMO will also investigate the general technology and vendor landscape again, possibly by issuing another RFI to the vendor and to other industry leaders, to benchmark the current technology and pricing directions.

Partnering with other groups within Cisco is critical for the success of the vendor management process. "We've learned that the way to succeed is to work closely with other Cisco groups," says Chuck Trent, director of information systems, VMO. "Without the shared ownership and commitment to success from procurement, legal, purchasing, and operations groups, the VMO could not achieve its goals."

THE MAKING OF A STRATEGIC VENDOR

Creating a strategic vendor is a complex process for both Cisco and for the selected strategic vendor. Because this process requires extra effort and attention, it is important to reduce the number of total vendors, and to distinguish between normal vendors and strategic vendors, or partners. The VMO defines strategic vendors as those vendors critical to Cisco IT or the position of Cisco in the marketplace. Ideally, Cisco strategic vendors are industry-leading in their sectors and are members of the Cisco Powered Network Program. In addition to selecting vendors based on their product or service, the VMO also evaluates the company's financial health and level of customer service and satisfaction. Once selected, strategic vendors share the risks and rewards of a mutually beneficial business partnership with Cisco. Many strategic vendors are granted master service agreements that facilitate purchases from client groups within Cisco. Cisco also works with its strategic vendors to help them develop skills and relationships that can help them improve their value and their position in the marketplace, and expects the same support from them.

Two years after its formation, the VMO's success can be measured in many ways:

Increased Flexibility and Simplicity - With standard contracts in place worldwide, Cisco can manage existing contracts and negotiate new ones more easily. Also, with standard, simplified contracts and a consistent vendor engagement process, legal and procurement organizations and internal client groups within Cisco spend less time managing vendor relationships. The VMO measures its success through process consistency, contract simplification, consistent contract terms and conditions, and contracts with lower cost commitments.

- **Lower Costs to Cisco** – Cisco now enjoys better pricing based on the higher volume of goods and services it purchases from strategic vendors. The small VMO has more than paid for itself during its short time in operation. Thanks to VMO efforts, IT cost avoidance, cost savings, and cost recovery totalled $33M through the first three quarters of FY04, and $64M over the life of the contracts. This achievement was recognized in August 2004, when the VMO received a quarterly IT team award for excellent business partnership. Brad Boston, CIO and senior vice president, of Cisco Systems, presented the award. Cisco views the VMO's success as providing vendor services at lower costs.
- **Lower Costs to the Vendor** – While vendors are providing the same services at lower costs, their own costs are also reduced. Cisco has reduced its number of vendors, and has consolidating contracts with a smaller number of strategic vendors, so these strategic vendors receive more business and less paperwork. Instead of having dozens of contracts with Cisco, with different billing approaches and terms and conditions, each vendor has a single contract, reducing contract management costs. Because Cisco is now spending significantly less on its contracts, it has more to spend with its strategic vendors.
- **Better Communication with Vendors** – Well-communicated, and consistent fair terms and conditions and SLAs reduce risk from both sides, and the creation of a global bidding process provides consistent criteria and communication with all vendors. "In the bidding process, we have created an environment where we communicate with one voice to all vendors," says Chan. "At the end of the bidding process, we offer to sit down with each vendor and show them their 'score', i.e., where they did well and where they didn't." This consistent feedback helps all vendors understand their strengths and weaknesses with respect to Cisco needs and expectations.

For strategic vendors that have contractual relationships with Cisco, the VMO has introduced a quarterly "vendor scorecard" that monitors the vendor's performance, against written expectations. If a problem arises, all parties are alerted in a timely fashion using clear escalation paths, opening up further lines of communication between Cisco and its vendors. "Previously, we'd get into situations where there would be no well-defined exit strategy," says Abdul Mumin, IT program manager, VMO. "For example, Cisco outsourced an activity based on a minimum 12-month commitment, and a vendor assumed the contract based on a cost-benefit analysis of 3 to 5 years. After 2 years, Cisco found another way of accomplishing this activity, and the vendor imposed penalties that were left indeterminate in the original contract." These situations can result in embittered and negative relationships. Now, Cisco and strategic vendors set all terms and conditions at the beginning of their relationship, including details on successor or cancellation costs, technology migration, acquisition clauses, and mutual account team expectations. This close communication helps ensure a flexible and open relationship between Cisco and its vendors, allowing both to learn from mistakes and to adapt to changing vendor and Cisco circumstances. The VMO and the vendor measure their success through quarterly reviews and scorecards based on the meeting of contract SLAs.

More Productive Partnerships with Vendors – For any business relationship to be successful, it must be mutually advantageous. Cisco and its strategic vendors have evolved their relationships. "We are making contracts more fair," says Chan. "Some contracts have business downturn clauses, so if a vendor's business slumps, Cisco will renegotiate the contract. We also conduct annual industry benchmarking, so if the price for this product or service is going down, Cisco pays a price reflecting current market conditions. By sharing the risk, we are trying to create 'win-win' scenarios."

Cisco and its strategic vendors are using their improved relationships to lead industry discourse on new technologies and services. In the service provider market, Cisco is both a significant customer and vendor, as well as a leader in adopting new technology. "Service providers perceive us to be 18 to 24 months ahead of other enterprises," says Chan. "Service providers showcase Cisco as the way of the future to other enterprises, and we try to take advantage of this position as buyers to advise and help business. We are members of service provider advisory boards and councils across the globe."

Cisco customers see the VMO as an attractive model. Since many Cisco customers are large, multinational enterprises, they share Cisco's interest in establishing and maintaining strategic vendor relationships. VMO managers are often invited to participate in executive briefing centre (EBC) meetings with customers to share their experiences, performance, and decision-making processes. The VMO measures its success by improved vendor performance during the contract, and improved vendor capabilities.

NEXT STEPS

Currently, the VMO numbers approximately 20 people worldwide, each working with numerous strategic vendors on a daily basis. Its organization has recently been added to the Cisco IT global shared services, which further expands its mandate. "Our organization is still maturing, so we are currently focusing on where we can add the most value," says Micheal Bollen, senior IT manager, VMO. "In the future, we want to automate more things, such as contract management, e-procurement, and how to keep internal clients and stakeholders up-to-date on vendor management."

QUESTIONS

1. What were the problems faced by Cisco IT? What measures will you take to solve the problems?
2. How Cisco found the solution to the problem?
3. Strategic vendors have played an important role in finding solution. Comment.
4. What Cisco should do to avoid re-occurrence of such issues?

3 Phuket: Entry Strategy of an Asian Car Manufacturer in the Swiss Market

Phuket is a leading Asian automobile manufacturer with its headquarters in Phuket Thailand. The company uses production facilities in Malaysia. Phuket is looking to establish itself in Europe and has chosen Switzerland as a test market. Phuket intends to set up an import company in Switzerland to build up and manage a network of motor dealers. Although Phuket is aware that there are not many capable dealers who are not already contracted to other manufacturers or to importers, it seems that many of these, representing a range of different car brands, may be unhappy with their current contract positions. This is because the car manufacturers have been taking advantage of their solid market positions and strong brands to dictate strict conditions in their contracts, affecting such features as showroom arrangements, service performance, sales of demonstration vehicles, and stock requirements. Dealers regard this behaviour as unfair, and Phuket thus sees an opportunity to take away some of these motor dealers away from competitors. With friendly contracts and attractive financial conditions the company hopes to acquire capable dealers with good locations or alternatively establishes a number of new dealerships of its own.

In terms of its finance and staffing, the new import company will be set up in a similar way to competitor companies, using Honda, in particular, as a benchmark. In the initial phase the following two models will be introduced:

- Phuket Saloon: 4 or 5 door (booted rear or fastback), 1.3 litre 4 cylinder engine with 75 hp or 1.5 litre 4 cylinder engine with 90 hp; average consumption 5.5 litres per 100 km, 6.2 litres for the larger engine; small car category, similar to VW Polo, Ford Fiesta, or Mitsubishi Colt.
- Phuket Persona: 4 or 5 door (booted rear or fastback), 1.5 litre 4 cylinder engine with 90 hp or 1.6 litre 4 cylinder engine with 113 hp; average consumption 6.3 litres per 100 km, 6.8 litres for the larger engine (these are low values for this category of car); lower mid-size car, similar to Opel Astra, Ford Escort, VW Golf.

For both models standard features are generous, and include ABS, double front airbags, and air-conditioning. The retail price will be lower than for comparable low priced vehicles from South Korea.

The automobile industry seems to have overcome the crisis that reached its climax in 1993. In 1994 growth in production and distribution was achieved in practically all markets. Experts assume that this positive trend will continue. But the markets in the different continents will develop differently, for reasons which are apparent. New trading areas, above all in Southeast Asia, and Latin America, are gaining in importance. But even in traditionally important markets as Western Europe, North America, and Japan, the figures are likely to be encouraging. One study has concluded that demand will rise by about 30% to almost 43 million vehicles per year until the end of the millennium. Europe will be part of this trend, with a yearly growth rate of 6%.

THE AUTOMOBILE MARKET IN SWITZERLAND

With 450 vehicles per thousand of population, Switzerland has the highest rate of car ownership in Europe. In the seventies and eighties the market was volatile, with Japanese producers challenging their European and American competitors with lower prices and more standard features. Today it is the ambitious South Koreans, like Hyundai, who are driving competition in the market. The turnover from new car sales is 7.6 billion Swiss francs in 1994. This represents around 266,000 new cars. In 2005 saw a growth in used car sales. Over 643,000 cars changed hands representing a turnover of 6 billion francs. Of these, 380,000 were sold by motor dealers and 263,000 were direct sales by individual car owners. In recent years the demand has been mainly for lower priced vehicles, costing up to around 15,000 francs. Used vehicles priced above 25,000 francs were difficult to sell. Exhibit 1 shows the market shares of the most important car brands in Switzerland.

Exhibit 3.1 Market share of the most important car brands for sales for new cars in Switzerland

VW 13.6%	Fiat 5.3%	Mazda 4.0%	Ford 9.0%
Opel 18.2%	Peugeot 6.4%	Audi 4.2%	BMW 4.6%
Renault 9.0%	Toyota 8.8%	Nissan 4.3%	Citroën 3.2%
Chrysler 3.0%	Subaru 4.2%	Honda 2.3%	

The area of Switzerland and Liechtenstein has 11,834 motor dealers, of which 6648 represent one or more brands. Most of these dealers have grown from one-man companies: some have now become extremely large dealerships. However, the majority of these garages have only 18 employees or fewer. Garages make on average 75% of their turnover on new cars, but with service and repairs 75% of their profit. For basic garage businesses, with service and repairs plus used car sales, a future without new car sales does not look encouraging. Turnover in these areas remained at the same level as in the previous year. However, in the last four years workshop capacity use has been falling: in 1990 it was 83%, by 1994 it had fallen to only 74%. The main factors for this trend are longer intervals for service and exhaust checks, the increasing renouncement of the owner for service checks and a smaller susceptibility to repairs. It should be noted too that the repair and maintenance of many types of car now requires special software: this means that only authorized dealers can carry out this work.

Industry experts estimate that there are some 500 to 1000 garages, and many will fall victim to the structural changes in the coming years. Importers are beginning to reorganize and tighten their dealer networks: only financially sound dealerships in strong locations are likely to survive. In the Swiss market too, the forecasts for new vehicle sales for 1995 are upbeat. The number of registered vehicles is expected to rise to between 270,000 and 280,000. But this short-term growth cannot hide the fact that the Swiss market is nearing saturation. Increasingly it appears that new cars are bought only to replace the existing ones.

People's need for individual mobility will continue, and the functioning of the economy will continue to depend on the use of both passenger and utility vehicles. However, the future of the automobile will increasingly be affected by changes in the environment: pressure will continue to grow for manufacturers to reduce petrol consumption and harmful emissions.

THE DISTRIBUTION STRUCTURE OF THE SWISS AUTOMOBILE MARKET

As private vehicles have not been mass-produced in Switzerland since 1975, earlier import restrictions intended to protect the home industry no longer apply, and the Swiss market is open to all manufacturers. Like Phuket, many other manufacturers have used Switzerland as a test market. Almost all new cars are imported by specialized import companies. Where these are not subsidiaries of the manufacturers, they have contracts with manufacturers guaranteeing the exclusive right to distribute the brand in Switzerland and Liechtenstein. The manufacturer undertakes not to deliver vehicles to any other Swiss business partner.

The Swiss industry has a traditional three-level structure: importer, regional dealership and local dealer. Originally, these three levels were quite separate and independent, both legally and economically. However, recently importers have followed a policy of forward integration, setting up their own dealers in good locations. Increasingly, too, the importers control the strategic decision-making, while at the same time leaving the dealers to bear the entrepreneurial risks.

Importers : There are basically two kinds of import company:

- Wholly-owned subsidiaries of the manufacturer, tied to the parent company brand: Honda, Mercedes Benz, GM, Ford, BMW, and Renault are imported by such subsidiaries.
- Legally and financially independent import companies working with one or more manufacturers. The manufacturer guarantees the company exclusive distribution for the Swiss market. Unlike the first type of importer, these companies are not committed to purchasing any specified number of vehicles, though they are required to promote sales. Important companies of this type include AMAG, the Emil Frey Group, and the Hugo Erb Group.

The dealer networks: The importers are free to determine how the vehicles are distributed and thus to set up their own networks of dealers. The traditional network consists of regional dealers ("A"-dealers) and local dealers ("B"-dealers). With over-capacity amongst garages, the importers do not find it necessary to offer especially advantageous conditions or to try to persuade dealers to change brands. A large majority of the dealers have no choice: they need the authorized dealer status for their brand.

(a) The regional dealerships, or "A" dealers, have contracts with the importers which give them responsibility for a clearly delimited regional market. Within these areas they are responsible for serving and supplying the local dealers, can sell directly to end-users (intra-brand competition with their own dealers), and must offer trouble free customer service. There is a limited amount of competition between the various regional dealerships representing the same brand. Despite the clear borderlines, in practice 'passive' selling (no advertising or acquisitions) outside this area cannot be avoided. Often the importers will not allow dealers to represent more than one brand. Exceptions can be made if the brands are not in competition with each other, because they target different market segments, or if the importer himself represents more than one brand.

(b) Local dealers, or "B" dealers, represent the lowest level in the distribution system. These are small garages which carry out maintenance and repairs, and represent one or two brands. Local dealers have no regional protection and have to engage in intra-brand competition, both with the regional dealership, and with other local dealers.

In addition there is a large number of independent garages which do not represent brands, and whose turnover comes mainly from repairs and used car sales. If a brand has a low market share, or if a brand's market share is falling, the decision to change brand allegiance, or to deal with more than one brand, can be a survival decision for a dealer. But for "A" dealers especially, it is an expensive undertaking. A large proportion of the dealer's investment will have been brand-specific and will have to be written off (special tools, stock of spare parts, visual and corporate identity).

Usually, the importers require the dealers to take over the visual identity of the manufacturer. National advertising is provided by the importers, regional advertising by the regional dealers ("A" dealers) responsible for the area, and local advertising in partnership between the regional and local dealers. In 1993 the automobile industry as a whole spent 253 billion francs on advertising in Switzerland. Some importers impose demands on dealers in terms of the product range; others leave this to the dealers. As far as stocks are concerned, the importers usually require the dealers to hold a certain number of new vehicles and demonstration vehicles in stock, and also impose requirements in terms of spare parts.

Usually the manufacturers and importers together determine the prices. The most important criteria are cost, elasticity of demand, and the behaviour of the competitors. In Switzerland prices are relatively high because price elasticity is weak and government requirements are relatively demanding. The importers price lists represent maximum prices. To offer lower prices and compete with each other, the dealers have to give up some of their margin. With high inter-brand and intra-brand competition, garages will offer up to 10% off list prices for a new car. With margins between 13% and 18%, dealers are unable to do better than this.

The importers take an active interest in making sure that dealers' personnel participate regularly in training. Regional dealers are sometimes given the freedom to develop their own distribution networks, choosing their own local dealers; otherwise the importer stipulates the local dealers. For efficient trouble-free business administration and information exchange importers generally recommend their computer networks to the dealers, and often require them to provide certain information.

The end user: Cars have developed from luxury vehicles to items of practical utility, and more recently have become lifestyle products. At the same time consumers have become more demanding. Even for small and mid-size cars, customers today expect high performance and comfort: low-priced basic models find fewer and fewer buyers. For this reason it is more and more frequent for a car to be manufactured only after an order has been placed. Brand loyalty is very high in the automobile industry. Garages estimate it at 70% to 80%. End users have become more and more dependent on the services provided by specialist dealers; other garages increasingly lack the infrastructure and the know-how to deliver the same services.

QUESTIONS

1. Carry out an industry segment analysis for the industry market of cheap automobiles.
2. Select the future generic business strategy and identify the industry segment(s) and the customer group(s) which will form the primary target.
3. State the network of the future competitive advantages.

4 Tata Sky: Training is the Key

Tata Sky is a satellite television provider that has redefined the television viewing experience for thousands of families across India. The service aims to empower the Indian viewer with choice, control and convenience through its wide array of programming choices and interactive features offered in DVD quality picture and CD quality sound. The company is a joint venture between the Tata Group and the STAR Group and operates under the Sky brand owned by British Sky Broadcasting.

Tata Sky was booming and racing to keep up. The company, a combination of Indian Tata Group and Britain's Sky television brand, was the second firm in India to offer direct-to-home satellite television and other services. After two years of rapid expansion, management wanted more speed, but bureaucracy and conflict were limiting efficiency.

"Because we are neither simply entertainment nor telecom nor consumer household, we have people with backgrounds in different industries and very different working styles," said Charanjit Lehal, senior training manager. "Nobody was speaking the same (figurative) language, and it was affecting efficiency—we could see a pattern of meeting after meeting, and quick decisions were not being made." Executives observed the following types of behaviors:

- People avoided each other instead of confronting problems.
- Employees returned from meetings with other functions complaining about the list of unrealistic projects they were being asked to accomplish.
- Team problems were being escalated to high-level executives rather than being resolved at an earlier stage.

THE TRAINING COURSE

After perusing dozens of training courses, Tata Sky learning and development team led by Mr Bhaskar Bhattacharya, vice president of learning and development, piloted three different workshops conducted by external trainers. Based on feedback and results, they chose to move forward with Vital Smarts Crucial Conversations Training in May 2008. Lehal found the skills taught in the course were clear. The tests and exercises were effective at engaging participants. He also liked how the action items required by the course helped each participant customize the principles to their specific needs. Based on the course's value, Lehal was able to secure executive approval by demonstrating how the results would lead to a return on investment.

In addition to the results and the skills, Lehal found the training integrated seamlessly across cultures. There was no cultural confusion between the American-based course and Tata Sky's Indian employees. "Dialogue is a necessity for any conversation," Lehal said. "The core content of the course has universal application." He acknowledged that, speaking generally, Americans may be direct in conversations while people from eastern cultures may build more background before coming to the main point. "While techniques differ, we still need to get on the table what you are trying to say and what I am trying to say, and that is what this course teaches," he said.

Lehal's experience was that with sufficient preparation cultural differences did not present significant challenges. Based on advice from a Vital Smarts master trainer, he also surveyed participants before they attended the course and built real-life examples for use in the course from their anonymous responses. This ensured they saw immediate application to their work environment. Lehal conducted two-day workshops at each of Tata Sky's four regional offices, focusing on the customer service function before moving to other functions. About eighty managers completed the workshop in 2008, with many more scheduled for 2009.

RESULTS

Tata Sky is seeing the change in behavior they hoped for after boosting its managers' communications skills. "This course is breaking down passive or aggressive cultures that had been found in various divisions," Lehal said. "It's become a very successful culture-building intervention." Some results from the training:

- Two teams had been struggling to cooperate. One reported that the other had been "moving to silence" and withholding their point of view, but is now "stepping up to crucial conversations."
- One manager told Lehal when she came into the training that she was looking for a new job because she was being made a scapegoat in her team. She was in "complete silence mode" and avoiding the issue. After the training she talked to her supervisor about it and is still with the company.
- The head of a service function was so impressed by the word-of-mouth on the course among his managers that he asked Lehal to conduct it for his senior team of general managers and vice-presidents.
- On a personal level, employees have shared with Lehal that the course has helped them sort out communication problems with their parents left behind when Tata Sky moved them to a new city. Or with their teenagers—certainly a challenge that transcends culture.

Following are testimonials e-mailed after the course:

- "I could relate the program the very next day at the office. On Friday during a conversation with the team, I could make out the 'silence' shown by one person and this tool helped me engage him into meaningful dialogue."

•"I feel [my] team has bonded once again."

•"I put crucial conversations skills into motion the very next day, and it has certainly helped clear the air."

When asked whether he would recommend crucial conversations, Lehal was somewhat surprised by the question: "What other workshop offers so much skill development? Such excellent audiovisuals? With so much of the course absolutely interactive? And is so well structured in terms of the workbook, videos, exercises, self-testing, and post-training? All these things I've recommended to my peers at other organizations."

QUESTIONS

1. What were the problems faced by the Tata Sky?
2. Why did the company select vital smart crucial training methods for the employee? Was it relevant and effective?
3. What was the outcome of the training programme?
4. If you were to select a training programme for your employer, would you use this training programme? Give your viewpoint.

5 The Tata Nano Project: Making of the World's Cheapest Car

The case discusses the making of Tata Nano, the world's cheapest car, manufactured by India based Tata Motors. On March 30, 2009, Tata Nano was launched with an ex-factory price tag of INR 100,000 (about US$ 2000). The case explains the design and development process of Tata Nano. The car was the result of a five year research and development project carried out by Tata Nano development team. While developing the car, Tata Motors and its suppliers constantly made efforts to reduce the costs while ensuring quality of each and every component including engine, steering, wheels, tires, windshield washing system, gear shifter, etc.

Analysts opined that Tata Nano had created a new segment in the passenger car market. However, they were concerned about the company's lack of capacity to fulfill high demand. They also argued that considering the low margins the company would get, it would take a long time for the project to break even.

THE PEOPLE'S CAR

On April 25, 2009, bookings closed for the much-awaited Tata Nano, the world's cheapest car, made by India-based Tata Motors Limited (Tata Motors). The bookings began on April 09, 2009 and the car received an overwhelming response from the Indian consumers. The company received a total of 203,000 bookings for the car. Tata Motors, the largest automobile company in India in terms of revenues, launched Nano, commercially on March 30, 2009 (The car with an ex-factory price tag of Rs.100,000 generated enormous interest among the public as well as industry experts.

The history of Tata Motors dates back to the mid-1900s. In 1945, Tata Motors was incorporated as Tata Engineering and Locomotive Company Limited (TELCO). The company was engaged in manufacturing locomotives and engineering products. Three years later, it launched a steam road roller in association with the UK-based Marshall Sons.

Nano – The Car: The Nano had a 623 cc rear engine and a rear wheel drive. The engine was a two-cylinder petrol engine. The fuel economy of the car was expected to be around 21 kilometers per liter under city driving conditions.

The Nano Project: The project to build the Nano started in 2003. Girish Wagh was selected as the leader of the 500-member team which was chosen to develop the Nano. Right from the beginning, the team members were asked to be as frugal as possible to maintain the low price target of the car.

Managing the Supply Chain: Although in the beginning, the auto part suppliers of Tata Motors were skeptical about the project, they were later convinced that they also could contribute to achieving the cost target as well as improve their own bottom lines.

TATA NANO VS. MARUTI 800

The Tata Nano's closest competitor in terms of price was the Maruti 800, made by Maruti Suzuki India Limited, a subsidiary of Suzuki Motor Corporation of Japan. Analysts pointed out the fact that the ex-showroom price difference of the standard models of the Tata Nano and the Maruti 800 was about Rs. 60,000 While Tata Motors launched the Tata Nano at the promised price of Rs 100,000 (ex-factory), most industry experts opined that the Nano would face many challenges in the near future. They said that the decline in the raw material costs between January 2008 and March 2009 had helped Tata Motors maintain the price target of the car.

What went wrong with the Nano? And what must Tata do to bring it back on track

Tata Motors racked up over 2,00,000 fully paid bookings, which with limited capacity translated into a potential four-year waiting list, at worst. The company could sell everything it made but just months before the Sanand plant in Gujarat was ready for full scale production, the highly-publicized incidents of the Nano catching fire battered the car's reputation. After touching a high of 9000 units in July 2010, sales have since fallen off a cliff to a shameful 509 units in November 2010.

What went wrong? It's a combination of many factors. The plant relocation messed up schedules and with the long-drawn-out rollout and even longer waiting lists, potential buyers began to lose interest. Also, the first round of bookings became a lottery for many and hence it was hard to gauge the true demand for the car. The booking system alienated many genuine buyers who could not buy the car. The company opened sales in select states only a year later. Till now, sales are open in only 12 states.

However, it's the spate of fires and the horrific sight of a Nano ablaze that is mainly responsible for scaring buyers away. Tata claims to have identified the cause of the fires and has introduced a raft of modifications and upgrades to sort out the problem. Some advertising experts say that Tata has been complacent after the huge bookings it received and didn't implement a comprehensive advertising strategy to keep the Nano brand pumped up. But after the problem of fires and falling sales, advertising has been reactive.

There are other softer factors which Tata did not bargain for. Many potential Nano customers want the car but don't buy it because they can't drive! Tata should have foreseen this by taking a leaf from Maruti's book. To tackle this issue, Maruti has heavily enlisted a lot of its first-time customers into Maruti-supported driving schools. Besides, many potential Nano buyers were not creditworthy and hence could not get loans.

This leads us to a larger question. Does Tata Motors know who the Nano customer really is? Tata is addressing an entirely new segment of people who never considered buying a car. This new segment, in which the Nano is the only player, will take time to develop. However, the Alto's record sales, helped in no small measure by the Nano's recent price hike (a cardinal mistake), suggests that if people can afford a not-so-one-lakh Nano, they don't mind spending a bit more on a tried-and-tested product.

However, one should not write off the Nano based on a few months of sales. These are very early days and the entire might of Tata Motors is behind this car to ensure its success. The company needs to quickly bring a Nano V2 with all the changes and improvements that have been on the anvil. Bringing forward the diesel launch would help too.

What Tata Motors has in its pocket are thousands of satisfied Nano buyers. They love the car's space and fuel efficiency, which the Alto can't match. If no more Nanos go up in flames, there's nothing better than positive word-of-mouth to restore customer confidence. The recent 4-year /60,000 km warranty will also help. It may be a long haul but we wouldn't be surprised if the Nano does emerge from this mess to eventually take its natural place on the sales charts.

LEARNING FROM TATA'S NANO MISTAKES

It's been a rough season for Tata Motors' much-publicized "people's car," the Nano. In November, while overall auto sales in India's booming economy rose more than 22%, Tata sold only 509 Nanos, down precipitously from the 9,000 it sold the previous July, news that's been trumpeted in disparaging headlines from New York to Sydney. There are no shortages of reasons for the Nano's poor showing: production delays, fires, the stigma attached to buying a "cheap" car. But the real problem is not with the car; it's with the hype surrounding it that tied Tata's hands.

Setting (or encouraging) high pre-launch expectations limits your ability to perfect your business model post-launch. But, this flexibility is essential to emerging-market innovation and product strategy. You have to get a lot of things right to successfully bring a product as novel as the Nano to market. First, you have to conceive of something people will actually want. (That's really three steps — thinking up something that's wanted, identifying who actually wants it, and working out the details of how and under what circumstances they will use the product.) You have to devise a way to produce it reliably and profitably at the price those people will pay. And you need to communicate a clear, targeted value proposition, differentiated from competing offerings. Tata has had trouble with just about every one of those steps, and this fact has played out very publicly.

Is there anyone who hasn't heard the story about how Ratan Tata conceived of the Nano as safe, affordable alternative for Indian families weaving in and out of New Delhi traffic perched precariously on the backs of motor scooters? Or how the famous 1 lakh price (variously valued at anywhere from $2,000 to $2,500, depending on exchange rates) was prompted by an offhand remark to a reporter? Expectations could not have been more public for what the Sydney Morning Herald's Amrit Dhillon referred to as "the pop star of the car world."

But, as pop stars come to understand, fame is fickle. On the one hand, the early hype predictably fuelled early demand. On the other, large initial demand required the company to build the car at scale from the outset, which proved publicly problematic when the company ran into problems purchasing land for a new factory in West Bengal. Production for the first 100,000 cars was delayed for more than 18 months.

Then it turned out that the car doesn't really sell for 1 lakh. In fact, the New York Times reports, a fully equipped Nano sells for only about $800 less than the Suzuki Alto, which "has a bigger engine, more storage space and a longer track record than the Nano." That last factor is particularly important in the wake of dramatic accounts of some Nanos bursting into flames, an unfortunate irony for a car touted as a "safe."

Nor, it seems, is the car popular with its original target market. Nano customers are not upgrading from motor scooters, Dhillon reports; they're people looking for a fun, trendy second car for running errands. A cheap car that's not really cheap. A safe car whose safety has been questioned. A poor people's car that poor people aren't buying. That sounds like a failure, certainly.

But really it's not. It's par for the course for almost every breakthrough innovation. There's nothing unusual about a company having to adjust the price, the production process, the marketing, or even the market of a breakthrough offering. The Nano's price changes, the new maintenance contract,Tata is rolling out to assure buyers of quality, the test drives it's introducing, the new smaller showrooms, and the new commercials — all widely discussed in the press — should not really be news.

In fact, we can think of only one example of a CEO who pre-announced an innovation that was going to change the world and actually delivered it. That's Steve Jobs of course. A far more common path to success is the one forged by E Ink, which early on envisioned several potential applications of its printing invention — billboards, radio-paper products, and e-books. Rather than pick one and go for broke, E Ink executives wisely (and quietly) made small-scale bets on all three approaches, spending a little to learn a lot about what would and wouldn't work and which path it should eventually pursue. Similarly, long before most people had heard of the low-power fridge "ChotoKool" Godrej & Boyce spent quite some time investigating people's refrigeration needs, designing and redesigning the product, and redoing its distribution strategy, carefully, slowly, and quietly.

It might not have been easy, but had Tata piloted the Nano quietly, on a small scale, perhaps through a limited production run in a small city like Durgapur in West Bengal or Ranchi in Jharkand, its engineering, pricing, financing, and marketing might have been adjusted far from the limelight to suit the needs of an optimal target customer. Then, like the "overnight sensations" who seem to have acquired instantaneous talent — but in fact spent years quietly perfecting their craft — the Nano might have made its debut to the wider world with less hype and greater effect. It might not have been a 1 lakh car or even an alternative to motor scooters. But when it first appeared in the mainstream, it would have been right product for the right price in the right market.

QUESTIONS

1. What was the motive behind bringing Tata Nano car?
2. What went wrong with Tata Nano after its launch in 2009?
3. What action Tata have taken to solve the problem?
4. Was Tata a hype or reality?
5. What were the reasons for fall in sale of Tata Nano. How will you overcome them?
6. What lessons can you learn from this case study?

6 Amway: The Role of Stakeholders

Amway is one of the world's largest direct sales companies. It is a global enterprise and is privately owned by the families that started the company in 1959. Amway manufactures markets and distributes more than 450 consumer products. Amway distributes a variety of products, including:

- Personal Care - fragrances, body care and hair care products
- Skin Care and Colour Cosmetics.
- Durables - cookware and water treatment systems.
- Nutrition and Wellness - food supplements, food and drinks.
- Catalogue Items - third party electrical goods.
- Home Care - laundry, cleaning and car care products.

Amway employs 14,000 people worldwide in its offices, manufacturing centres, warehouses, call centres or stores. It also works with around three million Amway Business Owners (ABOs) in more than 80 countries. These ABOs are the link between Amway and its products and the consumer. They also link Amway with communities across the globe. For more than 45 years, Amway Corporation has enabled people to have a business of their own. Amway has built up a strong regional structure around regional affiliates, for example, Amway UK and the Republic of Ireland. Operating through the regional structure, affiliate companies are responsible for:

- Forecasting (ensuring enough stocks are available to meet demand).
- Managing customer service and contact with customers.
- Efficient distribution to ensure products reach ABOs on time and in top condition.
- Product promotion and ABO support, for example, supplying brochures to ABOs.

Amway is an example of a business that recognizes its wider responsibilities. It recognizes that to be a good corporate citizen, it needs to support causes that matter to the communities in which it operates. The company has a range of social and ethical aims that are part of a 'Global Cause Program'. Amway's global vision is to help people live better lives. At the heart of this commitment is the "One by One Campaign for Children" that helps disadvantaged children from around the world. This program aims to support Amway's employees, ABOs and customers in putting time and money into helping disadvantaged children get access to medicine and education. Amway works with many different groups of people to carry out its business. This case study explores the relationship between Amway and its stakeholders. Stakeholders are groups or individuals who have an interest in the decisions of the company and its business. Stakeholders can be internal to the business, such as employees, or external, like suppliers, customers or the public.

A company may have shareholders who can be internal or external stakeholders. As a private company, the families who own Amway are its sole shareholders. It is important that Amway communicates regularly with its stakeholders. They can affect or be affected by the business. Amway uses different ways to communicate with its various groups of stakeholders. The method chosen depends on the message and the person receiving the message. Websites, emails and voice mail updates promote products and services to ABOs and customers and keep them up-to-date. Industry and trade memberships enable Amway to share and receive industry information. Publications target key sales messages, for example, its monthly newsletter "Amway Focus" help Amway to communicate to ABOs, consumers and guests about running Amway business and the products it can provide.

Amway is a direct selling company, selling products directly to consumers without going through traditional retail outlets or 'high street'. A supply chain links the finished products to end consumers. Amway has its own distinct supply chain, placing a strong emphasis on its ABOs. They are able to focus on individual customers and their needs. This supply chain is different from a more conventional supply chain that sells goods to final consumers through retail outlets. Amway's way of working depends on building lasting connections with the end consumer. Feedback provided by consumers and ABOs helps to shape future changes in products and the service provided. Suppliers must produce quality goods that Amway ABOs can sell with confidence. The goods should offer value for money and provide guarantees that they will meet Amway standards. Suppliers may contribute to the design and appearance of Amway products. ABOs operate independently as small businesses. They develop direct supply channels and sell products to friends and customers that they know or meet. They need to have a flexible approach to business. They require Amway to provide high quality, value for money products with a 100% satisfaction guarantee. ABOs determine for themselves how they will conduct business. This is a 'self regulatory' environment.However, they sign a contract to work within Amway's "Rules of Conduct and Code of Ethics". If ABOs do not conduct business within these rules, their behaviour could reflect back on the company. Consumers affect how Amway develops and promotes products. They do this by indicating their preferences and requirements through feedback. Amway can then make more of particular products or change the format of others. Consumer demand also influences how much stock Amway needs to carry. Consumers can show where Amway needs to address issues or concerns to improve the business.

With many different types of stakeholders, it is possible that different groups will have different key objectives or priorities. For example, a business needs to make a profit but customers want low prices. The company might find it difficult to support price cuts, as this would reduce its profit. These two priorities might be in conflict. How Amway affects its stakeholders? Amway's vision is 'helping people live better lives'. Amway's business plays a key role in the communities in which it operates. Amway has a global strategy for producing, distributing and marketing its products worldwide. It also has a strategy for promoting corporate social responsibility (CSR) in a global way. CSR refers to the role that a company plays in meeting its wider commitments as a citizen. Such commitments include supporting worthy causes and always acting in an ethical, honest way. Amway operates in many different markets worldwide and has a range of affiliates and ABOs. It therefore has to devise and communicate its plans for corporate social responsibility activities carefully to take account of different priorities and interests.

From the outset, Amway established some clear objectives. These were to:

- Build loyalty and pride among ABOs and employees.
- Enhance Amway's reputation as a caring organisation.
- Make a real difference to human lives.

This helps to maintain Amway's reputation with all its stakeholders. Amway contributes time, effort and money to support its business communities: It creates appropriate Amway products for ABOs to sell. It develops campaigns that support the business and social aims of the company. Getting the image right is vital in a business that relies on building relationships with individuals and the wider community. Amway regularly seeks to develop new products in line with market research aimed at finding out what customers want. Its employees volunteer at different charity organisations.It has shared $294 million (around £150 million) with non-profit organisations since the company began.

Amway produced its "Global Cause Program" in 2002 as the result of extensive research. Amway defines a global cause as 'a social issue affecting many people around the world engaged in a struggle or a plight that warrants a charitable response.' This program helps Amway to bring its vision to life. It declares what the organisation stands for and builds trust and respect in Amway brands. It also establishes corporate social responsibility as a high priority. In developing its global cause strategy, Amway also listened to what its ABOs cared about. Many favoured a cause to help children. This led to Amway's partnership with UNICEF's "Immunization Plus Program". This aims to provide vaccination against the six most serious diseases affecting children in the developing world. Amway's business image benefits from the relationship with UNICEF. UNICEF benefits from the fundraising Amway and its ABOs contribute.

Ethical business enterprises do more than simply provide goods and services for customers. They also make a real contribution to the communities in which they operate by creating employment and job security , providing products that give consumers good value for money and contributing to creating a more caring and cared-for community. Businesses operate in a competitive environment. They may compete on a number of factors such as price, range of products, quality, speed of service and customer service. Amway is a global enterprise. It must comply with the laws of the many different countries in which it operates. Its business ethics provide a framework to guide the behaviour of the company and its stakeholders. As part of its business values, it protects its consumers through the quality of the products and by offering guarantees of satisfaction. It promotes and supports ethical selling behaviour amongst the ABOs through its codes of conduct. However, in a highly competitive market where businesses are similar, Amway needs to find a way of achieving competitive advantage. Demonstrating a positive involvement in the community and attention to environmental issues can provide a business with competitive advantage. It shows that the company behaves in an ethical way, shares its values and enhances its image as a responsible organisation.

Amway recognizes that to respond to CSR issues, it must base its business on the principles of 'relevance, simplicity and humanity'. For example, Amway set up the 'One by One' program following discussions with various organisations involved in providing help to underprivileged communities worldwide. Amway is also active in a number of programmes to reduce its impact on the environment including supporting organic farms to grow the plants for its vitamin and mineral products. It provides training to employees to protect the environment, for example, encouraging reuse and recycling to conserve resources. It also encourages changing product formulations to be more concentrated and biodegradable, which reduces packaging and waste. It also undertakes use of sources of renewable energy, for example, a wind farm at its World Headquarters will provide 10% of energy needs. It measures environmental impact by auditing its activities to internationally recognized standards. All these activities carry a cost; therefore Amway needs to balance the costs of its corporate social responsibility programmes against not only the benefits of doing so, but also the cost of not doing so. Business practices that do not take account of ethical behaviour might lead stakeholders to reconsider their relationship with the company. Suppliers might stop trading or customers might stop buying (which would result in loss of revenues). At the company level, it might lead to infringement of the law or loss of reputation, which would influence the wider public.

QUESTIONS

1. Who are the stakeholders and what methods of communication does Amway use with each?
2. Explain how the ABOs operate their business and the potential issues?
3. Describe Amway's strategy and its impact on its stakeholders?
4. Using examples, discuss the meaning of ethical business?

7 Asos.com Strategic Growth in the Fashion Retail Industry

Asos.com is the UK's leading online fashion store for women and men. Launched in 2000, the online retailer targets fashion conscious 16-34 year olds. On asos.com there are 9000 products available at any one time, with 450 new fashion items added every week. These include women's fashion, menswear, accessories, jewellery and beauty products. Asos.com attracts 3.3 million unique shoppers every month and has 1.8 million registered users. An online service of this scale requires a substantial background operation to fulfill orders and to provide customer service. Five years ago, asos.com had just 550 square meters of warehouse space. Today, to meet growing demand, asos.com now has 32,500 square meters of warehouse space - equivalent in area to nearly five football pitches. In April 2005, asos.com employed 47 permanent staff. By February 2008, it had 250 employees. These human and physical resources are needed to meet rapidly increasing demand. Sales increased by 90% year on year for the 12 months to 31st March 2008. In April 2008, there was a daily average of 220,000 unique visitors to the asos.com website. The growth in sales translates into profit. Group profit is likely to be in excess of £7 million.

Asos.com is a public limited company (plc), that means the business is owned by shareholders and that its shares can be purchased by the general public. Asos.com shares are traded on the Alternative Investment Market (AIM), which is part of the London Stock Exchange. Joining AIM has several advantages for a growing company such as asos.com. AIM-listed companies do not need to comply with the strict rules that must be followed by businesses listed on the main London stock market. They do not need to meet any size threshold, either in terms of market capitalization or the numbers of shares that they issue. This means it is easier and cheaper to obtain an AIM listing. It provides smaller companies with a chance to raise capital through the sale of shares. This capital can be used to finance growth. As a limited company, asos.com is required by law to have a memorandum of association and articles of association. A memorandum of association sets out the name and purpose of the company and the number of shares it can issue. The articles of association sets out the rights of shareholders, the roles of directors and other factors that relate to the control and management of the company. These documents establish a company as a legal entity. Without this legal framework, the business would not be able to issue shares. The asos.com board consists of two non-executive directors and three executive directors. Non-executive directors do not have day-to-day operational responsibilities for the business. They are invited to join the board because they bring experience and qualities that can guide the strategic direction of the company.

All companies seek to grow. They want to increase profits for their shareholders. They also want to increase the overall volume of business because this can lead to significant reductions in costs. These are known as economies of scale. For example, as asos.com grows, it will require a larger warehouse and distribution operation. As it handles more sales transactions, it will find it easier to make these operations more efficient. It will also be able to get better deals from its suppliers through ordering goods and services in larger quantities. A company can grow in several ways. It can grow by simply selling more of its products. This is known as internal or organic growth. It can also grow by taking over or merging with other businesses. This is known as external growth. It is quicker to expand business through external growth. However, a company would need finance to fund any acquisitions. A company that seeks to grow through acquisition can adopt two main strategies. It can pursue a strategy of horizontal integration. This occurs when a company takes over, or merges with, a direct competitor. For example, when the supermarket chain Morrisons acquired the rival Safeway chain in 2004, it simply created a larger supermarket chain. This was a classic example of horizontal integration. Companies can also seek to grow through a strategy of vertical integration. This is when it acquires a business at a different stage in the chain of production. It may acquire businesses that were previously its suppliers or its customers. For example, a furniture manufacturer might purchase a chain of furniture stores so that it can sell its products direct to consumers. It would previously have looked to sell its products to this retail furniture business. Acquiring or merging with customer businesses is called forward vertical integration. The manufacturer could also choose to merge with one of its suppliers, such as a timber merchant. This would give it more control over one of its key inputs. Merging with suppliers is called backward vertical integration.

Asos.com has achieved rapid growth internally. It has not grown by acquiring other businesses. Instead, it has grown by increasing its customer base, number of brands and products available to buy at any one time. Moreover, it has grown rapidly without incurring the problems that this can cause for some businesses. At first glance, rapid growth might seem to be a positive occurrence. However, it can cause problems and a firm that grows too quickly can run into difficulties. A surge in demand generates additional costs. It costs money to fulfill orders. For example, a business may require extra staff to process orders or it may need to buy in more stock or supplies. A business may have to meet these expenses before it receives the proceeds from the additional sales, and this can lead to cash flow difficulties. Even if the company has enough capital to finance a surge in demand, it may still face problems. It may run into logistical difficulties and simply lack the short-term capacity to fulfill orders. It may not be able to make products quickly to meet demand. This sometimes happens in the run-up to Christmas, when a manufacturer cannot produce enough of that year's 'must-have' toy or gadget. A business that fails to meet demand risks losing customers. It can take a long time to repair a damaged reputation. Improving the business asos.com's strategy of organic growth has shown substantial results. It has managed to satisfy increased demand. The company has also increased its market share.

Asos.com has recognized that the conditions were right for an online retail business in the fashion retail sector. The company has used the Internet as the primary growth tool. It has tapped into the rapidly expanding online retailing market. As research in 2007 by the online retail consultancy Interactive Media in Retail Group (IMRG) showed total online spending in the UK reached £30.2 billion in 2006, the number of UK online shoppers grew from 16 million in 2003 to 25 million in 2006, an increase of 56 per cent over four years. Internet access grew by 45 per cent in the same period, with 42 million people having access in 2006 compared to just 29 million in 2003. The number of broadband connections more than tripled in four years, by 2006 there were more than 12.7 million UK broadband connections. Asos.com targets its offer at a specific market segment of young (16-34) fashion-conscious consumers. This market segment now accounts for 20% of the Internet shopping population in the UK. According to the market research organisation Mintel, women aged 20–24 are more likely than any other segment to spend their money on clothing and footwear. The average spends per head on clothing increased by 76% in 2006 to £1,208.

Asos.com offers an extensive and diverse range of products for men and women. Its departments cover its own brand clothing , high-street and designer brands , footwear and accessories, such as sunglasses, jewellery and swimwear. The clothing ranges also cater for narrow market segments, for example, for petite women (under 5'3"). As well as its own brand, asos.com also enters into collaborations with designer labels. This enables it to provide well-known brands that appeal to its young, fashion-conscious target market. Asos.com stocks over 400 brands which includes Diesel, All Saints, Fred Perry, Levis, Adidas, French Connection etc . However, asos.com would not have grown so rapidly if it did not offer a pleasurable shopping experience. The first step in any online business is to ensure that the website offers something of real value to consumers, something that cannot be obtained by visiting a store or a shop. One central question dominates asos.com's planning: why would consumers choose to buy clothes online when they could visit a shop and see, feel and try on different items? Asos.com had to create an online shopping experience that offered convenience, choice, interesting styles, competitive prices, all complemented with high levels of customer service such as prompt and reliable delivery.

Heavy investment in the website – and its underpinning technology – has been vital. Behind the technology and the website, asos.com has invested heavily in ensuring that customers get what they want from the online store. Internet shoppers have very high expectations. Asos.com knows that customers must be pleased with their shopping experience. Communication to support growth , the structure of business organisations usually alters as they grow. When a company is very small, a manager tends to take on most managerial functions. As the company grows, it often introduces new layers of management and organizes itself into specialist departments. As it has expanded, asos.com has developed a more hierarchical organisational structure, with individual departments responsible for specific functions such as warehousing, product design and merchandising. Asos.com works in a rapidly changing market. It must keep up with developments in web technology. Customers can now track their orders online. Shoppers can refine the products they view on asos.com, by choosing colours, sizes and brands to suit. The company tries to keep its website current by adding articles of interest to fashion conscious shoppers. This content is refreshed every week to retain the customer's attention. To enhance the shopping experience, asos.com has increased the size of product images on the web by 250%. It has also used a 'catwalk feature' for women's wear. This shows how the products fit and move to give the customer the best representation. The Asos.com 'Style Blog' is updated daily. This provides visitors to the website with features such as 'Daily Shop', 'Catwalk Trends' and the latest fashion and celebrity news.

The company uses a number of other communication channels to drive growth. It has increased the asos.com monthly magazine to 116 pages. The first three issues generated more than £1.5m in sales with an average response rate of 9%. This is higher than the industry average for this type of promotion. A menswear version of the magazine launched in May 2008, featuring practical style advice, entertainment news, band interviews and aspirational fashion stories to appeal to young male consumers. It emails a newsletter twice a week to 1.8 million people who have chosen to receive it. This significant investment in creative resources has helped to increase sales from the newsletter by 137% in 2007. As part of its PR campaign during 2007 there were 2,236 fashion editorial pieces about asos.com and its products in the consumer press. This was an increase of 59% against 2006. Asos.com takes a 'best friend' approach to help build customer relationships. This means that customers recommend other people. Customers feel they have a personal relationship with asos.com and therefore want to share this with their friends. This type of 'word-of- mouth' recommendation gives results above the industry average. Research on traffic to the asos.com website indicates that around 15% of customers visit the site following a personal recommendation. In the last customer survey, 73% of customers stated that they would recommend asos.com to a friend. Furthermore, in a survey to find out levels of use of the customer magazine, 60% stated that they share their copy of the magazine with at least two other people. As it continues to grow, asos.com needs to make sure that customers still receive the highest standard of service.

Many customers still prefer to deal directly with someone one to one. It has a team of 30 customer service advisers. This team responds by email to all customer enquiries, such as product questions, stock requests or delivery status. Asos.com has worked hard to reduce the average response time for customer enquiries from six hours to one hour. Asos.com has achieved a remarkable growth since it first began trading in 2000. Following the dot.com bubble of the late 1990s, many people doubted the potential of Internet-based retail businesses. It has taken careful planning to ensure that asos.com meets customer needs. The business has grown organically. It has expanded its market share, taken on more staff, and grown sales and profits. This growth has been achieved through systematically planned investment in both people and technology.

QUESTIONS

1. In what ways can a company benefit from growth?
2. What do you feel might be potential disadvantages of very rapid growth?
3. Describe, using examples, what is meant by horizontal and vertical integration.
4. What do you feel are the key things that asos.com did in order to achieve managed and successful organic growth?

8 Hostile Acquisition of Chilliano by Tangy Spices Ltd.

The Tangy Spices Ltd. has competence in Indian spices. The major destination markets for the Tangy spices Ltd. exports have been the Europe and America. The competence of Chilliano lie in Italian herbs and spices. Tangy spices Ltd, India's biggest spices marketer has decided to launch a hostile bid for Italy's major spice marketer Chilliano. This is a rare case of an Indian company making an unsolicited hostile bid for a foreign company.Tangy with this takeover will boost its operations in the world market, particularly in Europe and America – its major exports markets. It also wants to take advantage of the reach enjoyed by the Italian company in several countries where its own products are not being sold presently.

Hostile takeovers are extremely expensive. Acquirer need to be ready to pay extra price than market price of equity. It should be done when a cash-rich company sees strategic advantage in that acquisition. Indian companies can do the hostile takeover provided that takeover helps them to position much stronger in the market. Additionally, price paid for takeover should be in line with the strengths or values to be achieved from that takeover. So looking at this takeover, it seems if hostile takeover is done with proper long-term strategy than it is quite appropriate for the Indian companies.

The move of hostile takeover follows Chilliano's rejection to an agreement entered a year back. At that time Chilliano was suffering losses and it offered majority shares at a price of € 2.25. A total of 20% shares were transferred at that time. In one year Chilliano was able to turnaround its operations and the company made handsome profits in the last quarter. The promoters who have residual holding of 35% in the company are reluctant to transfer the shares now. They rejected the agreement with a plea that the earlier offer price of € 2.25 per share was not sufficient. So, it is a case where promoters either feel that they are not getting right value for their equity or they do not intend sell equity due to increased profitability of company in the recent past.

Tangy spices Ltd has revised its offer to € 2.95. By this lucrative offer some of the large shareholders of Chilliano revealed their interest for selling their stakes. On the other hand, promoters maintained their position on this matter. Through the process of buying of shares in the market the Tangy spices Ltd. gradually consolidated its holding in Chilliano to 45%. Being a major shareholder they were ready for a takeover. At the same time, Tangy spices Ltd. was trying hard to improve its position so that they do not leave any space for Chilliano's promoters in future.

QUESTIONS

1. What strategic alternative is followed by Tangy Spices Ltd?
2. Is the hostile takeover by an Indian company appropriate?
3. Why the Tangy Spices Ltd. is interested in this takeover?
4. Why the promoters are reluctant to transfer the shares after the agreement?

9 Expansion Strategy of Meters Limited

Meters Limited is a company engaged in the designing, manufacturing, and marketing of instruments like speed meters, oil pressure gauges, and so on, that are fitted into two and four wheelers. Their current investment in assets is around Rs. 5 crore and their last year turnover was Rs. 15 crore, just adequate enough to breakeven. The company has been witnessing over the last couple of years, a fall in their market share prices since many customers are switching over to a new range of electronic instruments from the range of mechanical instruments that have been the mainstay of Meters Limited.

The company has received a firm offer of cooperation from a competitor who is similarly placed in respect of product range. The offer implied the following:

(i) transfer of the manufacturing line from the competitor to Meters Limited;

(ii) manufacture of mechanical instruments by Meters Limited for the competitor to the latter's specifications and brand name; and

(iii) marketing by the competitor.

The benefits that will accrue to Meters Limited will be better utilization of its installed capacity and appropriate financial compensation for the manufacturing effort. The production manager of Meters Limited has welcomed the proposal and points out that it will enable the company to make profits. The sales manager is doubtful about the same since the demand for mechanical instruments in shrinking.

The Chief Executive is studying the offer. He thinks that for the time being, till the time new products are developed, they can accept the offer of other organization to manufacture their products for better utilization of capacity but we have to be cautious about competition/sales of products in the same category and that should be properly laid out in the agreement. However, in the long term, we should focus on new products developments and try to expand product range by including the manufacturing of electronic instruments.

QUESTIONS

1. What is divestment strategy? Do you see it being practised in the given case? Explain.
2. What is stability strategy? Should Meters Limited adopt it?
3. What is expansion strategy? What are the implications for Meters Limited in case it is adopted?
4. What are your suggestions to the Chief Executive?

10 Human Resources Management at Sahni Auto Industries

Sahni Auto Industries is a manufacturer and exporter of auto parts with an annual turnover of rupees one thousand crore. It employs about 200 persons in its factory in Punjab and its other offices in India and abroad. The personnel administration and human resources department of the company is headed by Mr. Amit Kapoor, the Chief Personnel Manager. Mr. Amit Kapoor, an automobile engineer joined the company 5 years ago as Product Development Manager. After a successful stint of 4 years as Product Development Manager, he was transferred to personnel administration and human resources department as the Chief Personnel Manager as a part of career development plan. Mr. Vikas, MBA in Human Resources from a renowned Business school, joined the company as Personnel Manager only 3 months back. He reports to Mr. Amit Kapoor, the Chief Personnel Manager. He handles all routine personnel and industrial relations matters.

One day, during informal discussion with Mr. Amit Kapoor, Mr. Vikas suggested him of linking human resources management with company's strategic goals and objectives to further improve business performance and also to develop organisational culture that fosters more innovative ideas. He also advocated creating abundant 'Social Capital' on the ground that people tend to be more productive in an environment which has trust and goodwill embedded unit rather than which is highly hierarchical and formal. Mr. Amit Kapoor disagreed with Mr. Vikas and told him that the role of human resources department was only peripheral to the business and all his suggestions about its strategic role were beyond the purview of personnel administration and human resources department. After this, Mr. Vikas started having number of arguments with Mr. Amit Kapoor on several issues relating to personnel and industrial relations since he felt that a person with a degree in Human Resources Management was in a far better position to run Personnel Administration and Human Resources Department. Mr. Amit Kapoor, the Chief Personnel Manager, had often shown his displeasure on Mr. Vikas's argumentative tendency and had made it known to the General Manager.

The General Manager called Mr. Amit Kapoor in his office to inform him that he has been elected for an overseas assignment. He further told him to find a suitable person as his successor; he even suggested Mr. Vikas as a possible candidate. Mr. Amit Kapoor, however, selected Mr. Balram, who was working as Training Manager in a Multinational Company for the last 5 years. Mr. Vikas, soon started having arguments with Mr. Balram also over a number of issues relating to industrial relations since he felt that he had no experience in handling industral relations matters. Mr. Balram now realised that Mr. Vikas was trying to make things difficult for him. After a series of meetings with the General Manager, Mr. Balram eventually succeeded in convincing him to transfer Mr. Vikas to an office outside Punjab. On learning about his impending transfer, Mr. Vikas wrote a letter to the General Manager joining details of various instances, when Mr. Balram had shown his incompetence in handling problematic situations. When asked for explanation by the General Manager, Mr. Balram had refuted almost all the allegations. The General Manager accepted his explanation and informed Mr. Vikas that most of his allegations against Mr. Balram were unwarranted and baseless. He further advised him to avoid confrontation with Mr. Balram. Mr. Vikas then wrote a letter to the Chairman repeating all the allegations against Mr. Balram. On investigation, the Chairman found most of the allegations true. He then called all the three - the General Manager, the Chief Personnel Manager and the Personnel Manager in his office and implored them to forget the past and henceforth to work in coordination with each other in an environment of trust and goodwill.

QUESTIONS

1. Identify and discuss the major issues raised in the case.
2. Comment on the recruitment of the two Chief Personnel Managers.
3. Would you justify Mr. Vikas's argumentative tendency with the Chief Personnel Managers? Give reasons for your answer.
4. Do you agree with suggestions offered by Mr. Vikas to Human Resources Management with the company's strategic goals? If yes, suggest prominent areas where Human Resources Department can play a role in this regard.

11 Avalon Consulting: Strategic and Operational Consulting Firm

Avalon Consulting, is an international management consulting firm that advises clients across the world on strategy, business transformation and innovation. It is part of the 1000-people Avalon Group which straddles the entire knowledge value chain. Apart from Avalon Consulting, the Group has three other entities - Avalon Global Research, a global market research firm geared to do very quick, high-level product, sector or country studies as well as full-fledged research exercises; Ugam Solutions, a leading provider of Marketing Analytics for global MR firms, management consultants and corporate; and Germinait Solutions, an artificial Intelligence software company focused on developing solutions that help business decision-makers make good timely decisions based on large volumes of data.

Avalon Consulting was founded in 1989 as Business Consulting Group and was rechristened in 2003 as Avalon Consulting. It has offices in Mumbai, Delhi and Chennai and serve clients in India, China, Europe, USA and the Middle-East. The company was set up with the objective of providing senior managers with a more effective resource to help resolve complex strategic and operational issues. Our reputation and credibility have been built through delivering practical and implementable solutions to clients - both domestic and international — covering both the manufacturing and the services sectors.

At Avalon, the work ethics and business credo are built on a fundamental respect for the client's time, business constraints and resources. This philosophy helps them in nurturing lasting client relationships and guarantees value maximization in all engagements. At Avalon Consulting, that strategy formulation is a deliberate search for a plan of action that will develop a business' competitive advantage and compound it.

Strategy is one of the most commonly used management terms, yet it is also the least understood. Often companies underestimate the power of good strategy or confuse tactical initiatives with strategy. Smaller organisations believe that strategy is only for the large companies while the truth is often the reverse. Senior management is often too close to the daily issues to be able to take a detached and clinical view of the long term. These are typical conditions where Avlon strategy team steps in to deliver results.

Avalon's strategy formulation exercise focuses on maximising client shareholder value while effectively managing risks. The process involves identifying the key success factors in any given situation and then designing an organisational framework to excel at each of these factors. Several disparate pieces of the organisational puzzle are addressed in designing the strategy – the core value proposition, product/business portfolio, organisation structure, leadership, skill sets, key operational processes and systems and so on – and combined under one unifying theme.

Strategy formulation can be a holistic exercise encompassing the entire organisation (corporate strategy) or can be localised (functional strategy) based on the magnitude of the problem or the company's appetite for change.

Avalon has engaged effectively with clients across the spectrum of business covering corporations, financial institutions, private equity companies, venture capitalists, government bodies and industry associations. They have executed assignments in over 50 countries around the world giving them wide geographical experience which enables them to maintain a global perspective while retaining the local flavour of individual markets.

The choice of configuration depends upon India based global advantages in business; relative gap between resources required and available for realising the business potential in a single business, in domestic market or globally; characteristics of the existing structure and management systems, whether suited for managing single or multiple businesses; and, orientation of the top management and cultural attributes of organisation, whether tuned to domestic market or outward looking. Given these factors, the configurations are sort of mutually exclusive, for Indian companies. Examples of Gujarat Ambuja as 'India-focused', ITC as 'India-diversified', and Infosys as 'global-focused', further illustrate the organism-like conception of configuration.

The quest is to realise and maintain the configuration in its internally consistent form. However, there could be variants, depending on company specific factors. The switch from one configuration to another, is inherently strenuous and uncertain, and needs to be precipitated by significant change with respect to one or more factors. In the case of Tatas, configurationally change is being enabled by the recognition of India-based global advantages in a majority of businesses and by dramatic change in resource position after initial public offering of Tata Consultancy Services and sharp upturn in steel and automobile businesses.

QUESTIONS

1. What is the philosophy of Avalon Consultancy group? How it helps them to build relationship with their customers?
2. Explain Avlon's strategy formulation exercise.
3. What are the areas where Avlon provides consultancy services?
4. Do they face any competition? How are they able to maintain their competitive edge?

12 Markstrat-Consulting Pvt. Ltd., Strategy and Business Consulting Firm

Markstrat-Consulting Pvt. Ltd, a New Delhi based a high calibre management strategy consulting company offering consulting services in areas of market entry strategies, marketing strategies for business growth, business and corporate strategies and provides effective and complete solutions to your marketing and business concerns in India. On the ground support of an experienced marketing consultant in India, it is necessary when a firm is contemplating to do business in India and wishes to enter peculiar Indian markets. It provides firm just that when they are set to explore Indian markets. Highly qualified, vastly experienced industry professionals and trained management consultants run this well-established consulting organization. Markstrat is a strategy and business consulting company offering services that embrace:

- Market opportunity assessment studies: Market studies comprising research about market size and structure, marketing research, demand potential forecasting and mapping of marketing and competitive environment.
- Market entry/marketing strategies: Advice in market entry strategies, formulation of marketing strategies for market and business growth.
- Strategic business alliances/partner search: Identification and evaluation of strategic business alliances including potential joint venture partners, contract or co-manufacturing partners and vendors/suppliers.
- Distribution partner search: Identification and evaluation of channel partners including country/regional distributors, importer/wholesaler and dealers.
- Distribution strategies: Channel related strategies, evaluation of distribution options, channel design, assessment of channel effectiveness and efficiency and channel development strategies.
- Corporate strategy: Formulation of corporate business strategies and strategic business plans.

Markstrat Consulting was set up in early 2000 with a view to providing advisory services to organizations desirous of utilizing professional knowledge and management expertise in areas of strategic marketing and in strategic management of business and administrative activities. In a short span, the company has taken long strides and takes pride in having serviced a plethora of domestic and international organizations in the private, SME's and multinational corporations to their complete satisfaction. As a testimony to the quality of services, over 95% of thier clients have repeated for their subsequent requirements pertaining to advisory services.

Markstrat Consulting is also the Indian consulting partner for Australian Business International Trade Services of NSW Business Chamber and Sydney, Australia. Markstrat-Consulting in association with Australian Business, regularly undertakes consultancy projects in India to assist Australian companies planning to pursue business interests in India. Markstrat-Consulting has also been assisting various companies from Germany, Singapore and Canada in their market entry strategies pertaining to India. Their esteemed associates are:

- Lombard Global, USA (www.lombardglobal.com)
- Global Intelligence Alliance, Singapore (www.globalintelligence.com)
- Dr. Winter Strategy Consulting, Germany

DEVELOPMENT OF BUSINESS MODEL FOR GERMAN COMPANY

A German company was interested in setting up business to manufacture and sell Kraft paper sacks in India. However, the company was not clear with regard to Indian market situation regarding prospects of world class multi walled paper sacks in India given the competition from cheap Indian products and Government of India's policy regarding foreign investment in paper sector. Given some bad examples of unsuccessful joint ventures in India, the company was apprehensive about the company management structure. Markstrat-Consulting conducted a detailed research to understand the paper sack market and growth prospects in India, prepared a detailed report encompassing Government's policy/procedures affecting investment and evaluated the options of management structure to recommend the best suited. The German company has benefited immensely from the advice and has set up business near Chennai.

MARKET ENTRY FOR HEALTHCARE PRODUCTS FOR A CANADIAN COMPANY

A Canadian company engaged in manufacture of healthcare products was planning to enter Indian markets through manufacturing or export route, however was not sure as to how would it strategize its market entry, given its high quality product and thus expensive offerings, and price sensitivity of most Indian markets, Markstrat-Consulting advised the company on the entry strategy with a suggestion to first export its products through a select distributor network so as to position products in the niche market. Four distributors of high-end healthcare products, one each in four major regions of the country were selected for alliance. Markstrat-Consulting located and recommended distributors who could comply with the positioning plans of the company and assisted the company in implementation of market entry strategy. It has been recommended that after the product is established in India, the manufacturing activity in India should be considered at an appropriate stage so to avoid high import tariffs.

REDEFINING MARKETING STRATEGIES FOR A GERMAN JOINT VENTURE COMPANY

A German Indian joint venture company had set up a manufacturing plant in India to produce plant performance enhancement equipment for Indian and export markets. Even after five years of production, the company could not reach a breakeven and was accumulating losses. Markstrat-Consulting was hired to advise the company to recommend a proper marketing strategy so as to develop the Indian market and to gain higher volumes so as to reach above eighty per cent capacity utilization. Markstrat-Consulting studied the entire business structure of the company and recommended a change in the product mix with emphasis on product development. Market expansion and market development strategies were prepared; marketing organization was restructured and fresh strategies were evolved to ensure intensive customer education and extensive penetration. The company has turned around and is well on its way to wiping out accumulated losses.

QUESTIONS

1. What kind of consultancy services are provided by the Markstrat?
2. Explain the market strategy developed by Markstrat or its German client. Do you think it was the right strategy?
3. What was the problem faced by German company and how Markstrat helped the company to overcome those problems.
4. What market entry was suggested for Canadian firm by Markstrat. So do you think it was appropriate strategy?

13 Davis Service Group: Growing a Company by International Acquisition

Successful businesses know when and how to adapt and change. This involves growing some areas of activity and cutting back on less profitable areas. Companies can often benefit from acquiring businesses operating in overseas markets. For example in Europe, the USA or the Far East, the availability of new customers or cheaper costs of employing people may give competitive advantage. This case study describes and analyses the growth of the Davis Service Group. The term group describes companies that are joined together with a shared ownership. The Davis Service Group provides textile maintenance services in the UK and Europe. This includes linen hire, work wear rental, dust control mat, laundry and washroom services. The Group operates across Europe from its London headquarters. It employs 17,000 people and has an annual turnover of more than £820 million. The Davis Service Group is a conglomerate. consisting of businesses focused on different markets. In 2001, the Davis Service Group consisted of three main operating companies each of which was the UK market leader in its own sector:

- Sunlight (textile maintenance) – hiring sheets to hotels, hospitals and private businesses. Sunlight was the original company from which the Group developed
- Elliott (building systems) – hiring modular buildings for temporary office space.
- HSS (tool hire) – operating through 450 outlets in the UK.

Although these companies were strong, they operated only in the UK which had become a mature market. This means that there are fewer opportunities for growth. Sunlight was the strongest performing part of the business with 45% of revenues at that time. Therefore, to improve return on investment to shareholders, the company chose to focus on the linen hire and textile maintenance part of the business and look for ways to grow it overseas. Davis Service Group had a number of options to choose from to follow its strategy of overseas growth. A strategy is a plan that a company develops and implements. Strategic choice involves deciding, what business sector or market to expand into, when to expand and how to expand, for example, whether to take over another company, set up a joint venture or set up a new company.

Expanding into other countries can be a good way to grow a company. In particular, expanding into other areas of the European Union (EU) provides many opportunities for a UK business. The EU currently has 27 member countries. It is a huge potential market. Any business in the European Union has over 500 million customers on its doorstep. Goods and services can flow freely in the single European market. This means it is much easier to do business in the EU. Trade within this area has risen by 30% since 1992. The development of fast transport links, for example, the Channel Tunnel, high-speed trains and cheaper air links, means people can travel to and across Europe more easily. The Internet and email enable companies to communicate instantly. British firms locating factories and offices in the EU are able to benefit from a skilled labour force. Within Europe, most member countries use a common currency – the Euro. This makes it easy to trade within this marketplace.

When a business decides to expand overseas, there are a number of factors which may present barriers that it needs to consider.

- Language: Language differences can lead to confusion. However, English is the main global business language spoken by many people within the EU.
- Currency differences: Most countries within the EU use the Euro. The UK uses the British pound. The value of the pound can go up or down against the value of the Euro. This can make it difficult for a business to predict what its costs and revenues will be. If the pound has a lower value than the Euro, a UK business would pay more for imported materials but receive less for its exported finished products. This would mean less profit.
- Cultural differences: Ways of behaving and doing things vary between countries and even within countries. In business, some behaviors such as buying decisions may be the same. In other cases it is important to respect local differences, for example, how you greet someone new for the first time.
- Legal and administrative differences: There may vary across countries, for example safety standards for buildings. However, there are international standards that create common requirements.
- Skill levels may vary between countries: In setting up a business that needs particular skills, it makes sense to focus activities in countries where those skills exist. Inorganic growth A business can develop by organic growth or inorganic growth. The term inorganic growth describes how a business grows by joining one or more companies together. This can be done by two firms joined by agreement. Mergers make it possible to share the resources of the two organisations and focus on the best activities of each. One company buys at least 51% of the shares of another company. This enables the company with the larger number of shares to have control over the other business and select which activities to keep.

Horizontal integration refers to a situation where two firms at the same stage of production join. If Sunlight joined another firm hiring sheets to hotels and hospitals in the UK, this would be an example of horizontal integration. In contrast, vertical integration joins businesses at different stages of production. For example, Sunlight could join with a company that makes hotel sheets. This shows backward vertical integration where Sunlight benefits from controlling the supply of the sheets it uses. This ensures quality control and on-time delivery. A business could also consider forward vertical integration. For example, it joins with a distribution company to economize on its transport costs. This could benefit Sunlight by showing its environmental responsibility. The advantage of vertical integration is that it gives the business greater control over the supply chain of its product or service. The Sunlight business was partially vertically integrated by including the cleaning and delivery processes in its service.

In 2002, the Davis Service Group acquired Berendsen, a company operating in Denmark, Sweden, Norway, Austria, the Netherlands, Poland and Germany. Berendsen was an ideal acquisition because, like Sunlight, it was the market leader in providing textile services in its geographical area. It was better for the Davis Service Group to take over Berendsen rather than set up a new rival company in Europe. Building on Berendsen's local experience and local market contacts, Davis Service Group could buy into established networks and customer relationships. When the Davis Service Group took over Berendsen, Berendsen was not performing financially as well as it could. Profitability was below that achieved by Sunlight. The Davis Service Group already had proven management systems in providing textile services. Taking over Berendsen, rather than merging with it, gave Davis Service Group the control to put the best systems in place at Berendsen. It was able to reduce operating costs, for example, closing down some locations where Berendsen had two outlets operating in the same area. Strengthen the management of the two companies led to saving fixed costs, by cutting out the central headquarters of the company. This put Berendsen in a stronger position to improve its sales and profits. Horizontal integration made sense.

Sunlight and Berendsen are specialist companies at the same stage of production. It was possible to pool the knowledge and expertise of the two companies so that both benefited. The factors that might have been barriers to international growth were easy to overcome in this acquisition These factors were:

- Language: Berendsen's business operates across several European countries and uses English as a common language.
- Cultural differences: Buying patterns and the culture in the areas where Berendsen operates are similar to the UK.
- Currency: The countries in which Berensden operates already used the Euro or had currencies linked to the Euro.
- Financing the takeover was straightforward: There was a close strategic fit with what Sunlight already did well, which was easy for shareholders and banks to understand. £150 million was raised through selling more shares to existing shareholders. The remainder of the £425 million to purchase Berendsen came from new bank borrowings.

The Davis Service Group successfully delivered the promised returns to its shareholders over the period 2002-2005 and has seen its share price rise accordingly. The next phase of growth involved some additional small takeovers of companies to strengthen the business position. The focus was on keeping the most efficient units in the growing company. These additional takeovers added a relatively small workload without the need for substantial investment.

Organic growth is when a company increases the turnover of the existing business. Much of the growth of Sunlight and Berendsen involves organic growth. These businesses are market leaders that have been able to learn a lot from each other and share good ideas and best practice. As part of the Group, these companies have increased their customers in the existing locations, as well as in other areas of the rapidly developing EU market. Trade and living standards in the EU are growing fast. Large global companies are opening up new sites and they require textile services from Sunlight and Berendsen. Countries like Poland, which joined the EU in 2003, are experiencing growth in key sectors such as manufacturing so more uniforms are needed. New EU legislation also provides an opportunity for Davis Service Group. For example, the need for protective uniforms for industrial workers provides plenty of new contract work for textile services. Organic growth – building on existing resources – is sometimes the only way to grow. For example, in many Eastern European countries that were part of the former Soviet Union, there are few companies suitable to take over. Most businesses in these countries had previously been government-owned. They had poor equipment and/or had no need to rent out textiles.

The Davis Service Group needed to grow. Of its original three divisions, the linen hire and textile maintenance services provided by Sunlight offered the greatest opportunities because of the strategic fit factors. The Group's other businesses were sold off to concentrate on the potential of the enlarged European textile maintenance business and to provide funds to invest further in this business. The Davis Service Group is an international business. However, it believes in giving local people responsibility for managing the markets they know best. It has a decentralized approach. The small London Head Office has just 17 people working there. Local managers manage local companies using their expertise in their own markets.

QUESTIONS

1. Describe two major ways in which a company can grow. Give examples to illustrate the two ways of growing.
2. Businesses grow when they have the resources to expand and opportunities exist for growth. Explain how the acquisition of Berendsen provided such a good opportunity for the Davis Service Group.
3. What aspects of European Union markets have particularly encouraged, horizontal growth of the Davis Service Group?
4. If the company were to expand into new areas of the globe, where would you recommend and why? What factors might encourage or discourage this choice?

14 Expansion Strategy of Bharti Airtel Limited

Bharti Airtel Limited, a group company of Bharti Enterprises, is among Asia's leading integrated telecom services providers with operations in India and Sri Lanka. The company had an aggregate of over 118 million customers as of end November 2009, including 116.01 million mobile customers. Bharti Airtel has been ranked among the six best performing technology companies in the world by *Business Week*. Founded in 1976, Bharti Enterprises has grown from being a bicycle manufacturer to becoming one of the largest Indian conglomerates. It is led by its founder Sunil Bharti Mittal, the group now covers retail, real estate, insurance, and food distribution but is best known internationally for its telecommunications and IT businesses. Across all the companies in the Bharti Group highly effective partnerships is probably the most visible common thread.

Bharti Airtel is India's leading telecommunications company and the largest telecoms operator in the world with over 210 million subscribers. It also provides mobile services across 19 countries in South Asia and Africa. It offers land-line telephone services and broadband internet access in nearly 100 Indian cities and also has a satellite TV business. Bharti Airtel is structured as four strategic business units – mobile, tele-media, enterprise, and digital TV. The mobile business offers services in India and Sri Lanka. The Telemedia business provides broadband, IPTV, and telephone services in 95 Indian cities. The enterprise business provides end-to-end telecom solutions to corporate customers and national and international long distance services to carriers. The digital TV business provides direct-to-home TV services across India. All these services are provided under the Airtel brand. Airtel's national high-speed optic fibre network currently spans over 113,326 km covering all the major cities in India. The company has two international landing stations in Chennai and Mumbai that connect two submarine cable systems – i2i to Singapore and Sea-Me-We-4 to Europe.

Launched in Delhi and Himachal Pradesh in 1995, Bharti Airtel has expanded at a breathless pace in the 16 years of its existence and analysts see that it has displayed remarkable capacity to scale up year on year and to execute its plans with high energy. For the first few years, Bharti Airtel followed a very similar growth strategy to other mobile operators around the world – buying licences, building networks, growing support activities such as customer care, billing and network operation, building its brand, offering competitive tariffs and the latest phones, and so steadily gaining more customers. This served the company well, but did not significantly differentiate it in the market or give it any major competitive advantage over its peers.

Facing the challenge of how to deliver telecoms at affordable (very low) prices to Indian customers in an industry that requires high capital investment, the breakthrough came at the end of 2002, when the management team recognised that to sell at the lowest prices in the world requires the lowest costs in the world. To achieve this it required a new business model under which Bharti Airtel took the hitherto unprecedented step in the telecoms services industry of just focusing on the things it does best – customer, brand and people management – and leaving everything else to people who can do it better.

To understand Bharti Airtel's success requires an understanding of India's unique telecom market and the firm's commitment to building strong customer trust and confidence. Bharti Airtel is already one of the most integrated telecom companies in the world and is on track to achieve its goal to become the "Most Admired Brand" in India. Bharti Airtel is the leading mobile telecom provider in a hyper-competitive and cost conscious market, which necessitates innovation and cost optimization.

From 2008 to early 2009, Bharti Airtel added 32 million new customers, and believes it can add another 100 million customers in a few years. At its current pace of nearly 100,000 new customers per day, this goal seems well within reach. In order to deliver the highest quality service at the lowest possible cost, the firm has had to embrace the business model that has helped make India an economic powerhouse: business process outsourcing (BPO).

The firm outsources many of its most fundamental functions and infrastructures, including its information technology (IT) operations to IBM, Nortel and Wipro; its communications networks to Ericsson and Nokia Siemens; and its contact centre operations to Nortel and Wipro. With 25 contact centres and 15,000 agents nationwide, Bharti Airtel needed to find a way to reduce the cost of delivering excellent customer service and handle millions of customer calls each month.

By outsourcing the majority of its activities – networks, IT, call centres, towers, distribution to global specialist firms in long-term partnership arrangements, Bharti is now able to operate a low-cost business model that supports the company's belief that it can 'bring the benefits of mobile telephony to millions and millions of lower middle class and poor consumers around the world.' And this focus on doing what it does best has allowed Bharti Airtel's entrepreneurial culture and customer-centricity to combine to create an organizational culture that is consistently opportunity minded.

Having honed its business model in India, over the past couple of years Bharti Airtel has been on a spending spree – adding operations in what it sees as other high-growth markets and its ambition is high as demonstrated by its belief that 'By 2015, Airtel will be the most loved brand in the daily lives of the African people.' Bharti Airtel, has successfully concluded a $10.7-billion deal to acquire the African assets of Kuwait's Zain, making *Bharti Airtel the world's fifth largest mobile phone services company*. The deal enables Bharti Airtel to extend its services in 15 countries across the African continent except Sudan and Morocco."Bharti is now among the five largest mobile operators in the world.

This will further strengthen the historic Indo-Africa economic and social ties and provide a big boost to South-South cooperation," said group chairman Sunil Mittal. " 42 million customers (which) is the customer base of Zain Africa, 3.6 billion dollars in revenue and just under 1.2 billion dollars in EBITDA is what Africa offers us at this starting point," added Mittal. Bharti now has a total user base over 180 million in 18 countries. Prior to this deal, Bharti had operations in India, Sri Lanka and Bangladesh. In order to expand its broadband market in India Bharti Airtel, Asia's leading integrated telecom service provider, had entered into a strategic partnership with Novatium. Novatium Solutions Private Limited is the leading provider of rich computing services in the country.

GROWTH STRATEGY FOR RURAL INDIA

Bharti Airtel was faced with the challenge of profitably serving the rural areas of India. It is an extremely daunting task due to a variety of factors: rural users' low incomes, a widely dispersed population, and a less than ideal public infrastructure (i.e., roads, electricity, etc.). Specifically, Bharti Airtel had to address the following conditions:

- The incomes of Indian rural residents are significantly lower than urban residents. The average revenue per user (ARPU) for rural residents was typically less than US$2 per month.
- Besides deploying a scalable network, Bharti Airtel also needed to establish a cost-effective marketing, sales, and distribution channel to provide service promotion and customer support.
- Counter to these challenges was a significant opportunity that the Indian rural market represented and Bharti Airtel's unique ability to address it.
- The future growth of the Indian mobile market is expected to be driven by rural customers, which account for about 70 per cent of the country's total population (1.1 billion people) with a teledensity of only 18.5 per cent as of September 2009. Indian urban mobile penetration is already over 100 per cent.
- Rural dwellers place a high value on communications. Contacting urban/overseas relatives and friends often requires a long and sometimes treacherous trip to the nearest town to reach a payphone.
- Various studies (e.g., fishermen in the Indian state of Kerala and grain producers in Niger) have shown that increased mobile service penetration in rural areas could have tremendous socio-economic benefits for the rural population.
- With its strong presence in the relatively untapped rural market (over 27 per cent market share as of September 2009), Bharti Airtel is well placed to continue growth with its focus on under-penetrated Indian regions with new revenue streams such 3G-enabled data services and pay-TV.

To extend its reach in India's rural markets, Bharti Airtel is focusing on innovative initiatives, including efficient infrastructure deployments, expanding its distribution network via partnerships, and customized content and tariffs.

- Bharti Airtel has launched microfinancing agreements in collaboration with Nokia and SKS Micro-finance. Under these partnerships, Bharti provides subsidized tariffs and subscriber identity module (SIM) cards to rural users, Nokia provides subsidized handsets, and SKS offers microfinancing.

- To expand coverage into rural regions, Bharti Airtel is sharing passive infrastructure services with Vodafone (42 per cent ownership) and Idea (16 per cent ownership) through its joint venture, Indus Towers. Sharing the infrastructure cost and usage between multiple operators has helped Bharti Airtel to reduce its operating and capital expenses.
- Bharti Airtel also formed a joint venture with the Indian Farmers Fertilizer Cooperative Limited (IFFCO). Its joint venture, IFFCO Kisan Sanchar, uses IFFCO's wide rural presence (present in 80 per cent of Indian villages) and appeal among the rural agricultural community to market and distribute Bharti's products.
- IFFCO Kisan Sanchar provides subsidized handsets and connections at competitive rates in rural areas. It also helps Bharti Airtel to identify and acquire suitable locations for deploying its cell sites. In addition, it offers tailored services including voice-based updates on crop prices, farming techniques, rural health initiatives, and "help line" services.

STRATEGY

Bharti Airtel first studies the commercial viability of a rural community (and the surrounding villages) based on parameters such as source of livelihood, average income, and involvement in frequent commercial transactions or travels. The company has developed a prioritized deployment strategy based on the specified criteria. Qualifying villages are first to receive a base station, which also caters to nearby communities. To help ensure efficient usage and profitability for each of these base stations, Bharti Airtel tracks the revenue generated per base station (instead of ARPU, which is considered less relevant in a rural context).

The following best practices have also been established:

- Bharti Airtel has adopted the strategy of direct communications to market its value proposition to rural customers. To make its services accessible, the company provides all of its marketing content in local languages. Vans are used to cover rural areas with staff who educate locals about mobile services and usage.
- The company has developed a shared phone service called Public Call Offices (PCOs) in rural regions to increase awareness about its brand and services.
- Bharti Airtel Service Centres have been set up in villages to address customer queries and complaints as well as act as sales and distribution points. These centres employ local people and offer sales and customer services using local dialects.
- Bharti Airtel has already established over 18,000 service centres in rural India, covering over 400 languages and local dialects. The company plans to expand this network.

SUCCESS FACTORS/METRICS/MONETIZATION

Bharti Airtel does not provide separate rural key performance indicators, but the following results have been publicly announced:

- As of April 2010, Bharti Airtel's network covered 440,000 villages in India, which, together with its urban services, accounted for coverage of approximately 84 per cent of India's total population.
- As of March 31, 2010, Bharti Airtel had added 9 million new customers to reach a total of 128 million connections. Ovum estimates that rural users accounted for 60 per cent of the company's net subscriber adds in that quarter.
- Despite Bharti Airetel's overall ARPU of just under $5, its mobile division's earnings before interest, taxes, depreciation, and amortization (EBITDA) margin was approximately 30 per cent, and its earnings before interest and taxes (EBIT) margin was approximately 19 per cent, which indicate a healthy return on overall (including significant rural) investments.

According to Mr Sanjay Kapoor , CEO, Bharti Airtell "In a country like India , which is so vast, with a very dismal penetration of fixed line broadband, I think wireless is the only solution. Like for the most Indian the first call, the voice call, was on a wireless devices; similarly for most of the Indians , the first access to Internet will also be through a wireless device".

QUESTIONS

1. How was the journey of Bharti Airtel Ltd.?
2. How the expansion has taken place in telecommunication and what role has been played by Bharti Airtel?
3. Bharti has diversified in other areas as well as a part of its expansion plan. How successful these diversifications were?
4. "Going international was the most logical step in the expansion". Comment based on the Bharti Airtel expansion strategy.

15 First Group: Managing External Influences

We all make use of the services provided by transportation companies. For example, you will probably have taken the bus in your home town, or travelled on a school bus or made an intercity journey by train. Some of you may have travelled on a tram or used a park & ride bus service. First Group plc (known as First) is the UK's largest surface transportation company. It has revenues of over £5 billion a year. It employs over 135,000 staff throughout the UK and North America and moves more than 2.5 billion passengers a year. First is the largest UK rail operator carrying 270 m passengers every year. This is one quarter of the passenger network of UK. First operates rail passenger services, which include regional, intercity and commuter services such as First Great Western, First Trans Pennine Express, First Capital Connect, First Scot Rail and Hull Trains. First is Britain's largest bus operator running every fifth local bus services. A fleet of nearly 9,000 buses carries around three million passengers a day in more than 40 major towns and cities, such as Manchester, Leeds and Glasgow. The company also operates First GBRF, a rail freight business and the Croydon Tram link network which carries almost 25 million passengers a year. In North America, First is the largest provider of student transportation carrying nearly 3 million students every day. First is the leader in providing reliable, safe, innovative and sustainable transport services.

Although First is a global business, it aims to be local in its approach. This means that local issues are dealt with by people that largely live and work in that location. This ensures a clearer understanding of what needs to happen and a more prompt response. External influences running a business would be simple if the directors and managers only had to think about what went on inside the business. They could concentrate on internal decisions, such as determining routes, timetables and operating buses. However, business planners have also to understand what goes on outside the business. Businesses are able to identify external changes that may affect it by carrying out a PESTEL analysis. This is a business tool in which each of the letters in PESTEL describes a type of change that takes place in the external business environment. Many of these external changes may be outside the control of the company, for example, new government legislation. Some changes may present a threat to the business, such as a competitor using new or improved technology. Social changes may bring opportunities, for example, migrant workers bringing new skills to the employment market. Environmental impacts, such as those caused by carbon dioxide (CO_2) emissions or the management of waste, are of particular concern to businesses like First.

A business must assess what external changes are likely and which it needs to react to or take advantage of. Business planners can then create strategies to help the business respond effectively. Business strategy refers to a plan or series of action plans for a group of related products. First's strategy relates to its transportation plans and takes into account all of the PESTEL factors in its environment.

Political factors: Transport services are at the heart of the UK economy – moving people to work, home and school, and goods to households and businesses. In the 1980s, the government started to privatize bus services in the UK. It believed that allowing private firms to compete to run bus services would keep prices low and ensure companies would try harder to give customers what they wanted. The result has been more efficient, innovative and sustainable bus services. Government operates at two levels – national and local. First believes in providing local solutions, therefore it concentrates on working closely with local government. For example, it provides a service to local schools and plans bus routes that are convenient for elderly people. A key government policy affecting all transport services relates to the reduction of CO_2 emissions. The UK government has signed the Kyoto Protocol. Countries which sign the agreement intend to reduce the emission of harmful gases. This can succeed only through partnership with business. A good example of this is the government initiative to encourage more children to use bus services rather than travelling to school by car. This will help to reduce carbon emissions. First is actively encouraging people to use the bus instead of their cars.

First has produced a Climate Change Strategy that shapes every action the company takes. This is part of First's vision – to 'Transform Travel'. It wants to change how people feel about public transport by delivering the highest levels of service and customer satisfaction. This involves recognizing its responsibility to reduce CO_2 emissions to as low a level as possible. Tram, bus and rail travel create less pollution than other forms of transport, but there is still room to improve. Key elements of First's Climate Change Strategy include:

- Improving the fuel efficiency of its vehicles.
- Purchasing vehicles with greater fuel efficiency.
- Using alternative fuels, such as biodiesel.
- Operational improvements through driver training
- New technology to monitor driver performance
- First aims to reduce its CO_2 emissions by 25% for its bus division and 20% for rail, both by 2020.

Economic factors: Businesses need to make money to continue to exist. They do this by listening to customers to ensure they keep their customers and attract new ones with good services that customers want and need. It is extremely important for businesses to respond to changes in demand from customers. For example, First has responded to increased demand in the Neath Valley in Wales by working closely with the Neath Port Talbot Council to run improved services. Another good example of responding to demand is the provision of high quality Yellow School Bus transport. Market research showed that parents and students wanted safer buses, so First designed special pilot services with the students in mind, based on the lessons learned from its US operations. Drivers are trained to work with students. Each day students step onto the same bus, can take the same seat and are looked after by the same specially trained driver. Vehicle safety features include padded seating, integrated seat belts, additional escape hatches and CCTV. First is working with the government via a specially appointed Yellow School Bus commission to investigate the possibility of rolling out specialized yellow school bus services throughout the UK.

Another economic factor affecting First's business is taxation. High tax on fuel encourages customers to switch from using cars to more economical bus and rail transport. Congestion charges in cities like London also encourage drivers to switch to other forms of transport. Of course, First does not want to replace the use of cars. Cars are an important means of transport and many families now have more than one car. However, many people are not aware of the environmental impact of, for example, a single person travelling to work in a large 'gas-guzzler' car. First's approach is to complement rather than compete with the car. First seeks to make it easy for people to switch between public transport and private car journeys. For example, in major cities where parking is inconvenient or expensive, First makes public transport easily available through its Park & Ride schemes.

Social factors: Social changes may have a major impact on business. The number of older people in the UK is rising. There are more people with bus passes in this country than ever before. The passes mean that users travel free, as the local authority pays First for providing the service. Many elderly people prefer to travel by bus because it is convenient and safe. Society's habits and tastes are changing. People are more aware of the importance of the environment and becoming 'green consumers'. Green consumers prefer goods and services that are 'environmentally-friendly' and which have less impact on the environment. The green consumer, for example, prefers to travel by bus or train than by air or in a large car. People are now more mobile and travel more. Statistics produced by the Department for Transport in 2007 pick out some of the major trends. These statistics show a positive picture for First. The market is growing and more people are realizing the benefits of a more environmentally-friendly form of transport.

Technological factors: Businesses are continually developing new technologies to provide the best solutions for the marketplace. Intelligent companies find out what the most appropriate technologies are for their businesses and use them. This is particularly true in transport. A good example of this is in the provision of buses that lower the floor for easy entry. These provide better accessibility for disabled and elderly people. First has invested heavily to meet government targets for the provision of low-floor buses. In 2006 First introduced FTR — short for 'Future'. These are state-of-the-art articulated vehicles that look like trams but have the flexibility of a bus and use normal roads. First has set up schemes using these vehicles in partnership with local authorities. First provides the bus service and the local authority the infrastructure, such as new road layouts and bus shelters. FTR vehicles are capable of carrying more people per journey, so fewer bus journeys are necessary. They are also more popular with customers resulting in fewer car journeys. This reduces the amount of fuel used, reduces CO_2 emissions and means less impact on the environment.

National Rail user increased, with 1.2 billion passenger journeys made a rise of 8% on the previous year. Passenger journeys on local buses in England rose by 4% in the year. Passenger journeys on light rail systems in England increased by 9%. In London, bus and light rail passenger journey grew by 6% in the year. Many regions in England saw increases in the number of bus passenger journeys. This resulted from the introduction of free bus fares for disabled people and those aged over 60. The average age of the national bus fleet fell from 8.4 years to 8.1 years. Average local bus fares in Great Britain fell by 3% in real terms. In First Group's rail division, First Scot Rail has set up ground-breaking alerting services for passengers, "Journey Check and Journey Alert". These enable passengers to receive up-to-date train information by text or email. These services provide a convenient way of letting people know if there are delays or alterations to train times so they can plan their journeys accordingly. Other technological solutions include the use of prepaid Smart cards to make payment on buses easier and faster.

Environmental factors: Today the environment is perhaps the most important external influence on any transport service. There is overwhelming evidence that human activities contribute to climate change. Government, consumers and businesses all want to see better environmental management. In 2007, First set out its Climate Change Strategy. The strategy sets targets to reduce CO_2 emissions in the short and long term along with plans to achieve these targets. The strategy identified some of the risks of climate change. These included the vulnerability of road and rail infrastructure to flooding and storm surges along the coast. It identified ways of managing these risks, for example, by working with transport network providers to monitor and maintain roads and rail. The strategy also identified opportunities. For example, First has set out ambitious targets of reducing its CO_2 emissions from its bus and rail divisions by 25% and 20% respectively by 2020. This gives First a clear advantage over its competitors.

Legal factors: Legal changes that affect business are closely tied up with political ones. Many changes in the law stem from government policy. Many of these laws are Europe-wide, for example, the standards for bus transport emissions. First makes sure that all its buses meet these requirements. First has to anticipate and prepare to meet future legal changes. From 2010, as part of an initiative called "Carbon Reduction Commitment", First and other transportation companies will have to buy carbon credits. These credits permit companies to generate specific quantities of carbon emissions. First had already prepared a budget to do this and has set out clear plans for anticipating how much CO_2 it will produce after 2010.

It is possible to see PESTEL factors as threats. However, First prefers to see them as opportunities. Social trends are creating increasing numbers of older passengers seeking comfortable easy-to-access buses. Government pressure is encouraging more and more individuals (particularly on school runs) to use public transport. Many people are seeking a 'greener' form of transport. A detailed PESTEL analysis helped First to make appropriate plans to rise to the challenges of a changing environment. First is able to move forward with confidence and grow its business.

QUESTIONS

1. What do the letters PESTEL stand for? Can you identify any links between some of these factors, for example between political and legal factors affecting a business? What other links can you make?
2. How does it benefit First to work closely with government in designing its transport service strategy? In your answer, show why it is important to work with local government.
3. Analyze how effective First has been in responding to changes in demand for bus services?
4. Evaluate the effectiveness of the way that First is meeting the challenge of providing sustainable solutions to transport needs.

16 Fun Spot Fun Park

Fun Spot Amusement Park & Zoo was a family amusement park located in Angola, Indiana, USA. Although it was small in comparison to parks in neighboring states, such as Cedar Point and Michigan's Adventure, it remained one of the most popular parks in the region. It also once boasted the only operating roller coaster (Afterburner) with an inversion in the state of Indiana.

Fun Spot boasts that it is one of only a few amusement centres in the nation that offers multi-level cement go-cart tracks – four separate tracks. In addition to go-carts, there are bumper cars, bumper boats, a number of other thrill rides and the children's section known as Kid Spot. The Kid Spot section includes a small carrousel; the Frog Hopper, a ride that drops its riders in small increments and then bounces back up; a kiddie's swing; a kiddies train and other rides.

Fun Spot Fun Park began as a small amusement park in 1985, with nothing more than a merry-go-round, a slide, pony rides, and an ice cream stand, Fun-Spot grew into a popular family attraction with 20 rides, a restaurant, and an outdoor performing arts theatre. Today, thousands of visitors flock to Fun-Spot—families, children of all ages, even senior citizens who enjoy strolling through the gardens and arbor. At Fun Spot, elementary school age children, teenagers and parents, will find plenty of fun and thrills at this mini-amusement park that packs a lot of excitement into a very small area. "There's something here for everyone," Gail Hart says. "Dozens of companies hold annual company picnics here. We have welcomed class field trips. And we even had one wedding here at the park!" "Here's the funny thing," Ron chime in. "We really don't know why we've been so successful! There is nothing else like Fun-Spot Fun Park in the area. We were just lucky." "I think it's the ambience of the park," Gail added, "that has brought so many visitors. We provide a 'total package' of entertainment. Plus, we try to change our rides and various attractions from time to time."

Ron and Gail Hart admitted that making every visitor happy is a priority. "That has always been our philosophy," they said. "And we've always been able to deliver on that because we've never allowed ourselves to grow too big too quickly."

QUESTIONS

1. Describe two critical factors impacting the strategic plan at Fun-Spot.
2. Would you consider Fun-Spot's mission statement to be market oriented? Explain.
3. At this point, how do Ron and Gail monitor Fun-Spot's business portfolio?
4. Into which quadrant of the BCG matrix does Fun-Spot fall? Why?
5. How might Ron and Gail implement a market penetration strategy at Fun-Spot?
6. In what way do Ron and Gail implement a product development strategy at Fun-Spot?

17 Growth Strategy: Hindustan Unilever Limited

Hindustan Unilever Limited (HUL), a 51% subsidiary of the Anglo-Dutch conglomerate, Unilever, is India's largest fast moving consumer goods (FMCG) company. HUL, had acquired a tremendous reputation as one of India's best-managed companies. Despite being the subsidiary of an MNC, HUL was perceived to be more Indian than foreign, in the way it managed its operations. HUL operated with considerably more autonomy than other subsidiaries in the Unilever system. HUL's origin went back to 1885 when the Lever Brothers set up 'William Hesketh Lever', in England. In 1888, Lever Brothers entered India by exporting 'Sunlight', its laundry soap. In the late 19th and early 20th century Unilever used to export its products to India. This process began in 1888 with the export of Sunlight soap, which was followed by Lifebuoy in 1895 and other famous brands like Pears, Lux and Vim soon after. In 1931, Unilever set up its first Indian subsidiary, Hindustan Vanaspati Manufacturing Company, followed by Lever Brothers India Limited (1933) and United Traders Limited (1935).The three companies were merged in November 1956 and the new entity was called Hindustan Lever Limited. HUL offered 10% of its equity to the Indian public, and it was the first among the foreign subsidiaries to do so.

The liberalisation of Indian Economy in 1991 and subsequent removal of regulatory framework allowed HUL to explore every single product and opportunity segment, without any constraints on production capacity. The 1990s witnessed a string of crucial mergers, acquisitions and alliances. In 1993, it acquired the Kissan business from the UBGroup and the Dollops Ice-cream business from Cadbury India. In one of the most talked about events of India's corporate history, the erstwhile Tata Oil Mills Company (TOMCO) merged with HUL, effective from April 1, 1993. In July 1993, Brooke Bond India and Lipton India merged to form Brooke Bond Lipton India Limited (BBLIL). Brooke Bond Lipton India Limited launched Wall's range of Frozen Desserts in 1994 and by the end of the year, HUL entered into a strategic alliance with the Kwality Ice-cream Group families. BBLIL merged with HUL, on January 1, 1996. HUL has also set up a subsidiary in Nepal, Nepal Lever Limited (NLL). The NLL factory manufactures HUL's products like Soaps, Detergents and Personal Products both for the domestic market and exports to India. In January 2000, as part of its divestment strategy, the government awarded 74% equity in Modern Goods to HUL . In 2002 it acquired the government's remaining stake in Modern Foods. In February 2007, the company has been renamed as "Hindustan Unilever Limited (HUL)", to stike the optimum balance and to take advantage of future benefits and synergies of alignment with the corporate name of "Unilever".

Vision of HUL: HUL's vision is to continuously innovate technologies to further reduce water consumption and further increase conservation in its operations. Simultaneously, HUL sites will progressively help communities, wherever required, to develop watersheds.

Mission of HUL: Unilever's mission is to add Vitality to life. We meet everyday needs for nutrition, hygiene, and personal care with brands that help people feel good, look good and get more out of life.

Corporate Purpose: Our deep roots in local culture and market around the world gives us our strong relationship with consumers and are foundation of our future growth. We will bring our wealth of knowledge and international expertise to the service of local consumers — a truly multi-local multinational. Our long-term success requires a total commitment to exceptional standards of performance and productivity, to working together effectively, and to a willingness to embrace new ideas and learn continuously.

The company offers products in over 20 distinct categories in home, personal care, food and beverages segments. HUL's brands like Lifebuoy, Lux, Surf Excel, Rin, Wheel, Fair & Lovely, Pond's, Sunsilk, Clinic, Pepsodent, Close-up, Lakme, Brook Bond, Kissan, Knoor, Annapurna, Kwality walls are household names across the country and span a host of categories such as soaps, detergents, personal care products, tea, coffee, branded staples, ice cream and culinary products. These products are manufactured over 40 factories across India and the associated operations involve over 2,000 suppliers and associates. Hindustan Lever Limited's distribution network comprises about 4,000 redistribution stockists, covering 6.3 million retail outlets reaching the entire urban population. Over the years, HUL had extended many of its popular brands with varying degree of success. Some extensions like Clinic All Clear anti-dandruff shampoo to hair oil category had been successful, while others like Ponds Toothpaste had been a dismal failure.

It primarily operates in India. It is headquartered in Mumbai, India and employs more than 16,000 people. The company recorded revenues of INR 196,910.2 million ($4,292.6 million) during the financial year end March 2011 (FY2011), an increase of 10.8% over FY2010. The operating profit of the company was INR 27,360.9 million ($596.5 million) in FY2011, an increase of 0.6% over FY2010. The net profit was INR 22,960.5 million ($500.5 million) in FY2011, an increase of 6.5% over FY2010.

Mr. M. S. Banga, Chairman, HUL explained: *"I believe that each extension must strengthen the core and the core must remain unchanged. When the core of the equity is in one direction and the product extension is in another and you graft the two, you are unlikely to succeed. The set of peripheral or extended values can be changed over time."*

In the early 2000s, as HUL struggled to generate growth, brand extension became an important strategic option. HUL extended its popular brands into the premium segment to increase its profits. By early 2003, HUL had launched a number of brand extensions with varying degrees of success. In 2003, in what seemed to be in response to intensifying competition in several segments, HUL decided to strengthen its already overwhelming presence in the talcum powder category where its brand, Pond's Dreamflower, was already the market leader. HUL also extended Lifebuoy, Vaseline and Fair and Lovely to Talc category. Senior HUL executives wondered if these brand extensions would yield the benefits they promised. Was HUL better off launching new brands?

QUESTIONS

1. HUL was perceived to be more Indian than foreign. Why?
2. What benefits were brought by liberalization which helped HUL?
3. Explain the "strategic intent" of HUL. Do you think it is inspiring to connect HUL with its customer and employeers.
4. HUL has developed a wide array of brands. Do you think this strategy has helped HUL to gain considerable market share?

18 Intel: Using Innovation to Create Competitive Advantage

We live in a digital age. Music, video, phone calls, information creation and information consumption are all, by and large, done digitally. A huge proportion of this happens on the Internet. People use the Internet and its content via computers: As Internet content becomes more sophisticated with, for example, film, music and podcasts, more computing power is needed. The computer chips inside computers need to keep pace with that demand. Intel is best known for producing the chips that deliver this increased computing power. Intel is the world's leader in silicon innovation. Transistors are the building blocks of computer chips that Intel has been making for 40 years. Intel has been working to make these transistors smaller so that more of them could be fitted onto the same area of silicon, making the chips more powerful. This came at a price. Until recently, the smaller the transistors, the hotter the chips tended to run. In 2007 Intel developed a breakthrough in the materials used to construct the transistors. Not only can these transistors work faster, they can also do this while generating less heat. Intel has started to use this new material for its latest generation of processors. These are made from transistors only 45 nanometers in size. This means over 2,000 of them could fit on the full stop at the end of this sentence. A 45 nanometer transistor can switch on and off approximately 300 billion times a second. A beam of light travels less than a tenth of an inch during the time it takes a 45nm transistor to switch on and off. Gordon Moore Intel's founder predicted that the number of transistors on a chip will double roughly every two years. Intel uses 'Moore's law' to inform its development strategies. This case study focuses on Intel's integrated mix of research and development (R&D) and manufacturing. This enables Intel to implement the 'tick-tock' strategy designed to put it ahead of its competitors and maintain that competitive advantage.

A business can develop its products either through product-orientated development or market-orientated development. Product-orientated development focuses on developing the production process and the product by new use of technology or innovation. A market-orientated approach identifies and analyses customer needs. It then develops products which meet them. Both approaches are important. Right from its early days, Intel realized the importance of combining product innovation with a market focused approach. Intel responds to both customer demand and product innovation. Its products are therefore 'user centric', that is, the product development meets the needs of the customer. Intel has anthropologists who study how people use technology in their lives. This information helps Intel's product design teams to understand what customer requirements are. Intel also has a development programme to increase the capacity of a microprocessor. This fits with the two-year cycle in which the microprocessor is adapted or a new product is launched.

Research and development can help to create new and better products, improve the methods for making the products and develop new market opportunities to sustain or accelerate growth. Research involves designing new ideas to solve a problem or to create an opportunity. An example is the development of a new microprocessor for a mobile phone to give it access to the Internet. Intel conducts research in two key areas: " Research into manufacturing capabilities and material". This type of research led to the introduction of the 45nm high-k metal gate silicon manufacturing technology. More broad research focused on what technology can offer. This can cover how to integrate multiple different types of wireless technology into a single device or how to use silicon technologies to act as sensors. The research reaches into areas such as robotics. Intel invests large sums in its research laboratories all over the world. Intel's leadership in silicon technology, combined with the R&D capability to develop new products and new ways of making products, makes it one of the leaders in its field. The result of this research is the creation of products customers want, which can be manufactured easily in large volumes. Examples include notebook computers containing Intel Centrino Processor Technology. Research generates many ideas but only the best will be chosen for development. Development involves converting good ideas into a commercial product, for example, by improving a microprocessor to run multiple computer programs at the same time. The development of the selected products must meet specific timetables for launch worldwide. The end products resulting from an intensive R&D program benefit the customer. These might include a smaller and faster computer or mobile phones at lower prices.

Technological advances can also mean less energy consumption, reducing the carbon footprint of consumers and businesses. Before manufacturing, Intel produces a 'blueprint' or design of what a particular microchip will be needed for. This outlines all the functions it will need to support, such as wireless capability or image software. The design has to answer key questions:

- What type of chip is needed and why?
- How many transistors can be built on the chip?
- What is the best chip size?
- What technology will be available to create the chip?
- When does the chip need to be ready? Where will it be manufactured and tested?

To answer these questions, Intel works with customers, software companies and Intel's marketing, manufacturing and testing staff. Intel takes all the responses to define a chip's features and design. The designs are put together in the form of a computer-simulated chip that can be tested using Computer Aided Design (CAD). The CAD system tests, for example, how the transistors turn on and off. It also tests how the chip performs an action such as launching a computer operating system.

Intel has been described as a 'manufacturing monster'. It can develop and bring a product to market faster than anyone else. Intel's production process is automated using sophisticated robotic equipment to ensure accuracy. This is a good example of production in the secondary sector of industry. Intel has plants around the world manufacturing different processors for different markets. It chooses locations where there is enough land to build such large plants. These need to be close to skilled labour, its markets and to customers. For example, Intel fabricates 45nm chips in New Mexico, Oregon and Arizona in the USA, as well as in Israel. Each new factory costs up to $3 billion (around £1.5 billion) to construct. The refitting costs for older plants can be over $1 billion (around £0.5 billion). Intel uses a methodology called 'copy exactly'. This ensures factories are built in exactly the same way, no matter where they are, and gives a consistent approach. This is critical when manufacturing such sensitive and highly complex devices. The manufacturing process requires the highest standards of 'clean environments'. This is thousands of times cleaner than in an operating theatre. Intel's employees wear special suits to ensure no dust or hair falls onto the wafers. The air is so clean that one cubic meter of air contains less than one particle of dust. The production process is a highly complex one. It takes an average of 200 people working full time for two years to design, test and have a new chip ready for manufacture.

Intel provides computer chips for many different market segments. A market segment is usually defined, for example, by age, gender or geographical position. Intel identifies its market segments by product use, e.g., notebooks, desktops, servers. Some products are for the business market, for example, desktop computers and laptops for companies. Other products are for personal use, for example, notebook computers for students. Intel is continually developing new approaches to keep it ahead of the competition. Vertical integration gives it a strong advantage. This means Intel does not outsource any of its work for research, development or manufacturing. For example, many companies do research and some development but give the product design to another company to produce. Intel does all three processes itself. Its manufacturing process is capital-intensive because of the specialist equipment. For example, Intel spent more than $7 billion (£3.5 billion) on manufacturing plants using the latest 45 nm process technology. Intel believes this investment is worthwhile, as this highly competitive approach gives it a competitive edge by ensuring quality, protecting its ideas, meeting its timescales.

Competitive advantage means a company has or does something better than its rivals. The 'tick-tock' strategy was announced in September 2006 by Intel's CEO, Paul Otellini. It is a blueprint for Intel to maintain its technology leadership and competitive advantage. It plans to take advantage of Intel's product research, development and manufacturing capacity to deliver improved products every year. This regular improvement will ensure continued market leadership. In 'tick' years Intel will introduce a new manufacturing process (of which the 45nm process is the latest). 'Tock' years will see the introduction of new designs (architectures) of CPUs (central processing units). Intel is competitive because it has a regular cadence (or rhythm) to the development of new products or improvements to existing ones. It integrates teams from R&D and all areas of manufacturing, all working to the same schedules. Intel is the only company that can combine and optimize manufacturing process technology, product design, leading-edge capacity, design tools, masks and packaging in-house. It sets the highest standards in high-quality clean production. The company invests vast sums in R&D and manufacturing. This makes it is difficult for rival companies to match Intel. Intel continually develops new technologies that combine product-led, user-led, and market-led features. It is also able to leverage its manufacturing capability. This means it can increase production to bring product to market in large volumes. Increasing volume and getting the product onto the market as quickly as possible are important elements in creating and maintaining a competitive advantage.

In order to protect its advantage it is essential that Intel registers intellectual property and patents in new product development. This registration is vital for Intel. This gives legal protection against copying by its competitors. The protected time allows it to sell its products without direct competition. These help to recover the investment costs of designing, researching and developing the new products. Since 1968 Intel has contributed to improving people's lives, work and leisure. The company's work is at the heart of the Internet, personal computing, mobile phones, games consoles and home entertainment systems. Intel products drive the technology we use in homes, hospitals, schools, offices, factories and airports. Intel's commitment to continual innovation and investment in research and development in product and manufacturing technology ensures competitiveness and growth. It also provides customers around the world with the latest developments.

QUESTIONS

1. Identify three key steps (innovations) in the development of microchip technology. In each case explain how the innovation has transformed people's work, life and/or leisure.
2. What is meant by (a) market-led and (b) product-led new product development? Give two examples to show how Intel has combined market-led and product-led approaches.
3. Show how research and development has enabled Intel to develop a new product that is aimed at a specific group of users.
4. Why is it so important for businesses like Intel to invest in R&D? Explain with examples how R&D has enabled Intel to gain competitive advantage

19 Kellogg's: Extending the Product Life Cycle

Businesses need to set themselves clear aims and objectives if they are going to succeed. The Kellogg Company is the world's leading producer of breakfast cereals and convenience foods, such as cereal bars, and aims to maintain that position. In 2006, Kellogg had total worldwide sales of almost $11 billion (£5.5 billion). In 2007, it was Britain's biggest selling grocery brand, with sales of more than £550 million. Product lines include ready-to-eat cereals (i.e., not hot cereals like porridge) and nutritious snacks, such as cereal bars. Kellogg's brands are household names around the world and include Rice Krispies, Special K and Nutri-Grain, whilst some of its brand characters, like Snap, Crackle and Pop, are amongst the most well known in the world. Kellogg has achieved this position, not only through great brands and great brand value, but through a strong commitment to corporate social responsibility. This means that all of Kellogg's business aims are set within a particular context or set of ideals. Central to this is Kellogg's passion for the business, the brands and the food, demonstrated through the promotion of healthy living. The company divides its market into six key segments. Kellogg's Corn Flakes has been on breakfast tables for over 100 years and represents the 'Tasty Start' cereals that people eat to start their day. Other segments include 'Simply Wholesome' products that are good for you, such as Kashi Muesli, 'Shape Management' products, such as Special K and 'Inner Health' lines, such as All-Bran. Children will be most familiar with the 'Kid Preferred' brands, such as Frosties, whilst 'Mum Approved' brands like Raisin Wheat are recognized by parents as being good for their children. Each brand has to hold its own in a competitive market. Brand managers monitor the success of brands in terms of market share, growth and performance against the competition. Key decisions have to be made about the future of any brand that is not succeeding. This case study is about Nutri-Grain. It shows how Kellogg recognized there was a problem with the brand and used business tools to reach a solution. The overall aim was to re-launch the brand and return it to growth in its market.

Each product has its own life cycle. It will be 'born', it will 'develop', it will 'grow old' and, eventually, it will 'die'. Some products, like Kellogg's Corn Flakes, have retained their market position for a long time. Others may have their success undermined by falling market share or by competitors. The product life cycle shows how sales of a product change over time. There are five typical stages of the life cycle. However, perhaps the most important stage of a product life cycle happens before product is born, namely the Research and Development (R&D) stage. Here the company designs a product to meet a need in the market. The costs of market research — to identify a gap in the market and of product development to ensure that the product meets the needs of that gap — are called 'sunk' or start-up costs. Nutri-Grain was originally designed to meet the needs of busy people who had missed breakfast. It aimed to provide a healthy cereal breakfast in a portable and convenient format. The different product life cycle stages of Nutri-Grain are discussed here:

- **Launch:** Many products do well when they are first brought out and Nutri-Grain was no exception. From launch (the first stage of product life cycle) in 1997 it was immediately successful, gaining almost 50% share of the growing cereal bar market in just two years.
- **Growth:** Nutri-Grain's sales steadily increased as the product was promoted and became well known. It maintained growth in sales until 2002 through expanding the original product with new developments of flavour and format. This is good for the business, as it does not have to spend money on new machines or equipment for production. The market position of Nutri-Grain also subtly changed from a 'missed breakfast' product to an 'all-day' healthy snack.
- **Maturity:** Successful products attract other competitor businesses to start selling similar products. This indicates the third stage of the life cycle — maturity. This is the time of maximum profitability, when profits can be used to continue to build the brand. However, competitor brands from both Kellogg itself (e.g., All Bran bars) and other manufacturers (e.g. Alpen bars) offered the same benefits and this slowed down sales and chipped away at Nutri-Grain's market position. Kellogg continued to support the development of the brand but some products (such as Minis and Twists), struggled in a crowded market. Although Elevenses continued to succeed, this was not enough to offset the overall sales decline. Not all products follow these stages precisely and time periods for each stage will vary widely. Growth, for example, may take place over a few months or, as in the case of Nutri-Grain, over several years.
- **Saturation:** This is the fourth stage of the life cycle and the point when the market is 'full'. Most people have the product and there are other, better or cheaper competitor products. This is called market saturation and this is the time when sales start to fall. By mid-2004 Nutri-Grain found its sales declining whilst the market continued to grow at a rate of 15%.
- **Decline:** Clearly, at this point, Kellogg had to make a key business decision. Sales were falling; the product was in decline and losing its position. Should Kellogg let the product 'die', i.e., withdraw it from the market, or should it try to extend its life?

When a company recognizes that a product has gone into decline or is not performing as well as it should, it has to decide what to do. The decision needs to be made within the context of the overall aims of the business. Kellogg's aims included the development of great brands, great brand value and the promotion of healthy living. Strategically, Kellogg had a strong position in the market for both healthy foods and convenience foods. Nutri-

Grain fitted well with its main aims and objectives and therefore was a product and a brand worth rescuing. Extending the Nutri-Grain cycle – identifying the problem Kellogg had to decide whether the problem with Nutri-Grain was the market, the product or both. The market had grown by over 15% and competitors' market share had increased whilst Nutri-Grain sales in 2003 had declined. The market in terms of customer tastes had also changed – more people missed breakfast and therefore there was an increased need for such a snack product. The choice of extension strategy indicated by the matrix was either product development or diversification. Diversification carries much higher costs and risks. Kellogg decided that it needed to focus on changing the product to meet the changing market needs. Research showed that there were several issues to address:

- The brand message was not strong enough in the face of competition. Consumers were not impressed enough by the product to choose it over competitors.
- Some of the other Kellogg products (e.g., Minis) had taken the focus away from the core business.
- The core products of Nutri-Grain Soft Bake and Elevenses between them represented over 80% of sales but received a small proportion of advertising and promotion budgets.
- Those sales that were taking place were being driven by promotional pricing (i.e discounted pricing) rather than the underlying strength of the brand.

Having recognized the problems, Kellogg then developed solutions to re-brand and re-launch the product in 2005. Fundamental to the re-launch was the renewal of the brand image. Kellogg looked at the core features that made the brand different and modelled the new brand image on these. Nutri-Grain is unique as it is the only product of this kind that is baked. This provided two benefits, the healthy grains were soft rather than gritty and the eating experience is closer to the more indulgent foods that people could be eating (cakes and biscuits, for example). The unique selling point, hence the focus of the brand, needed to be the 'soft bake'. Researchers also found that a key part of the market was a group termed 'realistic snackers'. These are people who want to snack on healthy foods, but still crave a great tasting snack. The re-launched Nutri-Grain product needed to help this key group fulfil both of these desires.. Kellogg decided to re-focus investment on the core products of Soft Bake Bars and Elevenses as these had maintained their growth (accounting for 61% of Soft Bake Bar sales). Three existing Soft Bake Bar products were improved, three new ranges introduced and poorly performing ranges (such as Minis) were withdrawn. New packaging was introduced to unify the brand image. An improved pricing structure for stores and supermarkets was developed. Using this information, the re-launch focused on the four parts of the marketing mix:

- **Product:** Improvements to the recipe and a wider range of flavours, repositioning the brand as 'healthy and tasty', not a substitute for a missed breakfast .
- **Promotion:** A new and clearer brand image to cover all the products in the range along with advertising and point-of-sale materials.
- **Place:** Better offers and materials to stores that sold the product.
- **Price:** New price levels were agreed that did not rely on promotional pricing.

This improved revenue for both Kellogg and the stores. As a result Soft Bake Bar year-on-year sales went from a decline to substantial growth, with Elevenses sales increasing by almost 50%. The Nutri-Grain brand achieved a retail sales growth rate of almost three times that of the market and most importantly, growth was maintained after the initial re-launch.

Successful businesses use all the tools at their disposal to stay at the top of their chosen market. Kellogg was able to use a number of business tools in order to successfully re-launch the Nutri-Grain brand. These tools included the product life cycle, Ansoff's matrix and the marketing mix. Such tools are useful when used properly. Kellogg was able to see that although Nutri-Grain fitted its strategic profile – a healthy, convenient cereal product – it was underperforming in the market. This information was used, along with the aims and objectives of the business, to develop a strategy for continuing success. Finally, when Kellogg checked the growth of the re-launched product against its own objectives, it had met all its aims to:

- re-position the brand through the use of the marketing mix
- return the brand to growth
- improve the frequency of purchase
- introduce new customers to the brand. Nutri-Grain remains a growing brand and product within the Kellogg product family.

QUESTIONS

1. Using current products familiar to you, draw and label a product life cycle diagram, showing which stage each product is at.
2. Suggest appropriate aims and objectives for a small, medium and large business.
3. Explain the difference between market orientated routes and product orientated routes in Ansoff's matrix.
4. Consider the decision taken by Kellogg to opt for product development. Suggest a way in which it could have diversified instead. Justify your answer.

20 Mott MacDonald: Creating Strategic Direction

In order to grow, a business needs to develop competitive advantage. This means that it is different or does things better than its rivals. This is known as differentiation. Differentiation helps an organisation to develop a unique business strategy. Managers need to make strategic decisions that create the right direction for their businesses. Decisions by senior managers at the top of a business influence decisions by other managers and employees. Mott MacDonald is a large global management, engineering and development consultancy. A consultancy contains experts who provide advisory services in a variety of fields. The Mott MacDonald Group was formed in 1989 when two consultancy businesses merged. Since then, the business has grown both organically by recruiting more staff in different fields and also by acquisition, that is taking over existing businesses in markets important to Mott MacDonald's development strategy. For example, in 2007 Mott MacDonald bought an educational consultancy in Romania, an environmental firm in the Netherlands and a power engineering company in the USA to help strengthen its core market sectors in these countries. Today Mott MacDonald's business spans 120 countries and employs more than 13,000 staff. Its experts work on thousands of projects across the world in many areas. These include transport, energy, buildings, water, the environment, health, education and communications.

Every project requires a different set of skills from Mott MacDonald's experts. Its projects address the challenges of environmental issues, such as flood protection or management of waste. It plans, manages and delivers projects to help its customers find more sustainable solutions. Mott MacDonald's customers are in both the public sector and the private sector. In the public sector, it works with organisations to provide services for central and local government. In the private sector, Mott MacDonald provides consultancy for private businesses. For example, in China the company is project managing the building of what will be the world's largest observation wheel – much bigger than the London Eye. Mott MacDonald has also been involved in over half the new wind farms in the UK, developed by privately-owned energy companies. These include one of the world's largest offshore wind farms off the coast of south-east England. At any one time Mott MacDonald works on thousands of projects around the world. These range from transport systems in Taiwan, healthcare initiatives in Africa or education planning in the USA. Mott MacDonald consultants advise on many aspects. For example, planning and design, quantity surveying, procurement advice and project management. This case study focuses on how Mott MacDonald stands out in its competitive environment by using the skills and knowledge of its people to achieve its business purpose.

All organisations need to have a purpose for the business. This is called the mission. A mission is a broad statement that identifies the long-term direction of a business. The mission helps to emphasize how different the business is from its competitors.The mission informs a company's business objectives. It becomes a focus for the whole organisation and helps to ensure long-term profitability. Mott MacDonald's mission is:"Providing customer satisfaction through professional excellence, giving commercial success and employee fulfillment". This mission shows that Mott MacDonald's employees directly support business growth. To achieve customer satisfaction Mott MacDonald employs the best experts across the market sectors it works in around the globe. These highly skilled consultants work in engineering, environmental science, economics, project management, health and safety, risk management, IT and education. Mott MacDonald values the contribution its employees make in satisfying customers and achieving its business objectives. To help its staff achieve professional excellence, Mott MacDonald promotes learning and development. It encourages its experts to help other staff develop their skills. It recognizes employee achievements, for example, through the Chairman's Award which acknowledges outstanding achievement in building customer relationships, and the Milne Award, which recognizes innovation. Mott MacDonald is an employee-owned company. This means employees can have a say in how the business is run and what its future plans are. They feel they can make a difference. This gives employees a clear link between meeting the customer needs and personal job satisfaction. In addition, they take part in a "Performance Pay Scheme (PPS)" based on the company's performance. Therefore the more employees contribute to the firm's success the more they benefit. These commitments helped Mott MacDonald to be recognized as the top consultant company of its kind in "The Sunday Times List" of the UK's "Top 20 Best Big Companies to work for" in both 2007 and 2008.

Employees need to know whether the business is achieving its mission. Therefore, Mott MacDonald measures its progress towards meeting its customer satisfaction target through customer satisfaction surveys. Customers recently rated the company at or above 8 out of 10 for every aspect of the service. These include how well Mott MacDonald responds to the customer's needs and the overall quality of service. The feedback helps Mott MacDonald to improve by focusing on customer satisfaction. This benefited the business, as shown by the 20% increase in revenue in both 2006 and 2007.

A mission sets out the purpose of the organisation where as a vision describes what the business wants to become in future and seeks to inspire its staff. Mott MacDonald's vision is "To be the consultant of choice in our global marketplace". For Mott MacDonald to become the consultant of choice, it has to set high standards that are achievable. In setting high standards, Mott MacDonald aims to be better than its competitors. Mott MacDonald's vision has two key elements – consultant of choice and operating globally.

- **Consultant of choice**: Mott MacDonald has four key stakeholder groups – existing customers, future customers, existing employees and future employees. Mott MacDonald wants to be 'consultant of choice' for both customers and employees. For customers, it needs to offer a unique mix of skill, expertise and customer focus. This helps to attract new customers and retain existing ones. Mott MacDonald operates in many market sectors and offers expertise in two that set it apart from many of its competitors - health and education. For employees, Mott MacDonald needs 20% more technical staff every year. It must compete to recruit the most able people. It seeks to achieve this by showing existing and potential employees that it offers a more attractive career path than other consultancies.
- **Global marketplace:** Mott MacDonald has its headquarters in the UK but operates across the world. For example, local managers run the businesses in India and North America. This means that local experts can meet local needs, and are also able to call on global skills and experiences. A project may need the experience of different consultants from around the world. For example, UK based consultants set up the first phase of the metro system in New Delhi. They supported and transferred knowledge to local managers. The local managers then ran the second phase of the project. To achieve its vision Mott MacDonald constantly develops its people to create the business capability its customers need.

An organization's values are the guiding principles that influence its activities. Values show how the organisation expects everyone within the business to behave. Mott MacDonald's values follow the acronym PRIDE: Progress, Respect, Integrity, Drive and Excellence.

- **Progress:** Mott MacDonald's activities create progress as its projects seek to improve the living standards of local communities and the well-being of the planet. It aims to promote sustainable development in its projects and to lead the development of the various professions in which it works. For example, Mott MacDonald's energy team helped a chemical factory in China drastically reduce its carbon footprint by treating its HFC-23 emissions to cut the equivalent of a colossal 4 million tonnes of CO_2 every year.
- **Respect:** Mott MacDonald recruits staff from markets around the world. It respects the local customs and cultures of the countries it works in and encourages all staff to respect each other regardless of background or origin. It encourages diversity in its workforce, benefiting from its employees' range of skills. For example, the specialist expertise of pharmaceuticals staff in India and Ireland is used to help on similar projects in the Middle East – this is a vital part of the company's global strategy.
- **Integrity:** Mott MacDonald promotes ethical behaviour. This means it only promises its customers what it knows it can deliver. Consequently, its customers are satisfied and not disappointed. It seeks to ensure that its communications are accurate and takes full responsibility for all aspects of its work, including promoting health and safety and sustainability.
- **Drive:** 'Drive' involves exceeding expectations. Mott MacDonald aims for continuous improvement. It benchmarks its performance against competitors. This helps it to exceed the targets it has set for customer satisfaction. For example, in

2006 it achieved a rating of 8.2 out of 10 for "Responding to Customer Needs", compared to 8.1 in 2005 and 7.8 in 2004.

- **Excellence**: Mott MacDonald wants its activities to be associated with excellence and innovation. In 2007 Mott MacDonald won over 50 awards for its roles on projects demonstrating innovation or excellence. One of its projects, "The Manchester Civil Justice Centre", has won 10 awards for its contribution towards sustainable building design including the Major Project of the Year at the inaugural Green Construction Awards.

PRIDE demonstrates the culture of the business. Mott MacDonald relies on its employees to fulfill its business objectives. Its culture helps employees to be responsible for their own development. This leads to growth of the people and the organisation. As part of its culture, Mott MacDonald also seeks to be a corporately responsible company. Part of this includes supporting sustainable business practice, such as reducing its carbon footprint. Employees of Mott MacDonald take the lead on many sustainability issues in projects they work on and as a company. It recently published its first "Corporate Responsibility Review (CSR)" which highlights initiatives to be worked on in the future and how the group seeks to achieve its corporate aims in a responsible way which includes:

- Setting targets to use less energy and paper in all of its offices.
- Reducing business travel by using video and telephone conferencing.
- Reviewing its energy supply contracts to find suppliers who support good environmental practice.

Mott MacDonald operates a rolling strategic plan that looks ahead over a five-year period and is updated every year. The five-year plan is an example of 'top down' planning - it sets targets and the direction for the company's business units. At the same time, the business units contribute to the planning process from the bottom-up through their annual business plans. As Mott MacDonald is an employee owned company, employees help to decide what areas they would like the business to focus on. This might mean the business takes on projects that do not provide a return on investment in the short term, but which help to position the business in the market in the longer term. For example, projects in China are likely to show bigger rewards as its economy grows.

The five-year plan covers all areas of importance to the business. These include financial growth, markets, services, customers, partners, sustainability and staff development. For each of these areas, Mott MacDonald has specific business objectives. By taking into account the mission, vision and values, business managers set SMART objectives. These help ensure that the business can measure its performance accurately. SMART objectives apply to projects too. For example, Mott MacDonald's engineering consultants supported a project in Malaysia where floods and traffic congestion have caused problems in the central business district of Kuala Lumpur, the capital. The solution is the Storm Water Management and Road Tunnel — by coincidence, also called SMART. This project is a world-first. The tunnel is 9.7 kilometers long and diverts the floodwaters away from the city centre. The 3 kilometer middle section of the tunnel also acts as a two-deck motorway to help relieve traffic congestion. When the tunnel is full with water, the road section closes. Mott MacDonald designed the dual-purpose section of the tunnel and helped solve the technical solutions to challenges linked with excavating out the entire tunnel. By providing expertise from across the Mott MacDonald Group, the consultants worked with the local teams to share knowledge and solve a local problem with a sustainable and innovative solution.

In considering the project, Mott MacDonald's experts needed to ask themselves key questions to ensure their objectives were SMART. The results of the project showed whether they had achieved them:

- S – What do we want to achieve? Kuala Lumpur needed continuous access to its business district.
- M – How will we know if it has achieved the right result? The traffic congestion and flooding will not happen again.
- A – Do we have the right resources to carry this out? Mott MacDonald helped to procure the specialized equipment for the excavation.
- R – Does it address the problem? The proposed solution solved both the flooding and congestion problems.
- T – What is the deadline? The first phase was to be completed in 2005 and the second in 2007. Stopping the flooding problems will massively reduce financial losses for the city.

Using SMART objectives to create the SMART solution helped to ensure that the project was completed on time and within budget when it was finished in 2007. Mott MacDonald's mission, vision, values and business objectives influence how it carries out projects. Mott MacDonald has positioned itself as consultant of choice for both customers and employees. It promotes investment in and development of its people to achieve its business objectives. Because it is an employee-owned business, everybody within the company is free to contribute his views upon its future. This has helped the business to become distinctive and achieve competitive advantage over its rivals.

QUESTIONS

1. Explain the difference between organic growth and acquisition.
2. What is meant by a performance pay scheme?
3. Analyze how Mott MacDonald's values influence its business activities.
4. Evaluate how a rolling five-year plan helps Mott MacDonald to identify which projects it will take on.

21 Parcel Force Worldwide: Customer Service as a Strategy

Parcel Force Worldwide is part of the Royal Mail Group Ltd. Royal Mail Group has three main operating brands:

- The Post Office Ltd provides counter services to the high street customer.
- Royal Mail manages the delivery of letters and packets.
- Parcel Force Worldwide provides express parcel delivery services for businesses and consumers.

Parcel Force Worldwide has over 30,000 business customers in the UK. It handles 200,000 parcels a day. It has a turnover of £382 million. In 2006-07, revenues grew by 7.3% over the previous year. With its 23 partners across 30 European countries and access to Postal Administrations through the Universal Postal Union. It operates in Business to Business (B2B) services, delivering parcels and supplies from companies to other companies, Business to Consumer (B2C) services, delivering parcels to individuals in their homes around the UK. Parcel Force Worldwide competes in a free or unregulated market. A free market is open to all. Any company can choose to operate in the market and customers can choose any supplier they wish. Suppliers therefore need to provide good value for money to keep customers and win new business.

In 2002, Parcel Force Worldwide was making a loss. In response, those managing the business decided to change the type of service it offered. Instead of unguaranteed parcel deliveries typically taking between two and four days, Parcel Force Worldwide decided to focus on time and day guaranteed, express delivery. This resulted in a reduction of the number of parcels handled (volume) but increased the value of each delivery to Parcel Force Worldwide. As a result of these changes, Parcel Force Worldwide also increased operational efficiency. The business, reduced the number of staff it employed, it closed some of its depots and opened a new technologically advanced sorting centre in Coventry. These changes enabled Parcel Force Worldwide to achieve its financial targets. It turned a loss-making business into a profitable one. However, it recognized that more could be done to improve efficiency. The business sought to improve staff attendance rates. It wanted to cut absenteeism – staff taking unauthorized or sick leave – and reduce the time lost as a result of accidents at work. To do this, Parcel Force Worldwide introduced a more decentralized approach to management. This gives depot managers greater decision-making accountability to improve the effectiveness of the operation in their local area. Most companies operating in the express parcel delivery market offer similar services. Parcel Force Worldwide remains competitive by differentiating itself in other ways. The business has developed a unique selling proposition (USP) based on high-quality customer service. This customer-orientated approach is designed to attract and retain key customers. Parcel Force Worldwide works in partnership with customers, such as the UK's examination boards, to develop and deliver services to meet specific needs. During exam season, Parcel Force Worldwide delivers millions of exam papers, scripts and coursework. This case study examines how a strategy focused on customer service can contribute to long-term business development.

Businesses have aims and objectives. Aims are the long-term targets of the business. Objectives are the steps that help to achieve these aims. Objectives should always be SMART - that is, they should be specific, measurable, achievable, relevant and set within a timeframe. This enables a business to assess what the objectives contribute to its overall aims and when they will be achieved. Businesses may set objectives to:

- Make the most of something - for instance, a business may want to increase growth, sales, profit and customer satisfaction.
- Reduce something adverse or unwelcome, for example, limit risk or reduce staff absence.
- Change the image or culture of the business, for example, changing the focus on internal operational issues from speed of service to a focus on customers' needs.

These objectives help to inform business strategies. By carrying out a SWOT analysis, a business can identify the best strategies to pursue. These strategies focus on different aspects of the business. For example, Parcel Force Worldwide has:

- Operational strategies to improve its efficiency and meet customer needs better promotional strategies to strengthen its brand presence in key markets.
- Growth strategies to expand its business outside its core national markets.

Parcel Force Worldwide's strategies have to take account of any changes in the external environment. For example, the parcel delivery industry has consolidated across the world. This means that there are now fewer global players, but each has a relatively larger market share. Parcel Force Worldwide needs to compete with these global rivals. To increase its market share, it needs either to grow its existing business or merge with other parcel delivery businesses. Customer service as strategy Parcel Force Worldwide operates within the tertiary or service sector. Customer service is important in this sector. This is because many tertiary sector industries provide similar products and services at similar prices. This makes it difficult to compete using a product orientated approach. In these types of markets, it is not easy to adjust the four elements of the marketing mix - product, price, promotion and place — to make a business stand out from its rivals. However, one way to gain an advantage is to offer high quality customer service. Customer service means talking and listening to customers. This helps a business anticipate its requirements and respond promptly to any problems. Parcel Force Worldwide does this because it wants to meet or exceed its customer expectations. It aims to be the UK's most reliable high value express carrier. This customer service focus provides Parcel Force Worldwide with a strong differentiator in the market. This helps it to keep its existing customers and attract new business. The key parts of this customer service are:

- Time – making sure that deliveries are on time
- Visibility – letting the customer follow a parcel through online tracking
- After-sales service – ensuring that any problems are dealt with courteously and promptly.

Parcel Force Worldwide has identified that its organisational structure is a key strength. Its people are essential to supporting quality customer service. For instance, drivers need to work with depot staff so that parcels are loaded in the right order for delivery. Staff needs to ensure that services are accessible by all customers. Society is now more diverse, with a larger proportion of the population aged over 60 and with more people from different ethnic backgrounds. Parcel Force Worldwide makes sure that:

- Drivers write delivery cards that can be easily read by people with sight problems or by those who do not speak English as a first language.
- Employees learn the best way of communicating with customers with disabilities, for example, by reading out information or writing it down.
- The company also needs to find out what its customers want so that it can provide additional services.
- It must talk to customers, both businesses and consumers.
- Pilot new products such as online or telephone services.
- Find out what its customers want who access services through the Post Office network.

For example, in this way, Parcel Force Worldwide discovered that some customers were concerned about the effects of carbon emissions on the environment. It therefore offers a 'carbon neutral parcel' option. The customer pays a few pence more to offset the carbon impact of delivering the parcel. Parcel Force Worldwide takes its corporate social responsibility (CSR) seriously. This means providing benefits for employees, customers and the communities in which it operates. Its CSR program focuses on health and safety, the environment, supporting local communities and diversity. For example it is reducing the carbon footprint of the business, supporting local communities through involvement in education and removing barriers to its services for all customers.

The implementation of customer service to improve its customer service, Parcel Force Worldwide has undertaken a 'gap analysis'. This is a detailed exercise that assesses "where the business is now ? where it wants to be ? what it needs to do to achieve that and how?" Parcel Force Worldwide is using this analysis to identify the key service touch points for customers. Customer service has an impact in six main areas of the business:

- **Deliveries to the customer** – providing timely delivery, prompt response to queries, clear documentation.
- **Re-deliveries** – ensuring clear procedures are in place.
- **Collections from customers** – providing a timely service with documentation.

- **End-to-end parcel location (tracking)** – an online service with easy-to-use screens means customers can find out when a parcel has been delivered.
- **Customer contact** – improving customer communications and providing help by web or by telephone.
- **Making claims** – making it easy for people to claim if things go wrong.

In each of these areas, Parcel Force Worldwide has identified best practice in the industry. It compares its performance by benchmarking itself against competitors. It then assesses how to improve its processes to achieve best practice. Parcel Force Worldwide aims to get each of these processes right in order to achieve customer service excellence. Evaluating the impacts, costs and benefits of customer service Research shows that it costs about five times more to gain a new customer as it does to keep an existing one. Parcel Force Worldwide therefore places an emphasis on retaining its existing customers. Its key objective is to have satisfied customers, who will use the service again in the future. Parcel Force Worldwide recognizes that its people are a key element in delivering customer satisfaction. All staff must be committed to a customer-orientated culture. This means that employees need appropriate training to ensure they have the skills to meet customer needs. This training also helps to develop a culture of improvement. A training programme costs money. However, the costs of not training staff can be even greater. This can result in loss of business, loss of revenue and, worse, loss of reputation. Parcel Force Worldwide measures customer service by using key performance indicators (KPIs). These set targets for factors such as response times, numbers of staff trained and levels of after-sales service.

Parcel Force Worldwide uses a balanced business scorecard to record progress against these targets. This measures where the business wants to be against actual performance in four key areas:

- **Financial** – includes operating margin, average unit cost.
- **Process** – includes on-time deliveries and collections, attempted deliveries.
- **Customer focus** – includes customer satisfaction scores, complaints.
- **Employee/teams** – measured by opinion surveys.

By tracking performance on a regular basis, Parcel Force Worldwide can identify areas that are performing well, as well as those that need to be improved. Parcel Force Worldwide aims not just to retain customers. It wants a bigger share of each customer's 'wallet' – the amount of money the customer has to spend on delivery services. Corporate customers may use several suppliers to give them choice and the option of a backup service if one cannot provide the right service. Parcel Force Worldwide aims to be the business that customers choose first – the 'business of choice'.

Parcel Force Worldwide is a major player in the parcel delivery market in the UK. It also provides international services by partnering with other providers around the globe. The parcel delivery market is highly competitive. Parcel Force Worldwide needs to differentiate itself from the competition. It has adopted a strategy based on quality customer service. This distinguishes its business from its competitors. It has improved efficiency and changed its focus from volume (the number of parcels carried) to value (what the customer wants - getting parcels there on time). Parcel Force Worldwide regards its people as its most important asset. It is developing the skills of its people to deliver high levels of customer service. By putting customers at the heart of its strategy, Parcel Force Worldwide aims to achieve competitive advantage.

QUESTIONS

1. Describe what is meant by a customer-orientated approach.
2. Explain how a SWOT analysis can help a business to improve.
3. Analyze the difference between B2B and B2C businesses.
4. Evaluate why it is important for a business to have a strong differentiator in an open market?

22 Skoda: SWOT Analysis in Action

In 1895 in Czechoslovakia, two keen cyclists, Vaclav Laurin and Vaclav Klement, designed and produced their own bicycle. Their business was named Skoda in 1925. Skoda went on to manufacture cycles, cars, farm ploughs and airplanes in Eastern Europe. Skoda overcame hard times over the next 65 years. These included war, economic depression and political change. By 1990 the Czech management of Skoda was looking for a strong foreign partner. Volkswagen AG (VAG) was chosen because of its reputation for strength, quality and reliability. It is the largest car manufacturer in Europe providing an average of more than 5 million cars a year – giving it a 12% share of the world car market. Volkswagen AG comprises the Volkswagen, Audi, Skoda, SEAT, Volkswagen Commercial Vehicles, Lamborghini, Bentley and Bugatti brands. Each brand has its own specific character and is independent in the market.

Skoda UK sells Skoda cars through its network of independent franchised dealers. To improve its performance in the competitive car market, Skoda UK's management needed to assess its brand positioning. Brand positioning means establishing a distinctive image for the brand compared to competing brands. Only then could it grow from being a small player. To aid its decision-making, Skoda UK obtained market research data from internal and external strategic audits. This enabled it to take advantage of new opportunities and respond to threats. The audit provided a summary of the business's overall strategic position by using a SWOT analysis. SWOT is an acronym which stands for:

- **Strengths** – the internal elements of the business that contribute to improvement and growth
- **Weaknesses** – the attributes that will hinder a business or make it vulnerable to failure.
- **Opportunities** – the external conditions that could enable future growth.
- **Threats** – the external factors which could negatively affect the business.

This case study focuses on how Skoda UK's management built on all the areas of the strategic audit. The outcome of the SWOT analysis was a strategy for effective competition in the car industry.

Strengths: To identify its strengths, Skoda UK carried out research. It asked customers directly for their opinions about its cars. It also used reliable independent surveys that tested customers' feelings. For example, the annual JD Power customer satisfaction survey asks owners what they feel about cars they have owned for at least six months. JD Power surveys almost 20,000 car owners using detailed questionnaires. Skoda has been in the top five manufacturers in this survey for the past 13 years. In Top Gear's 2007 customer satisfaction survey, 56,000 viewers gave their opinions on 152 models and voted Skoda the 'number 1 car maker'. Skoda's Octavia model has also won the 2008 Auto Express Driver Power 'Best Car'.

Skoda attributes these results to the business concentrating on owner experience rather than on sales. It has considered 'the human touch' from design through to sale. Skoda knows that 98% of its drivers would recommend Skoda to a friend. This is a clearly identifiable and quantifiable strength. Skoda uses this to guide its future strategic development and marketing of its brand image. Strategic management guides a business so that it can compete and grow in its market. Skoda adopted a strategy focused on building cars that their owners would enjoy. This is different from simply maximizing sales of a product. As a result, Skoda's biggest strength was the satisfaction of its customers. This means the brand is associated with a quality product and happy customers.

Weaknesses: A SWOT analysis identifies areas of weakness inside the business. Skoda UK's analysis showed that in order to grow it needed to address key questions about the brand position. Skoda has only 1.7% market share. This made it a very small player in the market for cars. The main issue it needed to address was: how did Skoda fit into this highly competitive, fragmented market? This weakness was partly due to out-dated perceptions of the brand. These related to Skoda's eastern European origins. In the past the cars had an image of poor vehicle quality, design, assembly, and materials. Crucially, this poor perception also affected Skoda owners. For many people, car ownership is all about image. If you are a Skoda driver, what do other people think? From 1999 onwards, under Volkswagen AG ownership, Skoda changed this negative image. Skoda cars were no longer seen as low-budget or low quality. However, a brand 'health check' in 2006 showed that Skoda still had a weak and neutral image in the mid-market range it occupies, compared to other players in this area, for example, Ford, Peugeot and Renault. This meant that whilst the brand no longer had a poor image, it did not have a strong appeal either. This understanding showed Skoda in which direction it needed to go. It needed to stop being defensive in promotional campaigns. The company had sought to correct old perceptions and demonstrate what Skoda cars were not. It realized it was now time to say what the brand does stand for. The marketing message for the change was simple. Skoda owners were known to be happy and contented with their cars. The car-buying public and the car industry as a whole needed convincing that Skoda cars were great to own and drive.

Opportunities: Opportunities occur in the external environment of a business. These include for example, gaps in the market for new products or services. In analyzing the external market, Skoda noted that its competitors' marketing approaches focused on the product itself. Audi emphasizes the technology through its tagline, 'Vorsprung Durch Technik' ('advantage through technology'). BMW promotes 'the ultimate driving machine'. Many brands place emphasis on the machine and the driving experience.

Skoda UK discovered that its customers loved their cars more than owners of competitor brands, such as Renault or Ford. Information from the SWOT analysis helped Skoda to differentiate its product range. Having a complete understanding of the brand's weaknesses allowed it to develop a strategy to strengthen the brand and take advantage of the opportunities in the market. It focused on its existing strengths and provided cars focused on the customer experience. The focus on 'happy Skoda customers' is an opportunity. It enables Skoda to differentiate the Skoda brand to make it stand out from the competition. This is Skoda's unique selling proposition (USP) in the motor industry.

Threats: Threats come from outside of a business. These involve, for example, a competitor launching cheaper products. A careful analysis of the nature, source and likelihood of these threats is a key part of the SWOT process. The UK car market includes 50 different car makers selling 200 models. Within these there are over 2,000 model derivatives. Skoda UK needed to ensure that its messages were powerful enough for customers to hear within such a crowded and competitive environment. If not, potential buyers would overlook Skoda. This posed the threat of a further loss of market share. Skoda needed a strong product range to compete in the UK and globally. In the UK the Skoda brand is represented by seven different cars. Each one is designed to appeal to different market segments. For example: the Skoda Fabia is sold as a basic but quality 'city car' , the Skoda Superb offers a more luxurious, 'up-market' appeal , the Skoda Octavia Estate provides a family with a fun drive but also a great big boot.

Pricing reflects the competitive nature of Skoda's market. Each model range is priced to appeal to different groups within the mainstream car market. The combination of a clear range with competitive pricing has overcome the threat of the crowded market. The following example illustrates how Skoda responded to another of its threats, namely, the need to respond to EU legal and environmental regulations. Skoda responded by designing products that are environmentally friendly at every stage of their life cycle. This was done by:

- Recycling as much as possible.
- Skoda parts are marked for quick and easy identification when the car is taken apart.
- Using the latest, most environmentally-friendly manufacturing technologies and facilities available. For instance, areas painted to protect against corrosion use lead-free, water based colours.
- Designing processes to cut fuel consumption and emissions in petrol and diesel engines.
- Using lighter parts making vehicles as aerodynamic as possible to use less energy.
- Using technology to design cars with lower noise levels and improved sound quality.

Outcomes and benefits of SWOT analysis: Skoda UK's SWOT analysis answered some key questions. It discovered that Skoda car owners were happy about owning a Skoda. The brand was no longer seen as a poorer version of competitors' cars. However, the brand was still very much within a niche market A change in public perception was vital for Skoda to compete and increase its market share of the mainstream car market. The challenge was how to build on this and develop the brand so that it was viewed positively. It required a whole new marketing strategy. Skoda UK has responded with a new marketing strategy based on the confident slogan, 'the manufacturer of happy drivers.' The campaign's promotional activities support the new brand position. The key messages for the campaign focus on the 'happy' customer experience and appeal at an emotional rather than a practical level. The campaign included the 'Fabia Cake' TV advert. This showed that the car was 'full of lovely stuff' with the happy music ('Favorite things') in the background. It recreates and redesigned website which is easy and fun to use. It also appealed to a young audience. It embodies the message 'experience the happiness of Skoda online'. Customers are able to book test drives and order brochures online. The result is that potential customers will feel a Skoda is not only a reliable and sensible car to own, it is also 'lovely' to own. Analysing the external opportunities and threats allows Skoda UK to pinpoint precisely how it should target its marketing messages. No other market player has 'driver happiness' as its USP. By building on the understanding derived from the SWOT, Skoda UK has given new impetus to its campaign. At the same time, the campaign has addressed the threat of external competition by setting Skoda apart from its rivals.

Skoda is a global brand offering a range of products in a highly competitive and fragmented market. The company must respond positively to internal and external issues to avoid losing sales and market share. A SWOT analysis brings order and structure to otherwise random information. The SWOT model helps managers to look internally as well as externally. The information derived from the analysis gives direction to the strategy. It highlights the key internal weaknesses in a business, it focuses on strengths and it alerts managers to opportunities and threats. Skoda was able to identify where it had strengths to compete. The structured review of internal and external factors helped transform Skoda UK's strategic direction. The case study shows how Skoda UK transformed its brand image in the eyes of potential customers and build its competitive edge over rivals. By developing a marketing strategy playing on clearly identified strengths of customer happiness, Skoda was able to overcome weaknesses. It turned its previously defensive position of the brand to a positive customer-focused experience. The various awards Skoda has won demonstrate how its communications are reaching customers. Improved sales show that Skoda UK's new strategy has delivered benefits.

QUESTIONS

1. What was the key weakness that Skoda was able to identify?
2. What strength did Skoda use to turn its brand weakness into an opportunity?
3. How has Skoda strategically addressed external threats?
4. What in your view are the important benefits of using a SWOT analysis?

23 Tarmac: How Roles and Functions Contribute to Competitive Advantage

A Nottingham County Surveyor, Edgar Purnell Hooley, discovered Tarmac by accident in the early 20th century. He found a barrel of tar had spilled onto the road at a local ironworks. This had mixed with waste slag from the furnaces. The result was a dust-free, strong surface. Hooley created and patented the product that could take the weight of the new automobile. In 1903 the Tarmacadam syndicate was formed, its name taken from the developer of the road construction system, John MacAdam. Tarmac's mission is 'to be the first choice for building materials and services that meet the essential needs for the development of the world in which we live.' Tarmac employs 12,500 people and has an annual turnover of £2.1 billion. It operates in many countries, including the UK, Poland, India and the Middle East. In 2005 it produced 76.8 million tonnes of aggregates. An example of Tarmac construction is the ceiling of Canary Wharf Station in London. Tarmac aims to provide customers with high quality products and services in line with its mission statement. This case study shows how Tarmac focuses on attracting and keeping the right staff and ensuring its employees have the right skills and expertise to grow the company.

In an organisation as large and diverse as Tarmac, there are many different jobs. The structure is complex, so individuals within the business need to understand their roles and responsibilities. This enables the whole workforce to work together and achieve Tarmac's aims and objectives. Operations are a key functional area at Tarmac. This is where a number of processes come together to make the products or services to satisfy customer needs. Tarmac Operations has support services in Human resources (HR) – This includes planning for and forecasting staff requirements, and managing recruitment and selection. The HR team ensures that managers apply HR policies and procedures consistently across the business. The development of staff is a key priority within Tarmac.

Finance manages and monitors the flow of money across the business. The finance team produces financial and management accounts and supporting information. Financial accounts deal with financial transactions, such as profit and loss accounts. These satisfy the organization's legal financial requirements. Management accounts look forward and contribute to the strategic decision making process by forecasting financial performance.

By understanding customer needs, the marketing function can inform the overall business strategy. It also ensures that Tarmac's image and brand reflect its high quality and success. The technical team looks for innovative solutions to keep Tarmac's profile high in the market. Within these functional areas, Tarmac has three main levels of staff:

- **Managers** - organize and plan their departments to exceed the expectation of internal end external customers. They work closely with other managers across the company to promote a range of benefits, including: continuous process improvements, improving accuracy, reducing the need to repeat work and driving up efficiency year on year.
- **Supervisors** - work with managers to ensure that operators apply procedures and practices consistently. This involves using best practice to create value-added services across the business.
- **Operators** - are responsible for day-to-day operations of the business. This is the level at which a graduate might enter the organisation in order to learn all aspects of the business. The role requires accuracy, efficiency and a high level of individual responsibility. Graduates can achieve rapid progress to more senior levels in the business.

Tarmac believes 'in bringing out the best in all our people, allowing them to realise their full potential'. It promotes and encourages a culture of learning and development throughout the organisation through its Organisational Development team. This team leads and coordinates training, learning and development opportunities. These enable people at all levels to acquire and practice high levels of skill and expertise. This means individuals can achieve their personal goals, as well as contributing to the wider mission and vision of the organisation.

The Operations function brings together raw materials with the production process to make products that customers need. It also shares ideas across the company about how to improve processes or achieve cost savings. This is known as best practice. The benefits are wide-ranging, such as increased efficiency and more effective management of health and safety and environmental issues. For example, Tarmac is implementing sustainable projects such as restoring quarries after use. It is also working with its suppliers to make the movement of goods more energy efficient. The Aggregate Products division within Operations has a typically hierarchical structure with seven levels. A graduate recruit 'shadows' a plant manager on entry into Tarmac. After 18 months, a graduate can expect to become a Zone Manager. A zone is a defined area of the business. A Zone Manager's job includes managing operational performance in that zone to meet or improve targets for cost, quality, delivery, safety and business integrity. The long-term aim is to develop high performance teams who work within a culture of quality and continuous improvement. Zone Managers have a set of agreed key performance indicators (KPIs). These show targets that they need to achieve. All staff in the zone needs to understand their roles in helping to meet these KPIs. It is the manager's job to help them get the best performance by

- Motivating the team through coaching and leadership.
- Identifying priorities for continuous improvement.
- Encouraging and rewarding staff who contribute improvement ideas and actions.
- Emphasizing the importance of developing skills and capabilities.

Tarmac employees have the opportunity to contribute their ideas on how to achieve results. This helps individuals gain a greater understanding of the business. They are more motivated because they feel a part of the whole structure and not simply a small fish in a large pool. Tarmac has a policy of getting involved with the communities in which it operates, so, for example, They have responsibility for monitoring impacts on the local environment.

Finance is critical to any business. All areas of the business need to have up-to-date information about its financial health. Financial reporting is a major part of this function. Tarmac has different routes for people to join the company, at both graduate level and through apprenticeship schemes. Graduate trainees enter this support function at Operator level. Standards of reporting and accounting need to be the same across all parts of Tarmac's business. This is so that the organisation has a clear and accurate picture of its performance. This is a huge task and good teamwork is essential to ensure that operators, supervisors, managers and the financial controller all follow the same practices.

Human Resources Management is an important asset to any business. It provides expertise in:

- Managing change and facilitating training and development.
- Recruitment, selection and employee relations
- Pensions and benefits
- Communicating with employees.

Tarmac aims to build the capacity and capability of its people to achieve their full potential. This strategy strengthens the business in the long term. An HR manager's role is to ensure that business managers apply HR policies and procedures consistently through all business units. This helps to develop partnerships across different teams, which supports corporate aims and objectives. It deals with improving employee performance and capability for the company and involves many different aspects. It includes ensuring appropriate numbers of staff, performance management, training and development, and dealing with absence. Tarmac needs to remain competitive so we need to evaluate how we do things on a regular basis. This means there is constant change, which is exciting. Businesses have to respond to rapidly changing markets and conditions in order to remain competitive and grow.

Competition from new or emerging markets, changing tastes and fashions, and changes to the law can all affect a business. Tarmac has put in place a programme of Change Management to respond to these issues and to improve performance and motivate staff. To make this happen, Tarmac is training managers to move from an autocratic (or top-down approach) to a coaching style of management. An autocratic manager tells people what to do and how to do it. This may be necessary if a job is urgent or needs to be done in a particular way, for example, for health and safety reasons. A coaching manager focuses on developing employees to manage themselves rather than managing every task. This means that they can find a way to achieve results and learn from the experience. This makes employees more motivated and better able to deal with future situations.

Tarmac's business involves much more than building and maintaining roads. It is a multinational business and serves different types of customers across its business activities. To maintain its competitive advantage, Tarmac needs to have employees with high levels of skill. To support this, it provides career development opportunities across a wide variety of job roles. Tarmac's change management programme ensures that managers work closely to develop their staff. The staff benefit from developing their skills and potential through Tarmac's positive commitment to progression. Tarmac benefits from the savings and quality enhancements arising from its process of continuous improvement.

QUESTIONS

1. What is a hierarchical organisational structure?
2. Describe the three levels of responsibility at Tarmac and the key roles for each.
3. Explain how organisational structure supports business aims and objectives.
4. Evaluate how key performance indicators help to drive business improvements.

24 The Tata Group: Challenges in Managing a Large Portfolio

Managing a portfolio of close to 100 companies is a mammoth task for any business house. Questions over acquiring newer firms and divesting non-performing firms need to be answered on a regular basis. These questions have become extremely important for the Tata Group as they have used the inorganic growth route extensively to scale up their international operations. This case looks at Tata's inorganic expansion and performs a portfolio analysis for the group identifying potential divestment targets.

The definition of growth has changed quite dramatically from the days when organic growth was considered the primary channel of progress. This is exemplified in the case of the Tatas where inorganic growth, through leveraged buyouts and sometimes audacious deals, has driven expansion over the last decade. With accelerated growth comes the challenge of integration and proper management of the portfolio of companies. The top management has to often answer the question mark over the business house's role in keeping all these companies under one roof.

The Tata Group is India's largest business group accounting for 5.2% of India's GDP and operates in over 80 countries with group revenue amounting to a whopping USD 62.5 billion in 2008.The group operates in seven broad sectors ranging from steel, automobiles, energy, chemicals, hotels and consumer goods to communication systems. Tata Steel, Tata Motors, Tata Consulting Services and Tata Power accounting for nearly 50% of the group revenue. The group profit has grown at a CAGR of 19.4% over the last decade and a half and the group revenue has grown at a CAGR of 16% over the same time period. Over the last decade, the Tata Group has had a clear focus on internationalization with contribution of international operations to the revenues having gone up to 61%. Today, the Tata Group comprises 96 companies, operates in 6 continents and employs approximately 350,000 people. Inorganic route has played a major role in this fast growth story.

Over the last ten years, the group's strategy has revolved around building a very strong presence in international markets. To quote Alan Rosling, Executive Director, Tata Sons "Internationalization is not a strategy; it is an imperative, a challenge or an objective". The group has made a conscious attempt to follow the inorganic growth route. Starting with the Tetley Acquisition in 2001 for USD 432 million, the group has made acquisitions in most of the sectors it operates in. The highlight of its international acquisition strategy was the USD 11.2 billion acquisition of Anglo-Dutch firm, Corus (the fourth largest in the global steel industry). Other significant acquisitions include the Tata Motors acquisition of Daewoo Chemical Vehicle Company, Tata Power buying a 30% stake in PT Kaltim Prima Coal and Indian Hotel's acquisition of Ritz-Carlton Hotels.

Merger &Acquisitions might be undertaken for horizontal acquisition to retain/ gain market leadership or to get a foothold onto international markets (market entry) or to leverage on synergies. Tata Chemical's acquisition of Brunner Mond (the second largest producer of soda ash in Europe) is a classic example of a horizontal acquisition. A market entry strategy can be used to tap the more advanced markets that help the company move up the value chain there by deriving higher margins. This was the major reason why Tata Steel decided to acquire Corus as it helped Tata Steel enter the value added steel market in Europe. In a merger/acquisition, the Tata Group brings along with it accumulated production experience, cost effectiveness of production processes and ability to differentiate products.

Going forward, the Tata Group is expected to pursue vigorously the M&A route to growth. Some of the markets which the group is looking at for inorganic growth include South East Asia, South Africa, United States and Europe. The group however should be careful about integrating all these companies under one roof. Focusing on methods to facilitate easy integration of companies while preserving the Tata culture will be of paramount importance in future acquisitions.

With accelerated inorganic growth comes the need to optimize the portfolio of companies held. Are there companies in their portfolio that have consistently underperformed as compared to the industry? This is explored using the BCG Growth Share Matrix.

The BCG Growth Share matrix uses the dimensions of relative market share and the market growth rate to establish a 2*2 matrix containing 4 main quadrants " Stars (high market growth, high market share), Cash Cows (low market growth, high market share), Question marks (high market growth, low market share) and Dogs (low market growth, low market share)". The ideal strategy is to hold on to the Stars and the Cash Cows, divest the Dogs and take a call on the Question Marks (hold/divest).

A detailed analysis (using the BCG Matrix) of the portfolio of companies in the Tata Group, is involved analyzing the sectors in which the Tata group operates as well as the companies in the Tata Group within each sector. The studies of the operational and financial performances of each company to understand their growth stories, special emphasis was laid on identifying the organic and inorganic growth routes pursued by each of these companies under the Tata umbrella. The conclusions drawn about these companies are based on analysis of the global strategy of the Tata group and on detailed conversations with top executives in the Tata Group.

The analysis reveals that Tata Steel, Tata Power, Tata Motors and Indian Hotels emerge as clear Stars (high market growth, high market share). Hence, they should be retained and the investment in these companies should be increased. Tata Chemicals and Tata Tea emerge as the Cash Cows (low market growth, high market share) and should be held on to for the time being. Some of the Question Marks (high market growth, low market share) are Tata Teleservices, Voltas and Tata Communications. These results are shown in Exhibit 24.1 below.

Exhibit 24.1 Portfolio Analysis of the Tata Group using the BCG Matrix

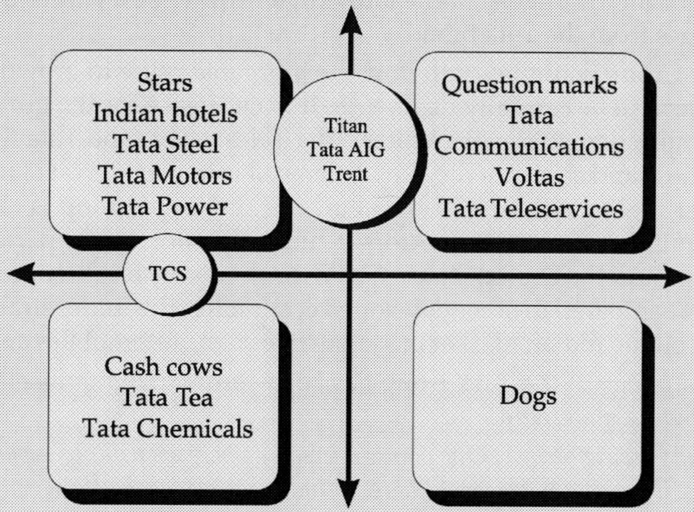

The profitability of the Tata Group in the telecommunications sector has shown a consistent decline from 10% in 2003 to 4% in 2006-07. Despite the telecom boom in India, the question on the presence of the Tata Group in the telecommunications sector warrants further discussion. For the Tatas, the broad objective behind entering any sector is to be among the top 3 in that sector. Despite having had a presence for many decades in the consumer durables segment, the Tatas have been unable to capture the leadership position in the segment through Voltas. Moreover, the growth registered by Voltas over the past few years has also been far from impressive which necessitates the need to critically evaluate its performance in this segment.

In addition, the question of operating so many companies under the Tata Group needs to be looked into. Does it make sense to have so many companies in the first place? Should there be a relook into the question marks like Voltas, Tata Communications and Tata Teleservices? These are hard questions that need to be answered as the group keeps going forward. With close to 100 companies under one roof, the question arises whether all of them should be under the Tata Group or should some be spun off.

Is there any advantage of being a part of the same business group? Business groups can add significant value. Firstly, business groups use funds and management talent from existing operations to start new ventures (thereby negating the need for venture capital firms). Secondly, large business groups can nurture in-house management talent that can be shifted across individual group companies. Thirdly, business groups create value by developing a common group brand that stands for world class quality and customer service. According to R Gopal Krishnan, Executive Director, Tata Sons; "The estimated value of the Tata brand is about INR 100 billion." For an individual company to use the Tata brand name, they need to meet a set of quality standards and business values. Hence, it is in the interest of the individual firms to be a part of the Tata Group to derive advantages from the Tata brand.

As the Tata Group continues to follow the inorganic route to growth, the challenges of integration need to be carefully dealt with. It is necessary for the group to take a look at some of their question marks like Voltas, Tata Teleservices and Tata Communications. Finally, given the brand equity of the "Tata" name, it is in the interest of newer companies to remain under the Tata Group. In the course of time, the group is expected to make many more acquisitions across the sectors it currently operates in, particularly in South East Asia, Europe and the United States. Given the relatively brighter prospects about the Indian economy compared to other developed economies, the future strategy also calls for a definite focus on the Indian market in sectors like steel, automobiles and infrastructure.

The future strategy of the Tata group has been summarized quite elegantly by Ratan Tata in the following statement:

"We have two guiding arrows. One points overseas, where we want to expand markets for our existing products. The other points right here, to India, where we want to explore the large mass market that is emerging " not by following but by breaking new ground in product development and seeing how we can do something that has not been done before."

QUESTIONS

1. Managing a large portfolio is a difficult task. How Tata Group has been successful in doing it?
2. "Internationalization is not a strategy". How do you perceive it and do you think it can be adopted by all firms?
3. M&A can be one of the strategies to enter into global market. Explain how Tatas have used this strategy and become successful.
4. What are the challenges faced by Tata Group when they adopted "inorganic route to growth".
5. Carry out SWOT analysis of Tata Group.

25 Strategic Management in Wal-Mart Retail

Michael Porter states that root of the problem lies in the lack of distinguishing between operation effectiveness and strategy. The expedition for productivity, quality and speed has resulted in management tools and techniques such as total quality management. benchmarking, time based competition, outsourcing, and partnering, reengineering, change management. In any organization, strategic management is the key to its success. There are many theories based on this assumption that without a proper strategy and planning, it is difficult for any industry to survive irrespective of its size. It is necessary to understand here that all the major corporate organisations have established themselves, thanks to superior strategic planning and implementation. The retail industry is making news everywhere with not only the traditional industries increasing their outlets but some major corporate industries also intruding into this industry like Reliance Fresh of Reliance Industries, More of Aditya Birla Group in India. Wal-Mart, a US based retail industry, which is known as the giant in the retail industry has survived and is still the huge enterprise in the world which deals with almost all the food and beverage (F&B) products, apparels, etc. It is not only the largest company in world but also the largest company in the history of world. The case study is divided into four sections to understand and answer as what makes Wal-Mart the best in the industry, (1) retailing industry at the time of Wal-Mart's innings, (2) Wal-Mart's competitive advantage and key components, (3) Wal-Mart's strategy and (4) Sustainable growth of Wal-Mart.

RETAIL INDUSTRY: WAL-MART SAYS HELLO!

Strategic decisions are ones that are aimed at differentiating an organization from its competitors in a way that is sustainable in the future. Porter strongly advocates that decisions in business can be classified as strategic if they involve some innovation and difference that results in sustainable advantage. According to Patrick Hayden et al. (2002) the retailing industry adopted the style of discounting on its merchandise after the Second World War. It is learnt that discount retailing was not the strategy at the time Kmart, Target and Wal-Mart first started operating their business. Frank states that when Sam Walton was franchising for Ben Franklin's variety store, invented an idea of passing on the savings to his customers and earning his profits through volume. Prior to Wal-Mart's entry into the market, Sidney and Hebert from Harrison founded Two Guys discount store in the year 1946 which dealt in hardware, automotive parts and later on groceries. Two Guys was the forerunner as compared to today's retailers like Super Target, Wal-Mart which succumbed to the economic recession. Another discount store set up by Eugene as E.J. Korvette, which is often cited as first discount store which did not raise from 5 & 10 cents roots and eventually declared bankruptcy due to inability to compete with the new entrants.

Porter states that combination of operational effectiveness and strategy is essential for superior performance which is the primary goal of any organization. He also says that a company can outperform its rivals only if it can operate in different ways which are not in practice. Much emphasis had been laid on strategic positioning like variety based positioning, needs-based positioning and access-based positioning.

Along with Wal-Mart, other stores that started operating were Target, Woolworth (Woolco) and K-Mart. However, Target has been functioning successfully, courtesy Wal-Mart, but other two failed in their operations and filed bankruptcy. Porters five forces model explains what strategic decisions should be made and on what basis. The model explains the basic strategies to be considered while starting a business like bargaining power of suppliers. While franchising of Franklin always looked for cheaper deals and thought of passing savings to the customers and earning through the margin on volume of bulk purchases. Through the way of discount stores, shoppers were given the cheapest price as compared to any other store. In regard to threats of new entrants, Wal-Mart has been constantly in the news for acquisition of other small retail shops in view of its expansion. But nevertheless it has stiff competition from likes of Super Target, Tesco, etc. it is the world's biggest retail industry.

KEY COMPONENTS OF WAL-MART BUSINESS MODEL

Wal-Mart is the leader in retailing industry with fiscal revenue of $244.52 billion in 2003 making it the world's largest corporation. Wal-Mart as of 2002 had 1,283,000 employees growing at 11.2%. The above data explains that strategy of Wal-Mart is extraordinary which manages and operates over 4150 retail facilities globally. The key components of Wal-Mart (The Value Chain), which offers cheaper prices than its competitors includes firm infrastructure like frugal culture, no regional offices and pleasant environment to work. Managements take lots of visits and it is learnt there are no rehearsals before any meeting which is usually scheduled on every Saturday. In any organization, human resource is the key to development and Wal-Mart efficiently manages its sources. Wal-Mart terms its employees as associates. Manager compensation is linked to the profit of store operated by him, within promotions, compensation offered to associates depending on company's profits and also offered some incentives on their performances. The workforce at Wal-Mart is not unionized as the company takes all the measures of their benefits and provides them training on related issues. Technology plays a vital role in development of the organization and Wal-Mart is well equipped with technological innovations like POS, store performance tracking, real time market research, and satellite system. Wal-Mart procurement measures like hard-nosed negotiations, partnerships with some vendors, centralized buying, planning packets, etc., helps at large the cause of providing the goods and services on cheap prices. The other factors that increase the margin of profit for Wal-Mart are inbound logistics with frequent replenishment, automated DCs cross docking, pick to flight, EDI, hub and spoke system. Wal-Mart strategy of operation is innovative with big stores in small towns with monopoly in the market at low rental costs, local prices, concentric expansion, merchandising in brand name, private labels, little space for inventory, store within store, etc. In relation to marketing and sales, merchandising is tailored from locals, spent less on advertising and the prices are fixed low and it depends on the store manager to fix the latitude of pricing. All the above factors combined together form the key components of Wal-Mart which not only increase the margin of profits through bulk sales but also boost the confidence of the customers with services like point of sale information system and everyday low prices.

WAL-MART STRATEGY

Wal-Mart dominates the American retailing industry due to number of factors like its business model which is still a mystery and its effectiveness in not letting the rivals let know about the weaknesses. Wal-Mart made strategic attempts in the its formulation to dominate the retail market where it has its presence, growth by expansion in the US and internationally, create widespread name recognition and customer satisfaction in relation to brand name Wal-Mart and branching into new sectors of retailing.

It is learnt that Wal-Mart strives on three generic strategies consisting of Focus Strategy, the Differentiation Strategy and overall cost leadership. Managers strive hard to make their organisations unique, distinctive and identify key success factors that will drive the customers to buy their products. Thus, firm specific resources and capabilities are crucial in explaining the firm's performance. The Resource Based View (RBV) explains competitive heterogeneity based on the premise that close competitors differ in their resources and capabilities in important and durable ways. The company's capability can be found through its functionality, reliable performance, like Wal-Mart superior logistics. Wal-Mart has firm infrastructure, well equipped in human resource with management professionals and technologically too.

Organisations thrive hard to be successful for which they needs to have better resources and superior capabilities. Wal-Mart has strong RBV with economically and financially very strong enough to stand still in the time of crisis. Dominating the retail market is its key strategy. Wal-Mart operates on low price strategy which is operated as everyday low prices (EDLP) which builds trust among the customers. The strategy lies in purchasing the goods at lower prices and selling the goods to customer at much lower prices, cutting the price as far as possible and increasing the profit by increasing the number of sales. This ferociously increases the competition in the market and Wal-Mart competes with all its competitors till it is dominant in the market.

Wal-Mart is expanding seriously and rapidly which is also its strategic goal. Wal-Mart employs over 1.3 associates, owns over 4000 stores out of which 3000 are in US and serves around 100 million customers weekly. Wal-Mart has acquired many international stores and merged with some super stores like ASDA in UK. Wal-Mart far flung network of retail outlets has ensured that Wal-Mart interacts with and has impact on virtually every locality within US. The expanded strategy has led the hunger of Wal-Mart to many European countries. It is learnt that three countries with no Wal-Mart stores became part of corporation's international presence wherein the domestic retail chains were taken over by Wal-Mart including 122 Woolco stores in Canada, 21 Wertkauf stores in Germany and 229 ASDA units in United Kingdom. The takeover strategy by Wal-Mart keeps the company at forefront when entering into the new market and the number of competitors is also minimized. The strategies have helped the Wal-Mart to rein in number one position in international countries making it the largest retailer in the world.

It is seen that Wal-Mart has significantly used the Porters five force model wherein through proper strategic planning and strategic implementation has led to removal of barrier entry, rivalry from competitors and pricing norms. In regard to substitutes, Wal-Mart in order to achieve its aim of customer satisfaction has selling goods under its own legal brand. Wal-Mart's big box phenomenon has changed the retailing industry in the United States which is often considered discount stores and makes profit through high volume of purchases and low markup on profits. Wal-Mart with its low cost and ever expanding strategy has made a dramatic impact since 1962 when Sam Walton first started his business. With this strategy, Wal-Mart has now over 4000 stores and outlets in US and other countries through acquisition and mergers.

SUSTAINABILITY IN DISCOUNT RETAILING : WAL-MART

According to Porter, operational effectiveness and efficiency are the key elements of success in any organization. A company can outperform its rivals or competitors in the market only with superior management and efficient control creating a difference from the others which eventually attracts customers. Porter defines operational effectiveness as performance of similar activities as its rivals but better than them. Wal-Mart is expert in manipulating perceptions. It is termed that low price is not the strategy of Wal-Mart but the advertisement manipulates the consumer perceptions by making them think that its prices are lower than its competitors' price using 'price spin'. Wal-Mart makes the consumer addicted coming to its stores by convincing them the prices are lower than in the other stores by selling itself cheaper by advertising that 'we have lower prices than anyone else' and placing a 'opening price point'. The 'opening price point' is the lowest price in the store which is kept at high visibility which makes consumer believes that the products in this store are really cheaper.

The SWOT analysis of Wal-Mart reveals that it is the most powerful retail brand, reputation for money, value, commitment, and provides wide range of products. It is growing at a brisk pace with expanding its horizon to other parts of world through acquisition and merger. Wal-Mart has good opportunities in markets of Europe and China and focuses on acquiring the market through acquisition of smaller stores and merger with leaders in the specific markets. Wal-Mart is always under threat to sustain its top position in market nationally and internationally. Global leader in the industry leaves the organization vulnerable to many socioeconomic and political problems of the country.

Sustainability at the top place is the most important job that makes its managers strives hard to frame the policies and strategy to compete with its rivals in the market. Slack, imitation, substitution and hold-up are some of the threats to any organization in retail industry. However, Wal-Mart with its visionary goal of attaining zero waste status and reaching 100% renewable energy has planned to launch number of sustainability initiatives. Imitation increases profits by increasing the supply. But imitation puts reputation, relationship at stake. James Hall reports that Wal-Mart is planning to open convenience stores as Tesco has started and operating in US called Fresh & Easy Neighborhood Markets. Such tactics will create mixed response among the consumers while degrading the reputation of the leader in market. Substitution reduces the demand for what a firm uniquely provides by shifting the demand elsewhere due to changes in technology. The threats of substitution can be subtle and unexpected like minimizing expenses through videoconferencing instead of air flights to long distance meetings with its managers of other stores, etc. Therefore, substitution is an especially effective way of attacking dominant rivals in the market. Substitution offers mixed responses after identifying and understanding the threats. The organization should fight the threat and merging with them, switching to different options of substitution to be in the market. Hold-up diverts the value to customers, suppliers or complementary who have some bargaining leverage which results in tough negotiations, contractual agreements and vertical integration.

Wal-Mart is having great network with almost over 7800 stores and Sam's Club locations in 16 markets worldwide. It employs more than 2 million associates and serves more than 100 million customers every year. According to Fishman Americans spend $26 million every hour at Wal-Mart which makes it believable that Wal-Mart is financially very strong and is capable of combating any threat from its rivals in the market. Wal-Mart is ever expanding its boundaries by way of acquisition and mergers. Thus Wal-Mart with such a vast network of stores and alliances in the forms of ASDA, Target and many other stores is well protected enough to sustain its top position in the retail industry.

QUESTIONS

1. How successful is the Wal-Mart in adopting the "discount retailing strategy". Did it face any challenges?
2. What generic strategies are adopted by the Wal-Mart. What steps have they taken to successfully adopt these strategies?
3. How Wal-Mart was able to sustain EDLP?
4. Sustainability at the top place is most important job of managers. How Wal-Mart managers were able to do it?

26 Turnaround Strategy in Avon

Avon Products, Inc. (Avon) is based in New York. The firm engages in the manufacture and marketing of beauty and complimentary products primarily in North America, Latin America, Europe, and Asia Pacific. Avon's products are classified into three product categories: Beauty, Beauty Plus, and Beyond Beauty. The Beauty category consists of cosmetics, fragrances, skin care, and toiletries; Beauty Plus includes fashion jewellery, watches, apparel, and accessories; and Beyond Beauty comprises home products, gift and decorative products, candles, and toys. The company sells and markets its products through a combination of direct selling, marketing by independent Avon representatives, and via its consumer Website, avon.com.

Avon was one of the prominent direct sales companies in the beauty products industry. Started in the late 1800s by David McConnell, the company sold a wide variety of beauty-related products to homemakers through its direct sales agents. However, by the 1980s, the company had lost its luster and performance began to falter. A failed diversification strategy made it the target of several takeover attempts. Turnaround efforts were initiated in the 1990s under then CEO James Preston and continued by his successor Charles Perrin, however, they failed to make a significant impact. Performance began to improve only after Andrea Jung became the CEO of the company in 1999.

Andrea Jung became president and CEO of Avon in 1999 and has totally revamped the company. Under her leadership, the company has updated its product line, launched new advertising, and created a new image. Avon's sales have increased by 30%, profits 40%, and the stock price has dramatically improved. Jung has been able to align the firm's core capabilities with its strategic targets which has led to phenomenal results. It appears that Jung has been able to establish a clear vision for the firm that has been incorporated in every aspect of the firm's operating system. This vision is shared by all employees and representatives of Avon priming the company for continued success.

Other strategies of Jung include cost cutting by reducing number of raw material suppliers, shifting production from smaller plants to larger ones, moving manufacturing from high cost nations like Great Britain to lower cost countries such as Poland. As mentioned in the Avon case study, the e-representative initiative also has helped Avon cut costs. The direct sellers are asked to fill in the order online.

Avon's brand has definitely resonated for women through the years. During the 1980s, the company began to diversify by investing in retirement properties and healthcare products, and launching catalogs for men and children. During the initial stages of this strategy, Avon started to remove itself from its core market of selling to women. The results were downward revenue trends and slow growth throughout the 1990's which resulted in several takeover bids.

Unfortunately, Sears Roebuck and JC Penny do not really resonate well with being a carrier of women's beauty supplies. The name "Sears" have been associated with appliance and not beauty products. The move of aligning with this companies and trying to sell higher end beauty products will only push Avon in the opposite direction that it should be heading, which is to move back towards tailoring to women domestically and globally.

Over the years, Avon has experienced several problems leveraging its brand in many of its product lines. As a result, positive net sales and earnings growth for the past five years have been in single digits and steadily declining year after year. Specific problem areas are stagnated sales, slow earnings growth, limited distribution capabilities and shift in personal care preferences and spending habits.

Andrea Jung's proposal to expand into certain retail markets will only perpetuate Avon's trend of declining net sales. The proposed plan will indeed create an additional distribution outlet and cater to this market segment. However, the question to examine is at what expense or cost will Avon endure making this decision? Avon has faced tremendous pitfalls marketing its product lines to effectively increase brand loyalty and recognition. Examples of this include the hair care product line. Avon did not effectively develop products for ethnic hair types. Additionally, Avon did not have a hair coloring product line. As a result, Avon suffered in building brand awareness and loyalty with the younger generation as well as the older generation that also demanded this product.

Avon has lost loyalty and brand recognition as a result of its decision to diversify into different industries and different product lines. This has resulted in a loss of market share drastically affecting annual profit margins. To examine the previous question of what cost will Avon endure deciding to move into the retail markets? It is clear and evident; the cost will be a further extension of the existing internal problems that Avon faces. Deciding to move into the retail market to create a store inside a store is not in Avon's best interest. This move would be a further expansion of Avon's previous decisions to diversify into markets that do not have synergy and thus will hurt the overall branding of the company. Finally, implementing Andrea Jung's proposal to enter the retail market would be detrimental to the already fragile state of Avon's brand awareness, recognition and loyalty.

Another factor for the underperformance of Avon in the late 1990s is its failure to develop the online business. For the fear of alienating its workforce, Avon downplayed the importance of developing the e-business. A company cannot ignore the environment and expect to be successful in the long run. Due to its internal struggle with the Internet strategy, Avon fell behind other less established companies in taking advantage of the explosive growth of the Internet.

Avon's approach should build on original direction and implementations however expanding as necessary to fit current trends and environmental assessments. The focus should be on existing internal structures to build, create and advance current product lines. Avon's focus should also exist in the field of technology to increase online selling opportunities, update the Internet technology and to re-brand themselves to be a leader of online sells. To accomplish this, strategy should focus on expanding kiosks globally and domestically. The expansion will leverage Avon by appealing to the market segment requesting additional distribution channels. This strategy will allow for trained beauty consultants to offer advice, education and samples thus increasing brand awareness and loyalty. Kiosks will have minimal start up cost and lower overheads. Focusing on product lines and catering to the needs and wants of each demographic group will prevent the previous pitfalls of lack of integration and decreased brand awareness and loyalty.

Keeping Avon's product offering separate and distinct will help existing challenges of branding. Focusing on technology improvements and online sales, Avon will have an opportunity to emerge as a leader in this area, thus adding additional channels of distribution and appealing to the overwhelming need.

Under Andrea Jung's leadership, Avon has faced a number of challenges. Some of these challenges were addressed successfully and others were not. In the early part of 2000, the management team had the daunting task of choosing an appropriate strategy for the immediate and long-term future for the company. One setback was a decrease in the firm's growth rate to single digits and stagnated earnings. Avon's CEO, Andrea Jung, was presented with a multitude of options that ranged from distributing through other departmental stores, establishing kiosks, to overhauling the firm's e-business. Jung was right in acknowledging that Avon's core competence is direct selling and its major strength is its brand name. By refocusing on the core competence, improving efficiencies, and adapting to the environment with new initiatives, Avon could overcome the hurdles of the past and turn the company in the new direction.

Avon's grand strategy under the leadership of Andrea Jung has its merits and is the grand strategy is properly focused and directed. Andrea Jung has clearly directed the successful transformation of Avon Products Inc. by defining its vision as the company for women. With grand strategies in-place she is revitalizing Avon's reputation as the world's foremost direct seller of beauty products while leading the company into exciting new lines of businesses, launching a series of bold and image enhancing initiatives, and expanding career opportunities for people around the world. The strategic plan in place has its merits and the grand strategy is properly focused and directed. Currently, Avon is the world's leading direct seller of beauty and related products, with $7.7 billion in annual revenues. Avon markets to women around the world through 4.9 million independent sales representatives.

Andrea Jung initiated expansion into markets outside US making Avon products available online, and began selling Avon products through retail channels. She also instituted a more upscale packaging to match the look of prestige cosmetic brands. She focused on a low cost/ low price strategy and focus to sale to low and middle income families. Andrea's new strategy was likely to improve Avon's financial performance and help build a competitive advantage. Her approach is sensible in light of what the competitors are doing and the position they hold in the marketplace.

Avon is highly backward integrated, self-manufacturing many of the items that they sell. This causes the competitive pressures of suppliers to be weak. Avon can get supplies from many parts of the world because they have entered foreign markets and produce products in different countries. A lot of Avon's supplies such as packaging, may be easily substituted if a supplier raised prices.

Under Andrea Jung's direction, Avon is focusing on developing nations especially China. Many developing countries are more receptive to direct selling by women since jobs with Avon are opportunities for women who want to be independent in the male dominated cultures. Avon has also recognized that the demographics has changed and recruiting younger women to sell to the younger customer base.

Competitive pressures stemming from customer buying power is moderate because switching costs are low and customers have the ability to fulfill their needs by switching brands. Buyers tend to be well informed about Avon's product prices and costs largely due to the Internet and this put customers at a position of higher bargaining power. Customers do not pose a threat of integrating backwards, because it would not be easy for women to develop their own make-up, perfume or skin care products. Due to the direct selling business model, there is an extremely large number of buyers. Another Avon objective that aims to alleviate pressures coming from competing sellers includes consists of reinventing their antiquated image. Realizing this, Jung endorsed the Williams sisters. Venus and Serena Williams were popular teen icons that portrayed the image where Jung hoped to achieve for Avon; young, powerful, and ambitious.

Andrea Jung's highly successful career would not be possible without effective and insightful management." Throughout Jung's ambitious expansion, her management style was to emphasize open communication, goal orientation, and feedback from her sales force." Avon routinely brings in the top performing sales reps from across the globe to Avon's headquarters in New York City in order to gather first hand feedback from the employees in the field. Ms. Jung herself even attempted to sell Avon's products as a traditional Avon lady. An attempt she acknowledges was not one of her more successful endeavours. The attempt however, showed Ms. Jung's commitment to understanding all aspects of the Avon business. A common theme in Ms. Jung's leadership speeches encourage women empowerment and promote a belief that more women will continue to hold key executive roles. Under Ms. Jung's leadership, Avon management supports flexible work schedules and encourages employees to create a healthy balance between work and family responsibilities.

There are a number of missteps that Avon has taken under Andrea Jung's leadership. They include partnering with companies that image does not adequately match Avon's and the company's problems with launching its online business segment. Recently, Avon announced plans to partner with Sears and JC Penney's. One of the potential negative aspects for Avon partnering with JC Penny and Sears would be the possible lowering of brand name for Avon. The company ran the risk of possible further reduction of its brand name." Since its inception Avon has worked very hard in tailoring its niche market towards women.

Based on demographic data, China holds 20% of the world's population. This represents a vast market of which Avon has only begun to cover. Avon should continue to focus on the expansion of retail outlet sales in China. Also, because the only sales in China are generated through retail outlets, Avon should further develop their Beauty Advisors training.

Europe should also be a continued focus for Avon. Industry leader, L'Oreal's attributes 50% of their total sales to the European market. Avon had a successful growth rate in Europe but only 23% of the total 2003 sales came from Europe. There is still room to expand in this market.

Based on one of the industry's key success factors, product innovation, Avon should focus even more resources on R&D especially in the areas of anti-aging products and teen products. Because 23 million teenagers have an average weekly disposable income of $85, Avon should continue with innovative teen marketing such as the current "Mark" brand but also work on products for problem teen skin.

Avon Products Inc under the leadership of CEO Andrea Jung is at a point where there are opportunities for growth for the organisation. However Ms. Jung appears to be indisposed towards taking steps to take advantage of Avon's position. Also her approach is flawed.

QUESTIONS

1. What is your assessment of Andrea Jung's performance as chief strategist at Avon Products? What has she done well? What overall grade would you give Andrea Jung for the job she has done as CEO?
2. What is Andre Jung's strategic vision for Avon? Do you approve of the company's new strategic direction? Why was it time for Avon to fundamentally change direction?
3. What is your assessment to the financial and strategic objectives Jung has set for Avon? Do they contain too much stretch? Too little stretch?
4. What have been the key elements of Avon's strategy been under previous CEOs? What new and different strategy elements have been initiated by Andrea Jung?
5. How well has Avon's new strategy been implemented so far? What are Avon's strategy successes so far? What problems or missteps do you see? How important has Susan Kropf been to Avon's implementation efforts? Was she a good choice as chief operating officer? Why or why not?
6. Has Andrea Jung been effective in evaluating the company's performances, monitoring new developments, and initiating corrective adjustments?
7. What additional actions would you recommend Andrea Jung take to help the company to achieve its long term strategic and financial objectives?

27 IKEA: Largest Furniture Retailer in the World

This case is about the internationally known home furnishing retailer IKEA the largest furniture retailer in the world. The purpose of the case study is to analyze the objectives and strategies used by IKEA, analyze the company financially, SWOT analyzing and discuss major issue that the company faced.

IKEA is a privately held, international home products retailer that sells flat pack furniture, accessories, and bathroom and kitchen items in their retail stores around the world. The company, which pioneered flat-pack design furniture at affordable prices, is now the world's largest furniture retailer. IKEA was founded in 1943 by 17-year-old Ingvar Kamprad in Sweden and it is owned by a Dutch registered foundation controlled by the Kamprad family. The company that was originated in Småland, Sweden, distributes its products through its retail outlets. As of August 2009, the chain has 301 stores in 37 countries, most of them in Europe, North America, Asia and Australia.

The IKEA Concept began when Ingvar Kamprad, an entrepreneur from the Småland province in southern Sweden, had an innovative idea. In Småland, although the soil is thin and poor, the people have a reputation for working hard, living frugally and making the most out of limited resources. So when Ingvar started his furniture business in the late 1940s, he applied the lessons he learned in Småland to the home furnishings market. Ingvars innovative idea was to offer home furnishing products of good function and design at prices much lower than competitors by using simple cost-cutting solutions that did not affect the quality of products. Ingvar used every opportunity to reduce costs, and he scraped and saved in every way possible-except on ideas and quality. The name IKEA comes from the initials of Ingvar Kamprad, I and K, plus the first letters of Elmtaryd and Agunnaryd, which are the names of the farm and village where he grew up.

IKEA vision statement is "To create a better everyday life for the many people." Mission. IKEA mission statement is "To offer a wide range of well designed, functional home furnishing products at prices so low that as many people as possible will be able to afford them." IKEA market positioning statement is "Your partner in better living. We do our part, you do yours. Together we save money."

The objectives of IKEA are:

- To produce cheap and affordable products for the public/customers.
- Better life for those who can't afford expensive products.
- Ensure the customer finds what they are looking for in store.
- Low prices.

Financial year 2010 was an unpredictable year with the effects of the financial crisis in 2009 still a reality for many of their customers. The conditions in our markets ranged from favourable to difficult. FY10 turned out to be a very good year for our retail operations, with growth in most markets, further increasing our market shares. Increasing sales, gross margin and improvements in the cost structure, adjusted for one-off items, led to a strong result. New stores, refurbishments and other investments were funded with our own cash flow.

Sales increased to 23.1 billion EURO in FY10, an increase of 7.7% compared to the previous year. The growth came both from existing stores, which grew by 2.4% and new stores. Sales grew in almost all countries, with China, Russia and Portugal showing the strongest increase. Gross margin improved to 46.1% from 44.6% in fY09. This increase was driven by higher sales and reduced costs in our supply chain, strongly supported by steps taken together with our suppliers.

SWOT ANALYSIS

Strengths	**Weaknesses**
• Powerful brand image. • Wide range of products and styles. • Hip, Swedish designs. • Cheap and affordable. • Furniture is easy to assemble and ship. • One stop shopping. • Friendly atmosphere/store layout. • Facilities: restaurant/daycare centre. • Strong global sourcing capabilities	• Assembling furniture yourself may be unappealing to certain groups of consumers. • Relatively few locations. • Store layout – a hassle for those who want a particular item only. • Swedish designs may not appeal to all American markets. • Advertising doesn't appeal enough to target market (young people). • Furniture is not built to last a lifetime
Opportunities:	**Threats:**
• Untapped markets (Midwest, corporate etc.).	• Indirect threats from Wal-Mart, Home Depot, Pier.

Contd...

• Educate consumers on IKEA through advertisements.	• The global economic crisis.
• Different type of stores such as outlets or high-end labels.	• Social trends – such as the slowdown in first time buyers entering the housing market. This is a core market segment for IKEA products.
• Increase online sales and Internet presence.	• Market forces – more competitors entering the low price household and furnishings markets. IKEA needs to reinforce its unique qualities to compete with these.
• IKEA can expand into many more cities in the world.	• Economic factors – the recession slows down consumer spending and disposable income reduces.
• Use the popularity among young people to expand to college markets.	
• Existing stores are few and large, new stores could be many and smaller.	

Major issues that faced by or may face IKEA:

- The high flow of visitors at one-time leads to many problems resulting from the lack of manpower who can meet this climax. In order to overcome this problem IKEA has used Beonic's Traffic Insight visitor flow system since December 2004, to ensure its checkouts are never short–staffed. Highly accurate Beonic sensors at each IKEA entrance track the number of people entering the 26,000 square meter store, ensuring that its checkout sales attendants are in position by the time customers reach the exit
- IKEA suffers from a lack of innovation and faces the possibility of offering a very similar product base. This is due in part to the lack of fresh blood in the organisation. IKEAs policy of hiring the same genre of people leads to inhibiting diversity and innovation to meet change in new markets. In order to overcome this problem KEA should broaden its selection base of hiring people. Whilst not changing the core competence required of key staff, a new emphasis should be placed on the hiring of people from a mix of backgrounds and personalities. This will promote diversity, infusion of new ideas and ensure the richness of the culture
- Not enough like-minded managers (Swedes) to manage stores. There are two options to solve this issue. Firstly, a solution would be to hire more Swedes with similar work ethos and cultural similarities. Secondly, another option is to promote successful managers from various countries to expatriate jobs in other geographies. This would not only achieve strong transplantation of talent but also build strong and committed global managers.

STRATEGIES USED BY IKEA

- **Low-cost leadership strategy:** IKEA has a unique business model that connects the needs of our customers with the possibilities on the factory floor. With a deep knowledge about life at home and the challenges most of us have with limited space and wallets on one hand and big dreams on the other, IKEA often develops its products directly on the factory floor. The starting point for product developers and designers is always the price. Together with our very skilled suppliers, we make sure to get the most out of the possibilities in the production plants. We adapt the sizes and constructions of our products so we can produce, package and transport them in the most efficient way. We also put a lot of effort into developing materials, to improve them and save resources. A limited range of articles and big sales volumes make it possible for us to keep costs and prices down. On top of this, our customers contribute to the low prices by collecting, taking home and assembling the products themselves. Today, they can even design their kitchen or wardrobe themselves using our computerized planner tools.
- **Product strategy:** Wide range of products according to the need of consumers. Products are available for different sections of the society. Products adaptation is carried out according to the need of different market. It has diversified product line and product depth. The low priced furniture store provides reassemble furniture and casual furniture. Most of IKEA's products are stylish that makes the company unique. Concept of flat packaging is used, which makes it easier to consumers to transport the furniture. IKEA designs its own furniture and it offers a variety of style for interested consumers to choose from.
- **Promotion strategy:** It uses high profile advertisement campaigns where it spends 70% of annual marketing budget in printing catalogs. The shoppers are guided properly when they enter IKEA stores. It also provides facilities for online shopping. IKEA provides home delivery service and after-sales service to the customers. It also undertakes online advertisements to further boost its sale on varioys sites.
- **Market development strategy**: It has started targeting new segments and enter new markets with existing products. The potential benefits of international expansion are increased market share, revenues, profit, and buyer awareness. IKEA is planning to open 10 new stores in Europe. Russia is a potential market for IKEA because the economy of Russia is expanding whereas Germany is the largest market of IKEA. North America market can be tough for IKEA as there are big competitors Like Fortunebrands, Jarden, Masco. IKEA planning to open 5 new stores in USA.

Asia is emerging as a large potential market for IKEA. IKEA has got permission to en to enter in INDIA. In 2011 IKEA has its store in Malaysia. China, Japan and Singapore are profitable markets to expand. Australia is a big market for IKEA, there is always demand for ready to assemble furniture and IKEA is planning to increase employees in stores there. IKEA is currently operating in all the states of Australia and planning to open more stores.

Potential market of IKEA: Currently IKEA is not operating in Latin America. (Mexico, Brazil, Chile, Ecudor. Africa can be a profitable market for IKEA (South Africa). In Asia, India is a big potential market. IKEA is planning to open new stores is China.

Competitive Advantage: IKEA used many methods to improve the competitive advantage. These are:

- Low price and good quality more than competitors.
- Good service
- High quality of design.
- Wide varieties.
- Good brand image in consumer's brains.
- IKEA has a special team develops new products, updating technology, promoting technological development.
- Most of IKEA's products are stylish that makes the company unique.

There are so many reasons that make IKEA so popular, for example, cooperating with the suppliers from all over the world, high efficientcy of logics, using "life system" to find what customer need, and so on. Follow the concept, IKEA tries their best to give the customers what they promised: low price, well-design, creating a better everyday life for many people. As a world famous international company, IKEA is like a fresh air in to new target markets such as Middle East, Australia and China. It not only brings new strategy and model to their competitors, but also brings the new lifestyle and service to the customers.

For the dilemma of IKEA in China market right now, IKEA should try to change the supply base to "supply-product-sale" base. Though the centralized procurement, flat-package, and more cooperation with local suppliers, IKEA can get more cost leadership. So IKEA can reduce the price and get the virtuous circle of "reduce price-increase demand-scale effect-reduce price". IKEA understands Middle East Australia and China markets more than before. With accelerating the speeds of expansion, IKEA will get more customers; the success of IKEA in these markets is only the problem of time.

QUESTIONS

1. What is your opinion about the "strategic intent" of IKEA? Can you suggest something different for them.
2. What are the major issues faced by IKEA? What steps should they take to overcome these?
3. IKEA has used many strategies to remain the market leader. Explain these strategies and suggest if some other strategy could be adopted by IKEA.
4. How can you improve the competitive advantage of your organisation? Compare them with IKEA.

28 Wilkinson: Marketing Strategy for Growth

Businesses must respond to change in order to remain competitive. Developing appropriate strategies which allow them to move forward is essential. Wilkinson is a prime example of a business that has responded to changing customer needs throughout its history. It is one of the UK's long-established retailers of a wide range of food, home, garden, office, health and beauty products. James Kemsey Wilkinson opened his first Wilkinson Store in Charnwood Street, Leicester in 1930. After the Second World War, the 1950s saw a rise in the use of labour-saving devices and do it yourself (DIY) . Wilkinson responded by making this type of product the focus of its sales. In the 1960s customers wanted more convenience shopping. Wilkinson started selling groceries and supermarket goods and created the Wilko brand. In the 1980s Wilkinson extended its range of low-cost products to include quality clothing, toys, toiletries and perfumes. In 1995 it opened a central distribution centre in Worksop, serving stores in the north of England and in 2004, a new distribution centre opened in Wales. In 2005 Wilkinson launched its Internet shopping service, offering over 800,000 product lines for sale online. Wilkinson currently has over 300 stores, which carry an average of 25,000 product lines. 40% of these are Wilko 'own-brand' products. Wilkinson's growth places it in the top 30 retailers in the UK. Recently it has faced increasing challenges from competitors, such as the supermarket sector. Wilkinson needed to combat this and identify new areas for growth. Over two years it conducted extensive market research. This has helped it create a marketing strategy designed to continue growing by targeting a new market segment – the student population. This case study focuses on how Wilkinson created and implemented this strategy, using the findings of its market research to drive the strategy forward.

To grow, a business needs to give consumers what they want, at a price they are satisfied with, when they want it and make a profit for the company. Wilkinson commissioned market research which identified key potential for growth in the student sector. It had to develop a strategy for growth that not only covered the specific requirements of this target group, but also linked closely with the company's overall aims and objectives. The key elements that need to be in place for business planning are:

- **Aims** – describe the overall goals of a business
- **Objectives** – are steps which managers decide need to be taken in order to achieve the overall aims
- **Strategy** – is a plan which outlines all the medium and long-term steps that need to be taken in order to achieve a given target
- **Tactics** – are what the business does in the short-term. These respond to opportunities and threats identified when preparing the original strategy.

Strategies may be to combat competition, to improve the position of the company in the market or to grow the business. The type of strategy required will depend upon several factors but the main influences include number and power of competitors, company strengths, size of business, financial position and government influences. Marketing strategy aims to communicate to customers the added-value of products and services. This considers the right mix of design, function, image or service to improve customer awareness of the business' products and ultimately to encourage them to buy.

An important tool for helping develop an appropriate marketing strategy is Ansoff's Matrix. This model looks at the options for developing a marketing strategy and helps to assess the levels of risk involved with each option. Marketing strategies may focus on the development of products or markets. Doing more of what a business already does carries least risk; developing a completely new product for a new audience carries the highest risk both in terms of time and costs. Based on its research, Wilkinson committed to a market development strategy to sell its products to a new audience of students. This is a medium risk strategy as it requires the business to find and develop new customers. It also carries costs of the marketing campaigns to reach this new group. The main focus of the strategy was to increase awareness of the brand among students and encourage them to shop regularly at Wilkinson stores.

Market research is vital for collecting data on which to base the strategy. Market research takes one of two main forms – primary research and secondary research. Primary research (also called field research) involves collecting data first hand. This can take many forms, the main ones being interview, questionnaires, panels and observation. Secondary research (also called desk research) involves collecting data which already exists. This includes using information from reports, publications, Internet research and company files. Both methods have advantages and disadvantages. The advantages of primary research are that it is recent, relevant and designed specifically for the company's intended strategy. The main disadvantage is that it is more expensive than secondary research and can be biased if not planned well. Secondary research is relatively cheap, can be undertaken quickly and so enables decision-making sooner. However, secondary research can go out-of-date and may not be entirely relevant to the business' needs. Wilkinson undertook primary market research using questionnaires from students across the UK and secondary research using government and university admissions data. The statistics revealed that there were three million potential student customers. They had a combined annual spend of around £9 billion per year. This research confirmed that the choice of focusing on the student market as a means of growth was valid.

Wilkinson undertook further research to identify how to reach students and persuade them to start shopping at Wilkinson stores. This information was used to formulate a focus strategy. This was aimed specifically at the needs of the student 'market segment'. Wilkinson involved 60 universities in research, using questionnaires distributed to students initially in Years 2 and 3 of a range of universities and then to 'freshers' (new students) through the University and Colleges Admission Service. This ensured the widest range of students was included to eliminate bias. It also gave a wide range of responses. From this initial group, students were asked a second set of questions. Participants were rewarded with Amazon vouchers to encourage a good take-up. The research focused on two areas, "student awareness of the Wilkinson brand and reasons why students were currently not using the stores regularly". The market research enabled Wilkinson to put together its marketing strategy. The aim was to ensure the student population began shopping at Wilkinson stores early in their student experience. This would help to maintain their customer loyalty to Wilkinson throughout their student years and also to develop them as future customers after university. Repeat business is key to sustained growth. Wilkinson wanted to create satisfied customers with their needs met by the Wilkinson range of products. A marketing campaign was launched which focused on a range of promotional tactics, specifically designed to appeal to university students. These included:

- Wilkinson being present at fresher's fairs – and giving free goody bags with sample products directly to students
- Direct mail flyers to homes and student halls, prior to students arriving.
- Advertisements with fun theme, for example, showing frying pans as tennis racquets.
- Web banners offering discounts of 15% with first purchase using the online store
- Gift vouchers and free wall planners.

The challenge was to get students into Wilkinson stores. The opportunity was to capture a new customer group at an early stage and provide essential items all year round. This would lead to a committed customer group and secure repeat business. Wilkinson wanted to know what would inspire students to shop at Wilkinson more and what factors would help to attract non-customers. The research provided significant primary information to analyze the effects of the campaign. Wilkinson used questionnaires collected from the first year undergraduates to gather qualitative data. In addition, Wilkinson obtained quantitative data from various other sources, including:

- **Redemption rates** – how many people used the discount vouchers when buying.
- **Sales analysis** – how much extra business did the stores handle
- **Footfall in stores analysis** – how many extra people went into stores.

This information helped Wilkinson to develop its plans for future marketing campaigns. It identified motivation factors for the student audience which would help to encourage future purchase. Key factors included products being cheaper than competitors and easy access to stores. Twenty-three per cent of students questioned gave 'distance from university' as a reason for not regularly visiting the store. The layout of the store was another major problem affecting repeat visits. These findings have been taken on board by Wilkinson in its future planning of store locations and layouts. Researching students' opinions after the campaign showed that awareness of Wilkinson brand had significantly risen from 77% to 95% of those interviewed. This brought it in line with Morrison supermarkets, a key competitor. 17% of students who received a goody bag at fresher's fairs used the 15% discount voucher. A further 58% intended to use the voucher. The campaign had either got students to enter the Wilkinson stores or increase their intention to visit the store. Of particular importance to Wilkinson was that the campaign had made the company more appealing to 67% of students interviewed. This fulfilled one of the main objectives of the campaign and was reinforced by figures from existing students. Prior to the campaign 13% shopped at Wilkinson at least once a month. After the campaign this had risen to 33%. The results of interviews with fresher students two months after the campaign shows which of the various marketing tactics Wilkinson used with the students had the greatest impact on their awareness.

Wilkinson's marketing strategy began with its corporate aim to grow and increase stores across the UK. It was facing increased competition from supermarkets and needed to identify an area to focus on. To pursue a growth strategy, Wilkinson used market research to identify new target customers. This enabled it to prepare marketing strategies to fit the audience. The campaign helped to achieve many of the business' aims, creating increased brand awareness and repeat visits. It also helped to inform the company's future strategies for growth. Market research gathered will help to formulate future plans for new stores. These will be in line with Wilkinson commitment to providing communities with affordable products across the country.

QUESTIONS

1. What is the difference between primary and secondary research? Identify one example of primary and secondary research carried out by Wilkinson.
2. Explain why Wilkinson needed a marketing strategy to help them to grow.
3. Evaluate the benefits of the marketing campaign to Wilkinson.
4. Analyze how effective the marketing campaign was in helping Wilkinson respond to competitive pressures.

Index